THE OXFORD HAND
MUTUA
CO-OPERATIVE,
AND CO-OWNED
BUSINESS

Jonathan Michie is Professor of Innovation and Knowledge Exchange at the University of Oxford, where he is President of Kellogg College, Director of the Department for Continuing Education, and Director of the Oxford Centre for Mutual & Co-owned Business. Jonathan is Chair of the Board of United World Colleges (UWC) Atlantic College, and a member of the UWC Council; and an 'Interdisciplinary' member of the Management & Business Panel for the 2021 Research Excellence Framework exercise. From 2004–2008 Jonathan was Director of Birmingham Business School. From 1997–2004 he held the Sainsbury Chair of Management at Birkbeck, University of London where he was Head of the School of Management & Organizational Psychology. From 1992–1997 he was at the Judge Business School in Cambridge where he was also a Fellow & Director of Studies in Economics at Robinson College.

Joseph R. Blasi is the J. Robert Beyster Distinguished Professor at Rutgers University's School of Management and Labor Relations in New Brunswick, New Jersey and Director of the Institute for the Study of Employee Ownership and Profit Sharing at Rutgers. An economic sociologist, Blasi studies the social history of the corporation and corporate governance with a special emphasis on organizations where rewards, power, and prestige are broadly distributed, as in the case of employee share ownership and profit sharing in business. Within the Institute, he also leads a national competitive Fellowship Program that grants research fellowships and gathers over a hundred research scholars in academic conferences on these subjects. He is co-author of *The Citizen's Share* (Yale University Press, 2013) and a frequent policy advisor on these issues.

Carlo Borzaga is full Professor of Economic policy at the University of Trento (Italy) and President of the European Research Institute on Cooperatives and Social Enterprise (Euricse). He also chairs the Master Programme in Management of Social Enterprises at the University of Trento and is a founding member of the EMES European Research network. Prof. Borzaga sits on the scientific committee of numerous Italian and European journals and is co-editor of the newly launched international *Journal of Entrepreneurial and Organizational Diversity* (JEOD). He has authored and co-edited numerous books and papers on labour economics and social and cooperative enterprises.

THE OXFORD HANDBOOK OF

MUTUAL, CO-OPERATIVE, AND CO-OWNED BUSINESS

Edited by

JONATHAN MICHIE, JOSEPH R. BLASI,

and

CARLO BORZAGA

OXFORD
UNIVERSITY PRESS

OXFORD
UNIVERSITY PRESS

Great Clarendon Street, Oxford, OX2 6DP,
United Kingdom

Oxford University Press is a department of the University of Oxford.
It furthers the University's objective of excellence in research, scholarship,
and education by publishing worldwide. Oxford is a registered trade mark of
Oxford University Press in the UK and in certain other countries

First published 2017
First published in paperback 2019

Published in the United States of America by Oxford University Press
198 Madison Avenue, New York, NY 10016, United States of America

British Library Cataloguing in Publication Data
Data available

Library of Congress Cataloging in Publication Data
Data available

ISBN 978–0–19–968497–7 (Hbk.)
ISBN 978–0–19–882882–2 (Pbk.)

Contents

List of Figures   xi
List of Tables   xiii
Abbreviations   xv
About the Contributors   xix
Introduction and Overview   xxiii
     JONATHAN MICHIE, JOSEPH R. BLASI, AND CARLO BORZAGA

PART I DIVERSITY AND COMPLEXITY OF MEMBER-OWNED ENTERPRISES

1. The Importance of Ownership   3
    JONATHAN MICHIE

2. Entrepreneurial Pluralism   14
    GIOVANNI FERRI AND ANGELO LEOGRANDE

3. Liberal Philosophies of Ownership   27
    STUART WHITE

4. Co-operative Principles and Co-operative Law Across the Globe   39
    HAGEN HENRŸ

PART II RATIONALE OF CO-OPERATIVE ENTERPRISES

5. Co-operation as Co-ordination Mechanism: A New Approach to the Economics of Co-operative Enterprises   55
    CARLO BORZAGA AND ERMANNO C. TORTIA

6. The Social and Political Dimensions of Co-operative Enterprises   76
    VICTOR A. PESTOFF

PART III HISTORY OF MEMBER-OWNED ORGANIZATIONS

7. A Worldwide Historical Perspective on Co-operatives
   and Their Evolution   97
   VERA ZAMAGNI

8. An American Historical Perspective on Employee Ownership   114
   JOSEPH R. BLASI AND DOUGLAS L. KRUSE

PART IV CO-OPERATIVES, MUTUALS, MEMBER-OWNED, AND EMPLOYEE-OWNED ENTERPRISES IN THE GLOBAL ECONOMY

9. Worker Co-operatives: Good, Sustainable Jobs in the Community   131
   VIRGINIE PÉROTIN

10. Credit Unions and Co-operative Banks across the World   145
    SILVIO GOGLIO AND PANU KALMI

11. Agricultural Co-operatives: A Struggle for Identity   158
    SAMIRA NUHANOVIC-RIBIC, ERMANNO C. TORTIA,
    AND VLADISLAV VALENTINOV

12. Social and Solidarity Co-operatives: An International Perspective   171
    GIULIA GALERA

13. Community Co-operatives and Co-operatives Providing Public
    Services: Facts and Prospects   184
    PIER ANGELO MORI

14. How to Think about Global Employee Ownership   195
    LOREN RODGERS

PART V POLITICAL, GOVERNANCE, AND ORGANIZATIONAL ASPECTS

15. Evidence: What the US Research Shows about Worker Ownership   211
    JOSEPH R. BLASI, RICHARD B. FREEMAN, AND DOUGLAS L. KRUSE

16. Enterprise Form, Participation, and Performance in Mutuals
   and Co-operatives 227
   ZOE ADAMS AND SIMON DEAKIN

17. Governance and Organizational Challenges 246
   PETER COUCHMAN

18. Are Co-operatives Small? Evidence from the World
   Co-operative Monitor 261
   CHIARA CARINI AND MAURIZIO CARPITA

PART VI NATIONAL CASE STUDIES

19. The Mondragón Experience 279
   XABIER BARANDIARAN AND JAVIER LEZAUN

20. Moving Towards 100% Employee Ownership Through ESOPs:
   Added Complexities in Add-On Transactions 295
   DANIEL TISCHER AND JOHN HOFFMIRE

21. Social Co-operatives in Italy 308
   SARA DEPEDRI

22. Co-operatives and the Transformation of the German
   Energy Sector 321
   MARKUS HANISCH

23. Co-operatives in Latin America 335
   MICHELA GIOVANNINI AND MARCELO VIETA

24. Developing and Sustaining Communities: The Role
   of Co-operatives 348
   LOU HAMMOND KETILSON

25. Shared Capitalism in the USA: Evaluation and Future Policies 361
   JOSEPH R. BLASI AND DOUGLAS L. KRUSE

26. Workers—and Consumers—of the World Unite! Opportunities
   for Hybrid Co-operativism 374
   MAURIE J. COHEN

27. The Worker Co-operative Form in the Home Care Industry
   in the USA 386
   DAPHNE BERRY

28. Raiffeisenbanks and Volksbanks for Europe: The Case
    for Co-operative Banking in Germany   398
    HOLGER BLISSE AND DETLEV HUMMEL

29. Statutory Employee Stock Ownership Plans in the USA   412
    COREY ROSEN

30. Employee Ownership in Britain Today   426
    ANDREW PENDLETON AND ANDREW ROBINSON

PART VII CORPORATE AND SECTOR CASE STUDIES

31. Corporate Governance Beyond Neoliberalism: Agency,
    Democracy, and Co-operation   445
    WILLIAM DAVIES

32. Co-operatives: A Development Strategy? An Analysis of Argan
    Oil Co-operatives in South-West Morocco   456
    ZAHIR DOSSA

33. Fair Trade and Co-operatives   470
    ALEX NICHOLLS AND BENJAMIN HUYBRECHTS

34. From Traditional to Innovative Multi-Stakeholder Mutuals: The
    Case of Rochdale Boroughwide Housing   480
    RUTH YEOMAN

35. The Emergence of Multi-Stakeholder Co-operatives in the
    Movement of Farm Machinery Co-operatives (CUMAs) in France   499
    FRANCK THOMAS

36. Agricultural Co-operatives in China   512
    LI ZHAO

PART VIII THE FUTURE OF CO-OPERATIVES

37. US Worker Co-operatives   527
    MARK J. KASWAN

38. The Essential Role of Co-operative Law and Some Related Issues   539
    ANTONIO FICI

39. Conversion from Stakeholder Value to Shareholder Value
Banks: The Case of UK Building Societies   550
DAVID T. LLEWELLYN

40. The Performance of Member-Owned Businesses Since
the Financial Crisis of 2008   570
JOHNSTON BIRCHALL

41. Creating Socially Sustainable Enterprise   585
DAVID ERDAL

42. The Co-operative Business Model: The Shape of Things to Come   598
CHARLES GOULD

Index   611

List of Figures

2.1	Extent of non-profit workforce on total workforce	16
2.2	Extent of co-operative workforce on total workforce	17
2.3	Extent of non-profit plus co-operative workforce on total workforce	18
2.4	Extent of family business workforce on total workforce	18
5.1	Different co-ordination mechanisms of the economic activity, and corresponding organizational forms	62
6.1	Investment per member in German co-operatives, 2014	79
13.1	A classification of co-operatives	186
17.1	The 'W' approach to board consultation	256
17.2	The Plunkett model of board competencies	257
18.1	Co-operatives in the World Co-operative Monitor Database by country	268
18.2	The 300 largest co-operatives and mutual organizations in the world, by turnover (left) and turnover on per capita GDP (right). For the year 2012	271
20.1	Non-leveraged ESOP	298
20.2	Leveraged ESOP diagram	299
22.1	Share of renewables in the German energy mix 2013	322
22.2	Development of German renewable energy sources, 1988 to 2012	323
22.3	EEG surcharge in cents/kWh, 1998 to 2015	325
22.4	Activities of energy co-operatives	327
22.5	Newly registered German energy co-operatives, 2006 to 2014	328
22.6	Investment per member in German co-operatives, 2014	328
25.1	Citizens' shares in the United States	363
25.2	How much is the typical citizen's share?	364
25.3	Employee ownership and income levels	365
25.4	Employee ownership in different parts of the economy	366
32.1	Value chain of argan oil co-operatives	459
32.2	Institutional hierarchy (Projet Arganier 2008)	460

34.1   The Mutual Organization Model   483

34.2   The RBH Mutual Organization Model   484

39.1   Diversity Index for financial service (D-Index): Ownership,
        competitiveness, resiliences, and geographic spread   555

39.2   Ownership Index: Banks, mutuals, and NS&I   556

39.3   Competitiveness Index: Mortgage balances outstanding and UK deposits 557

List of Tables

7.1	The 300 Largest Co-ops in 2012 (Numbers and Turnover)	100
14.1	Global Employee Ownership	199
18.1	The World Co-operative Monitor's Types of Co-operative Organizations	264
18.2	The World Co-operative Metrics Framework Structure	265
18.3	Main Figures of the Co-operatives and Mutual Organizations in the World Co-operative Monitor Database by Macro Geographical Region. Number of Organizations, Turnover, and Turnover on GDP Per Capita	269
18.4	Turnover (in Billion USD) of the European Co-operatives and Mutual Organizations in the World Co-operative Monitor Database by Country. Years 2010–2012	273
20.1	Illustrative Fair Value Calculation Before and After Add-On ESOP Transaction	303
20.2	Simplified Example of Floor Price Protection (Valid for 3 Years) Assuming 100,000 Shares, Repayment Rate of $7 p.a., and Pre-Transaction Company Value of $10m	304
22.1	Overview of Important Regulations and Their Consequences for Energy Co-operatives	329
22.2	A Typology of Factors with Impact on Ownership Costs of Electricity Co-operatives	330
22.3	Challenges and Co-operative Governance Solutions on Electricity Markets	330
27.1	Worker Attitudes/Outcomes by Type of Organization	396
28.1	Assets-Based Market Share (in per cent)	402
28.2	Cost-Earnings-Based Market Shares (in per cent)	403
28.3	Employees (absolute and in per cent)	403
28.4	Number of Credit Institutions and Their Branches (2015, in per cent)	404
28.5	PSD Banks and Sparda Banks (end of 2015)	405
28.6	Overview of German Co-operative Banks (2015)	406
28.7	(1) Number of Institutes and (2) Balance Sheet Average for each (in bill. €)	406

29.1   Estimated Number of ESOP Plans, Number of Participants,
       and Plan Asset Value, 2013   416

29.2   Estimated Growth of ESOPs, 2002–2013   416

29.3   Distribution of Plans by Industry   418

29.4   Difference in Post-ESOP to Pre-ESOP Performance, ESOP vs.
       Comparable Non-ESOP Companies   419

29.5   Percentage of Companies Having Other Retirement Plans   424

30.1   The Main Structures of Employee Ownership   430

30.2   Employee Ownership: Ownership and Governance Characteristics of
       Employee Ownership Groups   437

32.1   Framework of Internal and External Pressures Affecting Governance   461

32.2   Economic Data by Co-operative, by Member, and by Sector
       (numbers are in EUR)   464

37.1   Categories of Worker Co-operatives in the United States Based on
       Principal Motivation   535

39.1   Value Creation in SHV and STV Banks   562

ABBREVIATIONS

ACI	Alleanza delle Cooperative Italiane
AEA	American Economic Association
AGICES	National Fair Trade Network (Italy)
ALMO	Arms-length Management Organization
AMICE	Association of Mutual Insurers and Insurance Cooperatives in Europe
ANAP	National Association of Small Farmers (Cuba)
APF	Alaska Permanent Fund
APR	Asociaciones de Aqua Potable Rural
BBSO	Broad-based stock ownership
Bencoms	Community benefit societies
BERR	Department for Business Enterprise and Regulatory Reform
BSA	Building Societies Association
BVR	Bundesverband der Deutschen Volksbanken und Raiffeisenbanken
CCEDNET	Canadian Community of Economic Development Network
CEPS	Centre for European Policy Studies
CFL	Center for Family Life
CGSCOP	Confédération générale des sociétés coopératives et participatives
CGT	Capital Gains Tax
CHCA	Co-operative Home Care Associates
CHHA	Certified Home Health Agencies
CIAP	Installation in Farming Initiative
CIC	Community Interest Company
CICOPA	Comité International des Coopératives de Production et de Services Industrielles et Artisanales
Cogeca	General Committee for Agricultural Co-operation in the EU
Copa	Committee of Professional Agricultural Organisations
CPA	Agricultural Production Cooperative
CRM	Consumer relationship marketing

CSR	Corporate social responsibility
CSS	Social Solidarity Co-operative
CUCI	Cincinatti Union Co-op Initiative
CUMA	Coopératives d'Utilisation du Matériel Agricole
CUNA	Credit Union National Association
CWS	Co-operative Wholesale Society
DAWI	Democracy at Work Initiative
DAWN	Democracy at Work Network
DC	Defined contribution
DFE	Direct filing entity
DFID	Department for Foreign and International Development
DG	Deutsche Genossenschaftsbank
DZ	Deutsche Zentral Genossenschaftsbank
EACB	European Association of Co-operative Banks
EBITDA	Earnings before interest, taxes, depreciation, and amortization
ECB	European Central Bank
EEG	Renewable Energy Sources Act (Germany)
EFES	European Federation of Employee Share Ownership
EMT	Executive Management Team
ERISA	Employee Retirement Income Security Act (USA)
ERT	Worker-Recuperated Enterprises (Argentina)
ESOP	Employee Stock Ownership Plan
ESOT	Employee Stock Ownership Trust
Euricse	European Research Institute on Cooperative and Social Enterprises
EWOC	Eligible Worker Owned Co-operative
FAA	Argentine Agrarian Federation
FIT	Feed-in tariff
FNCUMA	National CUMA Federation
FPP	Floor price protection
FSC	Farmers' Specialized Co-operatives
GAO	General Accountability Office
GenG	German Cooperative Societies Act
GIC	General Interest Co-operative
GmbH	Bund Deutscher Konsumgenossenschaften

GNC	Groupement National de la Coopération
GSS	General Social Survey
HCRS	Household Contract Responsibility System
HPWS	High Performance Work Systems
ICA	International Co-operative Alliance
ICMIF	International Cooperative and Mutual Insurance Federation
IFAT	International Federation for Alternative Trade
ILO	International Labour Organization
INAES	National Institute of the Social Economy (Argentina)
Insee	Institut National de la Statistique et des Etudes Economiques
ISTAT	National Institute for Statistics
IOB	Investor-Owned Business
IOF	Investor-Owned Firm
IPO	Initial public offering
IRIS	Impact reporting and investment standards
IRS	Internal Revenue Service
JAC	Jeunesse Agricole Catholique
KAGB	Capital Investment Act
L3C	Low-Profit Limited Liability Company
LE	Leveraged ESOP
LHCSA	Licensed Home Care Services Agencies
LV	Locked value
MCC	Mondragón Cooperative Corporation
MEC	Mountain Equipment Co-operative
MGC	Mondragón Corporate Management Model
MOB	Member-Owned Business
NBER	National Bureau of Economic Research
NCEO	National Center for Employee Ownership
NEA	National Electrification Administration
NGO	Non-governmental organization
NIE	New institutional economics
NLE	Non-leveraged ESOP
NRWA	National Rural Water Association
NSTAC	Northern Saskatchewan Trappers Association Co-operative

OECD	Organization for Economic Cooperation and Development
OMOV	One member one vote
OV	Open value
P&G	Procter & Gamble
PA	Projet Arganier
PHI	Paraprofessional Healthcare Institute
QUEST	Qualifying Employee Share Trust
RBH	Rochdale Boroughwide Housing
REI	Recreational Equipment Inc.
RENETA	Réseau National des Espaces Tests Agricoles
ROE	Return on equity
SAR	Stock appreciation right
SAYE	Save as you earn
SCIC	Société coopérative d'intèret collectif
SHV	Shareholder Value
SICAE	Sociétés d'intérêt collectif agricole d'electricité
SIP	Share Incentive Plan
SMART	Simple, measurable, appropriate, realistic, and timely
SME	Small and medium-sized businesses
SOAS	School of Oriental and African Studies
SOE	State-Owned Enterprise
SPP	Simbolo de Requenos Productores
STV	Stakeholder Value
SUERF	The European Money and Finance Forum
SWIFT	The Society for Worldwide Interbank Financial Telecommunication
TEOCO	The Employee-Owned Company
UBI	Universal basic income
UBPC	Basic Units of Co-operative Production
UCIRI	Union of Indigenous Communities of the Isthmus Region (Mexico)
USFWC	US Federation of Worker Co-operatives
WFTO	World Fair Trade Organization
WOCCO	World Council of Credit Unions
WTO	World Trade Organization

About the Contributors

Zoe Adams PhD student, studying law at Pembroke College, University of Cambridge

Xabier Barandiaran Lecturer in the Faculty of Social and Human Sciences at the University of Deusto, working in the areas of governance, political communication, and social capital

Daphne Berry Assistant Professor of Management, Barney School of Business, University of Hartford, Robert Beyster Fellow, W.K. Kellogg Fellow

Johnston Birchall Emeritus Professor at Stirling University, Scotland. A social economist specializing in the study of member-owned businesses. Most recent books are *People-Centred Businesses; Co-operatives, Mutuals and the Idea of Membership* (Macmillan 2011), and *Finance in an Age of Austerity: The Power of Customer-owned Banks* (Edward Elgar 2013)

Joseph R. Blasi J. Robert Beyster Distinguished Professor, Rutgers University School of Management and Labor Relations and Research Associate, National Bureau of Economic Research

Holger Blisse Doctor/Researcher at the Department of Business Administration (Unit for Cooperative Studies) at the University of Vienna (Austria) (2009–2014)

Carlo Borzaga Professor at the University of Trento, and President of Euricse (European Research Institute on Cooperatives and Social Enterprises)

Chiara Carini Researcher, European Research Institute on Cooperative and Social Enterprises (Euricse, Italy)

Maurizio Carpita Full Professor of Statistics, Department of Economics and Management, University of Brescia (Italy)

Maurie J. Cohen Professor of Sustainability Studies and Director of the Program in Science, Technology, and Society at the New Jersey Institute of Technology and co-founder and board member of the Sustainable Consumption Research and Action Initiative

Peter Couchman Chief Executive, Plunkett Foundation

William Davies Reader in Political Economy, Goldsmiths, University of London

Simon Deakin Professor of Law and Director of the Centre for Business Research at the University of Cambridge

Sara Depedri PhD, Senior Researcher at Euricse (European Research Institute of Cooperatives and Social Enterprises), Trento, Italy

Zahir Dossa PhD, Massachusetts Institute of Technology

David Erdal Dr., Honorary Researcher, School of Management, University of St Andrews. Author of *Beyond the Corporation: Humanity Working* (The Bodley Head 2011)

Giovanni Ferri Professor of Economics, LUMSA University of Rome, Italy

Antonio Fici Associate Professor of Private Law at the University of Molise (Italy) and Senior Research Fellow at Euricse (European Research Institute on Cooperative and Social Enterprises)

Richard B. Freeman Ascherman Professor of Economics, Harvard University; Director, Science Engineering Workforce Project, National Bureau of Economic Research; Faculty Co-Director, The Labor and Worklife Program, Harvard Law School; Co-Director, Harvard Center for Green Buildings and Cities; and Senior Research Fellow in Labour Markets at the Centre for Economic Performance

Giulia Galera Senior researcher at Euricse (European Research Institute on Co-operative and Social Enterprises)

Michela Giovannini PhD, researcher at Euricse (European Research Institute on Cooperative and Social Enterprises)

Silvio Goglio Associate Professor, University of Trento

Charles Gould Director-General, International Co-operative Alliance, 2010–2018

Markus Hanisch Prof. Dr., Humboldt University Berlin, Department of Agricultural Economics, Cooperative Sciences Group/Economics of Agricultural Co-operatives

Hagen Henrÿ Adjunct Professor of Comparative Law at the University of Helsinki and Research Director at the Ruralia Institute of that university

John Hoffmire Director, Center on Business and Poverty, University of Wisconsin-Madison; Director, Impact Bond Fund, Saïd Business School, University of Oxford

Detlev Hummel Prof. Dr./Professor for Banking and Finance at the University of Potsdam (Germany)

Benjamin Huybrechts Professor, Centre for Social Economy, HEC Liège Management School, University of Liège

Panu Kalmi PhD, Professor, University of Vaasa

Mark J. Kaswan Department of Political Science, University of Texas Rio Grande Valley and J. Robert Beyster, Michael W. Huber, and W.K. Kellogg Fellow, Rutgers University School of Management and Labor Relations

Lou Hammond Ketilson Dr., Fellow in Co-operative Management, Centre for the Study of Co-operatives; Adjunct Professor, Johnson-Shoyama Graduate School of Public Policy, University of Saskatchewan, Canada

Douglas L. Kruse Distinguished Professor, Rutgers University School of Management and Labor Relations and Research Associate, National Bureau of Economic Research

Angelo Leogrande PhD in Economics, University of Bari 'Aldo Moro', Italy

Javier Lezaun Associate Professor in the School of Anthropology and Museum Ethnography and James Martin Lecturer in Science and Technology Governance at the University of Oxford

David T. Llewellyn Professor of Money and Banking, Loughborough University; Council Member, SUERF (The European Money and Finance Forum); Member, European Association of Cooperative Banks Think Tank; Chair of the European Banking Authority's Banking Stakeholder Group

Jonathan Michie FAcSS, DPhil, Professor of Innovation and Knowledge Exchange at the University of Oxford, Director of the University's Department for Continuing Education and President of Kellogg College

Pier Angelo Mori Professor of Economics, Department of Economics and Management, University of Florence

Alex Nicholls Professor, Skoll Centre for Social Entrepreneurship, Saïd Business School, University of Oxford

Samira Nuhanovic-Ribic PhD, Director of Social Business Incubator, Mozaik Foundation, Bosnia and Herzegovina

Andrew Pendleton Professor of Human Resource Management, Durham University Business School, Durham, UK; Faculty Fellow and Mentor, Beyster Program, School of Management and Labor Relations, Rutgers University, New Jersey, USA

Virginie Pérotin Professor of Economics, Leeds University Business School, Leeds, UK

Victor A. Pestoff Professor Emeritus, Ersta-Sköndal University College, Stockholm, Sweden; Guest Professor, Osaka University, Japan; and Adjunct Professor, Roskilde University, Denmark

Andrew Robinson Professor of Finance and Accounting, Leeds University Business School, Leeds, UK; Visiting Professor, Université Paris II-Sorbonne Universités, France

Loren Rodgers Executive Director, National Center for Employee Ownership (USA)

Corey Rosen Founder, National Center for Employee Ownership (USA)

Franck Thomas Deputy Director/National Federation of Cuma; studying co-operatives' innovations in rural France

Daniel Tischer PhD, Lecturer in Political Economy and Organisation Studies, Alliance Manchester Business School, University of Manchester

Ermanno C. Tortia PhD, Associate Professor at the Unversity of Trento, Department of Economics and Management. Affiliated to Euricse (European Research Institute on Cooperative and Social Enterprises, Trento)

Vladislav Valentinov Senior Researcher at the Leibniz Institute of Agricultural Development in Transition Economies, Halle, Germany

Marcelo Vieta Assistant Professor, Program in Adult Education and Community Development, Ontario Institute for Studies in Education of the University of Toronto, Canada

Stuart White Tutorial Fellow in Politics at Jesus College, Oxford

Ruth Yeoman Research Fellow, Kellogg College, University of Oxford

Vera Zamagni Professor of Economic History at the University of Bologna and at the Johns Hopkins University, SAIS Europe, Bologna

Li Zhao Assistant Professor at the Rural Development Institute of the Chinese Academy of Social Sciences

Introduction and Overview

JONATHAN MICHIE, JOSEPH R. BLASI, AND CARLO BORZAGA

This handbook analyses, describes, and explains the complex world of organizations that assign ownership rights and governance control to stakeholders other than investors. The complexity of this set of organizations results both from the different degree of control exerted by stakeholders in each typology, and from the different legislative and regulatory frameworks that govern these organizational forms.

This handbook covers the whole range of 'member-owned' organizations, whether consumer co-operatives, agricultural and producer co-operatives, worker co-operatives, mutual building societies, friendly societies, credit unions, mutual insurance companies, or employee-owned companies. Co-operatives can be owned by the consumers, the producers, the employees, or by other members—whether through single-stakeholder or multi-stakeholder ownership. By 'significantly employee-owned' we mean a business where a meaningful proportion of the company is owned by its employees, whether as individual shareholders or through a trust, or through some combination of the two—where 'significantly' is generally taken to be at least 25 per cent. The term 'employee-owned' or 'worker-owned' or 'worker co-operative' is typically reserved for a business where the workers own more than 50 per cent of the shares or ownership rights of the business.

This complex set of organizations is termed differently across countries: from 'mutuals' in the UK, to 'solidarity co-operatives' in Latin America, to 'employee-owned' and ESOPs (Employee Stock Ownership Plans) in the United States. In some countries, such organizations are not even officially recognized and thus lack a specific descriptor. For the sake of clarity, this handbook refers to 'member-owned organizations' to encompass the variety of non-investor-owned organizations, and in the national case-study chapters, the terms used will be those most widely employed in that country.

These alternative corporate forms have emerged in a variety of economic sectors in almost all advanced economies—since the time of the Industrial Revolution and the development of capitalism, through to the subsequent creation and dominance of the limited liability company. Until recently, these organizations were generally regarded as a rather marginal component of the economy. However, over the past few years, member-owned organizations have come to be seen, in some countries at least, as representing a newly attractive potential in light of their ability to tackle various economic and social concerns. The first international organization that explicitly recognized the importance of these organizations was the Labour Conference that in 2002 adopted the International Labour Organization (ILO) Recommendation No. 193 concerning the promotion of co-operatives. The interest in co-operatives grew further as a consequence of their relative resilience during the financial and economic crises of 2007–9.[1]

Thus, 2012 was designated by the United Nations as the 'Year of the Co-operative'. In addition, various documents have been researched and issued by the European Union Institutions that have pointed to the important potential role that could be played by non-investor-owned enterprises across European societies. These include the Communication of the Commission on the promotion of co-operative societies in Europe, where the Commission argued for a greater focus on this area within the new Member States and candidate countries, where despite extensive reforms the instrument of co-operatives is not fully developed. And the Report on Social Economy discussed by the Committee on Employment and Social Affairs of the European Parliament called on the Commission to take the specific features of the social economy (aims, values, and working methods) into account when devising European policies, and to incorporate the social economy into its policies and strategies. Another important such document, that pointed to the contribution of co-operatives to societal well-being, was that of the 'Europe2020' strategy, and this was followed by the European Commission launching their 'Social Business Initiative', which developed a similar message.[2]

This renewed interest in member-owned organizations has paved the way for a wider recognition of the importance of corporate diversity in contributing to the health and resilience of national economies, including for example by the 2012 Report delivered by the UK Commission on Ownership, which advocated a greater degree of corporate diversity, with a stronger member-owned and employee-owned sector, and with the UK's 2010–15 Coalition Government being committed—including in its *Coalition Agreement*—to strengthening the co-operative and social economy sectors, in part to create a more resilient financial services sector in reaction to the global financial and economic crises of 2007–9, which were generally seen as having been fuelled by the excesses of privately and shareholder-owned banks and other financial institutions.

This handbook is international in scope, includes contributions from the leading academics and practitioners from the relevant fields, and covers the various disciplinary areas—including economics, finance and accounting, management and business, law, politics, history, organizational studies, psychology, public policy, and industrial sociology. The approach of the collection is interdisciplinary. The chapters reflect the latest

---

[1] For a synthesis of the literature on mutual performance, combined with an elaboration of a theoretical framework for evaluating mutual performance, drawing upon data generated from a range of mutual organizations, see Tischer et al. 2016.

[2] Also noteworthy was the resolution by the European Parliament on the contribution of co-operatives to overcoming the crisis (A7-0222/2013).

academic research and thinking on each topic, as well as reporting the relevant policy debates. The strengths and weaknesses of the various alternative corporate forms are explored, with failures analysed as well as successes.

OVERVIEW OF THE CONTRIBUTIONS

The chapters in Part I of the handbook describe and analyse the diversity and complexity of member-owned organizations, with Chapter 1 by Jonathan Michie considering why ownership matters in the first place—from which follows the importance of who those corporate owners are, namely private (or family), external shareholders, or members. Following the 2007–8 global financial crisis and the subsequent years of stagnation and economic fragility across many economies, there remains little consensus as to what might constitute an alternative to the neoliberal order that led up to, and arguably caused, that global financial crisis of 2007–8, which in turn led to the first global fall in production and incomes, in 2009, since the 1930s. Chapter 1 considers what such an alternative might look like. The rise of capitalism led to the co-operative, Marxian, and other critiques of that emerging economic order. Likewise, the crisis of the 1930s led to Keynesianism and to social democracy being adopted across much of Western Europe, as well as to the new international order as fashioned at Bretton Woods. Similarly, Michie argues, the failure of what the late Andrew Glyn had termed 'capitalism unleashed' needs to herald fresh thinking, and a new era of global economic development—sustainable environmentally, economically, and socially. This will require a greater degree of diversity of ownership forms—private, state, and co-operative and mutual. Such diversity is needed to make the productive system more resilient. Such corporate diversity would also have the additional benefit of creating an environment in which it would become easier to tackle the problems of excessive corporate pay, and income and wealth inequality.

This analysis is developed further by Giovanni Ferri and Angelo Leogrande who, in Chapter 2, argue that policy debates are generally underpinned by an unacknowledged assumption that there is an archetypical form of enterprise, namely the private limited company, with enterprise forms differing from this archetype being viewed as anomalous, possibly the result of temporary or unusual conditions, and likely to naturally evolve into public companies (that is, private limited companies with their shares publicly traded). However, they argue, reality tells us that entrepreneurial pluralism is actually the norm rather than the exception, and that these 'non-archetype' enterprises do not in general disappear—and on the contrary often thrive. Furthermore, progress in the theories of industrial organization, corporate governance, stakeholder inclusion, and the common good all tend to suggest that entrepreneurial pluralism may be welfare enhancing. Against this background, Ferri and Leogrande consider and discuss the potential causes and effects of entrepreneurial pluralism. Specifically, they focus on mutual producer/consumer associations, social enterprises, co-operative enterprises, and family firms.

In Chapter 3, Stuart White discusses three liberal philosophies of ownership: right libertarianism, which advocates an expansive conception of private property and which holds that legitimate and strict rights to such property can emerge through the voluntary production and exchange of self-owning individuals on the basis of initial privatizations of external resources that can be very unequal but nevertheless just; left libertarianism, which modifies the right libertarian position by insisting on a (more) egalitarian initial distribution of external resources; and democratic liberalism, which makes all property rights subject to democratic judgements guided by principles of social justice which express an understanding of citizens' common good. The chapter discusses the implications of each philosophy for co-operatives and mutuals, and for the place of public policy in promoting these kinds of enterprises and related institutions.

Chapter 4 by Hagen Henrÿ considers the legitimacy of measuring co-operative law by the internationally recognized co-operative principles, and discusses the evolution of co-operative law across the globe over the past decades. Based on this, Henrÿ then suggests re-establishing the rationale for a co-operative law which distinguishes co-operatives from other types of enterprise, this rationale being the sustainable development enhancing diversity of enterprise types. The locus of competition and competitiveness needs to shift, he argues, from financial performance to the normative capacity of enterprises to contribute to sustainable development. Co-operatives have a competitive advantage in this respect. The chapter therefore suggests how to translate this capacity into the legal structure of co-operatives. This needs to be done against the background of current economic, political, sociological, and socio-psychological changes and challenges, of which globalization is both cause and effect, and which impact upon the co-operative values and upon the notion of (co-operative) law and of law-making.

The chapters in Part II consider the rationale of co-operative enterprises, starting in Chapter 5 with a consideration by Carlo Borzaga and Ermanno C. Tortia of co-operation as a mechanism of co-ordination. This, they argue, represents a new approach to the economics of co-operative enterprises—which is necessary because the interpretations hitherto produced on co-operative firms have been, in general terms, unsatisfactory. The reasons for this are to be found in the limitations of the dominant theoretical paradigms in interpreting the individual, collective, and social reality of co-operation. Recent theoretical developments, they argue, allow us to start dealing with the most relevant economic dimensions of co-operation, by: (i) recognizing co-operation as a peculiar and basic co-ordination mechanism of economic activity; (ii) considering collective and mutually beneficial entrepreneurial action, and not only individual action, as legitimate and fruitful; (iii) understanding economic motivations not only as self-interested and opportunistic, but also as intrinsically driven, as reciprocal, and as social. Starting from an analysis of the key market imperfections, Borzaga and Tortia develop a theory of co-operatives as enterprises that do not, as a norm, maximize net economic returns as their main objective, but instead pursue mutually beneficial and social aims.

In Chapter 6, Victor A. Pestoff analyses the social and political rationale of co-operative enterprises, and in particular their potential as providers of social services.

Co-operative enterprises have, he argues, a unique capacity to mobilize social capital and to provide relational goods that neither public nor private for-profit providers demonstrate to the same degree. This brings co-operative enterprises full circle in terms of their historical political role, as democratic pioneers, since they can now also contribute to reducing what is often today seen as a worrying democratic deficit. The chapter explores the political and social dimensions of co-operative enterprises that pursue multiple goals. It also introduces a dynamic model of co-operative development that can be fruitfully employed for analysing the social and political dilemmas faced by co-operative enterprises.

The chapters in Part III consider the history of member-owned organizations, starting with Vera Zamagni who argues in Chapter 7 that the birth of co-operatives in Europe in the middle of the nineteenth century shaped the presence of this form of enterprise and differentiated it from the established capitalist one over subsequent years, both in terms of internal organization and in terms of sectors of activity. This chapter highlights the diffusion of nineteenth-century types of co-operative across the world—including their successes and their limitations. Zamagni also analyses the novelties that emerged in the late twentieth century, and which helped contribute towards what is arguably a renaissance of the co-operative enterprise in the twenty-first century.

In Chapter 8, Joseph R. Blasi and Douglas L. Kruse provide a historical perspective on employee ownership in the USA, which as they demonstrate, plays a significant role in the US economy today, with this worker ownership taking a number of different forms. A large proportion of the US population (close to a fifth) currently own stock in the company where they work. Meaningful worker holdings are ubiquitous in high-technology companies such as Google in the Internet area, Microsoft in the software area, Gilead Sciences in biotechnology, and Qualcomm in mobile technology. As noted in Chapter 29 by Corey Rosen, the most intensive sectors of worker ownership in the USA are in around 10,000 companies with about 15 million workers having Employee Stock Ownership Plans, where about 4,000 of the firms are majority or 100 per cent worker-owned, and a compact but vibrant and growing sector of about 300 worker co-operatives with around 6,000 members.

The chapters in Part IV survey the co-operative, mutual, member-owned, and employee-owned sectors of the economy globally, starting with Virginie Pérotin's survey in Chapter 9 of worker co-operatives providing good, sustainable jobs across a range of communities. Her chapter examines the implications of the key international research findings of the last two decades for our understanding of why worker co-operatives are created, the objectives pursued by the founding and subsequent members, and the spillover effects of the performance of these co-operatives for the communities in which the firms operate. The chapter argues that worker co-operatives, by providing institutions in which employees control most aspects of their job and firm strategy (including pay and employment trade-offs) internalize a number of externalities to the conventional operation of firms. These co-operatives provide good, stable jobs in which employees' potential and creativity can flourish. In addition to promoting economic democracy, worker co-operatives thus offer sustainable and local employment, and are likely to have a number of positive effects on their communities' economies, public finances, and health.

The various national types of co-operative banking are considered by Silvio Goglio and Panu Kalmi in Chapter 10, including: credit unions (as in the UK), decentralized networks (as in Germany, Italy, and Austria), and centralized networks (as in France, the Netherlands, and Finland). This chapter considers the historical evolution that has characterized the different patterns with regard to national peculiarities (social and economic). The present process of hybridization in the sector is analysed, as is the potential for such hybrids to contribute towards a renewal of co-operative enterprises in the twenty-first century.

Over past decades, agricultural co-operatives have grown substantially in most developed and developing countries, often reaching dominant market positions. In Chapter 11, Samira Nuhanovic-Ribic, Ermanno C. Tortia, and Vladislav Valentinov enquire into the economic mechanism behind this growth, by elaborating on the relationship between co-operative identity and the outcomes of co-operative activities. They highlight the ability of agricultural co-operatives to co-ordinate large-scale production, to monitor work contributions and product quality, and to ensure economic independence of farmer members. Following the two principal streams in the economic literature, the chapter distinguishes between the conceptions of agricultural co-operatives as units of vertical integration and as firms characterized by common governance of collective entrepreneurial action with an ability to reduce transaction costs and economic risk. The chapter describes the financial and governance limitations of agricultural co-operatives, while taking account of institutional tools and models introduced to overcome such limitations. The chapter concludes by suggesting directions for enhancing the role of co-operatives in agricultural and rural development.

Over the past decade or so, in several countries both within and outside Europe, new types of co-operatives have emerged with specifically declared *social* goals. The development of these co-operatives is above all connected to the engagement of co-operatives in the supply of welfare and educational services, which are carried out beyond the 'boundaries' of each co-operative's membership. Their emergence is in contrast to the traditional model of co-operatives, which were based on a single stake-holding system; here we have the identification of both members and users, leading towards a greater openness, and a readiness to have additional bearers of interests, such as volunteers, sharing the duties and benefits of the organization. Drawing on country studies of Italy, Spain, France, Portugal, Greece, and South Korea, Chapter 12 by Giulia Galera focuses on these new types of co-operatives with declared social goals, which have in several countries become important providers of welfare services.

The community co-operatives that are also spreading today in many parts of the world are part of an evolutionary process that has seen the progressive shift of co-operatives' focus from specific social and professional groups to society as a whole. Since the term 'community co-operative' is relatively new, and similar institutions are named differently at different times, the first task is to elucidate the concept. Chapter 13 by Pier Angelo Mori discusses the differences between these new community co-operatives on the one hand, and the more traditional co-operatives on the other, reviewing the data, with a special focus on customer-owned providers of public utilities. The chapter closes with a discussion of the economic reasons why this new organizational mode is more likely to expand today than it has in the past.

Companies that wish to provide their employees with an ownership interest in their stock must adapt their plan design to the specifics of labour law, securities requirements, tax regimes, privacy laws, and other issues in their various countries. In Chapter 14, Loren Rodgers suggests guidelines for companies to design their plans by reviewing best practices in equity compensation. Rodgers argues that companies would be wise to begin with their ideal plan design and then adapt it to reflect legal requirements, taking into account that some companies must accommodate the requirements of multiple countries.

The chapters in Part V analyse the political, governance, and organizational aspects of co-operative and employee-owned and mutual businesses, starting in Chapter 15 with a consideration by Joseph R. Blasi, Richard B. Freeman, and Douglas L. Kruse of what the US research suggests about employee ownership. Sharing the fruits of labour with workers has led to initiatives of both profit-sharing and worker ownership. Several decades of research show that firms with worker ownership and profit-sharing tend to do better on average. A variety of studies, those comparing firms before and after they initiated worker ownership, those comparing workers in the same firm with and without worker ownership, and those looking at combinations of worker ownership and profit-sharing, reach the same conclusions. Evidence from large groups of firms and large samples of workers show that a supportive corporate culture is generally necessary for worker ownership to function best, and that cash profit-sharing in the short term tends to strengthen economic performance.

Mutuals and co-operatives have a distinct legal form which sets them apart from privately and shareholder-owned companies. Chapter 16 by Zoe Adams and Simon Deakin reviews the theoretical and empirical literature on the governance and performance effects of these differences in legal form. The chapter shows that it may be misleading to think of workers and customers as the owners of mutual enterprises, and that a more precise focus on the content of voice, income, and control rights in particular organizations must be undertaken in order to assess the implications of different legal structures for economic performance. The empirical evidence suggests that, on average, both worker- and customer-mutuals are more risk-averse and less profitable, but also more sustainable, than commercial entities structured as companies limited by share capital. However, the mutual form does not, in itself, guarantee that the firm is run in a more democratic and participative way, and the increasing use of mutuals in the public sector does not necessarily equate to increased involvement by workers and customers in decision-making. If the mutual form is not a panacea for the problems of accountability and sustainability affecting companies, it further follows that mutualization, while useful in some contexts, should not be favoured at the cost of wider reforms to corporate governance.

In Chapter 17, the Chief Executive of the Plunkett Foundation, which supports some of the world's smallest community-based co-operatives, looks at what the larger co-operatives can learn from these. Peter Couchman explores five different approaches that a co-operative can take—a trust based approach, the corporate governance based approach, the competence based approach, the values based approach, and an open co-operatives approach—and considers the implications of each.

There is a widespread belief that co-operatives are necessarily small-sized enterprises. However, there is evidence that in some cases co-operatives have larger dimensions in certain areas than other types of companies. Starting from this premise, Chiara Carini and Maurizio Carpita in Chapter 18 contribute to the existing literature by providing empirical evidence on the size of co-operatives in different areas of the world, and by analysing data from approximately 2,000 large co-operatives and mutual organizations from 56 different countries. These data are taken from the World Co-operative Monitor, a project promoted by the International Co-operative Alliance (ICA) in collaboration with the European Research Institute on Co-operative and Social Enterprises (Euricse). The purpose of the project is to take a step forward in measuring the dimensions of co-operatives, and to make an initial attempt at quantifying the economic and social impact of the largest co-operatives worldwide.

The chapters in Part VI report various national case studies. In Chapter 19, Xabier Barandiaran and Javier Lezaun analyse and report on the Basque town of Mondragón, which has given its name to one of the most significant experiences in co-operative organization and workers' ownership anywhere in the world. The Mondragón co-operative movement was founded in the 1940s with the establishment of a handful of educational institutions in and around Mondragón, and soon gave rise to a multitude of worker co-operatives, primarily in industrial manufacturing sectors. Today, the co-operative group encompasses more than 250 co-operatives, employing more than 74,000 workers across industrial and non-industrial sectors, and generating €12.5 billion in annual revenue.

The academic and practitioner literature on ESOPs has developed significantly over past decades, particularly with respect to their organizational impact (of improved corporate growth and productivity), and the different types of ESOPs (leveraged and non-leveraged). Yet, despite ESOPs being well conceptualized, the deals struck in the real world are often more complex endeavours than might be suggested by the literature. While there are examples of ESOP deals that effectively take firms into employee ownership in a one-stage process, it is often the case that ownership is transferred in multiple steps, which adds layers of complexity to the deal-making process. The focus here is generally on leveraged ESOPs where a worker-trust set up by a business receives a loan to buy company shares, with the loan being paid off by the company (rather than by the workers directly) out of its future revenues. ESOPs are unique in requiring no use of worker savings or investment to create employee ownership. In addressing this complexity, Daniel Tischer and John Hoffmire in Chapter 20 introduce and discuss various concepts of ESOPs, before providing a detailed description of what an 'add-on transaction' entails. In doing so, the authors are particularly interested in describing the key steps of such a deal, with a focus on the impact upon the business and on the employee-owners. The chapter provides valuable insights into the widely used practice of multi-tranche ESOPs. Understanding who the agents are that are involved in the process—as well as the impact and potential pitfalls of add-on transactions—is crucial factors in developing ESOPs as an alternative to external buy-outs.

In Chapter 21, Sara Depedri analyses social co-operatives as a new form that first emerged in Italy during the 1980s as a bottom-up phenomenon. The first regulation on social co-operatives was enacted in Italy through the 'Law 381/1991'. This chapter illustrates the emergence, the evolution, and the most recent trends of Italian social co-operation in order to identify the main traits that helped social co-operatives to become a successful organizational form for the provision of welfare services. The chapter also contributes to evaluating the added value of this co-operative form within its socio-economic context.

Over past decades, the discussion on climate change, together with catastrophic events in the power sector, has raised global interest in radical policy changes in these areas. Since the year 2000, Germany's 'Renewable Energy Sources Act' (EEG) has been a forerunner in triggering large-scale decentralized deployment of renewable energy. Although built on a relatively large social consensus, the consequences of the German 'Energiewende' have also raised conflicts between communities on the one hand, and investor-oriented project developers on the other. In Chapter 22, Markus Hanisch reviews the increasing role of energy co-operatives as a means to involve civil society, mitigate conflicts in planning, and distribute subsidies more evenly amongst a variety of often rural stakeholders.

Chapter 23 by Michela Giovannini and Marcelo Vieta focuses on co-operatives in four representative Latin American countries—Argentina, Chile, Cuba, and Mexico—highlighting their historical trajectories, evolutionary trends, and potential for further development. These representative countries reflect the range of co-operative development in Latin America, both historically and contemporaneously. Each country, for instance, shows different paths of co-operative development related to, amongst other factors, different levels of support by their governments, community-based responses to neo-liberal policies, and varying connections to broader social movements. The chapter also presents a number of experiences that are of particular interest today in the region, such as worker-recuperated enterprises, indigenous co-operatives, community-owned agricultural co-operatives, co-operatives managing general interest social services, and, most controversially, public services and work-for-welfare co-operatives created by the state.

Although globalization has many facets, a key aspect is the increasing domination of market relations over other kinds of social relations. This phenomenon has created an increased interest in alternative forms of economic development that are more consistent with community values, as well as an interest in the nature and importance of social relationships themselves—regardless of any possible contribution to economic success. Chapter 24 by Lou Hammond Ketilson provides numerous examples of the role that the social economy and, in particular, co-operatives play in developing and sustaining communities in Canada, which they do by building and strengthening physical, personal, and social infrastructures in remote, rural, and indigenous areas, as well as in urban settings.

In Chapter 25, Joseph R. Blasi and Douglas L. Kruse argue that US worker ownership, which is already significant, could and should be expanded through improved public policies. The USA spends about $1 trillion every five years on tax incentives for businesses. To expand worker ownership, the White House could develop an Office of Broad-Based Capitalism. Stock market companies should only be allowed deductions for executive pay if they have a broad-based worker-ownership plan for all employees. Moreover, all Federal business tax subsidies could be conditioned on a broad-based worker-ownership plan. However, worker ownership will never spread until earlier tax incentives for Employee Stock Ownership Plans (ESOPs) in stock market companies repealed by President George H. W. Bush, are reinstated with additional encouragements for all companies to make stock grants to workers. Finally, Congress needs to make it easier for small-business people retiring to sell the company to its employees, and for private equity firms to spin off their portfolio companies to the workers. These policy strategies can be adapted to understanding policy choices in other nations where corporate tax incentives play a role in their economies.

It has long been acknowledged that co-operatives can buffer economic insecurity, offset some of the vagaries of market capitalism, and enhance social solidarity. An interesting—and in many respects peculiar—facet of the history of co-operatives is how worker (or producer) co-operatives and consumer co-operatives have evolved along completely separate trajectories. Yet production and consumption are inextricably bound up in tight configurations. Moreover, no one is exclusively a producer or consumer, and we repeatedly and iteratively change roles, often numerous times during the course of a single day. We seem, though, to be at an auspicious moment to rectify this anomalous situation. Chapter 26, by Maurie J. Cohen, outlines the notion of multi-stakeholder co-operatives, and highlights how worker-consumer co-operatives can bridge this divide. These organizations can also inculcate democratic values and solidaristic social relations—which might contribute to a process of innovating a new system of social organization over the coming decades.

In the United States, the work that home health aides perform provides a valuable service to society. Changing views of care are necessitating care models in which people who are elderly or have disabilities receive care in their homes or communities. There is a growing gap between the sharply increasing need for those requiring care and the pool of people from whom caregivers are drawn, which is increasing much more gradually. The poor quality of home care jobs exacerbates this problem. Chapter 27, by Daphne Berry, examines worker attitudes across three home care facilities under different governance structures—a worker co-operative, a for-profit business with no participation or ownership by workers ('conventional'), and a not-for-profit business. The study uses data from multiple sources, describing worker attitudes across the different types of organization. The research shows that aides at the worker co-operative were significantly less likely to leave, and were more satisfied and committed to their jobs.

Co-operative banks have been an important part of the national banking systems in Europe since their creation as member-based organizations in the middle of the nineteenth century. Focusing on the Raiffeisenbanks and Volksbanks experiences in

Germany and Austria, Chapter 28 by Holger Blisse and Detlev Hummel recalls various phases in the history of these developments, concentrating on the switch from member-based to customer-oriented banks, and analyses possible strategies for reactivating a meaningful membership, to reposition these banks as responsible institutions for local and social problems.

As noted, an ESOP is the most common vehicle for broad-based worker ownership in the United States. The next chapter provides more detail about ESOPs. An ESOP is a legal trust that holds the shares of all the workers in a firm and thus makes it possible to have long-lasting employee ownership. Under US law, existing companies can contribute stock or cash to this trust in order to buy shares of company stock to establish worker ownership gradually. Such trusts can borrow funds to buy shares on behalf of workers in order to establish significant, majority, or even 100 per cent worker ownership in one single transaction. All company contributions to the employee trust, whether in cash or stock—or to repay loans used to buy stock for workers—give the company a tax deduction under US Federal Law. In addition, interest on the loan is tax deductible. These schemes are analysed in detail by Corey Rosen in Chapter 29. The international relevance of the ESOP is that it is an example of a trust mechanism that can pull together individual worker-ownership interests into one trust entity, thus helping to ensure the continuity of worker ownership.

Chapter 30 by Andrew Pendleton and Andrew Robinson reviews the development of new forms of employee ownership in Britain since the 1980s. It compares trust-based and direct forms of ownership, as well as hybrids of the two, drawing attention to the perceived benefits of each. The chapter then considers various influences on the development of these forms of ownership. The authors highlight the role of political factors within a broader context of economic change. Finally, drawing on a research project still underway at the time of writing, Pendleton and Robinson discern four main circumstances in which employee ownership is created, noting that those involved in ownership conversions vary according to these circumstances. This in turn impacts upon the forms of ownership and governance that are adopted.

The chapters in Part VII present various corporate and sector case studies. In Chapter 31, William Davies considers the themes of agency, democracy, and co-operation in relation to corporate governance. Corporate governance has long been theorized and criticized within the template provided by neoliberalism. This assumes that social relations will become most honest and productive when modelled on market relations. Yet this also results in a business culture of mistrust and endless audit. Participatory governance forms have certain advantages, which need to be clearly understood and articulated. Firstly, they treat dialogue as a better principle for relations within the firm than competition. And secondly, they treat ambiguity of value as a virtue, which can yield innovation. However, there is insufficient training, expertise, and practice for these advantages to come properly to light. As a result, we remain too often stuck with a dysfunctional model, whose failures are met with calls for more of the same.

Chapter 32's examination of the life cycle, institutional structure, governance, and policy environment of co-operatives in the Argan oil sector in south-west Morocco, by

Zahir Dossa, sets out the successes and setbacks of the co-operative model as a suitable tool for economic and social development in rural areas. Despite the positive development outcomes that Argan oil co-operatives reached, they strayed from four basic co-operative tenets: democratic decision-making, equitable profit distribution, open membership, and member education on co-operatives. Starting from this analysis, the chapter considers the relationship between the success of the Argan oil co-operatives on the one hand and their abandonment of the basic co-operative principles on the other. The chapter seeks to understand the conditions that make co-operatives feasible and effective in particular environments and how co-operatives, or employee-centric firms, can be adapted to their environments, or vice versa, in order to bring about economic and social development.

The co-operative and mutual model has been closely connected with the development of the Fair Trade movement, both in terms of producer groups and wholesale organizations. Both share key elements of participation and empowerment, and pay careful attention to economic development and fair governance. Chapter 33 by Alex Nicholls and Benjamin Huybrechts examines the development of Fair Trade globally, and explores some of these connections in detail.

The UK Government's agenda for public sector transformation has resulted in a growing number of public service mutuals. Despite this, there is little understanding of the transition experiences of such organizations, and the processes of organizational change necessary for becoming a mature public service mutual. Chapter 34 by Ruth Yeoman describes the transition experience of Rochdale Boroughwide Housing (RBH), a provider of affordable housing which is now a dual constituency mutual, jointly owned by staff and tenants. A key characteristic of the change was the need for individuals to craft new self-identities which held in tension the identity of being a co-owner with the identity of being a public service worker or tenant. Smith and Graetz's concept of 'paradox management' is used by Yeoman to investigate the proliferation of dualities in RBH, giving rise to dualistic thinking which generates new values from which individuals can craft positive self-identities, as well as develop the skills for managing a hybrid organization. Although the stresses and strains of change were not avoided, the co-owners of RBH have nonetheless created new individual and organizational capabilities which have the potential to not only sustain the organization, but to also raise the innovative and resilient capacities of the communities it exists to serve.

In French rural areas, in order to respond to economic and social needs, the co-operative movement has always developed entrepreneurship models based on democracy, solidarity, responsibility of actors, proximity, transparency, and consideration of future generations. Amongst others, the 11,500 farm machinery co-operatives (coopératives d'utilisation de matériel agricole, or 'Cuma') which are active in the French countryside can testify to this dynamism. Based on case studies, Chapter 35 by Franck Thomas outlines the current developments of collective entrepreneurship models in the context of territory-oriented agricultural activities in France.

Co-operatives have played a significant role in the agricultural sector in China, particularly since the promulgation of a first national co-operative law in 2007. Chapter 36 by Li Zhao offers an analysis of the diversity and dynamics of agricultural co-operatives in contemporary China. A multi-dimensional typology of co-operatives is proposed in order to provide a framework of analysis. This analysis enables one to understand the diversified driving forces, the operational patterns, and the organizational missions of agricultural co-operatives in China. The significant contribution provided by each type of co-operative to poverty reduction, work integration, and local community development is considered. The chapter concludes with a discussion on the challenges and opportunities for the future development of Chinese co-operatives.

The chapters in Part VIII consider the future of co-operatives, starting in Chapter 37 by Mark J. Kaswan with the United States, which has a long and proud tradition of co-operative labour arrangements. However, worker co-operatives today make up a very small proportion of the US economy. The chapter discusses the history and current extent of worker co-operatives in the USA, as well as the particular challenges and opportunities for growth and change in the worker co-operative sector. Kaswan also considers the character of the sector in terms of its principal objectives and orientation.

Co-operative identity is complex, and consists of several, at times interrelated aspects—which distinguish it from non-profit associations or for-profit companies. Co-operatives are characterized by a specific purpose, and when a legal entity has a defining feature that relates to the objective pursued, the organizational law of that entity has to define its particular identity in light of that objective. Given this, Chapter 38 by Antonio Fici considers the importance of co-operative law in stipulating the co-operative identity and preserving its distinguishing features. The chapter thus outlines the essential elements which characterize co-operative enterprises: the mutual purpose, co-operative transactions, co-operative activities with non-members, and the social function of co-operatives.

In Chapter 39, David T. Llewellyn's starting point is that there is merit in having a diversity of ownership structures and business models in a financial sector (not the least being in enhancing competition), and that mutuals, co-operatives, and similar ownership models have a substantial contribution to make to corporate diversity. The chapter considers the arguments that were used in the UK in favour of conversion of mutual building societies and insurance companies to shareholder value institutions. The chapter reviews the outcome. Llewellyn concludes that the arguments put forward for conversion were largely bogus at the time, and have since been found to be irrelevant, at best. Nonetheless, members of converting institutions voted for it—which is not surprising given that the 'windfalls' implied an inter-generation transfer of wealth from previous and potentially future members to the current cohort of members. Comparison is made between the UK and other European countries with regard to conversions, where we find that in most other European countries such conversions are not possible because residual net worth is regarded as being held in perpetuity within the institution, rather than as a saleable asset owned by the current cohort of members.

Chapter 40 by Johnston Birchall examines the performance of several types of member-owned business since the financial crisis of 2007–8. It summarizes evidence for three financial co-operative sectors (European co-operative banks, the worldwide credit union sector, and the UK building societies), finding that they have each proven to be less risky, more stable, and on a range of indicators more successful than conventional investor-owned banks. Birchall then examines the performance of retail consumer co-operatives, insurance mutuals, retailer-owned wholesalers, and employee-owned businesses. The wider benefits of having a significant member-owned sector are then considered. The conclusion is that resilience cannot be taken for granted—it has to be competed for in each industry sector, and the results will vary depending on the extent to which, in each sector, they can realize the 'co-operative advantage'.

Chapter 41 by David Erdal discusses evidence that the design of business as a human institution can be improved far beyond the current template of corporations owned by financial institutions, a template which led to the near collapse of the global economy in 2007–9, with costly consequences for future generations of taxpayers. Re-evaluating business theory from a perspective of human evolution leads to the recognition that human autonomy and voluntary co-operation in every business require the rights currently bundled as 'ownership'—the rights to information, influence, and wealth—to be allocated, not to financiers, but to the individuals directly co-operating as participants in the wealth-creation process. Evidence is discussed showing that member-owned enterprises perform as well or better than conventionally structured business in terms of human and economic sustainability, and that the problems of financing such enterprises are soluble.

In the concluding Chapter 42, Charles Gould argues that the future success of the co-operative business model will depend on its ability to distinguish itself, not only from the standard corporate form, but also from the variety of social economy options. The long-standing and globally accepted Statement on Co-operative Identity sets forth the accepted Principles that define a co-operative. With the *Blueprint for a Co-operative Decade*, co-operatives are now prepared to position themselves as the most participatory business model, and as leaders in sustainability, at a time when they are being widely adopted as priorities by the emerging generation.

REFERENCES

Tischer, D., Yeoman, R., Michie, J., Nicholls, A., and White, S. (2016), 'An Evaluative Framework for Mutual and Employee-Owned Business', *Journal of Social Entrepreneurship*, published online 31 May 2016. DOI: 10.1080/19420676.2016.1190396

PART I

DIVERSITY AND COMPLEXITY OF MEMBER-OWNED ENTERPRISES

CHAPTER 1

···

THE IMPORTANCE
OF OWNERSHIP

···

JONATHAN MICHIE

1.1 INTRODUCTION

THE ownership of productive assets plays a crucial role in the functioning of any economy, and also has profound implications for other aspects of social life, such as the
degree of wealth and income inequality, the quality of working life, and the functioning
of democracy.

The rise of capitalism was based originally on private (and family) ownership of productive assets, and then led to the development of 'limited liability', which facilitated
the creation and growth of shareholder-owned companies. This private ownership of
the nation's productive resources—the factories, farms, mills, mines, railways, and so
forth—placed great economic power in the hands of the new class of owners, which in
turn tended to bestow upon them political power and social influence. The resulting
inequality of income, harsh working conditions, and economic instability—where economic downturns left the unemployed with no means to support themselves—led to
various alternative visions for a non-capitalist society, where wealth and power would
be more evenly distributed, crucially through some alternative to private ownership of
the 'means of production'. For Robert Owen this would be based on co-operative and
mutual principles; for Marx it would be through the 'appropriation of the appropria-
tors', with the means of production owned collectively by society—operating in the first
instance through the state.

These alternatives to capitalist ownership led in the centrally planned economies to
state ownership and planning, and across most Western European economies to the
'commanding heights' of the economy being government owned and controlled—the
utilities (gas, electricity, and water), major infrastructure industries (railways, post, telecommunications), and other large-scale enterprises such as coal mining, steel, and so
forth. To these would be added companies—and even whole industries—that were seen

to be failing in private hands, and which therefore needed to be nationalized in order to keep them operating—such as, in different countries at different times, shipbuilding and car production.

Alongside these forms of state ownership, co-operative and mutual ownership flourished to varying degrees—in the UK the Co-Op held a major market share in food retail up until the 1960s, before gradually losing out to the big supermarket chains.

From the early 1980s, Thatcherism in the UK led to privatization, and this then spread globally. With the collapse of the Soviet Union, this whole historical era of state ownership was pushed back significantly. There followed an era of 'capitalism unleashed' (Glyn 2006), with a shift back to private ownership (by individuals and shareholders) of companies, away from public and state ownership; a rolling back of public regulation of industries and sectors; a financialization of society, whereby ever-more relations became marketized, with fewer and fewer free and subsidized goods; and a resultant increase in inequality of wealth and income in almost every country of the world.

This new era of laissez-faire capitalism led to the global financial crisis of 2007–8, which in turn created the first global recession since the 1930s, in 2009—with world output and income levels actually declining (rather than just the rate of growth declining, as had happened in the downturns during the 'golden age of capitalism' of the 1950s and 1960s). Five years on, in 2014, the global economy had still not fully recovered, and the UK's levels of output and income were still lower than they had been five years previously.

Yet despite this major failure of free market capitalism, there have been no major alternatives gaining widespread support along the lines of the planned economies so far described, or social democratic control of the 'commanding heights' of the economy. Neither has there been a generally accepted alternative to the failed ideology and theory of neoclassical economics and laissez-faire capitalism which justified and promoted the era of capitalism unleashed, as had occurred in the 1930s with Keynes's *General Theory of Employment, Interest and Money* (1936).

It is true that the claims of 'an end of history' have been generally derided—most forcefully and convincingly by Milne (2012). And there have been socialist and social democratic governments elected across South America, and also in some European countries and even US cities. But in general, outside South America, whichever political party was in office at the time of the global financial crisis tended to suffer the political backlash. There has been no global consensus to replace capitalism unleashed.

This chapter considers what this sort of alternative might look like—for the UK and globally, in the short term and longer term. Just as the rise of capitalism led to the co-operative, Marxian and other critiques, and just as the crisis of the 1930s led to Keynesianism and social democracy across much of Western Europe and a new international order as fashioned at Bretton Woods, so the failure of capitalism unleashed needs to herald a new era of global economic development—and one which is sustainable environmentally, economically, and socially. It will require a more equal ownership of wealth and productive assets than the extremely unequal situation that has been created by the past twenty-five years or so of capitalism unleashed. And it demands a greater degree of diversity of ownership forms—private, state, and co-operative and mutual. This is needed to make the productive system more resilient. It would also be a way of tackling the otherwise relentless spiral of ever greater inequality.

1.2   FAILURES OF THE CURRENT OWNERSHIP MODEL

The Ownership Commission was established in 2010 by the Cabinet Minister Tessa Jowell MP to review the state of ownership in the UK, to examine the extent to which it supports or inhibits successful, long-term value creation by business in all its ownership guises—recognizing that given the scale of Britain's economic challenges, it was time to reassess whether the balance of ownership obligations and rights had been struck correctly (Ownership Commission 2012). The independent Commission recognized there was a growing awareness that in Britain one ownership type—the shareholder-owned public limited company (PLC)—dominates all others, to a degree not seen in other countries, nor seen in Britain prior to the privatizations and demutualizations from the 1980s that resulted in an even greater dominance of the PLC model. This creates a two-fold problem. Firstly, as will be argued, this lack of corporate diversity creates systemic weaknesses. Secondly, the PLC model itself has become prone to short-termism, and a lack of proper stewardship has led to a series of problems including the ballooning of executive pay, often unrelated to genuine organizational performance (as opposed to financial returns which may be manipulated precisely to generate executive bonuses even when those manipulations are harming rather than supporting the underlying fundamentals of the business).

The Commission argued that there are three broad preconditions for good ownership. Firstly, a healthy economy needs diverse ways through which ownership can express itself and be applied to various business models. The consequent diversity will give the system more resilience and more opportunity to experiment with ownership forms as they are appropriate for different business models and purposes. It will also give investors and savers a greater diversity of choice. Secondly, an ownership culture is needed which enables and encourages decisions to be taken on the basis of long-term results and outcomes, and takes its responsibility for good stewardship seriously. This will lift investment and innovation, and also create a richer ecology of more long-lived organizations. And thirdly, owners are needed to participate and engage in the strategies and behaviours of the firms they own; 'absentee shareholders' are bad for everyone.

Britain has disproportionately more PLCs than other economies, and concomitantly fewer small and medium-sized businesses (SMEs), with nothing to compare with the German Mittelstand. Likewise, we have fewer customer-owned mutual and employee-owned companies than elsewhere. Different ownership structures are associated with different business models, and each needs a critical mass to be deployed effectively.

1.2.1 Capitalism Unleashed

'Capitalism unleashed'—which reigned over the twenty-five years or so from the early 1980s' Thatcher/Reagan era through to its creation of the 2007–8 global financial crisis and 2009 international recession—tended to prioritize money-making through the financial markets, which alongside the bonus culture that encouraged speculative behaviour, and the lack of strong public ownership and regulation, created huge inequalities in income and wealth, and an inherently unstable economic system. Hence the calls to 'rebalance the economy', with more emphasis on the real economic activities of providing goods and services, investment, and exporting, as opposed to the financial speculation of the banking sector, much of which has no economic or social use, and which on the contrary can prove horrendously costly in both economic and social terms when the speculation fails and the economy suffers.

The UK economy has suffered more than most countries from this dominance of the 'City of London', and from the resulting short-termism (Fine and Harris 1985; Kitson and Michie 1996). Hence Winston Churchill's desire to see manufacturing more successful and the financial sector 'less proud', and Keynes's critique of market contagion and economic stagnation.

The financial services sectors of all countries are characterized by a degree of diversity in terms of ownership types and business models. This variety of business models creates a corresponding diversity in forms of corporate governance, risk appetite and management, incentive structures, policies and practices, and behaviours and outcomes. It also offers wider choice for consumers through enhanced competition that derives in part from the juxtaposition of different business models. The diversity of ownership forms and business models generally includes a balance between public and private ownership, with the private sector being distributed between shareholder-owned PLCs, other private ownership such as private equity, and a range of 'stakeholder ownership' models including co-operative banks, mutuals, and credit unions. However, the UK financial services sector is dominated disproportionately by a single business model, namely the large, shareholder-owned PLC. The demutualizations of the late 1980s onwards withdrew around 70 per cent of assets from the mutual building society and insurance sectors, thus substantially reducing their critical mass. For an excellent discussion of the importance and role of corporate diversity in the financial services sector, and of the important role to be played by state-owned and by co-operatively and mutually owned banks in countries across the world, see Butzbach and von Mettenheim (2014).

This domination of the shareholder ownership model, whose purpose is to maximize financial returns to the shareholders, proved a lethal combination with deregulation which led to the creation of new financial instruments, rising debt levels, and a bloated financial sector—generally referred to as a process of financialization. Ever greater risks were taken to drive up financial returns and 'shareholder value', culminating in the global financial crisis of 2007–8, which in turn created the first global recession since the

1930s, during 2009, from which the UK and global economies are only slowly recovering. As the Bank of England noted at the time:

> Policy action is needed to reduce the structural problems caused by banks that are too important to fail (TITF). Larger UK banks expanded much more rapidly than smaller institutions in the run-up to the crisis and have received disproportionate taxpayer support during this crisis. That reflected a misalignment of risks on TITF banks' balance sheets, due to implicit guarantees on their liabilities. (Bank of England 2010: 11)

This has left a substantial legacy problem, which is likely to constrain bank lending for some time to come (Llewellyn 2010). Alongside the macroeconomic costs, the interests of individual consumers were sacrificed by managers who were focused primarily on shareholder value. One of the original champions of the concept of shareholder value, Jack Welch, by 2009 concluded that it had been 'the dumbest idea in the world'. Alan Greenspan, the former chairman of the Federal Reserve—and described by the *Financial Times* as 'a high priest of laissez-faire capitalism' (Guerrera 2009)—announced in 2008 that the global financial crisis had exposed a 'mistake' in the free market ideology which had guided his eighteen-year stewardship of US monetary policy: 'I have found a flaw,' Greenspan announced, referring to his economic philosophy. 'I don't know how significant or permanent it is. But I have been very distressed by that fact'.(Clark and Treanor 2008)

1.2.2 Diversity of Ownership and Business Models

A major contribution to ensuring the necessary systemic stability is to create a more diverse financial services sector. Diversity of ownership and business models promotes systemic stability and is also good for customers because of the resulting increased competition and choice, quality of service, and fairness.

Andy Haldane, former Executive Director of Financial Stability and now Chief Economist at the Bank of England, has described well the way in which one of the factors that lay behind the 2007–8 global financial crisis was that individual institutions had been diversifying, and that while this might be thought to reduce risk, it does not do so if all are diversifying in the same way, so instead the system as a whole becomes less diverse (Haldane 2009: 18–19). It is a classic fallacy of composition, that what is good for one institution acting alone does not necessarily apply when you consider all of them together. In addition to increasing risk through reduced diversity, this process also had the effect of shifting risk from the shareholder-owned banks that moved into investment banking, to the public sector, on account of the Bank of England's obligation to act as Lender of Last Resort.

The Centre for European Policy Studies (CEPS) produced two comprehensive studies of diversity in European banking (Ayadi et al. 2009, 2010). Both reports emphasize the advantages of having diversity in banking structures and models, and illustrate this with case studies of several countries. The purpose of these reports is not to argue that one model is superior to others, but precisely that advantages accrue through diversity. Their first report, *Investigating Diversity in the Banking Sector in Europe* found that 'The most important conclusion is that the current crisis has made it even more evident than before how valuable it is to promote a pluralistic market concept in Europe and, to this end, to protect and support all types of ownership structures' (Ayadi et al. 2009: 3).

Thus, in a situation of uncertainty and unpredictability, we cannot know which model will prove to be superior in all possible future circumstances, so we ought to be rather cautious before destroying any successful corporate forms. The global economy is a complex system. An important point about complexity is that many complex systems are intrinsically unpredictable, even if we know *everything else* about them. Thus, the problem is not just that the economic future is uncertain, but that it is fundamentally unpredictable.[1] As *The Economist* notes:

> Just as an ecosystem benefits from diversity, so the world is better off with a multitude of corporate forms. (*The Economist* 2010: 58)

Variety is the evolutionary fuel in economic development as well as in biology (as detailed, for example, by Hodgson, 1993). Diversity is desirable across the economy, and diversity within the financial sector itself—both a variety of corporate forms and geographical dispersion, with a strong local and regional presence—tends to support a broader variety of corporate forms in the rest of the economy, which in turn enhances competition and consumer choice (Gagliardi 2009). And promoting corporate diversity in the financial services sector itself contributes greater local presence, as the PLCs tend to be more London based. Thus, promoting mutuality within financial services not only creates a more competitive and robust financial services sector, it also brings the added benefit of fostering a more diverse economy more generally, in both corporate and geographic terms.

The financial crisis, which was largely caused by the activities of private-sector banks, resulted in the UK Government giving them a bailout of perhaps £80bn. In addition, the Government borrowed in order to provide the fiscal boost that was co-ordinated internationally to prevent a slide into global depression. These costs, along with the additional hit to Government finances that a recession causes, as tax receipts fall and unemployment benefits and other such payments rise, combined to create the fiscal deficit and accumulated debt that we are all having to pay for through increased taxes and cuts in services. Given the financial, economic, and social costs of that global financial crisis and concomitant recession, a key priority for policy needs to be to put in place measures to prevent a reoccurrence in the future. Otherwise such problems may well

---

[1] I'm grateful to Geoff Hodgson for making this point about uncertainty, unpredictability, and complexity (private correspondence).

recur, whether that be ten, twenty, or thirty years from now. (And there is evidence that the incidence and frequency of bank crises around the world has increased over time—see, for example, Eichengreen and Bordo, 2002.)

1.3 What Policy Reforms are Required?

The history of capitalism can be seen as having developed through distinct phases. The 30-year 'Golden Age of Capitalism' (Marglin and Schor 1992) from the post-Second World War reconstruction of the late 1940s through to the 1970s was one, broadly, of a Keynesian commitment to full employment and to public institutions, ownership, and regulation, nationally and internationally, to ensure relatively stable economic growth and to prevent the disparities of income and wealth from expanding beyond certain limits. The subsequent 30 years of 'capitalism unleashed' did the opposite: the buffers and other institutional arrangements that had been put in place to prevent extreme inequalities and instability were systematically rolled back and repealed. Not surprisingly, extreme inequalities and instability returned to the economic system and society. Although this era witnessed periods of rapid economic growth, generally driven by unsustainable financial bubbles fuelled by consumer credit or sub-prime mortgages, overall economic growth was nonetheless lower than in the previous Keynesian era.

The policy reforms required today need to be seen in this broad historical context. We need a new era of global economic development. There probably is a fair degree of consensus globally about what such a new progressive era would look like, although implementing reforms in the face of vested interests is always difficult, and there is not the head of steam necessary as there was, say, following the global defeat of fascism in 1945. The challenge is thus political as well as ideological and economic.

What is needed now is a genuinely global 'Green New Deal', with a return to international economic co-operation, along the lines of the new international economic order that was being pressed for before the collapse of the Golden Age of Capitalism. Wealth and income inequality needs to be tackled through progressive taxation of both income and wealth, alongside a culture change that recognizes the economic and social damage wreaked by inequality, to create the economic basis for sustainable growth. Piketty (2014) has detailed the way in which capitalism inherently generates inequality; tackling this is not only vitally important, but cannot be done through a few minor reforms—it will require an epochal shift in values, policies, and practices.

Shifting to environmental sustainability also demands a historic change in direction for the economy and society. Ecological outcomes need to be placed and embedded at the forefront of public policy and corporate decision-making. Privately owned and shareholder-owned companies should be encouraged to take long-term investment decisions and to behave responsibly, via new requirements on corporate governance, a new ethos and ideology across society, and competition from the public sector—with public ownership at national, regional, and local levels offering a ready alternative to private ownership where this is seen to be failing—and likewise competition from co-operative, employee-owned, and mutual businesses.

Ownership is therefore key. A new era of global economic development needs to be underpinned by public ownership of major economic sectors. Alongside this, a dynamic and entrepreneurial co-operative and mutual sector could deliver social as well as economic benefits. Private ownership should increasingly be seen as the exception, where there is an obvious justification for it—otherwise co-operative, mutual, and public ownership should become natural options.

The British economy certainly needs to be rebalanced away from the 'City of London', towards the creation of goods and services across the breadth of the country, with companies operating on the basis of long-term and sustainable decision-making—socially, environmentally, and economically sustainable.

A Green New Deal needs to be at the heart of this—over the next 30-year generational epoch. Such developments are needed globally, just as they are in individual countries. Global financial speculation needs to be reined in with a 'new Bretton Woods' era of responsible economic and financial institutions on an international scale, which prioritize stability and sustainability.

Greater corporate diversity is needed domestically and internationally, with stronger public and mutual ownership, operating at local, regional, national, and international levels. The commitment of the UK's 2010 Coalition Government to increase the corporate diversity of the financial services sector was welcome in theory, but proved worthless in practice, given their failure to take the necessary action—or even to measure the degree of corporate diversity over time. This measurement was instead undertaken by the Oxford Centre for Mutual and Employee-Owned Business, which found that far from the Government delivering on their commitment, the situation actually deteriorated (see Michie and Oughton 2013, 2014).

Privately owned and shareholder-owned companies need to be required to focus on their corporate purpose, creating and providing goods and services, rather than being used as simply the vehicle for private speculation and personal enrichment.

This sort of economic alternative is viable and quite possible, domestically for the UK and globally. It would be the natural next era in global economic development. If pursued consciously, it could lead to further eras of progress subsequently, rather than another lurch back to 'capitalism unleashed'. As the Golden Age of Capitalism was running out of steam in the early 1970s, alternatives were being promoted domestically and globally to take forward the social democratic project to a new era, in more far-reaching ways, from the 'wage-earner funds' in Sweden—which could have increasingly moved the bulk of the economy beyond a narrow capitalist outlook, with corporate ownership being increasingly collective, held on behalf of employees collectively—to the demands for a new international economic order that would have delivered fair prices to producers, in the same sort of way as the Fair Trade Movement is now attempting.

The challenge is twofold: firstly, we need a new political economy in place of the failed orthodoxy of neoclassical economics. And secondly we need public policy based upon an understanding of how markets actually work—namely, left to themselves, they create inequalities of income and wealth, inherent instability, and social and environmental degradation. Instead, for economic growth and development that is innovative and sustainable economically, socially, and environmentally, policy activism is required that includes in its armoury the innovative use of public ownership at local, regional, national, and international levels; progressive taxation of income, wealth, and expenditure; and reformed corporate governance to promote long-termism, including through the use of ownership stakes for employees and other stakeholders.

1.4 CONCLUSION

The Ownership Commission set out five pillars of good ownership:

i. *Corporate pluralism*: a plurality of ownership forms provides more opportunity to align the form of ownership with the appropriate business model, promotes more resilience to shocks within individual sectors and across the wider economy, allows savers and investors more avenues through which to save and invest, and gives consumers greater choice.

ii. *Owners have responsibility as stewards*: shareholders, trustees, investment management companies and directors have a stewardship obligation alongside their fiduciary responsibilities. Incorporation is a privilege, which should be associated with a business purpose that owners choose to pursue. Boards thus have both rights and responsibilities. 'Fiduciary responsibilities' should be widened so directors have a 'duty of stewardship' to deliver the business purpose, rather than at present just to 'have regard' to non-fiduciary obligations.

iii. *Ownership rights are contingent on accepting shared responsibilities*: owners can only expect to exercise their rights if they are committed to the organization and its purpose.

iv. *Owners have multiple aims, preoccupations, and interest*: the system must be careful not to prioritize the interests of short-term transactional owners.

v. *The more engaged owners and employees are with the business, the more likely it is to succeed*: employee engagement and participation enhances organizational performance.

The Commission went on to set out detailed recommendations for promoting this sort of good corporate ownership, including requiring directors to have a 'duty of stewardship', with similar measures to encourage long-term decision-making by institutional shareholders. The Commission also noted the success of German small- and medium-sized business with their access to largely state-provided long-term funding, research, and advice through the Fraunhofer Institutes, and a vibrant apprenticeship system. And, of course, the UK is almost unique as regards the ease with which their companies can be taken over including by hostile bids; a threat which adds to the short-term pressure on share price and dividend pay-outs, rather than being committed to long-term investment, research and development, and training.

In terms of the UK economy, the Labour Party Leader Ed Miliband was thus absolutely correct to identify predatory capitalism as one of the major problems for the UK economy (Miliband 2011). This needs to be tackled by productive firms being promoted, including through public and mutual ownership.

REFERENCES

Ayadi, R., Arbak, E., Valverde, S. Carbo, Fernandez, F. Rodriguez, and Schmidt, R. H. (2009), *Investigating Diversity in the Banking Sector in Europe: The Performance and Role of Savings Banks* (Brussels: Centre for European Policy Studies).

Ayadi, R., Llewellyn, D. T., Schmidt, R. H., Arbak, E., and De Groen, W. P. (2010), *Investigating Diversity in the Banking Sector in Europe: Key Developments, Performance and Role of Co-operative Banks* (Brussels: Centre for European Policy Studies,).

Bank of England (2010), *Financial Stability Report*, Issue Number 27, June (London: Bank of England).

Butzbach, Olivier and von Mettenheim, Kurt (2014), 'Introduction', in Butzbach and von Mettenheim, eds, *Alternative Banking and Financial Crisis* (London: Pickering & Chatto), 1–10.

Clark, Andrew and Treanor, Jill (2008), 'Greenspan—I was wrong about the economy. Sort of', *The Guardian*, 24 October.

Eichengreen, B. and Bordo, M. (2002), 'Crisis Now and Then: What Lessons from the Last Era of Globalisation?', NBER Working Paper 8716, National Bureau of Economic Research, January.

Fine, Ben and Harris, Laurence (1985), *Peculiarities of the British Economy* (London: Lawrence & Wishart).

Gagliardi, F. (2009), 'Financial Development and the Role of Co-operative Firms', *Small Business Economics: An Entrepreneurship Journal*, 32(4), 439–64.

Glyn, Andrew, (2006), *Capitalism Unleashed: Finance, Globalisation and Welfare* (New York: Oxford University Press).

Guerrera, Francesco (2009), 'Welch Rues Short-Term Profit "Obsession" ', *Financial Times*, 12 March.

Haldane, Andrew (2009), 'Rethinking the Financial Network', Speech to Financial Student Association in Amsterdam, April.

Hodgson, Geoffrey, (1993), *Economics and Evolution: Bringing Life Back into Economics* (Cambridge, UK and Ann Arbor: Polity Press, and University of Michigan Press).

Keynes, John Maynard (1936), *The General Theory of Employment, Interest and Money* (London: Macmillan for the Royal Economic Society).

Kitson, Michael and Michie, Jonathan (1996), 'Britain's Industrial Performance Since 1960: Underinvestment and Relative Decline', *The Economic Journal*, 106(434) (January), 196–212.

Llewellyn, David T. (2010), *The Global Banking Crisis and the Post-Crisis Banking and Regulatory Scenario* (Amsterdam: Amsterdam Centre for Corporate Finance, University of Amsterdam).

Marglin, Stephen A. and Schor, Juliet B., eds (1992), *The Golden Age of Capitalism: Reinterpreting the Postwar Experience* (Oxford: Clarendon Press).

Michie, Jonathan and Oughton, Christine (2013), 'Measuring Diversity in Financial Services Markets: A Diversity Index', Centre for Financial & Management Economics Discussion Paper No. 113, London: SOAS.

Michie, Jonathan and Oughton, Christine (2014), *Measuring Diversity in Financial Services Markets: An Update to the Diversity Index* (Oxford: Oxford Centre for Mutual & Employee-owned Business, Kellogg College, University of Oxford).

Miliband, Ed. (2011), Speech to the Social Market Foundation, London, November 17.

Milne, Seumas (2012), *The Revenge of History: The Battle for the 21st Century* (London: Verso).

Ownership Commission (2012), *Plurality, Stewardship and Governance: Report from the Ownership Commission* (London: Mutuo).

Piketty, Thomas (2014), *Capital in the Twenty-First Century* (Cambridge, MA: Harvard University Press).

The Economist (2010), 'The Eclipse of the Public Company', 21 August, 58.

CHAPTER 2

ENTREPRENEURIAL PLURALISM

GIOVANNI FERRI AND ANGELO LEOGRANDE

2.1 INTRODUCTION

WE notice that, either explicitly or implicitly, economic manuals and policy debates generally assume an archetypical form of enterprise: the private limited company (PLC), which is frequently viewed as a public company, a large listed enterprise with dispersed shareholders. Consequently, performance is measured in the ability to maximize profit. Instead, non-archetypical enterprise forms are described as anomalous, immature, and possibly the result of unstable constructions that are waiting to evolve into public companies.

We oppose such assumptions on both positive and normative grounds. First, we illustrate that the view based on a 'single enterprise model' is fallacious and that available data and literature strongly reject this hypothesis. Any country has a much richer configuration of enterprises and is not based just on one model. We demonstrate that, also in the most advanced market economies and even in the USA, the share of enterprises that do not merely maximize profits reaches a relevant size. Second, we argue that the theoretical approach that only considers the archetypical form of enterprise is misleading. Specifically, some scholars claim that in certain circumstances non-archetypical enterprises are superior,[1] and theory predicts that entrusting production to non-purely profit-maximizing enterprises can be efficient any time there is some form of market failure. Clearly, this is the case in labour and credit markets, where inescapable information asymmetries between the transacting parties permeate the market set-up. Such asymmetries cause non-trivial principal–agent problems that are impossible to tackle

---

[1] See, e.g. Borzaga and Tortia (2015) for a study on the superiority of co-operative enterprises in particular contexts.

via market incentives only. In addition to this, situations of imperfect competition—caused by technology-/network-induced economies of scale—provide further grounds where pure profit maximization reveals itself to be undesirable. Finally, market failures and imperfect competition tend to make the arena particularly unfitting for purely profit-maximizing enterprises. It is useful to interpret entrepreneurial pluralism in light of the Stakeholder vs. Shareholder theory debate (Ferri and Leogrande 2015).

The positive and normative argument we propose suggests that picturing a productive sector that is characterized by 'entrepreneurial pluralism' is both more realistic and more fruitful.

In this chapter, Section 2.1 collects information on the size of the non-archetypical enterprise sector in various countries, and demonstrates that the mainstream focus on the solely profit-maximizing PLC is strikingly ungrounded. Drawing on prominent contributions developed in recent decades, Section 2.2 builds the normative case for 'entrepreneurial pluralism' as the most promising approach to the theory of the enterprise. In the conclusions we summarize the chief findings and implications of the discussion and recommend affirmative action in favour of entrepreneurial pluralism.

2.2 Positive Approach: How Reality Does Not Conform to the 'Single Enterprise Model'

We claim that the single form—possibly linked to an evolutionary view of entrepreneurial forms—raises two empirical puzzles. First, the truth is, entrepreneurial pluralism is the norm rather than the exception, and wherever we look we can spot enterprises that are not even PLCs. Most of them are small in size[2] and wish neither to become large nor to list in the stock exchange. A large number of enterprises do not maximize profit—at least not as their sole objective. Second, we observe that non-archetype enterprises not only do not disappear but they often thrive.

We draw on the literature with the purpose of shedding light on potential causes and effects of entrepreneurial pluralism. We focus specifically on mutual producer/consumer associations, social enterprises, co-operative enterprises, and family firms.[3] Mutuality, the pursuit of a social goal or the purpose of serving members, obviously leads producer/consumer associations and social and co-operative enterprises to having different goals with respect to archetypical enterprises and, consequently, to

---

[2] A notable exception is agricultural co-operatives, where economies of scale lead to large dimension (Tortia et al. 2013).

[3] This way we underestimate non-archetypical enterprises where also state-owned enterprises (SOEs) belong: e.g. on Forbes Global 2000 data, Kowalski et al. (2013) find that SOEs are only 3 per cent of OECD firms but 46 per cent of BRICS firms.

deviate from profit maximization. This is also true for family firms since, due to their nature, they are subject to certain context constraints that tend to shape their aims at odds with those of PLCs and interfere with profit maximization. These context constraints span from the need to transfer the enterprise—an essential part of the family's wealth—across generations to having to cater to the stakeholders and the community around the firm's establishment (Cennamo et al. 2012; Miller et al. 2008; Mitchell et al. 2011).

Collecting cross-country data on the scope of non-archetypical types of enterprises is demanding. The search comes across the layer of institutional ignorance of these phenomena. There are no official statistics and one has to rely on occasional information sources. This fact is in itself revealing: 'In a performance-oriented society, what you measure affects what you do. If you have the wrong measures, you can wind up doing the wrong thing,' asserted Joe Stiglitz in presenting the Stiglitz-Sen-Fitoussi (2009) report on sustainability. In other words, non-purely profit-maximizing enterprises go unmeasured because they are generally considered trivial. To the contrary, we can demonstrate that these enterprises do matter.

Let us lay out some basic data. Salamon et al. (2004) estimate the size of the non-profit sector—only a part of non-archetypical enterprises—in 40 developed, emerging, and developing countries. On average, (median) 4.8 per cent (4.2 per cent) of the total workforce of these countries is employed in this sector (Figure 2.1). The maximum and minimum values have been registered, respectively, in the Netherlands (14.4 per cent) and in Mexico (0.4 per cent).

In turn, Coopseurope (2010) estimates the extent of the co-operative sector, which is not included in Salamon et al. (2004), in 31 European countries.

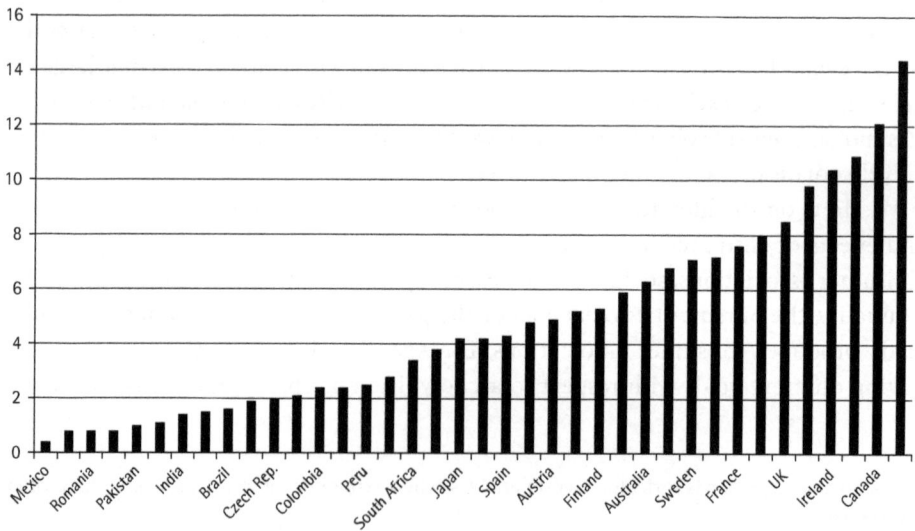

FIGURE 2.1 Extent of non-profit workforce on total workforce.

Source: Authors' calculations on data from CNP (2004).

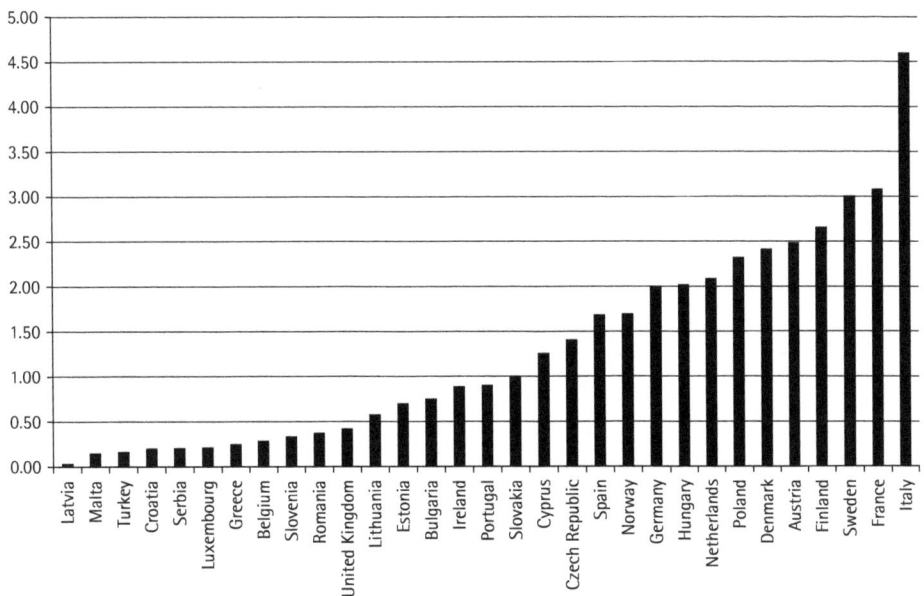

FIGURE 2.2 Extent of co-operative workforce on total workforce.

Source: Authors' calculations on data from Coopseurope (2010).

The co-operative share of the work force is 1.8 per cent with the peak in Italy (4.6 per cent) and the trough in Latvia (0.04 per cent; Figure 2.2).

By combining the two databases above we obtain data for 19 European countries. If we add the non-profit workforce to the co-operative workforce we come up with a weighted average of 7.7 per cent of the total workforce across this sample of countries, with a maximum of 16.5 per cent for the Netherlands and a minimum of 1.2 per cent for Romania (Figure 2.3).

The preliminary indication we obtain from examining the non-profit and the co-operative sectors is that we are not talking about peanuts. We are dealing with a close to 8 per cent average share of the workforce and this figure is twice as high in a strong economy like that of the Netherlands.

However, the largest contribution to the non-purely profit-maximizing sector derives from family businesses. Also in this case no official statistics are available and we therefore have to rely on occasional studies. Mandl (2008), for example, suggests that this phenomenon is quite substantial in Europe. The share of the workforce in family businesses is quantified for 12 EU countries, starting from a minimum of 25 per cent in Luxembourg, to reach intermediate values in the order of 50 per cent in Estonia, Ireland, Portugal, and Germany, and reaching a maximum of more than 90 per cent for Italy (Figure 2.4). However, we must keep in mind that these shares might be overstated as they are built not on the basis of true statistical investigations but by compiling the opinion of various experts.

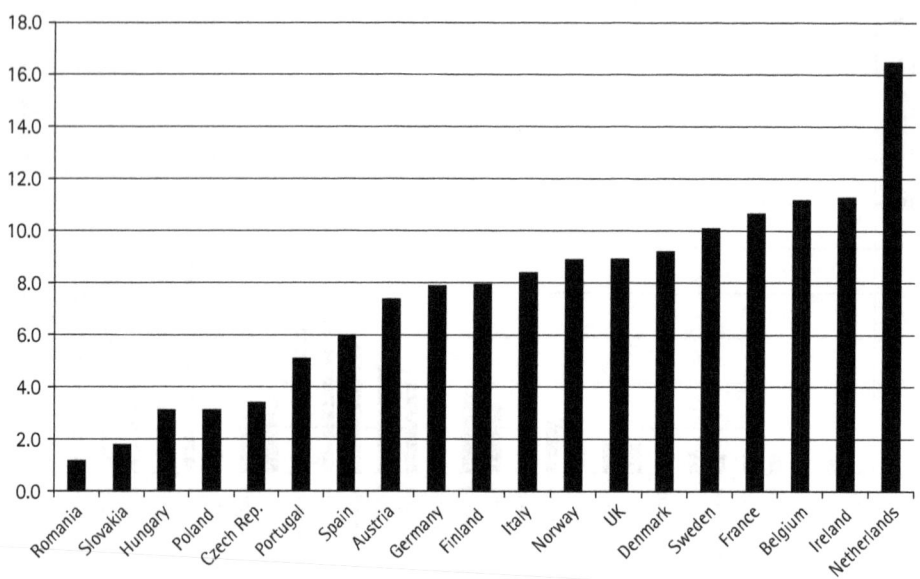

FIGURE 2.3 Extent of non-profit plus co-operative workforce on total workforce.
Source: Authors' calculations on data from CNP (2004) and Coopseurope (2010).

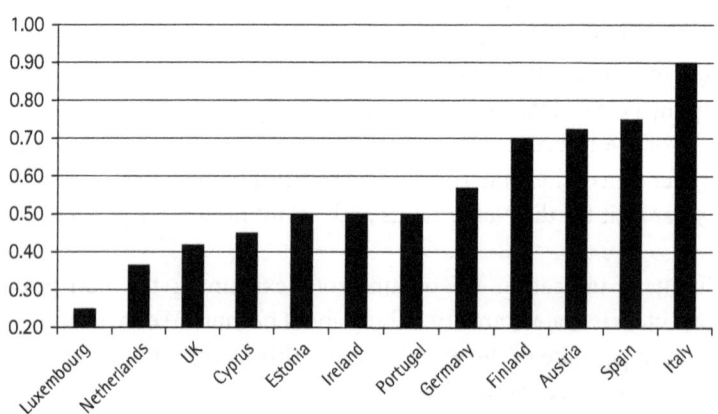

FIGURE 2.4 Extent of family business workforce on total workforce.
Source: Authors' calculations on data from Mandl (2008).

   This limitation prompts us to try to confirm the results through statistical investigations. For the USA, Astrachan and Carey Shanker (2003) estimate the family business workforce share at 27 per cent in 2000. More recently, Ferri et al. (2014) estimate the share for Italy at about 70 per cent in 2013. If we sum this data and look at the non-profit sector we see that in the USA more than one third of the workforce belongs to non-purely profit-maximizing enterprises. Analogously, when we sum family business, non-profit, and co-operative data in Italy we obtain a figure that is close to three-fourths.

A second important aspect we wish to point out is that we do not observe non-arche-typal enterprises disappear. On the contrary, they often thrive. If finding data for a single point is difficult, obtaining reliable time series is even more challenging. For co-opera-tives we can refer to ICA-Euricse (various years), which collects the turnover of the 300 largest co-operatives at the global level. If we compare the first available year, 2008, with the two most recent years, 2011 and 2012, we see the total turnover rising from $1.6 tril-lion to, respectively, $2.58 and $2.62 trillion. As a percentage of world GDP, the turnover of the global 300 largest co-operatives increased from 2.6 per cent in 2008 to 3.6 per cent in both 2011 and 2012.[4] Thus, there is no indication that co-operative enterprises are subsiding. With regards to family firms, we can notice that even *The Economist* (2014) reports that 'Companies controlled by founding families remain surprisingly important and look set to stay so.' The article also lists the ten biggest family firms that were fairly successful in 2013 at the global level.[5] Four are USA-based firms (Walmart, the largest, with $476.3 billion revenue, Phillips, Ford, and McKesson), one is German (Volkswagen), one is Anglo-Swiss (Glencore), one Korean (Samsung), one Italian (Exor), one Russian (Lukoil), and one Taiwanese (Foxconn). So, family enterprises also do not appear to be on the retreat.

2.3 NORMATIVE APPROACH: WHY 'ENTREPRENEURIAL PLURALISM' IS THE RIGHT WAY TO GO

On normative grounds, though hitherto unable to dent the mainstream view we have set out, progress in the theories of industrial organization, corporate governance, stakeholder inclusion, and the common goods all seem to suggest that entrepreneurial pluralism may be welfare enhancing. Entrepreneurial pluralism links with corporate governance models. Shareholder Value (SHV) and Stakeholder Value (STV) are the two corporate governance models that are juxtaposed in the economic literature (Freeman et al. 2010). The main difference between STV and SHV maximization relates to the different economic constituencies holding subjective rights and legitimate interests towards which the strategic choices of the management are consciously directed. While organizations maximizing STV have the ability to develop management systems that take directly into account the interests of (some of the) stakeholders, such as employees and customers (Freeman 1984), shareholders are the only ones to actually play a tangible

---

[4] For social co-operatives, there are signs of vitality in Italy. A 2014 Euricse and Alleanza delle Cooperative report finds that through the crisis (from 2008 to 2011) their total employees grew by 8.2 per cent (http://www.linkiesta.it/cooperative-sociali-italia, accessed 5 September 2016).

[5] *The Economist* considers family firms those where a family has the largest stake (at least 18 per cent) and power to appoint the CEO.

role in SHV maximization. Some management scientists have defined stakeholders as the essential economic actors for a firm's survivorship (Stewart et al. 1963), or as those who are related to the firm in order to achieve their personal goals (Rheman 1968).

Stakeholder theory is interdisciplinary (Freeman et al. 2010). Some authors question whether it is a comprehensive doctrine in the sense of Rawls (1993). They reject this idea and suggest stakeholder theory is an organizational theory (Orts and Strudler 2002; Phillips 2003). Stakeholder theory is divided into three fundamental parts: a descriptive, an instrumental, and a normative part. Descriptive stakeholder theory illustrates what managers and companies actually do. Instrumental stakeholder theory consists of research on the outcomes of specific managerial behaviour. Normative stakeholder theory relates to what managers or corporations should do (Donaldson and Preston 1995).

Stakeholder theory links in a pragmatic framework the old topic of business and society. It overcomes all the dichotomies between business and ethics and business and society through a common cognition enforced in the decision-making process (Jones 1995). From another point of view, business ethicists and philosophers who study the theory of the firm and economic organizations appreciate stakeholder theory for having linked philosophy and management (Jones and Wicks 1999).

In the economic literature the debate between shareholder theory and stakeholder theory is often referred to as the Friedman vs. Freeman debate (Freeman 1984). Nobel Prize scholar Milton Friedman proposed that SHV maximization, that is, present profit maximization, is the only way for corporations to reach valuable social goals. On this issue, many cite the 1970 *New York Times Magazine* article 'The Social Responsibility of Business is to Increase its Profits', in which Friedman argues that business has a single social responsibility, and that is to use its resources and engage in activities designed to increase its profits, so long as it can do so while respecting the rules of the game. In other words, as long as it engages in open and free competition without deception or fraud (Friedman 1970).

Both SHV and STV theories are compatible with a society based on individualism and freedom, along an anti-collectivist view, as Freeman explains in the paper 'Stakeholder Theory: A Libertarian Defence' (Freeman and Phillips 2001). The scholar describes stakeholder theory as a choice of the management based on an individual's fundamental freedom. Stakeholder theorists stress the libertarian perspective of STV and argue against shareholder economy as a model of political economy (Phillips 2003), as proposed by some authors (Barnett 1997; Hutton 1995; Rustin 1997).

Economists who study the nexus between leadership and stakeholders (Friedman and Olk 1995; Nwanko and Richardson 1996; Heller 1997; Roberts and King 1989) highlight that stakeholder theory can be seen as a form of managerial choice theory. Not only the development of leadership characteristics in a single economic organization, but also the relationships among leaders across organizations can be efficiently developed in an STV model. STV decision theory builds ethically oriented and efficient leadership (Friedman and Olk 1995; Andreadis 2002; Hall et al. 2004; Thomas et al. 2004; Fubini et al. 2006; Stenberg 2007; Clement 2005; Covey and Merrill 2006).

Having illustrated the commonalities, we can now focus on the differences between SHV and STV theories to explain entrepreneurial pluralism. To understand the methodologies behind managers' choices, we must refer to the model that directly affects their rationality and reasonableness, referring to STV vs. SHV maximization. The main contrast stems from the diversity and plurality of economic agents that are consciously involved in a firm's strategic management. While in STV theory various groups, such as employees, customers, and environmentalists, often have a moral claim, in SHV theory is that a single group constituted by the shareholders has a moral claim (Freeman 1984). Indeed, stakeholder theorists separate legal fiduciary and moral non-fiduciary duties (Boatright 1994). On philosophical grounds, the main contrast between STV and SHV theories is that the first is able to overcome Goodpaster's paradox of a business without ethics and an ethics without business (Goodpaster 1991).

Economic organizations produce externalities, and corporate governance models have a direct effect on how economic organizations manage their externalities. Externalities can be positive or negative. Negative externalities are social costs disrupting common goods such as savings, financial stability, and social order. Negative externalities are generally related to environmentally and socially valuable aims and can be efficiently dealt with via STV maximization (Wood and Ross 2006, Klassen 1993). Positive externalities can sustain common goods like trust, financial stability, and savings. Whether an economic organization maximizes SHV or STV directly affects these common goods. Stakeholder theory shows that STV maximization produces good results when it comes to governing externalities. The presence of one or more categories of stakeholders and their involvement in governance can help develop mechanisms for managing externalities.

In the literature, common goods are characterized by positive externalities and absence of rivalry. Traditionally, common goods are managed by public institutions but due to the privatizations of the 1990s many of them have been assigned to the market economy (Stiglitz and Hoff 2005). However, this picture is not complete. In the present state of economic development, not only state and corporations juxtapose public enterprises and private profit-oriented corporations; something the economic literature presents at length as the state vs. market debate. Indeed, we also observe economic organizations that lie in between and, although they operate in the market they are neither private, in the sense of profit maximizing, nor public, since they rely on the association or co-operation between economic actors. These economic entities generally abide by STV maximization, often applying a model of democratic stakeholder governance. We see these economic organizations engaged in the administration of certain common goods.

The administration of these common goods is more rational in the case of STV economic organizations than for SHV economic organizations, since only the former may overcome the problem of the tragedy of commons. In the economic literature, especially in the English tradition of economics and political economy, the management of commons has always been a tough question for economists. How can we manage common goods efficiently without disrupting them? Nowadays, after the great privatization wave, economists are trying to understand which management models of economic organizations can solve the new version of the old tragedy of commons problem. Indeed, this problem is the limiting case of a broader issue linked to the ability of entrepreneurial pluralism to generate positive externalities (Borzaga and Tortia 2015). In this sense, the tragedy of commons arises when in the administration of a public good—or of a good that provides positive externalities—no rule limits access to, and at the same time, no economic organization is responsible for, the management of that public good. According to the tragedy of commons, certain economic actors use a common good without limits and irresponsibly and, therefore, over time, diminish it. Common goods are destroyed when economic agents use them to maximize their subjective utility in a non-tuism scenario.[6] In other words, pure utilitarian maximization applied to the administration of a common good undermines the good.[7]

The ability of the STV model to reduce negative externalities and create positive externalities is higher than that of the SHV, since only in the former are all the stakes affected by managers' choices considered in the decision-making process. The literature shows various examples of economic organizations that are devoted to the administration of common goods or goods with positive externalities and that are managed based on an STV-maximizing approach (Argadona 1998, Hartman 1996). To conclude, the STV-maximizing model can solve the tragedy of commons.

Another debate which remains opened in the literature regards the efficiency of the STV vs. the SHV model. Allen et al. (2009) apply a mathematical model to the question and find that stakeholder-oriented firms have lower relative output but higher prices, which can lead to higher value. Other scholars argue that maximizing the STV multi-objective function can be less competitive than maximizing the SHV single-objective function (Jensen 2000, Sundaram and Inkpoen 2004). Starting with Friedman (1970) many economists—just because of their presumptions—assume that maximizing SHV is more efficient than maximizing STV.

Juxtaposing SHV and STV must be considered relating to the ability of the two theories to develop an efficient management system, where the economic organization can efficiently reach its goals. Therefore, we must also consider the externalities that these models produce and their ability to develop efficiency in economic organizations.

We must reject the hypothesis that SHV (STV) maximization is efficient (inefficient) per se. The 2007–9 financial crisis shows that firms that had maximized SHV, maximizing profit in a Wicksteedian non-tuistic utilitarian perspective (Wicksteed 1910), were key actors in the disruption of common goods such as savings and financial stability

---

[6] Non-tuism is a form of utilitarianism based on the absence of alterity in the definition of the economic game. In non-tuism economic subjects maximize the relationship with goods in the absence of relationships with other economic subjects.

[7] The disruption of the good is a 'tragedy' since it means that a resource has been destroyed by unreasonable and irrational behaviour of economic actors, and at the same time without any possibility of recovering the common good due to the fact that the absence of rivalry and limits in the access produce an absence of costs and prices.

and, at the same time, proved inefficient by going bankrupt and being punished by the market discipline.

The differences between the STV and SHV models regard corporate governance. They are related to historical, ethno-anthropological, and cultural reasons (Screpanti and Zamagni 2005). A key field of research in economics compares different types of legal, cultural, financial, and banking systems. Certainly many differences exist in the development of economies. Some authors refer to this as the 'varieties of capitalism' and state that such differences can represent an opportunity for economic systems. After the fall of the Berlin Wall, while some scholars declared 'the end of history and the last man' (Fukuyama 1992), others rediscovered that differences across market systems exist (Hall and Soskice 2001).

These varieties arise also for corporate governance models: as shown by Doidge et al. (2007) country characteristics explain much more of the variance in governance ratings (39 per cent to 73 per cent) than observable firm characteristics (4 per cent to 22 per cent). La Porta et al. (2002) show how legal determinants directly affect the finance–growth nexus and financial development. Others, instead, emphasize cultural, religious, and ethno-anthropological determinants when explaining economic performance (Alesina et al. 2003). In general, diversity is a resource. Barth et al. (2004) illustrate the great variety in banking regulation in different countries. We argued that STV and SHV are very different methods of corporate governance for economic organizations. While SHV economic organizations are pure corporations devoted only to profit, STV organizations are able to both obtain profits and increase social and relationship capital.

Preserving the diversity of corporate governance models and economic organizations is important since this diversity can support systems featuring a certain degree of heterogeneity that can continue to promote economic development and growth, even when some models fail. Thus, there are many reasons to defend the diversity of models in corporate governance (Michie 2014). Preserving heterogeneity and diversity means supporting 'entrepreneurial pluralism'.

2.4 CONCLUSIONS

We reached three main conclusions regarding the role of non-purely profit-maximizing enterprises. First, these non-archetypical enterprises tend to emerge and prosper where property rights are faltering and where market failures are pervasive. Second, the stakeholder/community orientation of these enterprises turns them into actors for the common good, something their archetypical homologues might (partly) satisfy only by adopting stringent corporate social responsibility norms. Third, failure to recognize the intrinsic merits of entrepreneurial pluralism may impoverish society. We reached the second and third conclusions through a discussion based on the comparison between Stakeholder theory and Shareholder theory. Finally, a lot still has to be done to take the public debate on entrepreneurial forms to a safe shore, and the economics profession should deeply revise its mainstream view on the matter. In order for this to be achieved affirmative action—an approach to avoid discrimination against non-archetypical enterprise forms—aimed at safeguarding entrepreneurial pluralism is needed.

References

Alesina, A., Devleeschauwer, A., Easterly, W., Kurlat, S., and Wacziarg, R. (2003), 'Fractionalization', *Journal of Economic Growth*, 8, 155–94.

Allen F., Carletti, E., and Marquez, R. (2009), 'Stakeholder Capitalism, Corporate Governance, and Firm Value', Working Paper 09-28, Wharton Financial Institutions Center, University of Pennsylvania.

Andreadis, N. A. (2002), 'Leadership for Civil Society: Implications for Global Corporate Leadership Development', *Human Resource Development International*, 5(2), 143–9.

Argadona, A. (1998), 'The Stakeholder Theory and the Common Good', *Journal of Business Ethics*, 17(9), 1093–102.

Astrachan, J. H. and Carey Shanker, M. (2003), 'Family Businesses' Contribution to the U.S. Economy: A Closer Look', *Family Business Review*, XVI(3), 211–19.

Barnett, A. (1997). 'Towards a Stakeholder Democracy', in G. Kelly, D. Kelly, and A. Gamble, eds, *Stakeholder Capitalism* (London: Macmillan), 82–95.

Barth, J. R., Caprio, G. Jr., and Levine, R. (2004), 'Bank Regulation and Supervision: What Works Best?', *Journal of Financial Intermediation*, 13, 205–48.

Boatright, J. R. (1994), 'Fiduciary Duties and the Shareholder-Management Relations: Or, What's So Special About Shareholders?' *Business Ethics Quarterly*, 4(4), 393–407.

Borzaga, C. and Tortia, E. (2015). 'Co-operation as Coordination Mechanism of the e-Economic Activity: A New Approach to the Economics of Co-operative Enterprises', Euricse Working Paper No. 78/15.

Cennamo, C., Berrone, P., Cruz, C., and Gomez-Mejia, L. R. (2012), 'Socioemotional Wealth and Proactive Stakeholder Engagement: Why Family-Controlled Firms Care More about their Stakeholders', *Entrepreneurship: Theory and Practice*, 36(6): 1153–73.

Clement, R. W. (2005), 'The Lessons from Stakeholder Theory for US Business Leaders', *Business Horizons*, 48(3): 255–64.

Coopseurope (2010), 'European Cooperatives'. Key statistics. Available at <http://www.coop-seurope.coop> (accessed 6 September 2016).

Covey, S. M. R. and Merrill, R. R. (2006), *The Speed of Trust: The One Thing that Changes Everything* (Free Press: New York).

Doidge, C., Karoyli, G. A., and Stulz, R. M. (2007), 'Why Do Countries Matter So Much for Corporate Governance? *The Journal of Financial Economics*, 86: 1–3.

Donaldson, T. and Preston, L. E. (1995), 'The Stakeholder Theory of the Corporation: Concepts Evidence and Implication', *Academy of Management Review*, 20(1): 65–91.

Ferri, G. and Leogrande, A. (2015). 'Was the Crisis Due to a Shift from Stakeholder to Shareholder Finance? Surveying the Debate', Euricse Working Paper No. 76/15.

Ferri, G., Pini, M., and Scaccabarozzi, S. (2014). 'Le imprese familiari nel tessuto produttivo italiano: Caratteristiche, dimensioni, territorialità', *Rivista di economia e statistica del territorio*, 2: 48–77.

Freeman, R. E. (1984), *Strategic Management: A Stakeholder Approach* (Boston: Pitman. Reprinted 2010 Cambridge University Press).

Freeman, E. R., Harrison, J. S., Wicks, A. C., Parmar, B. L., and De Colle, S. (2010), *Stakeholder Theory: The State of the Art*, New York: Cambridge University Press.

Freeman, E. R. and. Phillips, R. A (2001), 'Stakeholder Theory: A Libertarian Defence, Darden Business School Working Paper No. 01-03.

Friedman, M. (1970), 'The Social Responsibility of Business is to Increase its Profit', *The New York Times Magazine*, 13 September.

Friedman, S. D. and Olk, P. (1995), 'Four Ways to Choose a CEO: Crown Heir, Horse Race, Coup D'état, and Comprehensive Research', *Human Resource Management*, 34(1), 141–6.

Fubini, D. G., Price, C., and Zollo, M. (2006), 'The Elusive Art of Post-Merger Leadership', *McKinsey Quarterly*, 4: 28–37.

Fukuyama, F. (1992), *The End of History and the Last Man* (New York: Free Press).

Goodpaster, K. E. (1991), 'Business Ethics and Stakeholder Analysis,' *Business Ethics Quarterly*, 1(1), 53–73.

Hall, A. T., Blass, F. R., Ferris, G. R., and Messengale, R. (2004), 'Leader Reputation and Accountability in Organizations: Implications for Dysfunctional Leader Behavior', *Leadership Quarterly*, 15(4), 515–36.

Hall, P. A. and Soskice, D. W. (2001). *Varieties of Capitalism: The Institutional Foundations of Comparative Advantage* (Oxford: Oxford University Press).

Hartman, E. (1996). *Organizational Ethics and the Good Life* (New York: Oxford University Press).

Heller, F. (1997), 'Leadership and Power in a Stakeholder Setting', *European Journal of Work and Organizational Psychology*, 6(4), 467–79.

Hutton, W. (1995), *The State We're In* (London: Jonathan Cape).

ICA-Euricse (various years), *World Cooperative Monitor* (Trento: Euricse).

Jensen, M. C. (2000), 'Value Maximization and the Corporate Objective Function', *European Financial Management*, 7(3), 297–317.

Jones, T. M. (1995),'Instrumental Stakeholder Theory: A Synthesis of Ethics and Economics', *Academy of Management Review*, 32(1), 137–55.

Jones, T. M. and Wicks, A. C. (1999), 'Convergent Stakeholder Theory in Management Research, *Academy of Management Review*, 24(2), 206–21.

Klassen, R. D. (1993), 'The Integration of Environmental Issues into Manufacturing: Toward an Interactive Open Systems Model', *Production and Inventory Management Journal*, 34(1), 82–8.

Kowalski, P., Büge, M., Sztajerowska, M., and Egeland, M. (2013), 'State-Owned Enterprises: Trade Effects and Policy Implications', OECD Trade Policy Paper, No. 147, OECD Publishing.

La Porta, R., Lopez-de-Silanes, F., Shleifer, A., and Vishny, R. (2002), 'Investor Protection and Corporate Valuation', *Journal of Finance* 57, 1147–70.

Mandl, I. (2008), *Overview of Family Business Relevant Issues* (Vienna: Austrian Institute for SME Research).

Michie, J. (2014), 'The Need for Corporate Diversity', in J. Williamson, C. Driver, and P. Kenway, eds, *Beyond Shareholder Value. The Reasons and Choices for Corporate Governance Reform* (London: TUC Congress House), 64–8.

Miller, D., Le Breton-Miller, I., and Scholnick, B. (2008), 'Stewardship vs. Stagnation: An Empirical Comparison of Small Family and Non-Family Businesses', *Journal of Management Studies*, 45(1), 51–78.

Mitchell, R. K., Agle, B. R., Chrisman, J. J., and Spence, L. J. (2011), 'Toward a Theory of Stakeholder Salience in Family Firms', *Business Ethics Quarterly*, 21(2), 235–55.

Nwanko, S. and Richardson, B. (1996), 'Organizational Leaders as Political Strategists: A Stakeholder Management Perspective', *Management Decision*, 34(10), 43–50.

Orts, E. W. and Strudler, A. (2002), 'The Ethical and Environmental Limits of Stakeholder Theory', *Business Ethics Quarterly*, 215–33.

Phillips, R. (2003), *Stakeholder Theory and Organizational Ethics* (San Francisco: Berrett-Koehler Publishers).

Rawls, J. (1993), *Political Liberalism* (New York: Columbia University Press).

Rheman, E. (1968), *Industrial Democracy and Industrial Management: A Critical Essay of the Possible Meanings and Implications of Industrial Democracy* (London: Tavistock).

Roberts, N. and King, P. J. (1989). 'Stakeholder Goes Public', *Organizational Dynamics*, 17(3), 63–79.

Rustin, M. (1997), 'Stakeholding and the Public Sector', in G. Kelly, D. Kelly, and A. Gamble, eds, *Stakeholder Capitalism*, London: Macmillan: 72–81.

Salamon, L. M., Sokolowski, S. W., and Associates (2004), *Global Civil Society: Dimensions of the Nonprofit Sector*, Volume Two (Bloomfield, CT: Kumarian Press).

Screpanti, E. and Zamagni, S. (2005), *An Outline of the History of Economic Thought* (New York: Oxford University Press).

Stenberg, R. J. (2007), 'A Systems Model of Leadership', *American Psychologist*, 62(1), 34–42.

Stewart, R. F., Allen, J. K., and Cavender, J. M. (1963). 'The Strategic Plan', Research Report 168, Stanford Research Institute, Long Range Planning Service, Industrial Economics Division.

Stiglitz, J. E and Hoff, K. (2005), 'The Creation of the Rule of Law and the Legitimacy of Property: The Political and Economic Consequences of a Corrupt Privatization', NBER Working Paper No. 11772.

Stiglitz, J. E., Sen, A., and Fitoussi, J. P. (2009), Report of the Commission on the Measurement of Economic Performance and Social Progress, Institut national de la statistique et des études économiques, Paris.

Sundaram, A. K. and Inkpoen, A. C. (2004), 'Stakeholder Theory and the Corporate Objective Revisited: A Reply', *Organization Science*, 15(3), 370–1.

The Economist (2014), 'Family Firms. Business in the Blood', 1 November.

Thomas, T., Schererhorn, J. R., and Dienhart, J. W. (2004), 'Strategic Leadership of Ethical Behavior in Business', *Academy of Management Executive*, 18(2), 56–66.

Tortia, E. C., Valentinov, V., and Iliopoulos, C. (2013), 'Agricultural Co-operatives', *Journal of Entrepreneurial and Organizational Diversity*, 2(1), 23–36.

Wicksteed, P. (1910), *The Common Sense of Political Economy and Selected Papers and Reviews on Economic Theory*, L. Robbins, ed., Vols. 1 and 2 (London: Routledge).

Wood, D. and Ross, D. G. (2006), 'Environmental Social Controls and Capital Investments: Australian Evidence', *Accounting and Finance*, 46(4), 677–95.

CHAPTER 3

....

LIBERAL PHILOSOPHIES OF OWNERSHIP

....

STUART WHITE

3.1 INTRODUCTION

....

'LIBERALISM' is a capacious term. Liberals affirm the ideal of respect for free and equal personhood as the basis for legitimate authority and a just society. When it comes to thinking about the philosophy of ownership, however, it makes sense to think of there being a number of liberal philosophies based on different ways of interpreting this core ideal. My aim in this chapter is to set out in broad outline three philosophical perspectives on ownership within the liberal tradition. This treatment is far from exhaustive, but gives some indication of the range of possible liberal approaches.

I begin in Section 3.2 with an outline and brief discussion of the *right libertarian* philosophy of ownership. Section 3.3 elaborates the *left libertarian* philosophy of ownership. Section 3.4 presents the *democratic liberal* perspective. Each section sets out its respective philosophy of ownership in broad outline and then relates it specifically to co-operatives and mutuals. Section 3.5 concludes.

3.2 RIGHT LIBERTARIANISM

....

Liberalism is frequently understood as affirming the inviolability of the individual based on rights. As Robert Nozick famously puts it: 'Individuals have rights, and there are things no person or group may do to them (without violating these rights)' (1974: ix). In Nozick's view, rights are properly seen as 'side constraints'. They set direct limits on how we may act towards others. On this view, we may not violate a person's rights even to prevent an even graver violation of rights (Sen 1982).

According to Nozick, when individuals acquire income and wealth through certain procedures, then these 'holdings' are held as rights in this sense. The moral requirement on us, and thus on the state, is to respect and protect these rights. If the state attempts to 'redistribute' income and wealth through taxes and income transfers, it violates the rights people have in their holdings. It necessarily acts unjustly.

How, though, do individuals come to hold income and resources by right in the first place? What process generates 'entitlements' in this sense? Nozick's account places a central emphasis on voluntary production and exchange. Imagine an initial distribution of holdings under which everyone has rights to what they hold. Through their voluntary production and exchange they create a new distribution of holdings. Provided that this new distribution emerges in a way that is voluntary—no force or fraud—then it is just. This captures the principle of *justice in transfer* (Nozick 1974: 150–3, 160–4). Nozick's view here is strongly opposed to the idea that we should assess justice in distributions by how far they satisfy some 'patterned' principle such as 'each according to desert' or 'each according to need' (Nozick 1974: 155–64). What matters, for justice, is not how far the distribution satisfies a structural principle of this kind, but how far it emerges from a prior just distribution in the right way (through voluntary production and exchange).

Justice in transfer, however, cannot be the whole story about how people acquire rights to holdings. If a distribution is just because it emerged in the right way from a prior distribution that itself was just, what made *that* distribution just? Logically, at some point, we have to explain the justice of some initial set of holdings in a way that doesn't invoke voluntary production and exchange from a prior distribution that is itself assumed to be just. We have to introduce a theory of *original entitlements* to complement the principle of justice in transfer.

Nozick's account of original entitlements draws heavily on the theory of property presented by John Locke in Chapter V of his *Second Treatise of Civil Government* (Locke 1965 [1690]). First, Nozick claims that each individual originally has full private property in their own body and abilities (Nozick 1974: 167–74). This is the thesis of *self-ownership*. Whereas Locke's account of self-ownership involves some moral limits (because we are, in the most fundamental sense, the property of God, and may not destroy or wilfully negate God's property), Nozick claims that each of us has unlimited rights over our body and abilities. These include, for example, the rights to hire out our labour-power or to sell our rights over our body and abilities, to another permanently, thereby becoming their slave.

Second, Nozick claims that there is a legitimate way in which external resources, such as land, can become private property. In Locke's account, individuals can acquire private property rights in these initially unowned external resources by mixing their self-owned labour with them, subject to the condition that they do not annex more than they can use without products going to waste, and that they leave 'enough, and as good' for others (Locke 1965 [1690]: Chapter V, Sections 27–34).[1] Nozick has a lot of fun picking holes in

---

[1] Locke argues that in a non-monetary economy these conditions impose a significant limit on the size of individual holdings and, thus, on inequality in holdings. However, Locke also argues that the

Locke's labour-mixing idea, but he takes something from the spirit of Locke's 'enough, and as good' proviso. Specifically, Nozick claims that an act of privatization of an initially unowned resource is legitimate if it does not make anyone else worse off than they would be if external resources remained in their initially unowned state (Nozick 1974: 174–82).[2] If acts of privatization satisfy this condition—they are not harmful to anyone relative to the baseline of a world where all external resources remain unowned—we have what Nozick calls *justice in acquisition*.

So justice is generated by the establishment of valid ownership rights in the following way. Every person initially and fully owns their own body and abilities (self-ownership). People may also acquire full private property rights in initially unowned external resources, such as land. They do this when their privatization of a given external resource satisfies the above test for justice in acquisition. Once original entitlements have been established in this way, people then come to have rights in holdings through repeated actions of voluntary production and exchange (justice in transfer). If holdings are generated in an unjust way, for example through theft, then the *rectification principle* says that there must be appropriate rectification for this injustice (Nozick 1974: 152–3).

I have referred above to 'full' private property rights and this term needs explanation. In an extremely important article, Anthony Honoré argues that we can distinguish no fewer than eleven different 'incidents' that make up private ownership with respect to a resource (Honoré 1987). These are roughly as follows: (1) *possession*: exclusive physical control of the resource, implying no interference without permission; (2) *use*: personal use and enjoyment of the resource; (3) *management*: the power to decide how and by whom the resource is to be used, including power of contract; (4) *income*: the power to appropriate market returns on market deployments of the resource; (5) *capital*: the power to alienate the resource via sale or gift and to consume or destroy it; (6) *security*: immunity of expropriation of the resource; (7) *transmission*: power of bequest; (8) *absence of term*: no time limit fixed on holding of the resource; (9) *harm prevention duty*: the liberty to use the object is restricted by a duty not to harm others; (10) *liability to execution*: the resource can be taken from the owner in lieu of payment for the execution of her or his debts; and (11) *residuarity*: lesser interests in the resource return to the owner on their termination (e.g. if you lease out a room you own to someone for six months, rights to the room return to you at the end of the six months).

Honoré's objective is the analytic one of understanding what we mean, or can mean, by private property. He does not assert that all ownership relations must take the form of full private property, involving all eleven incidents. Nozickian property rights, however,

---

introduction of money allows for the legitimate emergence of much larger, and significant inequality in, holdings (Locke 1965: Chapter V, Sections 36–51).

[2] As Jonathan Wolff points out, there is an ambiguity as to whether Nozick's criterion is captured by either the question (a) 'Does this act of appropriation make anyone worse off than in a world where *this specific resource* remained unowned?'; or, (b) 'Does this act of appropriation make anyone worse off than in a world where *all external resources* remain unowned?' Wolff argues that Nozick probably means to apply the latter test. See Wolff 1991: 112.

are typically understood to be 'full' in the sense of involving all eleven incidents. Taken together, the forgoing principles, conjoined to this specific conception of private property, amount to one, particularly influential example of a right libertarian theory of economic justice.

To be clear, full private ownership rights constitute the legal baseline in this theory, but individuals are free to pool their resources in communes or worker-owned co-operatives if they wish. Nozick comments that worker-owned co-operatives might be less efficient than capitalist firms, but that even if this is so, they might arise if workers and/or consumers are willing to pay for them in the form of lower wages and/or higher prices (Nozick 1974: 250–3).[3] What is not acceptable, however, is to use state authority to require the co-operative form or to subsidize it. These measures would violate individuals' baseline private property rights.

Nozick's right libertarian theory has stimulated great controversy. It apparently allows for the emergence of significant economic inequality and poverty while ruling out the 'redistribution' that would mitigate them. Critics have identified a number of problems with the theory.

A first problem concerns the movement from theory to practice. Although the theory might show that a highly unequal capitalist society could be just in principle, it does not imply that any actually existing unequal capitalist society is just. This is because existing capitalist societies have been constructed on the basis of massive rights violations—enslavements, land grabs, and genocides—which have rarely, if ever, been subject to any adequate rectification. For the theory to have any real applicability to us, in our world shaped by enclosure and imperialism, we would first have to make appropriate rectification for historic injustices of these kinds (assuming such a thing is possible).

A second problem, internal to the theory, concerns the treatment of justice in acquisition. Nozick's account requires that nobody is harmed relative to the baseline world in which external resources remain unowned. But this criterion can be questioned on a number of grounds (G. A. Cohen 1995: Chapter 3). Perhaps most fundamentally, critics have asked why we should take the relevant baseline to be one in which all external resources are assumed to be unowned. Alternatively, for example, we could assume that the world is initially *jointly owned* (G. A. Cohen 1995: Chapters 3, 4). This means that nobody has an exclusive title to any external resource but also that use of any given resource requires the permission of everyone else, conceived as one of its joint owners. The distribution of welfare in this jointly owned world is likely to be different from that in the world where external resources are initially unowned. For example, those with limited productive capacity might be able to secure a higher level of welfare by using their power to withhold permission to use resources to bargain for a share of what the

---

[3] Nozick references the familiar arguments that worker-owned co-operatives will (a) invest less than equivalent capitalist firms because worker-owners lacking individual, transferable property rights in the enterprise will demand that capital outlays repay themselves over a shorter time horizon than an equivalent capitalist firm; and (b) restrict output and employment relative to a capitalist firm because worker–owners have an incentive to fix output to maximize average, rather than total, profit.

more productively capable produce. In this respect, joint ownership seems to imply a higher welfare threshold for legitimate privatization.

What this discussion points up is the essential ambiguity of the Nozickian approach to justice in initial acquisition. It is all very well saying that acquisition is legitimate when it makes nobody worse off, but what is the correct baseline against which to make the assessment of harm? Insofar as this remains unclear, so, too, does the legitimacy of any initial acquisition; and without a clear account of this, uncertainty applies to every claimed 'entitlement' (G. A. Cohen 1995: Chapter 3; Wolff 1991: 112–15).

3.3 LEFT LIBERTARIANISM

One weak point in right libertarianism, then, is its account of how people come to have legitimate private ownership of parts of the external world. *Left libertarianism* retains much of the framework of right libertarianism, but breaks with it on precisely this point (Steiner 1994; Vallentyne and Steiner (eds.) 2000).

In its simplest version, left libertarianism replaces Nozick's principle of justice in acquisition with a principle of equal division. When it comes to external resources, such as land, each individual has a right to an equal share. For purposes of implementation, this is often conceived as a right to an equal share of the market value of these resources. We are to think of the community as the fundamental owner of the resources. Individuals may pay the community to gain certain use–rights over them. The community might acquire this payment through an appropriate tax on the value of the resource (George 2009 [1881]) or through something like a commercial rental arrangement. The community consolidates these payments into a central fund and distributes them to citizens. One possibility is to use the fund to pay for public services, for example universal education. Another is to distribute the fund to citizens as cash, either in the form of a periodic income grant (a basic income) or as a one-off lump sum (e.g. a capital grant on reaching adulthood as proposed by Paine 1987 [1797] and Ackerman and Alstott 1999).

On the left libertarian view, the state still remains unjustified in adopting any general 'redistribution'. A just distribution, which the state may not tamper with without violating individuals' rights, is one that emerges from voluntary production and exchange from a position of justice in original entitlements. These just original entitlements include, as for the right libertarian, universal self-ownership. But they also include the right to an equal share of external resources implemented in the form of universal public services or a universal cash grant financed from an appropriate fee levied on those who use external resources.

There are many questions about the details of the left libertarian approach. Which resources count as external resources for purposes of the equal division principle? There is general agreement that natural resources count. But what about wealth produced by previous generations? Do 'job assets' count as external resources in the relevant sense (Van Parijs 1995: Chapter 4)?

In addition, not all left libertarians accept that equal division is the correct approach. Michael Otsuka argues for what one might call compensatory division (Otsuka 2003: Chapter 2). Recall that left libertarians affirm universal self-ownership. This means they regard each person as (initially) the rightful owner of their own body and abilities. Self-owning individuals might have radically unequal abilities to earn income and wealth. As a full self-owner, however, no individual is required to share the market-contracted fruits of their abilities with others (unless they make a contract to this effect). So universal self-ownership is consistent with, and may work to reinforce, a highly unequal distribution of labour income (which, in turn, can obviously translate through saving into inequalities in wealth and in capital income). Otsuka argues that original entitlements in external resources should be set to compensate for inequalities in self-owned capacities. At this point the left libertarian perspective starts to overlap with the democratic liberalism I will discuss in Section 3.4, though the left libertarian perspective retains a distinctive emphasis on somehow using rights over external resources to promote egalitarian distributional objectives rather than transfers derived from direct taxation of labour incomes (Fried 2004).

So far as co-operatives and mutuals are concerned, left libertarianism takes fundamentally the same view as right libertarianism. If people wish to establish co-ops or mutuals, they have every right to do so. However, the state may not require this particular form of enterprise, nor subsidize it. In practice, however, left libertarianism will likely be more favourable to co-ops and mutuals than right libertarianism. Some argue that worker-owned firms are likely to be more productively efficient than equivalent capitalist firms (Bowles and Gintis 1998: 36–9).[4] However, against a background of wealth inequality and credit market imperfections, workers find it difficult to get the capital needed to start a firm of their own (Bowles and Gintis 1998: 39; Hoff 1998). A left libertarian regime would apparently be better than a right libertarian regime in this respect. If, say, the equal division principle is applied in the form of a basic income or basic capital, then workers will have resources which will make it easier to gain credit to start co-ops. We would then expect to see more of them, particularly if they do have a net efficiency advantage.

3.4 Democratic Liberalism

Let us turn now to democratic liberalism. To understand this liberalism it helps to begin with the idea of a *deliberative democracy*. I will work here with a very basic account of the idea.[5] A political community is legitimate in its use of state power, according to this

---

[4] By 'worker-owned firm' here, I mean a firm in which workers have individual shares which they can trade on leaving the enterprise. Bowles and Gintis argue that firms of this kind are more effective in motivating workers, leading to higher labour efficiency than equivalent capitalist firms.

[5] For a fuller account, see J. Cohen 2009.

basic account of deliberative democracy, when certain conditions hold. The use of state power must be authorized by-laws which are themselves made in a sufficiently open, egalitarian, and contestable way. This implies a substantial set of civil and political rights to support egalitarian and contestatory political participation. In addition, the use of state power must be authorized by-laws that reflect deliberated judgements about what best secures the citizenry's common good. By common good here we mean, centrally, the shared basic interests that citizens have, such as interests in life, liberty, equal civic standing, and economic opportunity. Laws should express judgements about what best secures these shared basic interests.

What does this require? A great deal of 'liberal egalitarian' political philosophy aims to provide an answer to this question by identifying relevant principles of justice. A very influential example is John Rawls's theory of justice (Rawls 1999 [1971], 2001). Rawls's theory is an attempt to give democratic citizens guidance, in the form of principles of justice, on what it would mean to show equal consideration for their shared basic interests (J. Cohen 2003).

The subject of a theory of justice is what Rawls calls the *basic structure*: roughly, the set of institutions which fundamentally affects how society distributes the benefits and burdens that affect citizens' shared basic interests. It encompasses political institutions, but also economic institutions including, most importantly, the system of property rights. The picture we are often given in contemporary political debate is one in which market-generated inequalities of income and wealth are presented as presumptively just, and movements away from this distribution, through taxation and transfers, face the burden of justification. For Rawls and other democratic liberals this gets things badly wrong (Murphy and Nagel 2002). The right kind of economic system is an open question, and we must approach it as such, asking in an open-minded way what system will best secure our common good by satisfying what we take to be the relevant principles of justice.

Rawls famously argues for a conception of justice he terms *justice as fairness* which consists of two principles:

(a) Each person has the same indefeasible claim to a fully adequate scheme of equal basic liberties, which scheme is compatible with the same scheme of liberties for all; and

(b) Social and economic inequalities are to satisfy two conditions: first, they are to be attached to offices and positions open to all under conditions of fair equality of opportunity; and second, they are to be to the greatest benefit of the least-advantaged members of society (the difference principle). (Rawls 2001: 42–3)

Rawls argues that the first principle has a strict ('lexical') priority to the second; and that, within the second principle, fair equality of opportunity has priority over the difference principle. This conception of justice has liberal content in the emphasis it gives to certain 'basic liberties' and their priority. These include freedom of conscience, expression, and association, and political rights to vote and stand for elected office. So far as political rights are concerned, the first principle also requires that the basic structure uphold their 'fair value', meaning that citizens of equal ability and motivation have equal opportunity to influence government regardless of their social class (Rawls 2001: 46). For Rawls, however, private property in productive resources is not in the set of basic liberties. In addition, in contrast to right and left libertarians, Rawls does not view self-ownership as among, or entailed by, these liberties. Our basic liberties include rights of bodily integrity and freedom of occupational choice, but not the full set of rights constitutive of self-ownership.[6] Setting up a property rights system which includes taxation of labour incomes violates the libertarian principle of self-ownership, but is not a violation of the basic liberties.

Rawls's conception of justice is also liberal and, in one sense, egalitarian in affirming fair equality of opportunity. This centrally requires that institutions work to even out chances of occupational attainment across people from different socio-economic backgrounds (Rawls 2001: 43–4). The difference principle adds another egalitarian dimension. It requires that socio-economic inequalities, such as in income and wealth, be arranged so that they are to the maximum benefit of the worst-off group (which Rawls thinks of as the class of workers in, or available for, full-time employment with the lowest earnings prospects).[7]

On Rawls's view, our society's economic structure is to be settled by democratic choice after considering what institutions will work to secure the principles of justice. Key questions to ask are:

(1)   What sort of economic structure will work to maintain the first principle of justice, including the fair value of the political liberties?
(2)   What sort of economic structure will work to secure fair equality of opportunity?
(3)   What sort of economic structure will satisfy the difference principle?

Some have argued that a free-market capitalist economic structure will best satisfy principles such as these (Tomasi 2012). Rawls himself, however, claims that they are not well served either by a laissez-faire capitalist economy or by a command economy form of socialism. Nor does a system of 'welfare-state capitalism' go far enough, in Rawls's view, to satisfy these principles. welfare-state capitalism provides ameliorative assistance for those who lose out in market competition, but to really satisfy these principles more must be done to equalize citizens' claims over underlying assets. This might take the form of a 'property-owning democracy', which uses inheritance taxes and other

---

[6]   For relevant critical discussion of self-ownership, see Christman 1991 and G. A. Cohen 1995: Chapters 9 and 10. In terms of Honoré's framework, one might say that Rawls and other democratic liberals do assert a principle of self-ownership but one that involves fewer 'incidents' of private ownership than the libertarian conception, e.g. affirming the incident of 'management' but not that of 'income'.

[7]   See Freeman 2007: 106. Rawls abstracts from the issues of health and disability. For helpful critical discussion on this point, see Nussbaum 2006: Chapter 2.

measures to disperse privately owned wealth; or 'liberal socialism', which combines market allocation with public ownership of productive assets; or some hybrid of the two (Rawls 1999: 234–42, 2001: 135–40). Rawls contrasts property-owning democracy with welfare-state capitalism as follows:

> the background institutions of property-owning democracy, with its system of (workably) competitive markets, tries to disperse the ownership of wealth and capital, and thus to prevent a small part of society from controlling the economy and indirectly political life itself. Property-owning democracy avoids this, not by redistributing income to those with less at the end of each period, so to speak, but rather by ensuring the widespread ownership of productive assets and human capital … at the beginning of each period. … The idea is not simply to assist those who lose out through accident or misfortune (although this must be done), but instead to put all citizens in a position to manage their own affairs and to take part in social cooperation on a footing of mutual respect under appropriately equal conditions. (Rawls 1999: xv)

What does this framework imply for co-ops and mutuals? Rawls references John Stuart Mill's 'idea of worker-managed cooperative firms', commenting that this is 'fully compatible with property-owning democracy' (Rawls 2001: 176). In his *Principles of Political Economy*, Mill speculates hopefully that a general tendency towards reduced 'dependence' in social relationships will express itself in the gradual replacement of conventional capitalist firms by 'partnership, in one of two forms: in some cases, association of the labourers with the capitalist; in others, and perhaps finally in all, association of labourers among themselves' (Mill 1970 [1848]: 129). Referencing Mill's hopes, Rawls acknowledges that this hasn't happened, and poses some questions as to why it hasn't and whether a liberal state should promote Mill's idea (Rawls 2001: 178). Broadening the question a little, should a liberal state promote co-ops, mutuals, or similar institutions (e.g. enterprise democracy requirements)?

Note first that even if a liberal state does not purposively promote co-ops and mutuals, the relatively egalitarian distribution of wealth in a property-owning democracy might facilitate their formation relative to a right libertarian or similar basic structure. Again, the interaction between wealth distribution and credit markets could be important here.

Turning to active promotion of co-ops, mutuals, and related institutions, recall that liberalism is embedded here within a deliberative theory of democracy. The background supposition is of a citizenry concerned to legislate a basic structure according to informed judgements of the common good. But this, in turn, requires that citizens have a capacity and willingness for deliberative political participation. Imagine that enterprise democracy impacts positively on wider democratic citizenship (Pateman 1970). Then, as Rawls suggests, there could be a case for actively promoting democratic enterprises so as to secure the kind of political capacity and participation that deliberative democracy requires.[8]

---

[8] Empirical research suggests the impact of workplace democracy on wider political capacity and participation is complex. See Carter (2006) for a helpful overview.

Another possibility is that specific mutualistic forms of enterprise are in some way better suited to the economic interests of the worst-off (narrowly construed). For example, Martin Weitzman and James Meade have argued that certain very specific forms of profit- and revenue-sharing generate higher and more stable levels of employment relative to an otherwise equivalent capitalism in which workers are paid a fixed wage (Weitzman 1984; Meade 1989). If so, then a liberal state might have grounds to promote these forms of enterprise to satisfy the difference principle.

Third, if, as Rawls intends, one understands the position of the worst-off to be a matter of power and status, not only income and wealth, then a system that structures economic inequalities to the maximum benefit of the worst-off might well be one that places limits on acceptable inequalities of power and status within the enterprise.[9] This might ground a case for forms of 'workplace republicanism' (Hsieh 2005), or possibly employee ownership.

Finally, there might be contextual arguments for promoting co-ops and mutuals. Democratic liberals might wish to see a wider dispersion of wealth and, in principle, be indifferent as to how far this involves wider adoption of co-ops and mutuals. But starting from the situation in particular societies at particular times, it could be that promotion of co-ops and mutuals is the economically or politically most promising way towards the underlying goal of a more egalitarian distribution of wealth.

3.5 CONCLUSION

When we are asked to define liberalism's philosophy of ownership we must ask: which liberalism? Right libertarianism points to a society with potentially highly unequal amounts of private property, emerging through voluntary production and exchange, where the default ownership form is full private ownership in the sense clarified by Honoré. Left libertarianism qualifies this picture by insisting on a platform of initially equal external resource entitlements that are independent of voluntary production and exchange.

Democratic liberalism situates the question of property rights as a matter of democratic judgement of the common good, guided by principles of social justice. What follows from this perspective for ownership relations depends both on the exact specification of the principles and on what empirical research suggests is necessary or helpful to satisfy them. There is room for reasonable disagreement on both. It is therefore much harder to generalize about the sort of property relations supported by this perspective. John Rawls, a leading theorist of democratic liberalism, argues that justice requires either property-owning democracy, liberal socialism, or a hybrid of the two. This points towards an economy in which there is considerable collective effort to shape the

---

[9] For an important statement of the relational aspects of equality and social justice, focusing on status and power rather than the distribution of income and wealth, see Anderson 1999.

distribution of wealth and possibly also a significant degree of common ownership. This might provide an environment conducive for co-ops and mutuals to form; and there might also be arguments from within this framework to support deliberate promotion of these kinds of enterprises and related institutions.

REFERENCES

Ackerman, Bruce and Alstott, Anne (1999), *The Stakeholder Society* (New Haven: Yale University Press).

Anderson, Elizabeth (1999), 'What is the Point of Equality?' *Ethics*, 109, 287–337.

Bowles, Samuel and Gintis, Herbert (1998),'Efficient Redistribution: New Rules for Markets, States and Communities', in S. Bowles and H. Gintis, with Erik Olin Wright, eds, *Recasting Egalitarianism: New Rules for Communities, States and Markets* (London: Verso), 3–71.

Carter, Neil (2006), 'Political Participation and the Workplace: The Spillover Thesis Revisited', *British Journal of Politics and International Relations*, 8(3), 410–26.

Christman, John (1991), 'Self-Ownership, Equality and the Structure of Property Rights', *Political Theory*, 19, 28–46.

Cohen, G. A. (1995), *Self-Ownership, Freedom and Equality* (Cambridge: Cambridge University Press).

Cohen, Joshua (2003), 'For a Democratic Society', in Samuel Freeman, ed., *The Cambridge Companion to Rawls* (Cambridge: Cambridge University Press), 86–138.

Cohen, Joshua (2009 [1989]), 'Deliberation and Democratic Legitimacy', in Joshua Cohen, *Philosophy, Politics, Democracy* (Cambridge, MA: Harvard University Press), 16–37.

Freeman, Samuel (2007), *Rawls* (Abingdon: Routledge).

Fried, Barbara, (2004), 'Left Libertarianism: A Review Essay', *Philosophy and Public Affairs* 32(1), 66–92.

George, Henry (2009) [1881], *Poverty and Progress: An Inquiry into the Cause of Industrial Depressions and of Increase of Want with Increase of Wealth; the Remedy* (Cambridge: Cambridge University Press).

Hoff, Karla (1998), 'Market Failures and the Distribution of Wealth: A Perspective from the Economics of Information', in Samuel Bowles and Herbert Gintis, with Erik Olin Wright, eds, *Recasting Egalitarianism: New Rules for Communities, States and Markets* (London: Verso), 332–57.

Honoré, Anthony (1987), 'Ownership', in Anthony Honoré, ed., *Making Law Bind* (Oxford: Oxford University Press), 161–92.

Hsieh, Nien-hê (2005), 'Rawlsian Justice and Workplace Republicanism', *Social Theory and Practice*, 31(1), 115–42.

Locke, John 1965 [1690]), *The Second Treatise of Civil Government*, ed. Peter Laslett (New York: Mentor).

Meade, James (1989), *Agathotopia: The Economics of Partnership* (Aberdeen: University of Aberdeen).

Mill, John Stuart (1970 [1848], *Principles of Political Economy*, ed. Donald Winch, (Harmondsworth: Penguin).

Murphy, Liam and Nagel, Thomas (2002), *The Myth of Ownership: Taxes and Justice* (Oxford: Oxford University Press).

Nozick, Robert (1974), *Anarchy, State, and Utopia* (Oxford: Blackwell).

Nussbaum, Martha (2006), *Frontiers of Justice: Disability, Nationality, Species Membership* (Cambridge, MA: Harvard University Press).

Otsuka, Michael (2003), *Libertarianism Without Inequality* (Oxford: Oxford University Press).

Paine, Thomas (1987 [1797]), 'Agrarian Justice', in Isaac Kramnick and Michael Foot eds, *The Thomas Paine Reader* (Harmondsworth: Penguin), 471–89.

Pateman, Carole (1970), *Participation and Democracy* (Cambridge: Cambridge University Press).

Rawls, John (1987 [1797]), *A Theory of Justice: Revised Edition* (Cambridge, MA: Harvard University Press).

Rawls, John (2001), *Justice as Fairness: A Restatement* (Cambridge, MA: Harvard University Press).

Sen, Amartya (1982), 'Rights and Agency', *Philosophy and Public Affairs*, 11(2), 3–39.

Steiner, Hillel (1994), *An Essay on Rights* (Oxford: Blackwell).

Tomasi, John (2012), *Free Market Fairness* (Princeton: Princeton University Press).

Vallentyne, Peter and Steiner, Hillel, eds (2000), *Left-Libertarianism and its Critics: The Contemporary Debate* (Basingstoke: Palgrave).

Van Parijs, Philippe (1995), *Real Freedom for All: What (if Anything) Can Justify Capitalism?* (Oxford: Oxford University Press).

Weitzman, Martin (1984), *The Share Economy: Conquering Stagflation* (Cambridge, MA: Harvard University Press).

Wolff, Jonathan (1991), *Robert Nozick: Property, Justice and the Minimal State* (Oxford: Blackwell).

CHAPTER 4

....

CO-OPERATIVE PRINCIPLES AND CO-OPERATIVE LAW ACROSS THE GLOBE

....

HAGEN HENRŸ

4.1 INTRODUCTION

....

AT least for lawyers the reference to 'principles' in connection with the law on an enterprise type is peculiar. A presentation on the law of stock companies, for example, would not refer to the principles of stock companies. It is even widely assumed that there are no such principles. For many, this difference between co-operatives and capital-centred companies is essential.

Co-operatives all over the world have been guided by a set of identity-constituting principles ever since in 1844 the Rochdale Society of Equitable Pioneers formulated what became 'the' co-operative principles (Rhodes 1995: 4ff.). Since 1937, the International Co-operative Alliance (ICA) has formalized the co-operative principles in successive statements, the last being the 1995 ICA Statement on the co-operative identity (ICA Statement). For the purpose of this contribution, the term 'co-operative principles' comprises the definition of co-operatives, the co-operative values, and the co-operative principles as laid down in the ICA Statement.

Since the beginning of legislation on co-operatives in the mid-1850s in the United Kingdom (Snaith 2013), co-operative law and its implementation anywhere has been, directly or indirectly, influenced by these principles and assessed accordingly. A great number of national constitutions confer a special status to co-operatives. Many laws refer explicitly to them.[1]

---

[1] See introductory sections of the country reports in the *International Handbook of Cooperative Law* Cracogna et al. 2013.

This reference to the co-operative principles ensures a certain degree of similarity in the co-operative laws around the world. But the spreading of the co-operative principles (Bialosgorski Neto 2012; Rhodes 2012) has also led to various interpretations. Some of these interpretations depend on the nature of principles, others on national or cultural differences,[2] others still on the legal objective of co-operatives. Whereas the legal objective of stock companies is to maximize the financial return on investments, the legal objective of co-operatives as laid down in the ICA Statement is to satisfy the economic, social, and cultural needs and aspirations of co-operators. As these needs and aspirations vary in time and in space, the ways to satisfy them show greater variety than does the pursuit of the rather stable and uniform objective of stock companies. Consequently, the interpretation of the co-operative principles varies.

Co-operative laws reflect these variations.[3] Besides other classifications (see also, for example, Fici 2013b: 11ff.; Henrÿ 2012a: 59f.), one may distinguish between laws which are close to the co-operative principles, such as the Japanese consumer co-operative legislation and the Norwegian and the Portuguese co-operative laws; and others which, to varying degrees, depart from these principles. In its pursuit of developing co-operatives, the ICA intends to suggest a tool with which to evaluate the legal frameworks for co-operatives (ICA Blueprint 2013: 30).

As of the early 1970s, more and more national and regional law-makers have begun a qualitative variation by approximating through multifaceted, complex processes the features of co-operatives with those of stock companies, especially as far as the nature and structure of capital, management, and control mechanisms are concerned. They have started allowing, for example, limited investments in co-operatives, management qualifications to become those applied in stock companies, and control mechanisms based on economic/financial interests besides user interests.[4] The greatest risk for the co-operative identity lies in the possibility of such measures transforming the co-operative member–user relationship into an investor relationship. The full extent of this risk is difficult to assess as it would require an analysis of the effects of the—at times indiscriminate—application to co-operatives of laws designed for capital-centred companies, such as taxation law, competition law, accounting standards, and labour law, and/or the analysis of the effects of the by-laws of individual co-operatives.

This approximation of the features of co-operatives with those of stock companies is indicative of the difficulties in practice and in law of finding an appropriate balance between the economic and the social objectives of co-operatives. The reaction to these difficulties might lead to a new divide between co-operative laws: those which support the idea of co-operatives doing business as capital-centred

---

[2] For a recent account of differences, see Gijselinckx, Zhao, and Novkovic 2014.

[3] See *International Handbook of Cooperative Law* 2013. For older works, see Foreword to the *International Handbook of Cooperative Law* 2013 and European Union Study on the implementation of the Regulation 1435/2003.

[4] For a more detailed account, see Henrÿ 2014a.

enterprises, albeit in a different way (Australia, Northern European countries, and North America), and those which reflect the re-emerging social and solidarity economy idea (Central and South American countries and Southern European countries). The recent laws on the social (and solidarity) economy are signs of this divide and need considering,[5] even though the finality of these laws is not to regulate the organizational features of co-operatives. The extent of this divide will also depend on the outcome of the current globalization-driven readjustment of the welfare state systems in many countries and their possible transformation into welfare society systems (Henrÿ 2014b).

This chapter aims to develop the rationale for the protection of the co-operative identity (Section 4.2) and to point to some of the challenges legislators face when translating this rationale into law (Section 4.3). Its reference frame is the perception of the world as one global world. The chapter is to contribute to the implementation of the ICA Blueprint (ICA Blueprint 2013). The five themes defined therein, namely participation, sustainability, identity, legal framework, and capital, structure the line of thinking of the present chapter.

4.2 THE RATIONALE FOR THE PROTECTION OF CO-OPERATIVE IDENTITY THROUGH LAW

Some deny the risk of losing co-operative identity through legislation. Others deny the need for such an identity. Others, again, deny the need to protect the co-operative identity through law. Usually, the debate over this question is limited to exchanges of political arguments. These disregard the legal nature of the co-operative principles. The nexus between the two sets of arguments is determined by the legal principle of the rule of law, whereby legal reasons override political ones until such time as they are altered through a legally defined political process. This part of the chapter deals with both legal and political arguments.

4.2.1 Legal Arguments

By putting the co-operative identity at the centre of its Blueprint, the ICA (2013) expresses concern about the risk of losing the co-operative identity. Much of this loss is

---

[5] For example, in Ecuador: Ley Orgánica de Economía Popular y Solidaria y del Sector Financiero (2011); France: Loi relative à l´économie sociale et solidaire (2014); Portugal: Social Economy Law (2013); Spain: Ley de Economia Social (2013). See also the 2004 British Act on Community Interest Companies, the 2003 Finnish Law on social enterprises (Law 1351/2003), and the Italian Law on social enterprises 155/2006.

due to legislation which has deviated over the past decades from the co-operative principles. This concern is shared by many researchers.[6]

The question is: is there a legal justification for assessing law through principles which have been developed by private enterprises? This question is all the more pertinent as often, approximation of the features of co-operatives with those of stock companies has been requested by co-operatives.

The nature of the validity of the co-operative principles has evolved over time. Inherited from the Rochdale Society of Equitable Pioneers and further developed by the ICA, the political weight of the co-operative principles grew with the number of individual members represented by the ICA and the increasing economic and social impact of the co-operatives operating according to these principles. The co-operative principles remained, however, the principles of a non-governmental organization. This changed at the beginning of the century. In 2001, the United Nations General Assembly adopted the 'Guidelines aimed at creating a supportive environment for the development of cooperatives' (UN GA Res. A/56/73; E/2001/68. UN Guidelines). These Guidelines refer in Paragraph 11 to the ICA Statement. In 2002, the International Labour Conference adopted the International Labour Organization (ILO) Recommendation No. 193 concerning the promotion of co-operatives (ILC 90-PR23-285-En-Doc. ILO R. 193). It integrates the content of the ICA Statement. Thus, the co-operative principles became part of a legal instrument of an international organization.

The ILO R. 193 calls repeatedly upon legislators to provide for an adequate co-operative law (Paragraphs 6.; 8.(2); 9., 10.; 18. (c), (d)) in order to establish, re-establish, or maintain, as the case may be, the co-operative identity (Paragraphs 2.; 6.; 7.(2); 10. (1)). But it does not specify the details of such a law.[7] However, the definition, taken from the ICA Statement and contained in Paragraph 2 of ILO R. 193 is sufficiently precise, and the recommendation states the basis on which to construct the co-operative identity, namely the co-operative values and principles (cf. Paragraph 3 and Annex), which are also taken from the ICA Statement, and the equal treatment principle (Paragraph 7.(2)), the logic of which presupposes that co-operatives be distinct entities.

ILO R. 193 is legally binding as far as co-operative law is concerned.[8] As the arguments used to justify this opinion rely in part on the practice by legislators, they become weak when regional and national laws drift away from the obligation contained in ILO R. 193 to maintain the co-operative identity. Other than the legal validity of national law, the legal validity of public international law depends to a large extent on legal subjects

---

[6] For example, del Burgo, Chuliá, Cracogna, Fici, Henrÿ, Münkner, Somerville; Spear. Cf. also articles in Boletín de la Asociación Internacional de Derecho Cooperativo. Nos. 22, 1995; 25, 1996; 29, 1997-II: series of articles on co-operative legislation in European countries. Nos. 23/24, 1995: series of articles on the realization of co-operative principles in different national legislations. Nos. 26–27, 1996; No. 37, 2003: series of articles on new financing instruments.

[7] For more on the contents of ILO R. 193 as far as co-operative law is concerned, see Henrÿ 2012a: 51ff.

[8] For a detailed list of arguments, see Henrÿ 2013e.

abiding by it. We therefore need additional political arguments to convince legislators that the co-operative identity needs protection.

4.2.2 Political Arguments

Henry Hansmann is among those who deny the need for a protection of the co-operative identity through law. Building on his 1996 seminal work, *The Ownership of Enterprise* (Hansmann 1996) he predicts a few years later, together with Reinier Kraakman, 'The End of History for Corporate Law' (Hansmann and Kraakman 2000–2001). They foresee an organizational law for all enterprise types under which specifics, if any, could be regulated through by-laws. Antonio Fici's introduction to the *International Handbook of Cooperative Law* can be seen as the first *réplique* by a co-operative lawyer to Hansmann. Fici argues that 'the history of (comparative) cooperative law has yet to begin' in view of establishing 'the essential elements of the cooperative identity' beyond its considerable variations (Fici 2013b: 19). Fici thus continues contributing to designing this identity.[9] He rightly criticizes Hansmann and Kraakman for being selective by choosing the single criterion of the owners' control right and their right to appropriate the firm's profit (residual earnings) in order to arrive at the conclusion that there is no fundamental difference between enterprise types. Fici suggests, instead, distilling the much richer co-operative identity from a comparative study of the co-operative laws in their reciprocal relationship with the co-operative principles.

Indeed, the comparative study of co-operative law, which by its very nature has to cover as many laws as possible, has been neglected, in stark contrast with the universal recognition of the co-operative principles since the late nineteenth century. Notwithstanding sporadic comparisons, which served legislators especially during the early days of co-operative law-making, and later studies, which for practical reasons were limited geographically,[10] comparative legal science has never embraced the subject. Barnes's comparative study of the definition of co-operatives (Barnes 1954) stands out as one of few singular cases.

Fici's approach of distilling the 'essential elements of the cooperative identity' from a comparison of the co-operative laws, avoids the essence trap into which those who attempt to distil the identity of co-operatives from the co-operative principles alone risk falling. Co-operatives have no essence. Identity is the continuously changing, politically negotiated result of differentiation from the other. Contrary views are one of the major obstacles to rejuvenating the co-operative idea. But the co-operative laws not only derive from the co-operative principles and, in turn, shape and modify these principles. They also clearly distinguish co-operatives from other types of enterprises. They did so over a period stretching roughly from the 1850s to the 1970s (Alanen 1964: 217;

---

[9] For further articles by him, see Fici 2013b: 60.

[10] For more details, see Foreword to *International Handbook of Cooperative Law*, 2013.

Egger 1925), and many still do so today. This distinction constitutes and protects the co-operative identity. However, laws are subject to (legal) policy changes. If law dilutes the co-operative identity, as it has over the past decades in many instances, then the question 'why should the co-operative identity be protected through law?' needs to precede the question 'how can the co-operative identity be protected through law?'. This is a political question that goes beyond the scope of Fici's contributions. Hansmann and Kraakman evade the question by covertly limiting the purpose of legislation. Taking their position to its logical conclusion, one could argue that there is no need for organizational law at all, since the right to elaborate the rules on the organization and operations of business entities through by-laws may be derived from Human Rights instruments. But, beyond the immediate purpose of regulating the organization and operations of a business entity, legislation has a number of more mediate purposes. Legislation, for example, fulfils a pedagogical purpose by providing a template for those who want to organize their business. It also fulfils the purpose of informing third parties who might find it impossible to protect their interests if they were to scrutinize the by-laws of each and every business partner. In addition, legislation constitutes a public policy instrument in application of the legal principle of the rule of law. In general, this purpose of law-making is being overlooked by the proponents of more 'flexible' laws. Where this 'flexibilization' allows for the much needed autonomy of co-operatives, it adds to the general shift of the very nature of law from a social instrument to a private instrument (Henrÿ 2014a). It also adds to the attempts to introduce an empirical turn in legal science, which would have significant effects on the law/politics nexus and would be a set-back to trying to complement (again) the economic analysis of law with a juridical analysis of economics.

This section of the chapter deals precisely with legislation's public policy purpose. Public policy concerns express themselves in the objectives of various enterprise types. The law establishes functional relationships between the objective and the financial and organizational structure of specific types of enterprise. These relationships are the object of institution building.

Hence, behind the technical aspect of legal rules and regulations lies a political choice. The former president of the French Accounting Standards Authority, Jérôme Haas, summarized this in the following words (Reverchon 2014): 'Derrière la technicité de ces documents d'experts des choix de société se dessinent pour aider à sortir de la crise de la mondialisation financière: préférence pour le présent ou conscience du long terme, diversité de modèles socio-économiques'. If this is true for technical rules such as accounting standards, it must also be true for legal norms such as co-operative laws. Barnes (1954) expressed similar views. This idea is also relevant for the following discussion on diversity.

In its Blueprint (ICA Blueprint 2013) the ICA develops the rationale for each of its five themes and makes suggestions on how to reach the goals it sets. Here, the rationale for the protection of the co-operative identity will be derived from the epistemological connections between the co-operative identity as the central theme of the ICA Blueprint and three of its other themes, namely sustainability, participation, and capital. The following subsections will underline that

- the co-operative identity is a constitutive element of sustainability,
- participation is the means to (re)generate sustainability, and
- co-operative specific capitalization is the kernel of the co-operative identity.

In line with the purpose of this chapter, this is not an exhaustive discussion on the identity of co-operatives.

4.2.2.1 *Co-operative Identity and Sustainability*

Co-operatives contribute to sustainable development as part of their identity. There is a juridical link between the objective of co-operatives, economic, social, and cultural Human Rights (International Covenant on Economic, Social and Cultural Rights, UN Doc.993 UNTS 3 (1966)), and sustainable development (Henrÿ 2014c). In addition, the co-operative identity is a constitutive element of sustainable development.

Speaking of the identity of an enterprise type only makes sense in the presence of at least one other type of enterprise. Two is the minimum number for a diversity of enterprise types. The diversity of enterprise types is not only required by law, for example ILO R. 193, Paragraph 6, and recognized as a factor for resilience during economic crises, it is also an expression of diversity as the source of development in the sense of life. Without the possibility of development, there is no sustainable development. Sustainable development has been recognized by the International Court of Justice as a legal concept of public international law since 1997. This concept is contained in the resolutions of regional and international organizations, as well as in treaties and national constitutions. The ICA Statement (7th Principle), the UN Guidelines (Paragraph 2), and the ILO R. 193 (Paragraph 3 and Annex; Paragraph 4.(g)), all deal with this subject. The final declaration of the 2012 Rio Conference makes several references to the relevance of co-operatives for sustainable development (cf. UN Doc. 'The Future we want', Paragraphs 70, 110, and 154) (Henrÿ 2013b).

Diversity is at stake where 'the other' turns into 'the different'. The issue relates to the 'difference' between 'other' and 'different' (Henrÿ 2013a). Although it is constantly changing as a result of differentiation from the other, identity constitutes where the other ceases to be perceived in its difference and ceases to be treated with the intention to reduce this difference. The borderline between 'other' and 'different' is moving. Identity is not an absolute. Nothing absolute may therefore be derived from the co-operative principles. But those who claim that law should protect the identity of co-operatives must at least describe where the turning point from 'other' to 'different' is. It is obvious that a literal application of the co-operative principles would not only disregard the history of co-operatives but would also hamper the evolution of the idea of co-operatives. The '9 Cs' whereby (potential) members with a set of homogenous interests co-found, co-finance, co-administer/manage, co-control, co-own a rather single-purpose co-operative, co-determine and co-use the services it provides, are jointly liable for the losses, and share the benefits, are features of a past which might have or might not have existed. Non-member users, non-user members (employees/workers, investors— whether they are members or not, with or without limited voting rights, public entities, or supporters) make today for a wider group in multi-stakeholder (Mori 2014)/multi-purpose co-operatives. Many of the existing co-operative laws do not yet provide for the legal support of these phenomena.

However, the question remains: what are co-operatives? What constitutes their irreducible identity? The following is a suggestion for discussion: co-operatives operationalize joint self-help in response to otherwise unmet needs. These needs are determined by those who control the enterprise through which these needs are satisfied. Co-operatives transform into a different (company) type where (member) user control turns into investor control, where financial return in terms of dividends/interests or growth in value of the enterprise is ahead of human needs (ICA Blueprint: 14).

Furthermore, we need to consider the following points. The legislative measures which lead to the risk of losing the co-operative identity are meant to create equal conditions for all enterprise types in terms of financial performance.[11] However well reasoned these measures were in the past, their justification is not scientific and it is outdated. The justification is not scientific for three reasons: it swaps the roles of the financial and the real economy; it measures all types of enterprises by definitional criteria of one type, the capital-centred company; and it is incomplete as it does not leave sufficient room for qualitative assessments of the competitiveness as far as the social and societal performance of enterprises is concerned.

The justification is outdated as the relative weight of capital in the shift towards globalized knowledge production, distribution, and consumption decreases and the effects of globalization lead to a redistribution of the social costs of enterprising from the public to the private sector. The new measure for competitiveness is the normative capacity of enterprises to contribute to sustainable development. Where all types of enterprises assume already greater social and societal responsibility than in the past, they do so on the basis of soft law and as far as their operational outcomes are concerned. Co-operatives go further. Their legal structure juridicizes functional relationships between the aspects of the sustainable development and the structural features of co-operatives (Henrÿ 2013b; Henrÿ 2014c). This is especially the case with the aspect of social justice through the participation of stakeholders in the governance and control structure of co-operatives.

4.2.2.2 *Participation and Sustainability*

Participation in the decisions on what and how to produce and how to distribute the produced wealth is a Human Right (International Covenant on Civil and Political Rights, UN doc. 999 UNTS 171 (1966)). It is the main operational mechanism in the pursuit of the sustainable development goal with its four aspects, namely economic

---

[11] As for this intention, see for example the European Union Communication from the Commission, especially Para. 3.2. See also International Labour Conference 2001: Chapter II, 3.

security, social justice, biosphere stability, and political stability. Through participation, social justice (re)generates.[12] Social justice is a prerequisite for political stability. Political stability is a prerequisite for economic security. Without economic security, we cannot expect a concern for the biosphere.

The co-operative-specific participation of its stakeholders is probably the feature which distinguishes co-operatives best from other types of enterprises. As the knowledge economy dissolves the unity of economic and political spaces and, consequently, the state and the labour market partners find it increasingly difficult to organize democratic participation, participation in and through enterprises becomes ever more important. But, participation is difficult to put into practice and into law. The issue of participation reaches far beyond the one member/one vote co-operative principle.

Large memberships have been a challenge for some time. But they are no obstacle to participation (Birchall 2014). Plural voting rights have been introduced into many national and regional laws, based on a variety of criteria. Where plural voting rights are based on the volume of transactions, this might incite members to transact with the co-operative. Transactions are a key element of participation, not the least because they contribute to determining the services the co-operatives provide and the way in which this is done. This kind of plural voting rights attribution, however, bears the risk of putting economic interest before social. The same is true for the attribution of limited voting rights to investors.

New modes of participation must incorporate new (communication) technologies and techniques which facilitate physical meetings and allow for virtual meetings. They must accommodate the legitimate interests of those who have become part of many co-operatives besides the member–users, as well as new forms of co-operatives.

Besides representative democracy, deliberative democracy modalities are also being tested. They might be especially adequate in the social service sector. Collaborative forms might best meet the needs in multi-stakeholder co-operatives which formalize public–private partnerships and where public interests might require departing from the equal vote principle.

A new challenge for participation, but also an opportunity for new activities, is 'Big Data'. Regaining control over one's own data in the Internet might be a new reason for solidarity-based joint co-operative action. Some are already testing this possibility.

Finally, the co-operative value of self-help needs to be mentioned as the most fundamental means of participation. A careful reading of the definition of co-operatives as contained in the ICA Statement and in the ILO R. 193 reveals this value as a principle of participation. The definition reads: '[a cooperative is] an autonomous association of persons united voluntarily to meet their common economic, social and cultural needs and aspirations through a jointly owned and democratically controlled enterprise.' It is clear: the co-operative does not do anything for its members. The members do together something for themselves by means of the co-operative enterprise. This reading is widely missing.

---

[12] For further elements, see Henrÿ 2014a.

4.2.2.3 *Capitalization and Co-operative Identity*

Nothing in the co-operative principles prevents legislators from going beyond the traditional way of financing co-operatives through members. But, whatever forms of capitalization are introduced, member control must be guaranteed. The capital must serve the satisfaction of economic, social, and cultural needs. Laws must not allow investor interests to take precedence over user needs. Again, a clear borderline cannot be drawn for all cases.

4.3 CHALLENGES FOR LEGISLATORS

Section 4.2 presents the reasons why legislators should continue constituting and protecting the co-operative identity. While allowing for new forms of participation and capitalization, and while adequately balancing the various aspects of the objectives of co-operatives (economic, social, and cultural), legislators, in order to enhance performance and meet public needs, need to accommodate the legitimate interests of a larger group of stakeholders than the member–users group. For this to happen, legislators need information and guidance. The body of knowledge on the co-operative principles has grown over decades, but little has been published on the translation of those principles into law.[13] Such translation presupposes that they be reinterpreted to meet modern requirements and that they be specified as legal principles. The ICA has embarked on the reinterpretation of the co-operative principles and intends to issue Guidance notes (ICA Blueprint: 20, 23). The Study Group on European Cooperative Law (SGECOL)[14] is elaborating co-operative legal principles to serve as a bridge between the co-operative principles and co-operative law. The setting up of similar groups is currently being discussed in Central and South America, as well as in Africa. This could eventually lead to finding a global common understanding of such legal co-operative principles. The ICA has established a Cooperative Law Committee which is to collaborate with the equivalent regional committees of the ICA. These committees will assist the ICA in its work to improve the legal frameworks for co-operatives.

These initiatives will—and must—lead to a further harmonization of co-operative laws. Indeed, the harmonization of co-operative laws both at the regional (Henrÿ 2013e: footnote 2) and at the international level (example ILO R. 193) is a fact. This harmonization is the result of shifts of legislation from the national to the regional and international levels, in line with the constitution of supranational and international political orders (Henrÿ 2012b; Henrÿ 2013c; Henrÿ 2013d: 819/20). Both

---

[13] As for exceptions, see Cracogna 1992; Cracogna 1998; Münkner 1974; Münkner 1982. More recently, Fici 2013a.

[14] See Fajardo et al. 2012.

the European Union and the ILO recommend further harmonization (European Union Communication: Action 10; ILO R. 193, Paragraph 18). The harmonization of co-operative laws through the definition of common co-operative legal principles contributes to the preservation of diversity. The identity of co-operatives needs to be established against the capital-centred enterprise type, which already has a global legal framework.

4.4 Conclusion: Further Challenges for Legislators

Lawyers are yet to understand the impact of the radical paradigm shift from an international to a global world on law and law-making. Globalization is not another layer added to the national, regional, and international ones. It is a whole new category, which embraces all of the others and where time and space disappear, with the emergence of a de-materialized economy whose main means of production is not capital, but knowledge—that is, the main product itself—and where, because of telecommunication technologies disposing of labour, it is not a matter of the physical mobility of people. An immediate consequence for enterprise law, including co-operative law, is that enterprises dissolve in value chains connecting the various parts across the globe (interconnectivity), rather than assembling them into units (collectivity) which resemble the classical theatre with its unity of locality, action, and time. Digitalized production, the logistics of distribution channels, calls the very *raison d'être* of the classical model of enterprises into question.

Furthermore, as can be seen in the corporate social responsibility and social entrepreneurship debate, enterprises are being attributed what used to be a public role. On the other hand, entrepreneurial features are being introduced into public institutions. The public/private dichotomy no longer structures the political, economic, social, and societal. The legal structures of public and private institutions have become inadequate and dysfunctional, hence ineffective and inefficient. As far as the welfare state is concerned, we are moving from a welfare state to a welfare society composed of public institutions, private enterprises, and civil society organizations. Its efficiency will not only depend on the collaboration of these actors, but it will be a function of a successful hybridization of their respective legal structures into a new legal type of co-operative enterprise, such as social co-operatives, capable of pursuing general-interest objectives.

There is a socio-psychological dimension to this evolution, with consequences for the nature of law. It relates to group building. We are moving from an anthropocentric world view, favouring collective entities, to an egocentric world view, favouring connective orders. New technologies have already led to new ways of social networking. The singularization of production follows the move from the individualization to the singularization of human beings (Rosanvallon 2011).

As much as the international world is universal, the global world is diverse. Because there is no other world behind this one world (Dürr 2011), we come to understand that we depend not only on the (global) biosphere, but also on its correlate, namely the (global) noosphere. This and the dissolution of the unity of economic and political spaces signify that law-making de-nationalizes and de-internationalizes. A first step towards a global law (Cebada Romero 2013, Ferrajoli 2013) could be to use transnational mechanisms, such as the standard setting by the ILO.

A global co-operative law must be composed of different co-operative laws. It must be distinct from the uniform law on capital-centred companies. It must be the expression and guarantor of diversity.

References

Alanen, A. J. (1964), *Hannes Gebhard* (Helsinki: Yhteiskirjapaino).

Barnes, W. S. (1954), 'La société coopérative: Les recherches de droit comparé comme instruments de définition d'une institution économique', *Revue Internationale de Droit Comparé*, 569–84.

Bialosgorski Neto, S. (2012), 'The History of the Rochdalian Cooperatives in Latin America', in J. Heiskanen, H. Henrÿ, P. Hytinkoski, and T. Köppä, eds., *New Opportunities for Co-operatives: New Opportunities for People* (Mikkeli and Seinäjoki/Finland: University of Helsinki/Ruralia Institute), 64–71.

Birchall, J. (2014), *The Governance of Large Co-operative Businesses* (Manchester: Co-operatives UK).

Boletín de la Asociación Internacional de Derecho Cooperativo. International Association of Cooperative Law Journal, Nos. 22, 1995; 25, 1996; 29, 1997-II; Nos. 23/24, 1995; Nos. 26–27, 1996; No. 37, 2003.

Cebada Romero, A. (2013), 'El derecho internacional global: Una retórica útil para una transformación necesaria', *Revista española de derecho internacional*, 65(1), 15–42.

Cracogna, D. (1992), *Problemas actuales del derecho cooperativo*, (Buenos Aires: Intercoop Editora).

Cracogna, D. (1998), *Manual de legislación cooperativa* (Buenos Aires: Intercoop Editora).

Cracogna, D., Fici, A., and Henrÿ, H. eds. (2013), *International Handbook of Cooperative Law*, Heidelberg et al.: Springer).

Dürr, H.-P. (2011), Das Lebende lebendiger werden lassen: Wie uns neues Denken aus der Krise führt, München: Oekom).

Egger, A. (1925), 'The Co-operative Movement and Co-operative Law', *International Labour Review*, XII(5), 609–33.

European Union (2004), Communication from the Commission to the Council and the European Parliament, the European Economic and Social Committee and the Committee of Regions. Communication 23/2/2004 on the promotion of cooperative societies in Europe. COM/2004/0018 final.

European Union (2010), *Study on the Implementation of the Regulation 1435/2003 on the Statute for a European Cooperative Society (SCE)*, at http://www.euricse.eu/node/257 (accessed 7 September 2016).

Fajardo, G., Fici, A., Henrÿ, H., Hiez, D., Münkner, H.-H., and Snaith, I. (2012), 'New Study Group on European Cooperative Law: Principles Project', *Euricse Working Paper*, No. 024|12, at http://euricse.eu/sites/euricse.eu/files/db_uploads/documents/1329215779_n1963.pdf (accessed 7 September 2016).

Ferrajoli, L. (2013), *La democrazia attraverso i diritti* (Roma-Bari: Laterza).

Fici, A. (2013a), 'Cooperative Identity and the Law', *European Business Law Review*, 24(1), 37ff.

Fici, A. (2013b), 'An Introduction to Cooperative Law', in D. Cracogna, A. Fici, and H. Henrÿ, eds, *International Handbook of Cooperative Law* (Heidelberg et al.: Springer), 3–62.

Gijselinckx, C., Zhao, L., and Novkovic, S., eds (2014), *Co-operative Innovations in China and in the West* (Houndmills, UK: Palgrave Macmillan).

Hansmann, H. (1996), *The Ownership of Enterprise* (Harvard: Harvard University Press).

Hansmann, H. and Kraakman, R. (2000–2001), 'The End of History for Corporate Law', *Georgetown Law Journal*, 89, 439ff.

Henrÿ, H. (2012a), *Guidelines for Cooperative Legislation* (3rd revised edn) (Geneva: International Labour Organization).

Henrÿ, H. (2012b), 'Basics and New Features of Cooperative Law: The Case of Public International Cooperative Law and the Harmonisation of Cooperative Laws', *Uniform Law Review: Revue de droit uniforme*. Vol. XVII, 197–233.

Henrÿ, H. (2013a), 'Entreprendre autrement: Le droit coopératif n'y est pour rien', *Revue Economique et Sociale: Bulletin de la Société d´Etudes Economiques et Sociales*, 70, 93–103.

Henrÿ, H. (2013b), 'Sustainable Development and Cooperative Law: Corporate Social Responsibility or Cooperative Social Responsibility?', *International and Comparative Corporate Law Journal*, 10(3), 58–75.

Henrÿ, H. (2013c, in print), 'Armonizar los derechos cooperativos bajo las condiciones de la globalización. ¿Por qué? ¿Cómo?'.

Henrÿ, H. (2013d), 'Trends and Prospects of Cooperative Law', in D. Cracogna, A. Fici, and H. Henrÿ, eds, *International Handbook of Cooperative Law* (Heidelberg et al: Springer), 803–23.

Henrÿ, H. (2013e), 'Public International Cooperative Law: The International Labour Organization Promotion of Cooperatives Recommendation, 2002', in D. Cracogna, A. Fici, and H. Henrÿ, eds, *International Handbook of Cooperative Law* (Heidelberg et al.: Springer), 65–88.

Henrÿ, H. (2014a) 'Quo Vadis Cooperative Law?', *CCIJ Report* No. 72, 50–61 (in Japanese. English manuscript with author).

Henrÿ, H. (2014b), 'Introduction', in H. Henrÿ, J. Hänninen, S. Paksu, and P. Pylkkänen, eds, *Osuustoiminnasta valoa vanhuspalveluihin* [*Light for Elderly Care from Cooperatives*] (Sastamala/Finland: Vammalan Kirjapaino), 7–13.

Henrÿ, H. (2014c), 'Human Rights Concretely: Sustainable Development Enhancing Cooperative Law', *Herald of the Belgorod University of Cooperation, Economics and Law*, 2, 505–13.

ICA Blueprint (2013), 'International Cooperative Alliance Blueprint for a Cooperative Decade 2011–2020', at http://ica.coop/sites/default/files/media_items/ICA%20Blueprint%20-%20Final%20version%20issued%207%20Feb%2013.pdf (accessed 7 September 2016).

ICA Statement (1995), International Cooperative Alliance Statement on the Cooperative Identity, *International Co-operative Review*, 88(4), 85–6.

International Labour Conference, 89th session (2001), Report V(1): Promotion of Cooperatives.

Mori, P. A. (2014), 'Community and Cooperation: The Evolution of Cooperatives Towards New Models of Citizens' Democratic Participation in Public Service Provision'. *Euricse Working Paper* n. 63/14.

Münkner, H. (1974), *Cooperative Principles and Cooperative Law* (Marburg: Institute for Co-operation in Developing Countries).

Münkner, H. (1982), *Ten Lectures on Cooperative Law* (Bonn: Friedrich-Ebert-Stiftung).

Reverchon, A. (2014), 'Haut fonctionnaire Jérôme Haas', *Le Monde*, 23 mai, 16.

Rhodes, R. (1995), *The International Co-operative Alliance During War and Peace* (Geneva: International Cooperative Alliance).

Rhodes, R. (2012), 'British Empire: The First Global Cooperative Development Agency', in J. Heiskanen, H. Henrÿ, P. Hytinkoski, and T. Köppä, eds, *New Opportunities for Co-operatives: New Opportunities for People* (Mikkeli and Seinäjoki/Finland: University of Helsinki/Ruralia Institute), 51–63.

Rosanvallon, P. (2011), *La société des égaux* (Paris: Seuil).

Snaith, I. (2013), 'United Kingdom', in D. Cracogna, A. Fici, H. Henrÿ, eds, *International Handbook of Cooperative Law* (Heidelberg et al.: Springer), 735–57.

PART II

RATIONALE OF CO-OPERATIVE ENTERPRISES

CHAPTER 5

··

CO-OPERATION AS
CO-ORDINATION MECHANISM

*a new approach to the economics
of co-operative enterprises*

··

CARLO BORZAGA AND ERMANNO C. TORTIA

5.1 INTRODUCTION

··

IN this chapter we strive to offer a new interpretation of co-operative enterprises by introducing the concept of spontaneous co-operation as an autonomous co-ordination mechanism of the economic activity. Enterprises are interpreted as tools directed to organize the production of goods and services mixing three different co-ordination mechanisms: market exchange (gain from trade), authority, and co-operation. In this perspective, we evidence the specific nature of co-operative enterprises as organizations characterized by the dominance of the co-operation mechanism.

At a more basic level, we highlight that we still miss a clear-cut and general explanation of the existence of co-operative enterprises in economic theory. The neoclassical approach, by assuming self-seeking individuals and profit-maximizing enterprises, simply negates the relevance and the sustainability of co-operatives. On the other hand, the institutionalist literature, starting from Ronald Coase (1937), explains the existence of enterprises on the basis of the necessity to overcome specific typologies of market failure and imperfections, which in the most simple cases cause transaction costs to rise (see also Milgrom and Roberts 1990). This literature also explains the existence of co-operatives to some extent, positioning their emergence within the realm of market failures connected mainly with positional power on the market. However, co-operatives are generally considered by new institutionalist authors as 'transitional' organizations that will be overcome by regulation of markets and by heightened competitive pressure (Hansmann 1996). Alternative approaches, even when in favour of the spread of co-operative enterprises, are mostly empirical and focus mainly on specific types or characteristics of co-operatives, but fail to provide a general interpretation.

The shortcomings of existing theoretical elaborations have often led to overlooking the instances and dimensions under which co-operatives are not only able to overcome market failures, but are as much or more efficient than the other entrepreneurial forms. Oft-cited examples include the agricultural and credit sectors in which co-operatives have a prominent role, and the growth in numbers and dimension in some countries of co-operatives delivering social and community-oriented services. One negative consequence of the limited theoretical understanding has been the lack of attention paid by public policy in supporting and consistently regulating the co-operative forms.

Our contention is that theoretical flaws in economics are to be ascribed to the consideration of only two main co-ordination mechanisms of economic activity: exchange of equivalent values on the market, or 'gain from trade', and authority, or hierarchy (Heath 2006). Orthodox economics takes perfect markets as a condition that is either already given or that will generally be achieved through competition and/or regulation, except in the case of few public goods. However, imperfections on capital markets are positioned at the origin of investor-owned companies and these imperfections are, de facto, assumed to be the most difficult to overcome. In this case asset specificity gives rise to non-reducible and non-contractible asymmetries in information, contract incompleteness, and a clear incentive to behave opportunistically towards investors (Williamson 1973). These premises inevitably imply that enterprises controlled by investors (IOFs) are the only necessary form. The corollary to this conclusion is that, to overcome residual imperfections that are not overcome by the ownership of investors (e.g. in intra-firm relationships between owners and managers and between employers and employees), IOFs can resort to authority. We contend instead that the relative unimportance of imperfections in non-capital markets can be questioned, especially in sectors that do not provide pure private goods, such as collective goods.

In our framework, the market is not necessarily the best co-ordination mechanism, and authority is not always the best alternative to the market, as public choice theory claims. This is due to the persistence of market failures and power, contractual imperfections, and limitations, and of the connected transaction costs (Ostrom 1990). Also, market exchanges are not always conducive to optimal processes of production when intertemporal accumulation of knowledge, which has the potential to generate dynamic transaction costs and modify the boundaries of the firm, and collective action are needed to achieve the desired social and economic goals (Langlois 1992; Loasby 2006). Co-operation is able to introduce new ways to pursue entrepreneurial objectives since it emerges when a collective of economic actors voluntarily decides to join efforts and resources to increase welfare beyond what independent action would guarantee. Transactions managed through co-operation take place, not on the basis of an authority relation, but voluntarily and, differently from market exchanges, the participation in the transaction depends not on the equivalence between contribution and outcome (in terms of economic value), but on the reciprocity principle (Zamagni 2005). Due to the uncertainty surrounding the results of co-operative interactions, co-operation helps develop transactions when, under the veil of ignorance, equivalence between contribution and outcome can be expected, but not guaranteed, on the basis of fair procedures.

5.2 THE STATE OF THE ART
IN ECONOMIC THEORY

Traditional economic approaches to the study of co-operative enterprises, especially neoclassical economics, pre-eminently evidence the possible limitations of this organizational form by assuming self-seeking, non-co-operating economic agents, and maximization of monetary returns as the exclusive objective of worker co-operatives (Ward 1958). The conclusions of this approach have never been confirmed by empirical tests, showing inability to factor-in co-operation as a co-ordination mechanism (Bartlett et al. 1992; Craig and Pencavel 1992, 1994; Bonin et al. 1993).

Also, financial difficulties concerning the access to financial markets and self-finance represent the leitmotiv of critiques accusing co-operatives of being non-sustainable or dynamically inefficient entrepreneurial ventures. Furubotn and Pejovich (1970) and Vanek (1970) evidenced that, in worker co-operatives, the presence of non-recoupable assets conjugated with the truncated temporal horizon characterizing worker-members implies inefficient self-finance, which leads to underinvestment and undercapitalization. Indeed, co-operatives have often been found to rely more on the credit market than conventional enterprises, and to self-select into labour-intensive sectors, even if other contributions show the viability of co-operatives financed through the accumulation of divisible and indivisible reserves of capital (Bartlett et al. 1992; Podivinsky and Stewart 2006).

New Institutionalism demonstrated a superior ability in explaining the emergence and spread of co-operatives and reached wide consensus by showing, first, that co-operatives can play an important role in the presence of strong concentration of market power, that is monopoly power in the case of consumer and user (demand side) co-operatives and monopsony power in the case of agricultural, producer, and worker (supply side) co-operatives. Second, mutual benefit organizations can be the most effective solution when strategic investments are not carried out by investors, but by other classes of stakeholders, as happens in professional partnerships. Third, co-operative organizations are reported to perform well, at times better than conventional companies, when control rights can allow the reduction of organizational costs and better alignment of members' and organizational goals (Craig and Pencavel 1992, 1994, on US plywood co-operatives in Pacific Northwest). This evidence notwithstanding, most new institutionalist literature maintains that non-investor-owned forms of enterprise have a marginal role in contemporary economies and are transitory in the face of market completion, since they emerge due to failures on markets other than capital ones. Furthermore, the application of the same theoretical tools and methodology used in the analysis of investor-owned enterprises and the disregard of co-operation as a basic co-ordination mechanism has led to the idea that the working of co-operatives too is dominated by market exchanges and hierarchical control. Consistently, the economics profession has marginalized or altogether excluded teaching and analysis of co-operative enterprises (Kalmi 2007).

Taking a different perspective, we evidence, first, that non-investor-owned forms of enterprise are able to survive and spread in many sectoral and regional contexts in the absence of pronounced market failures, as in the case of contemporary agricultural, credit, and producer co-operatives. This evidence shows that market imperfections may be only one of the possible causes of their spread and resilience, therefore calling for new research evaluating their emergence and potential (Birchall 2013a, 2013b). Second, new institutionalism has not fully shown the benefits, but mostly the costs, that this kind of organization is able to generate. As some authors have noticed, higher costs do not necessarily imply inefficiency, as they can be functional to value generation or to increased non-monetary welfare (Dow 2003; Birchall 2010; Borzaga and Tortia 2010; Birchall 2013b). In providing a new and alternative explanation of the co-operative firm, we submit that the basic working mechanisms in co-operatives are different from those of other organizational domains concerning the way in which: (i) co-ordination among the involved actors is achieved; (ii) welfare is generated; (iii) the produced surplus is distributed.

We follow the Samuel Bowles (2004) framework and position the working of co-operative enterprises within the perimeter of the community, as alternative to markets and the state, as the relevant governance structure. We study under which conditions market failures cannot be overcome by increased market competition or by improved regulation and, second, how co-operatives are able, not only to overcome market and state failures, but also to generate higher surpluses and welfare thanks to non-traditional forms of co-ordination in the contexts of proximity, democracy, and community (Grandori and Funari 2008; Sacchetti and Sugden 2009).

5.3 CO-OPERATION AS A SPECIFIC KIND OF CO-ORDINATION MECHANISM

Spontaneous co-operation as a mechanism of associative nature, based on the mutual benefit of the participating actors and on trust and reciprocity as supporting behavioural dimensions, is added, in the realm of production and entrepreneurship, to market exchange and hierarchy, which have been sharing the dominant role in transmitted economic approaches (Williamson 1973). The recognition that collective action based on co-operation can be as much, or more, effective than market exchanges and hierarchy in achieving efficiency has spread only recently, thanks to the pioneering works by Elinor Ostrom (1990). She showed how, in the case of the management and exploitation of common pools of natural resources, co-operative effort can represent a more efficient alternative to both public and private ownership (Ostrom and Basurto 2011). Other authors have also considered the social advantages of associative and communitarian forms of governance (Valentinov 2007). Finally, this approach has just been applied to the study of enterprises, especially to co-operatives (Sacconi 2015; Sacconi and Ottone 2015; Tortia 2015).

Voluntary co-operation, as evidenced in the works by Joseph Heath (2006), can deliver adequate co-ordination without resorting to exchange or authority, or by using them in a functional and limited way. Market exchange is overcome because the parties do not exchange equivalent ownership rights on goods or services, but act on the basis of collective projects and objectives. Collective objectives are pursued, in many instances, on the basis of common forms of ownership, such as locked assets. Similarly, authority is also absent since co-operation is understood as horizontal co-ordination and, in its basic working, cannot be reduced to vertical relations between a dominant and a subordinate individual or group. In co-operative co-ordination, mutual benefit is pursued in order to increase welfare for the involved parties, and is sustained over time by exploiting existing trust relations, or by generating new ones, and by reciprocating behaviours (Sabatini et al. 2014). This form of social interaction either increases the total surplus produced (the production function is super-additive) or reduces possible costs that would arise in the absence of co-operation—for example, the costs of conflict, of opportunistic behaviours, and of negative externalities (Borzaga and Sacchetti 2015).

Co-operative effort or contribution is arranged before the achievement of the expected results. Insofar as the results are not controllable ex-ante, co-operative interaction is only partially enforceable, and implies that a precise equivalence between contribution and reward, which characterizes the exchange mechanism, cannot be guaranteed. The non-perfect predictability of outcomes and of distributive patterns requires that fundamental behavioural dimensions such as fairness, trust, and reciprocity acquire, in co-operative co-ordination, a more fundamental role than in other co-ordination mechanisms. Fairness becomes a necessary criterion in the evaluation of the quality of co-operative interaction, in accomplishing equitable distribution of outcomes, and in supporting participation in collective action (Guth et al. 1982; Kahneman et al. 1991; Tyler and Blader 2000). As an relevant oft-cited application, egalitarian wage structures do not represent anomalies any more, but can be correctly explained in terms of procedural and distributive fairness (Frank 1984; Leete 2000). Trust acts as facilitator and as transaction cost-reducing behavioural pattern. A significant degree of trust is necessary to support the ex-ante expectation that co-operative interaction will lead to mutually beneficial outcomes. Positive reciprocity, on the other hand, has been envisaged as the main mechanism through which fairness and trust are sustained, preserved, and invigorated over time (Axelrod 1984; Akerlof 1982; Fehr et al. 1993; Fehr and Gächter 2000; Zamagni 2005). Coherently, while opportunism is taken by all orthodox approaches to be one dominant behavioural trait in principal–agent interactions, and in relations among economic agents and conventional enterprises more generally (Alchian and Demsetz 1972; Williamson 1973), when co-operation becomes dominant, opportunism is downgraded to a non-fundamental behavioural distortion that can be tamed and overcome by proper working rules and governance solutions (Sacchetti and Tortia 2015).

5.3.1 Co-operation in the Organizational Context

A conception of the enterprise based on the co-operative mechanism refers primarily to the role of intrinsic motivation and non-self-seeking preferences (in line with deCharms 1968 and Valentinov 2007), while horizontal co-ordination based on trust, reciprocity, and fair procedures cannot be excluded any more (Fehr and Gächter 2000). This conception can be applied to co-operative firms, but also to other organizational and proprietary forms (private and public).

Co-operation as a crucial co-ordination mechanism in the organization of production has already been considered in several contexts, although to different extents and with different strength. For example, voluntary organizations require spontaneous co-operative effort as a driving force and cannot be managed by way of hierarchical control or market exchange in order not to dampen the intrinsic and pro-social motivations of volunteers (Titmuss 1970; Deci 1975; Rose-Ackerman 1996; Frey 1997; Ryan and Deci 2000). The relevance of co-operation is evident also in the case of donations, where horizontal co-ordination of donors mediated by the relevant non-profit entity is unavoidable if the desired results are to be reached. As said, collective action emerges as the crucial co-ordination mechanism in the literature on the management of common pools of natural resources and on the delivery of local public services (Ostrom 1965, 1990). Similar remarks concern the production of new knowledge in contemporary ICT services through the development of open-source software and publicly available online resources such as Wikipedia and Creative Commons, which have lowered ICT production costs and made the software industry less concentrated (Rifkin 2014).

Like market and hierarchies, co-operation exists in all organizational forms: public, private for-profit, and co-operative, with different functions and strength in each individual form. In publicly owned organizations, where authority is to be considered as the dominant co-ordination mechanism, co-operation is not fundamental. Nevertheless, it intervenes as a mechanism that reduces the costs of intra-organizational transactions by easing industrial relations, and facilitating the sharing of objectives by the different constituencies involved. Related arguments can be put forward in the case of private for-profit firms. This organizational form is more strongly dependent on relations based on gain from trade and systems of monetary incentives than publicly owned firms, as evidenced by the interpretation of the firm as nexus of contracts (Alchian and Demsetz 1972; Jensen and Meckling 1976). In private firms, co-operation has a similar function to that found in publicly owned organizations; it is not fundamental, but functional to reducing organizational costs by reinforcing trust and reciprocating behaviours (Akerlof 1982). Its importance has been widely stressed by managerial disciplines, especially in the relation between workers and managers, as related to the co-operative deployment of human resource management (McGregor, 1960; Aoki 1984; Roos et al. 1991; Appelbaum et al. 2000). In co-operatives, instead, co-ordination is more fundamentally based on spontaneous co-operation, which is not only functional to the reduction of organizational costs, but increases members' welfare beyond what independent production and simple market exchanges would guarantee. This is achieved through members' participation, which steers strategic objectives, production plans, and distribution patterns.

The impossibility of predicting exactly outcomes and rewards through the co-operative mechanism requires the design and implementation, both ex ante and in the course of action, of fair procedures and governance rules. The organizational importance of fairness is testified by the fact that fair interaction and procedures have been found to be the most relevant determinant of the well-being of the participating actors, both in co-operative enterprises and in other organizational forms. However, in co-operatives and in non-profit organizations they appear to take on a more fundamental and stronger role (Benz and Stutzer 2003; Benz 2005; Tortia 2008).

Co-operatives are less dependent on market exchanges than private for-profit firms because they tend to develop specific organizational mechanisms and accumulate resources, for example locked assets, that are directed to shield the membership against negative shocks and market fluctuations. Similarly, elements of authority in strategic decision-making and in the organization of production are not absent in co-operatives, but they do not represent the dominant co-ordination mechanism as happens in publicly owned organizations. Vertical relations are substituted, more fundamentally, by horizontal co-ordination.

Figure 5.1 shows how, at the vertices of the triangle, market exchanges, hierarchy/authority, and spontaneous co-operation concur in creating the space for entrepreneurial action. The three main enterprise forms are defined by the stratification and interaction of the three co-ordination mechanisms. The co-operative enterprise is closer to spontaneous co-operation than any other organizational form, but does not coincide with this vertex, since market exchanges and authority are present as well. Similar conditions are found in the cases of public and private for-profit enterprises, in which authority and market exchanges play, respectively, the most relevant, but not exclusive roles.

5.4 A New Approach to the Economics of Co-operative Enterprises

The consideration of co-operation as the dominant co-ordination mechanism allows us to develop a radically new theoretical approach to the study of co-operative enterprises, in light of the fact that existing theories have reduced co-operatives to the basic working of other dominant organizational forms.

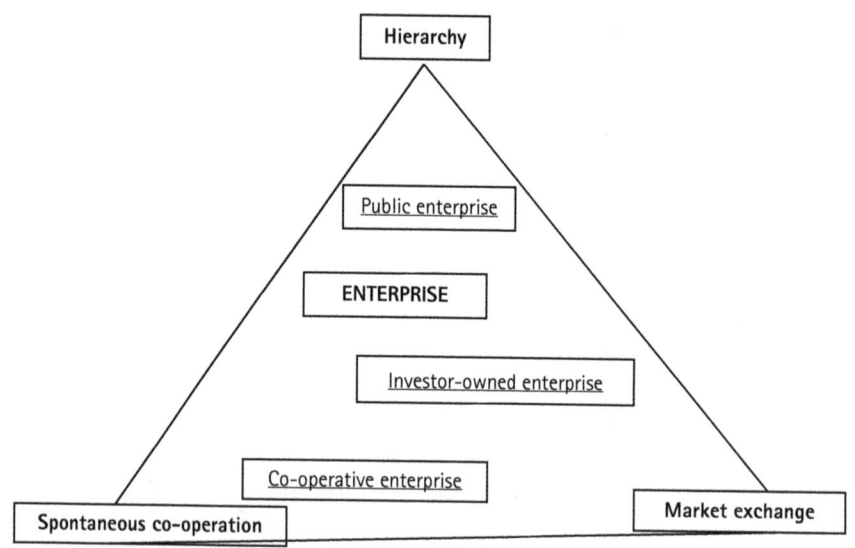

FIGURE 5.1 Different co-ordination mechanisms of the economic activity, and corresponding organizational forms.

Source: Authors' diagram

5.4.1 Features and Objectives of the Co-operative Form

In the process of revision of the economic theory of co-operative enterprises, newer and emerging approaches, such as evolutionary and behavioural economics, appear to be more compatible than orthodox economics with the institutional features and behavioural complexities of this entrepreneurial form. They promise to add crucial insights when co-operation is understood as a co-ordination mechanism. Behavioural economics, and its application in game theory and experimental economics, focuses on individual and collective behaviours informed by intrinsic and not fully self-interested motivations and preferences (Kahneman et al. 1991; Fehr and Gächter 2000; Degli Antoni and Sacconi 2011). While trust, reciprocity, and fairness can be widespread at the societal level and embedded in social capital (Guiso et al. 2006; Tabellini 2008), the conditions under which they become emergent organizational dimensions, are sustained and strengthened over time, and transmitted to or absorbed from the wider societal context and need deeper enquiry (Tyler and Blader 2000; Tortia 2008; Sabatini et al. 2014).[1] On the other hand, evolutionary economics focuses on structural and institutional change informed by adaptive behaviours, which can lead to the emergence and sustainability of new organizational routines and institutions based on co-operation and supporting mutual benefit as an evolutionarily stable and progressive organizational pattern. Among the main reasons for this result is the fact that such routines can overcome contract failures and internalize behavioural

---

[1] This approach is anticipated by contributions dealing with group selection (Bowles and Gintis 2011).

traits connected with trust, positive reciprocity, and fairness better than hierarchy and other traditional organizational solutions (Hodgson 1993; Gowdy and Seidl 2004; Borzaga et al. 2011).

In our framework, and contrary to the Ward (1958) model, the equivalence of the objective of co-operatives to profit maximization is not guaranteed. While monetary objectives tend to occupy most of the behavioural spectrum in profit-oriented enterprises, co-operatives promote additional goals that depend on their mutual benefit nature and on intrinsic and relational motivations. Individual objectives need to be conjugated with collective ones through the development of appropriate governance solutions. The different objective function also has implications in terms of distribution of benefits that accrue to different stakeholders through organizational routines informed by distributive fairness (Tortia 2008). Finally, especially in the presence of positive externalities of the organizational activity, the pursuit of social objectives too, once thought to be an exclusive feature of non-profit organizations, is not alien to co-operatives, as testified by the spread of social and community-oriented co-operatives in several countries.

These arguments imply that the welfare function maximized by co-operatives, which is not amenable to excessive simplification in terms of maximization of monetary returns, awaits finer definition (Thompson 2015). In co-operatives, standard monetary objectives, financial sustainability and growth, represent part of the process of need satisfaction that drives the working of the organization. However, the direct linkage between control rights and governance with the objectives of non-investor stakeholders is likely to imply that co-operatives do not in fact maximize net monetary returns alone, but satisfy, instead, a plurality of needs through monetary and non-monetary rewards related to the complexity of human motivations, and directed to increase also non-monetary well-being (Maslow 1943). The strongest implication of non-investor control is that, since capital no longer sets the objectives of the organization, it becomes a sheer instrument to the pursuit of members' objectives (Jossa 2012).

The absence of profit maximization does not imply inability to produce adequate added value and, therefore, in co-operatives profit maximization is not equivalent to maximization. Exemplifying, value-added maximization in producer co-operatives requires the pursuit of increased producers' remuneration, while profit maximization in investor-owned companies requires the remuneration of suppliers of inputs and rough materials to be minimized. As for demand-led co-operatives (mutuals and consumer, user, and banking co-operatives), their tendency to minimize profits and introduce better contractual conditions for clients and users can lead to maximum consumer surplus and minimum profits, even in the absence of sustained market competition. In more general terms, profit is normally a misleading measure of efficiency in co-operatives since it does not account for the whole value added produced by the organization, and for the necessity to increase consumer surplus in the presence of monopoly and monopsony power. Conversely, value added and social welfare may not be the best measure of performance in investor-owned companies, since these may tend to squeeze the remuneration of the contracted factors of production and consumer surplus in order to maximize profits.

Authority and market exchange are still present in co-operatives, as they can be functional towards achieving mutual benefit and social goals. Hierarchy is present in co-operatives, typically in the agency relation between the membership and managers, and between managers and employed workers. Authority is introduced as part of the governance structure to improve enforceability of contracts and effective implementation of investment and production plans, and distributive patterns. The required intensity of authority can vary widely with the type of co-operative enterprise, scale of operation, factor intensity (e.g. higher labour vis à vis capital intensity), and sector of activity.

Market exchanges are present as well, though their role is less paramount than in investor-owned companies. Co-operatives acquire their inputs and sell their output on the market, and this obvious connection makes them an integral part of decentralized market-led economies. On the other hand, over and above interaction with the market, membership rights and inclusive governance are intended to shelter members against excessively direct pressures (fluctuations and shocks) coming from the open market and from simple contractual transactions. Co-operatives are often created just to escape market failure, excessively harsh competition, and exploitative contractual relations based on positional power. As a notable example, worker co-operatives emerged historically to overcome negative contractual conditions on the labour market, such as exploitatively low wages due to monopsony, and arbitrary lay-offs; or to preserve the economic and social value of workers' competencies, as testified by the phenomenon of worker buy-outs (Vieta 2015). Second, credit co-operatives are most often created to eliminate usury and reduce credit rationing against small and financially 'opaque' producers, which can be deprived of collateral guarantees.

The non-traditional role of authority and market exchanges in co-operatives shows, once again, that we are dealing with a different organizational typology characterized by peculiar control rights and governance rules informed by co-operation as co-ordination mechanism. The different developmental logic of organizational routines and incentive systems has allowed co-operatives to realize peculiar institutions and governance structures, such as personal membership rights, the asset lock, and multi-stakeholder governance, to reach their mutual benefit goals. The dominance of the traditional co-ordination mechanisms is overcome thanks to participatory governance—as epitomized by the 'one member, one vote' rule—which emerged historically as the typical way in which groups of principals find compatibility between members' individual needs and preferences and align them to organizational objectives in a continuous two-way process of adaptation. The asset lock, whether compulsory or left to organizational by-laws, was introduced in most countries to guarantee the possibility of accumulating owned resources in indivisible reserves, which cannot be exchanged on the market, but, at the same time, cannot exist without relying on market exchanges in the acquisition-of-inputs and sale-of-output phases. Finally, thanks to multi-stakeholder governance, transactions are implemented starting from non-traditional premises through the involvement of groups of controlling and non-controlling stakeholders, by this means reducing the possible failures of simple contractual exchanges and exclusive decision-making power attached to one single group of patrons.

5.4.2 A Critical Review of the Limitations of Co-operative Enterprises

Orthodox economics finds the main limitations of co-operative enterprises in the distorted reactions to market stimuli and in the inefficient allocation of investment funds (Ward 1958; Furubotn and Pejovich 1970). New institutionalism, instead, has evidenced their difficulty as regards increasing the scale of operation and the cost-inflating nature of their governance, especially in terms of decision-making processes when a heterogeneous membership is involved. However, these limitations are largely dependent on the theoretical approaches and become less important when co-operation is considered the basic mechanism of co-ordination in co-operatives.

In the former stream of thought, the Ward (1958) model evidenced the so-called 'perverse effects' concerning the reactions of Yugoslav type worker-controlled enterprises to market stimuli (variation in product price and interest rate). Co-operatives would react to increased output prices by reducing supply and shedding labour and to increased cost of capital by increasing production and employment. These perverse effects have never been confirmed by empirical tests (Bartlett et al. 1992; Craig and Pencavel 1992, 1994; Bonin et al. 1993).[2] In our approach, the presence of perverse reactions to market stimuli can be overcome by introducing a fundamental role for collective action, instead of individual opportunism, and by hypothesizing the existence of formal and informal rules based on procedural fairness and reciprocating behaviours, factoring in employment stability for all worker-members as a fundamental objective of the organization (Miyazaki and Neary 1983; Jossa 2012; Albanese et al. 2015; Navarra and Tortia 2014; Pérotin 2014).

Second, within the same research stream, difficulties in the process of capitalization and in accessing financial markets represent the leitmotiv of many critiques accusing co-operatives of being financially inferior to investor-owned firms and non-sustainable. In the dynamic approach to the study of different property rights settings initiated by Furubotn and Pejovich (1970) and by Vanek (1970), underinvestment and undercapitalization derive from the presence of non-recoupable assets conjugated with worker-members' truncated temporal horizon. While no definitive results concerning the undercapitalization hypothesis have been reached, we submit that the financial structure of co-operatives shows radical differences relative to investor-owned firms. In most national systems of regulation, beside standard financial instruments (loan finance from financial intermediaries and bonds), capital in co-operative firms is more similar to a common good, that is a rival but non-excludable stock of accumulated resources, than

---

[2] While the Ward (1958) model assumes labour to be perfectly flexible in the short run, this assumption contradicts the pronounced tendency shown by worker co-operatives to protect employment levels in the short to medium run (Ellerman, 1986), as also testified by several empirical tests (Bartlett et al. 1992; Craig and Pencavel 1992, 1994; Pencavel et al. 2006; Burdin and Dean 2009).

to a private good. Members pursue collective goals in the presence of scarce (rivalrous) resources, while non excludability is due to the equality of membership rights and can be extended inter-temporally through the accumulation of common resources that are passed on from one generation of members to the next. In this case, intergenerational solidarity and reciprocity resemble the logic of trust games in that incumbent generations of members receive a given stock of capital from past generations and need to decide how much of it to hand over to future generations (Berg et al. 1995). This new theoretical frame needs to be developed following the tenets of institutional and behavioural theory, factoring in co-operation as financial co-ordination mechanism (Tortia 2015).

As concerns new institutionalist critiques, co-operatives are, as a norm, smaller than corporations since small size supports co-operation based on interpersonal relations. Personal interactions can lead to increased organizational welfare by favouring better circulation of information, creation of firm specific knowledge (both tacit and formalized), the reduction of opportunistic behaviours thanks to horizontal control and peer pressure, better quality of personal knowledge and relations, and the accumulation of localized social capital (Sabatini et al. 2014). They can also keep the interests, preferences, and objectives of the membership homogeneous and therefore reduce organizational costs in terms of decision-making. However, limited size can put co-operatives at a disadvantage compared to large private and public corporations due to lack of scale and scope economies, to the inability to control large shares of input and output markets, to enter capital-intensive sectors, and to innovate thanks to intensive R&D investments. While several counterexamples to the dominance of small size in co-operatives exist, this limitation can also be contrasted by introducing market and authority, alongside co-operation, as co-ordination mechanisms. Larger dimension can be achieved, in the latter case, through the development of networks, consortia, federations, and similar horizontal associative structures. In the former case, hybrid systems of ownership allow co-operatives in most countries to create, purchase, or otherwise control investor-owned companies, which are characterized by centralized governance and more direct access to financial markets (Spear 2012). In this way, co-operatives often reach a larger average dimension than privately owned companies. Other authors argue, instead, that limited size may not necessarily be a shortcoming of co-operatives. The concept of 'critical mass' is used by Michele Grillo (2015) to evidence that efficient size does not necessarily correspond to large size, because dimensional growth may be functional to increased market power, not to production efficiency. In this understanding, co-operatives, by not pursuing dimensional growth, can indirectly increase market competition and social welfare.

Finally, new institutionalists also evidenced the difficulty of co-operatives guaranteeing efficient governance due to their tendency to inflate organizational costs in terms of decision-making, especially when they are characterized by heterogeneous membership (Hansmann 1996). The problem of inflated decision-making costs can be faced, first, by improved adaptability of governance thanks to the development of appropriate organizational routines as systems of working rules, control mechanisms, and sanctions, even in the presence of pluralist and participatory decision-making (Ostrom 1990; Borzaga and Tortia 2010). Second, inclusion has the potential to increase overall surplus, not only organizational costs. Both monetary and non-monetary benefits can grow thanks to improved circulation of information, fair organizational protocols, and the reinforcement, rather than the weakening, of the intrinsic motivations of members. Third, mutual benefit and social, not purely individual self-seeking objectives pursued by co-operatives have been hypothesized to reduce negative external effects and social costs connected with contractual failures, through dedicated governance and increased resources devoted to social purposes (Borzaga et al. 2011, Borzaga and Sacchetti 2015).

New-institutionalist criticism addressed to co-operative governance is fully legitimate and can be thought to signal the existence of an evolutionary challenge forcing co-operatives to develop more refined and effective governance and working rules to face well-known break-down risks, as in the classic 'tragedy of the commons' situations, and to keep decision-making costs under control. As stated by Elinor Ostrom (1990: 45):

> Dilemmas nested inside dilemmas appear to be able to defeat a set of principals attempting to solve collective-action problems through the design of new institutions to alter the structure of the incentives they face .... But some individuals and/ or communities have created institutions, committed themselves to follow rules, and monitored their own conformance.

Complex processes of institutional adaptation in terms of creation and implementation of suitable governance are required if co-operatives are to keep the promise for which they have been created. Governance emerges as the context in which co-operation can accomplish its objectives and overcome the social effectiveness of other organizational forms, but also as the context in which co-operation can most easily break down. Hansmann (2013: 8) states:

> the principal question regarding enterprise ownership is which class(es) of patrons will be made the owners. The answer depends heavily on the governance structures that firms can and do adopt, which in turn depend on the legal and institutional environment .... The full potential of cooperatives should become much clearer when scholarship regarding their governance becomes both broader and deeper.

5.5 Applications of the New Framework

When co-operation is understood as an autonomous co-ordination mechanism of the economic activity, the whole understanding of the nature of co-operatives and of business enterprises more generally is renewed and widened, since the working of the organization is no longer exclusively seen in terms of trade and authority, but also in terms of collective ability to carry out co-operative projects by devoting effort and resources to them. As we observed, the implications are stringent: the dominance of the co-operative mechanism implies lower recourse to monetary incentives and relations based on trust more than on direction, thanks to a fundamental role for intrinsic motivations and procedural fairness, and to lower opportunism in intra-organizational relations. Market and hierarchy can still be useful, but not dominant, to pursue these objectives, for example when dimensional growth and wide delegation of decision-making are needed, or when co-operatives expand by acquiring conventional corporations.

The implications of this new organizational structure are highlighted through examples from real-world co-operatives. Contrary to what theories of organizational isomorphism claim, these examples clearly show that differences in control rights, objectives, and forms of governance impact the behaviour of the organization. Consistently with Williamson (2000), we can state that the impact of co-operative co-ordination runs all the way up from the most fundamental institutional layers to the surfacing layers. The deepest layers, which define strategic objectives and the patterns of appropriation, are found in control rights and governance; while the surfacing layers, which define the interaction between the organization and the external environment, correspond to working rules and organizational routines inscribed in organizational protocols, in managerial models and practices, and in the deployment of technology.

We start from producer co-operatives, more specifically agricultural co-operatives, which, according to new institutionalism, mainly emerge to overcome the monopsony power held by intermediaries and buyers. In the food industry, monopsonistic power can be present downstream in the activities carried out by farmers and growers. This phenomenon can push farmers to create co-operatives in order to gain direct access to and control over the market. However, the economic weight and the duration of agricultural co-operatives in many countries can hardly be explained by referring to market failures alone. Reference to efficiency gains, to the reduction of economic risk through the implementation of insurance mechanisms, and to the accumulation of knowledge that is generated by letting farmers co-ordinate while retaining independence in production are also needed. The non-standardized nature of agricultural production, which is connected with weather fluctuation and unpredictability, and with the intrinsically uncertain nature of its quality, requires pooling of resources to overcome economic risk, stabilize prices and production in the medium to long run, and create specialized know-how based on direct farmers' involvement. In many instances, contractual exchanges and authority alone would not be effective in guaranteeing the same degree of co-ordination and efficiency, implying lower resilience to external shocks (Tortia et al. 2013).

As a second example, we consider worker co-operatives. The ability to overcome monopsony power and to absorb negative shocks on the labour market allows this organizational form to achieve simultaneously adequate worker remuneration and stable employment, in that worker co-operatives have been observed in several contexts to resort to lay-offs less often than investor-owned companies (Craig and Pencavel 1992, 1994; Burdin and Dean 2009; Burdin 2014). The reasons for these behavioural differences are to be found in the overcoming of investor ownership and profit maximization, and in involvement processes. Since worker-members set the objectives of the organization, they can decide to choose employment stability as one of the most relevant goals and accept lower and/or fluctuating wages in order to absorb unpredicted demand or cost shocks. Internalization of the same contractual effects is more difficult in investor-owned companies. Contrasting interests and asymmetric information bedevilling the employment relation would heighten the problem of bilateral opportunism, abuse of authority and wage stickiness, making employment stability an unresolved issue (Miyazaky and Neary 1983: Albanese et al. 2015; Navarra and Tortia 2014; Pérotin 2014). Indeed, wage flexibility has been claimed long ago to improve resilience to negative macroeconomic shocks and to increase employment levels for marginal categories of workers (Weitzman 1986). Finally, involvement has been connected to higher productivity, thanks to a weaker need to implement stringent control and direction (Bartlett et al. 1992: Bonin et al. 1993: Appelbaum et al. 2000).[3]

Third, co-operative banks act as community banks in supporting small producers. They are examples of user-controlled enterprises and are reported to fundamentally reduce usury in developing countries and credit rationing in developed economies, especially in peripheral economic areas. Credit rationing is reduced by implementing relationship banking based on long-term interactions between the bank and its borrowers, who are often members. Locally based long-term relations are underpinned by embeddedness in gathering and processing soft information and allow the exploitation of local social capital in terms of social norms, trust, and peer monitoring (Birchall 2013a, 2013b). Again, the reduction of credit rationing is made possible by the substitution of the profit motivation with wider community-oriented objectives and norms, through dedicated regulation and constraints set by law, statutes, or by members themselves. This different goal-setting process positively contributes to endogenously driven socio-economic development (Borzaga and Tortia 2010). Net operating surpluses are reduced to increase members' welfare through lower interest rates on loans and higher interest paid on deposits. This reduction translates into increased consumer surplus even in the absence of sustained market competition, and in the creation of positive external effects in terms of economic and social value directed to the benefit of the community.

As a final example we discuss the pattern of institutionalization of social aims in the objectives of mutual benefit organizations. Social co-operatives have developed over the last three decades in several European and non-European countries. Differently from other co-operative forms, social co-operatives are able to involve a wide array of different constituencies in the definition and pursuit of their objectives thanks to three main institutional devices: (i) imposition of the non-profit distribution constraint and asset socialization through the asset lock; (ii) the requirement for the social goal of the organization to be made explicit in statutory rules; (iii) the formal introduction of multi-stakeholder

---

[3] Following the 2007 to 2014 financial and economic crises, co-operatives in general, and especially worker co-operatives, resorted to lay-offs less often than conventional corporations, confirming job protection as one of their dominant objectives. In Italy, since 2008, co-operatives have increased overall employment by 80 thousand units, while employment in private enterprises shrank by about 473 thousand units out of a national total of about 22 million. Still more remarkably, in co-operatives the number of permanent workers increased by about 100 thousand, while short-term contracts fell by about 20 thousand. About 50 per cent of the total increase in employment in co-operatives has been accounted for by socially oriented co-operatives (Euricse 2015).

governance. This way, entrepreneurial activity is widened to achieve community and social goals through collective action. Social co-operatives can be understood as part of the evolutionary pattern leading from traditional co-operative forms, which tend to pursue mono-stakeholder objectives only, to the pursuit of wider social aims, which are accomplished over and above mutualistic aims (Borzaga et al. 2011). Institutional innovation serves the role, in this case, of protecting and supporting non-self-seeking preferences and social motivations in order to achieve social aims that would be unattainable by other organizational forms. The non-distribution constraint, which makes co-operatives more similar to non-profit organizations, is no longer exogenous and unexplained, but is instead understood as a coherent institutional tool that underpins the preference given to collective action and social aims. Thanks to this salient process of institutional variation and spread, social and community oriented co-operatives have complemented, and in some cases substituted for, the public sector. They have enlarged the supply of social and community services beyond what the public sector and private providers would have been able to achieve, thereby showing the potential to contribute to much-needed welfare reforms in a long list of countries (Tortia 2010; Borzaga et al. 2015).

5.6 Conclusion

In this contribution, we have interpreted co-operation as a co-ordination mechanism of economic activity, focusing both on its advantages and limitations. We have also compared its role and functioning to the more traditional and much more studied mechanisms of authority and market exchange. Our approach represents a new scientific endeavour, since it can help explain the limitations of existing economic theory and the results of much empirical research. This approach is consistent with criticism against the prevalent socio-economic model of isomorphism based on two actors only: the market and the State. Our contribution, therefore, sets the stage for further and more analytical research in the economics of co-operation. Future theoretical, empirical, and experimental contributions will have the opportunity to analyse more closely the evolution of the institutional and governance structure of co-operatives, their ability to generate and distribute welfare among the involved constituencies, and the determinants of the well-being and collective choices and actions of their members.

References

Akerlof, G. A. (1982), 'Labor Contracts as Partial Gift Exchange', *The Quarterly Journal of Economics*, 97(4), 543–69.

Albanese, M., Navarra, C., and Tortia, E. C. (2015), 'Employer Moral Hazard and Wage Rigidity: The Case of Worker Owned and Investor Owned Firms', *International Review of Law and Economics*, 43(C), 227–37. doi: 10.1016/j.irle.2014.08.006.

Alchian, A. A. and Demsetz, H. (1972), 'Production, Information Costs and Economic Organization', *American Economic Review* 62(5), 777–95.

Aoki, M. (1984), *The Co-operative Game Theory of the Firm* (New York: Oxford University Press).

Appelbaum, E., Bailey, T., Berg, P., and Kalleberg, A. L. (2000), *Manufacturing Advantage: Why High-Performance Work Systems Pay Off* (Ithaca NY: Cornell University Press).

Axelrod, R. (1984), *The Evolution of Co-Operation* (New York: Penguin Science).

Bartlett, W., Cable, J., Estrin, S., Jones, D. C., and Smith, S. C. (1992). 'Labor-Managed Cooperatives and Private Firms in North Central Italy: An Empirical Comparison', *Industrial and Labor Relations Review*, 46(1), 103–18.

Benz, M. (2005), 'Not for the Profit, but for the Satisfaction? Evidence on Worker Well-Being in Non-Profit Firms', *Kyklos*, 58(2), 155–76.

Benz, M. and Stutzer, A. (2003), 'Do Workers Enjoy Procedural Utility?' *Applied Economics Quarterly*, 49(2), 149–72.

Berg, J., Dickhaut, J., and McCabe, K. (1995), 'Trust, Reciprocity, and Social History', *Games and Economic Behavior*, 10(1), 122–42.

Birchall, J. (2010), *People-Centred Businesses. Co-operatives, Mutuals and the Idea of Membership* (Basingstoke: Palgrave Macmillan).

Birchall, J. (2013a), *Finance in an Age of Austerity. The Power of Customer-Owned Banks* (Cheltenham, UK: Edward Elgar).

Birchall, J. (2013b), 'The Potential of Co-operatives during the Current Recession: Theorizing Comparative Advantage', *Journal of Entrepreneurial and Organizational Diversity*, 2(1), 1–22. Available at www.jeodonline.com (accessed 8 September 2016).

Bonin, J. P., Jones, D. C., and Putterman, L. L. (1993), 'Theoretical and Empirical Studies of Producer Cooperatives: Will Ever the Twain Meet?' *Journal of Economic Literature*, 31(3), 1290–320.

Borzaga, C., Depedri, S., and Galera, G. (2015), 'Emergence, Evolution, and Institutionalization of Italian Social Co-operatives', in A. Jensen, G. A., Patmore, and E. Tortia, eds, *Cooperative Enterprises in Australia and Italy: Comparative Analysis and Theoretical Insights* (Firenze: Firenze University Press).

Borzaga, C., Depedri, S., and Tortia, E. C. (2011), 'Organizational Variety in Market Economies and the Role of Cooperative and Social Enterprises: A Plea for Economic Pluralism', *Journal of Co-operative Studies*, 44(1), 19–30.

Borzaga, C. and Sacchetti, S. (2015), 'Why Social Enterprises Are Asking to Be Multi-Stakeholder and Deliberative: An Explanation around the Costs of Exclusion'. Working Paper, No. 075/15, Trento: Euricse. Available at http://www.euricse.eu/wp-content/uploads/2015/04/WP-75_15_Borzaga-Sacchetti.pdf (accessed 8 September 2016).

Borzaga, C. and Tortia, E. C. (2010), 'The Economics of Social Enterprises: An Interpretive Framework', in L. Becchetti and C. Borzaga, eds, *The Economics of Social Responsibility: The World of Social Enterprises* (London, UK: Routledge), 15–33.

Bowles, S. (2004), *Microeconomics: Behavior, Institutions, and Evolution.* (Princeton, MA: Princeton University Press).

Bowles, S. and Gintis, H. (2011), *A Cooperative Species: Human Reciprocity and Its Evolution* (Princeton, MA: Princeton University Press).

Burdín, G. (2014), 'Are Worker-Managed Firms Really More Likely to Fail?' *Industrial and Labor Relations Review*, 67, 202–38.

Burdín, G. and Dean, A. (2009), 'New Evidence on Wages and Employment in Worker Cooperatives Compared with Capitalist Firms', *Journal of Comparative Economics*, 37, 517–33.

Coase, R. H. (1937), 'The Nature of the Firm', *Economica*, 4(16), 386–405.

Craig, B. and Pencavel, J. (1992), 'The Behavior of Worker Cooperatives: The Plywood Companies of the Pacific North-East', *American Economic Review*, 82(5), 1083–105.

Craig, B. and Pencavel, J. (1994), 'The Empirical Performance of Orthodox Models of the Firm: Conventional Firms and Worker Cooperatives', *Journal of Political Economy*, 102(4), 718–44.

deCharms, R. (1968), *Personal Causation: The Affective Determinants of Behavior* (New York: Academic Press).

Deci, E. L. (1975), *Intrinsic Motivation* (New York: Plenum).

Degli Antoni, G. and Sacconi, L., eds (2011), *Social Capital, Corporate Social Responsibility, Economic Behavior and Performance* (Basingstoke: Palgrave MacMillan).

Dow, G. K. (2003), *Governing the Firm: Workers' Control in Theory and Practice* (Cambridge, MA: Cambridge University Press).

Ellerman, D. (1986), 'Horizon Problems and Property Rights in Labor Managed Firms', *Journal of Comparative Economics*, 10(1), 62–78.

Euricse (2015), 'Economia cooperativa: Rilevanza, evoluzione e nuove frontiere della cooperazione italiana', Euricse: Trento. Available at http://www.euricse.eu/wp-content/uploads/2015/09/00-ECONOMIA-COOPERATIVA.pdf (accessed 8 September 2016).

Fehr, E., Kirchsteiger, G., and Riedl, A. (1993), 'Does Fairness Prevent Market Clearing? An Experimental Investigation', *The Quarterly Journal of Economics*, 108(2), 437–59.

Fehr, E. and Gächter, S. (2000), 'Fairness and Retaliation: The Economics of Reciprocity', *Journal of Economic Perspectives*, 14(3), 159–81.

Frey, B. (1997), *Not Just for the Money: An Economic Theory of Personal Motivation* (Cheltenham-Brookfield: Edward Elgar).

Frank, R. H. (1984), 'Are Workers Paid Their Marginal Products?' *American Economic Review*, 74(4), 549–71.

Furubotn, E. G. and Pejovich, S. (1970), 'Property Rights and the Behaviour of the Firm in a Socialist State: The Example of Yugoslavia', *Zeitschrift für Nationalökonomie*, 30(5), 431–54.

Gowdy, J. and Seidl, I. (2004), 'Economic Man and Selfish Genes: The Implications of Group Selection for Economic Valuation and Policy', *Journal of Socio-Economics*, 33(3), 343–58.

Grandori, A. and Funari, S. (2008), 'A Chemistry of Organization: Combinatory Analysis and Design'. *Organization Studies*, 29(3), 459–85.

Grillo, M. (2015), 'Servizi pubblici locali e beni comuni', in L. Sacconi, and S. Ottone, eds, *Beni comuni e cooperazione* (Bologna: Il Mulino), 255–80.

Guiso, L., Sapienza, P., and Zingales, L. (2006), 'Does Culture Affect Economic Outcomes? *Journal of Economic Perspectives*, 20(2), 23–48.

Guth, W., Schmittberger, R., and Schwarze, B. (1982), 'An Experimental Analysis of Ultimatum Bargaining', *Journal of Economic Behavior and Organization*, 3(4), 367–88.

Hansmann, H. (1988), 'Ownership of the Firm' *Journal of Law, Economics and Organisation*, 4(2), 267–304.

Hansmann, H. (1996), *The Ownership of Enterprise* (Cambridge, MA: Belknap Press of Harvard University Press).

Hansmann, H. (2013), 'All Firms are Co-operative, and So Are Governments', *Journal of Entrepreneurial and Organizational Diversity*, 2(2), 1–10. doi: http://dx.doi.org/10.5947/jeod.2013.007 (accessed 8 September, 2016).

Heath, J. (2006), 'The Benefits of Co-operation', *Philosophy & Public Affairs*, 34(4), 313–51.

Hodgson, G. M. (1993), *Economics and Evolution: Bringing Life Back into Economics*, (Cambridge, UK and Ann Arbor: Polity Press, and University of Michigan Press).

Jensen, M. C. and Meckling, W. H. (1976), 'Theory of the Firm: Managerial Behavior, Agency Costs and Ownership Structure', *Journal of Financial Economics*, 3(4), 305–60.

Jossa, B. (2012), 'A System of Self-Managed Firms as a New Perspective on Marxism', *Cambridge Journal of Economics*, 36(4), 821–41.

Kahneman, D., Knetsch, J. L., and Thaler, R. H. (1991), 'Fairness and the Assumptions of Economics', in R. H. Thaler, ed., *Quasi Rational Economics* (New York, NY: Russel Sage), 220–37.

Kalmi, P. (2007), 'The Disappearance of Cooperatives from Economics Textbooks', *Cambridge Journal of Economics*, 31(4), 625–47.

Langlois, R. N. (1992), 'Transaction Cost Economics in Real Time', *Industrial and Corporate Change*, 1(1), 99–127.

Leete, L. (2000), 'Wage Equity and Employment Motivation in Nonprofit and For-profit Organizations', *Journal of Economic Behaviour and Organisation*, 43 (4), 423–46.

Loasby, B. (2006). 'Industrial Organization', in T. Raffaelli, G., Becattini, and M. Dardi, eds, *The Elgar Companion to Alfred Marshall* (UK and Northampton, MA: Edward Elgar), 371–8.

Maslow, A. H. (1943), 'A Theory of Human Motivation', *Psychological Review*, 50, 370–96.

McGregor, D. (1960), *The Human Side of Enterprise* (New York, NY: McGrawHill).

Milgrom P. and Roberts, J. (1990), 'The Economics of Modern Manufacturing: Technology, Strategy, and Organizations', *American Economic Review*, 80, 511–28.

Miyazaki, H. and Neary, H. M. (1983). 'The Illyrian Firm Revisited', *Bell Journal of Economics*, 141, 259–70.

Navarra, C. and Tortia, E. C. (2014), 'Employer Moral Hazard, Wage Rigidity, and Worker Cooperatives: A Theoretical Appraisal, *Journal of Economic Issues*, 48(3): 707–26.

Ostrom, Elinor (1965), 'Public Entrepreneurship: A Case Study in Ground Water Basin Management', Ph.D. dissertation, University of California, Los Angeles.

Ostrom, E. (1990), *Governing the Commons: The Evolution of Institutions for Collective Action* (Cambridge: Cambridge University Press).

Ostrom, E. and Basurto, X. (2011), 'Crafting Analytical Tools to Study Institutional Change', *Journal of Institutional Economics*, 7(3), 317–43.

Pencavel, J., Pistaferri, L., and Schivardi, F. (2006), 'Wages, Employment, and Capital in Capitalist and Worker-Owned Firms, *Industrial and Labor Relations Review*, 60(1), 23–44.

Pérotin, V. (2014). 'Worker Cooperatives: Good, Sustainable Jobs in the Community', *Journal of Entrepreneurial and Organizational Diversity*, 2(2), 34–47.

Podivinsky, J. M. and Stewart, G. (2006), 'Why Is Labour-Managed Firm Entry So Rare? An Analysis of UK Manufacturing Data', *Journal of Economic Behavior and Organization*, 56(2), 239–62.

Rifkin, J. (2014), *The Zero Marginal Cost Society: The internet of Things, the Collaborative Commons, and the Eclipse of Capitalism* (Basingstoke: Palgrave Macmillan).

Roos, D., Womack, J. P., and Jones, D. T. (1991), *The Machine That Changed the World: The Story of Lean Production* (New York: Harper Perennial).

Rose-Ackerman, S. (1996), 'Altruism, Non-Profits, and Economic Theory', *Journal of Economic Literature*, 34(2), 701–28.

Ryan, R. M. and Deci, E. L. (2000), 'Intrinsic and Extrinsic Motivations: Classic Definitions and New Directions, *Contemporary Educational Psychology*, 25, 54–67.

Sabatini, F., Modena, F., and Tortia, E. C. (2014), 'Do Cooperative Enterprises Create Social Trust?', *Small Business Economics,* 42(3), 621–41.

Sacchetti, S. and Sugden, R. (2009), 'The Organisation of Production and its Publics: Mental Proximity, Markets and Hierarchies', *Review of Social Economy*, 67(3), 289–311.

Sacchetti, S. and Tortia, E. C. (2015),'The Extended Governance of Cooperative Firms: Inter-Firm Coordination, and Consistency of Values', *Annals of Public and Cooperative Economics.* doi: 10.1111/apce.12058.

Sacconi, L. (2015), 'Beni comuni, contratto sociale e governance cooperativa dei servizi pubblici locali', in L. Sacconi and S. Ottone, eds, *Beni comuni e cooperazione,* (Bologna: Il Mulino), 175–214.

Sacconi, L. and Ottone, S. eds (2015), *Beni comuni e cooperazione* (Bologna: Il Mulino).

Spear, R. (2012), 'Hybridite des Co-operatives', in J. Blanc and D. Colongo, eds, *Les contributions des coopératives à une économie plurielle. Les cahiers de l'économie sociale: Entreprendre autrement.* (Paris: L'Harmattan), 33–60.

Tabellini, G. (2008), 'The Scope of Cooperation: Values and Incentives, *The Quarterly Journal of Economics*, 123(3), 905–50.

Thompson, S. (2015), 'Towards a Social Theory of the Firm: Worker Cooperatives Reconsidered', *Journal of Co-operative Organization and Management.* doi: 10.1016/j.jcom.2015.02.002.

Titmuss, R. (1970), *The Gift Relationship* (London: Allen & Unwin).

Tortia, E. C. (2008). 'Perceived Fairness and Worker Well-Being: Survey-Based Findings from Italy', *Journal of Socio-Economics*, 37(5), 2080–94.

Tortia, E. C. (2010), 'The Impact of Social Enterprises on Output, Employment, and Welfare', in L. Becchetti and C. Borzaga. C., eds, *The Economics of Social Responsibility: The World of Social Enterprises* (London, UK: Routledge), 55–72.

Tortia, E. C. (2015), 'L'impresa come bene comune: Il caso della accumulazione di capitale nelle imprese cooperative', in L. Sacconi and S. Ottone, eds, *Beni comuni e cooperazione* (Bologna: Il Mulino), 301–22.

Tortia, E. C., Valentinov, V., and Iliopoulos, C. (2013), 'Agricultural Cooperatives', *Journal of Entrepreneurial and Organizational Diversity*, 2(1), 23–36.

Tyler, T. R. and Blader, S. L. (2000). *Cooperation in Groups: Procedural Justice, Social Identity, and Behavioral Engagement* (Philadelphia, Psychology Press).

Valentinov, V. (2007), 'Why Are Cooperatives Important In Agriculture? An Organizational Economics Perspective', *Journal of Institutional Economics*, 3(1), 55–69.

Vanek, J. (1970), *The General Theory of Labour Managed Market Economies* (Ithaca, NY: Cornell University Press).

Vieta, M. (2015), 'The Italian Road to Creating Worker Cooperatives from Worker Buyouts: Italy's Worker-Recuperated Enterprises and the Legge Marcora Framework'. Euricse Working Paper no. 77/15. Available at http://www.euricse.eu/wp-content/uploads/2015/08/WP-78_15_Vieta.pdf (accessed 8 September 2016).

Ward, B. (1958), 'The Firm in Illyria: Market Syndicalism', *American Economic Review*, 48, 566–89.

Weitzman, M. (1986), *The Share Economy. Conquering Stagflation.* (Cambridge, MA: Harvard University Press).

Williamson, O. E. (1973), 'Markets and Hierarchies: Some Elementary Considerations', *American Economic Review* 63, 316–25.

Williamson, O. E. (2000), 'The New Institutional Economics: Taking Stock, Looking Ahead', *Journal of Economic Literature* 38(3), 595–613.

Zamagni, S. (2005), 'A Civil-Economic Theory of the Cooperative Enterprise' (*Per una teoria economico-civile dell'impresa cooperativa*), in S. Zamagni and E. Mazzoli, eds, Ver*so una nuova teoria economica della cooperazione* (Bologna: Il Mulino), 15–56.

CHAPTER 6

....

THE SOCIAL AND POLITICAL DIMENSIONS OF CO-OPERATIVE ENTERPRISES

....

VICTOR A. PESTOFF

6.1 INTRODUCTION

....

DURING the discussion of his report on *Co-operatives in the Year 2000* (Laidlaw 1980) at the International Co-operative Alliance's 1980 World Congress in Moscow, Dr. Laidlaw said he had two fears for the future of the co-operative movement. First, he feared for its democratic character, with less and less popular participation, and decision-making moving upwards; it was a question of how to handle 'bigness'—whether to use it for moving more power and influence to the central organizations, or for decentralizing and disseminating that power. When co-operative democracy vanished, he argued, the co-operative movement would be finished (ibid.). Moreover, a co-operative movement that did not educate its members and society-at-large about its values, would never change the world for the better.

His second fear concerned relations with Government. While he remained convinced that there were certain things that the state could and should do—for example, it must control the economy—it must also recognize its limits and work more closely with the third sector and co-operatives. In addition, Laidlaw spoke about four other things that the co-operative movement of the world should be doing in the year 2000. They included: 1) showing concern for food safety and security, 2) giving priority to worker co-ops, 3) recapturing the vitality of the consumer co-operatives of the last century, but in a different way and not necessarily in the traditional form, and finally, 4) building communities.

Expanding on Laidlaw's third priority, Borzaga underlined new opportunities for co-operatives and social enterprises in the changing landscape of the welfare systems in recent decades (2011). He noted that in his report to the ICA Conference in 1980, Laidlaw emphasized the evolution of co-operatives in the pursuit of general interest goals. But he questioned the ability of co-operatives to meet new social needs not adequately served by either the market or state. This opened up new spaces of action for co-operatives around the world, particularly as providers of welfare and social services. A decade after the turn of the century, Borzaga lamented that co-operatives in most countries were not able to meet the new challenges and opportunities in the past three decades, in spite of Laidlaw's clear analysis of them (ibid.). Nevertheless, Borzaga provided several examples of how Italian co-operatives and social enterprises successfully adapted to changing circumstances and were therefore able to develop many new welfare services not available from either the state or market (ibid.). This chapter argues that we can also find some clear examples of co-operatives developing social services, such as childcare in Scandinavia and healthcare in Japan. Such services of general interest express the social and political dimensions of co-operatives more clearly than their traditional commercial efforts as agricultural, consumer, credit, or housing co-operatives. But can these social service co-operatives provide a road map for the future of co-operatives, as suggested by Borzaga?

The International Co-operative Alliance (ICA), defines a co-operative as 'an autonomous association of persons united voluntarily to meet their common economic, social and cultural needs and aspirations through a jointly-owned and democratically-controlled enterprise' (ICA, www.ica.coop). The ICA's definition emphasizes the hybrid nature of co-operatives, and most of them combine several different types of goals—economic, political, and social. In fact, some might argue that their very *raison d'être* is to pursue both economic and social goals, not just a single goal. It is, therefore, natural that co-operatives attract the attention of various academic disciplines. However, given the differences between disciplines, economists quite naturally ask different questions than do political scientists or sociologists, even when studying co-operatives. Thus, the sociology or political science interest in co-operatives is not so much a question of the economic rationale for why they exist, but rather what and how they can contribute to society and how they can facilitate the functioning of democracy. This chapter explores the social and political dimensions of co-operative enterprise and frequently uses the Swedish consumer co-ops (Co-op and KF) to illustrate them. However, Co-op and KF also represent general trends for co-operatives elsewhere in European countries with well-established welfare systems.

The founder of the Grameen Bank warns against putting too much faith in hybrids that combine an interest in producing social value with the goals of enterprises in the mainstream market economy: 'In the real world, it will be very difficult to operate businesses with the two conflicting goals of profit maximization and social benefits. The executives of these hybrid businesses will gradually inch toward the profit-maximization goal, no matter how the company's mission is designed' (Yanis 2007:13). However, the unique capacity of co-ops to combine social and economic goals is seen as a strong advantage by many observers. They can combine sound economic practices, democratic control by members, the promotion of their members' interest, and good employment conditions, and thus they can provide a clear alternative to private firms competing on the market. The social and political dimensions of co-operatives clearly help to set them apart and make them different from their competitors. The active promotion of social values can provide them with a clear profile that helps to distinguish them from their competitors and can give them a competitive advantage, if properly understood and promoted. By contrast, the failure to promote their social values could erode their natural profile, making it harder for their members and ordinary consumers to distinguish between them and their competitors and thereby denying them a natural competitive advantage. Thus, the basic dilemma facing co-operative movements and other hybrid organizations is how to best combine their social and political goals with the demands of the market.

In brief, this chapter deals with the importance of adapting to major social change for sustainable organizational development, the impact of organizational growth and size on internal democracy, the importance of social goals for co-operative identity, and the need to develop methods to counteract the inherent instability often found in co-operatives. Some conclusions are reached about how to stabilize hybrid organizations in the final section. Together they provide a roadmap for rejuvenating co-operative movements by making membership meaningful once again. While it won't be easy, it can be achieved by focusing on members' most important daily needs, for example shifting their efforts from distributing goods and wares to providing enduring social services, involving members in the co-production of such services, and promoting multi-stakeholder models of democracy and social accounting in order to create greater trust in the provision of co-op social services. Together these ideas and concepts can help to provide a counterweight to major destabilizing factors facing co-operatives all over the world, and they can help to make membership meaningful again.

6.2 CO-OPERATIVES ARE HYBRID ORGANIZATIONS WITH MULTIPLE GOALS AND STAKEHOLDERS

A dynamic model for co-operative development is presented in this section to introduce the major stakeholders in co-operative organizations. This model is based on four separate and often opposing logics. Trying to maintain stability in organizations that have several rather than a single logic and several rather than one dominant stakeholder can be both challenging and problematic. This is so since one logic may at times crowd out the others and tend to dominate. But, when this happens for too long it can change the very nature of an organization or co-op.

6.2.1 A Dynamic Model of Co-operative Development

This section presents an interactive model of co-operative development that underlines the importance for co-operatives to adapt and adjust to major changes in society and their environment. It also points to the need for co-operatives as hybrid organizations to balance the claims of various stakeholders or strategic groups, so that no single group is dominant. Otherwise, there is a risk that the management might ignore the demands of some important stakeholders and only pursue one goal, such as maintaining its market shares or increasing its efficiency. If it did so, this could turn the co-op into a different type of organization and it would lose the support of some of its original stakeholders. This is seen clearly in the Swedish consumer co-ops, but is evident in the agricultural co-ops in Sweden as well. We need, therefore, to consider each environment or dimension in this interactive model more closely.

The four most important environments for co-operatives in industrial and post-industrial societies are the market, their members, their employees, and the public authorities. Together they set clear limits on the actions and decisions of co-operatives and their managers. Each of them can potentially act as a major constraint on the free-dom of co-operative leaders and their decisions. Each of them promotes their own par-ticular values and represents their own particular goals, which at times may come into conflict. Each of them is based on a separate logic, making it possible to speak of four competing logics or principles of co-operatives: the logic of (efficient) competition, the logic of (democratic) membership, the logic of (political) influence, and the logic of (personnel) management. Figure 6.1 depicts them.

Both members and employees comprise the internal environment of co-operatives, as they are part of the organization, while markets and authorities comprise the exter-nal environment of co-operatives, since they are outside the organization itself.

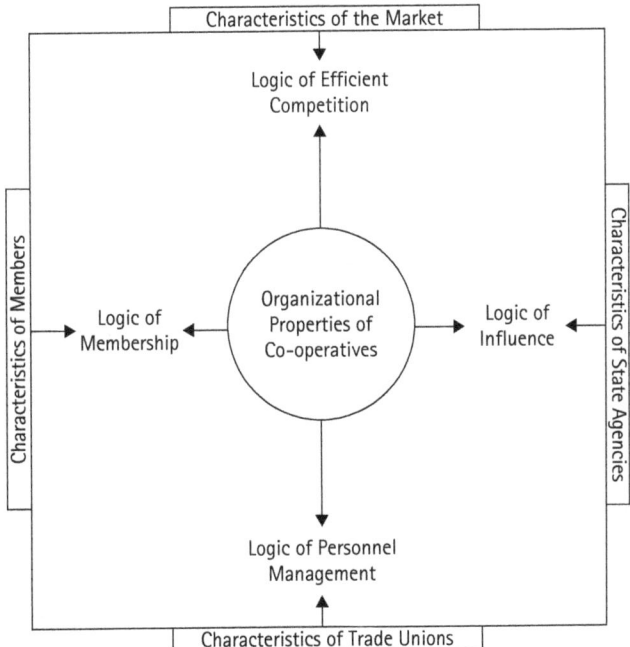

FIGURE 6.1 Investment per member in German co-operatives, 2014.

Source: V. Pestoff, 1991 & 1996.

At the same time, co-operatives can also be analysed in terms of their commercial and social/political dimensions. Here markets and employees comprise the commercial dimension, while members and authorities comprise the social/political dimension of co-operatives. The commercial dimension is something co-operatives share with other firms in the market while also competing with them at the same time. The social/political dimension of co-operatives is something they hold in common with other popular movements, non-governmental organizations, voluntary associations, and third-sector organizations, and is an expression of their purpose.

However, dominance of the logic of competition can result in an undermining of the logics of membership, influence, and personnel management, as seen in the repeated amalgamations of the Swedish consumer co-operative movement during the second half of the twentieth century. These amalgamations removed the last vestiges of democratic decision-making in most of the local consumer co-operative societies and thereby made membership in them trivial. Finally, at the beginning of the new millennium a mega amalgamation resulted in Co-op Norden and combined the activities of consumer co-ops in Denmark, Norway, and Sweden into a new Scandinavian consumer co-operative movement (Pestoff 2012).

6.2.2 Two Schools: A Democratic and a Business School

There are two main schools concerning the development and future of co-ops and they reflect the dilemma of co-operatives as hybrid organizations. According to the associational or democratic school (see Böök 1992; Craig 1993; Pestoff 1991, 2012, among others), co-operatives are primarily seen as associations that pursue social goals by economic means. In the business school (see Birchall and Simmons 2001, 2004; Gijselinckx 2012, among others), co-operatives are mainly business firms that have some unique social and associational features. The associational school focuses on the role of co-operatives as membership associations in a rapidly changing world, responding to their members' vastly changing needs and demands, as well as the need to strategically balance various stakeholders and goals (Pestoff 2012). The business school considers co-operatives as 'member-owned businesses' that need to modernize and professionalize in order to meet the growing competition from private firms (Birchall 2012).

Seen from the perspective of hybrid organizations, consumer co-ops face a number of fundamental democratic issues related to their unique identity as organizations that attempt to unite associative and business elements. This is reflected in (1) tensions between the associative and business parts of the co-ops or the logic of cooperation and the logic of bureaucratic organizations. When they come into conflict, the latter often squeezes out the former. This leads to a loss of co-op identity, declining member participation, less solidarity with the co-op movement, and eventually a loss of business. This, in turn, is related to (2) mobilizing members by facilitating and expanding possibilities for their participation in all parts of the co-op, both on the associational and business sides; which, in turn, reflects (3) the relationship between the members and the management of co-ops. This can be seen in attempts at (4) promoting innovations of organizational structure to facilitate communications and promote greater membership participation. Furthermore, this is also seen in (5) expanding the relationship with employees, perhaps even turning consumer co-ops into multi-stakeholder organizations; as well as (6) considering how co-ops should best account for their economic and social responsibility, and finally (7) taking account of women's changing gender roles as housewives, consumers, activists, board members, etc.

A second set of issues is related more closely to economic and financial aspects of co-operatives. It concerns (8) financing operational capital, investments, as well as (9) realizing economies of scale and other advantages, for example in co-operative networks and second- (or even third-) tier co-operatives. This has ramifications for the democratic challenges mentioned earlier, since it stretches the relationship between members and management in decision-making structures.

A final set of issues is related to cooperation with various organizations in their environment. Here it is important to consider (10) relations between the established and newer forms of consumer co-ops, including health and social service co-ops, energy and utility co-ops, ecological food co-ops, joint production and consumption co-ops; but also (11) promoting greater cooperation among and between co-ops of all kinds; and (12) relations with other types of voluntary associations and nonprofit organizations, including worker co-ops, labour unions, social enterprises, social movement organizations, and nonprofit agencies.

Given the nature, number, and complexity of the challenges facing co-operative movements around the world, we need to move beyond the opposition between the democratic and business schools in order to develop co-operatives in a more balanced fashion in the future. Recent trends make some of those issues all the more pressing, particularly in countries and societies facing major social and political change. The worldwide trend toward bigger, but fewer consumer co-ops is seen by some as an answer to economic exigencies, but if this is not combined with innovative organizational structures for effective member participation and reflexive renewal of the co-operative identity by members and management alike, it is likely to result in a loss of co-operative identity (Pestoff et al. 2017). Organizational democracy and business efficiency need to be balanced, amplifying the commitment of co-operative social responsibility to articulate an integrated vision (ecological, economic, and social) that responds to the current challenges and reaffirms its co-operative identity. This invites members to think about the roots of the co-operative in their local environment and as a key element in its future development. In order to build a cohesive culture, it is necessary for mature co-operatives to refer to and discuss their historical purposes to make their legitimacy more obvious, especially for newer and younger members. The need to strengthen organizational effectiveness requires an awareness of the co-operative identity, as well as its ability to act like a democratic organization of consumers (Böök 1992; Craig 1993; Pestoff 1991, 2012).

6.3 Adapting to Major Social and Political Changes

Historically, co-operatives have contributed to modernizing the political system in many countries, by providing access to grass-roots democracy for large groups of citizens, often long before the introduction of universal suffrage. But time marches on and their role as a provider primarily of goods and wares during the industrial age has become overshadowed more recently by the combination of their shrinking market shares, if not outright disappearance in some countries, along with their often unrealized potential as providers of social services in the post-industrial or service societies of the twenty-first century. Taken together, this poses a fundamental challenge to consumer co-ops worldwide. Should they continue to provide traditional goods, wares, and services or should they shift their focus to the continually expanding demand among members and citizens for good quality social services? This is made more acute by the retrenchment of the welfare state and privatization of public services. Much of the discussion that follows focuses on countries and societies with well-developed welfare states. Sweden is used here as a school-book example, but it bears relevance for developments in similar welfare states.

6.3.1 Major Social Change in the Twentieth Century

In today's highly developed welfare states, consumer co-operative movements are light years from the conditions that prevailed when they were established more than 100 years ago. Industrialization and urbanization are often seen as the prime drivers of early societal change. In brief, the transition from a rural, agrarian society to a post-industrial cosmopolitan society has been dramatic in recent generations, in Scandinavia in particular. Today's post-modern Western society is composed mostly of urban and suburban dwellers, many of whom live in multistorey and multi-family housing. Many are highly educated, hold jobs in highly advanced industries or services, and they are also highly interdependent economically, socially, and in other ways. They may travel greater distances by car or mass transportation to and from work every day than their ancestors normally did in a year or more. They take for granted things like hot and cold running water, showers, toilets, and in some cases even a jacuzzi, rather than having to dig their own wells or pump their own water. They also have electricity, a refrigerator and freezer, a stove, radio, TV, microwave, dishwashers, washing machines, etc. Given the informatics revolution, they come home to read their personal e-mail or chat on the Internet, and perhaps watch a DVD or download music or a film from the net, rather than 'spin yarns' or exchange local 'news' during their visit to town or to their church, as their ancestors did only a few generations ago.

Moreover, in the wake of industrialization and urbanization, Sweden and many other European countries have seen the rapid growth of trade unions and other forms of collective action; continual growth in the standard of living for most citizens; and the development of the welfare state and public bureaucracy to provide public services, particularly the social services that many citizens have become highly dependent on today. In terms of broad political changes in the twentieth century we note, among other things, the introduction of universal suffrage and parliamentarism; the Soviet Revolution and growth of Nazism in Germany; the Second World War and the Cold War, the fall of the Soviet Union and Communism; and the growth of new economic, political, and social structures and institutions at the European level brought about by European integration. Clearly, all types of co-operatives throughout Europe had to adapt and adjust to such broad sweeping social and political changes in order to survive. The question is: how well have they adapted to them and at what cost to their co-operative values?

6.3.2 The Historical Role of Co-operatives: Schools of Democracy

Alexis de Tocqueville regarded associations and their impact on society in a wider context nearly 200 years ago ([1830], 1945). He considered associations a 'school of democracy', without which the development of 'democratic habits of mind' would not be possible. According to de Tocqueville associations helped explain some major differences between the daily life he observed in the new world of America and that waiting for him back home in France (ibid.). Similarly, Putnam argued that associations, credit co-ops, unions, clubs, and even choirs made democracy work in Italy at the end of the twentieth century (1993).

From a Scandinavian perspective, Childs (1936, 1961) argued that co-operatives contributed significantly to forging a 'Middle Way' between the growing Fascist threat in Germany and the Soviet Revolution that many feared. Consumer and agricultural co-operatives in Sweden and Denmark provided a pragmatic and democratic alternative to both Fascism and Communism in a war-torn Europe in the 1930s and 1940s. Their decisions were usually made after long, careful consideration and deliberations, on the basis of one member, one vote. However, it is highly questionable whether a scholar would make such a statement today about the role of co-operatives in Scandinavian society, having gradually inched towards becoming an ordinary commercial business, particularly with the unrelenting amalgamations of the 1970s to the 1990s. Today, nearly two-thirds of the members in Swedish consumer co-ops no longer have a vote or say in the direction of the co-ops. They were in effect already disenfranchised by the first meta amalgamation in 1991, when membership lost its traditional meaning. There are only a few remaining local and regional co-op societies in Sweden where membership retains its original meaning, not just a watered-down card that gives points and eventual bonuses for purchases, just like for any of their competitors. Thus, they are no longer a 'school of democracy', nor do they comprise an alternative path of grass-roots democratic development for society at large.

Furthermore, the nature of the membership in the Swedish consumer co-operative movement has changed dramatically, from active to passive membership. In the 1960s, the Swedish consumer co-ops still required that members save their sales slips and report all their grocery and household purchases at the end of the year in order to get the annual dividend based on the amount they spent. By contrast, today these mundane tasks are replaced by a plastic card that electronically records all sales and provides bonus points on their purchases, similar to those provided by most other commercial chains. Thus, today 'membership' in a consumer co-op probably means as much or as little as 'membership' in American Express, the IKEA Family, or the H&M Club. There are no longer any democratic rights and responsibilities associated with membership in the larger, regional consumer co-ops. Thus, the Swedish consumer co-operative movement, Konsum & KF, has transformed itself into a huge international commercial conglomerate operating in several countries, but far removed from its origin as a popular movement that promoted social values, and that was democratically run. Swedish agricultural co-ops have followed similar developments and are now also international conglomerates, operating in several countries.

6.3.3 From Distributing Goods and Services to Providing Welfare Services?

A successful consumer co-op that continues to grow and expand its activities during several decades needs to occasionally examine the relevance of its social goals. It needs to ask, from time to time, how relevant its activities are for the well-being of its members and the community it serves. Do its goals and activities comprise an important part of their daily life? Are similar goods and services perhaps available on the local market at competitive prices? If such goods and services are provided by several competitors, what is the social value added by the co-ops? If there is little or no social value added, then such co-ops need to ask whether they should continue to provide such goods and services, or perhaps instead invest in providing some other goods or services that have a greater relevance for their members and the local community. Similarly, without clear democratic structures, co-operatives do not differ significantly from their competitors, and there is little reason to treat them as special organizational forms that somehow differ from their private competitors, nor to expect them to behave differently.

The social role of co-ops shifts from being a provider of goods, wares, and services in an industrial society to an emerging provider of services of general interest and enduring social services in today's post-industrial or service society. This development is made more acute by the retrenchment of the welfare state in most European countries in recent decades, combined with extensive privatization of public services promoted by the spread of New Public Management. Donati promotes 'relational sociology' as a new paradigm for the social sciences (2011). Its main cornerstones are civil society, relational goods, and social capital. Relational goods are not 'things' that can be appropriated by any single actor and can therefore not be bought and sold on the market. Rather they consist of social relations that are produced together by those who participate in them. Donati considers this an emergent effect which benefits the participants of such relations, in the form of social capital, as well as those on the outside, like family and friends, who share in its repercussions. Moreover, relational goods have a democratic character that distinguishes them from the goods and services produced by commercial organizations and the public administration (2014). Thus, they are goods that are not available on the basis of private ownership nor accessible to everyone indiscriminately.

Italy provides a good illustration of the rapid development of relational goods, particularly after Law 381/91. It recognizes two types of social co-ops, according to whether they manage social, health, or educational services (type A) or they undertake other activities that help integrate 'vulnerable persons' into the workforce (type B). In the latter type at least 30 per cent of the employees must be occupationally disadvantaged workers. The law also allows for volunteers to become full members of the social co-op and for the ownership structure of social co-ops to include several different categories of members, for example multi-stakeholder co-ops. This includes worker members who are remunerated; user members, that is, the recipients of the services supplied by the co-op or their family members; volunteer members, who work in the co-op without any form of compensation; financial members or suppliers of capital with limited rights to participate in the decision-making and governance of the organization; and legal entities (Borzaga 2014).

Data from ISTAT (Italian Institute of Statistics) show how the number of social co-ops has increased dramatically during the past 20 years, from approximately 2,000 in 1991, to nearly 3,900 in 1996, 7,363 in 2005, and 11,264 in 2011. Thus, the ninth Industry and Service Census in 2011 registered more than 6,500 social co-ops providing social services and 4,500 social co-ops for work integration. Moreover, in 2005 almost 40 per cent of the public expenditure for social services in medium and large Italian cities was managed by contracts awarded to social co-ops (ibid: 11). Thus, given a supportive environment, social service co-ops can clearly develop and thrive.

6.4 A CO-OPERATIVE ROADMAP FOR THE TWENTY-FIRST CENTURY?

As hybrid organizations, co-operatives experience institutional tensions that at times are strong enough to challenge their very identity. For example, if they are deeply embedded in the market and provide few, if any, social services to their members, they can more easily lose sight of their social purpose. They may focus on their market position and try to strengthen it, but often at the expense of their members, influence, and staff. However,

I maintain that democracy and the market could and should be more closely related, through intelligent organizational design. This would permit co-operatives to provide innovative solutions to contemporary social problems outside their traditional fields, in the form of co-operative social services. Here co-production and a multi-stakeholder model can provide important concepts, models, and institutions for understanding, developing, and promoting democracy at the micro-level in the daily lives of ordinary citizens, both as consumers and workers. Co-operatives could make a unique contribution to renewing social services, enriching work-life, and rejuvenating democracy. Co-operatives could provide a good example and set the best practices in social services, particularly in long-term or enduring social services (Pestoff 1998; Pestoff 2008).

6.4.1 Co-Production and Co-operative Welfare Services

One way to promote democracy in the daily lives of co-operative members and ordinary citizens would be to actively promote co-operative alternatives to both public and private for-profit provision of basic welfare services. Co-operatives and social enterprises can facilitate greater citizen participation in the provision of social services by promoting greater co-production and co-governance in public services. Co-production is the mix of activities that both public service agents and citizens contribute to the provision of publicly financed services. The former are involved as professionals or 'regular producers', while 'citizen production' is based on voluntary efforts by individuals or groups to enhance the quality and/or quantity of services they use. In complex societies there is a division of labour and most persons are engaged in full-time production of goods and services as regular producers. However, individual consumers or groups of consumers may also contribute to the production of goods and services, as consumer-producers (Ostrom 1999; Parks et al. 1981 & 1999). The participation of citizens in the provision of welfare services through co-operatives can make a unique contribution to democratic governance not found either in public services or private for-profit firms (Pestoff 2009). This also gives co-production the potential of a social innovation that can change the relationship between the professional providers of public financed services and their clients or citizens who use them (Pestoff 2016; Pestoff 2014).

There are four kinds or dimensions of citizen participation in the provision of public-financed welfare services, including economic, social, political, and service-specific participation (Pestoff 2006). In an interesting study, Vamstad (2007) compared four types of childcare providers: parent co-operatives, worker co-operatives, municipal services, and small-scale for-profit firms in two Swedish municipalities: Stockholm and Ostersund. It is clear that most forms for providing childcare may allow some degree of parent participation, however usually in a limited, ad hoc fashion. But, this study showed that parent co-operatives provide parents with unique possibilities for active participation in the management and running of their childcare facility, thus allowing parents to become active co-producers of high-quality childcare services for their own and others' children.

6.4.2 Internal Decision-Making—Multi-Stakeholder Co-operatives

The fact that co-operatives are democratic member-owned and member-run firms is normally reflected in their internal decision-making. Traditional models of co-operative democracy are based on the popular idea of 'one member, one vote', which is reflected in the statutes of most of the members of ICA. Yet, most of the co-operatives in the world are single stakeholder organizations, where the members who elect the board comprise a single category of stakeholders, while other stakeholders are unrepresented. In particular, both in consumer and agricultural co-ops, workers seldom gain a voice on the board and they lack a vote in important decisions. However, the debate in recent years has shifted focus to ideas of giving more representation to all major groups that contribute to an organization's or co-op's production or result, or what is known as a multi-stakeholder co-op. This is particularly notable in social service co-ops where more than one category is often represented on the board, either formally or informally.

As hybrid organizations, co-operatives normally combine two different functions or roles. The owners not only finance the co-op, they also supply the raw materials, provide the necessary labour or purchase its products. Thus, a single group of stakeholders 'owns' the co-op: they make all the decisions and thereby control it. Other stakeholders may contribute to the goods or services produced, but they do not own the co-op, nor do they have a voice in running it. So, they lack influence in its decision-making and have no claim to the eventual surplus produced. Therefore, some important stakeholders commonly find themselves excluded from influence in the management of the co-op and they have no share in its surplus or profit. This clearly influences the incentive structures available to major groups that contribute to creating the surplus, especially those who have no influence or ownership claim.

A multi-stakeholder organization is a firm or co-op that legally recognizes more than one type of stakeholder, gives more than one of them representation in its decision-making structures, and provides them with a share in the organization's surplus or profit. Multi-stakeholder co-ops, therefore, make several stakeholders its owners, create governance structures that include various groups in the co-op's internal decision-making, and provide them with a share in the surplus or profit. In addition, by virtue of doing so, they also contribute to the growth and spread of democratic attitudes and habits among the various owners, something uncommon in today's co-ops. Thus, multi-stakeholder organizations could conceivably play an important indirect role in inculcating and spreading democratic attitudes and habits among staff, since it would expose them to a different reality 40 hours per week for nearly 48 weeks per year for as long as they worked there. Multi-stakeholder co-operatives that provide public financed services, like the childcare co-ops mentioned in the following section, can provide an additional vehicle for inculcating and spreading democratic attitudes and habits among the general public. They too have the potential to make democracy a non-trivial aspect of the daily life of some citizens, in particular those who choose co-operative solutions for obtaining enduring social services like childcare, basic education, handicap care, and elder care. Thus, multi-stakeholder co-ops could include citizens in their daily lives, perhaps in several roles, as financiers, suppliers, workers, and consumers. This could contribute to making democracy a non-trivial aspect of the daily life of some ordinary citizens.

Consumer co-operative healthcare in Japan provides an example of fully fledged multi-stakeholder co-operatives. The membership comprises both lay and professional members. Statistics from 2007 show that only 1 per cent of them are healthcare professionals, like doctors, nurses, technicians, and administrators, while the other 99 per cent are ordinary healthy persons. Thus, medical co-ops in Japan seek to create a synergistic effect by involving different stakeholders working together in the same organization to attain common goals, that is, the promotion, maintenance, recovery, and/or restoration of each member's health. Furthermore, Japanese healthcare co-ops are governed by user-dominated boards of directors. In 2008, there were 1,934 lay members on the boards of medical co-ops representing the users, but only 739 paid board members representing the professional providers. Thus, over 70 per cent of the board members are ordinary lay members, not medical professionals. Taking the board of the Saitama Medical Co-op as an illustration: in 2008, the 23 user board members consisted of 21 housewives and two retired men; while the ten professional members consisted of three doctors, a nurse, and six executive directors representing healthcare providers (Kurimoto 2010). However, this does not imply a lack of tensions between professional and lay board members, but it can nevertheless be seen as an effort to bring these different interests together, facilitate a dialogue between them, and promote some degree of consensus in the management of co-operative healthcare.

6.4.3   Promoting a Dialogue Between the Staff and Clients

Vidal argues that the development of multi-stakeholder techniques is becoming necessary due to the asymmetric information often associated with social services, where the professional providers often have a monopoly on information. Consumers remain uncertain about the time and effort made by the providers of such services to maintain good quality standards. Consumers, quite naturally want greater insights into and more influence on the inputs of the services they depend on. It is, therefore, necessary to promote a dialogue between the providers and consumers of such services in order to reduce the tensions created by such a situation. Furthermore, when quality criteria are not certain, as is often the case with social services, a common understanding of what comprises good quality can be facilitated by a dialogue between the providers and consumers of such services (Hirschman 1970). Finally, consumers also need somewhere to complain if they are dissatisfied with the services.

Both parent and worker co-operative childcare in Sweden are organized as single stakeholder co-ops. Parent co-ops usually promote a multi-stakeholder dialogue by giving the staff a seat and voice on the board, but not a vote. Worker co-ops often create a special parent council, where parents can voice their concerns and make suggestions, but they are, however, not given a seat or voice on the board. In both cases we find attempts to promote a multi-stakeholder dialogue, but they fall short of formally investing other stakeholders with a vote on important decisions. However, voluntary associations that provide childcare are often based on a special pedagogics, for example Montessori, Waldorf, and Reggio-Emilio. Their boards usually combine representatives from both the staff and parents, thus qualifying them as multi-stakeholder organizations (Pestoff 1998).

6.4.4 Creating Trust in Welfare Services—A Competitive Advantage

We now need to turn our attention to trust in order to understand how co-operatives can create it in the absence of a non-distribution constraint. Trust could and should provide many organizations found in the third sector, such as social enterprises and co-ops, with a natural competitive advantage in the provision of welfare services, if correctly understood and actively put to use. Social enterprises take several different forms in Europe, including consumer co-ops, worker co-ops, and voluntary organizations. Consumer co-ops can engage their members in the provision of welfare services: they can empower them as co-producers and can provide them with greater influence and control than many other alternatives. Consumer co-ops can, therefore, create trust between the consumers and providers of social services. Worker co-ops usually result in more engaged, committed, and enthusiastic staff, which is often reflected in the quality of the services provided. Better quality services and more engaged staff can also result in greater trust between the consumers and providers of social services. Voluntary organizations that combine both the staff and clients as members function as multi-stakeholder organizations and can also contribute to greater dialogue, understanding, and trust between the consumers and producers of welfare services (Pestoff 1998).

Trust is the key to the future in business, in particular when it comes to social services. Private commercial firms, on the one hand, recognize this, but they often lack natural ways of generating trust. Rather, they must rely on advertising and other strategies to try to achieve what comes naturally to co-operatives. The growing interest in corporate social responsibility (CSR) and consumer relationship marketing (CRM) in business schools are two expressions of the need for private companies to create more trust. Co-ops, on the other hand, have it naturally, but often fail to recognize trust as a natural competitive advantage of the co-operative form.

6.4.5 Social Accounting and Audit

A co-op's economic goal is clearly seen and measured by the balance sheet, turnover figures, number of employees, number of shops, etc. But, its political and social goals are more difficult to measure. Social accounting provides a method that helps put an organization's social goals into a clearer focus (Gray et al. 1996). Its social goals should be found in its statutes, but they may need revising with time and changing circumstances. Many organizations outlive their original social goals and purpose, but they may find a new goal and purpose. Many organizations, especially those that survive for several decades, may need to revisit their statutes from time to time, in order to ensure their relevance and to relate them to changing circumstances and major societal changes. Similarly, without clear social goals and democratic structures for internal decision-making, co-ops cease to be co-operatives with any demonstrable differences that distinguish them from their private competitors (Pestoff 1998).

6.4.6 Closing the Circle at a Later/Higher Phase of Development—Helping Rejuvenate Grass-Roots Democracy

In a European context, we need to consider the future of democracy and the welfare state, as well as the role of voluntary associations and co-operatives in renewing both of them. Historically, co-operative enterprises have contributed to modernizing the political system of many countries by providing access to grass-roots democracy for large groups of citizens, often long before the introduction of universal suffrage. However, today co-operatives risk becoming historical relics and their offices, shops, and warehouses torn down or turned into cultural museums unless they can reinvent themselves and provide answers to tomorrow's growing unmet social demands, particularly with the retrenchment of the welfare state. Co-operative childcare in Scandinavia, social service co-ops in Italy, and co-operative health and elder care in Japan are but a few examples of their potential and rapidly expanding role as providers of essential social services in the twenty-first century. Moreover, co-operative enterprises demonstrate a unique capacity to mobilize social capital and provide relational goods that is not possible for either public or private for-profit providers. This brings co-operatives full-circle in terms of their historical political role as democratic pioneers, since they can now also contribute to reducing the growing 'democracy deficit' found in many parts of the world.

6.5 Conclusions and Discussion: Making Membership Meaningful

Several theoretical and practical issues of political importance are dealt with in this chapter. In brief, this chapter has dealt with the importance of major social change for organizational development, the importance of organizational growth and size for internal democracy, the importance of social goals for co-operative identity, and the need to develop methods to promote greater stability in hybrid organizations like co-operatives. In particular, a dynamic model of co-operative development has introduced the major stakeholders in co-operatives. This model was based on four separate and often opposing logics. Maintaining a stable balance in organizations that have several logics rather than a single one and several dominant stakeholders rather than just one can prove both challenging and problematic in the long run. Often a single logic will dominate, but if this happens for too long it can change the very nature of an organization or co-op. We have found clear evidence of this in the Swedish consumer co-ops, particularly in recent years.

Thus, nearly 20 years after the Centennial Meeting of the World Congress of the ICA in Manchester, it is perhaps time to reflect more seriously on the theme of a major policy report delivered at its hundredth Jubilee, with the ominous title *Making Membership Meaningful* (ICA 1995). All too often consumer co-operatives and other co-operative movements have done just the opposite. In recent times they have made membership meaningless, with the result that members eventually lose interest in them. Co-operatives in post-industrial society need to reinvent membership and relate it to activities and services that are more meaningful to their members in their daily lives in the twenty-first century. They need to develop a unique profile, one based on human needs and social values. They need to rediscover their political and social dimensions in order to emphasize and take advantage of their natural competitive advantage. It is by promoting their social values and responding to the growing demand for welfare services that co-operatives can play important economic, political, and social roles in a globalized economy. In this way they could also contribute to the development and renewal of democracy and the welfare state in the twenty-first century.

The provision of co-operative social services becomes increasingly feasible and necessary for rejuvenating and sustaining both the co-operative movements and the welfare state. Co-ops must adapt to the changing needs and demands of their members and the citizens. In doing so, they can revitalize themselves and renew democracy, both internally and externally. They can make membership more meaningful and citizenship more participative. They can once again serve as a school of democracy and help to democratize the welfare state from within.

The time has perhaps come in many post-industrial societies to ask whether consumer co-ops should perhaps consider selling off some or all of their stores and reinvest their collective resources in the development of welfare services, where co-ops could and should have a natural competitive advantage. In the post-industrial or service society of Europe, citizens are increasingly dependent on social services in their daily lives. This motivates closer collaboration between the established co-operative movements and new social service co-operatives of the type found in Italy, Japan, Sweden, and elsewhere, and/or more sustained efforts by established co-operatives to provide basic social services for their members and all citizens, not just sell goods and wares.

It is often argued that when an organization pursues multiple goals, some of which may conflict with others, and that when it attempts to combine the interests of multiple stakeholders, some of which may compete with others for scarce resources, it will be difficult for it to maintain its stability over time. Hybrid organizations are pulled in different directions, or torn apart by competing logics. Hansmann argued that the high transaction costs of decision-making in worker co-ops (1996) make them highly vulnerable and unstable. The present study, however, also illustrates risks of allowing a single logic to dominate for too long in hybrid organizations, especially if it comes at the expense of other competing logics. Does this study simply illustrate the impossibility of ever marrying democracy with the market, of democratic control in co-ops; or does it perhaps suggest the need to explore methods to ensure greater stability? Two methods were identified herein to help preserve organizational goals or prevent 'goal displacement', and to facilitate internal democracy. Both are highly central to maintaining democratic structures in co-operatives and other hybrid organizations with multiple goals and stakeholders. They are a regular social accounting and audit and multi-stakeholder representation in the internal decision-making of the co-op. These two methods, together with clear limits on the size of local co-ops and prohibitions against amalgamating them, would help to provide much greater stability to co-operatives and other hybrid organizations.

REFERENCES

Birchall, J. (2012), 'A "Member-Owned Business" Approach to the Classification of Co-operatives and Mutuals', in D. McDonnell and E. Macknight, eds, *The Co-operative Model in Practice: International Perspectives* (Glasgow: Glasgow: Co-operative Education Trust, Scotland), 67–92.

Birchall, J. and Simmons, R. (2001), 'Member Participation in Mutuals: A Theoretical Model', in J. Birchall and R. Simmons, *The New Mutualism in Public Policy* (London: Routledge), 202–25.

Birchall, J. and Simmons, R. (2004), 'What Motivates Members to Participate in Co-operative and Mutual Businesses? A Theoretical Model and Some Findings', *Annals of Public and Co-operative Economics*, 75(3), 465–95.

Böök, S-Å. (1992), *Co-operative Values in a Changing World; Report to the ICA Congress Tokyo, October 1992* (Geneva: International Co-operative Alliance).

Borzaga, C. (2011), 'New Opportunities for Co-Operatives and Social Enterprises in the Changing Landscape of the Welfare Systems.' Keynote speech at the International Co-operative Alliance's Research Conference, Mikkeli, Finland.

Borzaga, C. (2014), 'Europe in Transition: The Role of Social Co-operatives and Social Enterprises', Trento: Euricse Working Paper Series, n. 69/14.

Childs, M. (1936 & 1961), *Sweden: The Middle Way* (New Haven: Yale University Press).

Craig, J. G. (1993), *The Nature of Co-operation* (Montreal, New York, London: Black Rose Books).

De Tocqueville, A. (1830 & 1945), *Democracy in America*; 2 vols (New York: Knopf).

Donati, P. (2011), *Relational Sociology: A New Paradigm for the Social Sciences* (London, New York: Routledge).

Donati, P. (2014), The Ferment of a New Civil Society and Civil Democracy, in P. Donati and P Calvo, eds, *New Insights into Relational Goods* (Bologna: Department of Philosophy and Sociology: Recerca Revista de Pensament i Analisi, 14), 19–46.

Gijselinckx, C. (2012), 'Co-operative Answers to Societal Challenges: 9 Insights from 2 × 9 Cases', in M-J. Brassard and E. Molina, eds, *The Amazing Power of Co-operatives*, 403–18. Texts selected from the international call for proposals. Québec: International Summit of Co-operatives. Available at www.sommetinter2012.coop/site/summit-program/scientific-articles-selected (accessed 9 September 2016).

Gray, R., Owen, D., and Adams, C. (1996), *Accounting and Accountability: Changes and Challenges in Corporate Social and Environmental Reporting* (London: Prentice-Hall).

Hansmann, H. (1996), *The Ownership of Enterprise* (Cambridge, MA; Oxford: The Belknap Press of Harvard University Press).

Hirschman, A. (1970), *Exit, Voice & Loyalty* (Cambridge, MA: Harvard University Press).

International Co-operative Alliance (1995), *Making Membership Meaningful: Participatory Democracy in Co-operatives* (Saskatoon, CAN: University of Saskatchewan).

Kurimoto, A. (2010), 'Medical Co-ops: Evolution and Challenges', in CCIJ (ed.), *Toward Contemporary Co-operative Studies: Perspectives from Japan's Consumer Co-ops* (Tokyo: Consumer Co-op Institute of Japan), 136–64.

Laidlaw, A. F. (1980), 'Co-operatives in the Year 2000'. A Special Report commissioned by the ICA Central Committee; presented at the ICA Congress in Moscow, Soviet Union.

Ostrom, E. (1999), 'Crossing the Great Divide: Coproduction, Synergy, and Development', in McGinnis, M. D., ed, *Polycentric Governance and Development: Readings from the Workshop in Political Theory and Policy Analysis* (Ann Arbor, MI: University of Michigan Press).

Parks, R. B., Baker, P. C., Kiser, L., Oakerson, R., Ostrom, E., Ostrom, V., Perry, S. L., Vandivort, M. B., Whitaker G. P., and Wilson, R. (1981), 'Consumers as Co-Producers of Public Services: Some Economic and Institutional Considerations', *Policy Studies Journal*, 9, 1001–11, reprinted in M. D. McGinnis, ed, *Local Public Economies: Readings from the Workshop in Political Theory and Policy Analysis* (Ann Arbor, MI: University of Michigan Press, 1999), Chapter 17.

Pestoff, V. (1991), *Between Markets and Politics: Co-operatives in Sweden* (Frankfurt, Bolder: Campus Verlag, Westview Books).

Pestoff, V. (1998), *Beyond the Market and State. Social Enterprises and Civil Democracy in a Welfare Society* (Aldershot, UK; Brookfield, USA; Singapore & Sydney: Ashgate).

Pestoff, Victor (2008), *A Democratic Architecture for the Welfare State* (London & New York: Routledge).

Pestoff, V. (2009), 'Citizens as Co-Producers of Welfare Services: Preschool Services in Eight European Countries', *Public Management Review*, 8(4) (2006), 503–20, and reprinted in V. Pestoff, and T. Brandsen, eds, *Co-production. The Third Sector and the Delivery of Public Services* (London; New York: Routledge).

Pestoff, V. (2009), 'Towards a Paradigm of Democratic Participation: Citizens Participation and Co-production of Personal Social Services in Sweden', *Annals of Public and Co-operative Economics*, v. 80(2), 197–224.

Pestoff, V. (2012), 'Hybrid Tendencies in Consumer Co-operatives: The Case of Sweden', in D. McDonnell, and E. Macknight, eds, *The Co-operative Model in Practice: International Perspectives* (Glasgow: Co-operative Education Trust Scotland), 83–98.

Pestoff, Victor (2014), 'Hybridity, Innovation and the Third Sector: The Co-Production of Public Services', Ch. 13 in *Social Enterprise and the Third Sector. Changing European Landscapes in a Comparative Perspective*; J. Defourny, L. Hulgård and V. Pestoff, eds, (London & New York: Routledge).

Pestoff, Victor (2016), 'Democratic Innovations: Exploring Synergies between Three Key Post-New Public Management Concepts in Public Sector Reforms', Ch. 15 in *Social*

Entrepreneurship and Social Enterprises. Nordic Perspectives. L. Lundgaard Anderson, M. Gawell & R. Spear (eds) (London & New York: Routledge).

Pestoff, V., Kurimoto, Akira, Gijselinckx, Caroline, Vuotto, Mirta, and Hoyt, Ann (2017), 'Consumer and Service Co-Operatives as Economic Membership Associations', in D. H. Smith, J. Grotz, and R. Stebbings, eds, *Palgrave Research Handbook of Volunteering and Nonprofit Associations* (New York; London: Palgrave), Chapter 21.

Putnam, Robert D. (1993), *Making Democracy Work - Civil Traditions in Modern Italy* (Princeton, NJ: Princeton University Press).

Vamstad, J. (2007), 'Governing Welfare: The Third Sector and the Challenges to the Swedish Welfare State', Östersund: PhD thesis, No. 37.

Yanis, M. (2007), *Creating a World Without Poverty* (New York: Public Affairs).

PART III

HISTORY OF MEMBER-OWNED ORGANIZATIONS

A WORLDWIDE HISTORICAL PERSPECTIVE ON CO-OPERATIVES AND THEIR EVOLUTION

VERA ZAMAGNI

7.1 INTRODUCTION

THE historical development of co-operatives has not commanded an amount of research comparable to that of corporations, because co-ops have in general been smaller companies working in sectors that have not attracted much attention. Often, the history of co-operative enterprises has been part of the social history of self-promotion of the popular classes, together with the history of trade unions and of the political parties representing the working classes, rather than part of business history. Only in recent times has the *economic* importance of co-operation won more interest in academic and political milieus. Is this due only to the fact that a number of co-operative enterprises have managed to become large and build tightly connected networks? Recent consolidation of co-operatives is part of the answer, but to clarify the issue more thoroughly, it is necessary to sketch a quick outline of company history over time.

When companies appeared in Italian city-states in the Middle Ages, they were not standing alone, but belonged to associations of manufacturers (guilds) and merchants (chambers of merchants) which set the rules of the trade and administered justice (Bruni and Zamagni 2007). Such companies exercised responsibility towards their labour force and the surrounding society, for the well-being of which part of the profits were devoted. As companies started to enlarge and become active across oceans, such responsibility was lost, and companies started working only for the benefit of their capital owners, becoming therefore capitalist corporations without much interest in local low-profitability activities. Starting in the second half of the eighteenth century, the idea of promoting local businesses in an explicitly co-operative way started to spread in France, Austria, England, Spain, and Italy, as well as in the USA and Mexico. The first co-operatives were opened up by artisans (watchmakers), food producers (cheese), gardeners, and people who wanted to insure their houses against fire. This co-operative movement was part of a general effort by the working classes to self-help in order to counter the excessive growth of wealth concentration in the hands of capitalists.

Workable models of organizing these new businesses, however, were not developed until the middle of the nineteenth century, partly because the previous experiences had taught lessons, and partly because the capability of the working class to manage co-operatives had increased, both with regards to resources and to management. Co-operatives were rarely big business at the time, but they commanded the general interest of the working class, which multiplied their numbers, and the respect of economists and other intellectuals, who considered them an effective instrument for the progress of the economy of nations as well as for the improvement of the well-being of the working class. From different points of view, John Stuart Mill, Alfred Marshall, Leon Walras, Giuseppe Mazzini, Luigi Luzzatti, Giuseppe Toniolo, Sidney and Beatrice Webb, and George Holyoake, all agreed on considering co-operation a timely and viable model to overcome the shortcomings of capitalist corporations.[1]

Fordism has been the real antagonist of co-operatives.[2] Capital intensive plants, standardized production, huge numbers of employees, rigid assembly lines using unskilled labour, hierarchical chains of command, and all the well-known features of industrial corporations worked against the diffusion of co-operatives, especially in the manufacturing sector. As these huge capitalist corporations were the ones promoting growth in the twentieth century and because enough jobs were supplied by capitalist corporations, the working-class's interest in co-operatives diminished. What is even more relevant is that interest in co-operatives by economists and other intellectuals died out almost entirely. At most, co-operatives were seen as capable of filling in for businesses that were not desirable to capitalist corporations. The previous achievements of the co-operative movement were often maintained, but co-operatives seemed to have established themselves as marginal firms.

It is only in the late twentieth century, with the decline of Fordism, and the anti-social stance developed by many capitalist corporations, as well as the managerial strengthening of some co-operative enterprises, that such enterprises have had the opportunity to be reconsidered as appealing. Today, in advanced societies, most jobs are to be found in services rather than in industry, and in many services Fordism cannot be applied, hence co-operatives show a comparative advantage. Even in industry,

---

[1] For a general overview of the opinions of nineteenth-century intellectuals on co-operatives, see S. and V. Zamagni (2010), *Co-operative Enterprise Facing the Challenge of Globalization*, Cheltenham: Elgar.

[2] I have developed this argument in V. Zamagni (2012), 'Interpreting the Roles and Economic Importance of Co-operative Enterprises in Historical Perspective', *Journal of Entrepreneurial and Organizational Diversity*, 1: 21–36.

customization of products and quality, and intrinsic motivations by producers to respect traditions and the environment have come to weigh much more than before, with the consequence that in some branches of manufacturing co-operation today can be more attractive than in the past. Moreover, the footloose character of multi-nationals, their concentration on finance rather than on innovation, and their lack of attention to the environment and the social context have pushed many to reconsider working in small and medium sized firms, often self-managed by their employees, because they are more 'human' in their treatment of labour and more responsible as regards the social context where they are active. Finally, co-operatives have shown in more recent times a good ability to become larger and more efficient. According to an International Co-operative Alliance survey, the 300 largest co-operatives (or co-operative groups) of the world had annual revenues of $2.2 trillion in 2012 (see Table 7.1) and are mostly to be found in insurance (120), agro-industry (80), wholesale and retail (62), and banking (16).[3] Only 22 out of 300 co-operatives operate in other sectors (industry, utilities, and health).

In a world like the present one, in which opportunities for the diffusion of co-operative enterprises are growing, it is fundamental to understand the strengths and weaknesses of existing co-operative enterprises, as well as the basic features of the contexts that are most conducive to their consolidation. This will be done in the next two paragraphs by analysing first the birth and early evolution of the most important models of co-operation, and then the developments of co-operative enterprises in advanced countries in the last half a century.[4]

7.2 Birth and Early Evolution of Co-operative Enterprises

Co-operatives can be developed in any business, but they have been more successful in some. There are two possible ways of modelling co-operative enterprises: one based on who the members are and the other on the economic sectors in which the co-operative is active. The former approach subdivides co-operatives into the following four categories: *users* (consumer, utilities, banking, and insurance co-operatives); *producers* (agro-industry, retailers, and truck and taxi driver's co-operatives); *workers* (manufacturing and services); *community (social* co-operatives). This approach is more useful to the theorization of co-operatives and the identification of their comparative advantage,

---

[3] Co-operative banking has a market share in the European countries of around 20 per cent, but most of the co-operative banks are small and do not appear in the 300 largest co-ops list.

[4] Lack of space prevents the inclusion in this essay of the quite interesting history of co-operatives in the rest of the world. A general overview that however stops in the 1990s can be found in J. Shaffer (1999), *Historical Dictionary of the Co-operative Movement*, London: The Scarecrow Press.

Table 7.1 The 300 Largest Co-Ops in 2012 (Numbers and Turnover)

	Total		Insurance*		Other	
	No	Bln$	No	Bln$	No	Bln$
United States	86	564	39	370	47	194
Japan	17	348	10	11	7	337
France	41	329	10	67	31	262
Germany	31	251	15	83	16	168
Italy[#]	14	53	4	30	10	23
UK[§]	9	64	5	24	4	40
Spain	9	67	2	31	7	36
Canada[§]	10	46	5	13	5	33
Switzerland	7	73	2	6	5	67
Netherlands	15	110	6	47	9	63
Finland	10	50	4	16	6	34
Denmark	9	49	3	7	6	42
Sweden	6	28	3	13	3	15
Norway	8	26	3	10	5	16
Austria	3	24	2	19	1	5
Belgium	5	11	2	5	3	6
South Korea	2	53	1	2	1	51
New Zealand	5	25	–	–	5	25
Australia	3	7	1	2	2	5
Singapore	3	14	1	3	2	11
Ireland	2	5	–	–	2	5
Brazil	1	5	–	–	1	5
India	1	5	–	–	1	5
Saudi Arabia	1	1	1	1	–	–
Czech Republic	1	1	–	–	1	1
Argentina	1	1	1	1	–	–
Total	300	2210	120	761	180	1449

Notes: * For Insurance co-ops revenues from premium.

§ UK and Canada have one composite group each.

Italy has networks of organizations leaving single co-ops relatively small.

Source: Author's elaborations from the ICA databank.

which will not be adopted here (Zamagni 2012). The second approach follows the historical evolution of co-operatives more closely and is the one employed here.

As already mentioned, towards the middle of the nineteenth century, in many European countries the time was ripe to establish sustainable and reproducible co-operatives. For the success of its rules—most of which were later adopted by the majority of co-operatives—the English model must be analysed first. It is not by chance that England, the cradle of the Industrial Revolution, was the place where the early social movements that criticized capitalism emerged. England was also the cradle of 'social apostles', active in the organization of cultural and political movements in favour of the working class. Among them was Robert Owen (1771–1858). In 1799 in New Lanark he organized a model mill run with respect to the workers, and an entire village where all basic services were provided to workers and their families in a co-operative way. Many other attempts to build co-operative enterprises were subsequently made, but it was only in 1843 that a small group of weavers and other artisans under the leadership of Charles Howart launched a subscription to build a consumer co-operative in Rochdale, a small city in Lancashire. Strenuous efforts to raise enough capital to start the enterprise (£28 from 28 persons) led, on 21 December 1844, to the opening of a store on Todd Lane selling flour, butter, sugar, and oatmeal, thanks to the volunteer work of its members. According to its Statute, 'the objects and plans of this Society are to form arrangements for the pecuniary benefits and the improvement of the social and domestic conditions of the members'. The principles governing the operation of this co-operative store were the following: 1) sale for cash at fixed prices; 2) end of the year rebate proportional to purchases; 3) freedom of purchasing (members were not required to shop only at the co-op); 4) minimum interest on loans; 5) democratic government (one head, one vote; women too could be voting members); 6) ideological neutrality and tolerance.

This time it was a success. Housewives could accumulate a small treasure with the end of the year rebate and men found a place to meet and discuss their problems. In 1850, members already numbered 600. The following year, the store was opened every day with paid labour. The co-operative then added new sectors, giving work to many craftsmen. In 1855, a wholesale store was opened, the first of many, and the proliferation of subsidiaries began. A library was also opened as well as a meeting hall for men; schools and lectures were promoted, with a fund financed by 2.5 per cent of the operating surplus. The Rochdale Society of Equitable Pioneers eventually became a retailing giant, with an elegant, four-storey headquarters building and countless outlets (Holyoake 1893).

The Rochdale model was imitated throughout Britain and gained hegemony as British economists elaborated the principle of 'consumer sovereignty', especially when powerful wholesale societies were formed (the Co-operative Wholesale Society in Manchester in 1863 and the Scottish Co-operative Wholesale Society in 1868). These societies, however, opposed factory workers' sharing in the profits (even in factories linked to the societies themselves), for fear that this would mean higher costs of products. From a million members in 1877, consumer co-ops climbed to some 10 million members by the end of the 1930s, but other types of co-operative activities remained comparatively small. In

1919, a Co-operative College and the Plunkett Foundation for Co-operative Studies were created and in 1917 the Co-operative Party appeared. By 1940, the latter had reached more than 7 million members.

The second model is the workers' co-operative, which first developed in France. A society of carpenters was formed in Paris as early as 1831, followed by associations of goldsmiths, stonecutters, and bakers. In 1848, with the *ateliers nationaux* experiment under Louis Blanc, there were 255 such associations in Paris. The first legislation on their behalf was introduced that same year, creating a fund for workers' co-ops and giving them preference in public works' contracting. In 1884, a consultative chamber of workers' production co-operatives was formed with an original group of 29 societies; by 1904 this had grown to 200 (out of a total of 358 workers' co-operatives). Many of these co-ops originated in the conversion of existing capitalist enterprises into co-operatives. In the late nineteenth century, however, the French co-operative movement flourished mostly outside the manufacturing sector, with credit and farmers' co-operatives. In 1894, local and regional agricultural credit unions formed a central organization, the Crédit Agricole, which was later nationalized and then reintegrated to its original co-operative form.

The third model, from Germany, was the co-operative bank (labelled credit union in the Anglo-Saxon countries). In 1849, in Anhausen in the Rhine valley, Friedrich Wilhelm Raiffeisen, burgomaster and entrepreneur, founded the first rural mutual bank, lending only to members. Banks like it spread rapidly, and in 1876, a central German rural credit institute was formed, later to be named the Raiffeisen Bank of Germany. The majority of these banks were religiously inspired, but some were liberal. In 1910, they numbered 15,517, with 2.6 million members. In 1850, Hermann Schulze Delitzsch, judge and member of the national assembly in Berlin, founded the first urban mutual bank, called a popular bank. In 1859, there were already 111 of these, and in 1864 they formed a central institution. These second- and third-tier institutions helped individual co-operative banks consolidate and deliver services that they would not have been able to offer if they had remained isolated. By 1910, popular banks numbered 2,103, with one million members. Both Raiffeisen in the countryside and Schultze Delitzsch in cities subsequently extended co-operation to other fields. In 1913, Germany had over 35,000 co-ops with 6 million members. Their expansion continued in the Weimar period, and by 1933 there were 50,000 co-ops with 9 million members. The Nazi regime, however, put an end to this, dismantling all of the movement's central structures and subjecting the co-ops to direct government control; membership plummeted and it later proved difficult to reorganize the system.

The fourth model, the farmers' co-operatives, first developed in Scandinavia. The Danish Lutheran theologian and bishop Nicolas Friederich Gründtvigts (1783–1872) urged farmers in his diocese to promote farm co-ops and schools. After his death, these co-operatives grew considerably in the dairy farming and processing sector, which was becoming a Danish speciality. Starting in 1890, the dairy co-ops formed associations to export butter and, in 1901, the Co-operative Union of Danish Dairy Producers was founded, followed in 1920 by the Federation of Danish Dairy Producers, which virtually covered the entire industry. The co-operative formula began to spread to other sectors. In 1887, the first co-operative butchery and meat-packing operation began in Horsens. In 1890, the Central Office of Co-operative Butchers was created, followed in 1897 by the Danish Union of Co-operative Butchers. Comparable institutions took root in Sweden and Finland. In the latter country the movement started in the second half of the nineteenth century in farming and, in 1899, gave rise to the Confederation of Finnish Co-operatives, Pellervo (deriving from the Finnish word for 'field'), grouping 390 agricultural co-ops. The founder members included university professors, industrialists, and bankers who believed that co-operatives would serve not only to spread material well-being, but also to increase popular self-esteem and mass participation in the movement for economic and political liberation from Russia. Two apostles of co-operation devoted their entire lives to the movement: Hannes Gebhard, head of Pellervo, and his wife Hedvig, who was also a member of the Finnish Parliament. In 1902 a co-operative bank, Okobank, was created. Consumer co-ops followed; the largest of these, Sok, started in 1904 and now includes a large purchasing consortium, (Hankkija Maatalous Oy), forestry industry co-operatives (Metsäliitto), and mutual insurance societies.

By the end of the 1930s, Denmark had a co-operative membership covering almost half of its population, Finland 20 per cent, and Sweden 10 per cent. Only Britain and France matched these achievements, with around 20 per cent of the population being members of at least a co-operative in the former, and around 10 per cent in the latter. Germany had reached similar percentages (12–13 per cent) before Nazism.[5] Italy too had an important and highly diversified co-operative movement, which was not killed by fascism, but constrained into a State agency, leaving freedom of enterprise, but not of appointment of the governing body of co-operatives. At the end of the 1930s, roughly 7 per cent of the population were members of a co-op.

As the co-operative movement was growing in various countries, some of its leaders advanced the idea of promoting its international coordination. In 1867 in Paris, an attempt was made to organize an international meeting of co-operators, but the French government did not allow it for fear of disorders. Other attempts were made, but it was only in August 1895 that the meeting took place in London and the International Co-operative Alliance (ICA) was created. Nine of the 13 countries which participated were European, and the other four (the USA, Argentina, Australia, and India) derived their interest in co-operatives from Europe. The ICA, which soon evolved into an association of co-operative federations (single co-operatives could no longer join directly), acted mainly to defend the co-operative identity, not without difficulty, given the wars that set member nations in conflict with one another and the presence of authoritarian regimes that opposed the democratic functioning of co-operation.

The ICA also had to face the serious question of membership by organizations that were nominally co-operatives but actually companies under state control (particularly

---

[5] T. Menzani (2009), *Il movimento cooperativo fra le due guerre: Il caso italiano nel contesto europeo*, Rome: Carocci, 43.

in the Soviet Union). The difficult decision not to expel Soviet co-operatives was eventually taken, but the ICA had to defend itself against the attempts of the Soviet bloc's representatives to dominate the association. During the 1930s, the number of member federations plunged with the spread of dictatorships throughout Europe (in Italy, Germany, various Eastern European countries, Portugal, and Spain). At its Paris Congress in 1937, the Alliance nevertheless had the courage to reaffirm the democratic principles of the movement.

7.3 DEVELOPMENTS IN THE LAST FIFTY YEARS

After the Second World War, co-operation prospered in many countries. If we ask the question 'where have co-operatives been more successful in the recent decades?' the answer is not easy, because membership numbers are especially high in less developed countries (notably China and India), where co-ops are, however, mostly confined to agro-industry and rural credit banks. In developed countries, membership is not so massive, but co-operatives have consolidated their managerial profile in such a way as to be able to successfully compete with capitalist corporations. In this last half a century, what is first to be noted with reference to innovation in the field of co-operatives is the development of a brand new type of co-operative, the *social co-operatives* or *community co-operatives* (Borzaga and Defourny 2001). It is the only important co-operative model born since the nineteenth century and is largely the fruit of Italian creativity.

On 23 January 1963, the first co-operative for social assistance and solidarity was founded in Brescia (an Italian city north of Milan) under the leadership of the Catholic activist Giuseppe Filippini. The society, named after St. Joseph, had two distinctive features: bringing people together for social and cultural needs (training, education, assistance, recreation, and work for the disadvantaged); and acting not only for the benefit of its own members but also for 'others', as Filippini made clear at the first conference of the co-operative movement held in Italy in 1977. This pointed to an entirely new version of the mutualism that had existed before co-operatives. It implied a multi-stakeholder model of governance, a model previously unknown to co-operatives, in which the representatives of a number of different interest groups all have a say in decisions and a role in the governance structure. The co-operative boards thus comprise, not only worker-members, but also the beneficiaries of the co-ops' services and representatives of the local community. The Italian law 381/1991 instituted the *social co-operative*, a model which serves as the prototype of the social enterprise in Europe (Borzaga and Janes 2006). It has also inspired the introduction of a seventh principle of co-operation on the part of the ICA in its centenary meeting of 1995 in Manchester, which states: '7. Concern for Community: Co-operatives work for the sustainable development of their communities through policies approved by their members.'

Statistics concerning co-operatives have not improved substantially in this recent period, so it is not possible to offer comparatives tables that summarize the evolution of co-operation in the last 50 years. But from a more qualitative literature, it is quite possible to pinpoint the countries where co-operation has been more dynamic. Among these, a remarkable absence is that of the UK, the cradle of modern co-operatives. The major factors working against a strengthening of co-operatives in the UK are two fold: the lack of complementarities among co-operatives resulting from the predominance of consumer co-ops, and the inadequate strategy of the leader Co-operative Wholesale Society (CWS). CWS remained for too long stuck to the consumption model of a class of factory workers that was shrinking in favour of the middle class, which developed different consumption models, and its market share consequently plummeted. Not until 2001 did CWS merge with banking, insurance, and other co-operatives (mainly social, health, and community co-operatives) to form a new composite group, the Co-operative Group, which is busy recovering market share (Black and Robertson 2009).

A reference must also be made to the parable of British building societies, not least because they are a demonstration of the problems arising in the management of co-operatives in the present world. The origin of building societies reverts back to late eighteenth-century Birmingham, a city that was rapidly growing and hosted clubs and societies for co-operation. The first building society was founded by Richard Ketley in 1775, and implied the payment of a monthly subscription on the part of members into a fund used to finance the building of new popular houses for members. Soon there were hundreds of building societies in Britain, which developed also in Australia, New Zealand, and Ireland on the British model. In the USA, the savings and loans associations played a similar role, while in Austria and Germany some banks became specialized in mortgages and loans to the construction industry, but not all of them were mutual (often they were savings banks). In the 1980s, with the liberalization of financial markets, many of these building societies became de-specialized banks and a tendency to de-mutualize appeared, led by managers who wanted to profit from this. The first to de-mutualize in Britain was Abbey National in 1989, which was soon bought by Banco Santander, together with other demutualized building societies. In 1997, Northern Rock demutualized, adopting after that a highly speculative stance, which brought it to bankruptcy in 2008. It was bailed out by the British government, which came to control it and, in 2011 decided to privatize it. Today, less than 50 mutual building societies are left in Britain with 18 million members, while in Ireland they have practically disappeared.

As an opposite case to the British decline of co-operatives, we can quote Italy's flourishing co-operatives. The two basic features of the Italian co-operative movement are a multi-sector approach that has allowed synergies among various co-operatives, and an ideological non-neutral inspiration, which has seen the organization of three tight umbrella organizations: the socialist (and for a period communist) Legacoop, the Catholic Confcooperative, and the liberal AGCI (often referred to as red, white, and green co-operatives, the colours of the Italian flag). They have competed but also collaborated on major issues. Italian co-operatives have developed a special capability of acting together (inside the three umbrella organizations) by means of federations, consortia, and groupings, keeping each co-op relatively small (with exceptions), but acquiring market power through networking (Menzani and Zamagni 2010). In 2011, the three umbrella organizations decided to build an Alliance (ACI, Alleanza delle Cooperative Italiane), which is promoting a process of merger. The achievements of the Italian co-operative movement have been truly impressive: Italian co-operatives (Coop and Conad, plus other smaller groups) are market leaders in retailing, with one-third of the Italian retail market (small shops excluded). A similar percentage of the market is supplied by co-operatives in insurance and construction, while in agro-industry the impact of co-operatives is 25 per cent. Many other services also see a qualified presence of co-ops: in catering, logistics, transportation, facility management, as well as in banking. There are also some well-functioning manufacturing co-ops. Social co-operatives deliver more than 50 per cent of social services. In 2014, Italian co-ops directly employed 8 per cent of the Italian labour force and indirectly (through joint stock companies controlled by co-operatives or supplying co-operatives) more than 10 per cent of it.

Today France is certainly the European country where co-operatives are most strategic in at least three sectors: banking, agro-industry, and insurance. The Groupement national de la coopération (GNC) was founded in 1947 as the umbrella organization and followed a strategy of diversification. The greatest success was achieved in banking, where the Crédit Agricole freed itself completely from government controls in 1988 and obtained stock exchange listing for its holding company in order to conduct major economic transactions nationally and internationally. The holding company was at first entirely owned by the regional credit unions, which later sold part of their holdings but retained a majority stake. Today, the Crédit Agricole in its hybrid form (partly co-operative and partly capitalist) is the largest banking group in France and one of the largest in the world. When added to the popular, mutual, and saving banks (which have been turned into co-operatives) it appears that 60 per cent of French banking deposits are co-operative, while mutual insurance societies account for 40 per cent of the French insurance market. Agro-industry has also grown very strong and 75 per cent of French farmers are members of at least one co-operative.

Today retail co-operatives in France have a quarter of the retail market, but much more as a result of retailer co-ops than of consumer co-ops. The former had a total turnover of €39 billion in 2006, with 17,000 points of sale, mostly non-grocery (9,000 of them are pharmaceutical). The latter had a turnover of €3 billion and four main regional groups. In 2006, the largest French retailer co-op, Leclerc, built with the Italian retailer co-op Conad, the German Rewe, the Belgian private chain Colruyt, and the Suisse Consumer Coop the first European co-op, Coopernic. In 2014, this alliance was dismantled and two were born out of it: Coopernic, between Leclerc, Coop Italia (the wholesale company of the Italian consumer co-ops), plus the Belgian Delhaize; and Core, which gathers the former four partners of Leclerc but has been incorporated into a Belgian co-op. Workers co-operatives are also important in France; in 2007 there were some 1,800 of them with 50,000 employees and a €3.5 billion turnover.

The German co-operative movement had to start up almost from scratch after the war. This new beginning adhered to the same principle that governed the rest of the economy in West Germany, namely decentralization in the name of democracy. At a time when the European economy was strengthening and was emulating the US model of large corporations, this formula was not likely to allow a flourishing of the co-operative movement. Co-operative credit—the strongest of the movement's historical roots—succeeded in reorganizing, forming a single central institute (Deutsche Genossenschaftsbank, or DG Bank) in 1949, and a single national organization with a regional structure in 1972, the Bundesverband der Deutschen Volksbanken und Raiffeisenbanken (BVR). In 2001, as a result of successive mergers the Deutsche Zentral Genossenschaftsbank (DZ Bank) was created as the central institution of German co-operative banks, numbering around 1,100 in 2014, with 18 million members and about 24 per cent of German bank deposits.

The strategy for consumer co-ops, by contrast, proved inadequate. Between 1969 and 1972, German consumer co-operatives underwent a radical modernization with the creation of a central management organization (Bund Deutscher Konsumgenossenschaften GmbH), which in subsequent years renewed the retail network, intensified concentration, and began a campaign to transform the co-ops into public limited companies to facilitate financing. This change largely removed management activities from membership control. In 1975, the process of regionalization was well advanced; the eleven largest regional co-operatives accounted for more than 70 per cent of total sales by consumer co-operatives. However, the transition to a nationwide dimension proved to be difficult and concealed serious operational problems that management had kept hidden for a long time. When these problems emerged in 1989, bankruptcy was unavoidable (Fairbairn 1999). Today, Germany has a few consumer co-operatives, most of them small. Only three groupings are medium-sized (Coop Dortmund, Coop Schleswig Holstein, and Coop Nord Bayern). All in all, despite its significant presence in agriculture, banking, insurance, services, and small business, the German co-operative movement no longer commands the economic power that had distinguished it before the advent of the Nazi regime, mostly because of the weakness of its presence in the retail sector. However, thanks to the *Mitbestimmung* (co-determination, which implied that trade union representatives were sitting on the board of directors), the participation of workers in the governance of enterprises has been generalized in Germany in a way that is unknown in other nations of the world, although certainly in a form which differs from that of co-operative enterprises.

The case of Spain is special. Here too, the co-operative movement arose in the nineteenth century, when a series of powerful regional organizations were created. A nationwide federation came into being in 1928, but Franco's dictatorship marked a discontinuation and the movement barely survived and later only partially recovered. Spanish co-operation is known in the world, not for its national organization, but rather for the presence of a unique co-operative experience, Mondragón (Williams 2007). The foundation of the first co-operative in the Basque town that lends its name to it stemmed from the activities of a priest, José Maria Arizmendiarrieta, who became the parish priest of Mondragón in the 1940s. In 1943, he opened a vocational school for young people, and 1956 saw the founding of the first co-op, Fagor, which made stoves and radiators. It was the first of many, and by the end of the 1960s the Mondragón co-ops numbered 41. They were organized and financed by Caja Laboral, a bank which had been founded in 1959, the same year that the collective insurance company Lagun-Aro was activated. In 1969, a retailing society, Eroski, was created. Unlike anywhere else, Eroski is not a consumer but a worker co-op.

The original nucleus grew with the creation of a polytechnic school in 1962, and a research centre (*Ikerlan*) in 1974, both of which were incorporated into the University of Mondragón in 1997. In 1984, the need to reorganize led to the constitution of a group governed by a congress, which linked consortia of co-operatives together. As early as 1991, this organization gave way to a new structure based on product group divisions, with central departments responsible for finance, innovation, internationalization, and co-operative identity; a truly modern corporation, as marked even by the change in name to MCC (Mondragón Cooperative Corporation). In this way, Mondragón was to face the challenges of globalization (Reed and McMurtry 2009). Despite its undeniable success, and with the sole exception of the Eroski retailing chain which has achieved a certain degree of geographical diversification, the Mondragón group remains an enclave in the Basque country, where it accounts for 8 per cent of local output and 14 per cent of employment.

Among the smaller European countries, all the Northern ones (Finland, Norway, Sweden, Denmark, Netherlands) have a very strong co-operative movement, mostly present in retail, agro-industry, banking, and insurance.[6] There is another small European country with a large presence of co-operatives and it is Switzerland. The Swiss Union of Consumer Cooperatives, the country's first large co-operative organization, was founded in 1890. It was not until after the Second World War, however, that the movement was coordinated, with the institution of a single logo in 1960. In that year, there were some 400 consumer co-ops with 3,320 retail outlets, but a series of mergers brought the number of co-ops down to 40, then 18, and then 14. In 2001, the final merger was completed, forming the new Coop society, which is broadly diversified into other branches, and controls 15 per cent of the Swiss retail market. Coop, however, is not the only Swiss consumer co-operative. There is also Migros, larger in size, whose origin is atypical. Migros was founded as a limited company in 1925 by Gottlieb Duttweiler, a merchant with progressive ideas and a strong sense of social responsibility. In 1941, he transformed it into a co-operative, which is today Switzerland's leading retail organization, with 2 million members, 80,000 employees, and a presence in many other businesses. Co-operative credit is also important, with 1.4 million members and around 20 per cent of total bank deposits.

---

[6] Boscia, Carretta, and Schwizer (eds) (2010), *Co-operative Banking in Europe: Case Studies*, Basingstoke: Palgrave Macmillan.

The insurance sector deserves a special mention. The presence of mutual insurance societies in Europe is substantial: in 2008, more than two-thirds of all insurers in Europe belonged to the mutual sector, reaching 25 per cent of all the paid insurance premiums. They have an association—AMICE (Association of Mutual Insurers and Insurance Cooperatives in Europe)—with more than 100 direct members. In some countries their presence is much more substantial: in France and Germany mutual insurers cover around 40 per cent of the market. The market share at the world level is only slightly below the European: 24 per cent, with Japan at 38 per cent, and the USA and Canada at 30 per cent. There is a world organization: the ICMIF (International Cooperative and Mutual Insurance Federation), which was initially established by ICA in 1922, but became independent in 1972. With only five members at the start, in 2010 ICMIF reached 210 members, one-third in Europe, one-third in the Americas, and one-third in the rest of the world. These 210 members directly represent 600 organizations, and indirectly (through their national mutual trade organizations) represent 2,700 of them, including joint stock companies controlled by co-operatives. Mutual benefit societies, once the only ones to deliver health and assistance to their members, must also be briefly mentioned here. In the last half a century, they have had to measure themselves with the state monopoly of welfare in many European countries, but they have reacted creatively. In some countries (Germany, Belgium, the Netherlands, Czech Republic, and Slovakia), mutual benefit societies are running the compulsory health insurance covering from 80 per cent to 100 per cent of the population; in other countries (notably France) they provide complementary insurance against sickness or old age; and in others (UK and the Nordic countries) they still represent an alternative to the National Health system for those who want quicker services or higher pensions. All in all, in Europe 230 million people are covered by mutual benefit societies.

Moving out of Europe, only three cases will be presented, starting with the USA which, as Table 7.1 shows, presents the largest co-op, although the impact of co-ops in this country is substantial only in agriculture, insurance, and utilities.[7] In the second half of the nineteenth century, there was an extremely intense US co-operative movement in all fields, including innovative industries such as telephones, electricity, and water supply. A book on the history of co-operation in the USA was published as early as 1888, testifying to the movement's great early dynamism. A series of federations, institutes, and industry associations were formed. The strongest sector has always been that of farmer co-operatives. In 2009, US farmers' co-ops still had 2.2 million members and accounted for a third of the country's agricultural output. In the US credit sector, co-operation accounted for 91 million members and some 7,000 credit unions in 2009, with 7 per cent of the credit market. The other two sectors in which the co-operative

[7] A. Hoyt and T. Menzani (2012), 'The International Cooperative Movement: A quiet Giant', in P. Battilani, and H. G. Schröter (eds.), *The Cooperative Business Movement, 1950 to the Present*, Cambridge: Cambridge University Press, 23–62.

movement is powerful in the USA are insurance, with 1,000 mutual societies (the largest 39 alone administer premiums for $370 billion (see Table 7.1), and electricity, with around 1,000 co-ops serving 37 million customers and 40 per cent of the domestic market. Consumer co-operatives have retained only a niche role, such as that of REI (Recreational Equipment Inc.), which markets sporting goods and outdoor equipment, with 3 million members.

Overall, some 120 million Americans (well over a third of the total population) belong to at least one co-operative. A national co-operative organization was founded in 1916, as the Cooperative League of America. In 1922, when it incorporated the rest of the nation's co-operatives, its name was changed into Cooperative League of the USA. In 1985, it changed name again, to National Co-operative Business Association. In the 1990s, the organization persuaded Congress to enact a programme of support for rural co-ops (Ben-Ner, Burns, Dow, and Putterman 2000). What is also to be noticed is the existence of ESOP (Employee Stock Ownership Plan),[8] which was started in 1956 to allow employees to buy out the companies where they worked when the ownership was no longer interested in managing them. In the early twenty-first century, there are more than 11,000 ESOP companies, with 13 million workers.

Canada is an even more co-operative country than the USA. Co-operatives emerged in Canada at around the middle of the nineteenth century, at first in the consumer and farming sectors (McPherson 2009). Marketing co-operatives and creameries were established in many areas of the country and grew without interruptions. Today, they have become powerful corporations, accounting for over 40 per cent of total farm cash receipts. The first Credit Union was founded in 1900 by Alphonse Desjardins, the prototype of a large French-speaking movement that counts today, together with its English-speaking counterpart (the Canadian Co-operative Credit Society), more than 10 million members and 20 per cent of the market. Insurance, housing, and fishery co-operatives are also strong, as well as healthcare and childcare co-operatives. In the field of retail co-operatives, a remarkable example is MEC (Mountain Equipment Co-operative) established in 1971 in Vancouver for the sale of outdoor equipment and apparel, which in 2006 counted 2.3 million members and is leader in the use of Internet technologies as well as in running sustainability and ethical programmes (Walzer and Merrett 2000). Along with the services they render to their member co-operatives and second-tier organizations, the two Canadian umbrella organizations—the French-speaking Desjardins Group and the English-speaking Canadian Co-operative Association born in 1909 (McPherson 2009)—run programmes promoting co-operatives in the developing world. Today, 40 per cent of the Canadian population is a member of a co-operative, making Canada one of the most highly co-operative countries in the world.

Finally, the case of Japan must be mentioned. When the country opened up to the Western market economy in the nineteenth century, the co-operative movement started

---

[8] See D. L. Kruse, R. B. Freeman, and J. R. Blasi (eds) (2010), *Shared Capitalism at Work: Employee Ownership, Profit and Gain Sharing and Broad Based Stock Options*. NBER Conference: University of Chicago Press.

to spread in the 1870s, patterned after European models. The first legislation regulating co-operatives was enacted in 1900, and under it the movement flourished, reaching a million members by 1912 and nearly 3 million members in 1922. The authoritarian governments that followed, like the European dictatorships, put a brake on co-operatives, but post-war resurgence was rapid. Membership rose to 22 million in 1972 and 57 million two decades later. The strongest sectors are agriculture, consumer co-ops, and insurance (with 14 million members). Banking was also present, but it suffered deeply from the banking crisis of the 1990s. Farmers' co-operatives were the chosen instrument for applying government farm subsidies, performing a large number of diversified activities (supplying inputs, marketing of output, food processing, finance, insurance, building, and other rural services, including health, and cultural services). Japanese farmers' co-operatives became a power with over 10 million members. In fact, with a market share of 70 per cent at the end of the twentieth century, they dominate Japanese agriculture and maintain social cohesion in the countryside. On the consumer front, the Japanese Consumer Co-operatives Union was formed in 1951 and began producing under its own brand in 1960. It now has a market share of 5 per cent and is the third largest retailer in a highly fragmented market (Hasumi 2010). Half of the co-ops' total turnover depends on an original system of 'Han' groups that arrange for collective purchases and home delivery.

7.4 CONCLUSIONS

The co-operative movement, which is able to boast one billion members and at least 250 million jobs at the world level, should be better represented both at the political and at the cultural level. Indeed, when it was born in the nineteenth century, its originality and forcefulness were clear on both grounds. But then, on the one side, co-operation was for a long time confused inside the general political movements opposing capitalism and, on the other side, it was economically overwhelmed by Fordism. Now that history has made clear that there is no advancement without market economy, but that markets need not be populated only by Fordist corporations, there is room for a re-proposition of co-operation in new contexts. Co-operation today must not be limited to people living in the same place and forming small co-ops. Through the Web, co-operation can transcend physical boundaries and connect people across oceans for endeavours such as Wikipedia or crowdfunding, which were inconceivable back in time. Conceptualization as well as legislation must be adapted to these new dimensions and purposes of co-operation, as the European Parliament made clear in 2009.[9]

There are, however, some requirements distinguishing co-operative enterprises from capitalist ones that cannot be changed. A co-operative economic activity will always have to be participated in by a community of people, democratically run, and ready to

---

[9] European Parliament (2009), *Report on the Social Economy*, 26 January, A6-0015/2009, Referee Patrizia Toia.

distribute profits in a way that is equitable to all participants and respectful of workers (whether they are members or non-members), and of the natural and social contexts. In specific circumstances these requirements can be present also in enterprises incorporated differently from co-operatives and non-profit organizations, but in co-operatives they constitute their reason for existence.

References

Ben-Ner A., Burns, W. A., Dow, G., and Putterman, L. (2000), 'Employee Ownership: An Empirical Exploration', in M. Blair and T. Kochan, eds, *The New Relationship: Human Capital in the American Corporation* (Washington, DC: Brookings Institute Press), 194–210.

Black, L. and Robertson, N., eds (2009), *Consumerism and the Co-operative Movement in Modern British History: Taking Stock* (Manchester: Manchester University Press).

Borzaga, C. and Defourny, J., eds (2001), *The Emergence of Social Enterprise* (London: Routledge).

Borzaga, C. and Janes, A. (2006), *L'economia della solidarietà: Storia e prospettive della cooperazione sociale* (Rome: Donzelli).

Boscia, V., Carretta, A., and Schwizer, P. (2010), *Cooperative Banking in Europe: Case Studies.* (Basingstoke: Palgrave MacMillan).

Bruni, L. and Zamagni, S. (2007), *Civil Economy* (Oxford: Peter Lang).

Fairbairn, B. (1999), 'The Rise and Fall of Consumer Cooperation in Germany', in E. Furlough, and C. Strickwerda, eds, *Consumers Against Capitalism? Consumer Cooperation in Europe, North America and Japan, 1840-1990* (Lanham, MD: Rowman & Littlefield).

Hasumi, O. (2010), 'Consumer Coops in Japan: Challenges and Prospects in Transitional Stage', in The Consumer Cooperative Institute of Japan, ed., *Toward Contemporary Cooperative Studies: Perspectives from Japan's Consumer Coops* (Tokyo: Consumer Cooperative Institute of Japan), vii–xix.

Holyoake, G. J. ([1893], 3rd ed. 1900), *History of the Rochdale Pioneers* (London: Swan and Sonnenschein).

Hoyt, A. and Menzani, T. (2012), 'The International Cooperative Movement: A Quiet Giant', in P. Battilani, and H. G. Schröter, eds, *The Cooperative Business Movement, 1950 to the Present* (Cambridge: Cambridge University Press), 23–62.

Kruse, D. L., Freeman, R. B., and Blasi J. R. (2010), *Shared Capitalism at Work: Employee Ownership, Profit and Gain Sharing and Broad Based Stock Options* (NBER Conference: University of Chicago Press).

McPherson, I. (2009), *A Century of Cooperation* (Ottawa: Canadian Cooperative Association).

Menzani, T. (2009), *Il movimento cooperativo fra le due guerre: Il caso italiano nel contesto europeo* (Rome: Carocci), 43.

Menzani, T. and Zamagni, V. (2010), 'Cooperative Networks in the Italian Economy', *Enterprise and Society,* XI(1), 98–127.

Nowak, M. and Highfield, R. (2011), *Supercooperators: Evolution, Altruism and Human Behaviour or Why We Need Each Other to Succeed* (Edinburgh: Canongate Books).

Reed, D. and McMurtry, J. J., eds (2009), *Cooperatives in a Global Economy: The Challenges of Cooperation across Borders* (Newcastle upon Tyne: Cambridge Scholars Publishing).

Schaffer, J. (1999), *Historical Dictionary of the Cooperative Movement* (London: The Scarecrow Press).

Williams, R. C. (2007), *The Cooperative Movement: Globalization from Below* (Aldershot: Ashgate).

Zamagni, S. and Zamagni, V. (2010), *Cooperative Enterprise Facing the Challenge of Globalization* (Cheltenham: Elgar).

Zamagni, V. (2012), 'Interpreting the Roles and Economic Importance of Cooperative Enterprises in Historical Perspective', *Journal of Entrepreneurial and Organizational Diversity*, 1, 21–36.

CHAPTER 8

··

AN AMERICAN HISTORICAL PERSPECTIVE ON EMPLOYEE OWNERSHIP

··

JOSEPH R. BLASI AND DOUGLAS L. KRUSE

8.1 INTRODUCTION: THE COD FISHERY AND PROFIT-SHARING

WHEN the Revolutionary War for independence from Great Britain ended in 1783, the cod fishery, one of the mainstays of the colonial economy, was in dire straits. Cod were the fourth most valuable export of the colonies. The fish were caught off the coast of New England and to the north. The cod were dried and exported to Europe, particularly to Spain, Portugal, and southern Europe around the Mediterranean, Great Britain, and France, and to slave colonies in the West Indies. During the war, the British had destroyed many American ships, closed many European markets to American fish, and made life difficult for the fishermen who manned the cod ships.

Soon after taking office as first president of the United States, George Washington asked Secretary of State Thomas Jefferson to find a way to help citizens resurrect the cod fishery and make it prosper. Neither Washington nor Jefferson favoured direct state ownership or state subsidies and state control. They wanted a policy that would best fit the new American republic. To devise the policy Jefferson conducted the first research on inclusive capitalism in American history, working with Tench Coxe, who was the assistant secretary of the Treasury under Secretary of the Treasury Alexander Hamilton. Coxe, a well-known colonial political economist, asked Philadelphia shipper Joseph Anthony about work practices on the cod ships and was told in a 1790 letter from Anthony that 'they (the crew) were generally found the most attentive, when their Dependence was on a Share of what they Caught' rather than fixed wages not tied to productivity.

Broad-based profit-sharing had been the norm in both the cod and the whale fisheries for over a century in the colonies. The problem that most concerned cod fishermen and ship owners in rebuilding the industry was high tariffs on imports of equipment that they needed to operate the fishery. The high tariffs put a burden on the fishermen and owners of the ships, but they were important to support the Treasury. What was needed was a policy to encourage the cod-fishery sector, including the broad group of fishermen, to share the fruits of this industry without bankrupting the Treasury. Jefferson gave his analysis of the industry in a Report on the American Fisheries which he delivered to the Speaker of the House of Representatives on 1 February 1791.

On 16 February 1792, Congress passed and President Washington signed a new law that essentially gave tax credits to cod ships that went out during the fishing season based on the weight of the vessels. The tax credits were divided five-eighths to the crew and three-eighths to the owners of the ships, recognizing the tax burden that fell on both parties. This was probably the first time in American history that a tax credit was divided between the owners of capital and the workers in the industry in question. Moreover, as a condition for receiving the tax credit, President George Washington's law required a signed agreement between the captain and the crew, before the ship went to sea, in which the captain and owners of the ship additionally agreed to continue to practise broad-based profit-sharing on the entire catch. This was the first time in American history that worker capital shares, in this case in the form of profit-sharing, were a condition of a federal tax credit. The law stayed in force for decades. The case takes on added importance for surveying the contemporary scene because it demonstrates at the time of the Founders of the American republic that they perceived the importance of shares of financial participation in industry, in this case the fishing industry, just as they strongly defended the idea of land shares for farmers as the basis for a democratic republic (Blasi, Freeman, and Kruse, 2014: 1–9)

8.2 A CONSENSUS AMONG THE FOUNDERS DESPITE OTHER TERRIBLE DISAGREEMENTS

The founders of the United States believed that the economy should be structured with broad-based property ownership because wide ownership was essential for a democratic republic to exist. They saw this in contrast to European feudalism which they believed the British Crown was trying to impose on them to some extent. They believed that a republic required a strong middle class and equitable distribution of wealth in order to survive and be sustainable. To maintain the middle class, they supported policies to make capital ownership and capital income broadly available to citizens. This was originally done with land ownership but the idea was later connected to the idea of worker ownership. In a 19 June 1788 letter, Washington explicitly recognized the value of broad-based land ownership: 'It is also believed that it will not be less advantageous to the happiness of the lowest class of people because of the equal distribution of property.' During his administration as America's first president, in addition to the profit-sharing reform of the cod industry, Washington asked Jefferson to draft a liberal land policy to allow citizens to buy land at reasonable rates. Washington took radical action to broaden property ownership: one of his first acts after starting his presidency on 30 April 1979 was to reaffirm the Northwest Ordinance on 7 August 1789. This governmental act made the public land of what would later become seven states in the north-west available for cheap settlement by citizens, extending the idea of the landed republic. Certainly, there is no question that talking about liberty and broad-based property ownership was completely hypocritical for the Founders who limited their policies to males who were citizens, some of whom endorsed the great evil of slavery and the social exclusion of women from civil society. Our point, however, is to show how their broader vision created the ideological basis for the concept of broad-based property ownership in American society and helped to inform the development of worker ownership later, when, thankfully, many of these social exclusions would fall away as citizenship and the right to vote was extended.

John Adams, the staunchly abolitionist second president, repeatedly articulated his fear that concentrated property ownership would undermine the republic and he worked hard to distribute public land to landless citizens in his own state of Massachusetts. After the American Revolution, he favoured state laws to force families to divide their estates among all their children and thus prevent the large European feudal estates that developed when property went only to the eldest (male) offspring. Like other Founders, Adams closely read the seventeenth-century political philosopher James Harrington, whose book, *The Commonwealth of Oceana*, linked broad property ownership to the distribution of power and liberty in a republic. As the principal writer of the Massachusetts Constitution, Adams stressed the protection of property rights and the right to acquire property. Recognizing that natural human differences lead to inequality, Adams opposed mechanical plans to distribute property, but he still wanted property ownership to be as widespread as possible. His followers even proposed to change the name of the Commonwealth of Massachusetts to Oceana to underline the importance of broad-based ownership (Blasi, Freeman, and Kruse, 2014: 1, 26–30, 46–8).

Thomas Jefferson, the third president, argued that a higher proportion of broad-based property ownership reduced political corruption, and recommended that the Virginia Constitution make public land available to every citizen. When he was ambassador to France, he wrote to James Madison about the enormous inequality that he observed in France: 'But the consequences of this enormous inequality producing so much misery to the bulk of mankind, legislators cannot invent too many devices for subdividing property, only taking care to let their subdivisions go hand in hand with the natural affections of the human mind .... But it is not too soon to provide by every possible means that as few as possible shall be without a little portion of land. The small landholders are the most precious part of a state.'

Jefferson took specific actions to advance his agenda. He drafted George Washington's first policy on granting public land to landless citizens. He told James Madison in 1775 that those excluded from property ownership needed to have this 'fundamental right' returned to them. Like other Founders, he believed property owners were more likely to protect liberty because they had a personal economic ownership stake in the political system underlying their economic rights. He worried that the new nation would run out of land to make every citizen an owner. Jefferson and others developed the Northwest Ordinance of 1787, which offered land for less than a dollar an acre in what would later become Ohio, Indiana, Michigan, Illinois, Wisconsin, and part of Minnesota. It is considered by some historians of this period to be among the most important legislative acts aside from the Constitution itself. Among other things, it outlawed slavery and primogeniture in the entire region. As noted, Washington re-affirmed the Ordinance as part of the Constitution in 1789. In his 1801 Inaugural Address, Jefferson called for not taking 'from the mouth of labor the bread it has earned'. As president, Jefferson set up land offices and hired surveyors to accelerate the distribution of land to citizens. In his most radical move to underline the importance of the landed republic, he made the Louisiana Purchase of almost a million square miles of land from France, in part because this vast increase in the nation's territory advanced his vision of a homogeneous property-owning republic, 'the empire of liberty'. The Louisiana Purchase would later supply the land for all or part of some 15 US states (Blasi, Freeman, and Kruse, 2014: 1, 30–2, 48–51).

James Madison, the fourth president and in many ways the deepest thinker about the conflict between inequality and democracy, underlining again that his dream for America was in contrast to feudalism, wrote in his speech on the right of suffrage in 1821 that 'the United States have a precious advantage, also, in the actual distribution of property, and in the universal hope of acquiring property'. He warned that citizens would call for redistribution of property if they did not have the opportunity to be property owners themselves. Looking a hundred years into the future, Madison projected in 1829 that the acreage of fertile land would not keep up with the population, making the dream of 'every citizen a property owner' impossible to sustain. He sought new policies to maintain wide distribution of property ownership, meeting with others concerned about inequality of ownership, including Robert Owen, the proponent of various worker co-operative ideas. In a detailed essay in *The National Gazette* in 1792, Madison outlined a set of highly detailed new policies to solve this, which he viewed as the most serious problem facing the republic. Applying his ideas to contemporary public policy on worker ownership will be a major part of Chapter 15 on US policies and worker ownership (see also Blasi, Freeman, and Kruse 2014: 33–4, 51–2).

Before industrialization began, this idea of broad-based land ownership as the new country's approach to its political economy had strong political support. Until the Civil War, the idea of a far-reaching 'homestead act', first articulated by Democratic Senator

Thomas Hart Benton in 1809 and supported in Republican and Democratic Party plat-forms, was the most popular public policy in the entire nation, except for the estab-lishment of a postal service. In 1862, President Abraham Lincoln asked Speaker of the House of Representatives, Republican Galusha Grow, an anti-slavery representative from Lancaster, Pennsylvania, to steer a Homestead Act through Congress. Again, to advance the idea of broad-based property ownership, Lincoln took radical and far-reaching action. The act allowed citizens over the age of 21 to claim a homestead at little or no cost, by making available 20 per cent of public land and 10 per cent of the entire US land mass for that purpose. For the first time, women could be homesteaders, and they made up a significant proportion of homestead grants. The act led to homestead acts in many states, such as Texas (Blasi, Freeman, and Kruse 2014: 35–43, 53–6).

8.3 INDUSTRIALIZATION, THE NINETEENTH CENTURY, AND THE IDEA OF WORKER SHARES

The linchpin historical figure who straddled the Revolutionary tradition of dealing with inequality and democracy through broadened land ownership and the nineteenth- and twentieth- and twenty-first-century tradition of advancing worker ownership of indus-try was US House of Representatives Congressman Galusha Grow. Grow was a staunch anti-slavery Civil War politician from Lancaster, Pennsylvania. Echoing Madison's con-cern about the limits of land, Grow pointed out that the future of the broad-based prop-erty idea lay in ways of spreading shares of corporations to citizens, recognizing that corporate assets, unlike land, were limitless. Thus he saw broad-based capital shares in corporations as the next step in the property ownership / yeoman farmer ideal of the United States. This was developed further as business capital increased in importance. It was an important idea since the grants of 'public land' presumed that Native American land rights were less important. Corporate ownership shares would not have required dispossession of other peoples' land.

In the mid 1880s, John Bates Clark, one of the country's leading economists and the towering figure in economics after whom the John Bates Prize in Economics is named, argued in *The Philosophy of Wealth: Economic Principles Newly Formulated* (1886), that broad-based profit-sharing and worker ownership was the only private market econ-omy solution to the deep conflict of interests between labour and capital in a democratic society. He advised several doctoral students on their theses about worker ownership and profit-sharing at Johns Hopkins University that covered several regional geographic sectors of the United States. He made sure that articles on their findings appeared in the first issues of the newly created American Economic Association (AEA) economics journal (Clark was the third president of the AEA, while the author of one of the theses on capital shares, Richard T. Ely, was the AEA's sixth president).

In his 1915 presidential address to the AEA, John H. Gray, the sixteenth president of the AEA, laid out clearly the relation between ownership and the well-being of labour, while he strongly echoed the the broad-based property ideal of America's Founders:

> When the American Economic Association was formed about a quarter of a century ago, the prevailing system of economics taught that the state or organized society as such had nothing to do with economics. The sole function of the state was to preserve law and order, and to prevent physical violence to persons and injury to property. The philosophy did not provide for a condition of affairs in which the mass of workmen were unskilled, working for wages, and the instruments of industry were owned by another class of society for the most part devoid of technical knowledge.
>
> But it was not until the days of capitalistic industry and the enormous surplus resulting therefrom, with the consequent class cleavage and the creation of the great wage-earning non-propertied classes, that we began to discover that the majority of personally free adult males, because of economic conditions, were quite [as] unfree economically as many of those whose personal freedom was limited by law. Should the decline of real wages continue for many years, the tension is likely to become very great, for inequality, with the consequent lack of bargaining ability, tends to increase at an ever accelerating rate. Our free land has heretofore obscured the real tendencies of our economic development.
>
> On the other hand, it offered opportunities to vast numbers of people to make individual fortunes and rise to the capitalistic classes ... Whatever the final outcome may be it must accomplish two important results: give the workman a conscious share in the direction of industry; and it will also ... give him a share in the speculative gains and profits of the industry.
>
> With concentrated wealth and large production, in the absence of a wise and conscious social policy, increased population and consequent rise in rents will tend to shut out an ever increasing part of the population from dominion over or ownership in the natural resources and implements and tools of production.

Later, in 1892, Francis Amasa Walker, who served as the first president of the American Economic Association and later president of MIT, would actually form the American Association for the Promotion of Profit Sharing, in order to advance the idea of both profit and equity sharing in American industry. Walker authored one of the most important textbooks on political economy that treated these ideas sympathetically. Walker believed that both equity shares and profit shares would improve firm performance, and also believed that pure worker co-operatives could be successful if they found a place for entrepreneurial managers in building their competitive advantage.

From 1865 to 1989, social entrepreneurs, both from management and the labour movement, experimented with and invented approaches to, making profit shares and equity shares (employee stock ownership and worker co-operatives) available to regular workers and managers. Skilled workers organized co-operatives which first appeared in the USA in colonial cities in the late eighteenth century in reaction to efforts by master craftsmen to turn their apprentices into manufacturing labourers rather than train them to be autonomous worker–owners. Trade unions of different kinds, including the

Knights of Labor from 1884 to 1887, made share ownership a key part of their ideology, but actually put only limited organizational effort and resources behind it on the ground and were unable to develop worker-owned co-operatives as a large sustainable system. Unions abandoned this strategy in favour of collective bargaining by the time the American Federation of Labor was founded.

Ownership and profit-sharing systems initiated by business leaders had greater success in larger firms than workers' co-operatives at this particular time. Charles S. Pillsbury owned the largest grain mill in the entire world at the time. He showed that broad-based profit-sharing could work efficiently in this industry by broadening the concept to include most of the workers. Pillsbury also helped demonstrate that worker co-operatives could succeed with strong management talent and advice because he contributed his personal support and expertise to the famed Minneapolis worker co-ops that produced barrels to ship the flour of the Pillsbury flour mills. William Cooper Procter at Procter & Gamble in Cincinnati, Ohio, started a cash profit-sharing plan at the firm after hearing about both worker ownership and profit-sharing in the required political economy course of Professor Lyman Atwater at Princeton University. Procter later used a similar notion as John Bates Clark had suggested, and funded worker purchases of company stock with cash profit-sharing rather than wage investments, and later used sales of stocks at a discount and dividends on those stocks to fund worker share ownership. He worked hard to help the workers at Procter & Gamble (P&G) become significant shareholders in the emerging consumer products company in the late 1800s and early 1900s. They even elected members to P&G's board of directors. Elements of Procter's installment payments for worker stock, short-term company loans, discounts, matching company contributions, and funding worker ownership with cash profit-sharing and dividends are key aspects of the popular employee share-purchase plan today (which has discounts for share purchases), the widespread Employee Stock Ownership Plan or ESOP (which uses installments, worker access to company loans to buy the shares, and dividend payments), and worker acquisition of shares through 401(k) pension plans (where companies often match worker contributions in company shares) (Blasi, Freeman, and Kruse, 2014: 123–6, 129–41, 143–6).

8.4 Key Developments in the Twentieth Century

While space prohibits a lengthy detailed history, this review of major historical figures, events, and industrialists demonstrates that worker ownership, at least in the United States, was regularly on the business agenda. It did not inhabit a small isolated area of ideological discussion dominated by either the labour movement or the worker co-operative movement: it was seen as connected to broader discussions of political economy and religious concepts of what was right and just. Still, broader political and economic factors influenced support for the worker ownership idea. For Pillsbury and Procter the concept fit within fitted in with their notions of the Christian Social Gospel. For example, at the same time, the famous Christian theologian and Baptist pastor Walter Rauschenbusch, the undisputed leader of the Social Gospel movement, and well-known Congressional pastor Washington Gladden (who Procter invited to speak at P&G's 'Dividend Days' for workers), were writing that both worker ownership and profit-sharing were essential to implement the ideas of the Christian Social Gospel in light of the conflicts between capital and labour. Procter's teacher at Princeton, Lyman Atwater, studied at the Yale Divinity School, was a Congressional pastor, was an intellectual leader in the Social Gospel movement with articles on these issues in *The Princeton Review*, and served on the board of the Princeton Theological Seminary. The Bolshevik Revolution of 1917 created a political climate where establishment figures worried about the conflicts between labour and capital. On the economic front, the advent of corporate and individual income taxes after 1913 in the USA meant that every economic act by companies and individuals had either an incentive or a disincentive in the government tax system.

More major figures in business went on to put worker ownership on the national agenda. George Eastman probably created the first broad-based stock option in a high-technology firm, with Kodak in Rochester, New York, where he implemented both broad-based worker ownership and profit-sharing. Kodak was unquestionably the high-tech 'Google' of its day. The profit-sharing plan was unique in that it stressed powerfully the partnership between workers and public shareholders. Eastman assumed that for shareholders 'cash dividends up to 10 per cent are the equivalent of the employees' fixed wage'. He believed that dividends above 10 per cent were extraordinary, so Eastman told shareholders and employees that they would both share any dividends over the 10 per cent paid to shareholders. For example, an employee working for the company for five years at $15 a week in the early 1900s would get capital income in the form of a dividend of $81.90, or just over five weeks' pay, about 10 per cent on top of what was considered to be Kodak's generally fair, fixed wages.

The most activist and forceful and resourceful, yet little known and secretive corporate group pushing worker ownership, was the Special Conference Committee founded by John D. Rockefeller, Jr. in 1919. After the embarrassment and bad press of the violent and tragic Ludlow Massacre over worker rights at the Rockefeller Colorado Fuel & Iron Company, the Rockefeller organization decided to spearhead its own very energetic redesign of American capitalism from top to bottom. In a 'thinking-out-of-the-box move', also inspired by establishment concern over the Russian Revolution, John Rockefeller hired former progressive-leaning Canadian Minister of Labor William Lyon Mackenzie King as a special advisor on the effort. King much later was the widely admired and longest serving Liberal Prime Minister of Canada. With a doctorate from Harvard, King went on to write a book called *Industry and Humanity* on the idea that capital and labour were natural allies.

Rockefeller got very serious about this. The Special Conference Committee was made up of CEOs and heads of industrial relations for many of the largest corporations in the country, namely, AT&T, Bethlehem Steel, Dupont, GE, GM, Goodyear, International

Harvester, Irving Trust, Standard Oil of N.J., U.S. Rubber, US Steel, and Westinghouse. Lead by Standard Oil personnel relations executive Clarence Hicks, the group helped spearhead the 'welfare capitalism' movement whereby corporations would continue to focus more on employee welfare in order to gain employee trust, loyalty, and co-operation. The companies were encouraged to implement improvements in working conditions, paid vacations, sickness and injury insurance, profit-sharing, employee stock ownership, and non-union forms of company-sponsored employee representation, along with cafeterias, and recreational, and educational programmes.

In 1922, the Rockefellers funded the Industrial Relations Unit in the Department of Economics at Princeton University, along with other college programmes, to study these ideas and educate the rest of academia about them. In 1928, the head of the Rockefeller programme at Princeton University, Economics Professor Robert Foerster, came out with a report and book surveying the experience of corporations implementing employee stock ownership plans. He could not have made the connection between this effort and the Madisonian share idea in American history any more clear cut. Those who appreciated the larger issues of employee ownership 'would deplore the permanent growth of a wage earner caste, the coming of a class counterposed to another, the owning class, the acceptance by the workers of a status which has always bred discontent'. He proposed that 'from ancient times men have attacked the principle that the few should own and the many should serve, holding it to be a principle of instability, tending to subvert the state'. The question was how to apply the idea of 'scattered ownership ... by the many' to the large corporation.

The new Princeton book on employee stock ownership again used the privileged perch of the Special Conference Committee network and a respected national university in order to collect detailed information on about 400 corporations. The Standard Oil of New Jersey plan was considered the model lower-risk plan, with the company generously contributing half of employee payments for stock, and selling the stock at a third off the market price, with dividends on the stock being used to pay the stock off more rapidly. Employees had now become 44 per cent of all shareholders at Standard Oil, owned almost 5 per cent of the company, and elected company-sponsored non-union works councils by 1926. The study found that the plans spread quickly and easily and included virtually all employees. The machinery of having employees buy stock at the discount on installments worked smoothly. Using dividends to pay off the stock and less hazardous preferred stock helped reduce the risk.

Professor Foerster reported that employers were generally satisfied with the plans, typically seeing better employee–employer relations and reporting that the employee 'consciously or unconsciously takes a deeper interest, works a little harder, wastes less'. Some firms pointed to lower turnover. The researchers thought that some form of worker board representation made sense. Foerster found that a number of companies like P & G had elected worker representatives on the board of directors and that others had special worker shareholder meetings. This landmark study made clear that the corporations expected employee stock ownership to lead to greater efficiency and productivity.

Unfortunately, Rockefeller's initiative grew and peaked just before the Stock Market Crash of 1929 and the Great Depression. The Princeton study raised the issue of excessive risk to workers if stocks were to go down significantly. That is exactly what happened. To Rockefeller's credit, unlike some other companies, the Standard Oil employee ownership plan as noted, sold workers stock at a 50 per cent subsidy at a third the price, and was financed partly by dividends, a meaningful hedge against just the crash that happened. The plan had many grant-like qualities. Just after the collapse, the Princeton University Industrial Relations Section again looked at employee share ownership after the Depression with a new book, *Employee Stock Ownership and the Depression*. Basing the redesign of capitalism on employee stock ownership funded, in some corporations partly but in other corporations near completely, by worker savings, in spite of the discounts, was too risky an approach, given the unprecedented level of this crash and the unpredictability of crashes. The effort of John D. Rockefeller Jr's Special Conference Committee collapsed with the 1929 stock market crash (Blasi, Freeman, and Kruse, 2014: 65–70, 146–56).

The interest in employee share ownership initially waned after the Great Depression period. Unions were legalized in the United States for the first time in the 1935 Wagner Act, employer-co-ordinated non-union works councils were made illegal, and unions made their way to argue for 'fair shares' through collective bargaining about wages. During the next fifty years both union and non-union companies generally sought to give workers a share of increased productivity in fixed pay packages. Cash profit-sharing (shares in cash based on company profits) and gain-sharing (shares in cash based on an increase in sales or productivity or some other measure) became far more acceptable to some unions after collective bargaining was legalized and they could negotiate the terms in order to be sure the accounting for the plans and the benefits were really fair. Historian Sanford Jacoby in his book, *Modern Manors: Welfare Capitalism Since the New Deal* (1997) has documented how many non-union companies continued to foster employee stock ownership and profit-sharing in the forties and fifties, a phenomenon that exists right up to this day.

For most of American history, corporations that had employee stock ownership or profit-sharing simply did not look to the government for any leadership whatsoever. Various states amended their corporate laws in the early 1900s in order to make employee stock purchase plans easier to implement. After the Sixteenth Amendment to the United States Constitution in 1913 made the Federal Income Tax legal, the Federal government began to levy both corporate income taxes and individual income taxes, and some government opinion on the tax status of the share plans was absolutely necessary. The corporations advocating profit-sharing and employee stock ownership argued for and received tax incentives so that both the corporation and any worker contribution to these plans were exempt from corporate and individual income taxes under the Revenue Act of 1921. Shortly thereafter, as the capital gains tax rate differed from the ordinary income tax rate, employees could benefit from lower capital gains rates for employee stock ownership. As a result, very quickly after the period of corporate experimentation with profit-sharing and employee stock ownership from 1880 to 1920, most of the new formats to promote shares for workers were defined in Federal law and continued to receive some tax regulation and benefits. The tax benefits were modest because they mainly allowed deductions for the share idea that were common for deductions of all forms of compensation and capital gains.

Many corporations also continued to offer workers the opportunity to purchase company stock at a discount, building on the innovations in these areas pioneered by William Cooper Procter and John D. Rockefeller Jr. While it reached meaningful levels in some corporations, with generous plans and creative ways of funding the ownership (such as dividends and profit shares), employee stock ownership had not added up to a significant wealth stake for a majority of individual workers or a significant percentage of ownership for many firms. The 1929 Stock Market Crash highlighted that funding employee ownership principally with worker savings was simply too risky. There were often no basic standards of fairness for employee ownership plans, and some corporations simply reduced wages and offered workers shares as a kind of wage substitution ruse. The environment was ripe for someone to come along to begin to address all of these puzzles with a big insight and a broad policy stroke. That person was Louis O. Kelso.

8.5 The First Industrial Homestead Legislation: Louis O. Kelso and Russell B. Long

Kelso's archives indicate that he conducted a careful historical analysis on these issues for several decades. Louis O. Kelso was born in Denver in 1913 where he received training in finance and ultimately a law degree from the University of Colorado. As an associate professor, he then taught courses on the philosophy of law at the University of Colorado Law School. He served as a Naval Intelligence officer during the Second World War. Kelso went on to practise law focused on corporate and municipal finance in Denver, and later he headed his own law firm in San Francisco that specialized in financing purchases of corporations by their workers and inventing legal formats to make the ideas work. He set up Kelso & Company that early in its history assisted corporations in selling large stakes to their workers until it became a private equity firm after Kelso ceased to have a major operational role in the company.

His first book, *The Capitalist Manifesto* (1958), with former University of Chicago philosopher Mortimer Adler, synthesized his political philosophy insights while adding many novel creative financing techniques. The book remained in print for many decades. He practised law and worked as an investment banker and continued to write many books on these subjects. His collaborator and wife, Patricia Hetter Kelso, now heads The Kelso Institute in San Francisco, which makes his writings available to the public. His major contributions in the area of public policy were made in close collabo-ration with Louisiana Senator Russell B. Long, the long-time Chairman of the Senate Finance Committee and son of former economic populist Huey Long, Governor of Louisiana. Kelso is now best known for inventing the Employee Stock Ownership Plan, although it represents only one of his proposals for broadening capital ownership and a small part of his thinking on the broadened ownership idea. Louis Kelso died in 1991.

Kelso influenced a broad range of citizens. Senator Long called for 'establishing pol-icies to diffuse capital ownership broadly, so that many individuals, particularly pro-ductive workers, can participate as owners of industrial capital'. Again showing that the worker ownership idea was linked to the Founders' views on broad-based property ownership, Governor Ronald Reagan said, 'Ownership of land in most of the world had not been possible for the ordinary citizen …. The Homestead Act set the pattern for American capitalism …. Now we need an Industrial Homestead Act, and that isn't impossible.' Senator Hubert Humphrey asked the Joint Economic Committee to figure out how to get there and said 'the committee fully endorsed this goal by making it a recommendation in its 1976 *Annual Report to the President* "to provide a realistic oppor-tunity for more U.S. Citizens to become owners of capital."' In 1987, when President Ronald Reagan supported the most recent ESOP laws, he added: 'I've long believed one of the mainsprings of our own liberty has been the widespread ownership of property among our people and the expectation that anyone's child, even from the humblest of families, could grow up to own a business or a corporation … I can't help but believe that in the future we will see in the United States and throughout the western world an increasing trend toward the next logical step, employee ownership.' John D. Rockefeller 3rd would return to these questions that so caught his family's attention in the 1920s when he strongly endorsed Kelso's ideas in 1973 in a book called *The Second American Revolution*, again linking the idea of worker ownership and the ESOP to the Founders' notions of a middle-class ownership society. (1973).

The core of Kelso's idea was straightforward: in the modern period corporations mix increasing amounts of capital to finance machinery, technology, and various kinds of infrastructure with decreasing amounts of physical labour in order to create increas-ing wealth. Much of the initial capital is the result of profits from existing operations, namely retained earnings, and bank loans or bond issues. When the existing owners of corporations use this financing, they simply extend and concentrate their own owner-ship more. When new capital is purchased, he asked, might it not be possible for worker or citizen trusts to take out these loans and re-invest these profits to buy shares in the corporations, with the loan being repaid out of the income the capital produced, so that a broader group has access to the financing? Kelso reconceptualized the issue of worker ownership as a financing problem in investment banking. If Kelso were alive today, he would probably say that the two key issues explaining the low incidence of worker co-operatives were the risk workers have to endure in putting up their savings to finance these very risky businesses, along with the fact that worker co-ops need to secure large amounts of financing in order to compete with the standard capital intensive businesses.

Kelso collaborated with Senator Russell Long of Louisiana in 1973 to introduce the Employee Stock Ownership Plan, commonly known as the ESOP, as a part of Federal law, encouraged with tax incentives. In order to address the critical problem of risk and the fact that average workers cannot afford to use extra money to buy company stock, Kelso's thinking and the ESOP design provided grants of stock to workers that workers typically do not purchase with their wages or savings. Kelso was firm in holding that workers' wages were for living and that the share idea should not be based in any way on the stock being paid for by workers themselves. He thus reversed a key failure of employee stock ownership thinking before the Stock Market Crash of 1929 and created a principle around the alternative: workers would finance their ownership using the techniques other owners used to expand their own ownership, what he called self-liquidating finance, namely assets can pay for themselves out of income and profits if the financing is properly designed.

As it evolved, to address the problem of fairness, Kelso with Senator Long's help, made Employee Stock Ownership Plans part of the new Federal law whose goal was to regulate fair play for workers in retirement and savings plans, the Employee Retirement Income Security Act of 1974, called (ERISA). The law provides for how stock is fairly distributed to a range of workers in a corporation and how the rights of employee shareholders and investors are protected. ERISA was a bipartisan piece of legislation that grew out of retirement plan reforms initiated by President John F. Kennedy, supported by President Richard Nixon, and signed into law by President Gerald Ford. It passed the House and Senate unanimously. The Federal government created an enforcement machinery in the U.S. Department of Labor to monitor ESOPs for fairness, and in the U.S. Internal Revenue Service to monitor the tax incentives and to deal with occasional abuses that crop up with every piece of legislation. Kelso's main legacy in finance is his invention of a simple straightforward format to make lower risk employee stock ownership not dependent on worker savings possible. This has created a model that can be implemented in the context of this Federal law. Using his ESOP format, lawyers, accountants, investment bankers, and business consultants around the country can work with managers and workers to apply the idea and buy existing stock or even newly-issued shares which then become ESOPs. Kelso and Long also addressed the fact that tax laws now determined the ways businesses were organized. ERISA made both the principal payments and the interest ESOP worker trusts paid to banks to purchase capital, tax deductible to the ESOP corporation. It also allowed workers to put their ownership shares into accounts within the tax-sheltered trust, so that workers paid zero income or capital gains taxes on these ownership shares until they retired. Later Senator Long applied some of the ESOP tax incentives to an Eligible Worker Owned Cooperative (EWOC) that functioned like an ESOP. It is increasingly common that worker coops are using the financing techniques discovered by Kelso to use credit and leverage so that workers can own more capital wealth.

The ESOP addressed the thorny dilemmas that emerged from the past experience of a hundred years of implementing employee stock ownership and worker co-operatives in the USA and applied some of the hard lessons that were learned. Any corporation can set up a trust called an Employee Stock Ownership Plan.

Kelso and Long tackled the quandary that employee share plans had spread very slowly and did not often amount to significant wealth stakes for workers. Because ESOPs could take a major loan to buy a big chunk of corporations, the ESOP worker trusts could create much bigger amounts of worker wealth overnight compared to the more personally risky and the slowly growing stock purchase plans of the twenties. Later, entrepreneurs with small family businesses who wanted to retire could sell the company to an ESOP and be excused from capital gains tax under certain conditions. The question of fairness to workers was addressed by Federal rules that employee ownership plans had to include most employees in order to get the tax incentives. The plans had to grant ownership to individual workers at least according to their salaries. Detailed rules made clear that the highest paid employees in an ESOP could not be the principal beneficiaries of the ownership plan. Later on, older workers got the right to diversify their holdings in company stock well before retirement in order to reduce the risk even more. An important screen against overly risky ESOPs is the fact that private bankers have to review and approve the loans to corporations that establish ESOPs. As a result many weak companies can be sorted out of the process early.

As noted in Chapter 15 (Blasi et al. 2017), this effort has created the largest and, to date, the most durable pocket of meaningful employee share ownership in American history, the largest number of majority and 100 per cent worker-owned firms, and the ESOP financing idea offers pure worker co-operatives many financing solutions to their problems (Blasi, Freeman, and Kruse, 2014: 156–66)

References

Blasi, Joseph R., Freeman, Richard B., and Kruse, Douglas L. (2014), *The Citizen's Share: Reducing Inequality in the 21st Century* (New Haven: Yale University Press).

Blasi, Joseph R., Freeman, Richard B., and Kruse, Douglas L. (2017), 'Evidence: What the US Research Shows about Worker Ownership', in Jonathan Michie, Joseph R. Blasi, and Carlo Borzaga, eds, *The Oxford Handbook of Mutual, Co-operative and Co-owned Business* (Oxford: Oxford University Press), 211–226.

Clark, John Bates (1886), *The Philosophy of Wealth* (Boston: Ginn and Company).

Jacoby, Sanford (1997), *Modern Manors* (Princeton: Princeton University Press).

Kelso, Louis and Adler, Mortimer (1958), *The Capitalist Manifesto* (New York: Random House).

Rockefeller Jr., John D. (1973), *The Second American Revolution* (New York: HarperCollins).

PART IV

CO-OPERATIVES, MUTUALS, MEMBER-OWNED, AND EMPLOYEE-OWNED ENTERPRISES IN THE GLOBAL ECONOMY

CHAPTER 9

....

WORKER CO-OPERATIVES

good, sustainable jobs in the community

....

VIRGINIE PÉROTIN

9.1 INTRODUCTION

WORKER co-operatives are the least well-known part of the co-operative movement, perhaps because the idea of a business run by its employees sounds unrealistic to many people. It is commonly thought that worker co-operatives must be small, special firms in special industries, under capitalized, and probably short-lived. Until recently, this vision was supported to a certain extent by the partial empirical evidence available. However, a different picture is emerging from the more extensive data that has become available in the last decade. This evidence suggests that worker co-operatives are, in many ways, not as 'special' as we have long thought. Worker co-operatives are present in most industries, are not always less capital-intensive and tend to be larger on average than their conventional counterparts, and survive at least as well. This evidence suggests worker co-operatives are not simply niche organizations and have a broader role in a market economy than is often thought. In this chapter, I investigate the implications of these findings and other recent research evidence on worker co-operatives' finance arrangements and behaviour for our understanding of the role they play as viewed by their founders and supporters, and more broadly in the communities in which they operate.

The expectation that labour-managed firms are small and short-lived accords with the hypothesis put forward by theorists that labour-managed firms under-invest, to the point that they may disappear altogether (Furubotn and Pejovitch 1970; Vanek 1977). Although this hypothesis has been quite controversial, it has also been very influential. In practice, worker co-operatives are set up in ways that preclude under-investment (Alzola et al. 2010; Pérotin 2012). I will argue that the two main features ruling out under-investment that are found among employee-owned firms in market economies correspond to some extent to two different visions of the role of labour-managed firms, which co-exist in some countries.

Another controversial hypothesis from economic theory is the 'perverse supply response', according to which the labour-managed firm will cut output and jobs in response to an increase in the price of its product or service. Major studies looking at worker co-operatives from different traditions in three different countries (Craig and Pencavel 1992, 1993; Pencavel et al. 2006; Burdín and Dean 2009) in comparison with conventional firms have found recently that the co-operatives do not respond perversely to demand shocks. More importantly, these studies also show that while conventional firms respond by adjusting employment, worker co-operatives of all traditions adjust pay more than employment. I'll argue that members' control over major firm decisions is crucial to this behaviour and to the way they view the firm. Because worker control leads the firm to internalize some of the effects of its strategic decisions on stakeholders and create more sustainable jobs, it is also at the heart of the role worker co-operatives can play in their local communities.

The definition of a worker co-operative that I'll use here is that of a firm in which all or most of the capital is owned by employees in the firm, whether individually or collectively; where all employees have equal access to membership regardless of their occupational group; and where each member has one vote, regardless of the allocation of any individually owned capital in the firm. In other words, it is a worker-owned firm that applies international co-operative principles, but may be set up slightly differently in different countries. Potential differences especially concern financial arrangements, which as we'll see, can vary.

In the next section, I briefly review the new stylized facts that emerge from international data to show that worker co-operatives are, in many ways, not as 'special' as we have long thought. Section 9.3 examines (the lack of) incentives for under-investment in existing forms of labour-managed firms and the two main possible views of worker co-operatives that are reflected in the different traditions regarding co-operative financial arrangements. Section 9.4 looks at the implications of recent empirical research findings regarding employment, pay determination, and capital accumulation for the objectives pursued by worker co-operatives. In Section 9.5, I reflect upon the wider implications for the role of worker co-operatives in their local communities.

9.2 New Stylized Facts?

It is worth remembering that there exist many more worker co-operatives than is usually thought. In this, the champion country undoubtedly is Italy, where there are more than 25,000 worker co-operatives.[1] Spain is not far behind, with an estimated 18,000 worker co-operatives (Monzón Campos 2010).[2] France has about 2,800 (CG-SCOP

---

[1] Private communication from Alberto Zevi, October 2010.
[2] This estimate from 2008 does not include the 17,000 *sociedades laborales* (Monzón, ibid) which are majority employee-owned firms.

2016). Nevertheless, worker co-operatives remain a small minority of firms, and outside Italy and Spain represent an extremely small percentage of all businesses; for example, in early 2011 only 0.17 per cent of the firms that had employees in France were worker co-operatives.[3]

However, in many respects, worker co-operatives may actually not be as special as we have tended to assume. They are present in most industries, and although there is some clustering in certain industries, the industries concerned seem to vary from one country to another. For example, in France a larger proportion of worker co-operatives are found in manufacturing and construction, and a lower percentage in services, than among conventional firms (Pérotin 2016). But in Uruguay we find a lower share of the co-operatives than of conventional firms in manufacturing, and relatively more co-operatives in transport and services (Burdín and Dean 2009). Most people think worker co-operatives are generally smaller than conventional firms. It is true that we see very few very large worker co-operatives, and it is natural to think that the Mondragón co-operative group in Spain (which has about 85,000 employees in a range of industries) or the John Lewis Partnership in the UK (an employee-owned chain of department stores and supermarkets employing 76,500 people that jointly own the business) are simply exceptions. But very large firms are the exception among conventional firms as well. Thus, for example, 92 per cent of all firms with employees have less than 20 in the UK, 89 per cent in the USA, and 90 per cent in France; and only about 0.3 per cent of firms with employees have 500 employees or more in the UK and the USA, while for France the figure is 0.2 per cent. Only 0.03 per cent of firms have 5,000 employees or more in the USA, and 0.04 per cent have 2,000 employees or more in France.[4]

Size distributions of worker co-operatives and conventional firms are not always available in comparable form, but where we have the data, co-operatives do not appear to be smaller. The compared size distributions that are available for France (Pérotin 2016) and for Uruguay (Burdín and Dean 2009) indicate that worker co-operatives are less often micro-firms than conventional firms, and more often small or medium sized. In both countries the percentage of firms with 100 employees or more is greater for worker co-operatives than for conventional firms, and partial data suggest the percentage of firms with 1,000 employees or more is the same (about 0.1%) among the two types of firms in France or perhaps higher among worker co-operatives. On average, the co-operatives are larger than conventional firms in both France and Uruguay (Burdín and Dean 2009; Pérotin 2016), a feature that Pencavel et al. (2006) also observe in their extensive sample of large- and medium-sized Italian firms. This difference is probably due at least in part to the fact that it takes several people to form a co-operative, a constraint that is made explicit in the law regarding co-operatives in both France and Uruguay. Data on

---

[3] Author's computation from CG-SCOP (2011) and INSEE (2012).

[4] The figures for the UK and France concern 2007 (except for very large firms in France, which concerns 2011), that of the USA 2008. Author's computations from official data (see BERR 2008, US Census Bureau 2012, and INSEE 2012).

the Basque country of Spain presented by Arando et al. (2009) confirm that the differ-ence in size is already apparent at the creation of the firm, when newly formed worker co-operatives are larger than their conventional counterparts.

Worker co-operatives are also often thought to operate at a lower scale and to be less capital intensive than conventional firms, if only because the people who start labour-managed firms may be less wealthy than those who start conventional firms. However, Fakhfakh et al. (2012) observe that there is no statistically significant difference either in average capital (fixed assets) or in average capital intensity between the two types of firms in four out of the seven industries they study using a large representative sample of conventional firms with 20 or more employees and all the worker co-operatives in the same size band in manufacturing, construction, and services (in the other three indus-tries, the co-operatives do have lower average capital and capital intensity). Pencavel et al. (2006) find that in Italy the average capital level is higher among conventional firms, but the median capital is higher among worker co-operatives. They also find that capital intensity is more dispersed among worker co-operatives, a greater proportion of which have very high or very low capital to labour ratios.

In Italy, France, and the UK (and probably also other countries) it is not uncom-mon for worker co-operatives to survive for well over a century. International evidence on compared failure rates of conventional and labour-managed firms is patchy but suggests worker co-operatives survive at least as well as conventional firms (Ben-Ner 1988; Staber 1989; Dow 2003; Pérotin 2004). Burdín (2014) estimates Cox proportional hazard functions controlling for start-up conditions on Uruguayan data and provides robust evidence that, all else being equal, worker co-operatives survive better than other firms.

Although it concerns a small number of countries, this evidence has been obtained with data covering, for the first time, large representative or even exhaustive samples of firms. The picture of worker co-operatives that emerges, in relation to other firms, is not that of a niche type of business form appropriate only in a few very special cases.

9.3 FEATURES THAT PREVENT UNDER-INVESTMENT: TWO CONCEPTIONS OF WORKER CO-OPERATIVES

The idea that labour-managed firms must be short-lived was for a long time invoked as a possible explanation for their small numbers in market economies. One of the most famous and most controversial hypotheses put forward to explain the assumed ten-dency of labour-managed firms to disappear was that firms owned collectively by their employees would under-invest. This hypothesis was also consistent with the idea that labour-managed firms were inefficiently small. Proposed in different ways by Furubotn and Pejovitch (e.g. 1970) and Vanek (1977), the under-investment hypothesis hinges on the fact that, with collective capital ownership, property rights are truncated, in the sense that a worker-member who leaves the co-operative doesn't get a share of the present value of future profits as the owner of a tradeable share would (provided capital markets are efficient). As a result, co-operative members have an incentive to invest only in projects with inefficiently high and short-term returns, and may even consume the existing capital instead of investing. In the long run, the labour-managed firm will therefore operate at an inefficiently small scale (with increasing returns to scale), and may eventually shrink to the point of 'self-extinction' (Vanek 1977).

Although the hypothesis requires certain stringent assumptions to obtain and has been much criticized,[5] it is of interest because the remedies that have been proposed by economists against incentives to under-invest happen to have been present for a long time in existing employee-owned firms. Two main solutions to under-investment have been suggested. The one that is most often recommended by economists is having individually owned tradeable membership shares, so that members who leave the co-operative can get a share of all the future returns to investment that they helped finance. This arrangement can be observed among employee-owned firms that are set up as traditional joint-stock corporations whose shares are owned individually by the employees.[6] Many employee-owned firms that resulted from privatization around the world were set up in this way, as are other employee-owned firms in the USA, the UK, and elsewhere (though they may have adopted some clauses in their by-laws imposing equal shareholdings for all employees or equal voting rights regardless of capital holdings).

The other remedy is to have a compulsory profit plough-back rule, so that the collectively owned co-operative automatically accumulates capital. This rule can be found for example in the Mondragón co-operative group and in the laws governing worker co-operatives in Italy and in France (Alzola et al. 2010). Mondragón adopted its constitution voluntarily, and the provisions of co-operative law have been largely designed by the co-operative movement itself in Italy and France. Both this arrangement and employee-owned firms with tradeable shares co-exist, for example, in the UK.

It is not surprising, therefore, that no rigorous empirical evidence can be found in support of the under-investment hypothesis. Estrin and Jones (1998) find no evidence of under-investment in French worker co-operatives (though they argue the firms may be financially constrained by limited access to external capital). In another study, these authors even remark that French worker co-operatives may accumulate too much capital, at least some of the time (Estrin and Jones 1992). Fakhfakh et al. (2012) present

---

[5] For reviews of this debate see in particular Uvalić (1992) and Dow (2003). Another reason why the under-investment hypothesis is of interest is the insight that members who inherit collectively owned capital accumulated by previous generations may be tempted to appropriate that capital and demutualize. Demutualization has happened in the absence of an 'asset lock' prohibiting members from splitting the net assets even if the co-operative closes down, a provision present in most collectively owned worker co-operatives today (see Pérotin 2012 for a discussion of these issues).

[6] The cases where all the shares are held in trust and managed by elected representatives of the employees, as in some British and American employee-owned firms, are effectively closer to collective ownership.

descriptive evidence that, compared with other firms, French worker co-operatives invest as much or more, on average, in all the industries they study. Using two large comparative data sets covering ten industries, they find no evidence that the co-operatives produce at systematically lower scales, and no industry in which co-operatives produce at increasing returns to scale and conventional firms at constant or decreasing returns, as predicted by the under-investment hypothesis. Finally, Pencavel et al. (2006) show that Italian worker co-operatives' demand for capital responds in the same way as conventional firms' to product demand shocks.

While it resolves the under-investment issue, a tradeable membership shares arrangement may result in instability, especially among successful co-operatives. As the share price increases, employee-owners may be tempted to sell their shares to conventional owners, especially if they are close to retirement.[7] As a result, the firm may stop being employee-owned. Variants of this scenario have repeatedly been observed, in particular, but not exclusively, among the employee-owned firms generated by privatization. Collectively owned co-operatives that have mandatory profit plough-back rules don't suffer from this problem. However, the compulsory plough-back into collective capital may imply that the founding generation of members make a sacrifice by leaving in the firm some of the capital accumulated with their effort (subsequent generations inherit the accumulated capital, which compensates for leaving some with the firm). Mondragón, and perhaps some Italian co-operatives (Zevi 1982), remedy this problem by levying a non-refundable fee on new members, which goes towards the collectively owned portion of capital (Alzola et al. 2010).

Though instability may be a problem for advocates of employee ownership, there is nothing wrong in principle with worker entrepreneurs being able to do well out of their own business by selling it on. In this view of the labour-managed firm, the co-operative is created primarily for the benefit of the individual worker entrepreneurs. If it does well and benefits those entrepreneurs, it has achieved what it was there to do, even if it is not stable as an institution.

The mandatory plough-back rules in collectively owned worker co-operatives correspond to a different conception of the role of the co-operative. In this tradition, members do not necessarily leave the firm with only their initial investment—certainly in Mondragón, France, and Italy, members can accumulate some capital in individually owned shares and/or capital accounts. However, the co-operative is created to last, and the plough-back rule (together with an asset lock) ensures the firm is available for future generations of employee-owners. Our findings (Alzola et al. 2010) also suggest that this tradition may also have stronger provisions in place to avoid degeneration to the capitalist form. This process may take place over time as members who leave are replaced by equally productive non-members who do not share in profit until members form a

---

[7] If enough members stay with the firm, the market for membership may be restricted by arrangements for the existing membership to choose new members, as in the plywood co-operatives of the US Pacific Northwest (see Pencavel 2001).

minority of employees (Ben-Ner 1984).[8] The non-availability of tradeable shares may further remove incentives for degeneration. In this tradition, the worker co-operative is a collective good created to continue as a labour-managed institution and to be available for future members.

As we have seen, the plough-back rules have typically been devised by the co-operatives themselves or the co-operative movement in the countries where the rules have entered the law. In addition, anecdotal evidence indicates that individual co-operatives actually plough back a considerably greater share of profit in practice than mandated by law or by their own constitution—some two to three times more in Italy, France, and Mondragón (Alzola et al. 2010). This raises the issue of the objectives pursued by the worker co-operative.

9.4 THE OBJECTIVES OF THE LABOUR-MANAGED FIRM: A REAPPRAISAL

Another controversial hypothesis concerning labour-managed firms has been the 'perverse supply response'. This hypothesis derives from the traditional model of the labour-managed firm in which the worker co-operative maximizes income per member (Ward 1958; Domar 1966; Vanek 1970). In this model, members share both losses and profit, and as a result under the right assumptions, an increase in the price of output leads the firm to cut output—and therefore employment—in order to maximize the income of the remaining members. This hypothesis has long been criticized for several reasons. A number of authors have shown it does not stand up to small changes in the specification of the problem, like introducing more than one output or additional inputs (see Stephen 1982 for a discussion). More importantly, it has been pointed out that the predicted behaviour of the firm seems unrealistic—how do members choose who has to leave in order to increase the others' profit? It also misses the collective nature of the labour-managed firm. Yet the assumption that the firm maximizes income per member seems reasonable. It also explains the degeneration to the capitalist form (Ben-Ner 1984) that has been repeatedly observed among employee-owned firms.

A series of recent empirical studies comparing the response of pay and employment to product demand shocks among worker co-operatives and other firms suggest that there is no perverse supply response. Craig and Pencavel (1992, 1993, 1995) looking at the plywood sector of the Pacific Northwest in the USA, Pencavel et al. (2006) on Italy, and Burdín and Dean (2009, 2012) on Uruguay, all find that co-operatives do not exhibit any perverse

---

[8] Provisions against degeneration include rules imposing a minimum proportion of members among employees (Mondragón); sharing profit with non-members as well as members (France); and tax incentives for ploughing back all or most of the profit (Italy). See Alzola et al. 2010. For a more detailed discussion of these issues, see Pérotin 2012.

supply response to change in product prices or demand shocks, though their employment levels are more stable (less elastic) than conventional firms'. Furthermore, all find that when conventional firms primarily adjust employment, worker co-operatives primarily adjust pay.[9] The worker co-operatives behave as though employment is relevant to their objectives—whether as a simple labour supply constraint on the maximization of income per member, or as an argument of the objectives' function itself. It is remarkable that three groups of co-operatives that are arguably coming from at least two different traditions and in three different countries exhibit the same behaviour in relation to employment and pay adjustment. It is worth noting that a cut in pay in a recession in order to preserve jobs is completely incentive-compatible in a worker co-operative, since the worker members will decide on the allocation of any future profit and will be able to increase their income again. By contrast, a conventional employer may find it more difficult to provide a credible commitment to employees that pay concessions will be made up at a later date.

The evidence on pay and employment responses to changes in demand conditions is consistent with the idea that worker co-operative members are concerned with job security. Such a concern may explain why Italian, French, and Mondragón co-operatives all plough back substantially more profit than they are required to (Zevi 2005). Navarra (2013) argues that such a policy is a form of insurance against the risk of job loss. By adjusting pay rather than employment (and in the case of Uruguayan co-operatives adjusting only members' pay while preserving members' and non-members' jobs—Burdín and Dean 2009), members show they are prepared to take financial risks (Zevi 2005).[10] Rather than being extremely risk averse, as is sometimes suggested, co-operative members may simply prefer financial risks to job risks. I have argued elsewhere that the counter-cyclicality of co-operative creations, which is more pronounced than that of conventional firm creations, is due to co-operatives being formed when the risk of job loss increases in conventional firms (Pérotin 2006).

If income were the only thing that mattered to employee-owners, then a job in a conventional firm and a job in a worker co-operative would be equivalent. However, employment in a worker co-operative has a fundamental characteristic that makes it different from employment in a conventional firm—employees control the firm. This characteristic is valuable for several reasons that have to do with the particular nature of the employment relationship and the market failures that affect it. The first is that many non-pay characteristics of jobs, like working conditions, are local public goods (Freeman 1976) which may not be provided in the absence of a collective employee voice[11] so that their absence in other firms is not necessarily compensated for with

---

[9] This comparison does not imply anything about the relative pay levels of the two types of firm, even in a recession and for identical workers, because pay includes a share of profit in labour-managed firms, whether formally (as profit-sharing bonuses) or if pay is adjusted once the level of profit is known, before computing accounting profit. For a comparison of pay levels in co-operatives and conventional firms, see Clemente et al. 2012.

[10] Pencavel 2001 also remarks that it is likely that worker co-operative members are less risk averse than employees of conventional firms.

[11] Even though providing the right working conditions might reduce turnover costs for the firm (Freeman 1976).

higher pay. As Pencavel (2001) notes, workers more generally care about many non-wage aspects of their jobs, such as what they can refuse to do, whom they'll work with, etc. Worker-members' control of the firm allows these aspects, not only to be known, but also to be taken into account. By allowing employees more autonomy and recognition, worker co-operatives are also likely to foster intrinsic motivation (Frey and Jegen 2005), and more generally an environment in which their creativity can flourish.

Perhaps most importantly, control over the firm's strategic decisions protects employee-owners against moral hazard on the part of managers. For example, investment decisions, whether they maximize profit or the managers' utility or are simply ill-judged, may result in job losses. In looking at the performance effects of employee ownership, we have focused on the asymmetry of information in favour of the employee, which explains some of the incentive effects of ownership. From the point of view of the employee, the informational asymmetry that favours the firm is at least as important, given the job risks involved. Employee control means a job in a worker co-operative is a job whose risk the employee has some control over. This means that a job in a worker co-operative is likely to be much more valuable, all else being equal, than a job in a conventional firm, and the difference in value increases when the risk of job losses increases in conventional firms. It also implies that worker members may not just be concerned with job security generally, but specifically with the security of their job with the co-operative. By itself, this concern would be sufficient to explain the choice of income risk over job risk and profit plough-backs beyond the required minimum that have been observed among existing worker co-operatives.

Employment security may thus be more crucially involved in the objectives of labour-managed firms than has been assumed in the traditional theoretical model. Rather than pursuing a high income above all else, the co-operative may seek to ensure its continued existence in order to provide and preserve good jobs for its members. In this, control of the firm by its employees is an essential feature. Because it allows worker co-operatives to internalize some of the possible effects of management decisions, employee control also has implications for the communities in which the firms operate.

9.5 Economic Democracy and the Role of Worker Co-operatives in Their Local Communities

The fact that worker co-operatives seem to choose jobs over income stability means that they are likely to have more sustainable jobs. Worker co-operatives may create relatively fewer jobs than conventional firms in response to product price increases (since their employment level is less elastic).[12] However, the evidence we have seen clearly implies

---

[12] This does not imply that a worker co-operative's employment level will necessarily be lower than that of a conventional 'twin': for example, if the two firms started out with identical employment levels

that worker co-operatives preserve jobs better in deteriorating market conditions, when other firms are more likely to cut jobs. Co-operatives' probable higher overall productivity (Fakhfakh et al. 2012) and their ploughing-back profit and investing at rates at least as high as conventional firms do both provide further support for the presumption that co-operative jobs will be more sustainable. In addition, recessions increase the number of firm closures among conventional and labour-managed firms alike and decrease the number of creations among conventional firms, but increase creations of worker co-operatives, all else being equal (Pérotin 2006).

The descriptive evidence presented by Fakhfakh et al. (2012) shows annual changes in the firms' employment levels were the same or better in worker co-operatives than in other firms, in all ten industries studied. On average, worker co-operatives increased employment faster than conventional firms in four out of the seven industries that were studied over a period of modest growth (the increases being the same in the two types of firms in the remaining three industries). Among the four industries observed during the 1990s' recession,[13] Fakhfakh et al. (2012) report that the two types of firms cut jobs at the same rate in two industries; in one industry the co-operatives cut jobs at a significantly lower rate than conventional firms; and in the remaining industry the co-operatives even increased employment on average while other firms decreased.

If worker co-operatives preserve jobs better than other firms, this has potentially important implications for the wider community, because of the externalities associated with job preservation. Preserving jobs saves unemployment benefit, and may have a positive effect on tax revenue through the spill-over economic effects of preserved jobs on local communities. In addition to saving unemployment benefit, job preservation saves on other community resources such as social services. It is increasingly recognized that unemployment has both broader and more profound effects than its strictly economic consequences, in particular on health (e.g. Classen and Dunn 2012; Bambra and Eikemo 2009). If worker co-operatives preserve jobs better for their employees and help improve economic conditions in their local economies, they may thus also have a positive effect on public health in their communities. As we have seen, the key to the greater sustainability of jobs in worker co-operatives is the control that employee-owners have over the firm, which enables them to internalize the externalities of major firm decisions on their job risk and working conditions. Indeed, Burdín (2014) finds that employment stability explains a large part of the survival advantage of worker co-operatives relative to other firms in Uruguay. The simple fact of being in control may also affect worker owners' health in and of itself. Erdal (2000) attributes factors of this kind to his observation that mortality from cardiovascular causes was lower in a town with high co-operative employment than in comparable towns with conventional employment in Italy. There is increasing evidence that control, in particular in demanding jobs, significantly affects health and life expectancy by cutting the risk of coronary heart disease, psychiatric

---

and went through a downward shock first, the co-operative would enter the recovery with a higher level of employment than its twin.

[13] One of the industries appeared in both of the data sets used by Fakhfakh et al. 2012.

disorders, and other conditions (Kuper et al. 2003; Stansfeld et al. 1999). Higher accident rates have been reported among the plywood co-operatives of the US Pacific Northwest (Grunberg et al. 1996), which may be due to greater reporting and/or to employee-owners taking greater risks, as entrepreneurs sometimes do (Pencavel 2001). However, entrepreneurs have also been found to experience better health and greater well-being than employees (Stephan and Roesler 2010). Early results from a Scottish study suggest employees of employee-owned businesses may also have higher levels of well-being and job satisfaction than other employees in the UK (McQuaid et al. 2013).

9.6 CONCLUSION

Recent international evidence shows that worker co-operatives may not be as unusual as is often thought. Present in most industries, worker co-operatives are larger than other firms on average, are not necessarily under-capitalized, and survive as well as or better than conventional firms. Clearly the worker co-operative is not a niche business form appropriate only in very special circumstances.

Our examination of the financial arrangements that preclude under-investment has highlighted two different visions of the role of a worker co-operative—one in which the firm is set up for the benefits of its worker entrepreneurs, and the other in which the co-operative has a broader role as an institution designed to keep profit in the firm, and to last and provide future generations with an opportunity to control the firm in which they work.

Worker co-operatives of both traditions have been shown to choose employment stability, over income stability, in recent studies using extensive comparative data. Having control over the firm, its employee-members are able to choose to preserve jobs in which they have a say in determining working conditions and employment risk, and in which they are likely to be better motivated, more creative, and happier.

Worker co-operatives' ability to create more sustainable jobs, and their members' control over the affairs of the firm, which allows them to internalize some of the externalities of the firm's operation, are likely to have positive consequences for the communities in which they operate. The co-operatives may affect public finances and health positively by decreasing unemployment risk, both in the co-operatives themselves and in the community. The exercise of control may also, in and of itself, have positive effects on members' health.

The greater sustainability of worker co-operatives' jobs, and the likely effects on communities, suggest public support for worker co-operatives would be warranted. Existing co-operative movements have evolved several possible co-operative structures that ensure the continued existence of organizations that might receive public support (in the second tradition I have identified in this chapter). The small number of worker co-operatives in industrialized economies is not due to their incapacity for survival, but to the fact that very few are created in comparison with conventional firms. Public support at the stage of creation may make a significant difference to information and other barriers to entry, together with legislation that enables the worker co-operative to prosper as a stable business form (in particular by preventing degeneration and demutualization). We also know that the density of worker co-operatives in an area, year, and/or industry is an important determinant of further co-operative creation (Russell and Hanneman 1995; Pérotin 2006; Arando et al. 2009; Arando et al. 2012). Here, we should look more closely at the Italian and Spanish experiences to understand the critical ways in which the co-operative movement itself can foster the creation of more worker co-operatives to benefit local communities.

ACKNOWLEDGEMENTS

This chapter reproduces (with minor changes) an invited paper from May 2014 in the *Journal of Entrepreneurial and Organizational Diversity*. The DOI is http://dx.doi.org/10.5947/jeod.2013.009. The article can be accessed at: http://www.jeodonline.com/articles/invited-paper-worker-cooperatives-good-sustainable-jobs-community.

REFERENCES

Alzola, Izaskun, Arando Saioa, Fakhfakh, Fathi, Freundlich, Fred, Gago, Mónica, Pérotin, Virginie, and Zevi, Alberto (2010), 'Are Labour-Managed Firms All the Same? A Comparison of Incentives for Growth, Democracy and Institutional Sustainability in the Constitutions of Worker Cooperatives in Mondragón, Italy and France'. Paper presented at the 15th World Congress of the International Association for the Economics of Participation, Paris, July.

Arando, Saioa, Gago, Mónica, Podivinsky, Jan M., and Stewart, Geoff (2012), 'Do Labour-Managed Firms Benefit from Agglomeration?' *Journal of Economic Behavior & Organization*, 84, 193–200.

Arando, Saioa, Peña, Iñaki, and Verheul, Ingrid (2009), 'Market Entry of Firms with Different Legal Forms: An Empirical Test of the Influence of Institutional Factors', *International Entrepreneurship and Management Journal*, 5, 77–95.

Bambra, C. and Eikemo, T. A. (2009), 'Welfare State Regimes, Unemployment and Health: A Comparative Study of the Relationship Between Unemployment and Self-Reported Health in 23 European Countries', *Journal of Epidemiology and Community Health*, 63, 92–8.

Ben-Ner, Avner (1984), On the Stability of the Cooperative Form of Organization, *Journal of Comparative Economics*, 8(3), 247–60.

Ben-Ner, Avner (1988), 'Comparative Empirical Observations on Worker-Owned and Capitalist Firms', *International Journal of Industrial Organization*, 6, 7–31.

BERR (Department for Business Enterprise and Regulatory Reform) (2008), SME Statistics for the UK and Regions 2007, Table 1: UK Private Sector, Enterprise Directorate Analytical Unit, 2008. Available on http://stats.berr.gov.uk/ed/sme (accessed on 19 May 2011).

Burdín, Gabriel, (2014), 'Are Worker-Managed Firms More Likely to Fail than Conventional Enterprises? Evidence from Uruguay', *Industrial and Labor Relations Review*, 67(1), 202–38.

Burdín, Gabriel and Dean, Andrés (2009), 'New Evidence on Wages and Employment in Worker Cooperatives Compared with Capitalist Firms', *Journal of Comparative Economics*, 37, 517–33.

Burdín, Gabriel and Dean, Andrés (2012), 'Revisiting the Objectives of Worker-Managed Firms: An Empirical Assessment', *Economic Systems*, 36, 158–71.

CG-SCOP (Confédération générale des SCOP) (2016), Les chiffres-clés. Available on http://www.les-scop.coop/sites/fr/les-chiffres-cles/ (accessed on 10 September 2016).

Classen, Timothy J. and Dunn, Richard A. (2012), The Effect of Job Loss and Unemployment Duration on Suicide Risk in the United States: A New Look Using Mass Lay-Offs and Unemployment Duration, *Health Economics*, 21, 338–50.

Clemente, Jesús, Díaz-Foncea, Millán, Marcuello, Carmen, and Sanso-Navarro, Marcos (2012), 'The Wage Gap between Cooperative and Capitalist Firms: Evidence from Spain', *Annals of Public and Co-operative Economics*, 83(3), 337–56.

Craig, Ben and Pencavel, John (1992), The Behavior of Worker Co-operatives: The Plywood Companies of the Pacific Northwest, *American Economic Review*, 82(5), 1083–105.

Craig, Ben and Pencavel, John (1993), The Objectives of Worker Co-Operatives, *Journal of Comparative Economics*, 17, 288–308.

Craig, Ben and Pencavel, John (1995), 'Participation and Productivity: A Comparison of Worker Co-operatives and Conventional Firms in the Plywood Industry', *Brookings Papers: Microeconomics* (Special Issue), 121–74.

Domar, Evsey D. (1966), 'The Soviet Collective Farm as a Producer Cooperative', *American Economic Review*, 56(4), 734–57.

Dow, Gregory K. (2003), *Governing the Firm: Workers' Control in Theory and Practice*. (Cambridge, UK: Cambridge University Press).

Erdal, David E. (2000), 'The Psychology of Sharing: An Evolutionary Approach', PhD thesis, University of St Andrews (UK).

Estrin, Saul and Jones, Derek C. (1992), 'The Viability of Employee-Owned Firms: Evidence from France', *Industrial and Labor Relations Review*, 45(2), 323–38.

Estrin, Saul and Jones, Derek C. (1998), The Determinants of Investment in Employee-Owned Firms: Evidence from France, *Economic Analysis*, 1(1), 17–28.

Fakhfakh, Fathi, Pérotin, Virginie, and Gago, Mónica (2012), 'Productivity, Capital and Labor in Labor-Managed and Conventional Firms', *Industrial and Labor Relations Review*, 65(4), 847–79.

Freeman, Richard (1976), 'Individual Mobility and Union Voice in the Labor Market', *American Economic Review*, 66(2), 361–8.

Frey, Bruno S. and Jegen, Reto (2005), 'Motivation Crowding Theory', *Journal of Economic Surveys*, 15(5), 589–611.

Furubotn, Eirek G. and Pejovich, Svetozar (1970), 'Property Rights and the Behaviour of the Firm in a Socialist State: The Example of Yugoslavia', *Zeitschrift für Nationalökonomie*, 30(3–4), 431–54.

Grunberg, Leon, Moore, Sarah, and Greenberg, Edward (1996), 'The Relationship of Employee Ownership and Participation to Employee Safety', *Economic and Industrial Democracy*, 117, 221–41.

Insee (Institut National de la Statistique et des Etudes Economiques) (2012), 'Entreprises selon le nombre de salariés et l'activité', Répertoire des enterprises et des établissements—Sirene. Available on http://www.insee.fr/en/themes/tableau.asp?reg_id=0&ref_id=NATTEF09203 (accessed on 10 September 2016).

Kuper, H. and Marmot, M. (2003), 'Job Strain, Job Demands, Decision Latitude and the Risk of Coronary Heart Disease within the Whitehall II Study', *Journal of Epidemiology and Community Health*, 57: 147–53.

McQuaid, R., Canduela, J., Egdell, V., Dutton, M., and Raeside, R. (2013), 'The Growth of Employee Owned Businesses in Scotland', The Employment Research Institute, Edinburgh Napier University, February.

Monzón Campos, Luis, ed., 2010, *Las Grandes Cifras de la Economía Social en España* (Valencia, Spain: CIRIEC-España).

Navarra, Cecilia (2013). 'How Do Worker Cooperatives Stabilize Employment? The Role of Profit Reinvestment into Locked Assets', Department of Economics Working Paper No 1307, University of Namur (Belgium).

Pencavel, John (2001), *Worker Participation: Lessons from the Worker Co-ops of the Pacific Northwest* (New York, NY: Russell Sage Foundation).

Pencavel, John, Pistaferri, Luigi, and Schivardi, Fabiano (2006), 'Wages, Employment and Capital in Capitalist and Worker-Owned Firms', *Industrial and Labor Relations Review*, 60(1), 23–44.

Pérotin, Virginie (2004). 'Early Cooperative Survival: The Liability of Adolescence', in Virginie Pérotin and Andrew Robinson, eds, *Advances in the Economic Analysis of Participatory and Labor-Managed Firms*, Vol. 8, *Employee Participation, Firm Performance and Survival* (Bingley, UK: Emerald), 67–86.

Pérotin, Virginie (2006), 'Entry, Exit and the Business Cycle: Are Cooperatives Different?' *Journal of Comparative Economics*, 34, 295–316.

Pérotin, Virginie (2016), 'What Do We Really Know About Worker Cooperatives?' in A. Webster, L. Shaw, and R Vorberg-Rugh, eds, *Mainstreaming Co-operation: An Alternative for the 21st Century?* (Manchester: Manchester University Press), 239–260.

Pérotin, Virginie (2012), 'The Performance of Worker Cooperatives', in P. Battilani and H. Schroeter, eds, *A Special Kind of Business: The Cooperative Movement 1950-2010 ... and Beyond* (Cambridge: Cambridge University Press), 195–221.

Russell, Raymond and Hanneman, Robert (1995), 'The Formation and Dissolution of Worker Cooperatives in Israel, 1924–1992', in Raymond Russell, *Utopia in Zion: The Israeli Experience with Worker Co-operatives* (Albany, NY: State University of New York Press), 57–95.

Staber, Udo (1989), 'Age-Dependence and Historical Effects on the Failure Rates of Worker Cooperatives: An Event-History Analysis', *Economic and Industrial Democracy* 10, 59–80.

Stephan, Uke and Roesler, Ulrike (2010), 'Health of Entrepreneurs Versus Employees in a National Representative Sample', *Journal of Occupational and Organizational Psychology*, 83, 717–38.

Stephen, Frank (1982), 'The Economic Theory of the Labour-Managed firm', in F. Stephen, ed., *The Performance of Labour-Managed Firms* (London: Macmillan), 3–26.

US Census Bureau, (2012), 'Statistics about Business Size (including Small Business), Employment Size of Firms,Table 2a': 'Employment Size of Employer and Nonemployer Firms, 2008', Statistics of U.S. Businesses,. Available at http://www.census.gov/econ/susb/ (accessed on 10 September 2016).

Uvalić, Milica, (1992), *Investment and Property Rights in Yugoslavia* (Cambridge, UK: Cambridge University Press).

Vanek, Jaroslav (1970), *The General Theory of Labor-Managed Market Economies* (Ithaca, NY: Cornell University Press).

Vanek, Jaroslav (1977), *The Labor-Managed Economy* (Ithaca, NY: Cornell University Press).

Ward, Benjamin (1958), 'The Firm in Illyria: Market Syndicalism', *American Economic Review*, 48(4), 566–89.

Zevi, Alberto (1982), 'The Performance of Italian Producer Cooperatives', in D. C. Jones, and J. Svejnar, eds, *Participatory and Self-Managed Firms* (Lexington, Mass: Lexington Books), 239–51.

Zevi, Alberto (2005), 'Il finanziamento delle cooperative', in E. Mazzoli and S. Zamagni, *Verso una nuova storia della cooperazione* (Bologna, Italy: Il Mulino), 293–332.

CHAPTER 10

....

CREDIT UNIONS AND CO-OPERATIVE BANKS ACROSS THE WORLD

....

SILVIO GOGLIO AND PANU KALMI

10.1 THE MAIN FEATURES OF FINANCIAL CO-OPERATIVES

TODAY credit co-operatives represent a wide range of institutions, which reflect the needs of members and the specificities of national legislative frameworks. Their ability to adapt and grow in highly diverse economic and institutional environments has allowed them to become a substantial part of the banking industry. The sector embraces systems that are not entirely uniform in terms of legal and regulatory provisions, size, and organization: some are strongly integrated, others are more diversified. Each pattern has its strengths and weaknesses. Close co-ordination at central level can help overcome constraints and inefficiencies due to the small size of individual co-operative banks. On the other hand, entrepreneurial autonomy fosters competition, the quest for innovative solutions, and the ability to adapt to the needs of local economies. However, there are some crucial features that from the very beginning characterized credit co-operatives and still distinguish, even if with growing difficulty, the descending business model.

The most important of these features are democratic governance and mutualism. The democratic governance of credit co-operatives is based on three principles: the 'open door' principle, according to which everyone is eligible to become a member; the company capital consisting of shares of nominal value; and the 'one member-one vote' principle whereby, regardless of the number of shares, each member has only one vote in meetings. Ownership rights only stem from membership and are unrelated to the amount of shares, making takeovers highly improbable. Their mutuality rests on the commitment to devote their main activities to members, and to be not for profit, since they do not maximize profits, but the well-being of members. Other crucial features, stemming from the first two, are solidarity, local identity, and a stronger pledge to ethical behaviour.

These underlying principles determine the specialization and the business model of financial co-operatives, which rely heavily on relationship-based retail banking and the commitment to invest in the real economy and to create benefits for members, customers, and communities. The core values of this model are, among others, prudence, responsiveness, empathy, and transparency. Many potential effects may stem from this attitude: first, a tendency to adopt less risky strategies and to have much lower volatility of returns, with positive consequences for the financial stability of the territories where they operate; second, the propensity to defend consumer interests and maximize consumer surplus, offering simple and transparent products, fairly priced and well designed to meet local needs; and third, a lower inclination, during a credit crunch, to ration credit to customers and to raise loan interest rates, thanks to better capitalization and more prudent lending (Alexopoulos and Goglio 2013; Goglio and Alexopoulos 2014).

10.2 RAIFFEISEN MODEL VS. SCHULZE-DELITZSCH MODEL

The origin of co-operative credit dates back to the mid nineteenth century in Germany, immediately after the first co-operative of modern form, the Rochdale Pioneers' Equitable Society, was founded in December 1844. From the outset, the German movement attributed a central role to credit by proposing a new model of development for marginalized areas and small operators, who at the time were forced to resort to private lenders, often usurers. The first initiatives were undertaken in urban areas by Hermann Schulze Delitzsch. The essential requirements of his *Volksbanken*, or People's Banks, were the concept of *Selbsthilfe* (self-help), the general assembly as the main body of governance, and the election of the executive and control bodies following the 'one man, one vote' principle. Capital had to be constituted through participating shares acquired by individual members. The obligatory acquisition of one or more capital shares served both to restrict access only to people able to help themselves, and to stimulate members to form their own capital. Finally, the people's banks had to pay their members dividends deriving from operating profits, so as to attract people wanting to invest their savings and to encourage capital contributions.

The *Volksbanken* became definitively established from 1852 onwards and expanded also beyond German borders. Nevertheless, they were unable to take root in rural areas and to answer the needs of a peasant society. It was consequently necessary to re-interpret Schulze's model so that it matched rural realities. This challenge was taken up by Friedrich Wilhelm Raiffeisen who adopted some of Schulze principles, such as the *Selbsthilfe*, and, like all co-operative institutions, the democratic administration of the bank. Unlike the people's banks, his *Darlehenskassenvereine* had to restrict the geographical area in which they operated as much as possible, in order to allow members to have detailed knowledge of the economic and moral situations of co-members.

The models developed by Raiffeisen and Schulze-Delitzsch both envisaged credit co-operatives as the pivot of a complex system of associations operating in the area of consumption and production. However, although Raiffeisen started from theoretical considerations similar to those of Schulze, there was no homogeneity between their models. The basic difference sprang from the different ideal aspirations and from the overall purpose they attributed to co-operatives. For Raiffeisen, the co-operative creed drove a Universalist endeavour to render social co-living more harmonious: the tendency not to seek profit for its own sake but for the benefit of all members alike was a matter of principle based on Christian solidarity. On the other hand, co-operatives based on Schulze's model applied similar founding principles with a view to immediate economic utility, and were considered an essentially economic movement regardless of religious beliefs. The force of Schulze-Delitzsch's message lay in its pragmatic capacity to meet the needs of the lower middle class. This dispute was joined by Wilhelm Haas, who founded in 1883 the Union of Agricultural Co-operatives, with the approval of Schulze-Delitzsch, by then convinced that it was impossible to unite urban and agricultural co-operatives within a single federation. The underlying principle was, as Raiffeisen had argued, that rural society required an autonomous and independent co-operative union. Nevertheless, any religious vocation was regarded as superfluous; following the conviction that pure co-operation was possible by adapting Schulze's commercial ideas to the countryside (Goglio and Leonardi 2012).

10.3 ADAPTATIONS OF THE MODEL: THE CREDIT UNION MODEL IN THE USA AND CANADA

The credit union model was initially created at the beginning of the twentieth century in North America as an extension of the Raiffeisen model. The first credit unions were established in the Francophone regions of Canada, mostly Quebec. From these credit unions the powerful Desjardins Group later developed. In the Anglophone regions of Canada credit unions developed more slowly, in Atlantic provinces they started in the 1930s, and in the Western provinces mostly after the Second World War. Even today important differences between the Francophone and Anglophone credit unions remain, the former being organized in a tighter network and the latter often being larger and more independent.

The US credit union system developed rather independently. Its main sponsor was the wealthy Boston retail store magnate Edward Filene. Their formation speeded up considerably after Filene hired the attorney Roy Bergengren to lead the Massachusetts Association of Credit Unions in 1920, and a year later the Credit Union Extension Bureau was established. The Bureau promoted legislation initially at the state level. In the year 1934 a law enabling the formation of federal credit unions was passed. In the same year the Credit Union National Association (CUNA) was formed. Credit unions turned out to be fairly resistant in the Great Depression and this helped consolidate their position in the USA.

Between the 1930s and the 1990s, the US banking system was characterized by a greatly decentralized structure, and thousands of small and regional commercial banks coexisted with savings and loans associations. Credit unions were clearly the smallest in aggregate and by average size. However, their significance started increasing in the 1980s due to the Savings and Loans Crisis, when a large proportion of the savings and loans sector was either demutualized or went bankrupt. Credit unions, in turn, weathered the 1980s' recession and financial market deregulation rather well. A further development that increased their prominence was the liberalization of the common bond restrictions in 1998. Thereafter, credit union membership grew rapidly. As of 2015, credit unions in the USA have over 100 million members.

There are important differences between credit unions and European co-operative banks. First, membership has been, at least historically, rather different. While European credit co-operatives were territorially based and often included farmers as members, the membership of credit unions in the USA was typically defined by employer. Recent changes, including the decrease of the farmer population and the broadening of the membership in Europe and the liberalization of the common bond system in the USA, have brought the membership policies closer to each other. Another important difference is that credit unions only do business with their members, whereas European credit co-operatives typically also allow non-member customers. Moreover, credit unions are more focused on consumer lending, especially in the USA. Their network structure is much looser and competition among credit unions is common. Even though federal and state associations exist, their role is much smaller than in Europe (Desrochers and Fischer, 2005).

10.4 FURTHER DEVELOPMENTS OF THE MODEL: INTEGRATION IN FINANCIAL CO-OPERATIVES

Many types of co-operatives have a network structure, where individual co-operatives form second-level co-operatives that aim to support the functioning of primary-level co-operatives. They often have a variety of activities, including marketing, lobbying, educating members and their representatives, and organizing employee training. Probably in no other co-operative sector are networks as important as in the financial sector. In addition to the previously mentioned areas, in banking there are a number of other areas that require considerable economies of scale. Centrals of financial co-operatives have an important role as clearing partners in the payment system and as representatives of the banking group in matters towards the central bank, such as participating in the open market operations of central banks. Co-operative centrals also manage the liquidity within the system, allocating the savings from banks with deposit surplus to those with deposit deficit, investing the surplus in the interbank markets, and borrowing in the case of deficit. Centrals often have a credit rating that allows them to borrow from the market more cheaply than individual co-operative banks. Co-operative centrals are involved in many areas in which individual co-operatives would find it difficult to engage alone, such as organizing e-banking, credit cards, or mutual funds. Finally, co-operative centrals and their daughter companies are also engaged in large investment projects, for instance in corporate finance.

It is important to notice that co-operative centrals as such are nothing new. Already Raiffeisen had organized co-operative networks on a regional basis. These regional centrals for instance had an important role in auditing and training the personnel of local co-operatives (Guinnane 2001). However, due to the increase of non-traditional activities in co-operatives, the role of the centrals has become even more important. Their role has also become more important due to the actions of regulators and rating agencies. Regulators often prefer to deal with one contact point rather than with a network of independent banks. Similarly, rating agencies tend to prefer systems where there is a strong central and joint liability of the debts of banks within the network, and they have even assigned higher ratings for networks that have this type of structure.

Several benefits derive from network structures, as well as governance challenges (Ayadi et al. 2010). Without far-reaching network structures the viable minimum size for co-operatives would be likely to be much larger. Networks perform operations for which small co-operatives would not have required scale, and allow small co-operatives to focus on issues where small size yields better information and therefore competitive advantage, such as lending to local enterprises. Similarly, member participation in co-operative governance is likely to be more intensive when the size of the co-operative is smaller. For their part, networks are also effective in solving the governance challenges of co-operatives. First-tier co-operatives do not need to rely on monitoring by members only, but there is also supplementary (or perhaps primary) monitoring by the network. Especially when combined with the audit function, there are clear information benefits from getting the network to do the monitoring.

Sometimes networks of co-operative banks get involved in much riskier activities than banks at the local or regional level. Examples include varieties of corporate and infrastructure finance projects, investment banking activities, and internationalization of co-operative banks. While these services are often related to the needs of members in a dynamic environment, in some cases involvement in these services can be motivated by increases in managerial prestige and pay. Proper analysis of such risky undertakings often requires more elaborate governance systems and risk management methods than co-operative banks have available.

The degree of network integration varies considerably. Desrochers and Fischer (2005) differentiate between atomic, consensual, and strategic networks: the mature networks of financial co-operatives typically belong to the latter two. Examples of consensual networks include US credit unions, Italian Banche Popolari, and Spanish co-operatives. Most continental European co-operative groups, as well as the Desjardins Group in Quebec, form strategic networks. In fact, strategic networks have even more elaborate structures, including those with joint liability (Dutch Rabobank and Finnish OP Group).

10.5 INTERNAL AND EXTERNAL COMPETITION IN FINANCIAL CO-OPERATIVES

Traditionally, retail banking has been the core of co-operative banks' business. Their strength in this sector has hinged on their robust establishment in the territory, and vigorous participation in the life of the community, as well as on their ability to establish closer and more flexible relationships with small- and medium-sized firms and to monitor their profitability. These qualities often have off-set disadvantages of scale and generate system economies of various kinds; not necessarily economic ones. Recent times have seen an increase in competition in retail banking, mainly from commercial banks, trying to recover market shares and profits, often lost in the recent financial crisis, through relational finance. This policy is implemented not only by local banks, but also by big national and international banks, both by reinforcing local branches and through the acquisition of local banks. A second source of increased competition for co-operative banks arises from fellow co-operative banks.

This picture is correlated with local identity—the traditional source of strength of credit co-operatives—losing importance in the financial decisions of small firms and families vis-à-vis reasons derived by economic calculation. In this context, co-operative banks' pyramidal organizational structure—the historic reaction to their small-scale weaknesses—and their recent process of consolidating or defensive mergers, which aims to cut costs and possibly also diversify risks, can definitely create synergies. Nevertheless, they are altering some fundamental characteristics of the grass-roots initiative and of the co-operative movement. As a consequence, the competition between the two models of banking—one based on social cohesion and solidarity and the other on self-interest—is losing importance compared with a simpler and reductive competition in market excellence (Alexopoulos and Goglio 2011; Alexopoulos and Goglio 2013).

10.6 THE PERFORMANCE OF FINANCIAL CO-OPERATIVES: VARIOUS MEASURES AND THEIR SITUATION DURING THE CRISIS

Measurement of performance in financial co-operatives is considerably trickier than in investor-owned banks. Well-diversified investors only care about the returns on their investment, therefore the return on equity (ROE) provides a natural measure on the performance of investor-owned banks. However, the members of financial co-operatives, who are depositors and borrowers, in addition care at least about the following: loan rates, deposit rates, riskiness of the co-operative, and the quality of the services. In other words, it is difficult to gauge the performance of financial co-operatives using a single measure. The performance of co-operative banks vs. other types of banks has been studied in two ways: by analysing ratios (for instance, return on equity or assets, loan loss provisions to total loans, or cost-to-income ratios), and by means of formal efficiency analysis (for instance, stochastic frontier analysis). In both cases, a wide variety of approaches, samples, and even definitions of co-operatives has been used. In particular, we can distinguish among studies that compare the determinants of performance within co-operatives; studies that compare the performance of co-operatives and profit-maximizing banks; and studies that compare the performance of co-operative banks relative to profit-maximizing banks before and during the European financial and economic crisis that started in 2008 and is still evident in most parts of Europe at the time of writing (in 2015). Often these studies find quite contradictory results: for instance, there has been no consensus on whether co-operative banks were at a profitability disadvantage before the crisis, even though it seems clear that at least during the crisis co-operative banks no longer had poorer profitability (Ferri et al. 2015). Also, some studies found that co-operative banks are more efficient than shareholder banks (Girardone et al. 2009), whereas other studies concluded the opposite (Kontolaimou and Tsekouras 2010).

Co-operative financial organizations typically start out small and, at least traditionally, were viewed to have some advantages in their small size, including better information about borrowers and the possibility of imposing social sanctions on non-performing members. For a variety of reasons, including technological innovations, many observers have argued that lately the value of soft information in banking has decreased. For co-operative banks, a practical implication of this may be that the optimal size of co-operative banks has increased. This issue has been studied empirically most often in the USA, where the research has often uncovered evidence that suggests that credit unions would benefit from increasing their size (Wheelock and Wilson 2011; Wilcox and Dopico 2011). European co-operative banks have been studied much less in this respect. The few studies that exist typically do not find significant economies of scale or benefits from mergers (e.g. Lang and Welzel 1996). This difference in results may arise from different network structures: European co-operative groups are typically much more tightly integrated than US credit unions and this may help them operate on a smaller optimal scale.

The financial crisis that broke out in 2007–8 revitalized the interest in co-operative banks, largely because they were perceived to be more stable than profit-maximizing banks. Groeneveld and de Vries (2009) provided some early evidence that co-operative banks were less affected by the subprime crisis than large shareholder banks, and this view was further reinforced by Birchall (2013). Ferri et al. (2014a, b; 2015) provided an evaluation of the performance of co-operatives banks vs. savings and shareholder banks using quantitative analysis of large samples up to the end of 2011. One of their findings was that profitability of co-operative banks declined only marginally during the crisis, while the profitability of shareholder banks declined considerably, so that the pre-crisis wedge in profitability between co-operative and shareholder banks disappeared. Co-operative banks already had better loan quality than shareholder banks before the crisis, and this difference only became more pronounced during the crisis. Also the bank stability ratings of tightly integrated co-operative banks deteriorated much less during the crisis than those of shareholder banks. Lending by co-operative banks varied much less than that of shareholder banks, and co-operative banks also showed less responsiveness to monetary policy changes, both before and during the crisis. This suggests that co-operative banks have smooth lending cycles and can therefore be beneficial to overall economic stability (cf. Hesse and Cihak 2007).

However, it must be said that the record of co-operative banks during the crisis is not consistently positive, and many negative developments have occurred since 2011. Unsurprisingly, in countries where there has been severe economic disruption, co-operatives have also encountered grave difficulties. This applies to Cypriot co-operatives, which have been nationalized, and to Greek co-operatives, whose numbers have been drastically reduced by mergers. Some co-operatives also experienced trouble despite the fact they were located in less adverse environments. One of the earliest co-operatives to experience crisis was the Austrian Volksbank Corporation, which suffered severe losses in Eastern Europe as well as from other investments. The Austrian Volksbank Corporation has been restructured and partly taken over by the state. Another example of an organization that lost its co-operative character due to the crisis was the UK Co-operative Bank, which is now majority owned by external shareholders. In other countries, such as Italy, co-operatives that extended credit to the enterprises in their home regions during the crisis have suffered from the prolonged economic difficulties.

10.7 Corporate Governance Issues in Financial Co-operatives

The governance of a firm refers to the mechanisms for the internal control systems that make up the structure through which the objectives are defined, the means to reach the goals are determined, and the results are controlled. It involves a set of relationships among the shareholders, the boards of directors, the managers, and other stakeholders. The governance issue can be framed as an agency issue, where the separation between management and ownership, that is, between the decision agent and the principal, has an impact both on efficiency and profitability. For several reasons, this mechanism is more complex in the case of co-operative banks: members can be both depositors and borrowers, thus the board and the managers should represent the contrasting interest of both; the board and the managers should represent the more general interests of the community (the stakeholders); and respect the collective orientation and mutual interest.

Nowadays, the most urgent problems in the governance of co-operative banks stem from their growth. On the one hand, the increase in the number of members and the spread of ownership impact on the voting mechanism, make the individual position less important in the general assembly, and reduce member mobilization. This can result in decreasing internal control of the management and in increased free-riding by members who may feel disempowered as the institution adds new members. On the other hand, growth requires sophisticated professional management in order to deal with the new and more complex financial situations; but the qualitative and quantitative reinforcement of management may favour the separation of ownership and control, thus intensifying agency problems. The weakening of democratic control on management by the general assembly may lead to opportunistic lending policies, a misappropriation of co-operative funds on behalf of the management for its own use, or a substantial misalignment between corporate philosophy and needs and will of members. Therefore, why members are motivated to be on the board becomes a more relevant question; it is more likely that directors follow their own interests, turning collective action away from its initial goals and giving rise to collectively less efficient solutions.

Not only does growth make it difficult to encourage existing members to exercise their ownership rights and responsibilities to oversee management. Other reasons for the declining participation in board elections include insufficient knowledge of the subjects discussed and the claim that the board of directors formulates the co-operative's policies without taking into account the needs of members. In any case, absenteeism from general meetings deprives members of the possibility of understanding the reasoning behind the co-operative bank's operations. As a result, members judge the bank's performance mainly through their transactions, and ignore the true reasons that shape how transactions are run and the consequences of the policy that is adopted.

Finally, the weak participation of members in the governance creates an inertia in the turnover of managers that leads to a clear group-thinking problem: a group (the board) that secludes itself away from critics (and self-critics) and finds a rationalization for all its decisions (right or wrong) not only lacks creativity and innovation, but tends also not to perform correctly the role of agent with respect to the owners (members) and the stakeholders in general. Sometimes, it may represent the interest of only one group of stakeholders and, in other cases, only that of the board (Alexopoulos et al. 2013).

10.8 Regulatory Challenges of Co-operative Banks: Compliance Costs and Pressures to Adopt the Features of Shareholder Banks

The turbulent banking scene created by the crisis, in particular with the new Basel 2 and 3 requirements, has increased regulatory pressure on co-operative banks to strengthen both equity and profits, with a considerable impact on their internal organization. At the same time, the stricter regulatory framework that has been imposed and the institutional steps that have been taken towards introducing an EU banking union will introduce further challenges for co-operative banks. Since the costs of creating a union are expected to peak at a time when the banks will be required to build up their capital resources and finance economic growth, the underlying risk is that regulation will be seen again as a constraint to profit margins. In particular, the so-called stress-tests undertaken by the European Central bank (ECB) will probably increase the need to raise regulatory capital and ratios, even among major co-operative banks.

The aftermaths of this recapitalization process could be that co-operative banks will struggle between retaining profits and adopting a counter-cyclical behaviour, and financing local economy. Thus, members and 'loyal' customers will find themselves with limited access to a solution that was readily available till the recent past. As the distance created between members and their bank deprives members of an understanding that retained profits, that is, the traditional source of capital of co-op banks, is probably the safest way to secure the presence of a co-op bank in the banking arena, the recapitalization procedure may re-enforce the perception that a co-op bank is not that different from any other banking institution. This vicious cycle may, of course, become even more intensive if co-operative banks opt for the employment of 'alternative' recapitalization solutions that would increase their dependency on external debt (the market and its 'players'). This, in addition, would decrease their degree of freedom in their quest for ethical, socially responsible, development-oriented banking behaviour.

Also the new regulations designed for the banking system could have severe consequences for co-operative banks, since they do not include a proportionality principle, according to which the rules should be adapted for each type of bank based on its characteristics, in particular on small size. As an example, the strict impositions on the duties delegated to employees, for example one person should be devoted solely to the compliance, impacts on the minimal structure required to run a bank (Ferri and Kalmi 2014). The pursuit of economies of scale to reduce costs, especially personnel costs, will result in mergers and acquisitions, and an increase in size that may raise governance issues. This trend is likely to have a stronger impact on less integrated and centralized systems, such as in Germany and Italy, where single co-operative banks have a great deal of autonomy from federations (Alexopoulos and Goglio 2011).

10.9 Challenges faced by Co-operative Banks in Terms of their Mission and of Establishing New Co-operative Banks

As noted at the beginning of this chapter, co-operative banks, especially those of the Raiffeisenian variety, have been promoting the economic well-being of the economically disadvantaged. Nevertheless, over time, co-operatives seem to suffer from some mission drift. Being self-help organizations, co-operatives rely on economically stable middle-class members. Over time, this may lead to the exclusion of the poorest strata from membership. Thus, co-operatives need to constantly redefine their vision. An economic analysis of co-operatives starting from aggregating member preferences may justify the gentrification of co-operatives. However, it would be more consistent with co-operative values to have a more inclusive vision and co-operatives that include the economically disadvantaged in their field of membership. Many North American credit unions represent examples of this.

Retaining member participation in a situation where co-operatives are becoming larger in membership represents a second challenge. As explained, mergers are the result of a combination of technological changes and of pressures from the regulator, the supervisors, and often also from inside the group. Mergers tend to increase the distance between members and management. Co-operatives need either to consider new ways to incentivize members to participate in governance or to accept permanently lower participation. The dynamics of entry and exit in the co-operative population also pose important challenges. Even though co-operatives have advantages in the form of lower exit rates—as suggested by their greater resilience during times of crisis—they suffer severe problems of entry. In most countries, the main periods of entry of co-operatives took place in the late nineteenth and early twentieth centuries. As soon as nationally encompassing coverage of co-operatives was achieved, the internal non-competition rules of co-operatives discouraged the entry of new co-operatives. During that period, establishing credit co-operatives was relatively easy and minimum capitalization requirements, if any, were at low levels. Today the situation is completely different as there are stringent requirements for minimum equity capital and demanding operational requirements for banks. In some countries with small or no co-operative banks, including Belgium and Israel, there have been attempts to create new co-operatives, but these initiatives have proceeded very slowly. In the North American system, where financial co-operatives (credit co-operatives) are under their own regulatory framework, there is more entry, but even in this case it has been very limited. The lack of entry is worrisome, because in the long run the population cannot survive without new entry, even if the existing units were more resilient than their competitors.

Ultimately, the case for retaining co-operative banks rests on preserving the diversity in the financial markets. Indeed, it has been argued that greater diversity in the micro-level creates favourable conditions for macro-stability (Michie 2011). This stability can be threatened in two ways: either through the disappearance of co-operative banking organizations or through their continued nominal existence, but without any operational difference from shareholder banks. In the current situation, this diversity still exists in some countries (notably Germany and France), while it is under threat in others (e.g. Italy), and has practically disappeared in some others (the UK). In order to counter such worrisome trends it is necessary to find ways to revitalize co-operatives where they exist, and make sure new financial co-operatives can enter the market.

Acknowledgements

We thank Yiorgos Alexopoulos, Holger Blisse, and Eric Meyer for their kind help in answering our queries when writing this article.

References

Alexopoulos, Y., Catturani, I., and Goglio, S. (2013), 'Searching for a Model of Governance in Cooperative Banking', in J. Brazda, M. Dellinger, and D. Rössl, eds, *Genossenschaften im Fokus einer neuen Wirtschaftspolitik* (Berlin et al.: LIT Verlag), 707–31.

Alexopoulos, Y. and Goglio, S. (2011), 'Financial Cooperatives: Problems and Challenges in the Post-Crisis Era', *Journal of Rural Cooperation*, 39(1), 34–47.

Alexopoulos, Y. and Goglio, S. (2013), 'Introduction: Cooperative Finance and Sustainable Local Development', in S. Goglio and Y. Alexopoulos, eds, *Financial Cooperatives and Local Development* (London: Routledge), 1–18.

Ayadi, R., Llewellyn, D. T., Schmidt, R. H., Arbak, E., and Pieter De Groen, W. (2010), *Investigating Diversity in the Banking Sector in Europe: Key Developments, Performance and Role of Cooperative Banks* (Brussels: Centre for European Policy Studies).

Birchall, J. (2013), *Resilience in a Downturn: The Power of Financial Cooperatives* (Geneva: International Labour Office).

Desrochers, M. and Fischer, K. P. (2005), 'The Power of Networks: Integration and Financial Cooperative Performance', *Annals of Public and Cooperative Economics*, 76(3), 307–54.

Ferri, G. and Kalmi, P. (2014), 'Only Up: Regulatory Burden and Its Effects on Credit Unions'. Filene Institute Research Report.

Ferri, G., Kalmi, P., and Kerola, E. (2014a), Does Bank Ownership Affect Lending Behavior? Evidence from the Euro Area, *Journal of Banking & Finance*, 48, 194–209.

Ferri, G., Kalmi, P., and Kerola, E. (2014b), 'Organizational Structure and Exposure to Crisis among European Banks: Evidence from Rating Changes', *Journal of Entrepreneurial and Organizational Diversity*, 3(1), 35–55.

Ferri, G., Kalmi, P., and Kerola, E. (2015), 'Organizational Structure and Performance in European Banks: A Reassessment', in A. Kauhanen, ed, *Advances in the Economic Analysis of Participatory and Labor-Managed Firms*, Vol. 8 (Bingley, UK: Emerald Group Publishing), 109–41.

Girardone, C., Nankervis, J. C., and Velentza, E. F. (2009), 'Efficiency, Ownership and Financial Structure in European Banking: A Cross-Country Comparison', *Managerial Finance*, 35(3), 227–45.

Goglio S. and Alexopoulos Y. (2014), 'Cooperative Banks at a Turning Point?' *Journal of Entrepreneurial & Organizational Diversity*, 3(1), 1–8.

Goglio S. and Leonardi A. (2012), 'The Motivations of Economic Behavior: The Case of Cooperative Credit', *Journal of Entrepreneurial & Organizational Diversity*, 1(1), 65–84.

Groeneveld, J. M. and de Vries, B. (2009), 'European Cooperative Banks: First Lessons from the Subprime Crisis', *The International Journal of Cooperative Management*, 4(2), 8–21.

Guinnane, T. W. (2001), 'Cooperatives as Information Machines: German Rural Credit Cooperatives, 1883–1914', *The Journal of Economic History*, 61(02), 366–89.

Hesse, H. and Cihak, M. (2007), 'Cooperative Banks and Financial Stability', IMF Working Paper, 07/2.

Kontolaimou, A. and Tsekouras, K. (2010), 'Are Cooperatives the Weakest Link in European Banking? A Non-Parametric Metafrontier Approach', *Journal of Banking & Finance*, 34(8), 1946–57.

Lang, G. and Welzel, P. (1996), 'Efficiency and Technical Progress in Banking: Empirical Results for a Panel of German Cooperative Banks', *Journal of Banking & Finance*, 20(6), 1003–23.

Michie, J. (2011), 'Promoting Corporate Diversity in the Financial Services Sector', *Policy Studies*, 32(4), 309–23.

Wheelock, D. C. and Wilson, P. W. (2011), 'Are Credit Unions Too Small?' *Review of Economics and Statistics*, 93(4), 1343–59.

Wilcox, J. A. and Dopico, L. G. (2011), 'Credit Union Mergers: Efficiencies and Benefits', *FRBSF Economic Letter*, 28.

CHAPTER 11

....

AGRICULTURAL CO-OPERATIVES

a struggle for identity

....

SAMIRA NUHANOVIC-RIBIC, ERMANNO C. TORTIA,
AND VLADISLAV VALENTINOV

11.1 INTRODUCTION

....

THROUGHOUT history and across the world, agricultural co-operatives have lifted many farmers and communities out of poverty. When functioning in a supportive institutional environment, they have gone far beyond poverty alleviation and helped deliver sustainable and shared agricultural and rural development. In a purposive joining of interests, co-operatives continue to provide their members with the means to strengthen their market position by economizing on costs and dispersing the risks associated with pursuing productive activities individually. Co-operatives do this by integrating economic and social objectives in a participatory model of decision-making. Their uniqueness, therefore, lies in the intrinsic values which underpin this business model and turn co-operatives into enterprises that, in the long run, favour people over capital and long-term job security and financial stability over short-term pecuniary gain. Co-operatives can offer effective solutions to the failures of capitalistic firms and competitive markets.

Agricultural co-operatives, in particular, have been rather successful in protecting individual farmers from the interest of downstream and upstream market participants. Being an effective collective bargaining mechanism, co-operatives allow farmers to benefit from lower input and higher output prices while also strengthening their mutual social ties. In some regions their numbers and scope of impact are astonishing. In Europe, agricultural co-operatives have an aggregate market share of about 60 per cent in the processing and marketing of agricultural commodities and an estimated 50 per cent share in the supply of inputs. In the USA, co-operatives have a market share of about 28 per cent in the processing and marketing of agricultural products and 26 per cent in the supply of inputs (Borzaga and Galera 2012). These figures peak at around 70 per cent in some Northern European countries, especially in Finland, Denmark, and the Netherlands (European Commission 2012, Bijman and Iliopoulos 2014). The national federations of agricultural co-operatives, Cogeca (General Committee for Agricultural Co-operation in the European Union), and the Copa (Committee of Professional Agricultural Organisations), which federates the EU main agricultural unions, largely influence the positions taken by the national and European federations of all agro-industries. Copa represents over 13 million farmers and their families, whilst Cogeca represents the interests of 38,000 agricultural co-operatives. They have 77 member organizations from the EU Member States (Berthelot 2012).

While acknowledging the dimensional importance of the phenomenon, scholars and practitioners still face a dilemma when it comes to providing a 'fundamentum divisionis or ultimate discriminant' (Zamagni and Zamagni 2010: 30) between co-operative and non-co-operative enterprises. Due to a host of factors, in some contexts co-operatives have grown increasingly similar to their capitalist counterparts leading many to question the existence of a common co-operative identity that cuts across institutional settings and sectors. The conundrum surrounding the question of co-operative identity is not just a theoretical one: it also has practical ramifications.

During the past several decades, agricultural co-operatives have been subjected to the mounting pressures present in the agricultural and food industry, which stem from sector-specific characteristics and reflect disturbances in the wider institutional environment within which the sector functions (Swinnen and Maertens 2007). This development has left a mark on how other market actors perceive co-operatives, as well as on how co-operatives perceive themselves. Many co-operatives, including successful ones, struggle to understand how to strike a balance between being competitive in the market and staying true to co-operative principles. Nonetheless, the vulnerabilities of the agricultural sector to global market turbulence, as well as the features of productive processes, goods, and types of labour in agriculture underline why agricultural co-operatives are especially appealing in the face of recent challenges in global markets (Valentinov 2005, 2007; Tortia et al. 2013). The role of co-operatives in improving economic co-ordination both between and within agricultural organizations, and under such complex institutional circumstances, is critical to their long-term viability, especially in developing countries. When supported by proper development-oriented policy frameworks, agricultural co-operatives provide an organizational structure that helps offset the effects of unfavourable market conditions by consolidating the market activities of individual farmers. Furthermore, co-operatives are known to improve co-ordination along the value chain, the parts of which have grown more and more dependent on one another in response to structural changes in the agro-food markets (Bijman et al. 2011).

The main challenge of co-operatives stems from the need to balance the social and economic nature of these enterprises. Luckily, the distinctive structure and purpose of co-operatives can shed some light on how to strike this balance. The internal organizational structure, which is reflected in the specific ownership arrangement, the inclusive and participatory governance format, and the patronage-based benefit distribution helps differentiate this type of enterprise from other actors in agricultural markets. Agricultural co-operatives become localized enterprises when their orientation towards mobilizing small individual producers into an enterprise is successful and yields both pecuniary and non-pecuniary benefits to participating farmers. This aspect, which is strictly intertwined with the associative and embedded nature of co-operatives, supports endogenously driven processes of local economic development (Borzaga and Tortia 2009). Furthermore, agricultural co-operatives invest with a long-term perspective, and for this reason capital does not follow profit as is normally the case with investor-owned firms. Instead, capital follows a wider notion of benefits that accrue, not only to co-operative members, but to the community as a whole. This characteristic reveals the deeply idiosyncratic business philosophy of co-operatives.

To date, the relevance of the co-operative identity debate can be best understood by looking at the history of the co-operative movement which, particularly with regards to agricultural co-operatives, coincides with the history of localized reactions to the forces of industrialization, urbanization, and the rapid growth of market economies (Birchall 1997). Consequently, the co-operative movement itself has never been solely about strengthening the business dimension of co-operatives, but also about amplifying the ability of collective action as such to amend inequalities in social structures and consolidate the fabric of societies with weak social ties. The profound changes that have shaped the market economy as we know it today have revealed that there are systemic imperatives that contribute to reinforcing social inequalities, especially in the agricultural sector. Among other things, these inequalities include the inability of the institutional system and of the market to eschew the exclusion of weak social actors and the tendency to exacerbate exclusion and exploitation in the presence of the positional power derived from monopoly or monopsony. Marginalized groups can minimize the effects of these inefficiencies and inequalities by pooling their productive resources, thus strengthening their market position (Merrett and Walzer 2004).

By reviewing the most influential literature on the theory of agricultural co-operatives, we aim to elucidate the multi-layered nature of both the structure and purpose of co-operatives in the context of the ever-present debate about the true nature of co-operative identity. To this end, we pose two questions. The first concerns the nature of the co-operative enterprise and helps us underline the relevance of an old debate on whether co-operatives are a form of vertical integration, a firm, or a nexus of contracts and coalitions. By providing a historical overview of the theoretical responses to this issue, we will highlight the internal complexities of the ownership, the governance, and the benefits of the co-operative structure. The second question can be interpreted as an invitation to future research. We suggest that there is a need to reflect again on the role of co-operatives' embeddedness in their institutional context in the process of understanding and shaping co-operative identity.

Section 11.2 provides the basic economic argument for the emergence of agricultural co-operatives. Sections 11.3 and 11.4 highlight the major standpoints in the debate on whether co-operatives are firms or something else. Section 11.5 documents the recent evolution of this debate into the discussion on the new co-operative models emerging in response to the dynamics of global markets. Concluding remarks are presented in Section 11.6.

11.2 THE ECONOMIC RATIONALE FOR AGRICULTURAL CO-OPERATIVES

Agricultural co-operatives have a long history that goes back to the beginning of the nineteenth century. The co-operative movement first took shape in the United Kingdom, where consumer co-operatives emerged as a sustainable co-operative form by the middle of the nineteenth century, and then in continental Europe, where experiments involving worker and credit co-operatives surfaced. In that period, most countries formalized the presence of co-operatives through legislation. Initial co-operatives in agriculture were created in the second half of the nineteenth century in Europe. They later spread to North America first, and then to developing countries in different continents, becoming a means of rural development (Hoyt 1989; Ortmann and King 2007).

The economic theory of agricultural co-operatives is not as old, but it has a respectable history of its own. A discussion on whether a co-operative should have a firm-like status cuts across the early works on the theory of agricultural co-operatives. The first sign of a systematic inquiry into this question dates back to the writings by Nourse (1922) concerning early co-operatives and defending the idea that co-operatives are not much more than an extension of individual farmers' firms. Even in these early works, a critical question surfaced about the reasons why agricultural co-operatives emerge. This question has remained important as co-operatives continue to evolve in response to the needs of their members and in reaction to the pressures emanating from their institutional environment.

The explanation from the New Institutional Economics (NIE) tradition focuses on the cost perspective—that is, on how, by joining co-operatives, farmers avoid the relatively high 'market contracting costs' which they normally incur when they act alone in the market, and how, instead, farmers settle for relatively manageable 'ownership costs' associated with co-operative membership (Hansmann 1996; Ortmann and King 2007). In other words, viewed from this perspective, co-operatives serve as mechanisms guarding farmers against opportunistic behaviour on the part of downstream and upstream actors in agricultural markets. The price farmers pay for such a service is related to the costs associated with co-operative membership, which reside, for example, in free-riding and opportunistic behaviour by other members (Bonus 1986).

Another response to this critical question is to be found in the characteristics of the agricultural sector itself and, as such, echoes Nourse's argument of co-operatives being the logical extension of family farms. Productive processes in the agricultural sector are inherently uncertain and vulnerability of agriculture to a host of natural phenomena is just one of the factors causing overall uncertainty in this sector. Other factors include high monitoring and supervising costs of hired labour (Valentinov 2007). To increase efficiency of agricultural production one would need to take some control over natural phenomena and monitoring of hired workers in a single location, which are both difficult to obtain. Technological developments made the former possible, but often not cost efficient, which explains why the family farm is still a dominant actor in agricultural production. Although 'the family farm can be regarded as an organizational solution to the difficulty of monitoring and supervising workers' (Pollak 1985: 591), it has its own limitations. To begin with, family farms are limited in two areas: a) the geographical area that can be effectively supervised by family members; b) their ability to ever realize external economies of scale in production. Another limitation of family farms relates to the fact that firms occupying upstream and downstream positions do not experience fragmentation of production and the monitoring and supervision difficulties that instead characterize agriculture. Upstream and downstream organizations are, as a rule, hierarchically organized, presupposing much weaker constraints on firm expansion than family-based organization. Consequently, up- and downstream firms have significantly larger sizes than individual family farms. Historically, this has resulted in the tendency of family farms to exhibit a much more competitive industry structure than the upstream and downstream firms in the agri-food sector, whereby farmers have been put at an increasing disadvantage in terms of their ability to bargain with up- and downstream trading partners on an equitable basis. Inter-farmer competition can exert extreme downward pressure on prices, which can force individual owners to abandon the activity and sell their land or leave it unused. Moreover, the farmers' disadvantage resides not only in the danger of monopolistic pricing by up- and downstream firms, but also in their lower ability to combat opportunistic behaviour on the part of these firms. As indicated by Staatz (1987) and Hansmann (1996), farmers face significant risks of their trading partners exercising opportunistic expropriation of quasi-rents on their specific assets. The only alternative which is compatible with both the retention of independent small ownership and the achievement of adequate scale economies and market survival potential is the creation of collective governance forms in the form of agricultural co-operatives (Tortia et al. 2013). This intuition mirrors Bonus' (1986) view that the value of co-operatives' worth lies in their ability to balance two opposite forces, namely private, independent activities of farmers and joint activities of co-operative members. The core benefits of individual and independent farming are conjugated with the benefits of the collective organization like risk-sharing and transaction-cost-minimizing benefits. When these individual economic units come together under the co-operative framework, they form a separate legal and economic identity epitomized in a co-operative organizational form.

Still, are co-operatives firms or non-firms? And does it matter? Much of the identity debate derives its substance from these questions. Co-operatives emerge to rectify the problems specific to capitalistic firms in agriculture and this is why they are often perceived as non-firms.

11.3 AGRICULTURAL CO-OPERATIVES AS NON-FIRMS

Central to agricultural co-operatives in their focus on members as their *raison d'être* is to provide them with useful services (Valentinov and Iliopoulos 2013). The central role of members and their preponderance in terms of decision-making and benefit distribution led some early theorists to conclude that co-operatives have no independent economic identity of their own, since they are just a form of vertical integration. The most notable representatives of this view were Emelianoff (1942), Phillips (1953), and Robotka (1957). While each focused on a distinct issue in their independent analyses of co-operative nature and behaviour, all of them argued one thing: a co-operative is a mere service agency to its members, and decision-making rights and benefits can be reduced to individual member farmers. To Emelianoff (1942), the co-operative enterprise is nothing more than an aggregate of independent, profit-seeking economic units. In that light, Phillips (1953: 74–5) provocatively argued that 'the co-operative has no more economic life or purpose, apart from that of the participating economic units, than one of the individual plants of a large multi-plant firm'. The concept of vertical integration fits with Phillips's 'co-operative-as-an-extension-of-the-farm' when co-operative operations (e.g. marketing or transformation) are contrasted with farm production. At the heart of the 'co-operative as a form of vertical integration' view, which deals with integration strictly in terms of production, lies the idea that the co-operative operates at cost and has no profits or losses of its own. Indeed, the co-operative is non-profit relative to the farm and, in this specific sense, cannot be seen as an economic entity that is independent from the farm.

In our view, this theoretical standpoint can be overcome when account is taken of the process of horizontal, not only vertical, integration, since agricultural co-operatives are, as a norm, created not only to introduce new activities, but also to share risks, share and create new knowledge, and increase farmers' market power. The processes of collective decision-making underlying such outcomes cannot be fully reduced to individual farmers but, instead, create an emerging form of co-operative identity. We now turn to this second perspective.

11.4 CO-OPERATIVES AS FIRMS

The view that co-operatives can be analysed as separate and independent firms came in the article by Stephen Enke (1945), which acknowledged the existence of two separate categories of stakeholders within co-operatives, namely managers and members, and pointed out that it is managers, not members, who are tasked with everyday decision-making on what to maximize. Although his study dealt with consumer co-operatives, much of its propositions were also valid for agricultural co-operatives, especially with regards to the role of managers in balancing the interests of members.

The work of Helmberger and Hoos (1962) relied on organization theory to provide a broader interpretation of the concept of firm so as to include co-operative enterprises in the framework of analysis. They argued that the theory of the conventional for-profit firm needs to be accommodated to the specific characteristics of co-operatives to be useful for explaining their behaviour in the market. Another important contribution by Helmberger and Hoos was recognizing that co-operatives develop both short- and long-run behavioural models and tend to tie up an open or closed membership policy of the co-operative to what best suits members' interests. They concluded that it would be in the interest of members to expand the co-operative membership whenever the expansion yields the benefits associated with economies of scale, that is, as long as the co-operative allows for a reduction in the per-unit processing costs. One of the downsides of the Helmberger and Hoos approach is that it assumed nothing more than a single objective for a co-operative. Subsequent research showed that co-operative objectives are far more complex, both in their content and in the way in which they are set. Nevertheless, the Helmberger and Hoos model remained one of the most influential attempts at analysing agricultural co-operatives in the 1960s and 1970s.

Both 'co-operative as vertical integration' and 'co-operative as a firm' models assumed somewhat homogenous membership, thereby assuming no possibility of intra-organizational power struggles among different stakeholders or opportunism within membership categories. While the former assumed a scattered model of decision-making that essentially boils down to independent decisions by every individual economic unit, the latter propagated more centralized decision-making structures and placed more weight on co-operative managers as central decision-makers (Staatz 1987). A new view of co-operatives as a coalition of different participants emerged. Authors such as Kaarlehto (1955) criticized the existing approaches for neglecting the operational side of the co-operative–member relation. He argued that homogeneous membership cannot be so readily assumed and that if this assumption is relaxed to accommodate the realities concerning co-operative membership, conflicts both between farmer members and between farmers and management need to be factored in. Kaarlehto's contribution pointed out that, while the co-operative can be an instrument that ensures farmers' collective bargaining power vis-a-vis other market participants, it too has its own internal bargaining market where different participants struggle to have their individual interests prioritized over the interest of others.

We notice that this interpretation is the closest to more recent interpretations of entrepreneurial activity as a form of collective action, which implies not only benefits, but also costs due to diverging interests, opportunism, and power struggles in the presence of contract incompleteness and asymmetric information. The contemporary approach to economic action as collective action was initiated by Elinor Ostrom (1990), who applied it to the management of common pools of natural resources. It is now starting to be applied by some authors to instances of entrepreneurial action in a stricter sense and specifically to co-operative enterprises (Chapter 5 of this handbook; Tortia 2015).

11.5 BETWEEN FIRM AND NON-FIRM: NEW CO-OPERATIVE MODELS

Valentinov and Iliopoulos (2012) point out that from the 1980s onwards, agricultural co-operatives in the Western hemisphere entered a new era characterized by an unusually difficult and hostile business environment. Since then, the major challenges faced by co-operatives include fierce competition with powerful food and agricultural input conglomerates and financing shortages caused by deteriorating capital markets. These challenges laid bare a number of internal constraints that have become known as the property rights problems, also known as incentive problems (Cook 1995), which caused agricultural co-operative members to feel discouraged to invest significant risk capital (Cook and Iliopoulos, 2000) and unable to make efficient collective decisions (Iliopoulos and Hendrikse 2009). These problems resulted in numerous co-operative conversions into investor-oriented firms and liquidations as well as experimentation with new co-operative models (Cross et al. 2009; Chaddad and Cook 2004).

These structural transformations of co-operatives impart a new, quite practical, dimension to the scholarly debate on whether co-operatives are firms or non-firms. Chaddad and Cook (2004) transcend this debate by developing a continuum of co-operative models delimited by the traditional co-operative, on the one side, and the investor-oriented firm, on the other. The authors argue that co-operative models can be distinguished by how ownership rights are defined and assigned to the major stakeholders of the firm. Between the polar forms of the traditional agricultural co-operative and the investor-oriented firm, they identify five non-traditional co-operative models: proportional investment co-operatives, member-investor co-operatives, new generation co-operatives, co-operatives with capital-seeking entities, and investor-share co-operatives (ibid: 350).

Traditional co-operatives are characterized either by non-transferable and non-redeemable capital shares owned by members (mostly in Anglo-Saxon countries), or by reinvestment of net residuals into locked assets (mainly in Southern European countries). These features of the traditional structure of co-operative property generate various incentive problems. Free-riding derives from the utilization of common resources coupled with democratic membership rights, which engender incentives either to overuse common assets, as in the tragedy of the commons problem (Hardin 1968; Ostrom 1990), or to reduce work effort in an opportunistic way (Williamson 1973). The horizon problem has a dynamic nature and is connected with the emphasis of current members on present benefits at the expense of future ones (Furubotn and Pejovich 1970). The portfolio problem is more static in nature and refers to members' inability to differentiate their individual financial investments from co-operative investments.

Both the horizon and the portfolio problem arise in the presence of locked, socialized, non-transferable and non-redeemable assets. Finally, the control problem and the influence cost problem stem from the divergence of interests and preferences between members and managers in a democratically managed organization, and in the connected costs of ownership (Hansmann 1996; Valentinov and Iliopoulos 2012).

New co-operative models can ease the solution of the financial problems daunting traditional models by improving access to financial contributions by members and to financial markets. However, they also make the working and the objectives of co-operatives more similar to investor-owned companies, and can increase the danger of demutualization (Tortia et al. 2013). What all of these issues illustrate is that a balance needs to be struck between financial innovation and stability of the co-operative model, and between member participation and co-operative economic efficiency, a trade-off of sorts between democracy and efficiency. Evaluating the validity of this relationship, Jones and Kalmi (2012) warn that no definitive conclusions can be drawn before at least two issues are analysed carefully. Firstly, it is necessary to assess whether a co-operative is able to reflect on the composition of its own membership and develop appropriate democratic decision-making procedures and structures. They argue that in large co-operatives with heterogeneous membership it is of critical importance that proper representative democracy is carefully developed in order for different interests to be represented in decision-making processes. To preserve the democratic nature of their governance structure, the literature is somewhat critical of the possibility that co-operatives grow in size (Nilsson et al. 2009; Valentinov 2004). In fact, it has been shown that in large co-operatives, members often feel dissatisfied with the level of control they have over development trajectories and somewhat disconnected from management structures, which usually results in tensions between members and managers. Rather than dismissing altogether the idea that large co-operatives can have successful member control, Jones and Kalmi (2012) urge for flexibility in crafting a governance model that would combine members' need for exerting meaningful control over their co-operative and the amount of executive power vested in managers. In essence, they argue for meaningful rather than absolute control of the co-operative by its members.

The second central issue Jones and Kalmi suggest is the development of proper incentive structures for membership in co-operatives. Precisely because this matter is oftentimes taken as straightforward, it is rarely given enough attention. Instead, they argue, the functioning of the reward mechanism in the co-operative should be more clear and transparent. Recalling Dunn's (1988) seminal contribution, it is important to understand that at times there may be a deviation in how co-operative principles are translated into co-operative practices, but it is essential that every co-operative strives to approximate the two as much as possible. Dunn considers the three basic co-operative principles: the user–owner principle, the user–control principle, and the user–benefits principle, arguing that 'an organization that transforms the three basic principles into an operational reality can be said to be operating on a true co-operative basis' (Dunn 1988: 85).

11.6 CONCLUDING REMARKS

Following the framework used in Staatz (1987), Cook et al. (2004: 82–84) review the post-1990 literature on agricultural co-operatives and document a shift of focus from the study of co-operatives as a form of vertical integration towards the employment of so-called coalition and nexus of contracts approaches, both of which highlight the importance of increasingly heterogeneous co-operative membership and internal organizational dynamics. Recent research on governance structures in co-operatives draws on transaction cost, incomplete contracts, and agency approaches when analysing the choice between co-operative governance and other available alternatives, recognizing management as a separate co-operative actor unlike what Emelianoff suggested in the 1940s. Following the 1990 seminal contribution by Ostrom, also the study of entrepreneurial action as collective action and of the related decision-making costs in the presence of communalities in resource ownership promises to add new crucial insights. Finally, the interaction between the policy agenda and the development of co-operatives has also become an interesting research area.

The non-profit distribution constraint that is present only in some countries, typically in continental Europe, and the ideological element contained in co-operatives' social roles are both important qualifiers that have made co-operatives an interesting object of analysis within the wider field of social economics and its role in rural development, along with other non-profit oriented organizational forms. Indeed, agricultural co-operatives have been considered an essential part of the European social economy. The link between farmers' activities, agricultural co-operatives, and other non-profit organizations is important in as much as it enriches the discussion on the nature of the concept of social enterprises, especially when the economic justifications for the existence of both are taken into account. Both co-operatives and other non-profits revolve around the provision of missing collective goods, a pattern that has been especially strong in rural development (Valentinov and Iliopoulos 2013). For this reason, it remains crucial for co-operatives to be studied in relation to their immediate institutional and social environments and to other actors.

Agricultural co-operatives are different from conventional enterprises and corporations in the sector. Much of the current scholarly debate on the viability of agricultural co-operatives focuses on their economic functions and financial outcomes. Instead, we understand co-operative structures as a source of unique nature, identifying their ability to foster social trust and sustain equitable rural growth and human development. The entire conundrum surrounding the matter of co-operative identity in agriculture often revolves around proving or disproving the similarities and differences between co-operative and non-co-operative firms. The reality is that some co-operative models will be more firm-like than others. However, the most important thing is that co-operatives support their farmer-members in ways that investor ownership cannot imitate.

References

Berthelot, J. (2012), 'The European Agricultural Cooperatives, Promoters of the Unequal Globalization', Paris: Solidarité, Organization de Solidarité Internationale. Available from http://www.fao.org/fsnforum/member/jacques-berthelot (accessed 12 October 2016).

Bijman, J. and Iliopoulos, C. (2014), 'Farmers' Cooperatives in the EU: Policies, Strategies and Organisation', *Annals of Public and Cooperative Economics*, 85(4), 497–508.

Bijman, J., Muradian, R., and Cechin, A. (2011), 'Agricultural Cooperatives and Value Chain Coordination', in A. Helmsing and S. Vellema, eds, *Value Chains, Social Inclusion and Economic Development: Contrasting Theories and Realities*, (London: Routledge), 82–101.

Birchall, J. (1997), *The International Cooperative Movement* (Manchester: Manchester University Press).

Bonus, H. (1986), 'The Cooperative Association as a Business Enterprise: A Study in the Economics of Transactions', *Journal of Institutional and Theoretical Economics*, 142(2), 310–39.

Borzaga, C. and Galera, G. (2012), 'Promoting the Understanding of Cooperatives for a Better World', Trento: Euricse. Available at http://ica.coop/sites/default/files/media_items/Report_Venice2012_PRINT.pdf (accessed 11 September 2016).

Borzaga, C. and Tortia, E. C. (2009), 'Social Enterprises and Local Economic Development', in E. Clarence and A. Noya, eds, *The Changing Boundaries of Social Enterprises* (Paris: OECD), 195–228.

Borzaga, C. and Tortia, E. C. (2017), 'Co-operation as Coordination Mechanism: A New Approach to the Economics of Co-operative Enterprises', in J. Michie, J. R Blasi, and C. Borzaga (eds), *The Oxford Handbook of Mutual, Co-operative and Co-owned Business*, (Oxford: Oxford University Press), 55–75.

Chaddad, F. and Cook, M. (2004), 'Understanding New Cooperative Models: An Ownership-Control Rights Typology', *Review of Agricultural Economics*, 26(3), 348–60.

Cook, M. L. (1995), 'The Future of U.S. Agricultural Cooperatives: A Neo-Institutional Approach', *American Journal of Agricultural Economics*, 77(5), 1153–9.

Cook, M. L., Chaddad, F. R., and Iliopoulos, C. (2004), *Advances in Cooperative Theory since 1990: A Review of Agricultural Economics Literature* (Rotterdam: Erasmus University Rotterdam, Rotterdam School of Management).

Cook, M. L. and Iliopoulos, C. (2000), 'Ill-Defined Property Rights in Collective Action: The Case of US Agricultural Cooperatives', in C. Menard (ed.), *Institutions, Contracts, and Organizations: Perspectives from New Institutional Economics*, (London: Edward Elgar), 335–48.

Cross, R. M., Buccola, S. T., and Thoman, E. A. (2009), 'Cooperative Liquidation under Competitive Stress', *European Review of Agricultural Economics*, 36(3), 369–93.

Dunn, J. R. (1988), 'Basic Cooperative Principles and Their Relationship to Selected Practices', *Journal of Agricultural Cooperation*, 3, 83–93.

Emelianoff, I. V. (1942), *Economic Theory of Cooperation* (Ann Arbour, MI: Edwards Brothers).

Enke, S. (1945), 'Consumer Cooperatives and Economic Efficiency', *The American Economic Review*, 35, 148–55.

European Commission (2012), 'Support for Farmers' Cooperatives'. Available at http://ec.europa.eu/agriculture/ (accessed 11 September 2016).

Furubotn, E. G. and Pejovich, S. (1970), 'Property Rights and the Behaviour of the Firm in a Socialist State: The Example of Yugoslavia', *Zeitschrift für Nationalökonomie*, 30(5), 431–54.

Hansmann, H. (1996), *The Ownership of Enterprise* (Cambridge: The Belknap Press of Harvard University Press).

Hardin, G. (1968), 'The Tragedy of the Commons', *Science*, 162(3859), 1243–8.

Helmberger, P. and Hoos, S. (1962), 'Cooperative Enterprise and Organization Theory', *Journal of Farm Economics*, 44(2), 275–90.

Hoyt, A. (1989), 'Cooperatives in other Countries', in D. Cobia, ed., *Cooperatives in Agriculture* (New Jersey, US: Prentice-Hall, Inc.), 81–97.

Iliopoulos, C. and Hendrikse, G. W. J. (2009), 'Influence Costs in Agribusiness Cooperatives: Evidence from Case Studies', *International Studies of Management & Organization*, 39(4), 60–80.

Jones, D. C. and Kalmi, P. (2012), 'Economies of Scale Versus Participation: A Co-Operative Dilemma?', *Journal of Entrepreneurial and Organizational Diversity*, 1(1), 37–64.

Kaarlehto, P. (1955), 'Cooperation as a Form of Economic Integration', *Acta Agriculturae Scandinavica*, 5(1), 85–97.

Merrett, C. D. and Walzer, N. (2004), *Cooperatives and Local Development: Theory and Applications for the 21st Century* (Armonk, NY: M.E. Sharpe).

Nilsson, J., Kihlén, A., and Norell, L. (2009), 'Are Traditional Cooperatives an Endangered Species? About Shrinking Satisfaction, Involvement and Trust', *International Food and Agribusiness Management Review*, XII, 101–22.

Nourse, E. G. (1922), 'The Economic Philosophy of Co-operation', *The American Economic Review*, 12(4), 577–97.

Ortmann, G. F. and King, R. P. (2007), 'Agricultural Cooperatives I: History, Theory and Problems, *Agrekon*, 46(1), 40–68.

Ostrom, E. (1990), *Governing the Commons: The Evolution of Institutions for Collective Action* (Cambridge, Cambridge University Press).

Phillips, R. (1953), 'Economic Nature of the Cooperative Association', *Journal of Farm Economics*, 35(1), 74–87.

Pollak, R. (1985), 'A Transaction Cost Approach to Families and Households', *Journal of Economic Literature*, 23(2), 581–608.

Robotka, F. (1957), 'A Theory of Cooperation', in M. A. Abrahamsen and C. L. Scroggs, eds, *Agricultural Cooperation: Selected Readings* (Minneapolis: University of Minnesota Press), 121–42.

Staatz, J. M. (1987), 'Recent Developments in the Theory of Agricultural Cooperation', *Journal of Agricultural Cooperation*, 2(20), 74–95.

Swinnen, J. F. M. and Maertens, M. (2007), 'Globalization, Privatization, and Vertical Coordination in Food Value Chains in Developing and Transition Countries', *Agricultural Economics*, 37, 89–102.

Tortia, E. C. (2015), 'L'impresa come bene comune: Il caso della accumulazione ed uso delle risorse comuni nelle imprese cooperative', in L. Sacconi and S. Ottone, eds, *Beni Comuni e Cooperazione* (Bologna: Il Mulino), 301–22.

Tortia, E. C., Valentinov, V. L., and Iliopoulos, C. (2013), 'Agricultural Cooperatives', *Journal of Entrepreneurial and Organizational Diversity*, 2(1), 23–36.

Valentinov, V. (2004), 'Toward a Social Capital Theory of Cooperative Organization', *Journal of Cooperative Studies*, 37(3), 5–20.

Valentinov, V. (2005), 'The Organizational Nature of Agricultural Cooperatives: A Perspective from the Farm Problem Theory', *Journal of Rural Cooperation*, 33(2), 139–51.

Valentinov, V. (2007), 'Why Are Cooperatives Important in Agriculture? An Organizational Economics Perspective', *Journal of Institutional Economics*, 3(1), 55–69.

Valentinov, V. and Iliopoulos, C. (2012), 'Property Rights Problems of Agricultural Cooperatives: A Heterodox Institutionalist Perspective', *German Journal of Agricultural Economics*, 61(3), 139–47.

Valentinov, V. and Iliopoulos, C. (2013), 'Economic Theories of Nonprofits and Agricultural Cooperatives Compared: New Perspectives for Nonprofit Scholars', *Nonprofit and Voluntary Sector Quarterly*, 42(1), 109–26.

Williamson, O. E. (1973), 'Market and Hierarchies: Some Elemental Considerations', *The American Economic Review*, 63(2), 316–25.

Zamagni, S. and Zamagni, V. (2010), *Cooperative Enterprise: Facing the Challenge of Globalization* (Massachusetts: Edward Elgar Publishing Inc.).

CHAPTER 12

··

SOCIAL AND SOLIDARITY CO-OPERATIVES

an international perspective

··

GIULIA GALERA

12.1 THE SOCIAL COMMITMENT AND THE ECONOMIC FUNCTIONS OF CO-OPERATIVES

··

WHEN they first emerged as grass-roots organizations in the middle of the nineteenth century, co-operatives were spontaneous defensive reactions to the harsh conditions engendered by the Industrial Revolution or by rural poverty. Co-operatives were not merely economic institutions: they were also social institutions that recreated solidarity and collective self-help. Raiffeisen's idea of a Christianity of action, Schulze-Delitzsch's idea of self-help with the purpose of strengthening the individual, the Rochdale Pioneers' idea of emancipating workers, and Victor Huber's idea of active self-education are all examples of the strong non-economic social function of early co-operatives (Todev et al. 1993).[1] What mattered equally to the co-operative's precursors was the idea of a close and permanent link between the co-operative and its community (Girard and Langlois 2009). By combining the principles of economic security, social freedom, and political participation, co-operatives prospered in sectors where capitalist activity remained too weak to satisfy needs that were otherwise unmet. User and consumer co-operatives were established to minimize intermediation costs and retail prices;

[1] Todev et al., 'Quo Vadis Cooperative Movement in Eastern Europe?', in G. Turner, ed., *Economic Changes in Eastern Europe: Quo Vadis Cooperative Movement? Berliner Hefte zum internationalen Genossenschaftswesen, 1* (Berlin: Institut für Genossenschaftswesen an der Humboldt-Universität, 1993).

producer, especially agricultural, co-operatives to increase the weak market power of producers; worker co-operatives to provide members opportunities to self-manage their businesses. Credit co-operatives have emerged to ensure that people that are not bankable according to the traditional banking system, including small farmers and artisans, have access to credit; mutual aid societies have been set up by workers and communities to provide common insurance and assistance. By satisfying the needs of their members, co-operatives have contributed to improving the quality of life of large—and often disadvantaged—segments of society (Borzaga and Galera 2012a).

Whereas early co-operative initiatives were strongly rooted in a 'collective awareness' that sought to improve the well-being of communities (Defourny and Nyssens 2012), over the decades, co-operatives have become extremely diversified according to their location and field of operation. In many countries where markets are more developed, co-operatives have weakened their social commitment and, in some cases, they have evolved into entrepreneurial forms that differ from investor-owned enterprises solely due to their ownership rights, rather than by virtue of their social orientation (Borzaga and Galera 2012a). Conversely, in many Latin American countries, many co-operatives have kept their strong social commitment and contribute to alleviating poverty in a significant way (Mogrovejo et al. 2012). In several Latin American countries, co-operatives have historically been used to supply public or merit goods, with a consequent weakening of the members' centrality. Co-operatives have nonetheless played the key political role of democratizing the economy and coping with certain unresolved social concerns.

Unlike in Latin America, where co-operatives prospered as a key component of the social and solidarity economy, the establishment of public welfare systems prevented co-operatives from expanding in fields of general interest in several EU countries; the predominant assumption was that services that are of key public interest cannot be delivered in an entrepreneurial way. Co-operatives were thus confined to fulfilling key roles in given sectors of activity, including consumption, production, credit, and agriculture. From an international perspective, national legislations introduced to define and regulate co-operatives have thus clearly set the roles of co-operatives in specific fields of activity and have strictly regulated their membership. The predominant trend has been to acknowledge co-operatives as solely member-oriented organizations that are distinguished by a single stakeholding system. In essence, by introducing the observance of the mutuality principle and, in some instances, the economic orientation of co-operatives, most legislations have endorsed co-operatives' distraction from their social commitment. In some cases, legislation has even weakened the differences between co-operatives and companies, favouring a sort of 'companization' or hybridization of co-operatives (PECOL 2015).[2]

---

[2] The PECOL group of experts refers to 'mutual cooperatives' as co-ops aimed at satisfying their members' interests in obtaining or providing goods (including knowledge or other immaterial things), or services, or in working at the best possible conditions, which is an economic but not a lucrative purpose in a strict sense (PECOL 2015).

12.2 Interpreting the New Role of Co-operatives that Pursue Social Aims

Co-operative development is an ongoing process. The history of co-operatives corroborates that new co-operatives tend to emerge either when markets fail or when security systems created either by the State (mainly in industrialized countries, particularly in Europe), or by families or larger communities (particularly, but not exclusively, in developing countries) are no longer sustainable, leaving significant gaps in the provision of goods and services.[3] The political, economic, and social transformations that occurred over the past decades have provided co-operatives with new opportunities to reaffirm their ability to tackle social and economic concerns affecting local communities. In several countries, new co-operative forms have emerged to supply services of general interest beyond the 'boundaries' of co-ops' membership and thus fill gaps in the delivery of public services. This trend has undermined the traditional model of the co-operative, based on a single stakeholding system and on the identification of members and users, and led to openness and readiness for having additional bearers of interests that share the duties and benefits of the organization (Levi, 1999).[4] The new types of co-operatives that have been established over the past three decades are strongly rooted in forms of collective awareness, such as the need to promote social justice, protect the environment, support the social and professional integration of disadvantaged individuals, and sustain the development of marginalized and depressed localities. In new types of co-operatives pursuing social goals, collective benefits are not simply induced by economic activity; rather, they are a key feature that motivates members to undertake the activity (Defourny and Nyssens, 2012).

Laidlaw was the first observer who shed light on the revitalization of co-operatives' social commitment. In the speech he delivered in the year 1980 at the ICA Conference in Moscow, Laidlaw highlighted the ability of co-operatives to meet arising social needs and emphasized the new spaces of action opened up by the difficulties the welfare system faced worldwide. Laidlaw acknowledged the roles co-operatives could play in providing key services to the community beyond the traditional fields that co-operatives engaged in at a time when the global co-operative movement was experiencing a deep crisis that was mainly caused by the need to maintain co-operatives' distinctiveness from the private sector in the Western part of the world, and to escape the dominating influences of the State in communist and socialist countries (Galera 2004).

Along the same lines, by introducing the seventh principle, 'concern for community', the Statement of Co-operative Identity and Principles adopted by the ICA in 1995 endorses the revitalization of the social dimension of co-operatives. The rationale

---

[3] Ibid.

[4] Y. Levi, 'Communiy and Hybrid Multi-Stakeholder Cooperatives: A Comparison', *Review of International Co-operation*, 92 (1999), 83–94.

behind the introduction of the seventh principle is to counter co-operatives' tendency to emphasize the economic benefits of membership, which result from the distribution of surpluses in proportion to members' participation, over the social impact. By endorsing the connection between co-operatives and their communities, this principle highlights co-operatives' responsibility to care for the communities in which they operate (MacPherson 2012), thus acknowledging the inclination of some co-operatives to pursue general interest aims.

The evolution of the co-operative form towards the pursuit of social aims has occurred in different periods across an increasing number of countries with profoundly dissimilar characteristics. Differences across countries concern, among other issues, the prevalent co-operative traditions and cultures, how co-operatives are considered under national laws, and the status they enjoy at the national level. Such differences have contributed to shaping the new role of co-operatives in different ways across countries.

This said, the revitalization of the community dimension of co-operatives is expected to increase in importance over future years, both in urban and rural contexts in developed and in emerging economies, given the increasing complexity of society, the growing demand for social and health services, and the ongoing environmental degradation (Becchetti and Borzaga 2010).

12.3 A Worldwide Snapshot of Social and Solidarity Co-operatives

New co-operative forms, whose salient feature is community development, have emerged in a pragmatic way to care for elderly people, children, and disadvantaged persons, and to provide basic services, such as healthcare and other social support services. In Finland, Sweden, and Japan, where the existing legal systems do not pose obstacles to co-operatives that decide to take on new responsibilities, the evolution of traditional co-operatives towards a stronger social commitment has occurred naturally. Conversely, in countries like Italy, Spain, Portugal, France, and Germany, this evolution was technically not admissable due to the legislation in force: hence, the emergence of new co-operative forms presupposed either a legal adjustment or the introduction of new legislations, which would have to formalize the creation of new types of co-operatives. Depending on the country, new co-operatives have thus been recognized by law and named 'social co-operative', 'social solidarity co-operative', 'social initiative co-operative', 'solidarity co-operative', and 'collective interest co-operative society'.

The development of new co-operative forms has found great resonance initially in countries whose national legal systems presuppose that co-operatives perform a social function. However, more recently, co-operative evolution has also affected countries where such enterprises traditionally do not have a social orientation; but rather, have been designed to provide advantages primarily to their members (Beuthien 1989).[5] In Germany, for instance, recognizing this innovative co-operative trend has meant breaking with the strict observance of the mutuality principle and the clear economic orientation of co-operatives.

Over the last decade, this evolutionary trend has also cut across countries where co-operatives notably have a negative image, because they are often regarded as a relict of the previous Communist regime, thus contributing to their revitalization, for instance in Poland, Hungary, and Croatia. As an ongoing process, co-operative evolution is presently reaching many new EU members and candidate countries, like Serbia, that are facing severe social and economic problems. Also countries and regions outside Europe, such as Japan, South Korea, and Quebec, have been characterized by the strengthening of co-operatives' social commitment.

Interestingly, the fields in which the new social and solidarity co-operatives operate differ significantly, depending on various factors, including contextual characteristics, and limitations imposed by national legislations. While in some countries, the new co-operatives are engaged in the provision of welfare services, in others, they exclusively support work integration. Finally, in a third group of countries, co-operatives perform in a wide set of economic sectors with a view to supporting local economic development. The next paragraph provides a snapshot of the main fields of development of social and solidarity co-operatives in a selected number of countries and regions: Italy, Poland, France, Quebec, Japan, Portugal, Croatia Sweden, Greece, and Germany. The rationale for selecting these cases is that they show distinctive paths of development for co-operatives towards an explicit social commitment.

12.3.1 Co-operatives as Providers of Welfare Services

In Italy, which is characterized by a weakly developed welfare system when compared to other EU countries, the use of the co-operative form for the management of welfare activities of different kinds by groups of volunteers became rapidly widespread after beginning in the late 1970s. The newly established co-operatives responded to unmet needs and often relied mostly on voluntary work, especially in the start-up phase. These experiences played a role in raising awareness among public authorities about the importance of specific economic and social issues that had so far been largely ignored by public policies. Over the years, social co-operatives have thus succeeded in organizing tangible responses by instigating entrepreneurial action and by mobilizing a mix of resources. Social co-operatives have been formally acknowledged by law 381/1991, which allows for the broadening of the aims of co-operative enterprises and the prevalence of the general interest over the mutual aim. Specifically, according to this law, social co-operatives are created to 'pursue

[5] V. Beuthien, 'Wie genossenschaftlich ist die Genossenschaft?', in V. Beuthien, Genossenschaftsrecht: Woher—wohin?, Marburger Schriften zum Genossenschaftswesen 69, (Gottingen: Marburg IfG, 1989), 15.

the general interest of the community in promoting personal growth and in integrating people into society by providing social, welfare and educational services and carrying out different activities for the purposes of providing employment for disadvantaged people' (Law 381/1991). The law distinguishes two types of social co-operatives: social co-operatives that supply social services (A-type social co-operatives) and social co-operatives that integrate vulnerable persons into work (B-type social co-operatives). A-type co-operatives offer a wide range of services to different population groups, including the elderly, minors, the disabled, drug addicts, the homeless, and immigrants. Ever since they were created, social co-operatives have registered an average annual growth rate ranging from 10 to 20 per cent. Indeed, they increased in number from a little over 2,000 before regulation up to nearly double that number (3,900 units) in 1996, reaching 7,363 entities in year 2005 (ISTAT—National Institute for Statistics 2007). In 2011, there were 12,264 social co-operatives, which employed 365,006 workers,[6] and supplied about 50 per cent of the total provision of welfare services. The average was 32.41 employees per co-operative, which means that 613 people out of each 100,000 inhabitants in Italy are employed by social co-operatives. Other than ordinary workers, social co-operatives also employ a large number of volunteers, who amounted to 42,000 in 2011 (ISTAT 2011).

Unlike in Italy, where social co-operatives turned into a key welfare provider quite quickly, in Sweden, new types of co-operatives emerged in the 1980s in market niches, such as the childcare domain, where municipal services were lacking. Parents took these matters in their own hands by starting day care services according to their own preferences (Pestoff 1998) and, therefore, offered a pedagogical alternative to the childcare provided by local councils. Since 1985 parent co-operatives have been allowed to receive public funding and today they provide between 10 per cent and 15 per cent of childcare in Sweden (Vamstad 2012).

In Japan, health co-operatives have emerged to respond to the diversified needs of an increasingly heterogeneous society (Kitajima and Takato 2008). Traditional agricultural and consumer co-operatives started to engage in the social healthcare domain to support users' participation and contribute to building 'healthy communities'. Agricultural co-operatives (Koseiren) provide healthcare services in rural communities, where aged population rates are higher. Health co-operatives, dating back to 1948 when the Consumer Co-operative Act was enacted, provide medical services in urban areas and have a unique community approach to healthcare. Health co-operatives perform a prominent role: over the past 30 years, consumer co-operatives have established 120 health co-operatives representing nearly 3 million members (Restakis 2010).

12.3.2 Co-operatives as Tools for Social Inclusion

Work integration is the field where new types of co-operatives have developed the most. Work integration co-operatives are an institutional mechanism of supported employment that favours workers discriminated against by conventional enterprises.

---

[6] This figure includes permanent, external, and temporary workers.

Work integration co-operatives provide such workers with the appropriate on-the-job training to help them overcome their disadvantages (Borzaga 2007). Workers discriminated against include people who are 'disabled' as well as those who face systematic limitations preventing them from performing jobs according to accepted standards (Borzaga et al. 2001). Important and continuing barriers to employment include a lack of formal education, low skills and cognitive abilities, physical and mental problems, drug and alcohol abuse, and unstable housing arrangements (Deavers and Hattiangadi 1998).

The pioneering role of these enterprises is demonstrated by their early successes in implementing active labour-market policies bottom-up, before such policies became institutionalized and started to be adopted by public authorities (Defourny and Nyssens 2008). The philosophy of work integration co-operatives (B-type co-operatives), which emerged initially in Italy, was to empower and integrate marginalized people. Against this background, disadvantaged workers have been encouraged to participate in work integration co-operatives that offer them an opportunity to reassess the role of work in their lives and to gain control over their personal projects. This conception implies assisting disadvantaged workers, not only in developing an occupation, but also in acquiring specific values through democratic management structures (Borzaga et al. 2008). In Italy, B-type co-operatives are required by law to hire at least 30 per cent of their staff from disadvantaged categories. They are allowed to carry out any kind of economic activities excluding the production of social services. In exchange, their social security contributions are tax deductible and they may receive government subsidies.

Starting in 1991, other countries, including Portugal, Spain, Poland, Hungary, the Czech Republic, and Croatia, followed Italy's path and acknowledged the possibility of creating work integration social enterprises in the form of co-operatives (Borzaga and Galera 2012b).

In Portugal, where 'social solidarity' is a permitted area of activity for service co-operatives (Decree no. 323/81), and 'special education and work integration co-operatives' were recognized in 1982 (Decree no. 441-A/82, Article 3), as a result of the 1974 Portuguese democratic revolution, the legislature gathered the various existing forms of co-operative with a social purpose under a single definition in 1998 (Perista and Nogueira, 2006). To this end, a new form of co-operative was introduced: the 'social solidarity co-operative' (CSS),[7] which can offer welfare services and carry out work integration activities at the same time. Social solidarity co-operatives are supposed to play an active role against social exclusion, which is not limited to the rehabilitation of disabled persons, but covers also the support given to elderly people and the inclusion of both socially disadvantaged individuals and communities. This overlap of objectives was probably the reason for the scant success of this law; in 2014, as few as 108 social solidarity co-operatives were operating in Portugal (ICF GHK 2014).

In Poland, the development of social co-operatives specifically designed to provide employment opportunities for disadvantaged people started after the introduction of two pieces of legislation in 2003: the Act on Social Employment and the Act on the

---

[7] Cooperativas de solidariedade social.

Employment Promotion and Institutions of the Labour Market. Both acts contributed to the institutional and legal recognition of third-sector institutions and acknowledged social co-operatives as a special type of worker co-operative. The range of services that this type of co-operative can offer is very varied, and includes, inter alia, both social-welfare services and interventions to redevelop and care for green spaces. In its original formulation, the law required that 80 per cent of the co-operative's workforce belong to a category of disadvantaged individuals. Consequently, these co-operatives were more like sheltered workshops than work integration enterprises. This quota was subsequently reduced to 50 per cent, in order to ensure a more balanced composition of the workforce between non-disadvantaged and disadvantaged workers. There are currently approximately 1,000 social co-operatives in Poland (ICF GHK 2014a).

In Greece, Law 2716/99 on the 'Development and Modernization of the Ministry of Health's Mental Health Services' supports the development of co-operatives to promote the social and work inclusion of persons with psychiatric issues (Koi.S.P.E), whereas Croatia recognized social co-operatives in 2011 with the introduction of a new article in the Co-operatives Act (Official Gazette 34/11). This revision of the law was supported by part of the co-operative movement, which promotes employment inclusion projects through the use of work co-operatives. This is a first acknowledgment of a new form of co-operative, which, however, is still incomplete. By omitting to specify the characteristics that social co-operatives must possess, the legislature has left co-operatives entirely free to classify themselves as social co-operatives (ICF GHK 2014b). In the Czech Republic, Act 90 of 2012 on Trading Companies introduced the social co-operative form with the sole purpose of supporting the social and employment inclusion of disadvantaged individuals. According to this law, social co-operatives are also required to satisfy local needs through the optimal use of local resources. They must comply with a profit distribution constraint and have to be managed in accordance with democratic principles (ICF GHK 2014c). However, at the time of writing there is no information about any *ex lege* social co-operative that is operative in the Czech Republic. One explanation is the lack of engagement of practitioners and co-operative leaders in the process of drafting the new co-operative legislation. Another possible reason is that co-operatives are, to a certain extent, still regarded as a relic of the communist period.

12.3.3   Co-operatives as Vehicles for Local Development

In some countries and regions, the role of new co-operatives has been interpreted broadly as a means whereby local development can be supported. New co-operative models have been designed in Quebec, France, and Greece to offer avenues for partnerships to emerge between different actors, including civil society and public organizations in a variety of domains. These include the supply of general-interest services, as well as local development strategies in the agricultural domain and in depopulated rural areas.

In Quebec, starting from the ambulance transportation service, co-operatives have expanded to a number of sectors, by making use of the whole range of co-operative typologies, including traditional ones such as consumer, worker, and producer co-operatives, as well as a new type of co-operative: solidarity co-operatives. During the 1990s, there was a growth in the number of co-operatives that provided homecare services, particularly to elderly persons. The proliferation of solidarity co-operatives was linked to the necessity to answer a number of unmet needs at the local level: support local development strategies, contrast the closing of essential services in small villages, sustain the development of nursery schools, and support the insertion of disadvantaged people in the labour market (Girard 2002). Solidarity co-operatives are most numerous in the services sector with a notable concentration in social services, leisure and personal services, or homecare services. In many cases, they are innovative, not only because they gather diverse stakeholders, but also because of the way they structure or offer services. In 2008, there were more than 30 health co-operatives. Initially, the user co-operative model was the only avenue, but the advent of the solidarity co-operative model in June 1997 led to this form being favoured (Girard and Langlois 2009). Given their associative nature, solidarity co-operatives offer new avenues for partnerships to emerge between civil society, public organizations, and various local forces (Girard 2002).

Similarly, France has also witnessed the emergence of a new co-operative form: the société coopérative d'intèret collectif (SCIC).[8] The goal of the law, which was introduced in 2001, was twofold. On the one hand, the aim was to involve diverse stakeholders (workers, users, volunteers, and funders) by means of a democratic and participatory governance system which guarantees the permanence of the social goal of the enterprise. On the other hand, this organization was legitimized to benefit from the advantages of the associative model (access to public funding) and those of the producer co-operatives (ability to pursue commercial activities). Interestingly, the shift of associations towards an entrepreneurial stance is acknowledged by the law regulating SCICs, which prescribes that any declared association can be transformed into a SCIC without changing its legal status. By the end of 2013, there were 332 SCICs, with an average of ten employees and 95 members each (ICF GHK 2014d).

The French law prescribes a multi-stakeholder membership, that is, the existence of at least three member categories, each of which having a different relationship with the activity carried out. Workers and users must appear among the three categories. The opening of the membership to different stakeholder categories allows for a new partnership logic to be established among users, volunteers, workers, and local authorities. The experience of SCIC shows that many social enterprise initiatives have so far developed in the agricultural domain, where co-operatives were already undergoing an evolution towards a multi-actor model. As a result, such agricultural co-operatives saw in this new form of enterprise the opportunity to develop new activities aimed at supporting rural development according to a partnership logic in which local authorities could be engaged in the governing body of the co-operative.

---

[8] InfoScic, Société Coopérative d'Intéret Collectif, *Bullettin de liaison des acteur du Réseau Scic*, n°3, 2000, juillet.

In Greece, Law 4019/2011 on the 'Social Economy and Social Enterprises' introduced three categories of social co-operative (Koin.S.Ep.), which are expected to perform in a wide set of fields of general interest. These include: i) social co-operatives that promote the inclusion of vulnerable social groups. In this case, at least 40 per cent of the workforce must fall within the category of vulnerable persons; ii) social co-operatives providing social and welfare services to particular groups, such as the elderly, children, the disabled, or persons with chronic pathologies; and iii) social co-operatives that produce goods and services to satisfy the collective needs of the community in the broad sense (cultural, ecological, environmental, educational, etc.). In 2014, social co-operatives formed under the 2011 law amounted to approximately 530. Of these, however, only one or two hundred were fully operational, while the remainder were still at a preliminary planning stage (ICF GHK 2014e).

The major revision of the German Cooperative Societies Act (GenG) in 2006 has very clearly put new-style co-operatives with a social mission at the same level as traditional ones. Prior to that, the focus of the GenG was on the economic objectives of co-operatives and their members. With the revision, the act explicitly acknowledges co-operatives with an explicit social or cultural mission (Sozialgenossenschaften, Kulturgenossenschaften—although other forms of co-operatives can also focus on social objectives), and these can be incorporated as such. The policy towards these 'socially oriented' co-operatives is flexible: they can focus on non-market oriented self-help or solidarity activities by relying heavily on volunteer work. They can also be more entrepreneurial by establishing themselves in market niches that were not sufficiently serviced by traditional actors (see e.g. village shops in depopulated rural areas) (ICF GHK 2015).

12.4 Closing Remarks

Alongside the long-established co-operative enterprises (agricultural supply and marketing societies, credit societies, consumer societies, etc.), growing in the last decades into large-scale enterprises, new co-operative fields of development have emerged. The changing role of the state as regulator, rather than provider, and the emerging of new and unsolved social and environmental problems have significantly boosted the upsurge of new co-operatives and their successful entry into public-sector activities, thanks to their capacity of integrating different interests, such as member good and common good, as well as personal and societal gain (Lorendahl 1997).[9]

The expansion of co-operatives into new fields of activity that are of interest to local communities has been particularly significant in some countries and almost absent in others, and such development has occurred at different times. Whereas in some countries co-operatives now dominate the delivery of social services (e.g. Italy), in others

---

[9] B. Lorendhal, 'Integrating the Public And Cooperative/Social Economy, towards a new Swedish Model', *Annals of Public and Cooperative Economics*, 68(3) (1997), 387.

they compete with other organizational forms such as, for instance, associations in France. In some other countries, the emergence of new co-operative forms with a declared social focus is a recent development (e.g. Germany). In the Italian case, the role of legislation has been crucial in boosting the development of co-operatives pursuing an explicit social aim. Conversely, in some other cases, legislation has failed to support the widespread replication of new co-operative types (e.g. Portugal). In principle, the comparative analysis of co-operative legal evolution corroborates that legislation has been successful when it has managed to capture an ongoing evolution that was already taking place from the bottom up. This was the case in Italy and Quebec as far as both welfare delivery and work integration social co-operatives are concerned. This was also the case in agricultural co-operatives in France, which seized the opportunity offered by the SCIC legislation to create multi-partnership co-operatives in rural areas. On the contrary, when it was introduced top down, legislation normally failed to boost co-operatives' replication. This is precisely the case in the Czech Republic where no social co-operatives have so far been created, despite the existence of an ad hoc legislation.

As far as the fields of engagement of co-operatives are concerned, social services and work integration of people at risk of labour exclusion are still the main new fields of activity of co-operatives explicitly pursuing social aims. However, given their intrinsic characteristics, co-operatives are suited to develop also in many other areas that are of general interest.

In Europe, co-operatives have developed most rapidly where their expansion has been unhindered by inadequate regulation, their roles are fully recognized, and their operations have not been confined to specific sectors (Zamagni 2012). To develop co-operatives' full potential, co-operative law must recognize the roles of co-operatives and be flexible enough to permit co-operatives to operate in whatever industry in which they prove to be useful (Hansmann 2012). This includes sectors that benefit from public funding, have been traditionally public, and are of public interest, like the sector of general economic interest services. At the same time, to fully seize the opportunities offered by the current social and economic transformations that call for innovative and participatory modalities of production and consumption, management practices that are more consistent with the values and principles of co-operatives should be adopted. In essence, to reaffirm the collective awareness that boosted co-operative success in the nineteenth century, co-operatives pursuing explicit social aims should further strengthen their links with local communities and adopt inclusive governance models that allow for a fair representation of different stakeholders.

References

Becchetti, L. and Borzaga, C., eds (2010), *The Economics of Social Responsibility: The World of Social Enterprises* (London: Routledge).

Beuthien, V. (1989), 'Wie genossenschaftlich ist die Genossenschaft?', in V. Beuthien, *Genossenschaftsrecht: Woher – wohin?* Marburger Schriften zum Genossenschaftswesen 69 (Gottingen: Marburg IfG), 15.

Borzaga, C. (2007), 'Evoluzione recente, stato e prospettive della cooperazione sociale', *Impresa Sociale*, 76(3), 53–68.

Borzaga, C. and Galera, G. (2012a), 'Promoting the Understanding of Co-operatives for a Better World, Euricse Contribution to the International Year of Co-operatives', in *Conference Report Promoting the Understanding of Co-operatives for a Better World* (Trento: Euricse Publishing).

Borzaga, C. and Galera, G. (2012b), 'The Concept and Practice of Social Enterprise: Lessons from the Italian Experience', *International Review of Social Research*, 2(2), 85–102.

Borzaga, C., Galera, G., and Nogales, R. (2008), 'Social Enterprise: A New Model for Poverty Reduction and Employment Generation', Bratislava: UNDP Regional Bureau for Europe and the Commonwealth of Independent States.

Borzaga, C., Gui, B., and Povinelli, F. (2001), 'The Specific Role of Non-Profit Organizations in the Integration of Disadvantaged People: Insights from Economic Analysis', in R. Spear, J. Defourny, L. Favreau, and J-L. Laville, eds, *Tackling Social Exclusion in Europe: The Contribution of the Social Economy* (Aldershot: Ashgate), 267–86.

Deavers, K. L. and Hattiangadi, A. U. (1998), 'Welfare to Work: Building a Better Path to Private Employment Opportunities, *Journal of Labor Research*, 19(2), 205–28.

Defourny, J. and Nyssens, M. (2008), Social Enterprise in Europe: Recent Trends and Developments', *Social Enterprise Journal*, 4(3), 202–28.

Defourny, J. and Nyssens, M. (2012), 'Social Co-operatives: When Social Enterprise Meets the Co-operative Tradition'. Paper presented at the Euricse Conference, Promoting the Understanding of Co-operatives for a Better World, Venice.

Diario da Republica, 1.ª serie, nº 279, de 04.12.1981, Pág. 3172. Decree no. 323/81 of 4 December 1981.

Fajardo, Gemma, Fici, Antonio, Henrÿ, Hagen, Hiez, David, Meira, Deolinda A., Münkner, Hans-H., and Snaith, Ian (forthcoming), *Principles of European Cooperative Law. Principles, Commentaires and National Reports* (International Publications, Intersentia nv (Belgium)).

Galera, G. (2004), 'The Evolution of the Co-operative Form: An International Perspective', in C. Borzaga, and R. Spear, eds, *Trends and Challenges for Co-operatives and Social Enterprises in Developed and Transition Countries* (Trento: Edizioni 31), 17–38.

Girard, J. P. (2002), 'The Solidarity Co-Operative Movement in Quebec: A New Formula in North America'. Report prepared for the International Organization of Industrial, Artisanal and Service Producers' Co-operatives (CICOPA).

Girard, J. P. and Langlois, G. (2009), 'Solidarity Co-operatives (Québec, Canada): How Social Enterprises can Combine Social and Economic Goals?' in A. Noya, ed., *The Changing Boundaries of Social Enterprises* (Paris: OECD Publishing), 229–71.

Hansmann, H. B. (2012), 'All Firms are Co-operatives–and so are Governments'. Paper presented at the Euricse conference, Promoting the Understanding of Co-operatives for a Better World, Venice.

InfoScic, Société Coopérative d'Intéret Collectif, (2000), Bullettin de liaison des acteur du Réseau Scic, 3, juillet.

ICF GHK consulting (2014), *A Map of Social Enterprises and their Eco-systems in Europe. Country report: Portugal* (Brussels: European Commission).

ICF GHK consulting (2014a), *A Map of Social Enterprises and their Eco-systems in Europe. Country report: Poland* (Brussels: European Commission).

ICF GHK consulting (2014b), *A Map of Social Enterprises and their Eco-systems in Europe. Country report: Croatia* (Brussels: European Commission).

ICF GHK consulting (2014c), *A Map of Social Enterprises and their Eco-systems in Europe. Country report: Czech Republic* (Brussels: European Commission).

ICF GHK consulting (2014d), *A Map of Social Enterprises and their Eco-systems in Europe. Country report: France* (Brussels: European Commission).

ICF GHK consulting (2014e), *A Map of Social Enterprises and their Eco-systems in Europe. Country report: Greece* (Brussels: European Commission).

ICF GHK consulting (2015), *A Map of Social Enterprises and their Eco-systems in Europe. Country report: Germany* (Brussels: European Commission).

ISTAT, National Institute for Statistics (2007), *Le cooperative sociali in Italia: Anno 2005* (*Statistiche in Breve*: Rome).

ISTAT, National Institute for Statistics (2011), *9° Censimento dell'industria e dei servizi e Censimento delle Istituzioni non profit*, Rome).

Kitajima, N. and Takato, M. (2008), 'Health Co-operatives in Japan and the Nagano Health Co-operative', in C. Leviten-Reid, ed., Report of the International Conference, The Role of Co-operatives in Health Care: National and International Perspectives (Saskatoon: Centre for the Study of Co-operatives, University of Saskatchewan), 5–8.

Levi, Y. (1999), 'Community and Hybrid Multi-Stakeholder Co-operatives: A Comparison', *Review of International Co-operation*, 92, 83–94.

Lorendahl, B. (1997), 'Integrating the Public and Co-operative/Social Economy: Towards a New Swedish Model', *Annals of Public and Co-operative Economics*, 68(3), 387.

MacPherson, I. (2012), 'Co-operatives' Concern for the Community: From Members towards Local Communities' Interests'. Paper presented at the Euricse Conference Promoting the Understanding of Co-operatives for a Better World, Venice.

Mogrovejo, R., Mora, A., and Vanhuynegem, P. (2012), *El cooperativismo en América Latina: Una diversidad de contribuciones al desarrollo sostenible*, La Paz: OIT,. Available at http://www.ilo.org/wcmsp5/groups/public/---americas/---ro-lima/documents/publication/wcms_188087.pdf (accessed 12 September, 2016).

Official Gazette of the Republic of Croatia 34/2011, Decree no. 441-A/82, Article 3, *Co-operatives Act*.

Official Gazette of the Italian Republic, Law 381 of November 8, *Act on Social Cooperatives*.

PECOL, Study Group on European Co-operative Law (SGECOL), 'Draft Principles of European Co-operative Law' (draft PECOL) May 2015.

Perista, H. and Nogueira, S. (2006), 'Work Integration Social Enterprises in Portugal', EMES Working Paper, WP no. 04/06.

Pestoff, V. A. (1998), *Beyond the Market and State: Social Enterprises and Civil Democracy in a Welfare Society* (Aldershot: Ashgate & English Editions).

Restakis, J. (2010), *Humanizing the Economy: Co-operatives in the Age of Capital* (Gabriola Island, Canada: New Society Publisher).

Todev, T., Brazda, J., and Schediwy, R. (1993), 'Quo Vadis Co-operative Movement in Eastern Europe? in G. Turner, ed., *Economic Changes in Eastern Europe: Quo Vadis Co-operative Movement?* Berliner Hefte zum internationalen Genossenschaftswesen, 1 (Berlin: Institut für Genossenschaftswesen an der Humboldt-Universität).

Vamstad, J. (2012), 'Co-Production and Service Quality: A New Perspective for the Swedish Welfare State', in V. A. Pestoff, T. Brandsen, and B. Verschuere, eds, *New Public Governance: The Third Sector and Co-Production* (New York: Routledge), 297–316.

Zamagni, V. (2012), 'Interpreting the Roles and Economic Importance of Co-operative Enterprises in a Historical Perspective'. Paper presented at the Euricse conference, Promoting the Understanding of Co-operatives for a Better World, Venice.

....

CHAPTER 13

COMMUNITY CO-OPERATIVES AND CO-OPERATIVES PROVIDING PUBLIC SERVICES

facts and prospects

....

PIER ANGELO MORI

13.1 INTRODUCTION

....

THE first co-operatives running public utilities appeared at the turn of the nineteenth century, not much later than the three major types of traditional co-operatives, that is, worker co-operatives, consumer co-operatives, and co-operative banks. They were all engaged in power and water provision and were set up and controlled by customers similarly to consumer co-operatives and co-operative banks. Up to now they have lagged behind the main co-operative types and their present incidence is quite small. This is mainly the result of policies which led governments to take over most essential services. However, a new scenario is now taking shape which opens up new opportunities for co-operatives' entry into this sector. In this chapter we argue that customer ownership can help overcome some of the most challenging issues presently affecting public services, in particular, information asymmetries on service quality and regulation failures.

13.2 UTILITY AND COMMUNITY CO-OPERATIVES

....

Though there is a widely accepted idea of what a co-operative enterprise is, several concepts are actually in use that underscore different co-operative models. Therefore, before introducing utility and community co-operatives, we first need to shed some light on this issue.

A common feature of co-operatives in every country and period is their being democratic organizations, that is, controlled by their members according to the principle 'one head, one vote'.[1] This, however, is by no means enough to characterize a co-operative: there are other institutions that are run according to the democratic principle, and something else is needed for a definition. This further element is that to qualify as a member one has to perform some economic function related to the co-operative. More precisely, a co-operative's member must be either a customer of the firm's products or a supplier of some input[2] to it. Business organizations which meet these two requirements—democratic principle and functional membership—encompass most of those named co-operatives around the world. But there is another element that helps further delimit the concept and classify cooperatives: their aims.

For whose benefit are co-operatives run? There are two main cases to be distinguished. In every type of co-operative, members are the controlling party. In most cases they are owners too. Firm ownership in the usual sense comprises two elements, control rights and the right to appropriate the residual. However, in certain co-operatives members lack the right to appropriate the residual, as they act not in their own interest but in the interest of the community to which they belong. In one case the co-operative's aim is member benefit, in the other community benefit.[3]

Up until the late twentieth century, member benefit was the single aim of all co-operatives then existing, that is, *traditional* co-operatives. In the second half of the century there started to arise new ones that purported to act in the public interest, that is, *public benefit co-operatives*. With them, the concern for society became *explicit* and new models of co-operative organizations joined the traditional ones on the co-operative scene. A foremost example of this new class is the Italian social co-operative, which combines mutuality and the pursuit of community benefit (see Mori 2014, for details). The Italian social co-operative, however, is not the only model of public benefit co-operative. An entirely different philosophy is embodied, for instance, in Community benefit societies (Bencoms), which are one of the organizational types of co-operatives in the UK (Co-operatives UK 2009). Like traditional co-operatives they are owned and democratically controlled by their members but, unlike them, they are run for the exclusive

---

[1] While today most scholars and practitioners would agree that the democratic rule is a primary principle, in the past some, like, for example, Walras 1865, regarded it as a secondary feature and identified other principles as fundamental.

[2] Traditionally, the relevant inputs were required to differ from capital: besides providing a cooperative's equity, members were always required to perform a further economic function like work, purchase of consumer goods, borrowing, etc. This requirement is somewhat relaxed today, as pure investor-members are admitted in some of the new co-operatives (e.g. community finance societies, see Section 13.3), where the absence of economic functions other than that of investor is compensated for by the introduction of specific restrictions (e.g. asset lock) that differentiate these enterprises from capitalist ones.

[3] These are the pure cases but mixed cases are possible too.

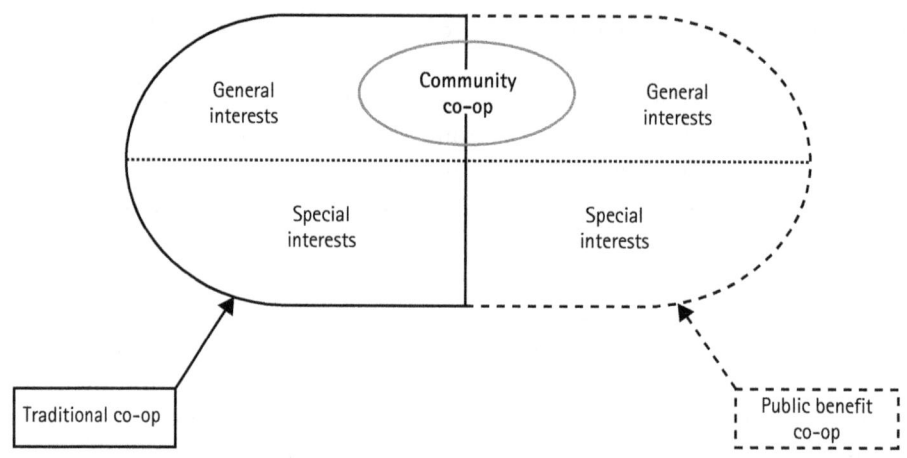

FIGURE 13.1 A classification of co-operatives.

(from Mori 2014)

benefit of their communities.[4] A definition of a co-operative encompassing also these new variants is thus the following: co-operatives are democratic business organizations owned by the suppliers of some input to them or their customers, and run for their mutual benefit or the community benefit.[5] Among them we further distinguish between customer-owned and supplier-owned co-operatives, according to whether their owners are customers of the firm's products or input suppliers.[6]

In summary, two major changes have marked the evolution of the co-operative enterprise. The first occurred at the turn of the nineteenth century and consisted in the enlargement of co-operatives' scope from the provision of special-interest to general-interest goods/services. The second change regarded the organizational mode, more specifically the enlargement of co-operatives' aims to include society's benefit. Four categories of co-operatives can be identified in these changes, each of which is characterized by a combination of an *organizational* type (traditional or public benefit) and a *product* type (general interest or special interest). The four categories constitute an exhaustive classification of co-operatives and are represented by the Venn diagram in Figure 13.1 (borrowed from Mori 2014).

Community co-operatives are business organizations that are citizen (community) owned and provide general-interest goods/services.[7] In Figure 13.1 they lie across the two subsets representing traditional and public benefit co-operatives, which means that they may take either organizational form. Utility/public services co-operatives are those that run public utilities/services. Utility/public services and consumer co-operatives have customer

---

[4] The role of mutuality (member benefit)—in particular whether it is necessary or not—is the subject of a debate that we are not able to review even summarily here for lack of space. We refer to Mori 2014 for further details.

[5] For more details see Mori 2014.

[6] The two functions are not mutually exclusive and may be both present at the same time. The prevalence criterion determines which of the two categories each co-operative falls into.

[7] For a full discussion we refer to Mori 2014.

ownership in common but differ in the business field (retailing vs. public utility/service). Community co-operatives are on the other hand owned by citizens and are not confined to public utilities, nor are they always customer owned (they may be supplier owned too). As a matter of fact, these classes, though closely related, do not coincide, and each would require a separate analysis, but space constraints do not allow us to examine them all. Here we focus on one of the categories showing stronger growth prospects at present, that of utility co-operatives. However, in dealing with them we will in a measure deal with community co-operatives too, since historically the two categories have largely overlapped.

13.3 Co-operation and Public Utilities: A Bird's-Eye View

Co-operatives providing public utilities first arose in the late nineteenth century, mainly in the electricity and water sectors (see Spinicci 2011). They were all customer owned and of the traditional type, that is, run solely for their members' benefit, but had a community streak too, which is why they are to be regarded as the forebears of modern community co-operatives (cf. Mori 2014). If customer-owned utility co-operatives were the first to arise, and still maintain prominence, they are not the only possible type; more recently supplier-owned ones have begun to appear too.

The renewable-energy co-operatives which are arising today in many parts of the world are not easy to classify on the basis of the customer vs. supplier ownership criterion (Mori 2013). A frequent pattern with these co-operatives is the following. A co-operative is established by a group of people who come together with some capital to be invested in a renewable generation project (wind, solar, etc.); the co-operative enters into feed-in tariff (FIT) agreements with a retailer which in turn applies preferential rates to the co-op's members.[8] Member benefit then comprises a return on capital (often subject to a dividend cap) and lower rates to individual members as customers of the external power supplier. If the benefit provided to members as power users is predominant, the economic function of power purchase is prevalent over the others and we are in the case of customer-owned co-operatives. Sometimes, however, member benefit from trade with the co-operative is limited or inexistent, as in the case of UK's community finance societies,[9] which invest in renewable energy,[10] and such co-operatives indeed fall into the category of supplier-owned ones.[11]

---

[8] See Willis and Willis 2012 with reference to Britain, but the same basic scheme is found with minor variations in other countries as well.

[9] A specific kind of co-operative in that country, see Cooperatives UK 2009, 32.

[10] For example, Baywind Energy Co-operative Ltd. in Cumbria (UK) http://www.baywind.co.uk (accessed 12 September 2012).

[11] There is an analogy between these and some producer co-operatives like, for example, agricultural manufacturing co-ops. In the latter, farmer–owners feed in their produce as an input for

In Europe, market liberalization has been a major stimulus for the entry of new co-operative providers into public services.[12] A comprehensive picture of what has been going on in this field is so far missing, but certainly the most relevant sector was and remains energy. New energy co-operatives have arisen in almost all European countries in recent years and in some of them (notably Germany) they are among the most dynamic actors in the market. Community renewable energy initiatives have cropped up in several countries: Germany, Austria, Britain, Denmark, Italy, and others (see Dubois and Saplacan 2010; Schreuer and Weismeier-Sammer 2010). In Germany more than 350 new electric co-operatives are reported to have arisen since the liberalization of the energy market in 1998 (Müller and Holstenkamp 2012).[13] Some of them are engaged in production without retailing, while others are customer owned and engaged in distribution too. In France, besides a large electric co-operative (Enercoop SCIC, 50,000 members), there exist various SICAE (*Sociétés d'intérêt collectif agricole d'electricité*) producing renewable energy with a total of about 250,000 customers. In Denmark wind power co-operatives total about 150,000 members and there exist over 2,500 small water co-operatives.[14] In Austria, 12 per cent of rural water services are co-operative-based (Bauby 2012). In Britain, community interest co-operatives (CIC) running wind, hydro, and photovoltaic power generation are spreading fast, but here too data is unsystematic.[15] In Finland, the majority of water companies with less than 1,000 customers, mainly located in rural areas, are co-operatives.[16] Outside Europe, the phenomenon is widely present too. In the United States electric co-operatives (supply only) are a very strong reality in the countryside where, according to the National Rural Electric Cooperative Association, they serve about 42 million people.[17] Still in the USA, most water systems classified by the U.S. Environmental Protection Agency as 'very small' (less than 500 customers) are customer owned through non-profit co-operatives, homeowners' associations, etc.[18] More rural electric and water co-operatives are reported in Argentina,[19] Canada, the

---

the co-operative's production, while in the former, members provide capital which is the major input for the co-operative's activity (but, differently from for-profit firms, within a democratic governance framework).

[12] For a survey of liberalization policies in public services in Europe, see Hermann et al. 2008. On liberalization in network industries, see Finger and Laperrouza 2011. Similar phenomena, though in a different institutional context, are reported in the USA (Wilson et al. 2008) and in some developing countries too (Yadoo and Cruickshank 2010).

[13] For more on Germany, see Mautz et al. 2008.

[14] The data is reported in Hukka and Katko 2009.

[15] More than 30 new establishments classified as co-operatives by Co-operatives UK are reported to have arisen since 2008 (Willis and Willis 2012). Energyshare.com reports many new projects in these fields throughout the country but no survey seems to have been made so far.

[16] According to Takala et al. 2011, there are about 1,400 in total.

[17] See section 'Co-op Facts & Figures' at http://www.nreca.coop (accessed 23 September 2016).

[18] According to a report by the National Rural Water Association (NRWA 2004).

[19] FACE (Federación Argentina de Cooperativas de Electricidad y Otros Servicios Públicos) reports that 10% of electric power is provided by co-operatives and 58% of rural customers are served by co-operatives. The total number of associates is over 180 co-operatives nationwide (http://www.face.coop/es/servicios/el-cooperativismo-en-cifras/ accessed 13 September 2016).

Philippines,[20] and other countries.[21] Cases of customer-owned co-operatives are also found outside the electricity and water sectors, as e.g. in telecommunications (Finland, USA, Argentina, and Bolivia; see Calzada and Dávalos, 2005) and in natural gas distribution (Canada),[22] but they are presently sparse and marginal. If this is the present picture, what are the sector's prospects?

13.4 PRIVATIZATION OF PUBLIC UTILITIES AND CO-OPERATIVES

A sharp line must be drawn between market liberalization and privatization with regard to the birth of new co-operatives in the field of public services. Liberalization has generally led to the entry of new market players, some of which are co-operatives. The energy sector is a significant example. On the other hand, the privatization of monopoly or restricted-entry markets has so far involved co-operatives marginally. In the face of this, there are quite a few reasons why the hand-over of monopoly services to *customer-owned* co-operatives should be given due consideration as a policy option.

The structure of the water and electricity sectors that took shape at the beginning of their history was to remain stable for almost a century. In Europe, the majority of public utilities were government owned for most of the twentieth century, and in a minority of cases private for-profit operators were active under a variety of arrangements with governments (Millward 2005). In the interstices of this bi-partite framework there stood the historical co-operatives providing public utilities—usually in marginal and poor areas—as exceptions to the rule. Starting from the 1970s a wave of utility privatization spread from the USA and Britain to the rest of Europe and other countries in the West.[23] The idea was that public provision ought to be replaced by private provision for two basic reasons: the supposed inefficiency of public provision and the need to finance new investments, typically in infrastructures.[24] Privatization has so far essentially meant the contracting out of services or the transfer of public enterprises to private investors, whereby services that were once publicly provided have started to be provided by for-profit enterprises, often in monopoly markets.[25] Privatization, however, has not

---

[20] NEA 2011 reports a total of 119 electric co-operatives.

[21] Even in some of the poorest LDCs like Nepal, Bangladesh, etc. (Yadoo and Cruickshank 2010).

[22] The Federation of Alberta Gas Co-ops comprises 81 natural gas utilities of which 59 are co-operatives, and claims to be 'the largest rural gas system in the world' (http://www.fedgas.com/ (accessed 13 September 2016).

[23] And some developing countries too (Yadoo and Cruickshank 2010). Here, however, we focus on developed countries.

[24] See Bognetti and Obermann 2008.

[25] Privatization often concerns monopoly markets. Liberalization brings competition into the liberalized market as government retreats; with privatization we often have government's retreat but no competition in the market (at most competition *for* the market).

lived up to expectations and quite soon started to reveal flaws, which have been fuelling widespread political opposition. As a consequence, a few initiated privatization projects came to a stop and new privatization plans have been blocked in several countries. Water is an emblematic case in this regard. The past fifteen years have witnessed the failure of a few water privatization projects in South America (e.g. Cochabamba, Bolivia, around the year 2000) and Europe (e.g. Wales in the same period). Moreover, campaigns have raged against water privatization in a number of countries (Hall et al. 2005).

What are the motivations for the growing opposition to privatization? Rate increases have certainly played a major role (as in the Cochabamba and Wales cases). Price regulation can in principle deal with this issue satisfactorily but in practice is often marred by several problems: governments and their agencies may not be competent enough, or sufficiently informed, or may not have sufficient power to regulate effectively; officials may collude with regulated firms, etc.[26] If the failures of regulation—and of price regulation in particular—are one of the main issues facing public utilities today, they are by no means the only one.

Another irksome issue is service quality, which public utilities share with many other productions with a public-good feature. The design and running of waste disposal sites is a significant example, but similar problems are exhibited by thermal power plants, wastewater treatment plants, etc. Why do people oppose disposal sites, incinerators, thermal power plants, and similar facilities? Part of the answer is to be sought in compensation mechanisms. If those who suffer negative externalities were fully compensated through monetary or other means—typically by those who enjoy the service but do not suffer its negative drawbacks or suffer them to a lesser extent—there would be no opposition. One problem then is the design of adequate compensation packages, but not the only one.[27] If location—and therefore the choice of the group of people affected by the externalities—is perhaps the biggest *ex ante* issue, an equally important issue is how the facility is run after establishment, for whenever service quality is subject to information asymmetries, there may arise substantial moral hazard problems (Abrardi et al. 2016).

Though facilities like waste disposal sites, incinerators, nuclear power plants, etc., involve significant health hazards, proper operation can abate risk to an acceptable level. Since for-profit enterprises have an incentive to save on operating costs,

---

[26] Criticism of utilities regulation dates back to at least the 1960s and has produced a huge literature, both in economics and political science, which cannot be reviewed even cursorily here. Broadly speaking, research has highlighted two main causes of regulatory failure: *inefficiency*, due to the agency problems besetting regulatory authorities, and *collusion* in various forms, like, for example, regulatory capture. Two titles for all: the survey by Noll 1989 on the former, and Rose-Ackerman 1999 on the latter.

[27] Much of the economic literature on the phenomenon is indeed about compensation packages, see, for example, Kunreuther and Kleindorfer 1986, Mitchell and Carson 1986, Easterling and Kunreuther 1995. For completeness we recall the opposite view, according to which money incentives may be detrimental to civic-duty motivations, as developed in Frey and Oberholzer-Gee 1997 and the ensuing literature on the crowding-out of pro-social motivations.

third-party monitoring of service quality is needed when the service is provided by them. Obviously, here we have a problem similar to the one that we have already encountered. If regulatory authorities are ineffective in controlling prices, they may also fail to effectively monitor service quality for the same basic reasons—inefficiency and collusion. As a consequence, private provision may result in excessive health hazards for the population.

All these facts contribute to the deadlock in which public utilities are mired today in several Western countries. On the one hand, a public finance crisis—most acute in some European countries—severely limits governments' ability to invest, and pushes them to attract private finance to the sector. This causes a thrust towards the contracting-out of services or the sale of public enterprises to for-profit entrepreneurs. On the other hand, citizens' trust in the public authorities which are to monitor or regulate service providers is low and this produces a thrust in the opposite direction, with the undesirable consequence that a complete stall sometimes occurs, as is presently the case for the water sector in Italy. A possible way out of such doldrums is customer ownership, which presents a few potential advantages over alternative organizational arrangements.

The first element to underline is the handling of information in customer-owned enterprises. Information asymmetries about service quality are, as we have argued, a relevant problem for public services. Customer-owned co-operatives allow the problem to be tackled in a radical way: service customers become owners of the service, and in this role they have a legal right of access to internal information, that they would not have in the face of a for-profit provider as simple customers (without being stockholders as well). Moreover, thanks to a co-operative's democratic governance, every citizen-member has the same formal powers as the others, while in for-profit corporations there may be considerable disparities, due to the concentration of capital, which facilitate the manipulation of information by some groups at the expense of others. Thus, transparency, though probably imperfect even in this context, is certainly easier to achieve in co-operatives than in for-profit enterprises, where information is typically private to the management and the controlling stockholders.

A second point is that a customer-owned co-operative's goal is not profit but customer satisfaction, which is likely to translate into higher welfare. As the economic literature shows, embedding consumption motives into the firm's objectives has a generally favourable impact on social welfare, both when the involved goods are public (e.g. Mas-Colell and Silvestre 1991) and private (Farrell 1985; Corneo 1997; Kelsey and Milne 2006, 2008). This fact has relevant implications for regulation. As we have argued, for-profit operators of a public utility need to be regulated by public authorities if they operate in monopoly or markets with limited contestability, but regulation may be ineffective owing to organizational inefficiency, lack of political clout, or collusion. By contrast, if it is citizens themselves who operate the service, the need for government regulation is alleviated (or even annihilated), since regulators can exploit customer-members' control of service operation to enhance the welfare of the whole customer community more effectively and at lower cost than with for-profit providers (in some cases regulation can even be waived altogether).

More complex is the comparison with the public enterprise. Public enterprises are not directly democratic but are controlled by elected governments and therefore are subject to a democratic governance of last resort. This makes them similar to citizen co-operatives, and the advantages of co-operatives that we have mentioned are in principle shared by public enterprises as well. The two modes of democratic governance, however, are different and this may affect the magnitude of these advantages. The literature is not much help here, as focused investigations on this point are still missing. We then limit ourselves to a few general remarks. Though both co-operatives and public enterprises are democratic in a sense, the two modes of democratic governance—co-operative and public—greatly differ between themselves: a citizens' control chain is shorter in the customer-owned co-operative than in the public enterprise, which presumably makes it less costly—thanks to the removal of political costs caused by meddling, corruption, etc.—and more effective. If, for example, customer-citizens want to fire the management of a public enterprise, they have no other means but to vote against their political patrons, a very indirect and diluted form of control, whereas citizen-members can directly vote against the management, or even sue it for misbehaviour. This observation suggests that co-operatives may be more effective in pursuing citizens' aims than their governmental counterparts, but new research is needed on the relative merits of the two forms of enterprise.

Customer ownership, however, not only has advantages but also some potential disadvantages. Two in particular deserve consideration. Co-operatives providing public utilities often have to make substantial investments (recall that one of the main motivations of privatization policies is governments' inability to finance new infrastructures). Customer ownership, as we know, combines democratic control and citizens' responsibility for the management and financing of service provision. This is likely to mean that capital must be raised from a dispersed ownership, which is likely to reduce the amount that can be collected. A further issue is the effectiveness of co-operative democracy. If it is not hard to accept that proper control of management can be exerted by members when they are few, doubts arise with regard to large memberships. Obviously, if control becomes less effective, investors' concentrated ownership becomes relatively more attractive.

In summary, customer ownership of public services has advantages and disadvantages, some of which, however, require further investigation. One point is nonetheless already clear enough. Despite its negligible diffusion to date, customer ownership is a serious alternative to both government ownership and contracted-out operation by for-profit firms—all the more valuable in the face of the privatization deadlock presently besetting public services in some countries. Historically, governments acted as a brake on the development of citizen co-operation, but now is the time for them to reconsider their policy. A change in policy-makers' attitude is indeed the trigger event that was missing in the past, and that could in principle propel customer ownership of public services beyond the niches where today it is entrenched.

REFERENCES

Abrardi, L., Colombo, L., and Mori, P. (2016), 'Customer Ownership and Quality Provision in Public Services under Asymmetric Information', *Economic Inquiry*, 54, 1499–518.

Bauby, P. (2012), 'Local Services of General Economic Interest in Europe: Water Services: What Are the Challenges?' *Annals of Public and Co-operative Economics*, 83, 561–83.

Bognetti, G. and Obermann, G. (2008), 'Liberalization and Privatization of Public Utilities: Origins of the Debate, Current Issues and Challenges for the Future', *Annals of Public and Co-operative Economics*, 79, 461–85.

Calzada, J. and Dávalos, A. (2005), 'Co-operatives in Bolivia: Customer-Ownership of the Local Loop', *Telecommunications Policy*, 29, 387–407.

Co-operatives UK (2009), *Simply Legal* (Manchester: Cooperatives UK).

Corneo, G. G. (1997), 'Taxpayer-Consumers and Public Pricing', *Economics Letters*, 57, 235–40.

Dubois, U. and Saplacan, R. (2010), 'Public Service Perspectives on Reforms of Electricity Distribution and Supply: A Modular Analysis', *Annals of Public and Co-operative Economics*, 81, 313–56.

Easterling, D. and Kunreuther, H. (1995), *The Dilemma of Siting a High-Level Nuclear Waste Repository* (Boston: Kluwer).

Farrell, J. (1985), 'Owner-Consumers and Efficiency', *Economics Letters*, 19, 303–6.

Finger, M. and Laperrouza, M. (2011). 'Liberalization of Network Industries in the European Union: Evolving Policy Issues', in M. Finger and R. W. Künneke, eds, *Handbook of Liberalised Infrastructure Sectors* (London: Edward Elgar), 345–65.

Frey, B. S. and Oberholzer-Gee, F. (1997), 'The Cost of Price Incentives: An Empirical Analysis of Motivation Crowding-Out', *American Economic Review*, 87, 746–55.

Hall, D., Lobina, E., and de la Motte, R. (2005), 'Public Resistance to Privatisation in Water and Energy', *Development in Practice*, 15, 286–301.

Hermann, C., Verhoest, K., Andersson, M., Brandt, T., Hofbauer, I., Schulten, T., and Thörnqvist, C. (2008), 'Varieties and Variations of Public Service Liberalisation and Privatisation', Leuven, Pique Policy Report no. 4.

Hukka, J. J. and Katko, T. S. (2009), 'Complementary Paradigms of Water and Sanitation Services: Lessons from the Finnish Experience', in J. E. Castro and L. Heller, eds, *Water and Sanitation Services: Public Policy and Management* (London: Earthscan), 153–72.

International Labour Organization (ILO) (2002), 'Recommendation Concerning the Promotion of Co-operatives', Recommendation no. 193, Geneva.

Kelsey, D. and Milne, F. (2006), 'Externalities, Monopoly and the Objective Function of the Firm', *Economic Theory*, 29, 565–89.

Kelsey, D. and Milne, F. (2008), 'Imperfect Competition and Corporate Governance', *Journal of Public Economic Theory*, 10, 1115–41.

Kunreuther, H. and Kleindorfer, P. R. (1986), 'A Sealed-Bid Auction Mechanism for Siting Noxious Facilities', *American Economic Review*, 76, Papers and Proceedings: 295–9.

Mas-Colell, A. and Silvestre, J. (1991), 'A Note on Cost-Share Equilibrium and Owner-Consumers', *Journal of Economic Theory*, 54, 204–14.

Mautz, R., Byzio, A., and Rosenbaum, W. (2008), '*Auf dem Weg zur Energiewende: die Entwicklung der Stromproduktion aus erneuerbaren Energien in Deutschland*', (Göttingen: Univeristät-Verlag Göttingen).

Millward, R. (2005), *Private and Public Enterprise in Europe: Energy, Telecommunications and Transport, 1830–1990* (Cambridge: Cambridge University Press).

Mitchell R. C. and Carson R. T. (1986), 'Property Rights, Protest, and the Siting of Hazardous Waste Facilities', *American Economic Review*, 76, Papers and Proceedings, 285–90.

Mori, P. (2013), 'Customer-Ownership of Public Utilities: New Wine in Old Bottles', *Journal of Entrepreneurial and Organizational Diversity*, 2, 54–74.

Mori, P. (2014), 'Community and Cooperation: The Evolution of Co-operatives Towards New Models of Citizens' Democratic Participation in Public Services Provision', *Annals of Public and Co-operative Economics*, 85, 327–52.

Müller, J., R. and Holstenkamp, L. (2012), 'Governance and Financing of German Energy Co-operatives'. Working Paper, Lüneburg: Leuphana University.

National Electrification Administration (NEA), *Annual Report 2011*, Quezon City: NEA.

National Rural Water Association (NRWA) (2004), 'Comparative Advantages of Alternative Forms of Public Ownership for Community Water Supply Systems', White Paper, Boulder (CO).

Noll, R. G. (1989), 'Economic Perspectives on the Politics of Regulation', in R. Schmalensee, and R. D. Willig, eds, *Handbook of Industrial Organization*, vol. II, (Amsterdam: North Holland), 1254–87.

Rose-Ackerman, S. 1999, *Corruption and Government: Causes, Consequences, and Reform* (Cambridge: Cambridge University Press).

Schreuer, A. and Weismeier-Sammer, D. (2010), 'Energy Co-operatives and Local Ownership in the Field of Renewable Energy Technologies: A Literature Review, RICC Report no. 4.

Spinicci, F. (2011), Le cooperative di utenza in Italia e in Europa (Trento: Euricse).

Takala, A. J., Arvonen, V., Katko, T. S., Pietilä, P. E., and Åkerman, M. W. (2011), 'The Evolving Role of Water Co-operatives in Finland', *International Journal of Co-operative Management*, 5, 11–19.

Walras, L. (1865), *Les associations populaires de consommation, de production e de crédit* (Paris: Dentu Libraire Éditeur).

Willis, R. and Willis, J. (2012), *Co-operative Renewable Energy in the UK* (Manchester: Co-operatives UK).

Wilson, E. J., Plummer, J., Fischlein, M., and Smith, T. M. (2008), 'Implementing Energy Efficiency: Challenges and Opportunities for Rural Electric Co-operatives and Small Municipal Utilities', *Energy Policy*, 36, 3383–97.

Yadoo, A. and Cruickshank, H. (2010), 'The Value of Co-operatives in Rural Electrification', *Energy Policy*, 38, 2941–7.

CHAPTER 14

....

HOW TO THINK ABOUT GLOBAL EMPLOYEE OWNERSHIP

....

LOREN RODGERS

14.1 INTRODUCTION

EMPLOYEE ownership is a global approach to business. This chapter focuses mainly on how to think about global trends in encouraging employee ownership using joint stock corporations. Other chapters focus on worker co-operatives. Some countries actively encourage stock plans, and those countries' motives are diverse. Some see employee ownership as a way to encourage society-wide entrepreneurial thinking. Others see broad ownership as a way to enhance social cohesion and reduce the gap between higher- and lower-income citizens. Countries that actively encourage employee ownership include the United Kingdom, which during the current decade has seen tripartisan support and a flurry of regulatory and legal activity, resulting in a 9 per cent increase in the number of employee-owned businesses in a single year (2014). Spain and Italy have long-standing worker co-operative movements with supporting legislation, and such companies are employers of large segments of those countries' work forces. South Africa has legislation that encourages employee ownership as a means to overcome the lingering social impacts of apartheid. Other countries essentially have no specific regulation, or legislation designed to support stock plans. Companies in Cambodia, for example, are free to set up stock plans using rules that apply to stock holders and to employees in general.

Regardless of the regulatory and legislative framework, every company that is interested in employee ownership must, regardless of its headquarters country, begin by making some foundational choices. Those choices will be driven by the company leadership's answers to some basic strategic and philosophical questions. Once the company has a clear vision for what it wants to accomplish with its stock plan, it needs to examine the legal and practical constraints in the country or countries where it will have stock plan participants, to determine whether and how it can achieve its goals.

Companies which have or hope to have employee-owners in more than one country face all of the issues that single-country employers face, as well as an additional set of legal and philosophical issues. This article begins with the foundational issues all companies should answer when building a plan, then translates those issues into twelve plan-design parameters. It next explores foundational issues specific to companies with stock plans that include employees in more than one country. Next, it provides an overview of the legal issues involved in creating a successful plan and examines best practices in maintaining successful plans. It closes by noting some recent developments in global employee ownership.

14.2 Foundational Issues for Single-Country Employers

Before it considers the parameters of plan design, the company's leadership needs to decide what its compensation philosophy is. The company leadership team should have discussed and have come to a consensus decision about a number of issues. Some of these issues apply to all businesses but have different implications for employee-owned companies, and others are specific to employee ownership:

Pay relative to market: Some companies choose an employee-centric model where they aim to have total compensation higher than the market. Others focus on minimizing labour costs. Others may pay above market for some segments of their work forces only. Any of these approaches is a legitimate business strategy, but employee ownership is most likely to be effective when the company intends to have all or much of the work force long-tenured and well compensated.

Components of compensation: One way to think of a compensation package is as composed of four broad categories: base pay, incentive pay, benefits, and non-cash perquisites that support quality of work life. Employee ownership may fall into the second category—stock options and other forms of equity plans are current-year or deferred compensation. It can also be a benefit. In the United States, employee stock ownership plans (ESOPs) are retirement benefits. Each company should have an explicit strategy about how it manages those four components. One National Center for Employee Ownership member company, for example, aims to have slightly below-market base pay, rich but highly variable incentive pay, generous benefits, and no perquisites.

Risk: The four components of the compensation system allocate risk between employees and the company. High base pay, for example, insulates employees from risk but increases the chances that the company will face losses during a downturn. Incentive pay and stock-based compensation, on the other hand, shift risk from the company to the employees. Risk is not inherently good or bad, but it does need to be managed. A shift to a riskier compensation package may well encourage some employees to leave the company, but if such risk is accompanied by increased potential for greater total compensation, others will be motivated to join or to remain.

The spectrum of riskiness is wide: the most risky approach from the employee perspective (and the least risky from the company's perspective) is to have employees invest their own money in the business, either by buying shares or exercising options, and to have to hold that investment at the same level of risk as all other shareholders. A lower level of risk would allow employees to purchase shares at a discount and sell them quickly. Even less risky would be a plan based on company contributions that holds company stock as its investment; periodic valuations of that stock (or the market, in the case of listed companies) would determine the value, including the possibility of a decline in value. Least risky would be a contribution-based plan that would only affect employees in the event that the stock rises in value, such as a stock appreciation right (SAR). Any plan that grants stock to workers is less risky than one where employees purchase the stock.

Employee voice: Although employee participation in decision-making at the company is not inherently tied to the legal form of the plan or its riskiness, in practice the design of the plan may have a substantial impact on the extent to which employees come to feel and act like owners. For example, when employees have small stakes for which they did not pay and fail to see the connection between their own job performance and the value of their shares, they are less likely to become actively engaged in the employee participation efforts.

Role of employee-owners: Very closely tied to the issues of risk and voice, companies are well advised to consider whether they want employee-owners to see themselves as employee-investors, employee-owners, or as employees only.

The company's public face: Companies that build a public image of employee ownership, such as the John Lewis Partnership in the United Kingdom or TEOCO (an acronym for 'The Employee-Owned Company') in the United States, need to ensure that their plans will be perceived by outsiders as a legitimate form of employee ownership. A company's brand could be deeply damaged by a news story purporting to show that its claims of employee ownership do not meet commonly held public expectations.

The company's future: Companies that are private and expect to remain so will have a vastly different approach to employee ownership than companies that are expecting to be acquired or to make a public offering.

14.3 DESIGN PARAMETERS
FOR OWNERSHIP PLANS

Once a company has come to conclusions about these foundational issues, it should translate those decisions into a configuration of the parameters of an ownership plan. Although some advisors recommend that the company makes its first draft of these parameters based on home-country law, regulation, or current practice, I strongly recommend that they make their first draft of these parameters based on their goals and compensation philosophy. Although it may be impossible or cost-prohibitive to design the plan the way they want, companies are more likely to find creative ways to accomplish their goals within the legal framework if they make their desired outcome the starting point.

Before introducing the parameters, a few definitions may be useful. 'Restricted stock' is actual stock that employees receive, but which they will forfeit if certain conditions are not met. These conditions may be continued employment or a measure of individual or group performance. 'Phantom stock' is a cash bonus, the size of which is determined by reference to the value of a share of stock. An employee may receive, for example, phantom stock set at the value of ten shares of stock as determined in six months. Restricted stock and phantom stock are full-value awards, because their value is determined with reference to the full value of a share.

Incremental value awards, by contrast, provide recipients with a value based on the change in the value of a share of stock over a fixed period. A 'stock option' accomplishes this by allowing an employee the right to purchase stock on a fixed date, but at the stock's price from a prior date. If I receive the right to purchase 5,000 shares of stock at today's price, and the stock has risen by $1.20 when that right becomes exercisable, then the value to me of those options is the amount of their increase in value, or $6,000. An SAR, is economically equivalent to a stock option, but it is a cash incentive payment that is determined by the increase in value of a set number of shares, so no actual stock is involved. The term 'stock purchase plan' refers to a wide variety of plans that facilitate employees purchasing shares, often by making voluntary deductions from payroll and often at a discounted price. Many types of plans involve 'vesting', which is a process that gives employees a nonforfeitable right to the award. Awards may vest gradually. Employees who fail to meet the vesting requirements, which may be based on tenure, individual performance, group performance, or a combination of events, will forfeit the unvested portion of the award.

Table 14.1 shows the twelve parameters that companies should consider when determining their ideal plan design.

The foundational issues should inform the way companies assemble these parameters. For example, a company that wants employees to have a low component of risk may want to avoid employee contributions and stock option plans, which tend to be more volatile than restricted stock or phantom stock. Companies whose public face involves employee ownership should ensure that a substantial portion of the work force and the company equity is in the stock plan.

14.4 Multi-Country Employers

Even before looking at the legal and regulatory issues in different countries, the leaders of companies that want to have employee-owners in different countries need to consider whether they want the ownership plan to help them build a unified global team. Many companies prefer to see their different country branches as playing various parts in a

Table 14.1 Global Employee Ownership

Parameter	Definition
1. Portion of work force	How much of the work force participates in the plan? All employees who meet basic eligibility requirements? All employees above a certain organizational level? Is there a different type of plan for different employees?
2. Portion of stock	How much of the company's stock is available for the stock plan? Any portion is possible. Public companies may have a fraction of a per cent, while many private companies are completely employee owned.
3. Cycle	The cycle of awards includes both how frequently employees receive them and when they can exercise those awards. Awards can happen sporadically, such as on hire, on certain anniversaries, or at the discretion of a supervisor. Other awards may be periodic, such as a quarterly option grant or an annual contribution. The term of the award may be short term (a year or less), medium term (up to three years), long term (three to ten years), or aimed at retirement.
4. Stock / stock-linked	Some plans (such as restricted stock, stock options, and stock purchase plans) involve actual shares of stock. Other plans (such as phantom stock and stock appreciation rights) provide a cash value that is determined by reference to the value of a share of stock.
5. Full value or incremental value	Some plans provide employees with the full value of a share of stock, while others provide that the employee will receive a value equal to the increase in the stock over a given period.
6. Employee contribution	Some plans require that employees spend some of their own money, while others are purely a benefit from the company.
7. Allocation	Stock plans may provide that all employees receive an equal award. Others provide all employees in a certain category (organization level, tenure, etc.) with equal awards. Others make awards proportional to compensation or to job evaluations.
8. Conditions / limits	Plans may be designed so that employees forfeit the awards unless certain conditions are met. These conditions may be based on continued employment, on individual performance, or on unit performance, often attainment of specific corporate or departmental goals.
9. Valuation	Private companies need to determine a mechanism and cycle by which the value of the awards will be determined. This is often done by an independent appraisal, or may be based on book value or a valuation formula.
10. Liquidity for employees	Public companies simply allow employees to sell shares on the market, but private companies must provide a mechanism by which employees can exchange their awards for cash. That mechanism may be a buy–sell agreement with the company, an internal market that allows them to sell shares to other employees, or specifying that the shares are not redeemable until there is a liquidity event such as a sale or a public offering.

(continued)

Table 14.1 Continued

Parameter	Definition
11. Governance	Some plans, especially those that grant actual shares in public companies, may specify that employees have the same rights as other shareholders. Stock-linked awards rarely have governance rights. Some plans, such as US ESOPs, specify a limited number of shareholder decisions on which employees have governance rights.
12. Ownership structure	Awards may be a form of compensation that cycles as people receive and exercise awards, never representing a significant portion of the company's equity. Alternatively, the stock plan may represent a path by which the ownership structure of the company changes, such as an original owner or owners transferring shares over time to the employee stock plan.

Loren Rodgers

division of labour, which means that each part may have its own philosophy for voice and compensation. Such companies are not seeking a unified team and do not need to think about building a stock plan (or stock plans) that make all employees around the globe feel a shared interest and sense of equality with all other employees.

If the company is striving to build a cohesive global team, it needs to consider a number of issues:

Labour market: Since prevailing compensation rates vary drastically from country to country, should the stock plan mirror those differences, or should it provide equal benefits to all employees, regardless of their home country? In some countries, many of a company's competitors will be offering equity compensation, while in others, there will be none.

Cultural norms: Some countries have a deeper cultural affinity to ownership and stock, while others have less of a tradition, and may value ownership less or even feel an aversion to stock ownership.

Strategy: A stock plan is likely to be a better fit in countries where the company is planning to grow versus countries in which its work force may stagnate or shrink.

Instead of trying to create a globally unified team of all employees, some companies instead pursue a strategy of 'matrix unification', in which similar categories of employees around the world have similar stock plans. Engineers, for example, may receive annual grants of restricted stock that do not require employee contributions and are exercisable after three years, giving them a low-risk, medium-term incentive. By contrast, managers may have blocks of options with a variety of exercise dates, giving them larger upside potential and encouraging them to consider a broader time horizon.

After companies have decided their approach to these multi-country foundational issues, they may need to adjust the twelve parameters. They often decide that they need to have multiple plans, each with their own set of parameters. There may be different plans for different employee categories among companies that are following the matrix unification approach, or they may have different plans in different countries if they are not aiming for globally unified employee ownership. Rosen and Schneider (2012) describe that process from the perspective of a US ESOP company.

After companies determine their design parameters, the next step is to determine how feasible it is to translate these parameters into a legal stock plan in the various countries where the company has employees.

14.5 Plan Design: Legal and Regulatory Issues

It is not possible to design a plan without legal counsel. The counsel should have specific experience in such plans and in the relevant countries, but that counsel should also understand and respect the company's goals. Since many legal professionals have their own favoured way of approaching projects, companies are well served to interview multiple law firms. Companies should show the prospective lawyers the design parameters they put together and ask them how feasible such a plan may be. If the plan is a poor fit for that country's legal system, companies should ask the prospective lawyers what the most feasible next-best plan might look like. Compare the various law firms' answers to these two key questions in making your decision about which counsel to work with.

The legal issues companies must face in adapting their design parameters to any given country encompass a number of areas.

14.5.1 Labour Law

In a number of countries, such as France, Hungary, and Hong Kong, benefits that the company provides may become an 'acquired right'. Such rights may be difficult to change or reduce, and they may be included in the calculation of termination benefits. A well-drafted award will often include a signed acknowledgement by the employee that the award is discretionary. Labour law may also make it difficult for companies to create plans that involve employees making voluntary deductions from their pay to acquire stock, as is usually the case in stock purchase plans, described by the Certified Equity Professional Institute at Santa Clara University (Certified Equity Professional Institute 2009).

Some countries' labour laws against age discrimination may make vesting rules based solely on age impossible, so a company may use age- and tenure-based vesting. Rules regarding the definition and rights of part-time workers can also force companies to change their eligibility rules when they bring their plans into a new country. Plans that have discretionary participation—for example, where supervisors may determine which employees participate in any given award cycle—may also have to ensure that they meet home country anti-discrimination requirements.

Finally, labour laws in some countries provide substantial rights to organized labour in the design and scope of stock plans.

14.5.2 Securities, Currency Exchange, and Foreign Ownership Laws

Since stock-based or stock-linked awards may be considered a security in various countries, the company may need to register the plan with the securities agency or make regular compliance filings. The company itself may need to become a registered broker. In some countries the company will need to either create a prospectus for participating employees or else file for an exemption.

Flows of local and foreign currency in and out of a country may be regulated, possibly involving paperwork for each individual transaction. When the employee exercises an award that involves the stock of a company outside the employee's home country, the employee may be required to report and receive approval from a regulatory agency. In some countries, these rules on currency flows may make stock plans that involve parent-company stock impractical, and laws concerning foreign ownership may have the same effect.

14.5.3 Taxation

Employees are liable for taxes on stock plan awards at different points in different countries, and although such taxes may not make plans infeasible, they can reduce or eliminate the perceived benefit. In some countries, for example, options are taxable to employees when granted or when they become vested. In other words, the employee may have tax due before he or she has received any cash benefit from the plan. As of this writing, for example, the government of Australia is discussing changes to the taxation of options, moving the employee's tax event from vesting to exercise.

Many companies provide tax benefits to company stock plans. Such plans bring their own set of requirements on plan design, and although they often result in greater after-tax benefit to employees, in some cases the restrictions imposed by such tax qualification may actually make the plan less attractive than a non-qualified plan.

Various countries also have different requirements for social insurance tax on stock plan awards. Countries may require withholding for income tax and/or social insurance taxes.

14.5.4 Employee Communications

Every country has its own set of required communications and standards for such communications. The documents most often included in award packages are an award agreement, an offer letter, the full plan document, possibly a prospectus, and a description of the tax implications of the award. Some countries have specific rules about whether plan communications may be delivered electronically and whether plan documents must be delivered in the home-country language.

14.5.5 Data Privacy Laws

Certain countries, and most notably the European Union, have strict laws guarding the privacy of personal data. These countries must certify that other countries have adequate protection for employee data before such data may be transferred to them. The United States, for example, does not yet meet these requirements, so data essential to the administration of equity plans may be impossible to share with company headquarters, if those headquarters are in a non-qualifying country.

After the legal issues have been researched, a company may well find itself facing some choices. It may need to determine if the set of parameters it desires is feasible and, even if so, if it is worth the set-up and maintenance cost. Companies are always well advised to consider the second-best plan to determine how well it meets company objectives.

14.6 Best Practices

This chapter does not attempt to enumerate all factors that determine a plan's success, but the areas that most frequently deserve increased attention from company leaders who want these plans to thrive include the following.

14.6.1 Benefit Levels

Company leaders often design plans by starting with the percentage of company equity they feel comfortable allocating to the stock plan. Since the success of the plan depends on how it is perceived by employees, not by the total percentage of stock in the plan, companies are well advised to begin instead with the perceptions and wishes of employees. While it is impossible to determine what level of value would be sufficient for employees, plan designers can gather many pieces of useful data:

- Forms and amounts of equity compensation paid in the home country, especially by competitors
- Employee surveys
- Exit interviews of departing workers

Both employee surveys and interviews with employees who choose to leave employment can provide valuable data, such as employees' level of risk aversion. Companies should also explore employees' perceptions of ownership, including their assessment of the financial value of stock, their positive and negative associations with the concept of ownership, and their appetite for accepting greater expectations of responsibility that come with some companies' transitions to employee ownership. Companies may also want to explore employees' expectations for their own tenure at the business: if many employees expect to remain for two to three years, companies need to decide whether to accept that (and possibly create short-term equity incentives), or whether to provide a reason for employees to stay longer by providing longer-term awards.

One approach many companies use is to determine a target amount of stock compensation as a percentage of base pay. Others put together projections that model the potential growth in value of various award programmes under optimistic and cautious scenarios.

14.6.2 Communications

Stock plans are not cheap. They require legal and administrative fees and considerable work by human resources or compensation staff to maintain. Companies often fall into the unfortunate situation of investing in a plan and then neglecting to spend the additional time and resources it would take to effectively communicate how the plan works, and its potential benefits.

Since the impact of the plan is fully dependent on changing employee behaviour, and since the plan will only change employee behaviour if employees are aware of the plan and understand it, failure to invest in communication and education often has the effect of reducing the return on the substantial investment the company is making in the plan. Research by the National Center for Employee Ownership and others suggest that in the typical company, employees perceive the plan as having less worth than its accounting value. In other words, companies are spending a dollar of benefit for 50 cents of motivational impact.

Companies that see the greatest benefit from their plans reinforce the value of those plans to employees through a careful network of communications that accommodates different learning modes: written communications, one-on-one meetings, videos, educational postings, etc. These companies also build references to the stock plan into other communications. The CEO may refer to the value of all employees' share accounts in an annual message to employees. The human resources department may create periodic 'small-bite' educational resources. References to employee ownership and planning milestones may be part of regular communications, company celebrations, and social events. A number of companies create peer-to-peer communications by involving non-management employees in creating and implementing educational programmes.

14.6.3 Business Literacy and Employee Participation

Suppose the stock plan and the communications programme succeed in motivating employees. The company needs to ensure that employee-owners know what to do with that motivation. A number of employee-owned companies train their work forces extensively on business literacy so that they can better determine the impact of what they do day to day on the profitability of the company.

A number of other companies create specific structures through which employees can engage in generating innovations and process improvements, or participate in decision-making through team hiring or representation on company boards.

14.6.4 Smooth Out the Incentive

Equity plans may cause trouble when employees have large blocks of awards, especially when these blocks are highly sensitive to stock price. An employee with a single block of stock options and no other equity awards only cares about the value of the shares during his or her exercise window and, in fact, such an employee is well served by wide swings in stock price. If he or she cashes in these options near the top of the swing, then the bottom of the swing causes the employee no financial impact.

Companies can reduce this challenge by providing full-value awards rather than incremental value awards. Other companies provide multiple tranches of awards or have awards vested in batches. Both strategies 'smooth out' the return curve for employees, aligning their interests more consistently with the fate of the company.

14.6.5 Predictability

One criticism of equity compensation is that some employees see it less as ownership and more as a lottery. Smoothing out the incentive will help with that, but a more fundamental answer is to make your stock plan transparent. A number of companies create trigger-driven stock plans and work hard to make sure the rules are widely known in advance. For example, all employees may receive an award valued at a fixed percentage of their base pay on their five-year anniversary. Or all employees who receive a top 25 per cent performance evaluation may receive a larger-than-typical stock award. The company may promise to provide a small but universal award each time the company crosses a progress threshold (the ten-thousandth customer, exceeding a revenue target, achieving a product-development milestone, etc.)

Other companies make their stock plans formula-driven. Most frequently, a key variable in the formula will be some measure of profitability. When EBITDA (refers in the USA to accounting to Earnings Before Interest, Taxes, Depreciation and Amortization), for example, exceeds some threshold, a percentage of the surplus may be used to determine a pool of allocable stock or other equity. That pool can then be allocated among the work force by a similarly transparent formula, which could be each employee receiving an equal share, or proportional to base pay, or connected to performance evaluations.

14.7 RECENT DEVELOPMENTS

The legal and business climate for employee ownership changes constantly, and this chapter does not attempt a current inventory of the state of specific countries around the world. For example, the Japan Employee Ownership Association launched in March of 2015, and Australia are currently in the process of re-examining their legal frameworks as regards stock plans.

In late 2014, the European Commission released a pilot project to support the development of employee ownership throughout Europe (Inter-University Centre for European Commission's DG Market 2014), *Promotion of Employee Ownership and Participation*. Early in 2015, the European Federation of Employee Share Ownership (EFES) released its own report reacting to the provisions in the pilot project and expressing its strong disagreement with the proposed legislation. The pilot project's legislation does not include financial incentives, and EFES argues that such incentives are essential for the successful growth of broad-based employee ownership in Europe.

The country with the most notable recent developments is the United Kingdom. In his retrospective on 2014, the UK Employee Ownership Association's Iain Hasdell noted that the number of employee-owned businesses in the UK increased by 9 per cent during 2014. Hasdell reflected on new tax incentives and the continued success of employee ownership in providing public services, and noted that employee ownership is on track to meet his goal of representing 10 per cent of the UK's economy by 2020 (Hasdell 2014).

In the UK employee ownership is a major issue across all three major parties. The Conservative Cameron government created a series of new incentives for broad-based employee ownership, including incentives for companies and business owners to use an ESOP-like mechanism to transfer ownership to employees in closely held companies.

In early 2015 the Labour Party issued the Hunt Review, which examines a wide variety of stock plans and other shared capitalism measures. Among other things, the review calls for a number of new incentives, including additional tax incentives for existing plans encouraging public companies to contribute shares to employees and/or encouraging employees to buy them at a discount, making existing plans that provide incentives for sharing equity with selected employees dependent on a commitment to move towards broader ownership, and creating additional tax benefits for companies that have more employee involvement in decisions (Hunt 2014).

14.8 CONCLUSION

Although requirements and benefits vary from country to country, many companies feel that stock plans are essential parts of their business success. Data on their performance suggest that they are often correct.

REFERENCES

Certified Equity Professional Institute (2009), *GPS: Global Stock Plans* (Santa Clara, California: Santa Clara University).

Hasdell, I. (2014), 'Mould in Our Hands', London: Employee Ownership Association. Available at employeeownership.co.uk/news/ceo-blog/mould-hands (accessed 13 October 2016).

Hunt, P. (2014), 'The Hunt Review', London: Mutuo. Available at www.mutuo.co.uk/wp-content/uploads/2014/12/Hunt-Review.pdf (accessed 13 September 2016).

Inter-University Centre for European Commission's DG Market (2014), 'The Promotion of Employee Ownership and Participation', October. Available at http://ec.europa.eu/internal_market/company/docs/modern/141028-study-for-dg-markt_en.pdf

Rosen, C. and C. Schneider (2012), 'International Ownership Plans for US ESOP Companies, Oakland', California: National Center for Employee Ownership.

PART V

POLITICAL, GOVERNANCE, AND ORGANIZATIONAL ASPECTS

CHAPTER 15

....

EVIDENCE

what the US research shows about worker ownership

....

JOSEPH R. BLASI, RICHARD B. FREEMAN,
AND DOUGLAS L. KRUSE

WHAT does empirical research show about worker ownership? The averages show that the key indicator of economic performance, productivity, and many other measures related to firm performance are higher for firms that operate with profit-sharing and employee stock ownership than for otherwise comparable firms that do not follow these practices. The averages also show that workers in firms with shares and participatory work relations have higher compensation, stay on the job longer, and offer more suggestions for improvement than workers in other firms.

15.1 STARTING POINTS

....

Several researchers, including the authors, have reviewed this work (Weitzman and Kruse 1990; Kruse and Blasi 1995; Bryson and Freeman 2007).[1] In 1995 Christopher

---

[1] The following studies reviewed research for the United Kingdom: Oxera Economic Consultancy, *Tax Advantaged Employee Share Schemes: Analysis of Productivity Effects, Report 1, Productivity Measured Using Turnover*. Prepared for Her Majesty's Revenue And Customs. London: Her Majesty's Revenue and Customs- HMRC, Report 33, August 2007a; Oxera Economic Consultancy, *Tax Advantaged Employee Share Schemes: Analysis of Productivity Effects, Report 2, Productivity Measured Using Gross Value Added*. Prepared for Her Majesty's Revenue And Customs. London: Her Majesty's Revenue and Customs- HMRC, Report 33, August 2007b; Oxera Economic Consultancy, *Tax Advantaged Employee Share Schemes: Analysis of Productivity Effects, Overview*. Prepared for Her Majesty's Revenue And Customs. London: Her Majesty's Revenue and Customs- HMRC, Report 33, August 2007c; and, Oxera Economic Consultancy, *Tax Advantaged Employee Share Schemes: Analysis of Productivity Effects, Appendices to Report 1*. Prepared for Her Majesty's Revenue And Customs. London: Her Majesty's Revenue and Customs- HMRC, Report 33, August 2007d.

Doucouliagos undertook a meta-statistic analysis of the evidence. Metastatistics is a technique widely used in medical science to put together results from many disparate studies to assess the magnitude and significance of coefficients from those studies in one fell swoop. It combines estimates from individual studies from different data sets, samples of different sizes and subject to different biases or data imperfections, into a single estimate covering all studies. The notion is that the imperfections across studies are random so that averaging gives a more accurate estimate of reality.

The scholars who have reviewed many studies plus newer studies not covered in the reviews—over 100 studies in total—find that firms with share arrangements average better outcomes than otherwise comparable firms without share arrangements. The magnitude of these effects is usually of the order of 2 per cent to 5 per cent. Meaningful profit-sharing generally has larger effects on output than employee stock ownership. Combinations of programmes—employee stock ownership and profit-sharing or a stock purchase plan and profit-sharing—have greater effects on output than individual programmes by themselves.

To turn to specific studies, there are five important studies of the effects of share approaches on outcomes outlined in the Appendix. The British government sponsored the first study, arguably the best existing study that uses standard production function methodology. The General Accountability Office (GAO) of the US Congress sponsored the second study. Both governments wanted to know whether policies that encouraged firms to introduce share approaches in their respective countries improved the productivity of firms, as proponents of the policies had predicted when the legislation was debated. Government sponsorship gave researchers access to financial and production information on firms that was not in the public domain.

The study commissioned by the British Government's Treasury department examined whether programmes that gave firms tax incentives to introduce individual stock ownership, profit-sharing, and employee stock options affected the economic performance of those firms. Because they were the government they had access to the private financial records of the companies. The quality of the data and number of firms covered 'made the study as close as we could imagine to giving a definitive analysis of tax-advantaged modes of shared capitalism on productivity'. The analysis covered a sufficiently large proportion of the United Kingdom's economy to suggest that broad-based employee ownership improved performance economy-wide (Oxera, 2007a, b, c, d).[2] A parallel study of publicly available information of corporations with broad-based capitalism in the United Kingdom by Alex Bryson of the London School of Economics and Richard Freeman gave comparable results and found that the effects were greatly influenced by management giving workers greater autonomy in decision-making (Bryson and Freeman 2010).

---

[2] In 2010 the UK commissioned another economic consultancy to review the evidence that supported these conclusions in the Matrix report. See Matrix Knowledge Group, *The Employee Ownership Effect: A Review of the Evidence*. London: Matrix Evidence, a division of Matrix Knowledge Group, 2010.

The General Accounting Office study examined 414 firms that set up Employee Stock Ownership Plans (ESOPs) in 1976–9 when ESOPs were just getting off the ground. The research design matched each ESOP firm with a similarly sized non-ESOP firm in the same industry. Again, the government had access to private financial information on the companies. This study found that a combination of employee stock ownership with a supportive corporate culture raised productivity, whereas ESOPs by themselves without a supportive culture had no statistically significant effect on output (United States General Accounting Office 1987).

The third study, by Joseph Blasi and Douglas L. Kruse, followed the design of the General Accounting Office study and looked at 300 privately held firms that set up ESOPs between 1988 and 1994 and compared each ESOP firm to similar companies of the same size in the same industry, but without an ESOP. It found that the ESOP firms had significantly higher sales growth and higher sales per worker, and were more likely to have survived through 1999 than matching firms without ESOPs (Blasi et al. 2013).

The fourth study was a field experiment in which researchers were allowed to randomly assign profit-sharing to several stores, helping overcome concerns that other factors could be responsible for any changes in performance. The stores where profit-sharing was established had increases in productivity and profitability, and decreased turnover, relative to a group of stores that were not assigned profit-sharing (Peterson and Luthans 2006).

The last study differs from the others by relying on management reports on quality of output, financial performance, and worker turnover, rather than on financial and production data. It gives a similar picture: firms do better when they combine a participatory company culture with profit-sharing and employee stock ownership (Kruse et al. 2010a—survey).[3]

Finding a positive relation between broad-based capitalism approaches such as employee stock ownership and profit-sharing and firm output across many studies shows that something real is going on with corporations that adopt profit-sharing or employee stock ownership. To get a better sense of what that real something was, in 2000 we initiated the Shared Capitalism Research Project at the National Bureau of Economic Research in Cambridge, Massachusetts (Kruse et al. 2010a).[4] In contrast to the studies just discussed, which obtained information from companies about their performance as firms, we sought information from workers about what was happening at their workplaces.

---

[3] Kruse et al. (2010a)—Survey designed by the University of California Berkeley Institute of Industrial Relations and conducted between May and October of 2003 of 2,806 establishments. On this California Establishment Survey, see Kruse et al., *Shared Capitalism*, 187–91. The book can be found at: http://www.nber.org/books/krus08-1/ (accessed 14 September 2016) and is available in print and online at the University of Chicago Press and online at Google Books.

[4] The National Bureau of Economic Research is the world's leading non-profit, non-partisan economic research centre.

15.2 THE NBER SHARED CAPITALISM STUDY

Our study surveyed over 40,000 employees in 14 corporations. The companies included large multinationals traded on major US stock markets, important high technology innovators (large and small), medium-sized corporations and smaller factories with ESOPs, and financial services firms and other service-oriented companies spread across just over 300 workplaces around the country and in their foreign divisions. Our initial plan was to pair firms that had profit-sharing and employee stock ownership with their closest competitors who paid workers solely with wages or salaries per unit of time, but this plan did not pan out. Fourteen firms with some form of broad-based capitalism agreed to participate in the study, but their competitors were unwilling to participate. We feared this would not give us enough contrast to reach firm conclusions about broad-based capitalism. To use the medical science analogy, we had firms that were trying the medicine but did not have evidence on the control firms without the medicine.

15.2.1 A Control Group for the Study

We recognized that to the extent that broad-based capitalist arrangements improved outcomes, the absence of firms without such programmes would likely bias downward estimates of those impacts (this assumes that the arrangements have a reasonably monotonic linear relation to outcomes). While it is always desirable to have a representative sample, second best is to have a sample biased in a given direction, since that means that if the results are in that direction, they understate the effect and thus provide a lower bound in what the relevant policy accomplishes. We obtained information from the US Government's General Social Survey national survey on workers in firms that had no employee stock ownership or profit-sharing in order to obtain a valid control group. The survey measures can be found in our earlier book *Shared Capitalism at Work* (Kruse et al. 2010b).[5]

15.2.2 What We Found

The first finding from the worker surveys in the NBER Shared Capitalism study was that shares and work practices varied widely inside and across these 14 companies. We gave each worker a score based on how much ownership he or she had in their company and how much he or she shared in profits and stock options. The scores varied substantially among workers. Some had a large ownership stake; some had little. Some were in establishments with a strong gain-sharing or profit-sharing programme; others were not.

[5] Kruse et al. (2010b), *Shared Capitalism*, 10–11, 24–34. The survey measures are in Appendix A, 387–401.

We then compared workers who had different shared capitalism scores but who were similar in their occupation, their fixed wages, supervisory responsibilities, tenure with the company, gender, age, disability, and so forth. Sometimes we analysed how economic outcomes varied among workers within the same company. Sometimes we analysed how economic outcomes varied among workplaces.

While we had too few companies in the NBER study to compare companies, as noted, we used the General Social Survey sample of workers, who are chosen at random from the country as a whole and are thus likely to represent single firms, to compare workers in companies with and without broad-based capitalism. We found that workers with higher shared capitalism scores, that is, the combination of worker ownership and profit-sharing, were more committed to their employer along a variety of dimensions than those with lower scores, and that these workers were better off in a host of important aspects of their work lives. In particular, workers with greater property in corporations in firms are more likely to stay with the company, are more loyal, are more willing to work harder, make more suggestions, and have better fixed pay and working conditions.

15.2.3 More Likely to Stay with their Firm

Management in most firms seeks to lower the rate of turnover. The reason is that recruiting, training, and integrating new employees into a work force costs money, time, and effort (see turnover cost calculator at http://www.cepr.net/calculators/turnover_calc.html (accessed 13 September 2016).

Our measure of turnover was whether workers intended to look for a new job—a strong predictor of actual future turnover behaviour. In the National Bureau for Economic Research study, 9 per cent of workers with high levels of profit-sharing, employee stock ownership, or stock options reported that they were likely to look for a new job compared to 15 per cent of employees with low levels of shared capitalist compensation—a difference of six percentage points in the likelihood of staying. Among individual forms of shares, profit- or gain-sharing was associated with the lowest turnover. But the combination with employee stock ownership had an even greater impact in reducing turnover (Kruse et al. 2010a: 152–7). To see if this result would fit the nation as a whole we examined responses to a similar question on the General Social Survey and found that 15 per cent of workers with profit-sharing, stock options, or employee ownership were likely to leave their firm compared to a fifth of workers without any form of broad-based capitalism–a difference of five percentage points.

15.2.4 Have Greater Loyalty and Pride Working
for the Firm

In the National Bureau for Economic Research study, 58 per cent of workers with a high level of shared capitalism reported greater loyalty to the firm compared to 46 per cent of workers with low amounts of such shares. The national General Social Survey asked a comparable question about whether workers were proud to work for an employer: 44 per cent of workers with a high level of shared capitalism reported a high level of pride compared to 29 per cent of workers without employee stock ownership or profit- or gain-sharing. Workers with profit- or gain-sharing expressed the highest loyalty, while those with employee stock ownership and stock options had somewhat more modest increases in loyalty that still exceeded that of workers without these forms of shares. Workers with the combination of the different forms, namely, employee stock ownership and profit shares, showed the greatest loyalty to their firm and greatest pride in working for it.

15.2.5 Express Greater Willingness to Work Hard

To obtain a measure of the work effort that employees give to their firm in the NBER study of 14 companies we asked: To what extent do you agree or disagree with this state-ment: I am willing to work harder than I have to in order to help the company I work for succeed? The proportion who strongly agreed was 36 per cent for workers with high levels of broad-based capitalism compared to 30 per cent for workers with no shared capitalism. (This comparison adjusts for differences in demographic and job character-istics, e.g. age, sex, tenure, occupation. The numbers represent the estimated likelihood of strong agreement for an average worker in the sample.)

Workers with profit-sharing and gain-sharing were at the top of the willingness to work hard ladder, whereas those who had just broad-based employee stock owner-ship and stock options did not differ from other workers. Remember that we are only comparing workers with stock shares versus profit shares without, for the moment in this discussion, taking into consideration the corporate culture of their companies. Employee stock ownership, as indicated by many other studies from the last 40 years, works mainly with a supportive corporate culture, and the types of and approach to employee ownership matter a lot.

15.2.6 Make More Suggestions

We asked workers in the NBER study how often they made suggestions to their firm and found that among those with some form of broad-based capitalism, 26 per cent made a suggestion at least once a month, compared to only 18 per cent among work-ers without shares. Employee stock ownership had a larger impact than profit-shar-ing on making suggestions, but the most effective practice, here as elsewhere, is shown to be combining employee stock ownership and profit-sharing with supportive work practices (Harden et al. 2010). Ownership gives workers a capital stake in the com-pany. Profit-sharing gives them short-term capital income. Employee involvement programmes of diverse sorts, such as worker town meetings, open door policies, self-directed work teams, and worker problem-solving committees, encourage workers to participate in decisions. Workers in firms with employee stock ownership and profit-sharing and supportive work practices not only make more suggestions than workers in other firms but they also report that management was more likely to heed their suggestions than did workers in other firms. Another US study found similar results (Dube and Freeman 2010).

One large company in the NBER project especially interested in innovation asked us to add questions to our survey of their corporation to find out whether their workers perceived a culture of innovation, or not, at their workplace. The responses to these questions showed that workers who had shares, a co-operative culture, and mutual monitoring were most likely to view the firm's culture as positively inclined toward innovation. One has to look beyond measurements of 'effort' in order to really understand broad-based capitalism in the new workplaces today, because a lot of the success of work teams in the current post-industrial economy has to do more with ingenuity and innovation than with sheer physical or mental effort. Citizens across the nation do a lot less heavy lifting and pushing and pulling and shovelling and carrying and putting things on and taking things off than they did 50 years ago. Much of this effort is now done by machines, so what happens in teams and between workers and with workers and customers is far more important. New research by Dan Weltmann indicates that the initial effect of employee share ownership on individual workers appears to kick in at very low thresholds in influencing the frequency with which workers make suggestions and whether they propose ideas for innovations rather than slight improvements. The effect on their overall company loyalty and their willingness to work on innovations appears to increase as share ownership expands (Weltmann, Blasi, and Kruse 2013).

15.2.7 Have Better Wages and Work Conditions

Do workers gain from a property stake in their firm? The question may strike some readers as a clumsy set-up to an obvious answer. However, some critics of employee shares believe that when workers have a stake in ownership, this stake comes at the cost of lower wages or other benefits, so that on a net basis, workers may not be better off with profit-sharing or employee ownership than otherwise. It is entirely possible that this is how shares could end up. In fact, some managers believe in what they call 'pay at risk' by putting the worker under the maximum possible pressure to earn even fair wages (Handel and Levine 2004). Our evidence dispels this criticism and supports the 'obvious answer'.

There is strong evidence that employee stock ownership and profit-sharing have meaningful impacts on workers' wealth. The NBER study found that workers with profit-sharing or employee stock ownership are more highly paid and have more benefits than other workers (Kruse et al. 2010a). This means that the substantial profit-sharing and gain-sharing and ownership stakes for the typical worker in these plans tend to come on top of (not in place of) fair fixed wages and benefits, as many other studies have found (General Social Survey 2006).[6] These workers also obtain more training and have greater job security than other workers, and enjoy better work conditions with greater participation in decisions, better treatment by the employer, and less supervision (Kruse et al. 2010a: 257–89). These better conditions are consistently linked to profit-sharing, although some of the conditions are also better for workers with gain-sharing, stock options, and employee stock ownership. Being eligible for profit-sharing or being an employee-owner by itself is associated with better wages and work conditions. But the size of a profit or gain share, the value of the employer stock ownership stake, and the size of the potential stock option profit are also associated with much better conditions for workers.

15.2.8 What About Those Free Riders?

The classic free rider objection to broad-based capitalism is that profit-sharing or employee stock ownership in a large group cannot succeed because each individual has an incentive to shirk. Since all workers presumably know that everyone thinks this way, the gist of this criticism is that ownership stakes and profit shares will fail to motivate

---

[6] General Social Survey (2006). The most recent evidence is from the 2006 General Social Survey where 70–80 per cent of a random sample of adult workers reported that they were paid at or above the market rate for their jobs if covered by profit-sharing, gain-sharing, employee stock ownership, or if they were holding employee stock options in their firm. See Kruse and Blasi (2007). The higher pay and benefits under these plans would appear to go against the economic theory of compensating wage differentials, which predicts that workers receiving employee ownership or profit-sharing will have lower regular pay, fewer benefits, and/or worse working conditions to compensate for the benefits of these plans. There were some publicized cases of workers making wage or benefit concessions in exchange for employee ownership or profit-sharing in the 1980s, but these constituted a very small fraction of plan adoptions (between 4 per cent and 7 per cent according to a General Accounting Office survey). On this, see U.S. General Accounting Office (1986). On concession bargaining with employee stock ownership, see Blasi and Kruse (1991): 325–8. Apart from these few concessionary situations, over 20 studies find employee ownership and profit-sharing are not linked to generally lower fixed pay or benefits, and are often found to exist along with higher base pay and benefits. This is found both in comparisons of matched ESOP and non-ESOP firms. On this, see Kardas et al. (1998), and Scharf and Mackin (2000). It is also found in pre/post comparisons of plan adoption controlling for state-level and industry-level wage changes and other company characteristics. See Kim and Ouimet (2009). ESOP companies are four times more likely than non-ESOP companies to have traditional pensions as noted in Kruse (2002). The pension assets per employee of ESOP companies are substantially higher than in non-ESOP companies with other types of defined contribution plans. On this, see Rodgers (2010). For detailed reports on the original data, see Rodgers and Keeling (20 September 2010a) and National Center for Employee Ownership (15 September 2010b), *ESOPs as Retirement Benefits–Supplemental Tables*, Oakland, CA and Washington, DC: National Center for Employee Ownership and Employee Ownership Foundation (15 September). Going against the idea that the higher pay levels simply reflect higher worker quality, average base pay of individuals goes up as workers join profit-sharing companies, and down as they leave them. See Kruse (1998): 105–53. Workers appear to be sharing in the average higher productivity of broad-based capitalism firms. As such, their higher total compensation may represent a compensating differential for their higher quantity and quality of work, and/or an efficiency wage that motivates and sustains high performance. See Akerlof (1984): 79–83.

anyone to work hard. One potentially important channel for overcoming the free rider problem is through worker co-monitoring—the process by which workers with an ownership stake and a profit share take on the responsibility of ensuring that fellow workers do their part at workplaces. Another way to think of it is mutual support, encouragement, coaching, or that good old-fashioned word, 'help'. While the notion that co-monitoring can reduce free rider behaviour is an old one in analysis of team production, until the National Bureau for Economic Research's Shared Capitalism Project, no major survey had documented co-monitoring behaviour, linked it to shares and the structure of work, and examined how it affected employee performance at workplaces.

We used both the NBER and the GSS surveys to study this issue. On the U.S. General Social Survey of workers across the United States, 77 per cent of workers said that they too could observe their co-workers' performance. On the National Bureau for Economic Research's 14-firm survey, 62 per cent of workers said that they could figure out what their fellow worker is doing. Given that most workers could observe the effort of co-workers, we next asked how likely it was that they would take action involving 'a fellow employee not working as hard or as well as he or she should'—anti-shirking behaviour, supporting the fellow worker. Workers varied a lot in their answers to this question. Some said it was very likely they would talk directly to the employer about their fellow shirking worker. Some said they would speak to a supervisor or manager. And some said it was very likely they would do nothing. The size of an employees' workplace was an important factor in these differences. In the NBER survey, in a workplace with less than ten employees, 44 per cent of workers said they would definitely respond in some fashion to seeing a fellow employee shirk, whereas in a workplace with over 100 workers, only 35 per cent said they would respond. Since getting a shirker to shape up has smaller benefits to other workers in a larger workplace, this is free-rider behaviour at work in monitoring free riding!

What we discovered was that workers with employee stock ownership or profit-sharing or gain-sharing were more likely to step forward and take action and support the shirking fellow employee than other workers without shares. In the 14-firm survey of corporations with some form of broad-based capitalism, the intensity of profit-sharing and gain-sharing was the most important factor in whether workers would take action. For shares of stock, workers took action against shirkers just as a result of owning any company stock or holding any employee stock options. In the General Social Survey, where some workers are in firms with no programmes at all, the presence of profit-sharing and gain-sharing and employee stock ownership was the most important determinant of anti-shirking behaviour. But it was the combination of the different share approaches with personnel practices that created an ownership culture that induced the most co-monitoring behaviour: being part of a team, having a high participation in decisions, being treated with respect by their supervisor, having formal training and job security, and being paid relatively well for their job. By contrast, when workers were paid large *individual* bonuses, they were less willing to get involved with a shirking co-worker. If you and I are competing for a bonus, why should I help you perform better?— the worse you do, the more likely I get the bonus. It is the team reward that generates co-operation and the willingness to take time and effort to press other workers to produce up to speed.

We added questions to the NBER survey to find out if the workers had ever actually seen a fellow employee not working as hard as they should, and what the employee had in fact done. We found that 35 per cent of the workers said that the employee who was not working well resented their intervention. But 45 per cent said that the other employee appreciated the action, and 40 per cent said the supervisor appreciated it. Over one-third said the employee's performance improved, but nearly the same proportion said the employee's performance did not improve, and one third did not know. However, our major finding was that the combination of worker ownership and profit sharing with a supportive corporate culture led to the great efforts by fellow employees to intervene with an support a shirking fellow worker.

15.3 THE NATION'S BEST EMPLOYERS

Every year the Great Place to Work Institute reviews the applications of major corporations who seek a place on the list of '100 Best Companies to Work for in America' that *Fortune Magazine* presents with great fanfare. Because being named one of the hundred best is an honour that can attract additional and better job applicants and help retain and spur current employees and bring companies lots of acclaim and attention, every year about 400 of the largest and most successful corporations apply for consideration and compete. The shares of half of the corporations applying are traded on the New York Stock Exchange and the NASDAQ, where they represent 20 per cent of the market value of the public stock market and 10 per cent of employment and sales of all stock market companies. Because of this, any study of shares among the applicants is a study of a major slice of America's corporations and the American economy. This study, entitled, 'Do Broad-based Employee Ownership, Profit Sharing, and Stock Options Help the Best Firms Do Even Better?' appeared in the *British Journal of Industrial Relations* (2016).

To determine the 100 Best Companies to Work For, the Great Place to Work Institute queries managements about their corporate culture and practices and obtains data on turnover and other aspects of work practices and corporate culture. The Institute then surveys a random group of each company's workers and asks them how they are paid— with cash profit-sharing, employee stock ownership, and broad-based stock options— and their attitude towards the company and behaviour at work. Between 2006 and 2008 over 1,300 corporations applied for the 100 Best Companies to Work For in America competition. Over 300,000 of their workers filled out the Great Place To Work Institute survey that ultimately determines whether a corporation makes the 100 Best list and where it is placed on the list. The Institute uses the survey responses to develop a comprehensive indicator of corporate culture called the Trust Index that measures workers' view of the credibility, respect, fairness, pride, and camaraderie of their company.

The Great Place to Work Institute gave us limited access to their data under strict confidentiality procedures to examine the relation between employee stock ownership, profit-sharing, work practices, and the performance of applicant firms. We sought to determine whether firms that gave their workers some property stake were disproportionately represented among applicants, and whether firms with greater degrees of shares and work practices performed better than their peer firms with weaker or no such programmes.

Since firms with exceptional human resource policies and corporate cultures self-select into the applicant pool, comparisons of outcomes within this group are likely biased against finding any effects for broad-based capitalism approaches such as employee stock ownership and profit-sharing. A firm that believed its practices merited recognition as among the 100 Best and that did not have profit-sharing or employee ownership presumably had other policies to reward and motivate workers (an especially well-designed promotion system? generous worker friendly-benefits?) that would compensate for the absence of those programmes. One can presume that many applicants were trying very hard to be 'the best' corporations.

It is interesting that a large proportion of the applicants for the 100 Best Company to Work For competition had some form of employee stock ownership or profit-sharing for their workers: 18 per cent had ESOPs; 18 per cent had cash profit or gain-sharing plans; 22 per cent had deferred profit-sharing plans. The average ESOP in the sample owned about 17 per cent of company stock. One-tenth of the companies were even majority worker owned. One in six companies granted stock options to a majority of their workers. Another 17 per cent of the companies granted stock options to between a quarter and half of all the corporation's workers. The average profit-sharing or gain-sharing plan provided a worker with a 7 per cent bonus on top of their pay.

We discovered that corporations with more extensive employee ownership and profit-sharing had higher scores on the Trust Index. The workers in these corporations rated their company as more credible, respectful of workers' interests, fairer, and as providing greater participation in decisions than workers at other firms. ESOPs and profit-sharing plans where profits added a lot to annual salary topped the list in the Trust Index. Workers with stock options did not differ much on the Trust Index from workers without those options. Corporations with more extensive broad-based capitalism had reduced voluntary turnover, increased employees' intentions to stay with the firm, and higher return on equity for the firm. Corporations that combined shares with participative work practices and a supportive corporate culture had the biggest pay-off in reduced turnover and higher return on equity. Finding these effects in the non-representative '100 Best Companies to Work For' sample strengthens the likelihood that the policies have a causal impact on employee well-being and firm performance (Kruse et al. 2011).

15.4 THE IMPORTANCE OF PARTICIPATIVE OWNERSHIP CULTURE

Every worker has the option to try harder, work harder, think more creatively, co-operate with fellow workers, or choose not to co-operate. Management cannot get into workers' minds and tap into this discretionary effort. This is a matter of free choice. It is either given or not given by the individual person through a complex set of perceptions, motivations, and judgements. Corporations can observe activity but corporate supervisors cannot control what goes on inside the head of the independent person who can grant discretionary effort or problem-solving capacity or not out of their own mind. In the post-industrial workplace much of what the worker has to do is not a matter of mere effort or extra time. If a worker has ownership of the company and finds that the corporate culture throws up barriers to his or her discretion to try harder through physical or mental or emotional or social effort, then it is difficult to imagine how broad-based capitalism can be tied to better performance.

The statistical evidence that firms in which workers have a property stake in their firm are more productive, induce more worker effort and responsibility, spur workers to innovate more, and produce diverse other benefits for workers and the corporation, shows that this is a viable organizational form of capitalism. It pays off, at least for those firms and workers that choose it. It is important to recognize that most research studies show that a very thin layer of shares—a stock option or two for every bank teller in a large publicly traded bank—is not going to make much difference. The impacts are larger when the programmes are meaningful, as they are in many closely held ESOP companies and some model publicly traded companies. But shares are not simply about workers getting more money in the pocket from an ownership or profit stake and firms benefiting with lower turnover, greater work effort, and higher production. It is also about the firm and its employees developing a culture that supports employee participation and co-operation between management and employees over the long term. The corporations and workers that do best combine shares and workplace practices in the context of a participative ownership culture. Our analysis found that giving workers more responsibility, having more teams and problem-solving groups, having a less hierarchical workplace where supervision involves more coaching than control, paying workers at or above the market rate for their fixed wages, and providing workers with greater training opportunities defined this culture.

One fascinating question is whether firms that adopt employee stock ownership or profit- or gain-sharing are likely to also adopt a supportive corporate culture. The answer is yes. Our national surveys show that workers in these firms report significantly more participation in solving company problems through employee involvement teams and self-directed work teams, and say they have more influence, and, in some cases, more training. Managers appear to be either increasingly inferring the better company culture or learning from each other as they compare one company to another. This is also underlined with new data on our *British Journal of Industrial Relations* study (See also, Kruse et al. 2008: 61, Table 1.6).

Extending these practices to more workers and firms, and strengthening the practices in workplaces where they exist, offer a road for normal workers to tap into the wealth embodied in corporate property.

APPENDIX

FIVE STUDIES OF THE RELATION BETWEEN SHARED CAPITALISM AND FIRM OUTPUTS

Study 1: UK Treasury Sponsored Study of British firms (2007). This study obtained data from confidential tax records that identified firms that had approved profit-sharing plans, Save as You Earn plans, and company share-option plans for 16,844 firms. It linked these data to company value added, employment, profits, and capital for 7,633 businesses. The study covered sufficient firms and years to permit the analysts to conduct a panel study of firms that entered or left the programmes as well as to compare firms with and without the programmes at a point in time, and to examine whether the effects differed among industries. The conclusion: 'on average, across the whole sample, the effect of tax-advantaged share schemes is significant and increases productivity by 2.5% in the long run'.

Study 2: General Accountability Office of the U.S. Congress (1987). This study examined 414 corporations which established ESOPs that were set up between 1976 and 1979 when ESOPs were just getting off the ground in the United States. The companies were mostly small- and medium-sized businesses whose stock was not traded on a public stock market. The average company was just under 10 per cent owned by its workers. The study matched the ESOP firms with non-ESOP firms in the same industry and of the same size, and compared outcomes three years after employee ownership started to two years before. The conclusion: By itself employee stock ownership did not change performance but the combination of employee stock ownership with a change in corporate culture was associated with an increase in productivity 'fifty-two percentage points higher than the change for firms that did not have such employee involvement'.

Study 3: Blasi–Kruse study of ESOPs set up between 1988 and 1994. These were small businesses with about 400 workers each. The study compared ESOPs to similarly sized businesses without broad-based employee ownership in the same industry a decade into the future. Workers in the ESOPs had a capital ownership stake of about $15,000, were five times more likely to have a traditional pension plan, were five times more likely to have a 401k plan, were four times more likely to have a profit-sharing plan, and seven times more likely to have another retirement plan than workers in the non-ESOP companies. The ESOPs had significantly higher sales growth and higher sales per worker than the companies without employee ownership. The ESOP corporations survived longer and had fewer bankruptcies. By 1999 almost 70 per cent of the employee ownership businesses were still in existence compared to only 55 per cent of the non-employee ownership companies. A 2002 follow-up on all ESOPs found similar results.

Study 4. This was a field experiment based on twenty-one fast-food franchises owned by one firm, where researchers were allowed to randomly assign profit-sharing to three franchises, and non-financial incentives (social recognition and performance feedback) to six franchises, with the remaining 12 as the control group. A pre/post comparison using monthly data found increased profitability and productivity, and decreased employee turnover in the profit-sharing franchises relative to the control group. In addition, profit-sharing had a more immediate positive effect on profitability and productivity as well as a greater long-lasting effect on employee turnover relative to the non-financial incentives.

Study 5: A 2003 survey of just over a thousand establishments in the State of California done at the Goldman School of Public Policy at the University of California at Berkeley came to similar conclusions. Managers' assessments of quality, financial performance, and the turnover of workers were best when a participatory company culture was combined with profit-sharing and employee stock ownership. This assumes that the arrangements have a reasonably monotonic linear relation to outcomes.

ACKNOWLEDGEMENTS

This chapter is adopted from Joseph R. Blasi, Richard B. Freeman, and Douglas L. Kruse (2013). Evidence, in Joseph R. Blasi, Richard B. Freeman, and Douglas L. Kruse (eds) *The Citizen's Share*, New Haven: Yale University Press, with the permission of Yale University Press.

REFERENCES

Akerlof, George (1984), 'Gift Exchange and Efficiency-Wage Theory: Four Views', *American Economic Review*, 74(2), 79–83.

Blasi, Joseph and Kruse, Douglas (1991), *The New Owners: The Mass Emergence of Employee Ownership in Public Companies and What it Means to American Business* (New York: HarperCollins).

Blasi, J., Kruse, D., and Weltmann, D. (2013), 'Firm Survival and Performance in Privately Held ESOP Companies', in Douglas L. Kruse, ed., *Sharing Ownership, Profits, and Decision-Making in the 21st Century: Advances in the Economic Analysis of Participatory & Labor-Managed Firms*, Volume 14 (Bingley, UK: Emerald Group Publishing Limited), 109–24.

Bryson, A. and Freeman, R. (2007), *Doing the Right Thing? Does Fair Share Capitalism Improve Workplace Performance?* (London: UK Department of Trade and Industry, Employment Relations Research Series, Number 81).

Bryson, Alex and Freeman, Richard (2010), 'How Does Shared Capitalism Affect Economic Performance in the United Kingdom?' in Kruse, Freeman, and Blasi, *Shared Capitalism at Work: Employee Ownership, Profit and Gain Sharing, and Broad-Based Stock Options* (Cambridge, MA: NBER), 201–24.

Doucouliagos, Christopher (1995). 'Worker Participation and Productivity in Labor-Managed and Participatory Capitalist Firms: A Meta-analysis', *Industrial and Labor Relations Review*, 40(1), 58–77.

Dube, Arindrajit and Freeman, Richard (2010), 'Complementarity of Shared Compensation and Decision-Making Systems: Evidence from the American Labor Market', in Kruse, Freeman, and Blasi, *Shared Capitalism at Work* (Cambridge, MA: NBER), 167–200.

Handel, David and Levine, David (2004), 'The Effect of New Work Practices on Workers', *Industrial Relations*, 43(1), 1–41, especially 6.

Harden, Erika E., Kruse, Douglas L., and Blasi, Joseph R. (2010), 'Who Has A Better Idea? Innovation, Shared Capitalism, and Human Resources Policies', in Kruse, Freeman, and Blasi, *Shared Capitalism at Work* (Cambridge, MA: NBER), 225–56.

Kardas, P., Scharf, A. L., and Keogh, J. (1998), 'Wealth and Income Consequences of ESOPs and Employee Ownership: A Comparative Study from Washington State', *Journal of Employee Ownership Law and Finance*, 10(4), 3–52.

Kim, E. H. and Ouimet, P. (2009), 'Employee Capitalism or Corporate Socialism: Broad-Based Employee Stock Ownership'. Washington, DC: U.S. Census Bureau Center for Economic Studies, Paper Number CES-WP-09-44, 2009.

Kruse, Douglas (1998), 'Profit-Sharing and the Demand for Low-Skill Workers', in Peter Gottschalk and Richard Freeman, eds, *Generating Jobs* (New York: Russell Sage Foundation), 105–53.

Kruse, D. (2002), 'Research Evidence on Prevalence and Effects of Employee Ownership', *Journal of Employee Ownership Law and Finance*, 14(4), 65–90.

Kruse, D. L. and Blasi, J. (1995). Employee Ownership, Employee Attitudes, and Firm Performance (Cambridge, MA: National Bureau for Economic Research Working Paper 5277).

Kruse, Douglas and Blasi, Joseph (2007), *Report on the 2006 General Social Survey on Shared Capitalism* (New Brunswick, NJ: Rutgers University School of Management and Labor Relations), Table 3.

Kruse, Douglas, Blasi, Joseph, and Freeman, Richard (2011), 'Does Shared Capitalism Help the Best Firms Do Even Better?' Cambridge: National Bureau for Economic Research, 2011, Working Paper 7745.

Kruse, Douglas, Blasi, Joseph, and Park, Rhokeun (2008), 'Shared Capitalism in the U.S. Economy', in Kruse, Freeman, and Blasi, eds, *Shared Capitalism at Work* (Cambridge, MA: NBER), 61 (Table 1.6).

Kruse, D. L., Freeman, R. B., and Blasi, J. R. (2010a), *Shared Capitalism at Work: Employee Ownership, Profit and Gain Sharing, and Broad-Based Stock Options* (Cambridge, MA: NBER).

Kruse, Douglas L., Freeman, Richard B., and Blasi, Joseph R. (2010b), 'Do Workers Gain by Sharing?' in Kruse, Freeman, and Blasi, *Shared Capitalism at Work* (Cambridge, MA: NBER), 257–89.

Peterson, Suzanne J. and Luthans, Fred (2006), 'The Impact of Financial and Nonfinancial Incentives on Business-Unit Outcomes Over Time', *Journal of Applied Psychology*, 91(1), 156–65.

Rodgers, L. (2010), 'Are ESOPs Good for Employees?' *Pensions & Benefits Daily*, 100(1), November: 1–5 (The Bureau of National Affairs).

Rodgers, L and Keeling, M. (2010a). *ESOPs as Retirement Benefits*, Oakland, California and Washington, DC: National Center for Employee Ownership and The Employee Ownership Foundation, 20 September.

Rodgers, L and Keeling, M. (2010b). *ESOPs as Retirement Benefits–Supplemental Tables*, Oakland, CA and Washington, DC: National Center for Employee Ownership and Employee Ownership Foundation, 15 September.

Matrix Knowledge Group (2010), *The Employee Ownership Effect: A Review of the Evidence* (London: Matrix Evidence, a division of Matrix Knowledge Group).

Oxera Economic Consultancy (2007a), 'Tax Advantaged Employee Share Schemes: Analysis of Productivity Effects, Report 1, Productivity Measured Using Turnover'. Prepared for Her Majesty's Revenue And Customs. London: Her Majesty's Revenue and Customs (HMRC), August, Report 33.

Oxera Economic Consultancy (2007b), 'Tax Advantaged Employee Share Schemes: Analysis of Productivity Effects, Report 2, Productivity Measured Using Gross Value Added'. Prepared for Her Majesty's Revenue And Customs. London: Her Majesty's Revenue and Customs (HMRC), Report 33, August.

Oxera Economic Consultancy (2007c), 'Tax Advantaged Employee Share Schemes: Analysis of Productivity Effects, Overview'. Prepared for Her Majesty's Revenue And Customs. London: Her Majesty's Revenue and Customs (HMRC), Report 33, August.

Oxera Economic Consultancy (2007d), 'Tax Advantaged Employee Share Schemes: Analysis of Productivity Effects, Appendices to Report 1'. Prepared for Her Majesty's Revenue And Customs. London: Her Majesty's Revenue and Customs- HMRC, Report 33, August.

Scharf, A. and Mackin, C. M. (2000), *Census of Massachusetts Companies with Employee Stock Ownership Plans (ESOPs)* (Boston: Commonwealth Corporation).

United States General Accounting Office (1986), *Employee Stock Ownership Plans: Benefits and Costs of ESOP Tax Incentives for Broadening Stock Ownership* (Washington, DC: U.S. General Accounting Office).

United States General Accounting Office (1987), 'Employee Stock Ownership Plans: Report to the Chairman, Committee on Finance, U.S. Senate,' Washington, DC: U.S. General Accounting Office, Report Number GAO-PEMD-88-1, October.

Weitzman, M. L. and Kruse, D. L. (1990), 'Profit Sharing and Productivity,' in *Paying for Productivity*, ed. Alan Blinder (Washington, D.C.: Brookings Institution), 95–141.

Weltman, Dan, Blasi, Joseph R., and Kruse, Douglas L. (2013), *At What Threshhold Do Employee Shares Have A Meaningful Effect?* (New Brunswick: Rutgers University School of Management and Labor Relations).

CHAPTER 16

....

ENTERPRISE FORM, PARTICIPATION, AND PERFORMANCE IN MUTUALS AND CO-OPERATIVES

....

ZOE ADAMS AND SIMON DEAKIN

16.1 INTRODUCTION

....

MUTUALS, co-operatives, and similar forms of social enterprise have a legal form which distinguishes them from commercial or 'for-profit' companies. In practice, it is not always clear how these differences in legal form map on to distinct approaches to corporate governance, or how far legal form and governance structure together are reflected in performance and distributional outcomes. There is some evidence that financial mutuals, for example, are more risk averse and less profitable, but also more stable and resilient, than commercial banks, and that employee ownership is associated with enhanced worker motivation and improved labour productivity. Overall, however, the empirical picture on the performance effects of different enterprise forms is not clear-cut. This may be because the fit between legal form and organizational structure and behaviour is not uniform across different sectoral and national contexts. There may be many factors driving the culture and practice of individual firms, of which legal form is only one. Legal structures are multi-functional and may be adapted to different ends. Thus the study of mutuals and co-operatives needs to take account of legal form, but also to consider the interaction of the law with a range of contextual factors.

In this chapter we review theoretical and empirical literature on the governance and performance effects of enterprise form. Section 16.2 outlines the nature of conceptual and theoretical debates concerning the effects of the mutual form and Section 16.3 provides an overview of the legal and incentive properties of different enterprise types. Section 16.4 reviews empirical evidence on performance outcomes and stakeholder participation in mutuals and other forms of social enterprise. Section 16.5 offers a concluding assessment.

16.2 Governance Structure and Legal Form

Business firms may be constituted in one of several legally defined enterprise forms. These include variants of the company limited by share capital, including the closely held private company and the publicly listed company; partnerships; producer co-operatives; mutuals; and types of social enterprise including the company limited by guarantee; and more recent innovations such as the US 'benefit corporation' and the British 'community interest company'. The choice of legal form has consequences for the financing of the enterprise, the balance of power, and the division of risks between different corporate constituencies or stakeholders, and the nature of managerial accountability.

In the company limited by share capital, residual rights of income and control together vest in the shareholders as a group, and they are often said as a result to be the company's 'owners'. The reference to 'ownership' needs to be qualified because it is more accurate legally to say that shareholders own their *shares*, which are corporate securities issued by the company in return for initial financial investments and are, in principle, tradeable as items of property in their own right. Ownership of a share confers voice, income, and control rights, which are generally proportionate to the extent of the investment made by each shareholder, and the tradability of the share confers liquidity, in particular where the company is listed and the shares are therefore exchangeable on the open market (Armour et al. 2009). However, ownership of a share does not confer a pro rata share of the firm's assets, which are vested in the legal person of the corporation or company (Ireland 1999; Robé 2011; Deakin 2012).

Nor is it meaningful to talk of shareholder ownership of the 'firm' understood as an organizational entity combining physical and human assets. This 'firm' or enterprise in this sense cannot be owned in its entirety by any one stakeholder group, whether the shareholders or otherwise (Deakin 2011). It is relevant here that 'corporation' or 'company' is not the firm as such, but the foundational legal concept which is used to structure it and to facilitate its operation through juridical mechanisms such as separate personality, limited liability, and delegated management (Robé 2011). In juridical terms, the company is a legal person or subject, not a *res* or thing that can be owned. The suggestion of some economists that the assets of the firm vest in the company and that the company, in turn, is a *res* owned collectively by the shareholders, does not reflect the juridical practice of modern company law systems (Deakin 2012).

It does not follow from what has just been said that the firm is *ownerless*. Shareholders have property rights in their shares which will under certain circumstances give them priority over other stakeholders in claims against the company's assets, but other stakeholders may also have property-type claims over these assets at points in the life cycle of the firm: collateral, in the case of banks, and preferred claims in the case of certain creditors, which may include the fiscal authorities and employees. Employees and creditors may also have voice rights which, in the event of a reorganization of the firm, may prevail over those of the shareholders. Property rights can take many forms, including income and voice rights as well as the alienation rights which shareholders have in common stock. Thus it is conceptually more correct to think of the company, not as the shareholders' property, but as a 'commons' in which there are overlapping and multiple property-type claims (Ostrom 1990; Poteete et al. 2010). The 'commons' provides a normative structure for the firm which operates simultaneously to define the rights of the different stakeholders and to enable the firm to be managed in their collective interests as a going concern (Deakin 2011; Talbot 2015).

It is necessary to consider the notion of ownership in the firm at the outset of a discussion of the properties of mutuals and other social enterprise forms, because just as it is a mistake to talk without qualification of shareholders owning the firm or company in which they hold stock, it is also a mistake to talk too loosely of worker or customer 'ownership' in the case of co-operatives and mutuals (Heath 2006). In the case of the company limited by share capital, the shareholders, as the company's members, have residual income and control rights, and this gives them certain powers and capacities, in particular the power to hold management to account, which other stakeholders or constituencies do not have in the case of the for-profit firm (Jensen and Meckling 1976; Fama and Jensen 1983; Armour et al. 2009). In the case of the professional partnership or producer-owned co-operative, these residual rights and powers vest in suppliers of labour; in the case of the mutual, they vest in customers (Hansmann 1996). However, the employees (in the case of the co-operative) and the customers (in the case of the mutual) are no more the firm's owners than the shareholders are in the case of the for-profit enterprise. Exactly what the rights of employees or customers are depends on the detail of the default terms of the legal forms which describe the various type of social enterprise and on the way in which those terms are customized by corporate by-laws or articles of association.

A feature which all forms of enterprise, whatever their legal type, have in common, is that they involve the combination of multiple inputs from suppliers of finance and labour, and a distinct role for management in the organization of the process of production (Robé 2011; Deakin 2012). The stakeholders—whether they are shareholders, creditors, or employees—generally have no direct right to intervene in the management of the firm. The law recognizes the role of managers in setting the strategy of the firm with a view to maintaining its viability over time as a going concern; to that end, they are insulated, up to a point, from pressures exercised by a given stakeholder group. Thus most legal systems provide that shareholders in a company limited by share capital do not have the right to manage the company; that power vests in the board which then delegates to officers and employees. The shareholders have the right to change the composition of the board by majority vote to elect new directors and may thereby change its strategic direction, and they may, by agreement or by virtue of a regulatory default rule, have powers over certain asset sales or in respect of change of control, but this is not equivalent to a right of management and does not confer a direct property right in the assets of the enterprise. The same principle applies, *mutatis mutandis*, to social enterprises constituted as mutuals and co-operatives.

It follows that mutuals and co-operatives are not necessarily going to be run more democratically, or managed in a more participative way, than for-profit firms. A mutual governance structure for the firm is not, in itself, a sufficient condition for meaningful stakeholder participation (Paranque and Willmott 2014). A number of more specific features of mutual firms need to be considered, including the precise channels through which managers can be held to account, and the nature of the asset lock placed on the capital of the firm, which affects the balance of risks and rewards across and within the different stakeholder groups.

As we have just seen, in the case of the company limited by share capital it is the shareholders exclusively who have the right to replace the board and thereby change the strategic direction of the firm, and only the shareholders can access the residual from production directly by receiving dividends, for example, or having their shares redeemed by the company for cash (share 'buy-backs' or repurchases). The rule of one-share, one-vote, which some systems recognize as close to being mandatory and others treat as a default rule which the shareholders can adjust (see Kraakman et al. 2009), ensures proportionality of risk and reward. Thus in the case of the for-profit firm, there is an alignment of residual risk and income rights.

Hansmann's influential theory of ownership in the firm argues that this alignment is efficient because it provides powerful incentives for the monitoring of management (Hansmann 1996). Which particular stakeholder group—investors, employees, or customers—is vested with the combined power and incentive to monitor management is a function of a number of factors. In the case of the for-profit firm, the vesting of residual income and control rights in the shareholders is justified by two considerations: their greater exposure to risk, which is a function of the non-contractibility of their claims, and the greater homogeneity of their interests viewed from the perspective of their own internal governance.

What the argument from risk means more precisely is that *governance* rights—rights of voice and control, and rights to the residual income generated by the firm—should vest in the group which is least able to *contract* for those rights in the market. Shareholders supply risk capital to for-profit firms, in a form which cannot be contracted because of uncertainty associated with the open-endedness of the investment. Their returns are entirely dependent on the success of the firm and hence in large part on the quality and effort of its management (Fama and Jensen 1983). By contrast, it is sometimes argued, the claims of workers and creditors can be more completely contracted for; there is no need to grant governance rights to banks which can protect themselves by taking collateral, and employees are protected by their contractual wages and salaries which are mostly fixed, in contrast to the variable element of shareholders' returns (Jensen and Meckling 1976).

The argument against homogeneity is that monitoring is best undertaken by the stakeholder group which has the least internal divergence of interests (Hansmann 1996).

Shareholders who invest for returns are motivated by financial considerations, it is argued, and as a result face low coordination costs when it comes to identifying a group interest and articulating it to management. Workers, by contrast, have multiple and heterogeneous interests, ranging from high wages to stable employment and satisfying work, which involve trade-offs of various kinds. This makes it more difficult for them to monitor managers effectively. Thus, in this theory, it is the internal governance or co-ordination costs which determine the relative efficiency of different enterprise forms.

Hansmann's theory generates two linked principles for the design of corporate law. The first is that it is inefficient to vest governance rights in more than one stakeholder group; the second is that governance and contract rights should be kept distinct. The law should allow the founders of the firm, or its members at any given time, to allocate control and income rights to the group which has the most to lose through market-based contracting and the most to gain by internalizing its risks through ownership, if not of the firm itself, then of the governance rights through which management can be held to account.

This view implies that in the case of the for-profit firm, it is costly for employees to be given voice rights which may conflict with or undermine those of shareholders. In practice, however, the managements of many firms constituted as commercial companies, whether closely held or publicly listed, seek to engage employees in participative initiatives, and some legal systems require them to do so by mandating codetermination in forms which include employee membership of a supervisory board or works council with consultation or, sometimes, veto rights over the way the firm is run as an organizational entity (Deakin and Adams 2015). Thus it is not obvious that stakeholder participation cannot be achieved within the legal structure of the for-profit firm. Going further, participation could be regarded as a necessity or prerequisite for certain types of complex, long-term co-operative ventures.

Conversely, it is not clear that mutuals and co-operatives will necessarily engage in more participative forms of management than commercial, for-profit firms. If it is the case that workers or customers have heterogeneous interests and that the costs of internal governance for employee- or customer-stakeholders are high, as Hansmann (1996) argues, it will be more costly to hold management to account in mutuals and co-operatives than it would be in the case of commercial firms. It is also possible that the absence of shareholder pressure on managers could reduce their incentive to engage in participatory initiatives with employees or customers which would increase the value of the firm but would mean a loss of power for management (Chai et al. 2015). If this were the case, we could expect mutual and co-operative forms of enterprise, paradoxically, to be both less productive and less democratic, in their internal mode of operations, than for-profit companies, in particular in legal regimes which encourage the shareholders to take a long-term view of their investments, as in the case of the concept of 'enlightened shareholder value', which has some relevance to the recent evolution of British company law (Keay 2013).

Also important when considering the internal dynamics of the firm, and the division of risks and rewards between the different stakeholders, is the nature of the asset lock which comes with particular legal forms. One of the functions performed by the juridical institution of corporate personality is the identification of a pool of assets which are distinct to the firm as opposed to its members, whether shareholders, customers, or workers, and which the firm can then use to bond with creditors and to put to use in meeting long-term strategic goals (Hansmann and Kraakman 2000; Hansmann et al. 2006). All enterprise forms, in one way or another, place restrictions on the power of any one stakeholder group, even those legally constituted as the firm's residual claimants, to deplete the firm's asset base. In the case of the company limited by share capital, individual shareholders cannot withdraw their capital at will (Blair 2003). They can only exit the firm by selling their shares to a third party, a transaction which leaves the underlying asset base of the firm unaffected. The shareholders can in principle, by a majority vote, liquidate the firm and retrieve its underlying assets. This capacity puts the shareholders in a powerful position to exclude other stakeholder groups from access to the income generated by the firm, and can as such pose a disincentive to workers and creditors making relational or asset-specific investments in the firm, through for example, firm-specific human capital or shared technological know-how. In practice, it is not unusual for the firm's capital to be protected against shareholder withdrawal by various means, which can include, for example, joint ownership of intellectual property on the part of suppliers and customers, the taking of collateral by banks, and the granting by law or contract of voice or veto rights to employees at the point where the firm is about to undergo a change of control or reorganization (Deakin 2011).

In the case of mutuals and co-operatives, the asset lock plays a role in protecting stakeholders from expropriation by one dominant group, and thus stabilizes the firm as a going concern. Thus the traditional mutual, in the form of the British building society, was characterized not so much by customer ownership, as by the strong asset lock placed on the firm's capital, which could not be directly accessed by the firm's depositor-members except in the form of returns on their savings, which were determined by the board and were also subject to external regulation in order to ensure that capital was not depleted. It was the removal of this asset lock through legally sanctioned demutualization in the 1990s which undermined and destabilized the traditional building society form, with largely negative outcomes for borrowers (Cook et al. 2002). It follows that when considering the properties of different legal forms, attention needs to be paid, not only to the identification of residual claims in each case, but to the detail of mechanisms of accountability, and to the division of risks and powers between management and the firm's stakeholders in general, and both within and between the different stakeholder groups.

More generally, there are grounds for thinking that multi-stakeholder governance, rather than legal structure alone, plays a role in determining the sustainability of social enterprises. Heterogeneity of interests within and across multiple stakeholder groups does not necessarily lead to higher governance costs where stakeholders have a shared commitment to a common social purpose (Wilson and Post 2011). Defining a social mission for the firm, over and above profit maximization, may serve to reduce internal governance costs associated with the exercise of authority and hierarchy within the firm (Levillain and Segrestin 2012). Work in the field of behavioural economics has emphasized the importance of non-instrumental aspects of human behaviour, such as reciprocity, and suggests that these behavioural qualities are capable of supporting frameworks in which the sharing of values and aims can prevail above the pursuit of self-regarding objectives. This perspective may help to explain why co-operative and deliberative approaches to governance are often found in the context of social enterprise forms (Borzaga et al. 2011; Borzaga and Sacchetti 2015).

Heterogeneity of interests may also bring benefits which outweigh high coordination costs. In particular, a diversity of interests within the firm may increase managers' access to complementary knowledge sources and lead to productive forms of deliberation (Middleton 1987; Evers 2001; Laville and Nyssens 2001; Campi et al. 2006). This suggests that involving diverse stakeholder groups in the decision-making process is a potentially effective strategy for social and other enterprises.

16.3 Legal Varieties of Enterprise Form

16.3.1 The 'Investor Mutual' or 'Capital Co-operative': The Company Limited by Share Capital

In companies limited by share capital, the investors enjoy exclusive rights to income (in the form of dividends and surplus assets in the event of company liquidation) and exclusive rights of control ('voice' rights exercisable in shareholder meetings and a number of powers to control the directors of the firm and its overall management). This form is most frequently found in for-profit industrial enterprises where the firm needs external capital in order to grow and sustain its operations. In this case, corporate law operates to align the interests of investors with the 'interests' of the enterprise by linking the investors' residual right to income to the firm's profitability. This creates an incentive for investors to monitor how the firm is managed, and the law creates governance and control mechanisms that facilitate this (Fama and Jensen 1983; Easterbrook and Fischel 1991).

The alignment between the incentive to monitor and the opportunity and means to do so is at the core of the claims made for the company limited by share capital, which because of the way it places shareholders at the centre of corporate governance, can be thought of as an 'investor mutual' or 'capital co-operative' (Hansmann 1996). Where shares can be openly traded on a public stock exchange, the mutual or co-operative element is downplayed as the shareholders are likely to be rentiers who have bought stock on the secondary market rather than investor-managers, and as such are not in the same position to exercise direct influence or control over management. However, the tradability of shares brings in other features of governance including the 'disciplinary' effect exercised on managers by stock price movements and takeover bids (Easterbrook and Fischel 1991).

16.3.2 Producer Mutuals and Employee Co-operatives

The 'producer' mutual was the traditional form taken by professional partnerships in sectors such as law and accountancy up until the later decades of the twentieth century, when it was displaced by the limited liability partnership which altered the balance of risk and reward by protecting individual partners from claims on their assets. The employee co-operative, in which residual income and monitoring rights vest in the workforce or a portion of it, is also an old form, but has enjoyed a revival in some countries including Britain as a result of successive privatization waves since the 1980s. It is now to be found across various industrial sectors and is the form taken by a number of public-sector spin-outs (Pendleton and Robinson 2015).

Support for the employee-owned mutual has come from a growing recognition that both equity finance and human capital play important roles in firm productivity. It is now more widely accepted that it is not just equity investors who face high levels of risk in terms of their investment into the firm; employees make firm-specific investments in terms of human capital to which a similar argument for ownership rights can be applied (Blair 1995). A more turbulent economic environment since the onset of the global financial crisis in 2008 has also encouraged some firms to adopt variants of employee ownership in an attempt to maintain worker support, given the need for recurrent changes to wage structure and frequent corporate reorganizations (Pendleton and Robinson 2015). In addition, the financial crisis has added fuel to the belief that shareholder-centric corporate governance encourages short-termism (Ownership Commission 2012). The assumption here is that employees' interests in the firm go beyond a short-term interest in profit maximization, so that employee ownership and participation can help stabilize the firm and encourage long-term strategic planning.

A further factor underpinning the popularity of this legal form is governmental and cross-party political support. Thus in Britain it has been associated with the recent Conservative Party discourse on the 'Big Society', but was also in line with several initiatives undertaken by previous Labour administrations. In the context of social services such as health and education, the idea of employee ownership has been used to minimize public opposition to, and facilitate employee co-operation in, privatization and marketization (Pendleton and Robinson 2015).

16.3.3 Consumer Mutuals: Co-operatives and Building Societies

In firms where residual claimant status is conferred on the organization's customers, the entity is often referred to as a consumer mutual or co-operative. This category includes organizations such as retail co-operatives, friendly societies, industrial and provident societies, credit unions, mutual insurers, and building societies (or in the US context, savings and loans corporations). These forms are frequently found in contexts where consumers have relatively weak market power and lack the information they need to secure their interests through contract. Many consumer mutuals originally emerged in low-income regions or localities in which profit-seeking corporations had a minimal presence, but where there was a social need for the provision of low-cost goods and services. The model is in principle most efficient when consumer interests are homogeneous, so that the costs of monitoring are low, and for this reason it is often adopted by organizations providing a limited range of goods and services, or serving a relatively small customer base with a shared regional, cultural, or religious identity (Hansmann 1996).

Regulation of particular types of organization can also be used to ensure that these conditions are maintained and thereby enable these organizations to operate in the areas where they are most needed. This was the case with the early building societies and mutual insurance firms. These organizations have been associated with a mutual 'ethos' driven by their origins in serving the needs of a local community, as part of which many of them sought explicitly to build loyalty between the firm and its local or regional customer base (Cook et al. 2002).

Arguably the most successful case of the customer mutual was the traditional building society. The British building society movement grew rapidly from its local beginnings, in part because of legislation which, from an early stage in the nineteenth century, protected the assets of 'permanent' societies and limited their corporate purposes. The law also placed restrictions on the use by societies of external financing, requiring them to rely on deposits by customer-members. The law overcame the potential ownership costs associated with the existence of heterogonous interests between lenders and borrowers by ensuring a high level of dispersal of the ownership rights, which was achieved by mandating a one-member, one-vote rule (not one-share, one-vote). This provides members with little incentive to be involved in governance, with the result that monitoring was mostly conducted by an external regulator. Low-cost exit for depositors meant that there was no need to compensate them for the risks of their 'investment' by providing them with residual rights linked to profitability. This meant that profits could be channelled into the business. In effect, the directors of building societies came to act as guardians of future generations of lenders and borrowers, rather than fiduciaries acting on behalf of current members. The decline in the building society movement from the 1990s was brought about by successive legal reforms which permitted building societies to demutualize in a way which removed the lock on assets and restrictions on external financing, thereby creating opportunities for investors seeking short-term financial returns (Cook et al. 2002).

16.3.4 New Legal Forms of Social Enterprise

A number of new enterprise forms have recently been introduced in ways which seek to accommodate the specific needs faced by social enterprises. These are often referred to as 'hybrid' forms as they combine aspects of the traditional non-profit and for-profit forms by expressly permitting combinations of economic and social purposes. Most such organizations prioritize the pursuit of a specific social mission as do traditional non-profit firms, but they also adopt sophisticated business models and pursue these objectives via corporate activity. They often require access to multiple financing options, which makes the traditional mutual unsuitable for meeting their needs. These organizations face novel governance challenges because they have to balance the interests of a number of different stakeholders, ensure loyalty to their social missions, generate sufficient profit to fund their activities, and also serve the interests of investors (Raz 2012).

In the USA, an attempt to accommodate these needs of social enterprises was made with the introduction of the 'L3C' in 2008 and the 'benefit corporation' in 2010. The low-profit limited liability company (L3C) was designed to encourage investment in socially beneficial for-profit ventures by empowering enterprises to pursue socially beneficial purposes which might not be compatible with the shareholder-centric mission of the company limited by share capital (Raz 2012). The L3C model permits the founders or members of the firm formally to reject profit-maximization as a corporate objective. It is intended to facilitate the flow of investment capital for use for social purposes, while leaving further issues of governance untouched and a matter for internal consensus.

The 'benefit corporation' was similarly introduced in order to allow firms to take decisions for non-financial reasons. It requires that the company make specific commitments to a social purpose in its constitution. This must involve a commitment to benefit the public. This new legal form sought to address many of the problems associated with traditional non-profits and mutuals by permitting firms to offer investors unlimited midstream and residual returns, thereby encouraging investment and improving financing prospects while enabling organizations to pursue a dual economic and social purpose (Reiser 2011). The model benefit corporation statutes impose various reporting obligations on the firm which are linked with the achievement of its social purpose. This was done in an attempt to increase transparency and improve the accountability of social enterprises to multiple stakeholders with interests in the purposes they pursue.

However, in the case of the benefit corporation there is no independent regulator or authority with powers of enforcement as there was in the case of traditional mutuals such as savings and loans corporations, and only shareholders have formal governance rights (Deskins 2012). Directors are protected from certain liabilities in order to enable them to balance competing economic and social considerations, but no guidance is offered to them in the exercise of this enhanced discretion. The definition of the 'social mission' is vague, and it has been suggested this model has failed to address the risk of 'mission-drift' in social enterprises (Raz 2012; Cummings 2012).

In the UK, legislation set up the 'community interest company' in 2004. A CIC must have the purpose of benefiting the community. In contrast with the benefit corporation, an independent enforcement authority was established, and a specific 'community interest test' applied to more precisely define the purposes which such firms were permitted to pursue. There is an ongoing requirement to satisfy the regulator that this test is met. The CIC otherwise operates in the same way as a normal commercial company, and is governed by both general company law and CIC-specific regulations. The idea is that CICs should operate as far as possible as 'conventional' for-profit enterprises, while nevertheless prioritizing social purposes over the pursuit of profit.

A CIC can be set up as a company limited by guarantee or as a private or a public company limited by share capital. The law permits CICs which are companies limited by share capital to offer dividends, but it imposes an asset lock which caps the value of dividends. It also limits the interest that can be agreed on any performance-related loans. This aspect of the regulations was designed to help CICs to remain committed to the community-related purpose and to address the danger of mission-drift. However, the limits imposed by the asset lock have been subject to a number of reforms since the CIC model was first introduced. Responses to government consultations addressing this issue suggest that the asset lock is seen as limiting flexibility in the design of firms' capital structures and restricting their ability to fund activities through equity investments. While a 35 per cent aggregate cap on dividends has been retained, the most recent reforms in October 2014 have removed the cap on dividends per share and have increased the limit on the performance-related interest that can be charged on loans. Although the enforcement authority enjoys extensive powers, it has expressly adopted a 'light touch' attitude since it was established. These changes have prompted concerns that investors seeking short-term returns will increasingly enter the market for CIC shares, undermining their social purpose.

16.4 Empirical Evidence on Participation and Performance in Mutuals and Co-operatives

Hansmann's model argued that the most efficient corporate types would show the most stability over time and would therefore gradually crowd out competing legal forms. He suggested that the investor-mutual would in most circumstances prove to be more efficient than the producer- or consumer-orientated version, and would come to dominate the market (Hansmann 1996). This view suggests that there is an inherent tendency towards monopoly and, ultimately, of sterility in the market for corporate form.

Another view is that diversity in the market for forms can be preserved by appropriate legislative limits on the conversion of mutuals and other social enterprise types into commercial companies (Cook et al. 2002). Different legal models serve different social and economic needs. It may be desirable for the law to intervene in order to maintain plurality so that the specific needs served by the different models are not left unmet. The experience of the 2008 financial crisis has lent support to the view that preserving a diversity of ownership structures in a sector of the economy may be a necessary prerequisite to the avoidance of systemic risk. A regulatory environment conducive to plurality should be more capable of weathering an uncertain market environment than the monoculture of corporate form that has characterized the financial services sector since the early 1990s (Haldane and Nelson 2012; Bholat and Gray 2013).

16.4.1 Consumer Mutuals and Building Societies

The demutualization of British building societies, including Halifax, Abbey National, Alliance & Leicester, Woolwich, Northern Rock, Bristol & West, and Bradford & Bingley, in the early 1990s, can be attributed to a combination of factors, including strategic decisions of the firms' managements, opportunism on the part of short-term investors ('carpetbaggers'), and legislative changes, not all of which had their intended effects (Stephens 2001; Hambach 2014). Some building society managers and related interest groups lobbied for legislation permitting demutualization on the grounds that it was needed to enable firms to respond to structural change in the market for residential property. Prior to demutualization, a series of regulatory changes had encouraged investor-owned banks, which were able to offer a diverse range of goods and services, to move into the residential mortgage market. This increased pressures on building societies to compete with the alternative model provided by the retail banks, and fuelled a belief that the legal restrictions associated with the mutual model were preventing them from adapting to a the new competitive and regulatory environment (Marshall et al. 2000, 2003; Klimecki and Wilmott 2011).

A series of reforms to the legal framework for financial mutuals, beginning with the 1986 Building Societies Act, gave building societies the option to offer shares to external investors, and provided for the possibility of demutualization. Building societies thereby became vulnerable to influence from opportunistic investors who began to put pressure on managers to pursue growth-centric business strategies, for which demutualization was deemed to be necessary.

There is also evidence that around this time, building society managers increasingly adopted a business ethic in line with the culture of the wider financial services sector (Marshall et al. 2000). The higher pay enjoyed by managers operating in the financial services sector appears to have increased the attractiveness of demutualization for building society executives (Marshall et al. 2003; Klimecki and Wilmott 2011; Shiwakoti 2012).

However, the failure of many of the demutualized building societies after 2008 casts doubt on claims that the investor-owned corporate form was appropriate for the sector. Both mutualized and demutualized building societies began to diversify their product lines around the same time, suggesting that demutualization was not necessary for a change of strategy (Stephens 2001). The collapse of the demutualized building societies was accelerated by sector-wide dependence on wholesale funding and securitization models which left firms vulnerable to external shocks, which duly arrived with the 'credit crunch' of 2007–8 (Klimecki and Willmott 2011; Bholat and Gray 2013). There is evidence that demutualization had an impact on the strategies that managers were choosing to pursue. It was already known, prior to the 2007–8 financial crisis, that commercial companies competing with mutuals in the same sector tend to pursue risk-ier strategies (Cook et al. 2002), and the post-crisis experience of demutualized firms bears this out (Klimecki and Willmott 2011).

There is also evidence that a particular combination of a weak regulatory environ-ment and ineffective monitoring contributed to the fragility of demutualized firms. The move to shareholder-centric governance encouraged firms to focus on financial returns, while institutional shareholders largely pursued a passive, hands-off role when it came to engaging with boards on issues of corporate strategy (Hambach 2014). The legal form adopted by demutualized firms encouraged a change in the way directors perceived and discharged their functions (Bholat and Gray 2013). The former building societies were very quickly faced with pressures to produce dividends and capital growth which impacted on the way that they were managed (Bholat and Gray 2013; Klimecki and Willmott 2011).

There is, conversely, evidence that consumer mutuals were on average less fragile than demutualized financial firms during the economic turbulence induced by the crisis of 2007–8. When liquidity froze in the 'credit crunch', mutual firms were less exposed to market movements because of regulations limiting the use they could make of whole-sale money markets. Their continuing reliance on savers' deposits meant that they were less likely to have pursued high-risk activities aimed at capital growth in the years prior to the crisis (Klimecki and Willmott 2011). There is also evidence that the 'mutual ethos' associated with long-term relations between building society members and the man-agement of the still-mutualized firms had acted as a 'check' on managerial opportunism in this period (Spear 2004; Bholat and Gray 2013).

16.4.2 Employee Ownership

The number of firms characterized by employee ownership of some kind has increased substantially in Britain since the early 2000s. Pendleton and Robinson (2015) report between 250 and 300 such firms, characterized by a range of different corporate gov-ernance structures. Drawing on a sample of 57 of these firms, they show that employee ownership is most frequently adopted as a result of privatization or business succes-sion, but can also occur where employees are allotted a portion of the share capital after an initial period of investor-ownership, or in the context of entrepreneurial start-ups. Since 2010, most of the rise in employee-owned firms has been in the context of pri-vatization, but the number of employee-owned start-ups has also risen (Pendleton and Robinson 2015).

In the context of a study of employee co-operatives, Ridley-Duff (2009) argues that the specific legal form appropriate to a given organization differs in accordance with the long-term growth priorities of the organization in question. This study showed how restrictions on financing influence firm behaviour. If a firm has growth ambitions, forms which allow for the issuing of share capital tend to be more efficient for the firm in ques-tion, and CICs with growth ambitions seem to benefit most if they form themselves as a company limited by share capital, rather than as a company limited by guarantee. While access to *external* equity financing does not appear to affect a firm's flexibility, access to capital—internal and/or external—seems to be important in all worker co-operatives. In addition, issuing external equity has been shown to help a firm weather an economic downturn, cement joint ventures with customers and suppliers, and facilitate business development. For all the companies investigated in the study, asset locks were generally perceived to be an obstacle to the pursuit of the firm's objectives (Ridley-Duff, 2009).

In order to sustain democratic organization and prevent loss of control to outside interests, the most effective ownership structure appears to require a combination of individual and collective ownership (Ridley-Duff 2009). Limiting the residual claims of employees to profit-linked income streams, without simultaneously adopting measures to encourage democratic decision-making and participatory governance, may result in a passive and complicit approach to management control. It also appears to preclude the incorporation of wider community and environmental concerns in corporate decision-making, as the employee's interest in governance remains closely linked with the pursuit of self-interest and profit maximization (Paranque and Willmott 2014).

Research in the USA supports the view that models based on employee ownership can have a positive impact on employee well-being, wealth creation, firm productivity, long term stability, and growth (Carberry 2011). Productivity is believed to be affected by the positive effects that ownership can have on employee motivation. Nonetheless, these effects appear to occur only when ownership is combined with increased decision-making opportunities, training in matters related to governance and financial performance, and an environment in which employee engagement is actively encouraged (Freeman et al. 2004). Some studies find that employee ownership can have a positive impact on corporate financial performance (Kaarsemaker 2006), but the relationship between employee ownership, corporate performance, worker productivity, and well-being is still relatively unexplored (Carberry 2011).

The evidence concerning public-sector spin-outs in the UK, particularly NHS trusts, suggests that drives to cut public expenditure have the potential to undermine the wider goals, including increased participation, of a policy of encouraging employee-mutuals (Pendleton and Robinson 2015). In the context of privatization, the workforces of NHS trusts have so far proved reluctant to embrace the employee-ownership model, due to a common perception of the risks involved. There is widespread belief that the gains from ownership do not offset the risks and uncertainties associated with ceasing to work in the public sector, such as the loss of pension and employment protection rights (Nuttall Review 2012; Birchall 2011; Mutuals Taskforce 2012). This might suggest that strengthening participation rights for employees is an essential complement to the process of privatization, and therefore to the ultimate success of the employee-owned model for privatized firms.

There is also evidence that stakeholder involvement has played an important role in ensuring the successful delivery of public services after privatization. Some organizations have adopted governance models that incorporate permanent user representatives in an attempt to ensure that responsiveness to community needs can be maintained after privatization (Hazenberg 2013).

16.4.3 Wider Social Impacts

There is evidence that the nature of the governance framework adopted by a firm can contribute directly to social cohesion by actively encouraging the participation of marginalized social groups in company decision-making. In the context of many charitable and social enterprises, this may form part of the firm's express objectives. In terms of social service delivery, inclusive governance may be a way to increase managers' access to information about social needs, enabling them to monitor the impact of their decision-making, and thereby increase the quality of social service provision (Borzaga and Sacchetti 2015).

Many mutuals, such as building and friendly societies, have traditionally operated in areas of social deprivation and have therefore maintained a strong link with the community in which they are located. The early building societies were able to offer low-cost mortgages and loans in socially deprived areas because the regulatory environment left them relatively insulated from the competitive pressures of the market. The highly regulated building society sector therefore played an important role in countering financial exclusion.

From this point of view, demutualization can be seen to have been a regressive step. Private limited companies offering financial services have moved out of socially deprived areas and smaller communities, concentrating branch closures on their local branches. In contrast, opening branches in socially deprived areas has been part of a deliberate strategy that many mutuals pursue. After demutualization, many former building societies also concentrated branch closures on deprived areas, and have since been criticized for having adopted 'plc' like behaviour in their attitude towards geographical coverage (Marshall et al. 2000, 2003). In contrast, of those mutuals that did not convert, many began to move into areas previously occupied by demutualized societies, in order to open new branches to help to meet local needs. Nonetheless, even these building societies engaged in branch closure, albeit at a slower rate, largely driven by competitive pressures originating in the regulatory changes of the 1980s. These closures have also been concentrated in under-serviced areas, significantly increasing the number of those at risk of financial exclusion (Leyshon et al. 2008).

The already limited scope for credit unions to fill the spaces left by the demutualized societies (Mitton 2008) has been further weakened by a 2011 reform relaxing the criteria for credit union membership and removing the requirement that there be a 'common bond' between members. This appears to be a continuation of the trend in policy-making that overlooks the geographical dimension of financial exclusion (Leyshon et al. 2008). The reform has also given credit unions new powers to charge members above cost in order to generate profit, and better enable them to compete with other organizations operating in the banking sector. It seems that legislative intervention to support the operation of the mutual model in deprived areas may be necessary to help to combat this growing problem of financial exclusion.

16.5 ASSESSMENT

An assessment of the implications of social enterprise for stakeholder participation and firm performance must take into account, but also go beyond, a consideration of legal form. Producer and customer co-operatives have legal structures which distinguish them from for-profit or commercial firms. For-profits are generally constituted as companies limited by share capital, in which equity investors have residual voice, income, and control rights. Similar residual rights vest in employees, in the case of producer co-operatives, and customers, in the case of mutuals such as building societies. However, these residual rights do not confer direct ownership of the firm, whether or not it is constituted as a social enterprise. It is necessary to look closely at the detail of property rights and accountability mechanisms when considering the role of legal structure in determining corporate governance. Thus the detail of the rules designed to prevent depletion of the assets of the firm ('asset locks') are important regardless of the identity of the residual claimants, while references to 'ownership' in the abstract tell us relatively little about the opportunity which employees or customers may have to participate in the management of the firm.

The empirical evidence suggests that financial mutuals are more stable and less risk-prone, but also more risk-averse, than commercial banks, implying that residual ownership does make a difference to firm performance. Employee share ownership has been shown to have positive implications for productivity in some contexts, although these positive effects are clearest where financial participation leads to, or is joined with, active involvement of employees and their representatives in aspects of the organization of the firm, and where employees have a voice in matters of strategy and planning. The use of the mutual form in the context of public–private transfers does not, without more, signify any increase in worker or customer involvement.

The introduction of novel legal forms, including benefit corporations and community interest companies, suggests that there is scope for innovation in the social enterprise sector, and that hybrids which combine a social mission with access to external capital may offer a way forward. For the time being, however, there is a lack of evidence on the consequences of these new legal forms, and it remains to be seen how far they offer a viable alternative to more established structures.

These conclusions suggest that the recent push towards mutualization needs to be treated with caution. The mutual form is not a panacea for the problem of how to achieve effective coordination within the multi-stakeholder enterprise, and where the rhetoric of mutualization is used to justify the transfer of assets out of public control, there is a risk of it being delegitimized.

REFERENCES

Armour, J., Hansmann, H., and Kraakman, R. (2009), 'What is Corporate Law?', in R. Kraakman, J. Armour, P. Davies, L. Enriques, H. Hansmann, G. Hertig, H. Kanda, and E. Rock, eds, *The Anatomy of Corporate Law: A Comparative and Functional Approach* (Oxford: Oxford University Press), 1–34.

Bholat, D. and Gray, J. (2013), 'Organizational Form as a Source of Systemic Risk', *Economics: The Open-Access, Open-Assessment E-Journal*, 7: 1–35.

Birchall, J. (2011), 'The Big Society and the "Mutualisation" of Public Services: A Critical Commentary', *Political Quarterly*, 82, 145–57.

Blair, M. (1995), *Ownership and Control: The American Corporation in the Twenty-First Century* (Washington, DC: Brookings Institution).

Blair, M. (2003), 'Locking in Capital: What Corporate Law Achieved for Business Organizers in the Nineteenth Century', *UCLA Law Review*, 51, 387–455.

Borzaga, C., Depedri, S., and Tortia, E. (2011), 'Organisational Variety in Market Economies and the Role of Cooperative and Social Enterprises: A Plea for Economic Pluralism', *Journal of Co-Operative Studies*, 44, 19–30.

Borzaga, C. and Sacchetti, S. (2015), 'Why Social Enterprises are Asking to be Multi-stakeholder and Deliberative: An Explanation around the Costs of Exclusion', Available at http://www.euricse.eu/wp-content/uploads/2015/04/WP-75_15_Borzaga-Sacchetti.pdf. (accessed 15 September 2016).

Campi, S., Defourny, J., and Gregoire, O. (2006), 'Work Integration Social Enterprises: Are they Multiplegoal and Multi-stakeholder Organizations?' in M. Nyssens, ed., *Social Enterprise: At the Crossroads of Market, Public Policies and Civil Society* (London: Routledge), 29–49.

Carberry, E. (2011), *Employee Ownership and Shared Capitalism: New Directions in Research* (Champaign, IL: Labor and Employment Relations Association).

Chai, D., Deakin, S., and McLoughlin, C. (2015), 'Corporate Governance, Gender Equality and Family-Friendly Practices in British Firms'. Forthcoming CBR Working Paper series.

Cook, J., Deakin, S., and Hughes, A. (2002), 'Mutuality and Corporate Governance: The Evolution of UK Building Societies Following Deregulation', *Journal of Corporate Law Studies*, 2, 110–38.

Cummings, B. (2012), 'Benefit Corporations: How to Enforce a Mandate to Promote the Public Interest', *Columbia Law Review*, 578–627.

Deakin, S. (2011), 'The Corporation as Commons: Rethinking Property Rights, Governance and Sustainability in the Business Enterprise', *Queen's Law Journal*, 37, 339–81.

Deakin, S. (2012), 'The Juridical Nature of the Firm', in D. Branson and T. Clarke, eds, *Sage Handbook of Corporate Governance* (London: Sage),

Deakin, S. and Adams, Z. (2015), 'Corporate Governance and Employment Relations', in J. Gordon and W.-G. Ringe, eds, *The Oxford Handbook of Corporate Law and Governance* (Oxford: Oxford University Press), available at: http://www.oxfordhandbooks.com/view/10.1093/oxfordhb/9780198743682.001.0001/oxfordhb-9780198743682-e-44.

Deskins, M. (2012), 'Benefit Corporation Legislation, Version 1.0—A Breakthrough in Stakeholder Rights?' *Lewis and Clark Law Review* 15, 1047–76.

Easterbrook, F. and Fischel, D. (1991), *The Economic Structure of Corporate Law* (Cambridge, MA: Harvard UP).

Evers, A. (2001), 'The Significance of Social Capital in the Multiple Goal and Resource Structure of Social Enterprises', in C. Borzaga and J. Defourney, eds, *The Emergence of Social Enterprise* (London and New York: Routledge).

Fama, E. and Jensen, M. (1983), 'Separation of Ownership and Control', *Journal of Law and Economics*, 26, 301–25.

Freeman, R., Kruse, D., and Blasi, J. (2004), 'Monitoring Colleagues at Work and Free Ride Problem: Profit Sharing, Employee Ownership, Broad Based Stock Options and Workplace Performance in the United States'. CEP Discussion Paper No. 467.

Haldane, A. and Nelson, B. (2012), 'Tails of the Unexpected'. Speech delivered at the University of Edinburgh Business School. Available at http://www.bankofengland.co.uk/publications/Documents/*speeches/2012*/speech582.pdf (accessed 29 October 2017).

Hambach, M. (2014), 'Bradford & Bingley Transformation and Decline: 1995–2010'. Ph.D. thesis, University of York, 2014. Available at http://etheses.whiterose.ac.uk/9037/ (accessed 16 Septermber 2016).

Hansmann, H. (1996), *The Ownership of Enterprise* (Cambridge, MA: Belknap Press).

Hansmann, H. and Kraakman, R. (2000), 'Organisational Law as Asset Partitioning', *European Economic Review*, 44, 807–17.

Hansmann, H., Kraakman, R., and Squire, R. (2006), 'Law and the Rise of the Firm', *Harvard Law Review*, 119, 1333–403.

Hazenberg, R. (2013), *Barriers and Solutions to Public Sector Spin-Outs* (London: Capital Ambition).

Heath, J. (2006), 'Business Ethics Without Stakeholders', *Business Ethics Quarterly*, 16, 533–57.

Ireland, P. (1999), Company Law and the Myth of Shareholder Ownership, *Modern Law Review*, 62, 32–57.

Jensen, M. and Meckling, W. (1976), 'Theory of the Firm: Managerial Behavior, Agency Costs and Capital Structure', *Journal of Financial Economics*, 3, 305–60.

Kaarsemaker, E. (2006), 'Employee Ownership and Human Resource Management: A Theoretical and Empirical Treatise with a Digression on the Dutch Context'. Doctoral Dissertation, Radboud University: Nijmegen.

Keay, A. (2013), *The Enlightened Shareholder Value Principle and Corporate Governance* (Abingdon: Routledge).

Klimecki, R. and Willmott, H. (2011), 'From Demutualisation to Meltdown: A Tale of Two Wannabe Banks', *Critical Perspectives on International Business*, 5: 120–40.

Kraakman, R., Armour, J., Davies, P., Enriques, L., Hansmann, H., Hertig, G., Kanda, H., and Rock, E. (2009), *The Anatomy of Corporate Law: A Comparative and Functional Approach* (Oxford: Oxford University Press).

Laville, J.-L. and Nyssens, M. (2001), 'The Social Enterprise: Towards a Theoretical Socio-Economic Approach', in C. Borzaga and J. Defourny, eds, *The Emergence of Social Enterprise* (London and New York: Routledge), 312–32.

Levillain, K. and Segrestin, B. (2012), 'A Mission-Centric View of the Firm: Lessons from Social Entrepreneurship', *R&D Management* Conference. Available at https://hal.archives-ouvertes.fr/hal-00733413/ (accessed 16 September 2016).

Leyshon, A., French, S., and Signoretta, P. (2008), 'Financial Exclusion and the Geography of Bank and Building Society Branch Closure in Britain', *Transactions of the Institute of British Geographers*, 33, 447–65.

Marshall, N., Willis, R., and Richardson, R. (2000), 'Mutuality, Demutualization and Communities: The Implications of Branch Network Rationalization in the British Building Society Industry', *Transactions of the Institute of British Geographers*, 25, 355–78.

Marshall, J. Neill, Willis, R., and Richardson. R. (2003), 'Demutualisation, Strategic Choice, and Social Responsibility', *Environment and Planning C*, 21, 735–60.

Middleton, M. (1987), 'Nonprofit Boards of Directors: Beyond the Governance Function', in W. Powell, ed., *The Nonprofit Sector: A Research Handbook* (New Haven, CT: Yale University Press).

Mitton, L. (2008), *Financial Inclusion in the UK: Review of Policy and Practice* (York: Joseph Rowntree Foundation). Available at http://www.jrf.org.uk/sites/files/jrf/2234.pdf (accessed 15 September 2016).

Mutuals Taskforce (2011), *Public Service Mutuals: The Next Steps* (London: Mutuals Taskforce).

Nuttall Review (2012) *Sharing Success: the Nuttall Review of Employee Ownership* (London: BIS, 2012).

Ostrom, E. (1990), *Governing the Commons: The Evolution of Institutions for Collective Action* (Cambridge: Cambridge University Press).

Ownership Commission (2012), *Plurality, Stewardship, and Engagement* (London: Mutuo).

Paranque, B. and Willmott, H. (2014), 'Co-operatives: Saviours or Gravediggers of Capitalism? Critical Performativity and the John Lewis Partnership', *Organization*, 21, 604–25.

Pendleton, A. and Robinson, A. (2015), 'Employee Ownership in Britain Today'. Interim Findings from the 2014-15 Employee Ownership Survey. Available at http://papers.ssrn.com/sol3/papers.cfm?abstract_id=2578921 (accessed 15 September 2016).

Poteete, A., Janssen, M., and Ostrom, E. (2010), *Working Together: Collective Action, the Commons, and Multiple Methods in Practice* (Princeton, NJ: Princeton University Press).

Raz, K. (2012), 'Toward an Improved Legal Form for Social Enterprise', *NYU Review of Law and Social Change*, 36(283), 238–308.

Reiser, D. (2011), 'Benefit Corporations: A Sustainable Form of Organization', *Wake Forest Law Review*, 46, 591.

Ridley-Duff, R. (2009), 'Co-operative Social Enterprises: Company Rules, Access to Finance and Management Practice', *Social Enterprise Journal*, 5, 50–68.

Robé, J.-P. (2011), 'The Legal Structure of the Firm', *Accounting, Economics and Law*, 1: Article 5.

Shiwakoti, R. (2012), 'Comparative Analysis of Determinants of Executive Remuneration in the UK Financial Services Sector', *Accounting and Finance*, 52, 213–35.

Spear, R. (2004), 'Governance in Democratic Member-Based Organisations', *Annals of Public and Co-operative Economics*, 75, 33–60.

Stephens, M. (2001), 'Building Society Demutualisation in the UK', *Housing Studies*, 16, 335–52.

Talbot, L. (2015), *Critical Company Law*, 2nd ed. (London: Routledge).

Wilson, F. and Post, J. (2011), 'Business Models for People, Planet (and Profits): Exploring the Phenomena of Social Business, a Market-Based Approach to Social Value Creation, *Small Business Economics*, 40, 715–37.

CHAPTER 17

GOVERNANCE AND ORGANIZATIONAL CHALLENGES

PETER COUCHMAN

> We are satisfied that DFB did not fail because it was a co-operative.
>
> (House of Commons 2010).

17.1 INTRODUCTION

THE co-operative model has always faced the challenge that the failure of any one co-operative tends to lead to accusations that the model itself is flawed. The same cannot be said of its private-sector equivalents.

This chapter takes a brief look at the options that a modern co-operative has in terms of its governance and organization. Whilst focused on the UK consumer co-operative experience, it does draw from other international comparators and structures. It is written against the backdrop of the 'catastrophic losses' (Myners 2014:7) of value from the Co-operative Group in the UK after its then subsidiary, the Co-operative Bank, got into trouble.

It argues that there are five approaches for a co-operative to consider for its governance and organization:

1) Trust-based approach
2) Corporate-governance-based approach
3) Competence-based approach
4) Values-based approach
5) Open co-operatives approach

17.2 TRUST-BASED APPROACH

For the majority of the time that modern co-operatives have existed, discussions on governance and organization have been quite limited.

It can be argued that this early approach was based on an assumption that the solidarity that had brought the group together was sufficient to ensure that its operation would be successful based on trust. Sadly, this was often not the case. The co-ops formed in the late 1820s experienced a high failure rate, many of which could be attributed to governance inexperience (Durr 1982).

The approaches adopted post-Rochdale had three main characteristics: firstly, a strong sense of trustworthiness and being able to rely on each other; secondly, high visibility of the inner workings of each society, with quarterly reporting or more to a very fine level of financial detail; thirdly, relatively simple structures with single shop or local clusters of shops models.

Over time, all three of these would be challenged. As co-operative societies became more complex enterprises, with multiple forms of business, in multiple locations, the ability of an individual member to fully understand the operation became harder. This complexity also meant that the inner workings became harder to understand as accounts retained the same level of detail, but for much larger enterprises.

The oversight of the first characteristic remained, but the main way that it was measured was the level of dividend paid to members. The perception was that a fall in the dividend level was an indication of wider problems. This approach was highly problematic as it gave boards of directors an incentive to hold dividends at artificially high levels in order to ensure their own re-election. Where the boards were employed full time, losing an election could have a massive impact on the individual's livelihood.

If trust was a weakness in the trust-based system, then its strength was co-operative education.

The Co-operative Movement was, from its earliest days, an educational movement. What marks its first 100 years is not just how much education mattered, but how it was constantly evolving. Robert Owen had stressed the importance of education: 'Any general character, from the best to the worst, from the most ignorant to the most enlightened, may be given to any community, even to the world at large, by the application of proper means' (Owen 1991: 40). William King, working from Brighton in the late 1820s integrated this with how to run a co-operative business, saying that the three essentials of a co-operative were 'Labour, Capital, Knowledge', adding that 'Our motto is "Knowledge and Union are power"' (Mercer 1947: 62). The Rochdale Pioneers went further with their broad vision 'That as soon as practicable, this Society shall proceed to arrange the powers of production, distribution, education, and government, or in other words to establish a self-supporting home-colony of united interests, or assist other Societies in establishing such colonies' (Fairbairn 1994: 5). By 1854, they were putting aside 2.5 per cent of their profits towards education.

Yet how this was delivered changed over time, from lectures to reading rooms to adult education classes to film. This reinvention of co-operative education by each generation continued between the wars, with Joe Reeves pushing the boundaries in the Royal Arsenal Co-operative Society. To him, the mission was clear: 'We cannot educate without a purpose, and our purpose shall be to prepare people to understand the profound implications of co-operation' (Reeves 1936).

Such education work both inspired people and prepared them for their roles within their co-op.

If we had to summarize the trust-based approach, it would be that an emphasis on solidarity between the members was at the core of its culture. This created a strong emphasis on educating members for the role that they could play. Its business structures were relatively simple; however, its engagement structures often evolved into complex methods of ensuring member engagement. For instance, the Royal Arsenal Co-operative Society had a layered democracy stretching from engagement on the shop floor to area-based groups to regional groups to the boardroom.

17.3 CORPORATE GOVERNANCE APPROACH

The enforced mergers or collapses of many societies can be seen as being due to having a performance feedback mechanism that was designed to incentivize the wrong behaviours, namely hiding instead of sharing poor performance, in order to maintain dividend levels.

Co-operatives were not alone in facing these challenges. In 1992, the Cadbury Report set out a series of recommendations on how a private-sector company should be governed. It, and subsequent reports, raised the governance bar for companies. A culture emerged of detailed reporting of governance processes and outcomes.

The question of how co-operatives should react to this was a controversial one. Some saw no need for reform, believing that co-operatives were better placed to manage themselves. Some objected to applying corporate models to co-operative structures. But others were bold enough to challenge this thinking by arguing that co-operatives should be operated to the highest possible standards.

This approach was not always popular. When the Chair of the working group on corporate governance at the Co-operative Union, Bob Burlton (Chief Executive of the Oxford, Swindon & Gloucester Co-op), presented the initial report to the movement in 1994, he made the point of bringing both his parents' and his own birth certificates to dispel the rumours about his motives for seeking changes to co-op society governance structures.

Although not perfect, the code and subsequent amendments did improve the operation of co-operatives. Annual Reports provided, in most cases, more information and boards were more conscious of their responsibilities. The Governance Code of the Co-operative Union encouraged a 'comply or explain' approach.

'Overall, the governance of large co-operatives is on a par with and probably superior to shareholder companies,' claimed Birchall in 2014 (Birchall 2014: 3).

Co-operative boards had procedures in place, but the question was to be whether this was enough. In this, some co-operatives proved themselves no different from the private sector in that they were able to comply with governance codes, report on these to shareholders, whilst then experiencing sudden shocks to their system that, with hindsight, originated in poor governance. These were failures, not of governance process, but of governance culture.

Organizational structures tended to be driven by management needs—a logical approach, but it did tend to see members as outside of the system and a source of problems rather than solutions. Elected members would, in many cases, see the relationship as being a confrontational one. Lord Myners spoke of elected members wanting to see managers as 'on tap but not on top' (Myners 2014: 23). Neither position was a healthy one.

The greatest weakness of this approach has been the gradual loss of co-operative education as a vital part of co-operative governance. The Co-operative College in the UK has attempted to keep this role alive, but it is very hard to do so when societies choose not to engage with any meaningful development of their members. The work in the 1990s to develop a comprehensive training programme for all societies and an Institute of Co-operative Directors to encourage professional standards, was replaced by individual societies making their own arrangements. During the recent governance crisis of the Co-operative Group, much was made of directors not being up to the task, yet there was little discussion of how the disappearance of co-operative education had contributed to this.

In summary, this model is still in wide use across the co-operative movement. Its strength has proved to be its focus on ensuring that proper process is in place. Its weakness is its ability to make co-ops more managerial and less focused on members. Such an outcome is not inevitable, but it does appear that it leads to a real struggle to maintain an appropriate balance between members and managers. The UK is not alone in this. The challenges faced by US food co-ops were dismissed with the following statement, 'Participatory organisations are like that. They mature, they become bureaucratized, they lose track of the larger world' (Cox 1994: 141).

17.4 COMPETENCY APPROACH

The corporate governance model tended to encourage co-operatives to look towards the corporate world for governance models. This placed great emphasis on what works in large organizations, rather than asking the much harder question of what works in co-operative organizations.

Co-operative boards have come in for a fair degree of criticism in recent years for what is seen as the amateur nature of their elected members. There was open criticism of having a plasterer or a nurse on the Co-operative Group board. Such commentators were silent when private-sector boards, filled with 'professionals', also got into trouble. A 2013 survey by McKinsey found that only 34 per cent of directors of public companies agreed that the boards on which they served fully comprehended their companies' strategies (Barton and Wiseman 2015).

Lord Myners was scathing of the quality of directors he found at the Co-operative Group: 'It places individuals who do not possess the requisite skills and experience into positions where their lack of understanding prevents them from exercising the necessary oversight of the Executive' (Myners 2014:17). On the other side of this debate are those who say that election by the members is an adequate test of the candidate's suitability for office.

The reality is that both camps need to reconsider their position. Those who say that election gives an endorsement and a mandate need to look hard at modern election procedures. The reality is that directors are elected having provided very little information to the members on their suitability for the role and very little that distinguishes them from other candidates. As one co-op activist put it to me: 'When I vote in the Labour Party elections I can tell instantly where each candidate stands from their electoral address and determine whether their position is the same as the one I wish to support. In Co-op elections, I can't. They all sound the same.'

The great Canadian co-operator George Keen said (in a less gender-aware time): 'A man can be an excellent co-operator and not be member of a co-operative society. Unfortunately he may be a member of a society and yet have none of the attributes of a co-operator' (Keen 1918: 6). The test of the system is for it to be visible to the members which candidates and board members are genuine co-operators.

The move is undoubtedly towards having boards which have appointed directors based on their competence. The disappointment in how this approach is evolving is not the process, but the definition of competence. Lord Myners has defined this as 'the need to put in place a Group Board that possesses the skills and experience, as well as the commitment to co-operative values, that will enable it to match in quality the boards of its primary competitors' (Myners 2014: 8). The emphasis would appear to always be on bringing those from outside the movement.

Aside from the question of how someone can have a commitment, let alone demonstrate a commitment, to co-operative values, but never have chosen so far to have any connection with the co-operative movement (a contentious issue), the question it raises is 'What are those skills and experiences?' If we define these narrowly as those which match our competitors' skill sets, then all we will do is replicate their actions and fail to build a distinctive market position.

Yet, a trend is beginning for a model in which a small board is elected for their business skills, whilst members are given a secondary role in which they can bring their co-operative knowledge to bear. The model has the strength of ensuring commercial expertise on the board. But this will come at the cost of having a co-operative organization simply seeking to copy its private-sector competitors rather than finding a uniquely co-operative position in the market place.

If the weakness of the previous model was to drive a wedge between board and managers, this has the potential to unite both against members.

Other co-operative failures suggest that the danger is even greater when this division is accompanied by an overconfidence of management being unchallenged. In a review of the failure of the Saskatchewan Wheat Pool, Fulton and Larson wrote of how managers, left unchecked, destroyed generations of co-operative capital building due to their own over-confidence. They made clear what should have checked this habit of senior executives overestimating the value of acquisitions: 'The relationship between CEO hubris and acquisition premium is greater when board vigilance is lacking' (Fulton and Larson 2009: 8).

The challenges of the Co-operative Group and the emerging solution to this is highly likely to ensure that it is this model which will be on the rise in the near future.

17.5 Values-Based Approach

The challenge is to find a way that captures the benefits of the newer models whilst not losing the original benefits of the co-operative model. No single action can do this, but a combination offers a distinctively different approach. The elements to focus on are:

1) The purpose of the co-operative
2) The role of members
3) Aligning governance with membership strategy and communications/marketing strategy
4) Ensuring that all interactions with the co-op are part of being a co-op
5) Restoring co-operative education
6) Ensuring that board competence is based on the three co-operative elements, not just technical retailing skills

17.5.1 Focus on the Purpose of the Co-operative

All around the world, larger co-operatives struggling with these issues are examples of much smaller co-operatives which have retained their connection to members and their interests. Alongside the struggles of many larger co-operatives has been the rise of community-based co-operatives, such as village shops, pubs, and football clubs.

Many of these are very small, but their connection to real community needs means that they have become highly influential with policy formers because they are seen to be focused on meeting the needs of communities. David Cameron, speaking as leader of the G8, said, 'I want our social investment funds to give people the opportunity to take them over and run them. This isn't some pipe dream. Already there are 311 community-owned shops, 18 community-owned pubs, as well as community-owned bookshops, cafes, swimming pools, bakers, farmers markets, even community-owned broadband networks' (Cameron 2013).

These co-operatives are using this community connection to deliver real value to their members, helping them to succeed where others fail. Often, they are built on the ruins where private-ownership models have failed. Despite operating on the margins, many achieve higher levels of sustainability than their private-sector peers. The survival rate after five years for village shops run as co-operatives in the UK is 99 per cent, compared to only 45 per cent for other start-ups (Plunkett Foundation 2014:9).

Larger co-operatives do not have the option to simply copy these smaller structures, but they need to ask the question 'What do we need to do differently in order not to lose the distinctive co-operative advantage that these smaller co-ops enjoy?'

At the core of this is the need to have a clear co-operative purpose. Just as corporations are clear that they must deliver value to their shareholders, the co-operative must be clear that it is there to meet the needs of its members. Former Plunkett Foundation Chief Executive Edgar Parnell summed this up perfectly when he argued that 'The function of a co-operative enterprise is to intervene in a specific marketplace in the sustainable interest of its members' (Parnell 2013a). It is not enough to operate in the same way as the market; the successful co-operative finds ways of operating in a distinctive way to meet member needs. Nor is it enough to do good deeds without being clear what the connection to achieving the co-operative's mission is.

So the first step towards building the modern co-operative organization is achieving this clarity of purpose on how you are going to benefit your members. Such clarity needs to be found in all parts of the organization, not just the boardroom. It has to be the driver for management and the culture for staff.

17.5.2 The Role of Members

Part of this will be the challenge to the member relationship. It is the realization that the achievement of value for members can only come from the members. Co-operatives do things with their members, not for or to them.

Members should be seen as a source of knowledge, loyalty, and communication, not as a burden to be borne by a weary management. The best co-operatives see this and build their strength on it. The lesser try and resemble their competitors. Young co-operative leaders at the Quebec Summit in 2014 went further than this in their communiqué when they called on major co-operatives to stop 'staffing the management teams of our cooperatives with subscribers to neoliberal philosophy' (Quebec 2014).

Whilst talk might be of how hard this connection to members is to achieve, the reality is that it has never been easier for larger co-operatives to do so. Social media, co-production, and the creative commons are all driving models of co-operative knowledge-sharing undreamt of by previous generations.

Connected to this is the realization that managers need to be recruited who understand this and build their approach around this. This is not a plea for no external recruitment—often external candidates will grasp the difference faster than those who have spent a lifetime in the movement. As the old Buddhist saying goes, 'A fish is the last to understand water'.

However, what it does mean is that recruitment processes should be geared to finding individuals open to this way of working; training programmes should equip people with the tools to enable this, the organization's culture should encourage it, and boards should recognize and reward it.

Many co-operatives have, on many occasions, developed an internal language about how co-operative they are without the rest of the world being aware of this. Such cultures will frequently talk of co-operative values, but fail to exhibit the behaviours connected to them. Lord Myners, in his review of the Co-operative Group, talked of 'a practice of hiding behind "values" in order to deflect or stifle criticism and protect self-interest' (Myners 2014: 8).

17.5.3 Aligning Governance with Membership Strategy and Communications/Marketing Strategy

The real difference with this model is that it realizes that governance cannot be separated from the membership strategy and the marketing/communications strategy. A co-operative that attempts to compartmentalize its operations will fail to unlock the value that its co-operative identity offers.

17.5.4 Ensuring That All Interactions With the Co-op are Part of Being a Co-op

The Plunkett Foundation developed an approach for smaller co-operatives which could be applied equally to larger ones. It is called 'The Journey' and seeks to get people thinking outside the traditional approaches to governance. It invites the enterprise to go on a journey looking at their own enterprise from an outside perspective. The stages are:

17.5.4.1 *Approaching the Outside*

The journey begins in the outside world. When someone approaches the co-operative (either in the physical world or online), what do they see? Does it look remarkably like the competition in a way that is hard to distinguish? Or does it announce proudly what it is and how this difference will deliver for the customer?

17.5.4.2 *The Shopfloor*

The step beyond this is in whatever form the shopfloor takes. Here, there is a rich opportunity to engage in a dialogue with the customer. The genuine co-operative shopfloor explains its co-operative identity, demonstrates the difference that it will make to the customer, seeks the customers' views on whether it is succeeding in this, and invites them into membership. It will recognize that, in most forms of business, the customer will return regularly, so the message will need to evolve and develop in order not to simply become wallpaper. The more the messages connect with the concept that the co-operative is shaped by its members, the stronger the incentive for the customer to connect with it.

17.5.4.3 *The Staff*

The next step is when the customer connects with the staff. Are they ambassadors for their co-operative, proud of what it is achieving, well treated by it and members themselves? Or is it just another job and not a very exciting one at that? This interaction offers opportunities on a range of levels, from informing the customer and seeking their views, to recruiting the person as a member or recognizing that they already are. It is also worth remembering that the number one reason that people don't join something is that they were never asked.

17.5.4.4 *Becoming a Member*

The transition into membership is a vital one. Throw a sharebook along with a poorly written standard letter at the new member and the chances are that the book will stay in the bottom drawer, the member will never participate, and their money will stay firmly in their pocket. Reaching out with a welcoming vision of what they can expect is vital, but not easy. Too little and the interest is not aroused. Too much and they are overwhelmed.

This is also the time when governance first appears. What are their roles and responsibilities? How can this be presented in a way that attracts, not repels. For some the answer is a copy of the rulebook. This isn't always the best motivator (although it should be available). Even worse are the traditional rulebooks calculated to confuse. I can recall one co-operator complaining that the Plunkett model rules 'aren't like how we normally do our rules as they appear to be written so the members will understand them'.

The new member is in a golden period where they aren't sure what having joined means, but they will lapse into old ways if they are invited to the ball but no-one asks them to dance.

Central to making the recruitment and development confusing is for the co-operative itself not to be clear what the membership offer is in the organization. Setting this out is vital. The most common error is for this to be designed by those already heavily involved with years of activity behind them. Such people tend to forget that this is not how they first saw the co-operative all those years ago. A language is needed which connects with where the person is currently on their journey, not where they might be.

17.5.4.5 *Communicating with Members*

Communication from a co-operative needs to carry out a whole range of different functions. It needs to celebrate what has been achieved and to give credit to the members in that success. It needs to encourage the member to become more involved without overwhelming them. More than anything else, it needs to encourage interaction. It needs to demonstrate that the co-operative wants to engage with the member and is willing to offer multiple ways of doing so. It needs to suggest that there is a real chance that the member's contribution will be valued and acted upon. This was always the case, but in a modern world that offers so many other ways to engage, it is now even more vital.

17.5.4.6 *Educating Co-operators*

No co-operative can live in the past. Things which once were important can often be of no value now. Learning to let go is a vital part of shaping a co-operative future. Yet there are some things which should never be let go of and some of these, unfortunately, have been. No more so than in the case of co-operative education.

The co-operative of the future will need to reinvent co-operative education, just as their forebearers did, in a way which inspires current generations and prepares them for the contribution they can make.

17.5.4.7 *Engaging the Member*

The modern co-operative needs to find ways for the member to engage in the simplest ways possible, given the way that communication has evolved in the world. Yet, the time will come when some of the members decide to engage with the more formal parts of a co-operative's democratic structure. The starting point for this tends to be the members' meeting.

This wonderful tradition is normally anything but a meeting belonging to the members. Its format tends to be based on a model developed by the German Freemasons in the seventeenth century to control the meeting and conduct the business as speedily as possible. The top table has control, and member contributions are likely to be made brief, with right of reply always resting with the top table. There is little incentive for the person to travel some distance to a meeting at which, if they are lucky, they can ask one or at best two questions.

It doesn't have to be this way. Whilst some formal business needs to be transacted (approval of minutes, accounts etc.), these are actually quite limited and nothing dictates what else goes on in between formal items. One Scottish meeting combined its members' meeting with a Cèilidh, interleaving agenda items with dances. This may be extreme for some, but there is no reason why more time cannot be given to interactive activity rather than just formality. It should be an event where members feel that they have helped to shape their society, challenged its current running, and explored its future.

17.5.4.8 *Electing Members*

Central to this governance challenge is the role of the elected member. Co-operative democracy is facing the same challenge that many other forms of democracy are facing. It is no longer acceptable for someone to be elected and to 'believe' that they therefore have free rein to represent the electorate for their term of office. People want a different relationship. As the Argentinian Democracy OS slogan puts it, they want, 'No representation without a conversation' (Mancini 2014).

Few co-operatives have adapted to this new world so far. The best have to be adept at using market research far more effectively to ensure that there is some member voice within the boardroom. The challenge of recognizing the changed role of the elected member is still at its early stages.

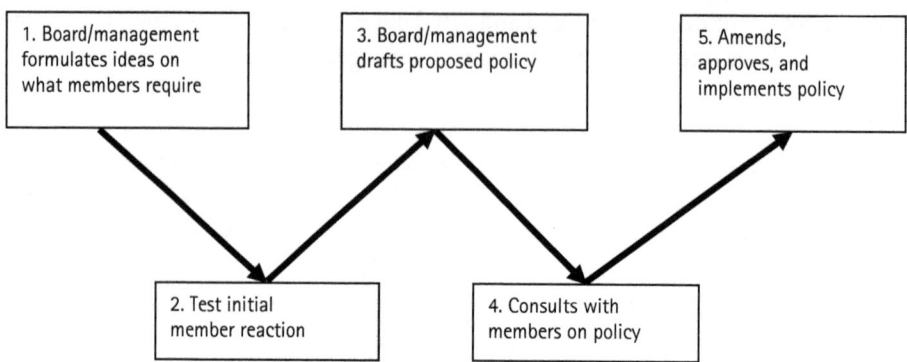

FIGURE 17.1 The 'W' approach to board consultation.

Source: Model developed by co-operatives in Quebec.

A model developed several years ago by co-operatives in Quebec, such as La Coop Fédérée, has explained its thinking as a 'W' (Figure 17.1). Directors in this model do not assume being elected by the members means that they are guaranteed to understand what members want. Instead of this, directors need to test their assumptions with members before considering their actions, then testing those planned actions before proceeding. A longer process, but far more engaging.

Modern communication has removed all excuse for members not to be consulted or engaged on any issue which doesn't involve commercial confidentiality. Even on these, the strategy behind such decisions can be open. Such an approach should not be seen as a chore, but as an opportunity to engage far more brains in a process than an elected handful. The Co-operative Movement is one of a number of organizations which evolved models of engagement that were radical in the nineteenth century, but which will either have to reform or die in the twenty-first century.

The challenge is how to generate a sense of ownership among the members that leads to them trading with, sharing knowledge with, and helping to shape their co-operative.

17.6 PULLING IT TOGETHER: A PLUNKETT APPROACH

Sir Horace Plunkett offers a solution developed over 100 years ago for the agricultural co-operatives of Ireland. He argued that, to succeed, they needed the Three Betters—Better Farming, Better Business, Better Living. Taking these out of the agricultural context, but using the headings used by Sir Horace himself, we can translate this into:

Technical—access to the best knowledge of how to succeed in the sector in which you are operating.

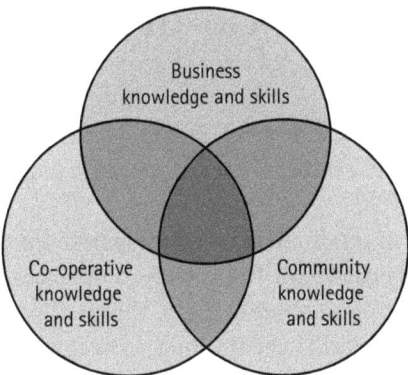

FIGURE 17.2 The Plunkett model of board competencies.

Source: Adapted from model developed by Sir Horace PlunkettSource.

Economic—access to the best knowledge on how to run a co-operative.
Social—access to the best knowledge on how to stay connected to the communities
that you serve.

Sir Horace is not alone in seeing the importance of this grouping of three. The great
Swedish co-operator, Sven Åke Böök said, 'A viable co-operative is characterized by a
combination of a strong economy, a living democracy and a relevance to the community
at large. These are mutually interrelated and support each other' (Böök 1992: 160).

Those who would argue that a board's competency should only be based on the technical, condemn their co-operative to failure. Indeed, in the case of the Co-operative
Group, its failure was at least as much in the economic and social sphere as it was in the
technical.

Sir Horace knew the price of failure if you did not manage to balance these three
needs. He saw it in Ireland:

> A material bias was given to the movement, the old idealism and enthusiasm melted
> away; the co-operative spirit, which ensures the essential loyalty of members to their
> societies and which the deeper thinkers among us know was, even from an economic
> point of view, of more vital importance then the practical work our organisers had
> to concentrate upon, was very insufficiently cultivated. That is the weak spot of the
> movement; by the restoration of the co-operative spirit can it alone be saved for the
> great work which lies before it. (Plunkett 1925)

His warning to Theodore Roosevelt on the implications of only focusing on the economic was even more stark: 'Once a co-operative society becomes a soulless corporation, its days are numbered' (Plunkett 1910: 48).

So the debate on competency should be welcomed, but it needs to be competency in
all three areas, not just the technical (Figure 17.2).

17.7 OPEN CO-OPERATIVES

There is one more model that is emerging. Still in its early days, it is either the greatest opportunity for, or the greatest threat to the co-operative model in 100 years. The jury is still out on which.

The networked world has produced ways of co-operative communication that previous generations could only dream of. The formal co-operative structure was created to enable people who wished to co-operate to do so. The question being asked is: Do people co-operating in the modern world need the long-term commitment that a co-operative requires? It is the same form of revolution that was seen in the 1960s which challenged whether marriage, with its 'until death us do part' commitment, was the only way of structuring a loving relationship.

Such models form around groups which come together for a clear purpose, with a high degree of trust and co-operation between them, carry out activities which would traditionally have been seen as an enterprise activity, but with no formal structure or expectation that they will continue co-operating indefinitely.

Talking of this new economy, Robin Murray said, 'It is nothing other than a co-operative economy that is now growing with the speed and diversity of a tropical forest. It is informal and astonishingly inventive. It shares many of the same values and practices of formal co-operatives, and opens up numerous possibilities for a meshing between them' (Murray 2011: iii).

At first look, such informality will have no interest or relevance to existing co-operatives. Yet to ignore their rise is to ignore the tremendous sense of ownership they unlock from participants. The motivating of a group to achieve specific tasks also offers great learning for existing co-operatives. What the existing will struggle with is the idea that also this can be built up and then allowed to vanish into the ether when the task is achieved.

Some pioneers of this world see the possibility of more permanent co-operative forms. When Michele Bauwens, of the P2P Foundation, talks of open co-operatives, he says that the criteria for such a co-operative is:

1 That co-ops need to be statutorily (internally) oriented towards the common good
2 That co-ops need to have governance models including all stakeholders
3 That co-ops need to actively co-produce the creation of immaterial and material commons
4 That co-ops need to be organized socially and politically on a global basis, even as they produce locally. (Bauwens 2014)

Josef Davies-Coates stresses the link between old and new, defining open co-operatives as 'Co-ops that combine best practices from the international co-operative movement with best practices from the open source software and hardware communities are now possible. Soon anyone will be able to set up an Open Co-op and invite all their stakeholders to help finance, govern and organise the co-op online' (Davies-Coates 2014).

The current examples are highly task driven and often use multi-stakeholder models. Multi-stakeholding has been an uneasy model for many in the co-operative. Whilst used effectively by some, such as Mondragón-based Grupo Eroski, it has been rejected by others, such as Edgar Parnell (Parnell 2013b). Open co-operatives appear to use it for a different purpose, as the participants see themselves as co-creators and are not tied to the concept of passive consumer or salaried staff. In many ways, their view of such structures is closer to the Rochdale Pioneers' early views, which did not distinguish between consumer co-operation and worker co-operation.

For the existing co-operatives, open co-operatives offer a chance to rethink how they connect to their members. For the new, it offers a different way from the formal traditional movement. For the Co-operative Movement it offers the opportunity to seek a convergence with other social movements, such as the creative commons and the transition movement, to find new relevance in the modern world. Alternatively, the movement may choose to distance itself from this informality and cut itself off from a new generation of enterprises.

17.8 CONCLUSION

Every co-operative has to face the issue of governance and organization. To fail to do so is to guarantee failure. Yet how they do so will define not only their business operation, but also whether they succeed in their co-operative mission.

REFERENCES

Barton, D. and Wiseman, M. (2015), 'Where Boards Fall Short', *Harvard Business Review*, 93(1/2) (January-February), 98–104.

Bauwens, M. (2014), 'Open Co-operatives'. Available at http://p2pfoundation.net/Open_ Cooperatives (accessed 15 September 2016).

Birchall, J. (2014), *The Governance of Large Co-operative Businesses* (Manchester: Co-operatives UK).

Böök, S. A. (1992), *Co-operative Values in a Changing World* (Geneva: International Co-operative Alliance).

Cameron, D. (2013), Speech at the Social Impact Investment Forum, 6 June. Available at https://www.gov.uk/government/speeches/prime-ministers-speech-at-the-social-impact-investment-conference (accessed 15 September 2016).

Cox, C. (1994), *Storefront Revolution: Food Co-ops and the Counterculture* (New Jersey: Rutger).

Davies-Coates, J. (2014), 'Open Co-ops: Inspiration, Legal Structures and Tools', *Stir to Action*, Available at http://stiraction.com/open-co-ops-inspiration-legal-structures-and-tools/ (accessed 15 September 2016).

Durr, A. (1982), *Co-operation in Early Nineteenth Century Brighton* (Brighton: Polytechnic History Workshop).

Fairbairn, B. (1994), *The Meaning of Rochdale: The Rochdale Pioneers and the Co-operative Principles* (Saskatoon: University of Saskatchewan).

Fulton, M. and Larson, K. (2009), The Restructuring of the Saskatchewan Wheat Pool: Overconfidence and Agency, in M. Fulton and B. Huet, eds, *Cooperative Conversions, Failures and Restructurings: Case Studies and Lessons from U. S. and Canadian Agriculture* (Centre for the Study of Co-operatives: University of Saskatchewan).

House of Commons Environment, Food and Rural Affairs Select Committee (2010), *Dairy Farmers of Britain* (London: House of Commons).

Keen, G. (1918), The Responsibilities and Opportunities of Members (Brantford: Co-operative Union of Canada).

Kelly, Sir C. (2014), *Failings in Governance and Management: Report of the Independent Review into the Events Leading to the Co-operative Bank's Capital Shortfall* (Manchester: Co-operative Bank).

Mancini, P. (2014), 'No Representation Without a Conversation'. Available at http://blog.democracyos.org/post/76769137533/no-representation-without-a-conversation (accessed 15 September 2016).

Mercer, T. W. (1947), *Co-operation's Prophet: The Life and Letters of Dr. William King of Brighton, with a Reprint of the Co-operator, 1828-1830* (Manchester: Co-operative Union).

Murray, R. (2011), *Co-operation in the Age of Google* (Manchester: Co-operatives UK).

Myners, P. (2014), *Report of the Independent Governance Review* (Manchester: Co-operative Group).

Owen, R. (1991), *A New View of Society and Other Writings* (London: Penguin).

Parnell, E. (2013a), *Co-operative Principles Plus*. Available at http://www.co-oppundit.org/purpose-and-function.html (accessed 15 September 2016).

Parnell, E. (2013b), *Co-operative Principles Plus*. Available at http://www.co-oppundit.org/markets-1.html (accessed 15 September 2016).

Plunkett, H. (1910), *The Rural Life Problem of the United States* (New York: Macmillan).

Plunkett, H. (1925), 'The I.A.O.S—The Founding of a Great Movement and the Evolution of Ireland's Agricultural Policy'. Typescript of speech, Plunkett Foundation Library.

Plunkett Foundation (2014), *Community Shops 2014: A Better Form of Business* (Woodstock: Plunkett Foundation).

Quebec Summit 2014 Young Co-operative Leaders, 'Cooperate to Transform Society'. Available at https://docs.google.com/forms/d/1bXgp-lepIlVwInlaMHRR3_HLQLPTx_Y2_ZD1N0_2slc/viewform?c=0&w=1 (accessed 15 September 2016).

Reeves, J. (1936), *Education for Social Change* (Manchester: Co-operative Union).

CHAPTER 18

....

ARE CO-OPERATIVES SMALL? EVIDENCE FROM THE WORLD CO-OPERATIVE MONITOR

....

CHIARA CARINI AND MAURIZIO CARPITA

18.1 INTRODUCTION

....

THERE is a widespread belief that co-operatives, especially in some sectors, are small-sized, under-capitalized, and probably short-lived enterprises. In the past, even in the academic world, some researchers (Vanek 1977) have brought attention to the problem of the undercapitalization of co-operatives, especially in certain sectors, such as production and labour. Empirical studies, however, have highlighted the fact that co-operatives have larger dimensions in certain areas than other types of companies (Estrin and Jones 1998; Pencavel et al. 2006). Moreover, in recent studies, data collected in Spain, Italy, and France have shown that co-operatives can be found in most sectors of activities, and they are not always less capital-intensive than other enterprises. They also survive at least as well as their conventional counterparts (Pérotin 2014). Though previous studies demonstrate the existence of large co-operatives, the problem is that they focus on specific business sectors and specific countries, and generally cover only European and/or American countries, while data for other regions are still lacking. Indeed, despite the fact that during the last several years the importance of the co-operative sector and its impact around the world have been increasingly studied and highlighted, the economic and social dimensions are yet to be fully understood and demonstrated. Despite this growing interest, the real economic dimensions of co-operatives worldwide remain fragmented. This gap leads to a lack of understanding of the real economic dimensions of co-operatives, something that could be avoided if a more nuanced view of how co-operatives actually contribute to the socio-economic welfare of different countries were to be acknowledged.

Despite such requirements, standardized, harmonized, and complete statistical data on co-operatives are scarce. Moreover, the application of existing metrics to measure and capture the influence of co-operatives often proves inadequate, as they are largely founded upon an enterprise paradigm into which co-operatives do not fit. The need for statistics on co-operatives is twofold. On the one hand, data are required to fill a significant gap in knowledge about the true size and demeanour of the global co-operative economy in all its diversity. On the other hand, data—including the specific methodologies utilized to gather and analyse data, the indices, metrics, and the approaches themselves—influence how co-operatives behave and how we assess performance in non-co-operative sectors (Carini et al. 2015).

Having said that, in the absence of data, a realistic estimate of the economic impact of co-operatives is required in order to demonstrate that they are neither small nor marginal organizations, which goes to show that a valid model—one that is different from the for-profit model which is dominant in today's world—exists.

However, this estimation requires an effort that involves defining the target population, identifying the most appropriate tools for data collection, and, finally, providing a definition of the indicators that are used to assess the economic and social development of co-operatives. With regard to this last point, particular attention needs to be paid to the contribution that these institutions make to the functionality of economic systems. The activities of co-operatives appear to be strongly interconnected with the definition of local endogenous development, especially because co-operatives can combine the economic objectives democratically defined by members who contribute to the bottom-up development process within their communities (Borzaga and Galera 2012).

Starting from this premise, this chapter aims to contribute to the existing literature by providing empirical evidence on the economic size of co-operatives and mutual organizations in different areas of the world.

In the following paragraphs, data from approximately 2,000 co-operatives and mutual organizations from 65 different countries will be analysed. These data are taken from the World Co-operative Monitor,[1] a project promoted by the International Co-operative Alliance in collaboration with the European Research Institute on Co-operative and Social Enterprises (Euricse) in order to take a step forward in measuring the dimensions of co-operatives and to make an initial attempt at quantifying the economic and social impact of the world's largest co-operatives.

This chapter is structured as follows: Section 18.2 presents the aims and the methodological issues faced by the World Co-operative Monitor project. Section 18.3 presents the main results of the 2014 edition of the project in terms of the economic impact of co-operatives and mutual organizations around the world. Section 18.4 presents a deeper analysis of European co-operatives and mutual organizations. The final section articulates the main conclusions of the research.

---

[1] www.monitor.coop (accessed 16 September 2016).

18.2 THE PROJECT WORLD CO-OPERATIVE MONITOR: METHODOLOGICAL ISSUES

The World Co-operative Monitor is an international project started in 2012 by the International Co-operative Alliance.[2] It aims at monitoring, with the scientific and technical support of Euricse, the economic and social impact of the largest co-operatives and mutual organizations in the world. The project is continuing the work started by the Alliance with the Global 300, which brought together economic information about the 300 largest co-operative and mutual organizations in the world, broadening its goals and reviewing its methodology.

The idea behind this new project is to define a new process of data collection, integration, and analysis, culminating in the creation of a regularly updated database containing economic, but also employee, member, and other organizational data, to monitor and demonstrate both the economic and social impact of the largest co-operatives worldwide. The project involves several researchers and experts from different countries who actively contribute to the success of the project by providing methodological support and data collection.[3]

The aim of this project is to collect robust economic, organizational, and social data—not only related to the top 300 co-operative and mutual organizations worldwide, but also on an expanded number of co-operatives—in order to represent the co-operative sector in its organizational, regional, and sectorial diversity. That said, when looking at the methodological issues, providing a clear and agreed-upon definition of the population under study is the first challenge faced by researchers.

For the purpose of this project, it is important for the boundaries of the population under study to be understandable worldwide and, most of all, for them to reflect the characteristics of co-operative organizations in different areas of the world and in different contexts. The process of defining and classifying is not trivial. Researchers working on these aspects face two main issues: (a) the diversity of national legislation and (b) the variety of co-operative forms. Comparative studies (Roelants 2009) show that the legislation concerning co-operatives varies widely from country to country—much more so than legislation regarding profit enterprises. In particular, national laws often do not consider all forms of co-operatives, and they are restrictive about various aspects, such as the minimum number of members or the rules limiting the distribution of profits.

In addition to legislative diversity, it is also necessary to consider the organizational diversity within the co-operative sector. In recent years, researchers have studied the varied and multi-faceted nature of co-operative organizations (Fici 2013; Hansmann

---

[2] www.ica.coop (accessed 16 September 2016).
[3] For the complete list of the researchers and experts involved in the project, visit the project's website: www.monitor.coop

1988), highlighting how they vary in the relationships between the co-operative and its members and in terms of the type of activity they carry out. The variety of existing organizations that refer to the co-operative model has been schematized for the purpose of the project in the typologies shown in Table 18.1.

Regarding mutual organizations, there is a longstanding debate over how to classify a co-operative organization. A recent report by the European Parliament follows the mainstream definition by stating: 'Mutual societies are voluntary groups of persons (natural or legal) whose purpose is primarily to meet the needs of their members rather than achieve a return on investment. They operate according to the principles of solidarity between members who participate in the governance of the business' (European Parliament 2011). So, the main difference between these organizations consists in their willingness to trade with everybody or only with members (Birchall 2010). For the purpose of the World Cooperative Monitor, mutual organizations have been considered as a representative part of the movement by reason of their member-owned business nature

Table 18.1 The World Co-operative Monitor's Types of Co-operative Organizations

Co-operative type	Definition
Co-operative	An autonomous association composed mainly of persons united voluntarily to meet their common economic, social, and cultural needs and aspirations through a jointly owned and democratically controlled enterprise. Members usually receive limited compensation, if any, on capital subscribed as a condition of membership.
Mutual	Private co-operative type organization providing insurance or other welfare-related services. Consider also micro-insurance and mutual organizations with both voluntary and compulsory membership.
Co-operative of Co-operatives/mutuals	Co-operatives composed mainly of co-operatives/mutual organizations that carry out an economic activity for the production of goods or the provision of services of common interest for their members. It periodically publishes its own financial statements.
Co-operative group	A co-operative group: 1) is composed of organizations that operate as a single economic entity, 2) regularly publishes a consolidated financial statement, 3) includes mainly co-operatives, 4) acts according to co-operative principles and values, and 5) is controlled by co-operatives.
Co-operative network	A co-operative network: 1) is composed of organizations that operate as a single economic entity, 2) does not publish a consolidated financial statement, 3) includes mainly co-operatives, 4) acts according to co-operative principles and values, and 5) is controlled by co-operatives.
Non-co-operative enterprise	Non-co-operative enterprise in which co-operatives have a controlling interest.

Source: World Co-operative Monitor: Exploring the Co-operative Economy—2014 report.

Table 18.2 The World Co-operative Metrics Framework Structure

ORGANIZATION DESCRIPTION: Metrics that focus on operational models, type of the organization, sector of activity, and location.	OPERATIONAL IMPACT: Metrics that describe the organization's members, employees, and volunteers.
PRODUCT DESCRIPTION: Metrics that describe the organization's products and services.	PRODUCT IMPACT: Metrics that describe the performance and reach of the organization's products and services.
FINANCIAL PERFORMANCE: Reported financial metrics.	GLOSSARY: Definitions for common terms that are referenced in the metrics.

Source: World Co-operative Monitor: Exploring the Co-operative Economy—2014 report.

(Birchall 2011) and in the longstanding relationship with the International Co-operative & Mutual Insurance Federation (ICMIF). Another reason for considering mutuals in this study comes from the recent debate about the process of demutualization. The process has been defined as the transformation of a co-operative to a shareholder-owned company, considering mutuality as a founding principle of every co-operative organization. In this way, the only difference between mutuals and co-operatives is that the members of mutuals derive their rights through their customer relationship instead of through direct investments (Galor 2008).

Considering this population, the aim of the World Co-operative Monitor is to collect a set of SMART[4] indicators grouped into six categories (Table 18.2) and inspired by the Impact Reporting and Investment Standards (IRIS), a universal language of impact-related terms and metrics for social, environmental, and financial performance reporting promoted by the Global Impact Investing Network (GIIN 2011).

The enquiries of the World Co-operative Monitor focus mainly on three sections: organizational description, financial performance, and operational impact. In the organizational description section, there are questions designed to collect general data on organizations, such as the name, the year of founding, the location of the organization's headquarters, the organization type, the sector of activity, and so on.

Looking at the financial performance section, the choice of economic data to be collected is based on an analysis of the most recent developments of scientific thought concerning the measurement of the economic performance of co-operatives (Austin et al. 2006; Beaubien 2011; Beaubien and Rixon 2012; Lerman and Parliament 1991; López-Espinosa et al. 2009; Marin-Sanchez and Melia-Martì 2006).

Looking at the operational impact section, the questionnaire focuses mainly on the governance and ownership structures, as well as on employees. The choice of collecting

---

[4] SMART stands for *Simple, Measurable, Appropriate, Realistic and Timely.* For more than three decades, the acronym 'SMART' has been widely used and read in various ways in management (Doran 1981).

data related to members is justified by the objective for which a co-operative is formed. A co-operative, indeed, aims at satisfying the specific need(s) of its members through the provision of a service. For this reason, the availability of data on the members of a co-operative (especially regarding type, gender, age, and level of education) can be helpful for understanding a co-operative's organizational structure and its decisions. Collecting data on employment allows us to measure the non-economic impact of a co-operative and to make comparisons with other forms of companies, especially in relation to national or international employment levels.

The methodology used for data collection offers a new process with respect to the methodology used by the Global 300 for data collection, integration, and analysis. This innovative process culminates in the creation of a regularly updated database containing not only economic data, but also employee-related and other social data about the largest co-operatives in the world. In selecting the tools for data collection, a dual strategy involving the following elements was used: (a) the definition of an integration process to create a single database from existing databases and other data collected by national associations, research institutes, and other organizations, and (b) the development of a questionnaire used for the collection of data.

With regard to the first strategy, in recent years, several federations, associations, and research institutions around the world have launched projects to collect economic data in order to publish lists of the largest co-operatives at the national or sectoral levels. To these the databases developed by private companies that allow for the collection of economic data on co-operatives in different parts of the world are added.

From a methodological point of view, the acquisition of existing databases and charts is instrumental to the pursuit of the second strategy. In fact, although the existing databases show diversity in terms of hedging and of the economic indicators collected, their integration provides a good starting point for building a list of co-operatives to whom the questionnaire may be applied. The questionnaire includes questions on the indicators presented in the previous section. The strength of this second strategy is the collection of data from the primary sources of such information, the organizations themselves. This approach allows researchers first to collect data already available in databases and classification lists and then, thanks to the international adoption of common definitions, ensures the greater consistency and robustness of the data collected.

18.3   THE 2014 WORLD CO-OPERATIVE MONITOR REPORT

The 2014 edition of the World Co-operative Monitor collected economic and social data on the largest co-operatives and mutual organizations in the world for the year 2012.

The research team focused on consolidating the results collected during the previous years and on improving the processes for data collection, integration, and analysis.

Data are based mainly on three different sources: existing rankings and lists published by national apex associations, the Amadeus Bureau Van-Dijk database,[5] and the World Co-operative Monitor questionnaire.

With respect to the existing rankings, data were derived from lists obtained from ten different countries[6] and from the insurance sector ranking published by the International Cooperative and Mutual Insurance Federation (ICMIF). Additionally, data from European co-operatives with a total turnover in 2012 of over USD 100 million were extracted from the Amadeus-Bureau van Dijk database and included in the data set. In addition to the above-mentioned data sources, co-operatives were invited to submit their data directly to the World Co-operative Monitor through an online survey, after which the information was integrated into the global database. Although the number of surveys collected during the first five months of 2014 was relatively small, the data represent 185 co-operatives from 51 countries, 19 countries more than the previous year.

Looking at the results of the 2014 edition of the project,[7] data collected by the World Co-operative Monitor highlight the existence of co-operative and mutual organizations that, to all intents and purposes, can be considered to be economic giants: data were collected on 1,926 co-operatives from 65 countries with a total turnover of USD 2,623.1 billion in 2012, which is equal to an average turnover of USD 1.36 billion per organization.

Going into detail, 68.2 per cent (1,313 organizations across 42 countries) of the surveyed organizations reported a turnover of at least USD 100 million, with an average turnover equal to USD 1.98 billion, and 31.8 per cent reported a turnover of at least USD 500 million, with an average turnover of USD 4.09 billion.

Looking at the top 300 co-operatives and mutual organizations in terms of turnover, the data show that 84 per cent of the turnover (i.e. USD 2,205.7 billion) was generated by the top 300 co-operatives and mutual organizations. On average, in 2012, the top 300 co-operatives in the world recorded a turnover of USD 7.35 billion, with the average turnover increasing to USD 17.04 billion if one considers the top 100, and to USD 57.54 billion if one considers the top ten co-operative and mutual organizations.

A by-sector analysis of activity shows that there are large co-operatives and mutual organizations in each of the sectors monitored. Data show that about one-third (27 per cent) of the 1,926 co-operatives are active in the agriculture and food industry sector, another third (27 per cent) in the insurance sector, 21 per cent in the wholesale sector,

---

[5] https://amadeus.bvdinfo.com (accessed 16 September, 2016).

[6] Colombia, Finland, France, Italy, Japan, the Netherlands, New Zealand, Spain, the United Kingdom, and the United States of America.

[7] Data shown in this chapter are taken from the report Euricse (2014) *World Co-operative Monitor: Exploring the Co-operative Economy—Report 2014*. Available online at: www.monitor.coop/.

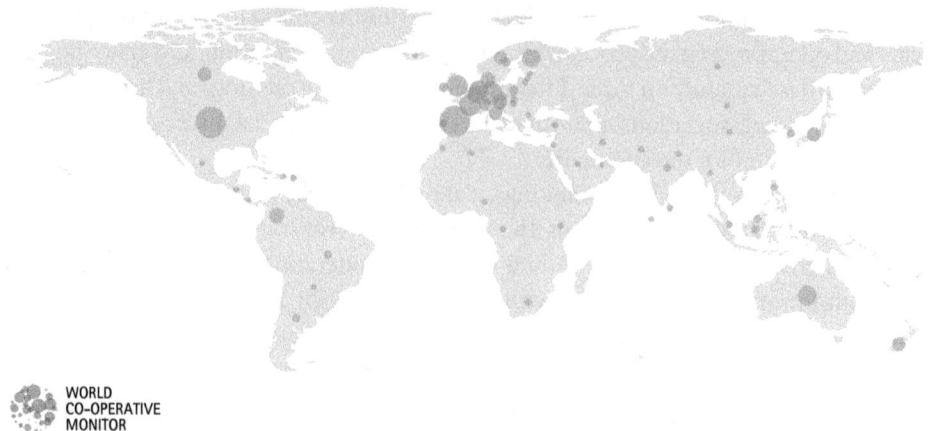

WORLD
CO-OPERATIVE
MONITOR

FIGURE 18.1 Co-operatives in the World Co-operative Monitor Database by country.
Source: World Co-operative Monitor: Exploring the co-operative economy—2014 report.

8 per cent in industry, 5 per cent in the financial sector, 3 per cent in social health services, and the remaining 9 per cent in other services.

Taking into account the three main sectors, the insurance industry is the one that
contributed the most to the overall turnover in 2012: co-operatives and mutual organizations active in this sector produced USD 1,156.48 billion, with an average turnover of
USD 2.23 billion. Agricultural co-operatives declared a total turnover of approximately
USD 600 billion, with an average turnover of USD 1.15 billion. Finally, co-operatives
active in the wholesale sector contributed USD 563.86 billion, which, on average, is USD
1.39 billion per co-operative. Among the remaining sectors, also of note is the size of
90 co-operatives active in the financial sector, which, according to the data collected,
recorded USD 164.96 billion, with an average revenue of USD 1.85 billion.

An analysis by macro geographical region highlights the existence of large co-
operatives and mutual organizations all around the world,[8] with a stronger concentration of co-operatives, as shown in Figure 18.1, in Europe; some countries of the
Americas, such as the United States, Canada, and Colombia; in some Asian countries,
such as Japan, and in Oceania.[9] Nevertheless, as shown in Figure 18.1, the data also
include large co-operatives and mutual organizations in Latin America, Asia, and, to a

[8] The composition of macro geographical regions adopted is the one proposed by the Statistical
Office of the United Nations. http://unstats.un.org/unsd/methods/m49/m49regin.htm (accessed 16
September 2016).
[9] In interpreting this data, please consider that the higher number of large co-operatives in such
countries can be attributed to both the strong presence of co-operatives in these regions and the
availability of several existing rankings and, for the European region, the availability of the Amadeus
database. This could possibly lead to the inclusion of a higher number of co-operatives in Europe than in
the rest of the world. The future goal of the project is to ensure adequate coverage of the co-operatives in
all continents.

lesser extent, given the major problems related to data collection, Africa. Furthermore, the data show that the 2014 edition of the project, compared to the two previous editions, saw an increase in the number of co-operatives from countries not represented in the previous year, including Congo, Costa Rica, the Dominican Republic, Iran, Iceland, Israel, Kenya, Morocco, Myanmar, Mongolia, Nepal, Pakistan, and Paraguay.

In detail, as shown in Table 18.3, the highest numbers of large co-operatives and mutual organizations were recorded in Europe: 1,244 organizations (64.6 per cent of the organizations monitored), which together generated a turnover of USD 1,385 billion (52.8 per cent of the total turnover), with an average of USD 1.11 billion per organization. Next are the Americas, with 439 organizations, which generated USD 742 billion, with an average turnover of USD 1.69 billion per organization. For the Oceania region, data were collected on 141 co-operatives with a total turnover of USD 54 billion and for Asia 93 organizations with a total turnover of USD 441 billion and an average turnover of USD 4.74 billion per organization are reported on. Finally, for Africa, nine co-operatives were surveyed for a total turnover of 1 billion, corresponding to an average turnover of production valued at USD 116.8 million.

Looking at these data, there are two main conclusions to be drawn. First, the importance in economic terms of the European co-operatives and mutual organizations cannot be understated. Of the top 300 co-operatives in terms of turnover, 57 per cent are found in Europe; 32.7 per cent in the Americas, particularly in the United States and Canada; 8 per cent in Asia; and 2.7 per cent in Oceania.

Second, the high average turnover of co-operatives and mutual organizations in Asia, compared to those in other areas of the world, is easily explained: among the top ten organizations in terms of turnover, five are Asian. Among them is Zenkyoren, a Japanese

Table 18.3 Main Figures of the Co-operatives and Mutual Organizations in the World Co-operative Monitor Database by Macro Geographical Region. Number of Organizations, Turnover, and Turnover on GDP Per Capita

		Turnover, 2012		Turnover on GDP per capita, 2012	
Region	Number of organizations	Total (billion USD)	Average (million USD)	Total (thousands USD)	Average (thousands USD)
Africa	9	1	116.8	4,082.0	453.56
Americas	439	742	1,690.4	158,764.7	361.65
Asia	93	441	4,737.1	144,526.4	1,554.05
Europe	1,244	1,385	1,113.7	330,244.7	265.47
Oceania	141	54	380.5	11,705.9	83.02
Total	1,926	2,623	1,361.7	649,323.7	337.14

Source: World Co-operative Monitor. Exploring the co-operative economy—2014 report.

co-operative active in the insurance sector, which in 2012 reported a turnover equal to USD 77.61 billion. The other four organizations all exceeded USD 50 billion.

So far, this chapter has discussed data about turnover in absolute terms. However, in order to analyse and compare the economic dimensions of the co-operatives and mutual organizations in different parts of the world, it is appropriate to assess the size of the organizations in relation to the economic reality of the country or region in which they operate. The average turnover for the smaller co-operatives active in Africa, and those in some sub-regions of Asia, cannot be automatically interpreted as a lower contribution by co-operatives in these regions. Instead, it must be related, in order to draw useful considerations, to the purchasing power of the population in the country in which the organization operates.

As a first attempt to measure the economic dimensions of an organization while taking into account the wealth of the country in which it operates, we computed the ratio of the turnover to the per capita gross domestic product (GDP) of the country.[10] The terms 'GDP' and 'per capita GDP' have different meanings: GDP describes the overall output of all final goods and services produced within a country during one year, whereas the per capita GDP measures the purchasing power of an economy in an internationally comparable way. Therefore, the ratio turnover on per capita GDP measures the turnover of a co-operative in units of the purchasing power of an economy in an internationally comparable way.

As shown in Table 18.3, the picture of the economic size and distribution of co-operatives and mutual organizations which emerges when we use the ratio of the turnover to GDP is different to that which emerges when we use turnover data in absolute terms. In particular, the average values of the ratio of the turnover to GDP show that the average contribution of African co-operatives (USD 453,560) is not only higher than that of European (USD 265,470) and American (USD 361,650) co-operatives, but also higher than New Zealand and Australia-based ones (USD 83,020). Furthermore, the index greatly reduces the difference, compared with data recorded using the turnover in absolute terms, between the average values of the Asian co-operatives and mutual organizations (USD 1,554,050) and the African ones.

The different results given by these two indices are very clear if one is looking at the map of the top 300 co-operatives based on the two indices. The map on the left in Figure 18.2 shows that the 300 largest co-operatives and mutual organizations in the world, in terms of turnover, are distributed among 23 countries, while the 300 largest co-operative and mutual organizations in terms of turnover compared with per capita GDP are distributed among 32 countries, and a greater weight is given to some of the large co-operatives in countries in the developing world, particularly those in South America and Africa.

---

[10] Please note that this ratio is not proposed to compute the percentage of turnover on the GDP, so it should not be interpreted as the contribution of each co-operative to the national GDP.

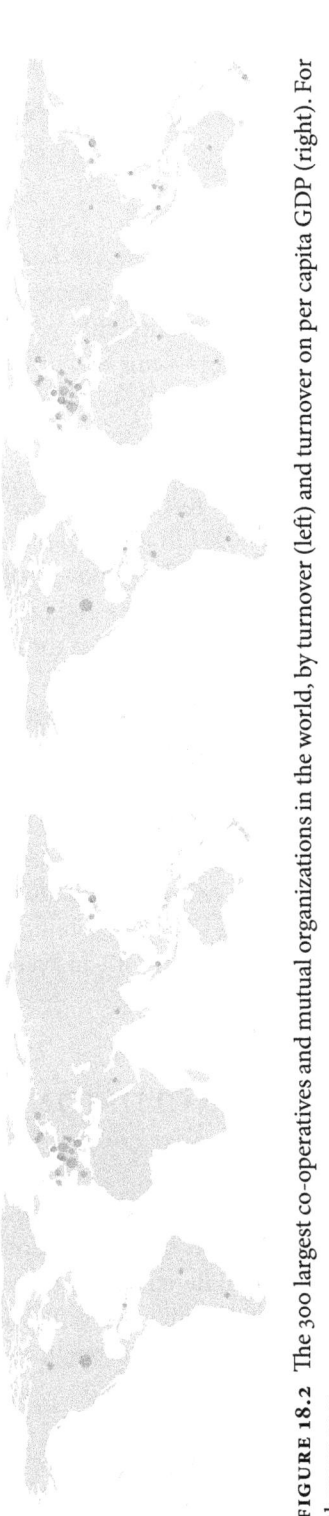

FIGURE 18.2 The 300 largest co-operatives and mutual organizations in the world, by turnover (left) and turnover on per capita GDP (right). For the year 2012.

Source: World Co-operative Monitor: Exploring the co-operative economy—2014 report.

18.4 European Co-operatives in the World Co-operative Monitor Data

To conclude this analysis, this section is intended to provide additional data about co-operatives and mutual organizations monitored in Europe. As noted in the previous section, Europe is the geographic area where we monitor the largest number of co-operatives and mutual organizations. This is not only because of the high number of co-operatives, but also due to the minor problems encountered during the data-collection process. For this reason, it is already possible to analyse the economic dynamics of the co-operatives in this region for the years 2010 to 2012.

By focusing on the 702 European co-operatives and mutual organizations for which economic data for the years 2010 through to 2012 are available,[11] we see that these bodies have generated a total turnover of USD 1,199.27 billion, an increase of 4.3 per cent compared to 2011, and 5.5 per cent compared to 2010. As shown in Table 18.4, among the countries under review, France, Germany, The Netherlands, Italy, and the United Kingdom were the ones that, in 2012, had contributed the most to increasing the total turnover.

In 2012, European co-operatives in the wholesale sector generated a total turnover that amounted to USD 382.13 billion (31.9 per cent of the total turnover), which is equal to an average turnover of USD 1.9 billion and an increase of 10.42 per cent compared to 2011 and of 3.64 per cent compared to 2010. As for the insurance sector, co-operatives recorded a turnover of USD 348.92 billion (−4.1 per cent compared to 2011 and −0.8 per cent compared to 2010), with an average turnover of USD 38.8 billion. Finally, the agricultural sector produced USD 264.34 billion (+12.3 per cent compared to 2011 and −23.2 per cent compared to 2010), with an average of USD 37.8 billion per co-operative.

18.5 Conclusions

The data from the World Co-operative Monitor presented in the previous paragraphs provide some preliminary information on the real economic size of the largest co-operatives and mutual organizations in different areas of the world. First, the data show that the 1,926 co-operatives and mutuals monitored generated a total turnover of USD 2,623 billion, and the top 300 organizations, when computed alone, accounted for USD

---

[11] Data presented in this section include data on 111 Italian co-operatives; this also includes 70 Italian co-operatives that are not included in the data presented in the preceding paragraphs, because, at the time of publication of the World Co-operative Monitor reports, no data were available.

Table 18.4 Turnover (in Billion USD) of the European Co-operatives and Mutual Organizations in the World Co-operative Monitor Database by Country. Years 2010–2012

	2010		2011		2012	
	Total	Average	Total	Average	Total	Average
France	344.19	3.34	354.66	3.44	358.84	3.48
Germany	272.58	2.02	256.32	1.9	273.7	2.03
The Netherlands	102.18	1.5	113.04	1.66	120.31	1.77
Italy	87.28	0.79	86.96	0.78	84.41	0.76
United Kingdom	74.75	1.59	78.16	1.66	82.47	1.75
Denmark	55.78	1.27	58.01	1.32	64.15	1.46
Spain	54.87	1.12	56.22	1.15	58.31	1.19
Finland	49.38	1.5	55.5	1.68	57.42	1.74
Austria	32.43	1.01	32.13	1	31.73	0.99
Belgium	28.66	0.54	27.58	0.52	31.22	0.59
Other countries	34.62	1.28	31.32	1.16	36.7	1.36
Total	1,136.75	1.62	1,149.83	1.64	1,199.27	1.71

Source: World Co-operative Monitor. Exploring the co-operative economy—2014 report.

2,205.7 billion. Looking at these data, it is clear that co-operatives and mutual organizations are not necessarily small-sized enterprises: there are co-operatives and mutuals that generated a turnover comparable to that of large for-profit corporations located in different countries and sectors.

Second, the use of turnover on GDP as an indicator to compare the turnover to purchasing power of the population allows us to highlight more clearly the existence of large co-operatives and mutual organizations, not only in Europe, the Americas, and the Far East, but also in Africa and some areas of South East Asia. This also allows scholars to gather useful information from the comparison of data across countries.

Recognizing that the lack of accurate knowledge about the economic and social impact of co-operatives affects the world's view of how important these organizations are, the World Co-operative Monitor project proposes and promotes the need for an improved methodology for data collection and analysis of co-operatives worldwide.

The results achieved so far are only the first, and they highlight the potential of the project and the need for co-operatives to play a greater role and to become more involved. Currently, based on the available data, it is only possible to describe the economic dimensions of the organizations. Therefore, in order to give visibility both to the economic and to the social impact of the largest co-operatives and mutual organizations in the world, the World Co-operative Monitor research team intends to gradually collect data that can describe how those co-operatives contribute to the welfare of the countries in which they operate in terms of employment, facilities, and so on. However, to be successful, the project cannot ignore the contribution of co-operatives themselves. Co-operatives can actively participate in the project, first by completing the questionnaire on the website of the World Co-operative Monitor and then by spreading the word about the project, thereby contributing to a wider dissemination of its goals and objectives.

Conscious of the challenges of data collection, the World Co-operative Monitor Research Group is working to create a network of research centres and associations that can play an active role in data collection. This can promote the project among co-operatives at the national and regional levels. The goal for the future is to encourage these institutions to create national or regional observatories for co-operatives based on the methodology presented in this chapter.

References

Austin, J., Stevenson, H., and Skillern, J-W. (2006), 'Social and Commercial Entrepreneurship: Same, Different, or Both?' *Entrepreneurship Theory and Practice*, 30(1), 1–22.

Beaubien, L. (2011), 'Co-operative Accounting: Disclosing Redemption Contingencies for Member Shares', *Journal of Co-operative Studies*, 44(2), 38–44.

Beaubien, L. and Rixon, D. (2012), 'Key performance Indicators in Co-Operatives: Directions and Principles, *Journal of Co-operative Studies*, 45(2), 5–15.

Birchall, J. (2010), 'A "Member-owned Business" Approach to the Classification Of Co-operatives and Mutuals', in D. McDonnel, and E. Macknight, eds, *The Co-operative Model In Practice: International Perspectives* (Glasgow: Cooperative Education Trust).

Birchall, J. (2011), *People-Centred Businesses: Co-operatives, Mutuals And The Idea Of Membership* (London: Palgrave Macmillan).

Borzaga, C. and Galera G. (2012), 'Promoting the Understanding of Cooperatives for a Better World'. *Euricse*. Available from www.euricse.eu/publications/promoting-the-understanding (accessed 16 September 2016).

Carini, C., El-Youssef, H., and Sparreboom, T. (forthcoming), 'The Importance of Statistics on Co-operatives: Why and How Should We Collect Data?' in L Brown, S. Novkovic, C. Carini, E. Hicks, L. H. Ketilson, J. Gordon-Nembhard, R. Simmons, and D. Rixon, eds, *Tools to Measure Performance and Impact of Co-operatives* (City: University of Saskatchewan Press).

Doran, G. T. (1981), 'There's a S.M.A.R.T. Way to Write Management's Goals and Objectives', *Management Review*, 70(11), 35–6.

Estrin, S. and Jones, D. C. (1998), 'The Determinants of Investment in Employee-Owned Firms: Evidence from France', *Economic Analysis*, 1(1), 17–28.

European Parliament (2011), 'The Role Of Mutual Societies In The 21st Century', Brussels. www.europarl.europa.eu/activities/committees/studies.do?language=EN (accessed 16 September 2016).

Fici, A. (2013), 'Co-operative Identity and the Law', *European Business Law Review*, 24(1), 37–64.

Galor, Z. (2008), 'Demutualization of Co-operatives: Reasons and Perspectives'. Available at www.coopgalor.com/i_publications.html (accessed 16 September 2016).

Global Impact Investing Network (2011), 'Data Driven: A Performance Analysis for the Impact Investing Industry', IRIS Data Report, 2011. Available at iris.thegiin.org/data-and-benchmarking (accessed 19 October 2016).

Hansmann, H. (1988), 'Ownership of the Firm'. *Journal of Law, Economics and Organization*, 4(2), 267–304.

Lerman, Z. and Parliament, C. (1991), 'Size and Industry Effects in the Performance of Agricultural Cooperatives, *European Review of Agricultural Economics*, 6(1), 15–29.

López-Espinosa, G., Maddocks. J., and Polo-Garrido, F. (2009), 'Equity-Liabilities Distinction: The Case for Co-operatives', *Journal of International Financial Management & Accounting*, 20(3), 274–306.

Marin-Sanchez, M. and Melia-Martì. E. (2006). 'The New European Co-operative Societies and the Need for a Normalized Accounting in the European Union', in J. Chamard and T. Webb, eds, *Symposium on Accounting for Co-operatives Proceedings* (City: Saint Mary's University), 66–88.

Pencavel, J., Pistaferri, L., and Schivardi, F. (2006), 'Wages, Employment and Capital in Capitalist and Worker-Owned Firms', *Industrial and Labor Relations Review*, 60(1), 23–44.

Pérotin, V. (2014), 'Worker Cooperatives: Good, Sustainable Jobs in the Community', *The Journal of Entrepreneurial and Organizational Diversity*, 2(2), 34–47.

Roelants, B. (2009), *Cooperatives and Social Enterprises: Governance and Normative Frameworks* (Brussels: CECOP Publications).

Vanek, J. (1977), *The Labor-Managed Economy* (Ithaca, NY: Cornell University Press).

PART VI

··

NATIONAL CASE STUDIES

··

CHAPTER 19

....

THE MONDRAGÓN
EXPERIENCE

....

XABIER BARANDIARAN AND JAVIER LEZAUN

19.1 INTRODUCTION

....

THE Basque town of Mondragón has given its name to one of the most significant experiences in co-operative organization and workers' self-management anywhere in the
world. Founded in the 1950s, the Mondragón co-operative movement began with the
establishment of a vocational training school and quickly expanded through the creation of a group of industrial firms. Since then, the Mondragón network of co-operatives
has continuously expanded in terms of the number of firms it includes and the range
and scope of the economic activities it encompasses. Today, the co-operative group
comprises over 100 firms employing more than 74,000 workers and generating €12.5
billion in annual revenue (Mondragón 2016). It includes a wide variety of co-operative
firms—from tiny enterprises with a handful of members to large industrial companies
employing thousands of workers around the world—alongside a series of supporting and
auxiliary organizations. Incarnating a tenacious commitment to the dignity of the individual worker and the sovereignty of labour, Mondragón represents an object lesson in
the potential and predicament of a co-operative experience in constant adaptation to the
conditions of an increasingly globalized market economy.

We begin the chapter by describing the local historical context in which the first
Mondragón co-operatives were launched, as well as the values that animated their founding. Next we will describe the organizational architecture of the Mondragón system at the
level of the individual co-operative firm and of the co-ordinating corporation or group.
We will then analyse the rapid expansion and internationalization experienced by some
of the largest Mondragón co-operatives since the 1990s, and the impact of these processes on the equilibrium between co-operative and capitalist principles in the organization of production. Finally, we will discuss the impact of the current economic crisis on
the Mondragón group, and on the operation of its unique system of inter-co-operative

solidarity. We will conclude by reflecting on the future prospects for this long-lasting and far-reaching experiment in workers' ownership and democratic self-governance.

19.2 CONTEXT AND FOUNDING VALUES

In the 1940s, Spain was a country traumatized by the sequels of a terrible civil war, living in poverty under a harsh dictatorship, and forcibly isolated from the rest of the world. Political associations and trade unions were banned (with the exception of the state-sanctioned 'Vertical Syndicate'), and civil society was subjected to extensive police surveillance. In the Basque provinces, General Franco's regime adopted an even more coercive profile, with an active policy of repression against any expression of Basque identity and autonomous social organization.

It was in this context that the seeds of the Mondragón co-operative movement were planted. The driving force was a young priest, José María Arizmendiarrieta, who arrived in the town in 1941 after completing his studies at the diocesan seminary of Vitoria, a leading centre of social Catholic thought in Spain (Lannon 1979; Molina and Miguez 2008). Like other nearby towns in the valleys of Gipuzkoa, Mondragón combined an industrial tradition—centred around the company Unión Cerrajera and its Apprentice School—with deep cultural ties to its rural hinterland. Arizmendiarrieta would draw on this particular blend of communitarian values and economic entrepreneurialism to instigate the creation of a series of co-operative ventures with the primary aim of providing the youth of the region with improved education and employment opportunities (Molina 2005).

Intellectually, Arizmendiarrieta borrowed his philosophical and organizational principles from a series of ideological currents of the time. Paramount among them was the social doctrine of the Catholic Church, which, since Pope Leo XIII's 1891 encyclical *Rerum Novarum*, had asserted the dignity of labour and the right of workers to organize. To this doctrinal bedrock Arizmendiarrieta added the influence of French 'personalist' thinkers (Jacques Maritain and Emmanuel Munier in particular), and his own familiarity with Basque traditions of communal organization, especially those that had flourished around the town of Eibar, a significant manufacturing centre and hub of socialist activism throughout the period leading up to the Civil War, and the for co-operative forms of organization advocated by Basque nationalist unions in the 1920s and 1930s (Azurmendi 1984; Olabarri 1985; Zelaia 1997).

Arizmendiarrieta's initial efforts were focused on the establishment or renewal of local educational institutions. In 1943 he led the creation of a vocational training school (*Escuela Profesional*), and in 1948 he inspired the establishment of a local cultural and educational association (*Liga de Educación y Cultura*). These activities culminated in 1952 with the opening of a new and expanded technical training school. Educational initiatives soon spilled over into industrial enterprises. In 1956, a group of employees of Unión Cerrajera and former students of the *Escuela Profesional* created the first industrial co-operative: Talleres Ulgor (later Fagor Electrodomésticos), dedicated to the fabrication of heaters and gas stoves. Over the following decade, a growing number of firms began to be established around Mondragón and nearby towns: Arrasate (1957), Urssa (1961), Lana (1962), and Ederlan (1963) were some of these initial ventures, often the result of spinning off product lines from already existing co-operatives (Ormaetxea 1998).

The movement soon diversified beyond its manufacturing origins. Critical stepping stones in the growth of what would eventually become the Mondragón Co-operative Group were the creation in 1958 of a system of social provision (*Lagun-Aro*), the founding in 1959 of a co-operative savings bank and credit institution (*Caja Laboral Popular*), and the establishment in 1965 of the ULARCO group, a first attempt to co-ordinate the activities of individual firms and develop mechanisms of inter-co-operative solidarity (Altuna and Urteaga 2014). The consumer co-operative Eroski was established in 1969, and would eventually become the largest firm of the group by number of employees. Beginning in 1970, co-operatives dedicated to applied research, such as Ikerlan, or professional services, such as LKS, emerged to provide R&D services to the industrial firms. The educational and training infrastructure continued to grow alongside the rest of the Group. A new polytechnic school was founded in 1962, and in 1997 the multiple initiatives in higher education were merged to create the University of Mondragón.

While deeply imbued with the ethical and organizational vision of Arizmendiarrieta, the early experiences in co-operative life did not follow a preordained plan, nor even a specific managerial philosophy. They expressed, first and foremost, a form of *practice*— the practice of establishing and sustaining entrepreneurial activities that sought to do justice to a holistic view of the worker as person, and relied on a robust model of collective self-governance. One of Arizmendiarrieta's best-known maxims was that 'the only good idea or word is that which can be turned into action', and the Mondragón experience is best understood as an ongoing experiment in co-operative work and management, rather than the result of any pre-existent programmatic formulation (cf. Gupta 2014).

In fact, it was only in 1987, after several decades of co-operative experience and long after Arizmendiarrieta's death in 1976, that the Mondragón movement began to codify its own principles. That year the first Co-operative Congress adopted the ten 'basic principles' guiding the Mondragón co-operative experience. These were (based on Ormaechea 1991 and 1994):

1. Free Membership (*Libre Adhesión*): there are no barriers to membership for those who want to be part of the Mondragón experience, provided they respect its basic principles;
2. Democratic organization: equality of worker–members (*socios cooperativistas*) expressed in the election of the co-operative's representative bodies (one *socio*, one vote);
3. Sovereignty of labour: labour (*trabajo*) is the transformative factor in society and in human beings and is therefore the basis for the distribution of wealth;
4. The instrumental and subordinated character of capital: capital is an instrument, and should be subordinated to labour;

5. Self-management: worker–members should be provided with opportunities and mechanisms to participate in the management of the firm;

6. Pay solidarity: a fair and equitable return for labour;

7. Inter-co-operation: a commitment to co-operation among different co-operative firms;

8. Social transformation: a commitment to transform society by pursuing a future of liberty, justice, and solidarity;

9. Universalism: the Mondragón experience is part of the broader search for peace, justice, and development of the international co-operative movement;

10. Education: a commitment to dedicate the necessary human and economic resources to co-operative education.

These ten principles have been enshrined as the movement's founding values, a distillation of Arizmendiarrieta's original vision. Their value as a description of the actual *ethos* of the tens of thousands of *socios* that compose the Mondragón co-operatives is, of course, a more complicated matter. In a recent study of how grass-roots worker–members interpret these principles, Heras-Saizarbitoria (2014) found a significant gap between the ideals expressed in this declaration and the day-to-day reality of co-operative life. Worker–members, Heras-Saizarbitoria argues, 'predominantly view [the principles] as part of the organization's *rhetoric*, as a representation of the formal macro-organization that is Mondragón—mainly of the Corporation, rather than their original co-operative. This is *talk* that is detached from daily decision-making and actions' (Heras-Saizarbitoria 2014: 656; emphasis in original; see also Taylor (1994) for an account of how the rhetoric of 'efficiency' has impacted democratic decision-making in the Mondragón cooperatives).

This cleavage between ideals and everyday organizational life has a strong generational dimension: while the founding generation saw these ten principles as the enunciation of a lived experience of co-operative life, younger cohorts of worker–members increasingly treat them as part of Mondragón's corporate self-presentation. 'Worker-owners' commitment to the cooperatives and to cooperativism is still fairly strong,' Cheney wrote in 1999, 'but it appears to be declining, especially for new *socios* and for some segments of the veteran work force as well' (Cheney 2002: 126–7). Before we get ahead of ourselves, however, let us take a closer look at the organizational architecture of Mondragón, and at some of the co-operative group's most significant transformations over the last three decades.

19.3 ORGANIZATIONAL STRUCTURE

As we mentioned earlier, the evolution of the Mondragón co-operative movement has not followed a preordained plan and does not reflect a fixed managerial philosophy. Organizational structures have evolved and adapted to changing economic circumstances as the number of co-operatives grew and the range of their activities expanded. By the late 1970s, however, a distinctive organizational architecture was in place, a set of standard governance mechanisms that applied to all the existing co-operatives and served as a template for the creation of new ones.

Each co-operative is an autonomous and legally independent entity; its membership in the Mondragón Co-operative Group is always a voluntary choice. Worker–members (*socios cooperativistas*) create the firm or join it by contributing their own private capital. The amount of these contributions varies from firm to firm, and is decided by each co-operative's General Assembly (*Asamblea General*). The Assembly is the ultimate sovereign power in the co-operative. It offers every worker–member the opportunity to participate on an equal footing (one member, one vote) in the formulation of the firm's strategy and in the election of its representative bodies.

The first and most significant of these bodies is the Governing Council (*Consejo Rector*). Composed of worker–members elected by the General Assembly, this is the standing governing body of the co-operative, and is in charge of overseeing the fulfilment of the policies agreed by the Assembly. One of the key responsibilities of the Governing Council is to select and appoint the co-operative's general manager (*gerente*), who in many cases is recruited from an external (sometimes non-co-operative) firm. In large and medium-sized co-operatives, the general manager and key operational directors make up a Management Council (*Consejo de Dirección*), which runs the firm on a day-to-day basis and is expected to work in close alignment with the Governing Council.

Another important body in the governance of some co-operatives is the Social Council (*Consejo Social*). Composed of *socios* elected by the General Assembly, this is a consultative body tasked with representing the interests of members as *employees* of the firm. The Social Council is expected to counterbalance the managerial focus of the Governing and Management Councils—a function that is particularly significant if we consider that the Mondragón co-operatives do not recognize trade union representation for their worker–members. The strength of the Social Council, however, and the forcefulness with which it represents members qua employees, varies greatly from co-operative to co-operative (see Kasmir (1996) for an analysis of the relationship between Mondragón and other forms of labour militancy in the region).

Finally, a Monitoring Commission (*Comisión de Vigilancia*) performs an arbitration and auditing role in some co-operatives, although nowadays the audit function *sensu stricto* is typically sourced from specialist firms.

These bodies constitute the governance architecture in every one of the Mondragón co-operatives, but, as with any architecture, everyday life inside these structures adopts in each organization a very particular shape. Individual co-operatives tend to express distinct and idiosyncratic cultures. The level of worker–member participation in the day-to-day management and governance of the firm, for instance, varies greatly across co-operatives. In many firms, attendance at the General Assembly rarely exceeds 50 per cent of the *socios*, unless a critical strategic decision, such as a plan to create a foreign subsidiary, is on the agenda. Otherwise, and in the absence of a sudden change in the fortunes of the firm, strategic decisions are left in the hands of the Governing Council, which would generally make all important decisions in consultation with the Social Council. In other words, this is, at its best, a well-functioning system of worker *representative* democracy, which is no mean feat when compared to the level of worker participation and decision-making power in capitalist firms.

In addition to conforming to the standard governance architecture, all the co-operatives in the Mondragón group share a series of structural features. Perhaps the most striking one is the commitment to pay equity, expressed nowadays in a maximum salary differential ratio of 1 to 9 (in gross terms: the net value ratio is close to 6.5). The co-operatives also share the Mondragón Corporate Management Model (*Modelo de Gestión Corporativo*), which lays out in detail the core principles of the Mondragón experience and sets criteria for designing and evaluating management processes in the different organizations that make up the Group (see Mondragón 2013 for its most recent iteration; see also Heras-Saizarbitoria and Basterretxea 2016 for an analysis of how managerial discourse in individual cooperatives differs from that of the supra-cooperative bodies).

Up to the late 1980s, co-operatives were grouped geographically—or, in some cases, by historical or cultural affinity (Ormaetxea 1998). A fundamental, if informal, governing function was played by the financial arm of Mondragón, Caja Laboral Popular, which effectively operated as the co-ordinating entity of the group as a whole. In 1991 the system of relations between co-operatives was formalized in a new entity, the Mondragón Cooperative Corporation (MCC). Membership of MCC was (and remains) a voluntary choice of the individual co-operatives. At the time of its founding, more than 100 co-operatives joined MCC. They were grouped in three large divisions: financial, manufacturing, and distribution—a fourth division, knowledge (research, training, and professional services) was added later on. In 2008 the group changed its name from Mondragón Cooperative Corporation to Mondragón, or Mondragón Corporation.

To co-ordinate the operations of the group, the Mondragón Corporation has created a series of supra-co-operative governing bodies. The Co-operative Congress (*Congreso Cooperativo*) is the ultimate decision-making body for the Mondragón Group as a whole. It typically meets once every four years, but can be convened extraordinarily by the Standing Committee, the General Council, or through a petition signed by 15 per cent of the worker–members of the Corporation. Delegates to the Congress (a total of 650) are chosen by the members of all the co-operative firms.

The Standing Committee of the Corporation (*Comisión Permanente*) oversees the implementation of the policies agreed by the Congress. Its members are not elected by the Congress, but by the four Divisional Councils, composed of Governing Council members from firms in the respective sectors. Each of the four divisions has a representation on the Standing Committee proportional to its relative share of the total membership of the Corporation.

The Corporation's General Council (*Consejo General*) is the executive body of the Group. It is composed of a Council President and four Vice-Presidents, each representing one division of the group. Since the creation of MCC there has been a lively discussion about the concentration of power in the executive bodies of the Corporation.

The General Council, and particularly its vice-presidents, have a degree of authority—and a level of access to operational information—that makes it difficult for the Congress, let alone the General Assemblies of individual co-operatives, to hold their decisions to account. It is also important to note that, at the level of the Corporation, there is no equivalent to the Social Council of the individual co-operative. Many studies have noted a strong managerial focus in the supra-co-operative structures on the Mondragón Group, and a lack of a counterbalancing power (other than the unwieldy Congress) capable of asserting alternative interpretations of the mission and strategic orientation of the group (see, for instance, Bakaikoa et al. 2004; Cheney 2006).

Since the founding of MCC in 1991, some co-operatives have chosen to leave the group and chart their own independent paths. In 2008 two large and successful co-operatives—Irizar, dedicated to the manufacture of coach vehicle bodies, and AMPO, specialized in the fabrication of stainless steel and high alloy castings—decided to sever their ties with the Corporation. Departures from (and returns to) the group are not uncommon. For instance, ULMA, a large co-operative group in its own right, left the Mondragón Corporation in 1993, only to return in 2002. These changes in the composition of the Mondragón co-operative movement are simply an expression of the fact that individual co-operatives, via their respective General Assemblies, remain, in the last instance, fully sovereign actors.

The glue that connects the co-operatives, beyond their formal membership in the Mondragón group, is their commitment to, and reliance on, a series of mechanisms of inter-firm solidarity. These include a common system of social security, managed by the *Lagun-Aro* co-operative group (*socios* of co-operative firms are considered self-employed by Spanish law and are therefore excluded from statutory unemployment protection and other forms of state support for wage workers), access to the credit facilities of the Caja Laboral co-operative bank, and, most importantly, a series of mechanisms that redistribute profits and obligations within the Group. When they decide to join the Group, co-operatives agree to dedicate a percentage of their profits (variable depending on the division) to inter-co-operative funds intended to support firms in times of crisis and provide professional development opportunities for worker–members. The co-operatives are also committed to finding employment for worker–members whose firms are in the process of downsizing, a feature of the Mondragón system that significantly reduces the impact of economic crises on the aggregate levels of employment.

In summary, it is not easy to characterize the Mondragón system in any straightforward fashion. The relationship between the individual firm and the co-operative group is always complex and finely balanced, acquiring specific features for each co-operative and changing over time. Turnbull has described the Mondragón system as an example of 'network governance' in action (Turnbull 2002), and this is a good shorthand description for what is essentially an equilibrium in constant evolution. Furthermore, the fact that a large majority of co-operatives are situated in close geographic proximity means that formal networks of membership are always overlaid with a dense web of personal and familiar relationships that add a particular flavour to the organizational life of co-operatives and their governance processes.

19.4 Mondragón's Internationalization

The Mondragón co-operatives were born within an autarchic Spanish economy that offered very few opportunities to expand abroad and plenty of protection from foreign competition. By the mid 1960s, some industrial co-operatives, particularly those in the machine tool sector, had begun to make inroads into foreign markets, but the internationalization of the Mondragón Group did not start in earnest until the opening of the Spanish economy that followed the country's admission into the European Union (then the European Communities) in 1986, and the completion of its full membership in the European Single Market in 1992.

With the liberalization of the Spanish economy, the Mondragón Corporation made a strategic choice for the internationalization of production. The 4th Co-operative Congress, held in 1993, identified this as one of the Corporation's priorities, a decision that was reflected in the MCC General Council's 1994 Co-operative Strategic Plan for Internationalization (*Plan Estratégico Cooperativo de Internacionalización*). This was a time when the Basque Country was littered with the ruins of once powerful industrial firms, and it was widely understood within Mondragón that co-operatives would suffer an identical fate unless they were able to compete successfully in international markets. The primary economic *raison d'être* of the co-operatives—the maintenance of secure, quality employment in their local communities—required a radical and proactive internationalization strategy.

The formula chosen for this internationalization has presented Mondragón with challenges as well as opportunities. Large firms operating in mature markets—the case of the home appliance manufacturer Fagor Electrodomésticos, which we will discuss in more detail later on, is emblematic in this regard—pursued a strategy focused on transferring manufacturing capacity to lower-wage markets via affiliate or subsidiary firms in those countries, while keeping higher-value operations in the home co-operative (Clamp 2000; Errasti et al. 2003; Luzarraga and Irizar 2012). At the same time, co-operatives that operated primarily as suppliers of large multinational companies—those in the automotive sector are the best example—had to relocate production to maintain their proximity to strategic clients. To give a sense of the scale of this process: in 2014 Mondragón co-operatives or their affiliates owned 18 production plants in China, ten in Mexico, nine in the Czech Republic, seven in Brazil and six in Poland. In some cases, the Mondragón group has acted as the broker of new international ventures, for example through the creation of Mondragón industrial parks in Kunshan (China) and Pune (India). Today, several of the Mondragón industrial co-operatives are among the most competitive and export-driven firms in Spain. Companies such as Orona (lift manufacturing), Fagor Ederlan (automotive components), or Danobat (machine tools), to name just a few, operate successfully in highly competitive international markets, proving on a daily basis that co-operative principles of organization and ownership are compatible with the highest standards of economic performance.

The rapid expansion and internationalization of Mondragón has led to a diversification of the typology of membership and a greater heterogeneity of employment contracts within co-operatives—something that has become a burning issue for the present and the future of the movement (Errasti et al. 2003). In addition to the traditional worker–members (*socios cooperativistas*), the co-operatives have increasingly employed workers, particularly on short-term contracts, who do not enjoy the rights and obligations of membership. In some cases, co-operatives also employ limited-period worker–members (*socios colaboradores*), who possess the same participation rights as a permanent worker–member but do not enjoy the same social-security protections. If one considers only the workers employed by the co-operatives themselves (and not those of affiliated companies), worker–members represent currently about 80 per cent of the total workforce in Mondragón industrial firms. A significant proportion of workers without member status are concentrated in the distribution division, particularly in the consumer co-operative Eroski. The firm's rapid expansion in the Spanish market has been driven by the acquisition of capitalist food retailing and distribution firms, whose workers have often remained mere employees of Eroski (even when they have been given the option of investing capital and becoming worker–members). Today, less than half of Eroski's 36,000 employees are worker-members (Mondragón 2014).

It is however a fourth category of employment, that of workers in local and foreign subsidiaries, that best exemplifies the repercussions of Mondragón's breakneck international expansion. In 2014, foreign subsidiaries accounted for more than 11,000 of the Group's employees. These workers are, however, not members, that is, owners of capital in their respective firms, nor do they have any say in the decisions made by the parent co-operative. They remain employees of capitalist firms. As Bakaikoa et al. noted a decade ago that, 'the working conditions and labour relations of these affiliated companies depend not so much on the nature of the parent company, in this case of the co-operatives, but on the conditions extant in the country where each offshoot business is located' (Bakaikoa et al. 2004: 78; see also Clamp 2000). In other words, the expansion of Mondragón co-operatives in China, Brazil, or the Czech Republic, for instance, has unfolded in conventional capitalist terms. As a result, '[t]he Mondragón system has created a new organizational paradigm based on a dual employment model wherein, apart from the co-operatives themselves, there are conventional companies dependent on the former' (Bakaikoa et al. 2004: 79).

Many factors explain the emergence of this dual or 'coopitalist' model. For one, the legal principles that sustain the Mondragón model of governance and ownership in the Basque Country have generally no equivalent in foreign jurisdictions. Furthermore, there is sometimes little appetite among employees of affiliates or subsidiaries to become co-operative owners—which would require them to invest their own capital and become responsible for the management of the firm (and liable for its losses)—even in the rare instances when the possibility is presented to them (see Errasti 2015 for a discussion focused on Mondragón's subsidiaries in China).

Individual co-operatives and the Mondragón group as a whole have made efforts to extend their governance model to subsidiary firms. Some co-operatives have encouraged their own subsidiaries to transform themselves into 'mixed co-operatives'. This legal figure, included in the Basque Co-operative Law of 1993, allows co-operative-members to control a majority of votes in their firm's General Assembly, while making room for the representation of external investors in the co-operative's Assembly and General Council. This essentially allows a parent co-operative to transform a subsidiary into a mixed co-ooperative and become a shareholder in it, thereby safeguarding its original investment as the new firm become increasingly autonomous and self-governing (see Flecha and Ngai 2014 for examples). The Mondragón Group has also promoted the adoption by affiliate and subsidiary companies of elements of its Corporate Management Model, and in some cases it has facilitated the dissemination of best governance practices to the capitalist firms that are part of the Mondragón network. Yet it remains the case that, while the Mondragón co-operatives have been highly efficient in exporting technological capacities and operational management skills to foreign markets, they have been less successful in exporting the values and governance models that give them their distinctive identity back home (Azkarraga 2007; Errasti 2015). Or to put it differently, the internationalization of production has very quickly outpaced the ability of Mondragón co-operatives to extend their founding principles beyond their communities of origin. The goal of a 'democratic multinational enterprise' (Errasti et al. 2003) remains as elusive as ever.

In summary, liberalization of the global economy has presented the Mondragón movement with a particularly complex set of challenges. On the one hand, it has created new conditions for the success, or even survival, of individual co-operatives, and many have become highly adept at navigating multiple production and distribution markets around the world. At the same time, this process has brought into sharper relief the fact that preservation of co-operative employment and ownership at home often depends on the intensification of capitalist methods of production and labour utilization abroad. This essential tension is now at the heart of the Mondragón experience. The way this tension is confronted will determine the future identity of the Mondragón co-operative movement, and its relevance for other experiments in co-operative organization around the world.

19.5 MONDRAGÓN IN CRISIS

The economic crisis of the last decade has hit Mondragón hard. The most visible symptom is perhaps the bankruptcy of Fagor Electrodomésticos in 2013. The direct heir to the original Ulgor co-operative, Fagor Electrodomésticos was the group's flagship co-operatives, with 5,600 employees (2,000 of them worker–members) and eighteen production plants in six countries. Over the decade that preceded its demise, and during a period of massive growth in the Spanish construction sector, Fagor Electrodomésticos more than doubled its production capacity. In 2005 it acquired the French firm Brandt to become the fifth largest domestic appliance manufacturer in Europe (Errasti 2013).

The striking fact about the case of Fagor Electrodomésticos is not only that a co-operative of such significance and size could put itself in an unsustainable financial position, but that the Mondragón Group, via its General Council, refused to provide additional financial support and effectively abandoned one of its largest and most emblematic co-operatives to the bankruptcy court. At the same time, the collapse of Fagor Electrodomésticos showcases some of the strengths of the co-operative group. Prior to the ultimate decision to force the firm's bankruptcy, worker–members across the Mondragón co-operatives had agreed to significant pay cuts in a last-ditch effort to keep the firm afloat. In May 2013, for instance, the Co-operative Congress approved the establishment of a €70 million re-structuring fund (*Fondo de Restructuración y Empleo Societario*) that drew on contributions from all the co-operatives in the group. Once the General Council decided, a few months later, not to infuse any additional funds into the firm, other mechanisms of inter-co-operative solidarity kicked in, particularly the commitment to find employment within the group for worker–members made redundant by the bankruptcy. Today, a majority of the former *socios* of Fagor Electrodomésticos have been relocated to other Mondragón co-operatives. The situation is wholly different, however, for the thousands of employees of the co-operative and its subsidiaries who were not members, and as a result are not protected by the group's safety net (Errasti et al. 2016).

The crisis of Fagor Electrodomésticos has revived long-standing discussions within the Mondragón co-operatives and in their immediate communities about managerial competence and oversight, the pace and goal of internationalization, and the relationship between individual firms and the corporate group (Ortega and Uriarte 2015). This is, of course, not the first time Mondragón has faced economic difficulties. In the late 1970s and for much of the 1980s the industrial co-operatives confronted a very serious recession. In their classic study of the Mondragón co-operatives in the 1980s, William and Kathleen Whyte (1991) dealt at length with the challenges that the worldwide recession posed to the co-operative movement, and to Fagor Electrodomésticos in particular. At the time, the firm introduced radical changes in its mode of operation—most significantly, a new compensation policy for worker–members that linked individual returns (the Mondragón alternative to a worker's salary) to the economic performance of the firm (up to that point individual returns had been linked exclusively to the evolution of the Spanish consumer price index). Since then, individual returns in Fagor and other co-operatives have been calculated through a complex formula that includes as a key factor the evolution of the co-operative's cash flow, used as a proxy indicator for the economic fortunes of the firm.

Economic crises, in other words, have significantly transformed and transfigured the Mondragón experience, and the current period of adjustment will similarly have profound implications for the organization and *ethos* of the co-operative movement. Economic difficulties not only test the competitiveness of individual co-operatives and the competence of their governing bodies, they also reveal the moral mettle of worker–members, and their commitment to the values and principles that have animated this co-operative experience over the last 60 years.

19.6 RE-FOUNDING MONDRAGÓN

In a recent document, the Mondragón Group identifies, among others, the following strategic goals for its immediate future:

1. To achieve a more intense experience of the Co-operative Principles and Values, on the basis of the centrality of the individual and of labour in co-operation;
2. To encourage a form of leadership that is visionary and demanding, and coherent with the Co-operative Principles and Values;
3. To encourage forms of co-operative solidarity that will allow transformation—not the perpetuation of unsustainable economic realities;
4. To open the Corporation to other initiatives that might share similar values and objectives;
5. To encourage an integrated education of individuals in values and skills;
6. To develop a more open and transparent communication policy. (Mondragón 2014).

These commitments reflect the hard lessons Mondragón has learned from its recent travails, and suggest some of the changes the group will pursue in the coming years. The reference to 'the perpetuation of unsustainable economic realities,' for instance, is a clear reference to the demise of Fagor Electrodomésticos, and implies that the core principle of inter-co-operative solidarity will be increasingly complemented by a determination to allow the termination of co-operative initiatives that prove unable to compete in their respective markets.

As we have suggested, Mondragón's recent upheavals should be seen within the long trajectory of continuous transformation that has characterized the movement since its inception. In fact, the challenges that Mondragón faces today are to some extent the result of its own success—if we measure success by the ability of firms founded on the principles of workers' ownership and democratic governance to compete effectively and expand significantly within the parameters of an increasingly globalized capitalist economy. This success has transformed the conditions under

which the Mondragón co-operatives must operate, not least by shaping the expectations of their worker–members. Sixty years after the establishment of Talleres Ulgor
there are few traces of the political and economic context that justified the launch of
this radical co-operative experience. In 1956, per capita gross domestic product in
Spain was barely 40 per cent of the average for West European countries; Spain was
politically and economically isolated from the rest of the world, suffering under a
dictatorial regime that repressed any form of labour militancy and took special aim
at any expression of Basque national identity.

In the late 1950s, Spain started a process of economic liberalization that would
eventually lead to greater openness to the flows of the global economy. In the wake of
Franco's death in 1975, the country underwent an equally profound political transformation. In 1979, The Basque Country approved its Statute of Autonomy and gained
significant powers of self-rule, particularly in economic and fiscal policy. The socio-
economic transformation of the region in the intervening years has been dramatic.
Today, GDP per capita in the province of Gipuzkoa, in which the vast majority of
Mondragón co-operatives are concentrated, is 34 per cent higher than the Spanish
average; even more significantly, it is 28 per cent higher than the average of European
Union countries. The productive structure of the territory differs starkly from that of
Spain, with a disproportionate emphasis on high-value manufacturing, engineering
services, and exports. Even during the current economic downturn, the situation in
Gipuzkoa and the rest of the Basque Country is comparatively benign—while still high
(over 12 per cent at the time of writing), unemployment in Gipuzkoa is about half of
the Spanish average. All these facts owe a great deal to the activity and success of the
Mondragón co-operatives.

This is, in other words, a prosperous part of the world, albeit one that has experienced more than its share of political turmoil and violent conflict over past decades.
The challenge for the Mondragón group has been to adapt to a social and economic
environment that no longer resembles the conditions of penury and isolation that
justified and energized this co-operative experiment. It is undeniable that the relative
affluence of the region has eroded the co-operative spirit. *Socios* in the Mondragón
co-operatives are cut from the same cloth as other members of their communities:
they often value the material returns they obtain from their participation in the co-
operatives—greater job security, higher pay—above and beyond their commitment
to the principles and values that drove the foundation of those co-operatives in the
first place. Or rather, they are inclined to think of those two dimensions—personal
benefit and commitment to a co-operative enterprise—as discrete and separate
aspects of their working life. In the case of the largest and oldest firms, new worker–
members are joining organizations that were founded long before they were born,
and which are now orders of magnitude bigger than the co-operatives their predecessors created. The worker–members are, furthermore, subject to the same processes of
cultural and ideological change as any other member of their societies. As Azkarraga
et al. note in their examination of the transformation of the Mondragón movement,

'[t]he process of de-ideologization has affected the whole of society and, as members of that society, the cooperative social body as well' (Azkarraga et al., 2012: 78).

Mondragón, we have argued, is not a co-operative, not even a supra-co-operative corporation. Members of the first generation of worker–members often used a phrase to describe their efforts: they were participating in a 'co-operative experience', *una experiencia cooperativa*. This is perhaps the most useful way of understanding Mondragón: not as a series of established firms, or a corporation with a particular organizational model and management formula, but as a form of practice rooted in specific local conditions—a form of practice that has evolved over time, has had its accomplishments and failures, and that at its fullest embodies and actualizes a founding commitment to the emancipatory power of co-operative associationism and workers' ownership (Sarasua 2010).

Criticism of the shortcomings of this practice have characterized the Mondragón co-operatives since their origins, and in this article we have identified some of the most salient targets of reproach. Yet the fact that these criticisms exist and persist reflects the strengths as much as the weaknesses of the movement. For it means that the practical realization of the Mondragón experience can still be held up to the standard established 60 years ago with the creation of the first co-operatives, that the ideal of a non-capitalist mode of economic existence founded on a personalist understanding of the worker is still operative, even if sometimes it resonates with barely audible force. Alongside the economic success of most of the firms in the Mondragón Group, this is perhaps the most significant achievement of the movement: the very longevity of this experiment in co-operative self-management, and its value as an example of both the potentialities and the dilemmas that will confront any such endeavour when it operates in a world dominated by a very different, often incompatible set of values.

References

Altuna, R. and Urteaga, E. (2014), 'Los inicios de la experiencia coopeativa Mondragón', *REVESCO. Revista de Estudios Cooperativos*, 115, 101–31.

Azkarraga, J. (2007), *Mondragón ante la globalización: La cultura cooperativa ante el cambio de época* (Eskoriatza: Lanki Ikertegia).

Azkarraga Etxagibel, J. A., Cheney, G., and Udaondo, A. (2012), 'Workers' Participation in a Globalized Market: Reflections on and from Mondragón', in M. Atzeni (ed.), *Alternative Work Organizations* (Basingstoke: Palgrave Macmillan), 76–102.

Azurmendi, J. (1984), *El hombre cooperativo: Pensamiento de Arizmendiarrieta* (Mondragón: Caja Laboral Popular).

Bakaikoa, B., Errasti, A., and Begiristain, A. (2004), 'Governance of the Mondragón Corporacion Cooperativa', *Annals of Public and Cooperative Economics*, 75(1), 61–87.

Cheney, G. (2002), *Values at Work: Employee Participation Meets Market Pressure at Mondragón* (Ithaca, NY and London: Cornell University Press).

Cheney, G. (2006), 'Democracy at Work Within the Market: Reconsidering the Potential', *Research in the Sociology of Work*, 16, 179–203.

Clamp, C. A. (2000), 'The internationalization of Mondragon', *Annals of Public and Cooperative Economics*, 71(4), 557–77.

Errasti, A. (2013), 'Tensiones y oportunidades en las multinacionales coopitalistas de Mondragón: El caso de Fagor Electrodomésticos, sdad. coop', *REVESCO: Revista de Estudios Cooperativos*, 113, 30–60.

Errasti, A. (2015), 'Mondragón's Chinese Subsidiaries: Coopitalist Multinationals in Practice', *Economic and Industrial Democracy*, 36(3), 479–99.

Errasti, A., Bretos, I., and Etxezarreta, E. (2016), 'What Do Mondragon Coopitalist Multinationals Look Like? The Rise and Fall of Fagor Electrodomésticos S. Coop. and its European Subsidiaries'. *Annals of Public and Cooperative Economics*, 87(3), 433–56.

Errasti, A. M., Heras, I., Bakaikoa, B., and Elgoibar, P. (2003), 'The Internationalisation of Cooperatives: The Case of the Mondragón Cooperative Corporation', *Annals of Public and Cooperative Economics*, 74(4), 553–84.

Flecha, R. and Ngai, P. (2014), 'The Challenge for Mondragon: Searching for the Cooperative Values in Times of Internationalization', *Organization*, 21(5), 666–82.

Gupta, C. (2014), 'The Co-operative Model as a "Living Experiment in Democracy"', *Journal of Co-operative Organization and Management*, 2(2), 98–107.

Heras-Saizarbitoria, I. (2014), 'The Ties That Bind? Exploring the Basic Principles of Worker-Owned Organizations in Practice', *Organization*, 21(5), 645–65.

Heras-Saizarbitoria, I. and Basterretxea, I. (2016), 'Do Co-Ops Speak the Managerial Lingua Franca? An Analysis of the Managerial Discourse of Mondragon Cooperatives', *Journal of Co-operative Organization and Management*, 4(1), 13–21.

Kasmir, S. (1996), *The Myth of Mondragón: Cooperatives, Politics, and Working Class Life in a Basque Town* (Albany: SUNY Press).

Lannon, F. (1979), 'A Basque Challenge to the Pre-Civil War Spanish Church'. *European History Quarterly*, 9(1), 29–48.

Luzarraga, J. M. and Irizar, I. (2012), 'La estrategia de multilocalización internacional de la Corporación Mondragón', *Ekonomiaz*, 79(01), 115–46.

Molina, Fernando (2005), *José María Arizmendiarrieta (1915-1976): Biografía* (Mondragón: Euskadiko Kutxa).

Molina, F. and Miguez, A. (2008), 'The Origins of Mondragon: Catholic Co-operativism and Social Movement in a Basque Valley (1941–59)', *Social History*, 33(3), 284–98.

Mondragón, 'Humanity at Work: Corporate Management Model', 2013. Available at http://www.mondragon-corporation.com/wp-content/themes/mondragon/docs/Corporate-Management-Model.pdf (accessed 28 October 2016).

Mondragón (2014), *Mondragón del futuro. 1ª fase: Diagnóstico y líneas de actuación*, (Mondragón: Mondragón Corporation,).

Mondragón (2016), *Annual Report 2015*. Available at http://www.mondragon-corporation.com/eng/about-us/economic-and-financial-indicators/annual-report/ (accessed 9 January 2017).

Olabarri, I. (1985), 'Tradiciones cooperativas vascas', in J. Intxausti, ed., *Euskal Herria: Historia y sociedad* (Donostia: Caja Laboral Popular), 298–307.

Ormaechea, J. M. (1991), *La experiencia cooperativa de Mondragón* (Mondragón: Grupo Cooperativo Mondragón).

Ormaechea, J. M. (1994), 'Los principios cooperativos de la experiencia', in *Textos Básicos de Otalora* (Aretxabaleta: Otalora).

Ormaetxea, J. M. (1998), *Orígenes y claves del cooperativismo de Mondragón*, 2nd edition (Mondragón: Caja Laboral Popular).

Ortega, I. and Uriarte, L. (2015), *Arrasateko Kooperatibagintzaren Erronkak eta Dilemak: Fagor Etxetresnak Kooperatibaren Krisiaren Ondotik* (Eskoriatza: Lanki Ikertegia).

Sarasua, J. (2010), *Mondragón en un Nuevo Siglo: Síntesis reflexiva de la experiencia cooperativa* (Eskoriatza: Lanki Ikertegia).

Turnbull, S. (2002), *A New Way to Govern: Organisations and Society after Enron* (London: New Economics Foundation).

Whyte, W. F. and Whyte, K. K. (1991), *Making Mondragón: The Growth and Dynamics of the Worker Cooperative Complex* (Ithaca: Cornell University Press).

Zelaia, A. (1997), *Kooperatibak Euskal Herrian* (Bilbao: Udako Euskal Unibertsitatea).

CHAPTER 20

·····

MOVING TOWARDS 100% EMPLOYEE OWNERSHIP THROUGH ESOPS

added complexities in add-on transactions

·····

DANIEL TISCHER AND JOHN HOFFMIRE

20.1 INTRODUCTION

·····

THIS chapter focuses specifically on financial transactions to create ESOPs rather than the background and research on ESOPs in the USA. While many countries have co-operatives or similar member or employee-owned firms, the USA has many debt-financed ESOPs. Since being established in 1973, Employee Stock Ownership Plans have been the most influential approach to transferring ownership to employees in the USA, partly because, with the company providing the collateral required through a trust, employees are not required to finance the purchase of shares themselves. As noted by Corey Rosen in Chapter 29 on ESOPs, the *National Center for Employee Ownership* (NCEO)[1] estimates that at the end of 2015, there were about 9,300 employee-owned companies in existence that have used ESOPs and similar plans to transfer varying percentages of their stock, estimated at about $1 trillion to about 15 million employees who are participating in the schemes. Projections based on their database also suggest that a significant proportion of ESOP plans will be 100 per cent employee owned.

With some exceptions (see Alam et al. 2003), much of the academic and practitioner literature conveys ESOP transactions to be simple, one-stage transfers of shares

·····

[1] A Statistical Profile of Employee Ownership (2015). http://www.nceo.org/articles/statistical-profile-employee-ownership (accessed on 21 September 2016).

to employees or a trust that administers the shares on behalf of employees. In reality, multi-stage ESOP transactions are the norm, because few companies can afford to borrow, collateralize, and fund a 100 per cent buy-out of the existing owners at fair market value.[2]

This chapter will explore ESOP transactions. In doing so, we will provide a background on ESOPs and the two main types of ESOP transactions—leveraged and non-leveraged—before zooming in on add-on ESOP transactions.

20.2 ESOPs: Purpose and Background

The purpose of an Employee Stock Ownership Plan is to enable employees to participate in the ownership of their company without having to invest their own money, thus extending ownership to even the lowest-paid employees. Under US corporate law, corporations can be divided into C corporations and S corporations. A C corporation pays US federal corporate taxes at the corporate level, whereas an S corporation passes corporate income to individual shareholders who then pay the taxes. Retiring or departing owners of a closely held C corporation who wish to cash out their ownership and sell to a buyer[3] benefit from a readily available market for their shares (Miller 2010) by virtue of selling them to the ESOP and the tax advantages that come with ESOPs (Freeman and Knoll 2008; NCEO 2014a). An ESOP has the mandate to primarily invest funds in employer stock and is overseen by the Internal Revenue Service and the US Department of Labor.

The ESOP is either the recipient of company stock contributed by the company itself or receives money to buy shares in the company. The shares are not directly held by employees but in a trust, which is the holder of record for all shareholder purposes and allocates a proportion of shares according to income or an alternative basis (Hoffmire et al. 1992). Using a trust structure to manage the ESOP has two clear benefits: 1) an additional layer of governance to monitor corporate management, and Board of Director actions are aligned to the objectives of the ESOP participants; and 2) it exempts ESOP participants from paying income tax on the allocated shares at the time they are awarded.[4]

There is a breadth of research suggesting that ESOP ownership has positive impact on company performance and growth, job safety, employee satisfaction, retirement assets

---

[2] A notable exception to this is when owners gift their ownership to employees; however, this is a relatively rare event.

[3] A company where more than 50% of stock is owned by five or fewer players and tax is payable both at corporate level (on profits) and at the level of those (on dividend income) owning a stake in the company. For the definition of an S corporation, see http://www.irs.gov/Businesses/Small-Businesses-&-Self-Employed/S-Corporations/ (accessed 17 September 2016). New 2015 legislation before the US Congress would extend the tax benefits of C corporations for owners selling to the workers, to S corporations.

[4] Income is taxed in the event of shares being distributed, or sold back to the company at market value, unless employee-owners roll over their ESOP accounts into Individual Retirement Accounts.

and compensation (Blasi et al. 2015; Kim and Quimet 2009), especially in those companies that are majority-owned by ESOPs and those with participatory management (Kramer 2010). While ESOPs can be a motivating factor for employees, management, and owners, mutual agreements need to be reached between the involved parties, thus representing employee-owners' interests (Kruse et al. 2003).

Critics often cite the inherent risk of ESOPs being used as quasi-retirement plans because, unlike other retirement schemes that aim to diversify investments, ESOPs concentrate retirement assets in one firm; thus a firm's default could have serious financial implications for employee owners. While it reflects useful commentary at a theoretical level, research has shown that in reality ESOPs are often resilient to crisis and have lower default rates than comparable non-ESOP companies Blair et al. (2000). In addition, Kruse (2002) has shown that ESOP plans that are combined with other 401(k) retirement plans result in a considerably higher value of employee stock per participant ($27,244) when compared to other defined contributions plans.

The mechanisms by which ESOPs operate vary depending on a number of factors including whether they are leveraged or not, and whether new shares are issued or existing shares transferred. Still, the underlying functionality is broadly similar. Most ESOPs are leveraged and many involve financing from an external source, usually a bank or financial lender; however, it is useful to first explore the mechanics of a non-leveraged ESOP.

20.2.1 Non-Leveraged ESOP (NLE)

NLEs are financed directly by the sponsoring company which contributes newly issued or existing stock, or contributes cash to the ESOP to finance the purchase of shares directly from shareholders exiting the business. This configuration is often used as a way to gradually build enough equity to facilitate a leveraged transaction for a larger percentage ESOP transaction.

A NLE can be used by owners wishing to transfer ownership to employees by making use of the tax advantages an ESOP enjoys, particularly the deduction in the current income tax for the amount of the contribution and the possibility to defer capital gains tax by the seller if the ESOP holds 30 per cent or more of the outstanding stock of the company immediately after the transaction, and as long as within twelve months[5] of the ESOP creation the seller uses the proceeds to invest in the correct types of replacement securities, as outlined in Section 1042 of the US tax code. These types of transactions can only be used in closely held C corporations. Once the transaction is finalized, the C Corp. status can be changed to that of an S Corp. to benefit from lower tax levels on the income which is only payable at the individual level.

---

[5] The actual timetable is within the 15 months that begin 3 months before the transaction and end 12 months after the transaction.

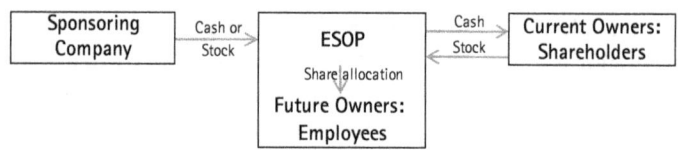

FIGURE 20.1 Non-leveraged ESOP.

Source: Adapted from ESOP Association (2016).

Essentially, the set-up of the plan only involves five parties: the owner/seller, the company, the ESOP, the trustee for the ESOP, and the employee participants. As illustrated in Figure 20.1, the company finances the ESOP by contributing cash used by the ESOP to buy stock from the seller of the company, or by contributing shares to the ESOP directly from the company. The shares are held by the ESOP trust which allocates shares to employees based on equitable principles, for example income. An employee accumulates shares until exiting the company, which is when the employee, through the trust, essentially sells shares back to the company or the ESOP for a value determined by an outside appraiser.

The biggest downside of the NLE is that, in most cases, transferring ownership in such a way can be a lengthy process because the funds available within the company are limited, and thus may only allow small percentages of the shares to be transferred annually. In certain situations, the value of a company may increase while a NLE transaction rolls forward, even if the company is not gaining in profitability. This might stretch the time to move to 100 per cent employee ownership to an even longer period. Alternatively, a company might issue new shares and gift them to an ESOP to dilute the seller's interest; however, in most cases where this happens, the volume of shares issued are limited to lift ESOP ownership above specific thresholds, for example, from 25 per cent to above 30 per cent to qualify for tax deferral under Section 1042 (only in closely held C corporations) (NCEO 2014b).

20.2.2 Leveraged ESOP (LE)

Broadly speaking, LEs tend to be more complicated than NLEs. Leverage or debt financing is the key mechanism that allows the ESOP to buy shares the same way any other investor would buy them—by levering the future earnings of the company to pay for it. The advantage to the owners is mainly that it enables them to sell a larger volume of shares or stake in the company to the ESOP in one single transaction as would not be possible in NLEs because of the limited funding.

Figure 20.2 illustrates the basic mechanism. The leveraged ESOP (LE) is 'leveraged' because it is financed by an external loan from a third-party provider (banks or alternative lending sources)[6] or through a seller loan. In either case, the loan is often guaranteed

---

[6] Alternative lending sources include, for example, finance companies, insurance companies, mezzanine debt funds, and sellers themselves.

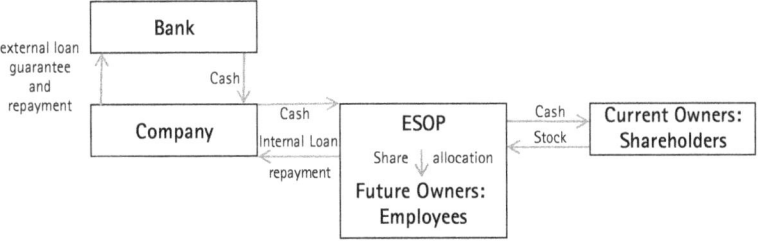

FIGURE 20.2 Leveraged ESOP diagram.

Source: Adapted from ESOP Association (2016).

by the company and/or the seller. The company usually loans the same amount to the ESOP which enables the ESOP to purchase a pre-determined (by the value of the loan) number of shares from the current owners. The internal loan is amortized (or repaid) by the ESOP as dividends paid on the company stock are tax deductible if used to repay principal debt or interest. The company often uses the money saved through tax advantages to repay loans over a shorter number of years than would have otherwise been contemplated. In practice, the internal and external loan repayment schedules do not need to be the same.

The amount of stock transferred is likely to be larger than the amount transferred in NLEs because debt financing makes larger deals possible. The price of the shares is determined by an independent valuator, and not by the owner of the stock. Moreover, the seller may have to pledge some or all of the proceeds of the transaction to the third-party lender as collateral for a period of time. Employees receive share allocations each year as the loan is repaid.

Still, although leveraged ESOPs speed up the process of transferring ownership to employees, it remains unlikely that, even with external funding, 100 per cent of ownership may be transferred in a one-off transaction, but when this does happen, it usually takes a combination of external financing and subordinated seller notes.[7] However, doing so may result in over-leveraging which may have a negative impact on future company performance because debt repayments are financed through the reallocation of the operating cash flow from productive uses such as investments.

Sometimes, owners and ESOP participants are happy with a minority, for example 30 per cent, stake in the company being transferred to employees. Still, as suggested earlier, since 30–40 per cent of ESOPs own, or will eventually own 100 per cent of the company, we need to focus on the mechanisms that allow this and that are regularly used to increase employee ownership in multiple stages.

---

[7] A seller note is issued by the buyer (the ESOP) bearing the terms of repayments and interest payable to the seller to bridge a funding gap between the purchase price and the financeable asset base of the company to be purchased.

20.3 ADD-ON ESOP TRANSACTIONS

Indeed, multi-stage ESOP transactions are a common type of ESOP deal because of the limitations of both leveraged and non-leveraged ESOPs. Because it usually requires multiple tranches of ESOP transactions to take a company to 100 per cent employee ownership, ESOP transactions are seldom as straightforward as suggested by the frequently used neat diagrams representing the mechanism (as we did in this chapter). Instead, ESOP transactions become, usually, more complex, with each transaction that is added to the process of a multi-stage ESOP. Some of these issues are discussed in sections that follow.

As outlined, not all ESOP transactions transfer 100 per cent of shares from the current owners to the employees at one time. It is much more common that the initial ESOP only involves the transfer of a minority stake. In smaller firms, the first tranche might transfer up to 50 per cent of ownership to the ESOP; in larger companies, that percentage might be lower. In this light, our discussion will assume that the ESOP holds 30 per cent of company shares after the first stage.

20.3.1 Outlining a Typical Series of ESOP Transactions

At the beginning of any negotiation the various parties involved would get together to set out the goals and the steps of the ESOP transaction: seller(s), management, the ESOP trustee, and other advisors.[8] The ESOP representative(s) would not have been involved in the early stages of the initial transaction negotiation process because, especially if an outside trustee is contemplated, there was no trust to represent at the time that the transaction was first contemplated.

Following the successful completion of the initial ESOP transaction, it would be reasonable to assume that add-on transactions follow the same process, and while they do to some extent, there are some changes to the process and the people involved. The complexities arising in an add-on transaction will be discussed later in the chapter, so the following discussion really is meant to give an overview of the process and involved parties.

1) Once the goals are clearly understood by the parties, for example raising ESOP ownership from a minority to a majority stake, sellers would outline their objectives, as well as some initial terms and conditions. The proposal would then be reviewed by the ESOP trust, management, and possibly financial advisors.

2) In turn, the ESOP's financial and legal advisors, and perhaps the trustee, would submit proposals to be reviewed by stakeholders to be negotiated, and due diligence discussions would be held.

---

[8] If the company is unionized, unions may also be involved in the negotiation process.

3) The process moves forward with the formal analysis of the particulars of the pro-posed deal, including firm valuation, terms, and conditions, and conditions for the new ESOP holding (in this case 70 per cent). The principal issues at this stage are that the valuation satisfies the sellers, and, most importantly, that the financial viability of the company to service the debt used to purchase stock for the work-ers is confirmed. Changes in majority ownership will require additional research into new governance procedures to ensure employees are adequately represented (see next section). Moreover, pre- and post-transaction cash flow and shareholder returns will be analysed to outline the feasibility of the transaction and the impact on employee-participants' share values.

4) A draft company presentation and proposed transaction outline will be handed over, usually by advisors, to the company before being presented to shareholders. Simultaneously, management and, at times, financial advisors, would co-ordinate lending partners, and negotiate consent for funding by the lending institution(s).

5) Selling shareholders and their advisors would respond to the proposed transac-tion's terms and conditions and term sheets. Alternatively, when sellers propose the sale at certain terms, ESOP financial advisors would assess whether these terms are fair to the ESOP. The negotiations are then finalized between the parties involved in the transaction, including the price of the transaction and the terms and conditions of the sale to the ESOP.

6) The last step includes the finalization of legal documents required for the transac-tion before the transaction can be closed and funded. In the end, the trustee must be comfortable with the price and the matters that influence price.

20.3.2 Internal Consideration: Changing Power Relations in Negotiating Add-On Transactions

Once the initial first-stage ESOP transaction has been completed, the owner may decide to sell a further stake in the company by repeating the process. Whereas in the initial transaction the owner was the sole decision-maker (and theoretically could impose employee-ownership on the company), an add-on transaction involves the initial owner and the fiduciary[9] representing the ESOP and its now new and current employee-owners in negotiating a deal. This has implications for the parties involved because the board of directors and the ESOP trust have (potentially varying) fiduciary duties to shareholders and ESOP participants, thus requiring them to carefully represent their interests during negotiations and to respect the boundaries between settlor and fiduciary functions.

Effectively, changes in the ESOP ownership percentage can bring about change in control of the ESOP trustee and ultimately the board of directors, potentially influencing

---

[9] The fiduciary is a person who holds assets in trust for another party and manages that asset solely in the interest of that party and not for his or her own profit.

the long-term success of the company. In support, the Department of Labor argues that when an ESOP purchases a controlling stake, it must actually gain control within a reasonable period of time,[10] limiting the control and influence of the initial owners. Moreover, one might want to change ESOP trustees when subsequently completing a change of control ESOP transaction. A trustee to this transaction may require additional qualifications, and must understand what it means to be independent from and able to control the board of directors to ensure decisions are made in the interests of the ESOP participants.

Moreover, the involvement of the ESOP trust at this stage is important because the add-on transaction, financed via debt, lowers the overall value of the firm, thus reducing the value of shares allocated to employees, as illustrated in Table 20.1. While this may have no immediate implications for most employees, employees who are leaving the firm at this point in time will face a decline in the value of shares accrued. Because of this, agreements often (for moral reasons) include provisions called *floor price protection* (FPP) to protect those participants from the impact transaction debt may have on the future value of stock[11] and once agreed 'this right should not be amendable or forfeitable by the ESOP'.[12] However, setting an FPP creates a conflict with the remaining employee-owners as they do not benefit from the FPP and instead may prefer exiting employees to be paid less to keep the cash in the company in order to generate higher company value in the future. Still, while there is some ambiguity as to the law,[13] the Department of Labor will usually side with those affected.

Table 20.2 illustrates this dilemma. Assume a company worth $10m with 100,000 shares does an add-on transaction. Because they are older, 10 per cent of the employees are eligible to have their share price protected for three years. The post-transaction value in this example drops by 30 per cent for unprotected shares as a result of debt taken on to finance the deal. In subsequent years the price per share of that stock is forecast to increase by $7 annually. Shares with FPP however are valued higher and, assuming that all eligible employees sell shares just after the transaction is done, the cost would be $30 per share, with an overall cost of $300,000 to the ESOP value. Without FPP, the $300,000 would remain with the company and ease the debt load (i.e. through earlier repayment), in which case the share price would recover more quickly. In this scenario, shares without FPP would reach a value of $105.80 after four years, meaning that all remaining employees' ESOP allocation has increased by 5.8 per cent in value. In the case of FPP being implemented, remaining participants would see a reduction in the value of their allocation of $2 in year 4.

[10] Alam et al. (2003), 'An Update on Multi-Stage ESOP Transactions', *Journal of Employee Ownership Law and Finance*, 15(4): 37–60.

[11] J. Demetrius et al. (2012), *Floor Price Protection in ESOP Transactions*, NCEO Issue Brief, Oakland: NCEO.

[12] Alam et al. (2003), 'An Update', 44.

[13] Ibid., 39.

Table 20.1 Illustrative Fair Value Calculation Before and After Add-On ESOP
Transaction

In thousands of US dollars firm value	Indicated value pre-add-on transaction		Indicated value post-add-on transaction	
Discounted cash flow		9,600.0		9,800.0
Guideline company		10,300.0		10,400.0
Concluded firm value		10,000.0		10,100.0
Less: debt (interest-bearing)	–	500.0	–	3,000.0
Add cash and cash equivalents		2,000.0		200.0
Add: securities, available for sale		500.0		200.0
Less: non-operating accounts	–	200.0	–	150.0
Total adjustments to firm value		1,800.0	–	2,750.0
Marketable value of equity		11,800.0		7,350.0
Less: discount for limited marketability at 10.0%	–	1,180.0	–	735.0
Fair market value of equity		10,620.0		6,615.0
Divided by: outstanding shares		500,000		500,000
Fair market value of equity per share	$	21.24	$	13.23

Source: Adapted from Levine and Briggs (n.d.).

20.3.3 External Consideration: Investment Bankers' Push for a Successful Deal

Moreover, the involvement of external parties, specifically financial advisors, becomes more complex. Instead of predominantly having to deal with the concerns of one party (i.e. the initial owner selling part of his or her stake in the company), advisors could now have to advise multiple parties, and crucially, establish communication with all parties involved for the purpose of negotiation. While some of this can be streamlined by having a clear and mutually beneficial understanding between buyers (ESOP and management) and sellers, the financial implications generally demand the involvement of more outside expertise. More so than in almost any kind of transaction, advisors need to be careful about whom they represent. In cases where parties, for example sellers and management, defer rights to the ESOP advisor, the ESOP advisor would need to have a legal allegiance that is exclusive to the ESOP during the negotiation of the terms of the contract. The employee-owners, in particular, could be represented separately by a lawyer or a union. The following discussion focuses predominantly on the role of investment

Table 20.2   Simplified Example of Floor Price Protection (Valid for 3 Years) Assuming 100,000 Shares, Repayment Rate of $7 p.a., and Pre-Transaction Company Value of $10m

	Value of shares		Forecasted value in year following			
	Pre-transaction	Post-transaction	Year 1	Year 2	Year 3	Year 4
Value of each share	$100	$70	$77	$84	$91	$98
Value of price protected shares	$100		$100	$100	$100	
Cost of FPP per share		$30	$23	$16	$9	
Projected cost of FPP at 10% eligibility		$300,000	$230,000	$160,000	$90,000	
Share price forecast without FPP			$80	$89.30	$97.90	$105.80

Source: Calculation adapted from Burdette et al. (2013).

bankers (or financial advisors) taking account of the market that developed in the USA for these types of ESOP transaction specialists.

Unlike investment banks specializing in commercial business mergers and acquisitions, the role of ESOP financial advisors in an (add-on) ESOP transaction is different to the extent that the deal is struck between multiple parties to the business.[14] While ownership is transferred from one party to the other in an ESOP transaction, the purchasing party is not external, nor does the selling party necessarily relinquish all ownership rights.[15] This means that while both parties are logically interested in cutting the best deal financially, alternative motives come into play: for example, the initial owner may want the company to be set up for a sustainable future instead of maximizing the sales value. Equally, the ESOP has fiduciary responsibilities to employees and, while this requires them to cut the best deal, the nature of reaching that deal might, again, not involve cut-throat negotiations with the seller, but should be reached on a mutual basis. In fact the price is set by an independent evaluation and thus negotiations are (rightly) limited. In this respect, the involvement of the investment banker/financial advisor is partly comparable to that of a *mediator*. Still, financial advisors'

[14]   J. Hoffmire (1990), 'Practitioner Conduct: The Need for Open Debate, *The Journal of Employee Ownership Law and Finance*, 2(2), 1–8.

[15]   Even in add-on transactions, the initial owner(s) may still hold the majority stake within the company.

key responsibilities remain: 1) to do the compilation of financial information and 2) to run complicated financial models, for example on the projected future value of the ESOP shares and debt repayment schedules, all within the bounds of coming to a fair price confirmed by an independent valuation.

Investment bankers often negotiate the terms of the loan with potential lenders and select the most suitable lender that will finance the ESOP's purchase of stock from the selling parties. Because non-ESOP leveraged buyouts of companies and other transactions in the USA are frequent, investment bankers are common players in business interactions. While they are not involved in every ESOP transaction in the USA, people in other countries who use investment bankers less might dislike the idea of involving investment bankers. However, their involvement is important in a) minimizing the costs of the debt repayment and b) pushing the project forward because, unlike lawyers and other advisors who are paid on an hourly basis, investment bankers often only get paid if the transaction is finalized. This often means that they have to invest resources up front without the guarantee of seeing a return on the investment, and thus it is in their interest that the add-on ESOP transaction is successful. This is not to say that lawyers and advisors want them to fail, because if they repeatedly failed to close a deal, their reputations would suffer; however, their compensation is essentially guaranteed and not success related, and thus they could bill many hours without the transaction needing to be finalized.

At the same time, investment bankers cannot propose financing options that are against the interest of the ESOP but would benefit the investment bankers instead. In ESOP transactions, the trustee of the ESOP and management of the ESOP company review the details of the finance solution presented by the investment bankers and make a decision on whether the deal can go ahead or not. The involvement of the trustee in reviewing the terms and size of the debt finance proposed also ensures that the deal is not overleveraged, because that would be against the interest of current and future employee owners.[16]

20.4 CONCLUSION

We have summarized the complexities arising from initial and add-on ESOP transactions, which are much more common practice than is suggested elsewhere. Having said this, it was not our intent to dissuade people about ESOP transactions; on the contrary, our aim was to enhance the understanding of the processes and the changing relationship of parties involved.

---

[16] The Department of Labor might equally object to overleveraging because of its impact on the value of the ESOP as a pensionable plan.

For sellers of stock to workers through an ESOP, it is important to realize that terms and conditions of an add-on transaction must be aligned with the (financial) interests of the existing ESOP participants represented by a trustee and subject to Department of Labor oversight. Doing so, there need not be any unacceptable financial implications for the seller, because the price is set by an independent agent. Indeed, a seller who understands the requirements can possibly encourage a quick sale and thus limit the costs arising without deterioration in the relationship with the trustee and employee-owners.

Equally, fiduciaries representing employee-owners should understand that it is their legal obligation to have financial and legal experts advising on the transactions. This is not someone taking responsibility who should not be involved; it has merely to do with having experts to examine the legal requirements and provide oversight. Similarly, the fiduciary must ensure that the evaluation on the suitability of the transaction given by the investment banker is proportionate and not overleveraged to minimize any potential adverse effects on the future performance of the now worker-owned firm. Indeed, because they are paid on success, investment bankers have an interest in speeding up processes and reaching an agreement quickly, and this could reduce lengthy debates with lawyers who are paid by the hour. In ensuring that the best deal is struck with lenders using the expertise of investment bankers, ESOP participants often benefit from lower interest payments and thus an increased value of their shares in the future.

Moreover, the Department of Labor has set up safeguards to ensure that add-on transactions benefit employees and not just the others involved in the process; the level of debt and the impact on short-term firm value must not adversely affect the value of shares for employees, and equally must not overleverage the employee-owned business with debt (as often is seen in private equity-led leveraged buy-outs). This is crucial to maintaining the idea behind ESOP transactions as a benefit to employees by allowing employees to buy companies without having to use their own savings or collateral.

References

Alam, V., Brown, G., and Johanson, D. (2003), 'An Update on Multi-Stage ESOP Transactions', *Journal of Employee Ownership Law and Finance*, 15(4), 37–60.

Blair, M., Kruse, D., and Blasi, J. (2000), 'Is Employee Ownership an Unstable Form? Or a Stabilizing Force?' in T. Kochan and M. Blair, eds, *Corporation and Human Capital*, Washington, DC: The Brookings Institution 241–98.

Blasi, J., Freeman, R., and Kruse, D. (2015), *The Citizen's Share*, Yale: Yale University Press.

Burdette, D. Urbach, J. and van Heyde, J. (2013), 'Second Stage ESOP Transactions'. Available at http://www.esopassociation.org/docs/default-source/new-south-chapter/second-stage-transaction.pdf?sfvrsn=0 (accessed 18 September 2016).

Demetrius, J. et al. (2012), *Floor Price Protection in ESOP Transactions*, NCEO Issue Brief, Oakland: NCEO.

ESOP Association (2016), 'What is a Leveraged ESOP?' Available at http://www.esopassociation.org/explore/how-esops-work/learn-about-esops/leveraged (accessed 21 September 2016).

Field, E. (1997), 'Money for Nothing and Leverage for Free: The Politics and History of the Leveraged ESOP Tax Subsidy', *Columbia Law Review*, 97(3), 740–85.

Freeman, S. and Knoll, M. (2008), 'S Corp ESOP Legislation Benefits and Costs: Public Policy and Tax Analysis', Organizational Dynamics Working Paper 08-07: 1–15.

Hoffmire, J. (1990), 'Practitioner Conduct: The Need for Open Debate', *The Journal of Employee Ownership Law and Finance*, 2(2), 1–8.

Hoffmire, J., Willis, J., and Gilbert, R. (1992), Practice Note: Questions and Answers Regarding ESOPs for Family Businesses', *Family Business Review*, 2(2): 173–80.

Kim, E. and Quimet, P. (2009), 'Employee Capitalism or Corporate Socialism? Broad-Based Employee Stock Ownership', U.S. Census Bureau, *Center for Economic Studies*, Paper No. CES-WP- 09-44.

Kramer, B. (2010), 'Employee Ownership and Participation Effects on Outcomes in Firms Majority Employee-Owned through Employee Stock Ownership Plans in the US', *Economic and Industrial Democracy*, 31(4): 449–76.

Kruse, D. (2002), Research Evidence on Prevalence and Effects of Employee Ownership. Presented in Testimony before the Subcommittee on Employer-Employee Relations, Committee on Education and the Workforce, U.S. House of Representatives, 13 February.

Kruse, D. et al. (2003), 'Motivating Employee-Owners in ESOP Firms: Human Resource Policies and Company Performance', *NBER Working Paper No.* 10177, December.

Levine, S. D., and Briggs, P. H. (n.d.), 'Redemption Approach to Leveraged ESOP Transactions'. Available at http://www.esopassociation.org/docs/default-source/carolinas-chapter/redemption-approach-to-leveraged-esop-transactions.pdf (accessed 21 September 2016).

Miller, S. (2010), 'The ESOP Exit Strategy', *Journal of Accountancy*, 209(3), March, 32–7 http://www.journalofaccountancy.com/issues/2010/mar/20092046.htm (accessed 18 September 2016).

NCEO (2014a), 'How an Employee Stock Ownership Plan (ESOP) Works'. Available at http://www.nceo.org/articles/esop-employee-stock-ownership-plan (accessed 18 September 2016).

NCEO (2014b), 'ESOP Tax Incentives and Contribution Limits'. Available at http://www.nceo.org/articles/esop-tax-incentives-contribution-limits (accessed 18 September 2016).

CHAPTER 21

....

SOCIAL CO-OPERATIVES IN ITALY

....

SARA DEPEDRI

21.1 INTRODUCTION

....

THE term 'social co-operatives' was coined in Italy during the 1970s to define those co-operative firms that produce social services and have a dominant social aim. The fact that this new term has firstly emerged in Italy can be explained by the strong co-operative culture, the grass-roots movement, and the social and economic change which characterized the country in those years. In the 1970s, co-operative firms had developed successfully in all sectors of activity and with a variety of co-operative forms (consumer or users co-operatives, producer and agricultural co-operatives, worker co-operatives, co-operative banks, etc.). The active participation of citizens in the co-operative movement therefore reached certain social capital dimensions and contributed a relevant added value to society and the economy. While developing in size and number, co-operatives also intercepted and responded to the new needs of their members and of society as a whole. As a consequence, some co-operatives started to distinguish themselves for their interest in social services' provision and for the strengthening of their social function. They started to assume a new role as welfare providers and suppliers of general-interest services and work integration of disadvantaged people.

This evolution was supported by the simultaneous development of the welfare system, with an increasing demand for social services not covered on the supply side by public bodies. Social co-operatives were therefore a self-organized solution to social problems and appeared in Italy as a bottom-up phenomenon, whose recognition and institutionalization was enacted only in 1991 by Law 381.

Understanding the emergence, the evolution, and the main traits of Italian social co-operatives seems to be the best way to describe this relevant co-operative form.

This chapter illustrates the Italian experience and the most recent trends of Italian social co-operatives in order to outline the main traits that helped social co-operatives become a successful organizational form for the provision of welfare services and to define the added value this co-operative form provides to the economy and to society. As described in other chapters in this book (see, for example, Galera 2017), following Italy's path other countries have experienced the emergence of social co-operatives or social enterprises. In some cases, these countries have also replicated and adapted the Italian model of social co-operatives or the Italian law on social co-operatives to their social and cultural context and to their welfare systems. For these reasons, looking at the Italian experience and analysing step by step its evolution and its ability to adapt to new challenges and needs is particularly useful.

21.2 EMERGENCE AND LEGAL RECOGNITION

The emergence of social co-operatives was essentially a response to the deficiencies and inefficiencies of both the market and the State in the provision of social services (Borzaga and Ianes 2006; Borzaga and Tortia 2010).

When in the 1970s the Italian welfare system started to face the first symptoms of financial crisis, the supply of social and personal services was limited, mainly public, standardized, and poorly managed. With the exception of the provision of health and education services, most public spending was allocated in the form of cash benefits (mainly pensions). The crisis and the lack of clarity of responsibilities between different governmental levels impaired the needed growth in social services. Remarkable changes took place also in family structures and dynamics owing to the changing role of women and a shift from large to nuclear families. Thus, from service-providers, families progressively started to become generators of new intangible needs. Such needs could hardly be addressed by the existing public services. Additional factors that played a role in expanding the demand for social services include demographic changes, social exclusion, and youth unemployment.

Against the inability of the Italian welfare state to face the increasing new needs of society, groups of citizens self-organized in order to provide the required services. They set up new voluntary organizations and innovative entrepreneurial initiatives that aimed at integrating disadvantaged people into the labour market. Over the years, such initiatives grew dramatically and stimulated a collective thinking about the organizational solution that could best exploit the contribution coming from civil society. Since associations and foundations were legally prevented from carrying out economic activities in a stable and continuous manner, when new needs started to arise and grow intensively, several spontaneous groups of citizens that voluntarily committed themselves to providing social services decided to institutionalize their activity through the co-operative form.

This choice was also supported by the increasing attention of some co-operatives to local social needs and by the strengthening of co-operatives' social function. New co-operatives were therefore evolving from member interest-oriented organizations to providers of social services to people in need and for general purposes. Expanding co-operatives' supply of social, educational, and work integration services was possible also thanks to co-operatives' assembly into unitary movements: national federation and local consortia became widespread and assumed the role of co-ordinating the activity of local co-operatives and promoting start-ups.

The diverse forces and initiatives that stimulated the emergence and the rapid diffusion of social co-operatives highlighted the will and the need for regulating this new co-operative form with tailored legislation. At the beginning of the 1990s, in fact, around two thousand of such co-operatives were already operating. Many practitioners and representatives of the movement were involved in the processes both of identifying the key features of social co-operatives and institutionalizing this new type of enterprise. In 1991, Law 381 acknowledged the new co-operative form as a 'social co-operative'. According to this law, social co-operatives are created to 'pursue the general interest of the community in promoting personal growth and in integrating people into society by providing social, welfare, and educational services, and carrying out different activities for the purposes of providing employment for disadvantaged people'. The law distinguishes two types of social co-operatives: social co-operatives supplying social services (A-type social co-operatives), and social co-operatives integrating vulnerable persons into work (B-type social co-operatives). In this latter case, at least 30 per cent of the employees must be certified as disadvantaged workers. The law does not allow B-type social co-operatives to produce social services, but these organizations can operate in all other sectors of activity. This restriction explains the specialization of both types of social co-operative and, finally, the rapid development of successful organizations.

Among the main traits recognized by law, the conception of social co-operatives as collective organizations is notable. The law allows for the simultaneous involvement of different categories of members in the ownership structure: from workers to users, from voluntary members to financing members, from individuals to legal entities. This helps social co-operatives identify unmet needs that arise in local communities and ensures that the general-interest aim dominates over the entrepreneurial and commercial dimension. This characteristic also ensures multi-stakeholder membership of social co-operatives and encourages the involvement of the local community. Furthermore, as co-operative enterprises, the decision-making process of social co-operatives is democratically driven.

The last of the main traits that legally define social co-operatives consists in the non-profit distribution constraint. Social co-operatives are allowed to achieve profits, but a consistent part of such profits must be accumulated into locked assets by law. Evidence from Italian social co-operatives shows that they tend to spontaneously accumulate all their profits in the asset lock in order to increase economic and financial stability and to expand. Finally, the law foresees the indivisibility of assets, which means that members are not allowed to privately appropriate assets generated by the entrepreneurial activity through reinvested net residuals.

In addition to specifying the main organizational traits, Law 381/1991 also recognizes the relevance of social co-operatives in supporting social policy and, therefore, gives local public authorities the opportunity to stipulate contracts with both A- and B-type social co-operatives. The law implicitly recognizes that public bodies and social co-operatives pursue similar objectives and encourages collaborative relations. Two other laws regulating local public bodies—Law 142 and Law 241 of 1990—played a role in paving the way for the development of collaborative relations between social co-operatives and municipalities. In particular, by foreseeing the possibility that municipalities entrust to social co-operatives the supply of social services, Law 142 created the conditions for the definition of contractual relations between public entities and social enterprises (Borzaga and Ianes 2006). However, social co-operatives and municipalities remain distinct entities. Although local governments are explicitly regarded as key partners of social co-operatives, and a process of entrusting social services from public bodies to social co-operatives is progressively taking place, public authorities normally do not join social co-operatives' membership.[1] In essence, social co-operatives continue to emerge and develop as bottom-up and autonomous organizations.

In conclusion, the enactment of Law 381 on social co-operatives represents both a clear and comprehensive model of institutionalization of social co-operatives and the first important step in the recognition of this new and relevant phenomenon. As a consequence, in the following years the law paved the way for the extraordinary growth of social co-operatives.

21.3 An Unstoppable Growth

The second phase of the evolution of social co-operatives in Italy is characterized by the inflexible growth of these phenomena. Data corroborate that Italy is one of the countries where social enterprises have developed steadily over the last 20 years. Since 1991, social co-operatives have been registering a 10 to 20 per cent average annual growth rate. Indeed, they increased in number from a little over 2,000 before regulation up to nearly double that number (3,900 units) in 1996, reaching 7,363 entities in year 2005 (ISTAT—National Institute for Statistics—data). In 2011, there were 12,264 social co-operatives, which employed 365,006 workers,[2] 30,534 of which were disadvantaged workers. These social co-operatives supplied about 50 per cent of the total provision of welfare services. There was an average of 32.41 employees per co-operative, which implies that 613 people

---

[1] In any event, the law excludes the possibility that social co-operatives are controlled by public bodies.

[2] This figure includes permanent, external, and temporary workers.

for every 100,000 inhabitants in Italy were employed in social co-operatives. In addition to workers, social co-operatives also employ a large number of volunteers, who in 2011 amounted to 42,000 (ISTAT 2015).

ISTAT data show that 3.3 million users had services delivered to them by social co-operatives in 2005.[3] These primarily included educational services (these services were delivered by 45 per cent of the A-type social co-operatives); home based care and residential services for the elderly (respectively, supplied by 37 per cent and 36 per cent of A-type co-operatives); recreation and entertainment (32 per cent of A-type co-operatives); preschool education (22 per cent); and healthcare (23 per cent) (Table 2, ISTAT 2005). The relatively low incidence of healthcare services is explained by two main factors: public ownership of most healthcare facilities in Italy and the relatively high capital-intensity of healthcare, which is hardly achievable by such types of organizations. At any rate, the relevance of social co-operatives to healthcare services has been steadily increasing over the years. Some co-operatives are clearly multi-service providers. Recent investigations on a representative sample of Italian social co-operatives (ICSI, Enquire on Social Co-operatives in Italy 2007) confirm these figures (see for example Borzaga and Depedri 2013): social co-operatives mainly provide social services (75.2 per cent of the total) and educational services (72.7 per cent), but they also provide recreation (49.3 per cent) and healthcare services (39.7 per cent). According to Euricse estimations, the total number of users of social co-operatives reached 5,000,000 in 2011, out of which 2,935,586 were people in need (ISTAT 2011). These included, among other groups, drug addicts (2.5 per cent), people with disabilities (31 per cent), people affected by severe diseases (20.3 per cent), and poor people (27.3 per cent).

In 2011, social co-operatives had a turnover of 11.2 billion euros and an invested capital of 8.3 billion euros (Euricse 2013). Available data show that 72.4 per cent of all social co-operatives declared revenues up to 500,000 euro, while large-sized co-operatives' (16 per cent of the total) revenues were over one million euros (Euricse 2015). Most of the revenues came from supplying services to public bodies (74 per cent in A-type social co-operatives and 53 per cent in B-type). Increasingly, private revenues and the supply of goods and services to private firms has characterized work integration social co-operatives especially (43 per cent of their revenues comes from private sources) (Borzaga and Depedri 2013).

Social co-operatives entertain strong relations with public institutions and are substantially financed by public resources. The high percentage of income derived from public funding has permitted acceleration in their expansion and consolidation. Outsourcing the production of general-interest services to social enterprises has indeed implied a key shift to a more stable public engagement with social enterprises as social-service providers. Social procurement has contributed to greater efficiency and a significant increase in the supply of services.

---

[3] So far no 2011 ISTAT data about the users of social co-operatives are available.

21.4 FACING CHALLENGES

After the big expansion in their number and size and in the added value produced by social co-operatives, recent years have seen social enterprises facing new challenges triggered by both exogenous and endogenous factors.

When looking at exogenous dynamics, the main challenge for social co-operatives comes from the recent crisis. The drop in activity of business firms and a reduction in market demand have certainly influenced social co-operatives that are particularly integrated into market dynamics and which collect resources from private clients. As data demonstrate (Unioncamere 2014), despite the constant growth of the previous decades, since the crisis the number of social co-operatives has increased by only 324 units in 2009 and 98 units in 2010, while the year 2011 witnessed, for the first time ever, a decrease in the number of social co-operatives. Nonetheless, data does not seem dramatic or negative when we look at other dimensions: the number of people employed in social co-operatives has increased by 15.1 per cent in the period 2008–13, while the total employment in Italy declined by 1.2 per cent (Euricse 2015). These contrasting trends are partially explained by the sector of activity in which social co-operatives supply their services, but also by the diverse policies and strategies promoted by social co-operatives to face the crisis. On the one hand, the phenomenon of mergers between social co-operatives cannot be considered marginal. Market pressure and increasing business risks were threatening some social co-operatives and the ability to ensure job opportunities and service provision to people in need. Consequently, social co-operatives occasionally opted for mergers, thereby negatively influencing the number of existing social co-operatives without compromising the number of people employed. Merging of social co-operatives has also allowed the differentiation of activities and achievement of scale economies. On the other hand, the number of start-ups probably resized over time, due to the increasing competition on the market and with similar organizations, and also the need for a better planning of spaces available for new social co-operatives.

Another endogenous phenomenon pushed in the same direction: the sovereign debt crisis, which induced severe contraction of usable resources coming from local authorities, the externalization of social services, and change in public–private partnerships (Borzaga and Fazzi 2011). While the shortage of public resources tends to compromise the form of some social co-operatives that depend totally on public funding, it also makes it urgent to establish relationships with public and government bodies other than public procurements for whom price is the main discriminant. Social clauses are increasingly established by local government, and new forms of partnership are developing. At the same time, social co-operatives are encouraged to find new sources of revenue by dealing with the private market and with private citizens and by experimenting with new financing instruments.

With regard to the other challenges coming from endogenous dynamics, the first risk that social co-operatives faced involved isomorphic pressures. Social enterprise culture and managerial practices have sometimes been excessively influenced by the public ones, due to a continuous interaction of social enterprises with public policies and the need for social co-operatives to adopt public standards. These trends have sometimes weakened the civic activism that marked the first social enterprise initiatives and reduced the propensity to innovate (Borzaga and Galera 2014). The reaction of many social co-operatives has been a loosening of the ties with public bodies and the search for new sectors of activity and innovation strategies. Data from recent years demonstrate social co-operatives' ability to be open to innovative sectors of activity and their propensity to invest in new service and process innovation. Today, social co-operatives appear able and eager to identify new services and fields of activity. These new fields go beyond their traditional core activities and include culture, environment, social tourism, and social housing. Process innovation has also occurred, as social co-operatives have made increasing use of networking through company groups and agreements. These include consortia, co-operatives groups, network contracts,[4] product societies, project partnerships, and temporary enterprise associations that aim to clarify and coordinate the roles and interdependency among the various actors in the production chain. These initiatives have also encompassed social inclusion activities targeting disadvantaged groups by means of agreements between social co-operatives and for-profit enterprises.

Social co-operatives also face a second endogenous challenge since they are frequently exposed to problems when it comes to efficiently managing their governance. Firstly, due to the average age of social co-operatives, a generational change is needed. While the continuous growth of social co-operatives has allowed the involvement of new and young employees and members, the main challenge concerns the change in the management. In fact, in the past, social co-operatives were generally founded by leaders and philanthropists, whose intrinsic personal and social motivations significantly influenced the soul and the mission of their social co-operatives. Today, replacing the presidents and the managers of social co-operatives is frequently hard, since it is difficult for incoming managers to benefit from the same social recognition that workers and members granted to founding managers. As a consequence, many social co-operatives must therefore develop and experiment with new governance models and decision-making processes.

At the same time, the growth in size and number of members of social co-operatives and the need to increasingly involve citizens and stakeholders' representatives in the membership also call for a renewal of governance models. The predominant governance model in social co-operatives is actually that of the multi-stakeholder: the data from a recent investigation on a sample of Italian social co-operatives shows that 69.7 per cent of social co-operatives has more than one category of patrons in their memberships and one third includes, at the same time, workers, volunteers, and other classes of stakeholders on the boards of directors. As a strategy to also involve organizations in informal

---

[4] A new law (no. 40/2007) on the network contract was passed by the Italian Parliament in 2007.

processes, social co-operatives promote networks and collaborate with local institutions, citizens, and representatives of the community in order to co-ordinate their objectives and activities. Notwithstanding these strategies, more complex governance models are also needed and social co-operatives are starting to innovate in this direction.

21.5 LOOKING AHEAD

If the origins of social co-operatives help explain the motivations for their emergence and their social and economic role in welfare systems, and if the evolution of social co-operatives describes the ability of these organizations to find new solutions to emerging problems, looking ahead will allow us to understand the long-term sustainability of this phenomenon and describe the most desirable scenario. Two main approaches must be followed when looking at the Italian model of social co-operatives in a constructive way: the first one consists in understanding the strengths that in the past ensured the efficiency and the effectiveness of these organizations and understanding the way in which these traits can be renewed, innovated, and enforced. The second consists in forecasting the evolution of markets, social policies, and citizens' needs and thus in depicting the possible action of social co-operatives.

By following the former approach, earlier analyses have already tried to categorize the main traits and strengths of social co-operatives (e.g. Depedri 2010). As a rule, social co-operatives draw their force from their governance structure, which allows the involvement of citizens and a better knowledge of users' and citizens' needs; from their connection with the local community, which increases the ability to collect resources from the community and among the free resources like voluntary jobs and donations; from the enjoyment of trust and reputation among their stakeholders, which stabilizes revenues and increases co-planning and long-term partnerships; from their ability to strengthen local social capital; and from developing intrinsic motivations, altruistic behaviours, and willingness to co-operate among citizens, which increases co-operation and improves outcomes. These factors also represent the levers for increasing welfare effects beyond the economic value of production (Borzaga et al. 2010). It is in fact demonstrated that the economic aim of social co-operatives (and social enterprises in general) is the maximization of their added value, where the latter is intended as the maximization of the well-being of users, the achievement of effectiveness, and the maximization of the social impact on the various stakeholders with which the organization relates.

The long-term sustainability of social co-operatives and their future therefore seem to require investment in and reinforcement of their main traits and the comparative advantages that distinguish social co-operatives from other (both private and public) organizations. Social co-operatives need to move even more towards the community, to stress their social impact, and to reinforce their visibility and their networking with all categories of stakeholders. Today, social co-operatives must find strategies to advantageously involve the main stakeholders and to increase their embeddedness in the community.

The option of multi-stakeholder governances, as previously described, can be a solution for increasing the commitment of diverse stakeholders, but also for enriching communication, knowledge, and trust. Likewise, social co-operatives must increase their entrepreneurial dimension without compromising their social aims and, therefore, need to find the perfect balance between governance structure, business activity, and social impact. Enforcing the entrepreneurial dimension entails investing resources, supporting some entrepreneurial risk, being innovative, finding new market opportunities and activities, networking in order to create stable relations and achieve scale economies, having dedicated and specialized groups for research and development, formalizing processes that avoid bureaucracy and favour flexibility, finding partners in the finance market, and asking to be evaluated on the basis of the social impact produced, instead of on the financial risk of the activity proposed. This evolution will further enforce the ability of social co-operatives—especially when compared to public agencies—to be flexible, innovative, efficient, and reactive to the emerging needs of citizens.

These last considerations help us approach the second type of analysis over the future of social co-operatives. It is, in fact, possible to predict the evolution of social co-operatives by not only looking at their potential but also at the observable needs of the market and the welfare system. Whether or not the role of social co-operatives has always been to meet some social needs of citizens, social co-operatives today have to identify emerging demands, new social needs, and their trends. Some matters can be considered urgent, at least in the case of Italy. Among the traditional sectors of welfare, education, and health, we probably see the lowest presence of social co-operatives today. The public monopoly that has characterized these services and the high fixed costs have influenced the low level of development of social co-operatives in offering education and health services (by managing hospitals, nurseries, clinics, and schools). The tightening of public expenditure and the decreasing quality of public services have started solicitation of private initiatives by citizens. Community-interest co-operatives (an emerging organizational form in Italy) and social co-operatives themselves can develop by directly providing these services or by taking on the management of them as they are externalized by public bodies.

Among other sectors of activity which promote social effects and community interests, disused public buildings can represent a further opportunity for social co-operatives. The added value of social co-operatives consists in those cases in investing in structures and real estates that are no longer productive and in using them to supply social-interest services by also involving the community as a whole in the decision-making process. Moreover, social co-operatives are increasingly called on to respond to the emergency of unemployment. While B-type social co-operatives are traditionally working with disadvantaged workers, the presence of new classes of disadvantaged people on the labour market, such as young people and over 50-year-olds, forces social co-operatives to plan new strategies and training activities for job placement. New networks with both public and private organizations, increasing flexibility, and a better understanding of the professionals required by the market represent some opportunities for enlarging the activity of social co-operatives.

These examples have been introduced with the aim of opening up the debate on the future of social co-operatives. Opportunities are very concrete and are increasing over time. Social co-operatives must identify these opportunities and, in some cases, transform their structure in order to become even more dynamic and entrepreneurial and be able to take full advantage of such opportunities. Renovation will allow social co-operatives to maintain their efficiency and effectiveness and, when possible, increase their social impact and their role in the economy.

21.6 Conclusions on the Economic Role and the Social Impact of Italian Social Co-operatives

As a final thought, we want to briefly outline the social impact of social co-operatives. The economic role and the social impact of co-operatives have been mentioned often in this contribution and it is therefore necessary to better define the added value produced by social co-operatives.

First and foremost we should keep in mind that social co-operatives provide the general-interest services that public agencies and for-profit enterprises fail to deliver for a number of reasons, including budget constraints, incapacity to identify new needs arising in society, and market failures (such as those induced by information asymmetries or positive externalities, that is, difficulties in internalizing the entire value produced). Social co-operatives have been pioneers in developing new services and experimenting with new solutions to better meet those needs. As already highlighted, social co-operatives often emerge in areas in which neither private organizations nor public service providers are present and therefore have a relevant social impact for local stakeholders.

Secondly, social co-operatives play a crucial role in job creation. Not only do social co-operatives supply job opportunities to disadvantaged people, but they generally supply good job opportunities thanks to their adaptability and flexible labour relations. Social co-operatives develop new activities and contribute to generating employment in sectors presenting high employment potential, such as the social and community-oriented sectors. Indeed, the social enterprise model, and especially the social co-operative, is engaged in developing new forms of work organization enhancing workers' participation in decision-making processes. In addition to this, social co-operatives frequently facilitate the hiring of hard-to-employ workers, such as women with children, and contribute to creating innovative models of industrial relations (Borzaga and Tortia 2006, Borzaga and Depedri 2005, 2013). Nor is the role of social co-operatives limited to providing jobs, but instead they are reported to provide good quality jobs, in terms of stability, involvement, intrinsic incentives supplied, welfare, etc. (Depedri et al. 2012).

Thirdly, social co-operatives are demonstrated to attract a mix of resources, including those that are unexploited and that would otherwise not address welfare and development goals. Therefore, inputs increase without additional costs and the relationship between inputs and outcomes improves and greater efficiency results. Social co-operatives frequently produce a distributive function, that is, they over-produce services, externalities, and outcomes thanks to the employment of volunteers, highly motivated workers, donations, and re-investment of profits.

In addition to this positive relation between inputs and outputs, data also demonstrate that social co-operatives frequently allow for the saving of resources. Analyses of social enterprises that supply social services have demonstrated these organizations' ability to decrease the costs of production compared to public bodies, as well as the conspicuous social return on investment generated by these organizations. Furthermore, and with specific regard to Italian social co-operatives, work integration of disadvantaged people into social co-operatives is demonstrated to reduce costs for the public administration, on average by 5,000 euros per year per person (Borzaga and Depedri 2013). These elements demonstrate the fact that social co-operatives represent efficient solutions, in addition to improve peoples' well-being, and reduce marginalization.

A further beneficial impact of social co-operatives is generated by the positive externalities engendered. Social co-operatives increase local well-being and enhance the production of social capital (Sabatini et al. 2014). They promote inclusive governance models that empower the local community in strategic decision-making, supporting a model of endogenously driven local development (Borzaga and Tortia 2009). Social co-operatives contribute to taking economic activities with a social goal out of the informal economy and help foster social cohesion and enhance the level of trust within society and the economy (Borzaga et al. 2008). All these aspects confirm the role of social co-operatives as innovative agents of economic development.

As a general conclusion, this analysis of Italian social co-operatives demonstrates the socio-economic role that these organizations are increasingly covering at the local and at the national level, and the significant social impact that they produce on behalf of their diverse stakeholders. Social co-operatives in their history and evolution over this 30-year experience have demonstrated that they are reactive and flexible organizations, which are able to stimulate co-operation among citizens, to organize resources in an entrepreneurial way, to answer problems by finding innovative solutions, and to generate a unique added value for societies and economic systems.

References

Borzaga, C. and Depedri, S. (2005), 'Interpersonal Relations and Job Satisfaction: Some Empirical Results in Social And Community Care Services', in B. Gui and R. Sugden (eds), *Economics and Social Interaction: Accounting for Interpersonal Relations* (Cambridge: Cambridge University Press), 132–53.

Borzaga, C. and Depedri, S. (2013), 'When Social Enterprises Do It Better: Efficiency and Efficacy of Work Integration Social Co-Operatives', in S. Denny and F. Seddon, eds, *Social Enterprise: Accountability and Evaluation around the World*. London: Routledge), 85–101.

Borzaga, C., Depedri, S., and Tortia, E. (2010), 'Testing the Distributive Effects of Social Enterprises: The Case of Italy'. in G. Degli Antoni, and L. Sacconi, eds, *Social Capital, Corporate Social Responsibility, Economic Behaviour and Performance* (Basingstoke: Palgrave MacMillan), 282–305.

Borzaga, C. and Fazzi, L. (2011), 'Processes of Institutionalization and Differentiation in the Italian Third Sector', *Voluntas: International Journal of Voluntary and Nonprofit Organizations*, 22(3), 409–27.

Borzaga, C. and Galera, G. (2014), 'New Trends in the Nonprofit Sector in Europe: The Emergence of Social Enterprises: Advances in Public Interest Accounting', v. 17, 89–110.

Borzaga, C., Galera, G., and Nogales, R. (2008), *Social Enterprise: A New Model for Poverty Reduction and Employment Generation* (Bratislava: UNDP-Regional Bureau for Europe and the Commonwealth of Independent States).

Borzaga, C. and Ianes A. (2006), 'L'economia della solidarietà: Storia e prospettive della cooperazione sociale (Roma: Donzelli).

Borzaga, C. and Tortia, E. (2006), 'Worker Motivations, Job Satisfaction, and Loyalty in Public and Non-Profit Social Services', *Non-Profit and Voluntary Sector Quarterly*, 35(2), 225–48.

Borzaga, C. and Tortia, E. (2009), 'Social Enterprises and Local Economic Development', in A. Noya and E. Clarence, eds, *The Changing Boundaries of Social Enterprises* (Paris: OECD Publishing), 195–228.

Borzaga, C. and Tortia, E. C. (2010), 'The Economics of Social Enterprises: Toward a New Interpretation', in L. Becchetti and C. Borzaga, eds, *The Economics of Social Responsibility: The World of Social Enterprises* (London: Routledge), 15–33.

Depedri, S. (2010), The Competitive Advantages of Social Enterprises', in L. Becchetti, and C. Borzaga, eds, *The Economics of Social Responsibility: The World of Social Enterprises* (London: Routledge), 34–54.

Depedri, S., Tortia, E. C., and Carpita, M. (2012), 'Feeling Satisfied by Feeling Motivated at Work', in J. Heiskanen, H. Henrÿ, P. Hytinkoski, and T. Köppä, eds., *New Opportunities for Co-operatives: New Opportunities for People*, Proceedings of the 2011 ICA Conference (University of Helsinki, Ruralia Institute), 136–53.

Euricse (2013), 'Le cooperative italiane negli anni della crisi'. *Secondo rapporto EURICSE*. Trento: European Research Institute on Co-operative and Social Enterprises, 2012. Available at http://euricse.eu/sites/euricse.eu/files/db_uploads/documents/1390832942_n2470.pdf (accessed 19 September 2016).

Euricse, (2015), *Terzo rapporto EURICSE* (Trento: European Research Institute on Co-operative and Social Enterprises) (in print – online book).

Galera, G. (2017), 'Social and Solidarity Co-operatives: An International Perspective', in *The Oxford Handbook of Mutual and Co-Owned Businesses* (Oxford: Oxford University Press),

ISTAT (2005), 'Le Cooperative Sociali in Italia'. Rome: Istituto Nazionale di Statistica, 2015. http://www3.istat.it/salastampa/comunicati/non_calendario/20071012_00/testointegrale. pdf. (accessed 19 September 2016).

ISTAT (2015), 'Istituzioni pubbliche e nonprofit', in Annuario Statistico Italiano. Rome: Istituto Nazionale di Statistica. Available at http://www.istat.it/it/files/2015/12/C23.pdf (accessed 14 October 2016).

Sabatini, F., Modena, F., and Tortia, E. C. (2014), 'Do Co-Operative Enterprises Create Social Trust?' *Small Business Economics* 42, 621–41.

Tortia, E. C. (2010), 'The Impact of Social Enterprises on Output, Employment, and Welfare', in L. Becchetti, L. and C. Borzaga, eds, *The Economics of Social Responsibility: The World of Social Enterprises* (London: Routledge), 56–73.

Unioncamere (2014), 'Cooperazione, non profit e imprenditoria sociale: Economia e lavoro'. Centro studi Unioncamere,.

CHAPTER 22

CO-OPERATIVES AND THE TRANSFORMATION OF THE GERMAN ENERGY SECTOR

MARKUS HANISCH

22.1 INTRODUCTION

GERMANY is the largest industrialized economy in Europe and the fourth largest world-wide. Accordingly, the national consumption of energy and the associated emission of greenhouse gases is quite high. However, the German government has set relatively ambitious targets to implement renewable energies (Federal Environmental Agency 2015), with a 50 per cent share of renewable energy in electricity consumption by 2030 and 80 per cent by 2050 being envisioned. In the last decade, the German energy sector has been transforming towards sustainable energy production based on renewable sources. This shift, along with improving energy efficiency, has been helping Germany to meet the emission targets agreed upon in international climate negotiations.

German citizens have been playing an active role in implementing this energy transformation. After the Chernobyl catastrophe of 1986 and the Fukushima catastrophe in 2011, anti-nuclear concern finally led to a complete nuclear opt-out following new energy legislation. The Renewable Energy Act of 2000 initiated the transformation of the German energy sector and promoted the installation of renewable energy plants with fixed feed-in tariffs. In 2013, over 25 per cent of German electricity consumption was covered by renewable sources, with wind energy accounting for the largest share, followed by biomass, photovoltaic, and hydro energy (Bantle 2014). By using renewable energy sources, Germany has been able to avoid greenhouse gas emissions to the extent of around 148 million tons of CO_2 or 16 per cent of the total emissions in 2013 (Federal Ministry for Economic Affairs and Energy 2015b; see Figure 22.1). Even though it had

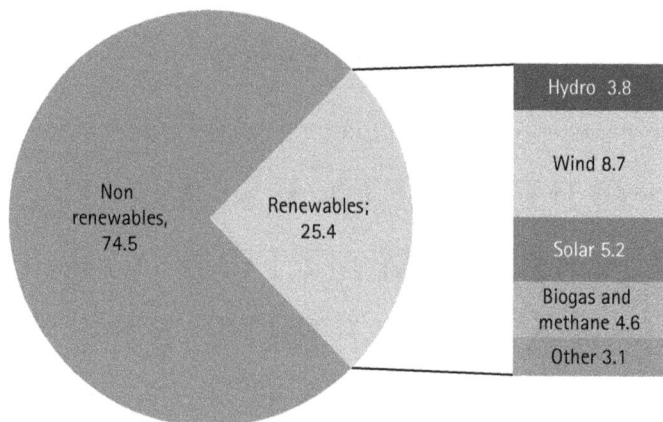

FIGURE 22.1 Share of renewables in the German energy mix 2013.

Source: Federal Ministry for Economic Affairs and Energy 2015.

been argued that the energy transformation and the nuclear opt-out might lead to a serious supply gap, today Germany has become a net exporter of energy.

This change towards renewable energy has been led by citizens rather than by large-scale energy providers. Around 30 per cent of investments in the renewable energy sector, for example, have been made by private people or community enterprises (trend: Leuphana Universität Lüneburg 2013). Therefore, it is not just a change in the production technology—from fossil to renewable energy sources—that has been taking place, but also a change in the organizational forms of energy provision (Holstenkamp and Müller 2013). The German energy transformation has been said to be going hand in hand with a decentralization and democratization of energy production. There is ample scope for citizen participation at the production level, for example by participating in or establishing local energy co-operatives and citizen-owned wind parks (Yildiz et al. 2015). Between 2006 and the beginning of 2014, about 900 such energy co-operatives were newly established, with co-operative members investing €1.5 billion (DGRV 2014). On the consumer side, households as well as industry can buy different energy mixes from a variety of energy traders, including co-operative, municipal, and private traders and renewable and non-renewable electricity varieties.

From a development perspective, this energy transformation has often been perceived as an opportunity for job creation and regional development, especially in remote and sometimes indebted rural communities. At the local level however, the planning and installation of renewable production plants has also prompted conflicts regarding land use as well as the choice of specific technological and organizational forms (Becker et al. 2014).

Recognizing the various kinds of citizen participation in current German energy production and distribution, the focus of this chapter is on co-operatives as one specific form of citizen ownership.

22.2 FOUNDERS' FINANCIAL INCENTIVES: THE RENEWABLE ENERGY ACT (EEG)

A precondition for the emergence of energy co-operatives was the liberalization of the German energy sector in 1998. After liberalization, however, the energy market still maintained its oligopolistic character, with four large companies controlling 90 per cent of the market share (Laird and Stefes 2009).

The Renewable Energy Act (Erneuerbare-Energien-Gesetz: EEG) was introduced in 2000 as a reform of the previous Feed-in Law (Stromeinspeisegesetz: StrEG). The act markedly increased the incentives and economic stability conditions for the founding of renewable electricity projects. It has been argued that this change of the regulatory framework contributed greatly to the successful development of the renewable energy sector in Germany (Laird and Stefes 2009). Following the enactment of the EEG, especially wind, photovoltaic, and biomass energy production increased significantly (see Figure 22.2).

The core idea of the EEG is to share the cost of implementing new environmentally friendly technologies among all energy consumers, according to their energy usage. It is aimed at supporting renewable energy projects which otherwise would not be economically feasible. In order to lower market-entry barriers, especially for small and medium-sized producers, the larger grid operators are obliged to preferentially feed-in electricity from renewable sources.

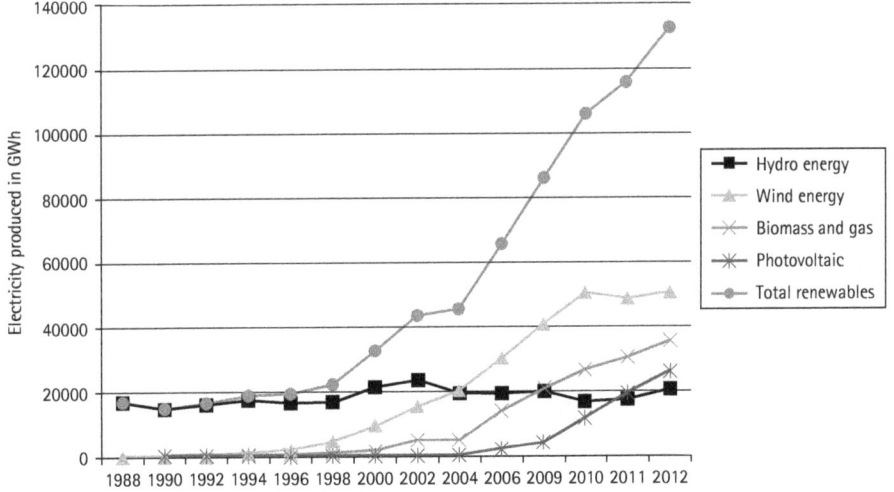

FIGURE 22.2 Development of German renewable energy sources, 1988 to 2012.

Author's illustration, data source: Bantle 2014.

From the perspective of electricity producers and investors, the EEG guarantees above-market-price feed-in tariffs for renewable electricity through to 2020, differentiating between technologies and regions. For instance, in 2000 the average payment for solar energy was 50.6 cents/kWh and for wind energy 6.19 to 9.10 cents/kWh. Nevertheless, ever since then, the feed-in tariffs have gradually been reduced, especially for solar energy, as installation costs have gone down and the additional cost burden for consumers has rapidly increased.

Since 2000, the EEG has been subject to a range of reforms and adjustments that depended on the political parties in power at the time, the economic situation, technological progress, and new experience gained from implementing the law. An important amendment to the law was enacted in 2012, resulting in a new form of payment for renewable energy called the market premium, which is calculated as the difference between the average monthly stock market price for energy and the legally fixed feed-in tariff for the different kinds of production technologies (wind, biomass, photovoltaic). The goal of this instrument is to increase the direct marketing of renewable energy by targeting more market-oriented production.[1] Thanks to this tool, electricity producers can choose between the 'classical' payment or the market premium (Federal Ministry for Economic Affairs and Energy 2012). In 2014, a consequent reform of the EEG further reduced feed-in tariffs and set limits to the newly installed energy production capacities. The direct marketing of energy and the price premium payment became compulsory for all larger renewable energy plants, and starting in 2017 it will be compulsory for all energy plants. Another minor reform of the law took place in 2016, introducing a tendering procedure for plants above 750 kW.

Regarding electricity consumers, the cost of the programme has been incorporated into the electricity bill through a surcharge per unit of use, which was 6.24 cents/kWh in 2014, accounting for more than 20 per cent of the total electricity bills paid by private households. Consequently, private households bear 35 per cent of the costs for the EEG, tallying up to €8.3 billion out of €23.6 billion in 2014 (Bantle 2014; see Figure 22.3).

A reduced surcharge of 10 per cent of the energy bill or 1 per cent of the full amount of energy costs is given to energy-intensive industrial electricity users. This exemption applies to around 4 per cent of all industrial users. The EEG has been critically discussed by both politicians and the public. According to recent studies, 90 per cent of Germans consider the energy transformation to be important or very important, but around 50 per cent feel that their share in the overall costs is too high (Bantle 2014). Whereas some point to the increasing cost for private energy consumers and the uneven distribution of financial burdens, others see the success of the EEG in promoting an urgent change towards sustainable energy production (International Energy Agency 2013). Conflicts that have arisen from the rapid extension of renewable energy production under the EEG are discussed in the next section.

---

[1] Usually producers sell their energy to a local grid operator. With direct marketing, however, they sell it directly to the end user.

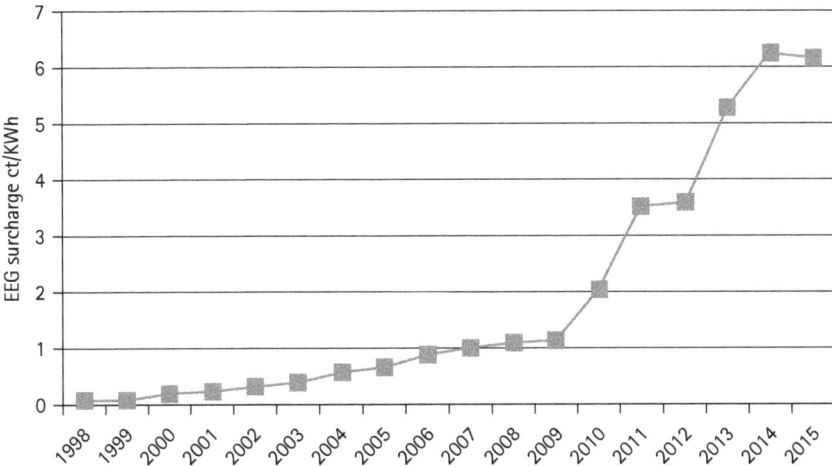

FIGURE 22.3 EEG surcharge in cents/kWh, 1998 to 2015.

Source: Federal Ministry for Economic Affairs and Energy 2012 and Netz-Transparenz 2015.

22.3 CONFLICTS OVER RENEWABLE ENERGIES

In Germany, as elsewhere, conflicts at the local level have arisen regarding the implementation of energy projects. This is true not only for fossil but also for renewable energy projects, even though a majority of the population seems to agree with the ongoing energy transformation and its objectives. The use of any kind of renewable energy source can adversely affect residents by, for example, spoiling the landscape, causing unpleasant smells, noise pollution, or the depreciation of the value of real estate. Another critical issue associated with energy transformation is the need for extension and renewing of grid lines (Becker et al. 2014). In Germany, this issue has become a typical example of the Not In My Back Yard problem, where a population in principle agrees to the necessity of implementing a certain measure but not in their immediate proximity. Becker et al. (2014) develop a typology of local conflicts around energy policies, distinguishing between:

1. Conflicts over distribution: regarding the distribution of financial benefits generated by new energy plants and the right to use the produced electricity.
2. Conflicts over procedure: concerning the planning and decision-making process in implementing renewable energy plants, e.g. access to information, transparency, participation of citizens.
3. Conflicts over land use: considering the impact on the landscape and adverse effects on residents, such as noise pollution.

4. Conflicts over identity: regarding the overall identity of a region, e.g. being seen as a touristic region vs. energy region.
5. Conflicts over technology: regarding the acceptance of specific technologies, such as renewable vs. non-renewable.

A particular case of conflicting interests over renewable energy production is biogas, which is produced from liquid manure, crop residuals, as well as from maize, cereals, or sugar beets. Usually biogas plants employ cogeneration systems to produce both heat and electricity. Since with fixed feed-in tariffs biogas production has become a profitable business for farmers, maize production has increased significantly. It is estimated that 1,157,000 ha arable land were used for the cultivation of plants, mainly maize, for biogas production in 2013. Such intensive maize cultivation can, however, cause environmental problems, such as high nitrate concentrations, and alter the landscape by, for example, replacing pastures (Scholwin et al. 2014). Moreover, controversies have arisen regarding the moral implications of using potential food crops for the production of energy, especially with increasing world-market prices for staple foods and conflicts over land resources (Bayerischer Rundfunk 2015; Süddeutsche 2014). Particularly in Eastern Germany, land prices have increased over the last 15 years, one factor being the subsidized returns to biogas production that have attracted investment in agricultural land.[2] Not only biogas plants but also large solar parks can directly lead to land conflicts between investors and farmers or residents over land use (Süddeutsche 2012).

In light of such conflicts over land use and distribution of income, energy co-operatives are perceived as organizational forms for increasing citizen participation in the planning, management, and organization of renewable energy projects. Participatory planning and investment can help to avoid the costs of conflict settlement and reduce potential resistance against projects for energy transformation. Through co-operative organization, local populations become the owners, managers, and beneficiaries of their own energy plants (Becker et al. 2014). In the next section, we briefly examine how this new co-operative organizational form has been recently employed in Germany.

22.4 Co-operatives in the German Energy Sector

Holstenkamp (2012) defines energy co-operatives as all co-operatives whose main purpose is to carry out activities in the energy sector without limitation to a distinct stage of

---

[2] As a result of the increasing awareness of the negative side effects of biogas production, in 2014 the EEG was reformed to limit further increase of biogas production and promote the use of waste and crop residuals instead of potential food crops.

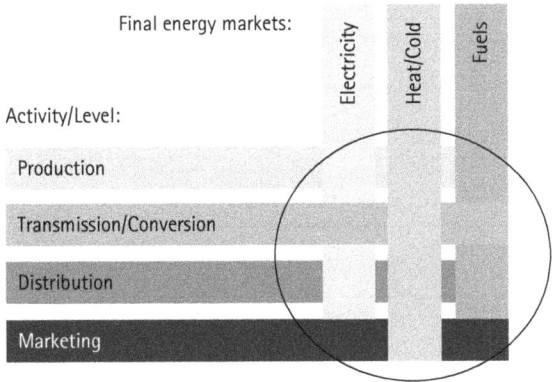

FIGURE 22.4 Activities of energy co-operatives.

Source: Holstenkamp 2012.

the energy value chain. In practice, energy co-operatives engage in a variety of quite different activities and business areas along the energy value chain, from heat and energy production to the operation of regional grids (see Figure 22.4).

German energy co-operatives have been increasingly diversifying their activities to areas such as trading and marketing of energy, the construction and operation of facilities, undertaking research, and offering consulting and planning services. According to a Deutscher Genossenschafts- und Raiffeisenverband (DGRV) survey in 2014, 95 per cent of the new energy co-operatives are active in energy production, 16 per cent in heat production, 16 per cent in the operation of heat grids, and 4 per cent operate electricity grids. Electricity co-operatives mainly invest in photovoltaic installations, which require a lower investment volume compared to wind or hydro energy projects. Different scholars have suggested classification systems to categorize energy co-operatives based on various indicators, including their historical and regional development or the value chain approach (Yildiz et al. 2015; Holstenkamp 2012).

By the end of 2014, there were 973 registered energy co-operatives in Germany; of these, 892 had registered after 2006. Energy co-operatives are the strongest growing co-operative sector in Germany, constituting 11 per cent of all registered co-operatives there. Among all newly founded co-operatives, the share of energy co-operatives reached 64 per cent in 2012. However, the number of newly registered co-operatives has been decreasing since 2011; the reasons for this adverse trend are discussed in Section 22.6 (see Figure 22.5).

On average, German energy co-operatives have been founded with 43 members. But the total number of members per co-operative has been increasing rapidly: by 2014 most energy co-operatives had between 50 and 200 members. More than 90 per cent of German co-operative members are private persons, with other members being farmers, banks, and enterprises, as well as public entities or churches. In nearly 75 per cent of current co-operatives the minimum investment requirement per individual member is less than €500. The average investment per individual member is €738

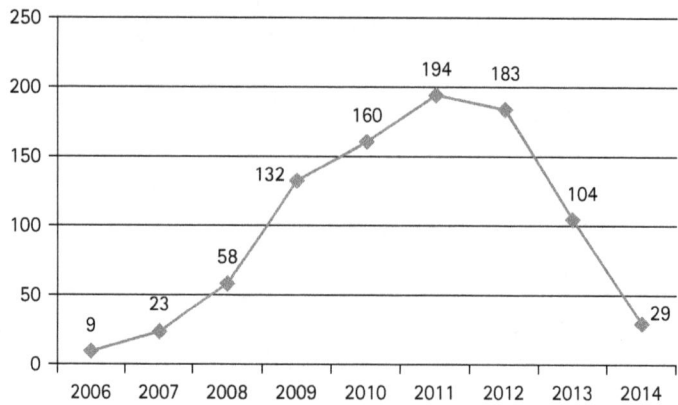

FIGURE 22.5 Newly registered German energy co-operatives, 2006 to 2014.

Author's illustration, data source: Müller and Holstenkamp 2015.

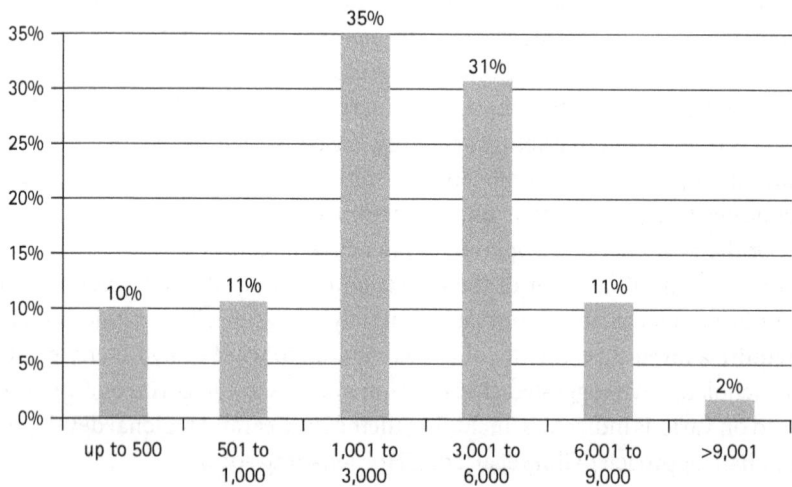

FIGURE 22.6 Investment per member in German co-operatives, 2014.

Source: DGRV 2014.

(DGRV 2014). These numbers indicate that a large number of people can participate in and contribute to the ongoing energy transformation with relatively small amounts of capital.

According to calculations by the German co-operative association DGRV, the 145,000 members of energy co-operatives hold altogether €470 million equity capital and have invested around €1.67 billion in renewable energies. On average, German energy co-operatives had an annual turnover of €337,000 and paid a dividend of 4.26 per cent in 2013. However, in the same year, half of the co-operatives did not pay any dividend at all, because their dividend distribution only commences a few years after foundation. After less than one decade in which energy co-operatives had formed, energy co-operatives

Table 22.1 Overview of Important Regulations and Their Consequences for Energy Co-operatives

Year	Act	Consequences for energy co-operatives
1998	Liberalization of the energy sector	More stable and non-discriminatory environment for small-scale energy producers
2000	Implementation of EEG	Reduced risk of investing in renewable energy projects and long-term financial incentives
2006	Reform of co-operative law	Reduced administrative burdens and decision-making costs, especially for small co-operatives
2012/2014	Amendment of EEG	Reduced economic incentives and higher risks for investments in renewable energy
2013	KAGB	High administrative burdens for co-operatives and increased information and counselling costs

Source: Author's compilation.

today produce 830,000 MWh of electricity, enough for 230,000 households with about one million energy consumers (DGRV 2014).

A recent survey profiling co-operative members indicates that the majority of energy co-operative members are men above 35, who are highly educated and belong to higher income groups. Members exhibit a strong interest in actively participating in and influencing local energy policy while also generally supporting renewable energy and decentralization policies (Yildiz et al. 2015).

The legal framework for co-operatives in the energy sector is dynamic with respect to sector-specific regulations as well as co-operative-specific regulations. An overview of the major legal changes that have impacted energy co-operatives in Germany is provided in Table 22.1.

The next section discusses the question of how renewed interest in energy co-operatives can be explained from a theoretical perspective.

22.5 THEORETICAL PERSPECTIVES ON GERMAN ENERGY CO-OPERATIVES

Energy co-operatives emerge in complex and dynamic settings of legal regulations, economic prospects, political targets, and social expectations. Müller and Rommel (2010) identify a set of political, economic, social, and technological factors that have favoured the founding of energy co-operatives in Germany, claiming that they may ease local participation in energy projects and associated planning decisions. Such co-operatives may also enable collective decision-making and help to economize on energy producers´ agency and risk costs (Müller and Rommel 2010: see Table 22.2.)

In addition, co-operatives may have an advantage in solving some current problems in the German energy market. Compared to other organizational forms, co-operatives may benefit from increasing public awareness about the importance of citizen partici-pation in energy transformation, provide a counterweight to traditionally monopolistic energy market structures, and realize competitive advantages for offering green energy, as renewables can be characterized as credence goods (Sagebiel et al. 2014: see Table 22.3).

Recent studies based on choice experiments show that consumers are willing to pay a significant price premium of up to 16 per cent for renewable energy (Kaenzig et al. 2013). At the same time, it has been shown that consumers are willing to pay a higher price for electricity produced locally by municipal energy providers like co-operatives. In the end, consumer willingness to pay for electricity seems to increase with greater

Table 22.2 A Typology of Factors with Impact on Ownership Costs of Electricity Co-operatives

	Collective decision cost	Agency cost	Cost of risk
Political factors	(1) Revised co-op law		(4) Renewable Energy Act, (5) Regulation and unbundling
Economic factors	(2) Need for local investment and jobs	(6) Differentiation of energy, (7) Interaction producer and consumer	(8) Externalities of renewables
Social factors	(3) Entrepreneurial civil society	(9) Change in owner– tenant relationship	
Technical factors	(10) Small-scale generation		

Source: Müller and Rommel 2010.

Table 22.3 Challenges and Co-operative Governance Solutions on Electricity Markets

Challenge on electricity market	Co-operative governance solution
Monopolistic market structures	Participation and democratic control, reducing regulation costs
Energy transition and sustainable consumption	Activity space for commitment/initiatives, reducing information costs
Electricity (from renewables) as a credence good	Transparency; local suppliers embedded in social networks, reducing enforcement and information costs

Source: Sagebiel et al. 2014.

amounts of renewable energy available and with shorter distances between households and energy providers (Sagebiel et al. 2014). At present, at least 10 per cent of all households in Germany already choose more costly electricity tariffs that are entirely based on renewable energies. It follows that energy co-operatives can be seen as offering a way for citizens to express their preferences and actively promote the energy transformation from the bottom up. Local energy production is preferred because consumers feel that they have better control over the process and outcome of green energy production. In this situation, co-operatives can enhance trust, increase transparency, and reduce the information and enforcement costs of the energy transformation (Sagebiel et al. 2014).

22.6 THE FUTURE OF THE GERMAN ENERGY TRANSFORMATION

As shown in Figure 22.5, the number of newly founded co-operatives decreased from 104 registered in 2013 to only 29 in 2014. Is this the end of the founding boom in the energy co-operative sector? And what are the reasons for this adverse trend?

Two institutional factors for the current reluctance to register new energy co-operatives can be identified: the amendment of the Renewable Energy Act in 2014 and a new financial regulation mechanism, known as KAGB, implemented in 2013.

The fixed feed-in tariffs, together with a rapid expansion of renewable energy production, have led to an increase of electricity prices for end consumers. Therefore, politicians have decided to limit energy costs for citizens by reducing feed-in tariffs and limiting newly installed capacity for renewable energies. High energy prices are also seen as a threat to Germany's competitiveness in international markets. Following this line of argument, the 2012 and 2014 EEG reforms gradually transformed a system of fixed feed-in tariffs to one that is market-based in combination with a price premium. This system change has weakened planning security for new renewable energy plants and increased transaction costs for new co-operative energy plants.

The other institutional factor at play here has been the introduction of compulsory direct marketing of energy oriented towards prices set at the stock exchange. This is a potential disadvantage for small energy producers with less professional management and lower risk-taking ability. Moreover, starting in 2015, a public tendering procedure will become compulsory for new photovoltaic plants larger than 750 kW, competing for land. In the future, feed-in tariffs will not be fixed by the government but will be determined by this tendering procedure (Federal Ministry for Economic Affairs and Energy 2015a). This will pose a significant market-entry barrier for co-operatives mainly investing in photovoltaic plants. The tendering procedure will carry a high administrative burden for local initiatives, because large energy producers will find it easier to come up with cost of application writing, mitigate the risks of application rejection, and diversify their production portfolios (Bundesverband Erneuerbare Energien 2015). At present, initial experience with tendering in this context is being gathered, and it is expected that law-makers will have to deal with a number of protests and critical evaluation studies on the subject.

A need for stronger financial regulation emerged after the financial crisis began in Europe and law-makers in Brussels intend to better control financial investments and portfolio management companies in order to avoid risky speculation in the financial sector. This has resulted in another concern for energy co-operatives. The so-called Kapitalanlagegesetzbuch (KAGB) or Capital Investment Law, implemented in July 2013, is a result of new European legislation regarding the control of investment funds. Probably only a few had suspected that this regulation would affect energy co-operatives. However, energy co-operatives also need to collect capital among their members prior to investment. Under certain conditions, energy co-operatives may be treated like investment funds before law, and fall under the control of the Federal Financial Supervisory Authority (BaFin), leading to higher administrative burdens. In 2014, many co-operatives became concerned, as they could not meet the required professional standards for managing funds, according to which co-operative managers need to have theoretical and practical knowledge about their particular business area, as well as experience in financial management. This is why the KAGB was expected to have a negative impact on co-operators. Since March 2015, however, most of the problems with the KAGB have been resolved, as exemptions for smaller energy plants have been agreed upon between co-operative associations and institutions for the control of investment funds (Bühler 2015).

Considering these problems together, there remains much to do for policy makers to support a decentralized energy transformation process and continue the promising beginning of democratization of the energy sector. At present, the founders of the next generation of energy co-operatives remain in a cautious position of waiting for the next reforms in Brussels and Berlin. Meanwhile, the first signs of a restructuring process among energy co-operatives have also been observed. Experts expect both mergers and acquisitions to occur and strategic networks to emerge. Technological progress, framed through paradigms such as 'Industry 4.0' and 'smart grids technology', and the need to better position local energy providers in more and more internationalizing markets appear to be the current drivers of these processes. In the future, the products of energy co-operatives will have to diversify towards a product mix between photovoltaic energy, wind, biomass, and the use of excess heat. Where this cannot be achieved through the growth of a single co-operative, co-operatives are likely to do what they always have done: join forces at the regional and federal-state levels (as has been the case with Thuringia and Bavaria), or group together with the aim of creating virtual power plants at the federal level.

References

Bantle, C. (2014), *Erneuerbare Energien und das EEG: Zahlen, Fakten, Grafiken (2014): Anlagen, installierte Leistung, Stromerzeugung, EEG-Auszahlungen, Marktintegration der erneuerbaren Energien und regionale Verteilung der EEG-induzierten Zahlungsströme*. Bundesverband der Energie- und Wasserwirtschaft. BDEW Pressestelle. Available at https://www.bdew.de/internet.nsf/id/83C963F43062D3B9C1257C89003153BF/$file/Energie-Info_Erneuerbare%20

Energien%20und%20das%20EEG%20%282014%29_24.02.2014_final_Journalisten.pdf (accessed 20 September 2016).

Bayerischer Rundfunk, Biogas: Nachhaltigkeit mit Nebenwirkung | BR.de, 2015. Available at http://www.br.de/themen/wissen/dossier-energiealternativen-biogas100.html (accessed 20 September 2016).

Becker, S., Bues, A., and Naumann, M. (2014), 'Die Analyse lokaler energiepolitischer Konflikte und das Entstehen neuer Organisationsformen: Theoretische Zugänge und aktuelle Herausforderungen', EnerLOG Working Paper, No. 1.

Bühler, H. (2015), 'Beurteilung der Geschäftsmodelle unter Berücksichtigung des KAGB'. Presentation held at the conference, Bundeskongress genossenschaftliche Energiewende, 3 February. Berlin, Germany.

Bundesverband Erneuerbare Energien (2015). 'Regierungspläne für Solarausbau bremsen die Energiewende. Available at http://www.bee-ev.de/3:1813/Meldungen/2015/Regierungsplaene-fuer-Solarausbau-bremsen-die-Energiewende.html (accessed 20 September 2016).

DGRV (2014), *Energiegenossenschaften, Ergebnisse der Umfrage des DGRV und seiner Mitgliedsverbände.*

Federal Environmental Agency (2015), 'Treibhausgas-Emissionen in Deutschland'. Available at http://www.umweltbundesamt.de/daten/klimawandel/treibhausgas-emissionen-in-deutschland (accessed 20 September 2016).

Federal Ministry for Economic Affairs and Energy (2012), 'BMWi - Erneuerbare Energien - Das Erneuerbare-Energien-Gesetz'. Available at http://www.erneuerbare-energien.de/EE/Redaktion/DE/Dossier/eckpunkte_der_eeg_novelle.html?cms_docId=75588 (accessed 20 September 2016).

Federal Ministry for Economic Affairs and Energy (2015a), *Gabriel: Erste Ausschreibungsrunde Photovoltaik-Freiflächenanlagen kann im Februar 2015 starten.* Available at http://www.bmwi.de/DE/Presse/pressemitteilungen,did=687578.html (accessed 20 September 2016).

Federal Ministry for Economic Affairs and Energy (2015b), *Zeitreihen zur Entwicklung der erneuerbaren Energien in Deutschland: unter Verwendung von Daten der Arbeitsgruppe Erneuerbare Energien-Statistik (AGEE-Stat).* Available at http://www.erneuerbare-energien.de/EE/Redaktion/DE/Downloads/zeitreihen-zur-entwicklung-der-erneuerbaren-energien-in-deutschland-1990-2013.pdf?__blob=publicationFile&v=14 (accessed 20 September 2016).

Holstenkamp, L. (2012), 'Ansätze einer Systematisierung von Energiegenossenschaften'. Working Paper Series in Business and Law, No. 11.

Holstenkamp, L. and Müller, J. R. (2013), 'Zum Stand von Energiegenossenschaften in Deutschland Überblick: Ein statistischer Überblick zum 31.12.2012'. Working Paper Series in Business and Law, No. 14.

International Energy Agency, (2013), *Energy Policies of IEA countries–Germany. 2013 Review.* Available at http://www.iea.org/publications/freepublications/publication/Germany2013_free.pdf (accessed 20 September 2016).

Kaenzig, J., Heinzle, S. L., and Wüstenhagen, R. (2013), 'Whatever the Customer Wants, the Customer Gets? Exploring the Gap between Consumer Preferences and Default Electricity Products in Germany', *Energy Policy*, 53, 311–22.

Laird, F. N. and Stefes, C. (2009), 'The Diverging Paths of German and United States Policies for Renewable Energy: Sources of Difference', *Energy Policy*, 37(7), 2619–29.

Müller, J. R. and Holstenkamp, L. (2015), 'Zum Stand von Energiegenossenschaften in Deutschland: Aktualisierter Überblick über Zahlen und Entwicklungen zum 31.12.2014'. Working Paper Series in Business and Law, No. 20.

Müller, J. R. and Rommel, J. (2010), 'Is There a Future Role for Urban Electricity Cooperatives? The Case of Greenpeace Energy'. Paper presented at the 7th Biennial International Workshop, Advances in Energy Studies, October 19–21, Barcelona, Spain, 185–95.

Netz-Transparenz (2015), *EEG-Umlage*. Available at http://www.netztransparenz.de/de/EEG-Umlage-2010.htm (accessed 20 September 2016).

Sagebiel, J., Müller, J. R., and Rommel, J. (2014), 'Are Consumers Willing to Pay More for Electricity from Cooperatives? Results from an Online Choice Experiment in Germany', *Energy Research & Social Science*, 2, 90–101.

Scholwin, F., Grope, J., Schüch, A., Gödeke, K., Reinhold, G., Vetter, A., Reinhardt, G., Vogt, R., and Müller-Lindenlauf, M. (2014), *Dossier: Biogas aus Energiepflanzen Potenziale und Flächen, Anbauprioritäten und Kosten, Natur und Landschaft*. Available at https://www.dbfz.de/fileadmin/user_upload/Download/Dossier_III_-_Biomethan.pdf (accessed 14 October 2016).

Süddeutsche (2012), *Kottgeisering und die Solaranlage—Dorffrieden statt Energiewende*. Available at http://www.sueddeutsche.de/muenchen/fuerstenfeldbruck/kottgeisering-und-die-solaranlage-dorffrieden-statt-energiewende-1.1320052 (accessed 20 September 2016).

Süddeutsche, (2014), *Lebensmittel in Biogasanlagen—Strom aus dem Supermarkt*. Available at http://www.sueddeutsche.de/wissen/lebensmittel-in-biogasanlagen-strom-aus-dem-supermarkt-1.2167766 (accessed 14 October 2016).

trend:research GmbH, Leuphana Universität Lüneburg (2013), *Definition und Marktanalyse von Bürgerenergie in Deutschland: Bremen, Lüneburg*. Available at https://www.buendnis-buergerenergie.de/fileadmin/user_upload/downloads/Studien/Studie_Definition_und_Marktanalyse_von_Buergerenergie_in_Deutschland_BBEn.pdf (accessed 14 October 2016).

Yildiz, Ö., Rommel, J., Debor, S., Holstenkamp, L., Mey, F., Müller, J. R., Radtke, J., and Rognlih, J. (2015), 'Renewable Energy Cooperatives as Gatekeepers or Facilitators? Recent Developments in Germany and a Multidisciplinary Research Agenda', *Energy Research & Social Science*, 6, 59–73.

....

CHAPTER 23

CO-OPERATIVES
IN LATIN AMERICA

....

MICHELA GIOVANNINI AND MARCELO VIETA

23.1 INTRODUCTION

....

IN Latin America the economic sphere located between the state and the market has been growing since the 1980s as a response of civil society to growing inequality, unemployment, and social marginalization. Its historical roots, however, can be traced back to pre-Columbian collectives and co-operative-like models that were later influenced by participatory organizational models introduced by European colonizers and settlers. The modern co-operative movement began at the end of the nineteenth century, thanks to European immigrants who were bringing experiences from developments in their homelands. However, older experiences had already been documented in Venezuela, Mexico, and in Argentina by the middle of the nineteenth century, where forms of embryonic co-operatives such as benevolent societies and mutual associations had been active since the first half of that century. By the beginning of the twentieth century, the movement in Latin America had started to advance and was being strongly influenced by utopian, socialist, and even anarchist schools of thought, as well as from trade unionism and the social doctrine of the Catholic Church (Coque 2002). However, it should be kept in mind that these experiences were characterized by discontinuity and heterogeneity, with different impacts at the regional and national levels.

Studies carried out in the 1990s described the co-operative sector in Latin America as composed of a number of organizations varying between 30 to 50 thousand, with the total number of members estimated to be between 17 and 23 million, depending on the source consulted. These varying data bear witness to one of the greatest weaknesses of the co-operative sector in Latin America: the lack of structural studies and consistent longitudinal data collected over time. Furthermore, data are partial because of the lack of legal recognition that these organizations have in several Latin American countries, where they are active de facto as informal organizations due an absence of enabling legal frameworks.

According to recent studies carried out by the International Labour Organization (ILO) and the International Co-operative Alliance (ICA), co-operative enterprises in Latin America have been reinforced in recent years by the economic crisis, particularly as a response to the neoliberal model in countries throughout the region, as the number of co-operatives continues to increase. Indeed, a wave of new co-operatives, especially worker co-ops, has emerged in recent years in countries hardest hit by the crisis of the neoliberal model, such as Argentina, Uruguay, and Brazil (Vieta and Ruggeri 2009). However, on the whole, a great heterogeneity characterizes Latin American countries' co-op movements concerning origins, dimensions, legal recognition, economic impact, and number of organizations. Co-operatives, and more generally the social and solidarity economy sector, have recently started to capture the attention of policy makers and scholars, but existing specialized research institutions are still recent and policies still, in the main, insufficient to completely support the potential of co-operatives as fundamental actors of socio-economic development.

23.2 CHILE

Despite its relative importance, the social and solidarity economy sector in Chile still lacks recognition and visibility. This is all the more true if looking at the few national studies on this sector. Chile's co-operative sector is somewhat better understood, however. ICA Americas estimates that in 2014 there were almost 1,000 active co-operatives in the country with more than 1,700,000 members.

From a conceptual viewpoint, the development of the social and solidarity economy in Chile has been influenced by three main trends (Radrigán and Barria 2005): the 'social economy' concept, mainly deriving from the European (and especially French) school of thought; the 'third sector' or 'non-profit' concepts, influenced mainly by the US stream of thought; and the 'social and solidarity economy' concept. The latter was coined in Latin America with the aim of differentiating it from the traditional co-operative sector, which some argue is becoming more and more similar to the traditional for-profit sector, especially in the case of large agricultural co-operatives.

The main organizations belonging to the social and solidarity economy in Chile are community organizations, co-operatives, trade associations, indigenous organizations, mutual societies, non-profit enterprises, non-profit foundations, and trade unions (UNDP 2012). The origins of the modern social and solidarity economy in Chile can be traced back to the nineteenth century, when charity organizations based on solidarity principles started to develop, often supported by the Catholic Church (Irarrázaval et al. 2006). At the time in Chile, these charity organizations were carrying out all of the charitable social assistance and solidarity activities connected to the process of economic and political consolidation that the country was undergoing in the immediate decades following independence. Later on in the nineteenth century, legal recognition was given to foundations and *corporaciones* (a type of association) as non-profit organizations, established by the Civil Code of 1855.

The co-operative movement started to emerge several decades after independence, incorporating the influences brought by the European experience. The first Chilean co-operative, a consumer co-operative called La Esmeralda, was founded in 1887. The co-operative movement was also influenced by the emergence of the trade-union movement, which originated in this period mainly due to the spontaneous efforts of miners in the northern part of the country (Del Campo and Radrigán 1998). Other influences derived from mutual societies, initially linked to typography workers that were replicating the European mutual model.

The first legal recognition for Chilean co-operatives came in 1924, followed by specific legislation for agricultural co-operatives in 1929. In the period between 1925 and 1963, the state created a Department of Mutuals and Co-operatives, headed by the Ministry of Work and Social Security. This department supported the creation of co-operatives in several sectors: agriculture, drinking water, housing, and electricity. However, more structured support for the co-operative sector was still lacking as the state mainly sustained single and isolated initiatives. President Eduardo Frei Montalva (1964–70) made an important contribution to sustaining and growing the co-operative sector: although a coherent programme was still lacking, in this period co-operatives became an instrument supporting the government's reformist policies. During Salvador Allende's presidency (1970–73) the number of co-operatives continued to expand into new and differentiated sectors of activity, such as worker housing, and users' co-operatives. However, the military coup of 1973 marked the breakdown of all civil society movements and organizations, as well as the repression of individual freedoms. During the dictatorship, solidarity economy organizations suffered their worst period, affected by the neoliberal economic system that intervened in their internal structure. Many of the existing organizations were forced to cease their activities and, due also to the economic crisis at the beginning of the 1980s, many co-operatives went bankrupt.

With the restoration of democracy, civil society and social economy organizations were restored in order to address societal needs. However, the national constitution continues to be the same document inherited from the military regime, strongly framed in neoliberal terms. Nevertheless, with the restoration of democracy, there was a resurgence of civil society initiatives and a review of the legal framework for social and solidarity economy organizations, but there has been no clear break with the legislation introduced during the period of the military regime. While the government in Chile has changed its role in recent decades from a welfare model (*modelo asistencialista*) to a neoliberal model where the meeting of social needs tends to be left to the private sector (*modelo subsidiario*), the social and solidarity economy sector in the Chilean context has been developing within a framework of political and economic transformation.

Nowadays, some interesting co-operative experiences are active in the provision of general-interest services, especially concerning drinking water. Indeed, more than 1,500

Rural Drinking Water Associations (Asociaciones de Agua Potable Rural, APR) are active all over the country (Villarroel 2012), constituting almost 17 per cent of the total number of co-operatives in the country (Ministerio de Economía 2014). These organizations take the form of co-operatives or committees and perform an interesting community model of water provision, in a country where water provision has been privatized since the period of the military regime (Gobierno de Chile 1981). Today, several of these community-based organizations, some of them active since the 1960s when they were founded thanks to the direct intervention of the state, represent an actual alternative to the private model of water provision. Moreover, they are also providing a plurality of complementary services to communities, such as public libraries or public spaces open to community participation and initiatives.

Other remarkable initiatives are emerging, not without difficulties, in the context of waste recycling. These organizations assume different legal forms, such as micro-enterprises or associations, and they are collectively and democratically managed. They are supported, up to different degrees, by local municipalities and NGOs, given their importance from the environmental and social points of view. Recent attempts at the institutionalization of recyclers' organizations have been useful in order to reduce the stigmatization these people suffer, raise their chances of finding materials to be sold, and in some cases, slightly improve their working conditions (Giovannini 2014).

23.3 ARGENTINA

In Argentina, social and solidarity economy organizations, especially co-operatives, have a long and storied history. Already by the middle of the nineteenth century a growing urban working class was engaged in forming mutual associations, benevolent societies, and renters' associations. With its first formal co-operative society founded in 1875, the Argentine co-operative movement was the 'first to begin in a country outside the industrialized countries of Europe, Australia, Canada, Japan, and the United States' (Shaffer 1999: 139). Historically, as in Chile, social economy organizations and co-operatives in Argentina were linked to the country's ties to Europe, and particularly with the waves of immigrants from Spain, Italy, and other countries who arrived from the beginning of the last quarter of the nineteenth century with new ideas of how to organize social, economic, and working life (Montes and Ressel 2003). The Argentine co-operative movement has also been pushed and pulled between the interests of local people seeking socio-economic autonomy, state policies that at times sought to protect and at other times deregulate the economy, and influential multinational and corporate interests. One of the most robust co-operative sectors in Latin America, today around 9,300,000 Argentines belong to almost 29,000 producer, consumer, credit, insurance, housing, and worker co-operatives, the latter amongst the largest sectors in the world with over 22,500 worker co-ops that have surged over the past two decades (Las cooperativas argentinas 2012; Vuotto 2014).

The first national legislation for co-operatives was passed in 1905 (Shaffer 1999). A more robust legislative framework was passed as Law 11.388 in 1926, updated by the third government of Perón as Law 20.337 in 1973 and is still in effect today (Olivera 2006). Merging the co-operative sector with the broader social economy, the National Institute of the Social Economy (Instituto Nacional de la Economía Social, INAES) is the body regulated by the Ministry of Social Development to oversee co-operatives and other social economy organizations in the country. Over the years, Argentina has developed a rich and diverse network of co-operative federations (175 as of 2012), co-operative education and training institutes (such as the Centro Cultural de la Cooperación), and even a well-regarded co-operative movement publishing house (InterCoop Editora).

The agricultural sector saw an early growth in co-operatives by small farmers seeking to survive and share in production and marketing in the midst of landholder oligopolies. These early co-operatives were important for the rise of Argentina's Socialist Party and the Argentine Agrarian Federation (Federación Agraria Argentina, FAA) (Olivera, 2006). Today over 1,000 agricultural co-operatives exist and range from first-degree small farm co-ops, to second- and third-degree co-ops, to some of the largest co-operatives in Argentina, such as the SanCor dairy co-operative.

Consumer co-operatives would also emerge in the first years of the twentieth century, with the most famous and influential, El Hogar Obrero (The Workers' House), founded in 1905 as an initiative of the Socialist Party. El Hogar Obrero accompanied the rise of the growing working class and labour movement and has been involved in social housing, credit provisioning, tourism and recreation, and grocery stores (Ronchi 2012). Public utilities, such as water, electricity, and telephone services would also gain influence throughout the Argentine territory, especially in the smaller provincial towns. Savings and credit co-operatives also have a long history in Argentina and were mainstays in small towns and cities throughout the country until the neoliberal policies beginning in the 1970s that put many of them out of business. Banco Credicoop emerged in the late 1970s from the merger of 44 credit unions during the military dictatorship, and still remains the major co-operative presence in the country's banking sector (Martí 2006).

The first worker co-operative was founded in 1928 by a small group of construction workers. Because of the historically strong role of unions and the relatively early introduction of social security in the 1940s during the two first presidencies of Juán Perón, worker co-operatives had a slower initial uptake compared to other co-operative forms until the 1990s and the introduction of neoliberal reforms that gutted many decades-old workers' benefits (Vuotto 2012). Partially in response to the weakening of labour rights and increased closures of businesses, by the mid-to-late 1990s worker co-operatives began to surge in the country, from 392 worker co-ops in 1984, to 4,264 in 1997, to over 11,371 by 2008 (INAES 2008; Levin and Verbeke 1997). In the period during and after the 2001–03 socio-economic crisis, this surge included the rise of worker-recuperated enterprises (*empresas recuperadas por sus trabajadores*, ERT) and especially worker co-operatives linked to the delivery of social assistance programmes (Vuotto 2012).

Argentina's ERTs began to emerge in the late 1990s as workers' direct responses to structural adjustments, labour reforms, and ultimate market failures of that decade. With a weakened union movement and an increasingly unresponsive state overwhelmed by growing life precariousness, employees working in failing or bankrupt firms began occupying and then self-managing their workplaces, almost always transforming them into worker co-operatives. The emergence of ERTs hit its peak during the country's social, political, and financial crisis years of 2001–03 as more and more businesses dismissed workers and began to fail. ERTs have proven to be effective responses for saving small- and medium-sized firms (SMEs) in Argentina, a new form of labour organizing linked to the country's new social movements for socio-economic justice that arose during these years, and have become viable solutions to informal work, stubborn unemployment, and precarity (Vieta 2014). As of early 2016, almost 16,000 workers were self-managing 367 ERTs throughout most of the urban economy in sectors as diverse as printing and publishing, media, metallurgy, foodstuffs, construction, textiles, tourism, education, health provisioning, shipbuilding, and hydrocarbons and fuels (Ruggeri 2016). Many ERTs have also been contributing to the socio-economic needs of surrounding communities by, for instance, allowing social and cultural initiatives to operate within the firm, while some ERTs invest part of their surpluses to community economic development (Vieta 2014).

Another reason for the large surge of worker co-operatives in Argentina has much to do with the national government's delivery of 'social containment' initiatives for the under- and unemployed that began to be implemented during the recessionary and crisis years of 1997–2001. More recently, these social assistance initiatives have expanded into municipal infrastructure construction programmes spearheaded by the presidencies of Nestor and Cristina Kirchner (2003–15), such as Manos a la Obra (Hands to Work) and Argentina Trabaja (Argentina Works). By 2009, Argentina Trabaja included the formation of worker co-operatives as employment-generating mechanisms via state contracts for public works and maintenance tasks. Creating more than 7,300 new worker co-operatives by March 2011 (Vuotto 2012), some have called these 'assistentialist' uses of co-operatives that create further dependency and have claimed that they are, in reality, work-for-welfare programmes delivered by the downsizing neoliberal state via local groups of under- and unemployed social assistance recipients without adequate training for members in the intricacies of self-management or co-operative values (Dinerstein 2007). However, there is also evidence that some of these new worker co-operatives have become viable labour-managed businesses, and have shown an increased willingness by the state in recent years to more diligently invest in local community development.

23.4 MEXICO

Conceptually, the main term employed in Mexico to identify the sector located between the public and the for-profit sector is the 'social and solidarity economy'. The discourse implied by this term tends to stress the processes of economic and political change that these organizations can contribute to, together with an emphasis on the contribution given by indigenous peoples with their ancestral practices of solidarity and reciprocity. In Mexico, unlike in other areas of Latin America, the term 'social enterprise' is also employed, reflecting the influence of the North American school of thought, even though this concept is still not predominant.

The Mexican social and solidarity economy comprises about 50,000 organizations with around 8,000,000 members (Rojas Herrera 2013), even though these estimates are approximate, and reliable studies on the sector are still lacking. These estimates report that workers employed in the sector represent 18 per cent of the active population, and that the social and solidarity economy sector contributes to 5 per cent of Mexican GDP (Rojas Herrera 2013). While most of these organizations belong to the agricultural sector, the social and solidarity economy also comprises associations that do not necessarily have a productive nature, as well as informal organizations. This makes it difficult to provide a comprehensive picture of the social and solidarity economy and justifies the limited contribution that the sector is able to make to GDP. It is worth noting that the general economic weakness of the sector is also testified by the paucity of supportive second-degree organizations, which are still very few in number and gather only a minority of associates.

Historically, the social and solidarity economy sector in Mexico has its roots in pre-Columbian times and in the solidarity and reciprocity practices of indigenous peoples. One example is that of the *cajas indígenas,* that administered savings, credit, and social provision for members (Rojas Coria 1982 [1952]). The co-operative movement was influenced by the Catholic Church, especially concerning savings organizations, and by artisans' guilds (Rojas Coria 1982 [1952]). The first mutual savings bank, based on the principle 'one head one vote', opened in 1839 in Orizaba, Veracruz (Shaffer 1999). By the second half of the nineteenth century the first legislative provisions were incorporated into the Commercial Code of 1889.

Article 25 of the Mexican constitution provides for support to the social and solidarity economy sector, including all those organizations 'devoted to the production, distribution and consumption of goods and services that are socially necessary'. This category comprises *ejidos,*[1] community organizations, workers' organizations, co-operatives, and other forms of enterprises belonging in part or completely to their workers. This constitutional provision, however, remains largely unattended, in spite of the recent approval of a law in support of the social and solidarity economy. Indeed, Mexican institutions have been favouring the expansion of the national and foreign for-profit sector, even in those sectors of activities that the Constitution declares fields of activity of the public sector, and this tendency appears to be accentuated with the recent neoliberal reforms brought by the government of Enrique Peña Nieto (2012–present). Accordingly, real institutional support of the sector has been lacking and this shortage of specific public

---

[1] The *ejido* is a form of communal land tenure: the *ejido* land titles are legally held by the community and each *ejidatario* receives a piece of land. All decisions regarding every piece of land are taken in the general assembly of *ejidatarios.* Most *ejidos* include plots of land destined for communal use.

policies has produced scarce access to funding opportunities, poor training in entrepreneurialism, and a consequent high informality of productive activities in the sector.

The main objectives of the new Social and Solidarity Economy law (2012) are to establish mechanisms able to support the organization and expansion of the social and solidarity economy sector, where the responsibility of this support is taken by the state; and to define rules for the organization and empowerment of the sector as a mechanism that can contribute to socio-economic development through employment generation, strengthening of democracy, redistribution of resources, and generation of social patrimony (art. 2). The law has also created a National Institute of Social Economy, an autonomous institute that will be part of the Secretariat of the Economy, with the aim of defining and implementing public policies to support the social economy sector. However, the real impact of this institute appears limited, given its reduced dimensions and the scarcity of funds available to it.

Next to traditional agricultural or large co-operatives, and in spite of the scarce institutional support, several autonomous initiatives are developing from civil society. Among a number of innovative initiatives, it is worth mentioning community enterprises developed by indigenous peoples who are seeking an alternative approach to development, mixing their ancestral knowledge and culture with modern practices. Self-managed community organizations seem to be a particularly effective vehicle for promoting *buen vivir*, an indigenous conception of well-being based on reciprocity and solidarity between human beings and the natural environment (Giovannini 2015).

23.5 CUBA

Cuba's co-operative movement is fairly recent in comparison to the rest of Latin America, and has been closely linked to the Cuban state. This has raised questions for some in the global co-operative movement, such as the ICA, concerning Cuba's respect for the co-operative principle of autonomy and independence. Nevertheless, it is undeniable that since the Revolution of 1959, co-operatives have had an important economic role in Cuba, especially in the agricultural sector. The country's recent economic reforms have also introduced a promising new initiative for 'non-agricultural' or 'urban' co-operatives (DuRand 2013).

Before the Revolution of 1959 Cuba's co-operative sector was small; co-ops were more akin to collective associations due to the lack of national co-operative legislation. While the 1940 Cuban constitution did offer state support for co-operative development, the promised support for co-op development failed to materialize. In 1950, the Agricultural Development Bank managed to finance a small agricultural co-operative sector, and co-operative legislation eventually came into effect in 1951 (Shaffer 1999). However, the reality for pre-Revolution co-operatives was stark since 73.3 per cent of Cuba's land was owned by 9.5 per cent of the island's property owners and multinational interests (Nova González 2013).

It was not until 1959 and Fidel Castro's decree that *campesinos* were vital for the Revolution that co-operatives began to take off: co-ops were viewed by the Revolutionary government as a way to return social wealth to the people. For the next half century, this happened almost exclusively in the agricultural sector (Nova González 2013). The first post-Revolution co-operatives emerged from the agrarian reforms of 1960 and the redistribution of land to *asociaciones campesinas* (agricultural associations), eventually becoming the first post-1959 co-operatives in the province of Pinar del Río. Sugar-cane co-operatives also emerged for a time from the nationalization and redistribution of large-estate-owned sugar plantations to previously landless peasants, but most of them reverted back to state ownership after 1962, however, due to inexperience in running co-operatives (Nova González 2013). By 1961, the National Association of Small Farmers (Asociación Nacional de Agricultores Pequeños, ANAP) was established, which has been over the decades an invaluable source of co-operative education and capacity building.

Soon after the Revolution, an increasing number of credit-granting institutions and banks dissolved or left Cuba. By 1960 it was decided, therefore, to create Credit and Service Co-operatives (*Cooperativas de Créditos y Servicios*, CCS). Essentially producer co-operatives, CCSs were formed voluntarily by farmers that had received land from the Revolution's agrarian reforms (Nova González 2013). Still existing today, CCS members work their own land and collaborate to purchase supplies from and sell products to the state and local markets, sharing marketing, training, and equipment purchases while defraying infrastructure costs and gaining access to credit. In 2013, there were 2,489 CCSs representing 348,080 members farming roughly 35 per cent of agricultural land (Holm 2014).

Fifteen years later, Agricultural Production Co-operatives (*Cooperativas de Producción Agropecuaria*, CPA) were introduced at the First Congress of the Communist Party when it was decided to develop and promote advanced farming methods among farmers who had received land from the agrarian reforms. CPAs are voluntary worker co-ops made up of farmers who contribute their means of production and/or land to the co-operative, which they then work collectively. As Nova González explains: '[u]nlike CCSs, CPA members [sell] their resources to the co-operative, [receive] payment for them, and become collective owners and workers' (2013: 281). By 2013, there were 996 CPAs representing approximately 48,336 members farming close to 9 per cent of Cuba's agricultural land (Holm 2014).

In 1993 a new type of agricultural co-operative, Basic Units of Co-operative Production (*Unidades Básicas de Producción Cooperativa*, UBPC), was introduced shortly after the beginning of the Special Period as a direct response to the crisis and the need for food security (Holm 2014). Formed from the break-up of large state farms, UBPCs were intended to 'change the relation of production' in the agricultural sector, promoting 'the self-sufficiency of members and their families through co-operative efforts[,] ... rigorous association between worker income and production[,] ... and management autonomy' (Nova González 2013: 284). Technically set up like worker co-operatives, UBPCs have in actuality become hybrid state enterprise co-operatives.

Initially, state farmland was given to their former workers for free (in perpetual usufruct tenure), and workers then purchased equipment and infrastructure over time via soft loans. Some urban *organopónicos* (urban organic farms that feed large sectors of Cuba's cities and towns) have also taken on the UBPC model. Because of their lack of full autonomy and due to strict government quotas, however, UBPCs have not produced as efficiently as CCSs and CPAs and experienced a decline in recent years. In 2013, there were 1,989 UBPCs representing approximately 121,481 members farming nearly 30 per cent of agricultural land (Holm 2014).

Until 1993, most of Cuba's agricultural land was under state control, and was characterized by industrial agricultural methods imported mostly from the Eastern bloc, including cheap access to machinery and oil in a subsidized exchange for sugar, tobacco, and other Cuban commodities. By 1989, 15 per cent of Cuba's agricultural land was co-operatively owned and the rest state-owned. During the Special Period things changed dramatically out of necessity. Taking up organic and permaculture-based farming methods and low-technology harvesting, by 2003 well over 70 per cent of Cuba's agriculture was under co-operative control (Holm 2014: 788). Cuba's agricultural co-operatives have gone a long way in recent years in bringing food security to the island after the effects of the Special Period and the embargo, only recently lifted in late 2014.

Since 2011, Cuba has been expanding its co-operative sector, now including what it calls 'non-agricultural', or 'urban-based' co-operatives. After the release of a draft of plans for substantial economic reforms in 2010, and after wide public consultations between December 2010 and February 2011, the Sixth Congress of the Communist Party put into effect *Los Lineamientos* (Policy Guidelines) in April 2011, committing Cuba to a massive restructuring of the economy. The *Lineamientos* have set the stage for a new form of socialist economy where 'non-state enterprises' are encouraged, opening up space for *cuentapropistas* (the self-employed), *trabajadores asalariados* (non-state salaried workers), a regulated private sector, as well as a non-state social-economy sector populated by new non-agricultural co-operatives (Vieta 2012). The vision of the *Lineamientos* of the Cuban Communist Party was to increase the non-state employment sector from 16 per cent to to 35 per cent of Cuba's workforce (2010 figures) by the end of 2015. This would mean that by 2016, if this projection holds, Cuba will have 1,800,000 non-state workers employed either as *cuentapropistas, trabajadores asalariados*, or *cooperativistas* (co-operators) (Piñeiro Harnecker 2011).

There is evidence that the *Lineamientos'* stimulation of growth of new co-operatives is taking root. Moreover, towards the goal of clarifying the economic sectors where co-operatives will be permitted, as well as the organizational form that non-agricultural co-ops may adopt, new co-operative legislation was passed by the National Assembly in December 2012 stipulating that, among other things, co-operatives: will be independent of the state; will set their own prices on some goods and services not deemed essential for national interests; can emerge from the conversion of state enterprises or start-ups; can hire wage-labour for up to 90 days, after which they must become members; are to share in profits and pay social security for workers; and will be funded by loans, state funds, and member contributions (Gaceta Oficial 2012). Since 2012, and promising a new direction for Cuba's brand of socialism, non-agricultural co-operatives have emerged in sectors such as commerce, retail, food provisioning and gastronomy, transport, commercial services, construction, and, more recently, public utilities. By July 2013, 124 new urban co-operatives were formed; by April 2014, 452 (Rodriquez Delis 2014).

23.6 Conclusion

Latin America's social and solidarity economies and their co-operative sectors have long histories and have made vital contributions to alternative economic arrangements. Throughout Latin America, in differing national conjunctures and circumstances, co-operative economics have merged with indigenous knowledge, labour movements, and social and solidarity economy initiatives. Worker-recuperated firms and worker co-operatives, rural and producer co-ops, consumer and public utility co-operatives, social services delivery organizations, and other forms of co-ops have been making lasting impacts throughout the region for over a century, most recently offering viable alternatives to the neoliberal model as a 'made in Latin America' co-operative movement. From out of these co-operative experiments, often federated territorially in some way, some states have also gone far in supporting national co-operative and social economy movements for local community development. Such has been the approach taken up in Brazil in the past decades, for example, with the close ties there between the state (via the National Secretary of the Solidarity Economy), many of the country's unions, and the rural and urban co-operative movements. As the cases of Chile, Argentina, Mexico, and Cuba reviewed in this chapter demonstrate, increasingly Latin American co-operatives are emerging from or linking to a people-centred solidarity or popular economy rooted in broader economic justice and participative democracy.

References

Coque Martínez, J. (2002), *Las cooperativas en América Latina: Visión histórica general y comentario de algunos países tipo*, CIRIEC, 43, 145–72.

Del Campo, P. and Radrigán Rubio, M. (1998), *El Sector cooperativo Chileno: Tradición, experiencias y proyecciones* (Santiago de Chile: CONFECOOP-CCA).

Dinerstein, A. C. (2007), 'Workers' Factory Takeovers and New State Policies in Argentina: Towards an "Institutionalisation" of Non-Governmental Public Action?'. *Policy & Politics*, 35(3), 529–50.

DuRand, C. (2013), 'Cooperative Cuba: Centre for Global Justice', Available at http://www.globaljusticecenter.org/cooperative_cuba (accessed 20 September 2016).

Gaceta Oficial de la República de Cuba (2012), 'Ley de cooperativas no agrícolas'. Ministerio de Justicia de la República de Cuba. Accessed at: http://www.cuba-economia.org/documentos/legislacion-economica/gaceta_53_cooperativas_no_agricolas (accessed 20 September 2016).

Giovannini, M. (2014), 'De la economía popular a la economía social y solidaria: El Caso de los Recicladores de Base en Santiago de Chile'. Euricse Working Papers, 73/14. Available at http://www.euricse.eu/wp-content/uploads/2015/03/1417514040_n2605.pdf (accessed 20 September 2016).

Giovannini, M. (2015), 'Indigenous Community Enterprises in Chiapas: A Vehicle for Buen Vivir?'. *Community Development Journal*, 50(1), 71–87.

Gobierno de Chile (1981), Código de aguas. Accessed at: http://www.dga.cl/Paginas/default.aspx (accessed 20 September 2016).

Holm, W. (2014), 'Sustainable Paths to a Just Economy: Cooperatives in the Land of Martí'. Texts selected from the international call for papers for the Quebec 2014 International Summit of Cooperatives. Available at https://www.sommetinter.coop/sites/default/files/library/pdf/articles-scientifiques/2014_50_holm.pdf (accessed 1 February 2014).

INAES (2008), *Cantidad de cooperativas por actividad*, Instituto Nacional de Asociativismo y Economía Social (Buenos Aires: Ministeria de Desarollo Social, Gobierno Nacional de la República Argentina).

Irarrázaval, I., Hairel, E., Wojciech Sokolowski, S., and Salamon, L. (2006), *Estudio comparativo del sector sin fines de lucro–Chile* (Santiago de Chile: Johns Hopkins University/UNDP).

'Las cooperativas argentinas crecieron un 49per cent en los últimos 3 años', *Cooperativismo en Movimiento*, Buenos Aires: Centro Cultural de la Cooperación, 2012. Available at http://www.centrocultural.coop/blogs/cooperativismo/2012/07/28/las-cooperativas-argentinas-crecieron-un-49-en-los-ultimos-tres-anos/ (accessed 20 September 2016).

Levin, A. and Verbeke, G. (1997), 'El cooperativismo argentino en cifras: Tendencias en su evolución: 1927-1997'. Publicación del Centro de Estudios de Sociología del Trabajo, n. 6. (Buenos Aires: Universidad de Buenos Aires). www.econ.uba.ar/cesot/docs/documento 6.pdf (12 October 2016).

Martí, J. P. (2006), *Impactos de la integración regional del MERCOSUR sobre el movimiento cooperativo* (Buenos Aires: Cooperativas e Inegración Regional Mercosur).

Ministerio de Economía, Fomento y Turismo (2014), 'El cooperativismo en Chile', Gobierno de Chile. Available at http://www.aciamericas.coop/IMG/pdf/el-cooperativismo-en-chile.pdf (accessed 20 January 2016).

Montes, V. L. and Ressel, A. B. (2003), 'Presencia del cooperativismo en Argentina', *UniRcoop*, 1(2), 9–26.

Nova González, A. (2013), 'Agricultural Cooperatives in Cuba: 1959–Present', in C. Piñeiro Harnecker, ed., *Cooperatives and Socialism: A View from Cuba* (Basingstoke, UK: Palgrave Macmillan), 279–91.

Olivera, G., ed. (2006), *Cooperativismo agrario: Instituciones, políticas públicas y procesos históricos* (Córdoba, Argentina: Ferreyra Editor).

Piñeiro Harnecker, C. (2011), 'Empresas no estatales en la economía cubana: Potencialidades, requerimientos y riesgos', *Revista Universidad de la Habana*, 272, 45–65.

Radrigán Rubio, M. and Barría Knopf, C. (2005), *Situación y proyecciones de la economía social en Chile*, Programa Interdisciplinario de Estudios Asociativos-PRO-ASOCIA (Santiago de Chile: Universidad de Chile).

Rodriguez Delis, L., 'Cooperativas no agropecuarias: De una experiencia a una novedad en Cuba', *Granma*, 30 April, 2014. Accessed at http://www.granma.cu/cuba/2014-05-19/cooperativas-no-agropecuarias-de-una-experiencia-a-una-novedad-en-cuba (accessed 20 September 2015).

Rojas Coria, R. (1982 [1952]), *Tratado de cooperativismo Mexicano* (Mexico City: Fondo de Cultura Económica).

Rojas Herrera, J. J. (2013), 'Fortalezas y debilidades de la economía social en México y sus perspectivas de cara a los retos que impone el modelo neoliberal', in L. Oulhaj and F. J. Saucedo Pérez, eds, *Miradas sobre la economía social y solidaria en México* (Puebla: Universidad Iberoamericana Puebla).

Ronchi, V. (2012), *La cooperazione integrale: Storia di 'El Hogar Obrero': Avanguardia dell'economia sociale argentina (1905-2005)* (Rome: Edizioni di Storia e Letteratura).

Ruggeri, A., ed. (2016), *Las empresas recuperadas por los trabajadores en los comienzos del gobierno de Mauricio Macri: Estado de situación a mayo de 2016* (Buenos Aires: Facultad de Filosofía y Letras, Universidad de Buenos Aires,).

Shaffer, J. (1999), *Historical Dictionary of the Cooperative Movement*, (London: The Scarecrow Press).

Sixth Congress of the Communist Party of Cuba, Resolution on the Guidelines of the Economic and Social Policy of the Party and the Revolution, 18 April 2011. Available at http://www.cuba.cu/gobierno/documentos/2011/ing/l160711i.html (accessed 20 September 2016).

UNDP (2012), *Desarrollo humano en Chile: Bienestar subjetivo: El Desafío de Repensar el Futuro* (Santiago de Chile: United Nations Development Programme).

Vieta, M. (2012). 'The Coming Cooperative Economy? Reflections on Two Recent Field Trips'. *The Bullet*, 2012, eBulletin of the Socialist Project n. 667. http://www.socialistproject.ca/bullet/667.php (accessed 20 September 2014).

Vieta, M. (2014), 'Learning in Struggle: Argentina's New Worker Cooperatives as Transformative Learning Organizations', *Relations Industrielles/Industrial Relations*, 69(1), 186–218.

Vieta, M. and Ruggeri, A. (2009), 'Worker-Recovered Enterprises as Workers' Co-operatives: The Conjunctures, Challenges, and Innovations of Self-Management in Argentina and Latin America', in D. Reed and J. J. McMurtry, eds, *Co-operatives in a Global Economy: The Challenges of Co-operation Across Borders* (Newcastle Upon-Tyne: Cambridge Scholars Publishing), 178–225.

Villarroel, C. N. (2012), *Asociaciones comunitarias de agua potable rural en Chile: diagnostico y desafíos* (Santiago de Chile: Gráfica Andes).

Vuotto, M. (2012), 'Organizational Dynamics of Worker Cooperatives in Argentina', *Service Business*, 6(1), 85–97.

Vuotto, M. (2014), 'La economía social y las cooperativas en la Argentina', *Voces en el Fénix*, 38, 46–53.

CHAPTER 24

···

DEVELOPING AND SUSTAINING COMMUNITIES

the role of co-operatives

···

LOU HAMMOND KETILSON

24.1 INTRODUCTION

···

COMMUNITIES are often destabilized by the impact of globalization (Bauman 1998; Scholte 2000). Livelihoods and ways of life may be undermined, particularly in remote rural and indigenous communities as well as marginalized urban populations. Although globalization has many aspects, a key marker is the increasing domination of market relations over other kinds of social relations. This phenomenon has created an increased interest in alternative forms of economic development more consistent with community values, as well as an increased attention to the nature and importance of social relationships in themselves and as preconditions for economic success. The development of the social economy (Lévesque 1998; Quarter 1992) has been central among the responses to economic problems.

'Social economy' is a term for which multiple definitions exist, reflecting and inviting diverse theoretical approaches (Shragge and Fontan 2000; Bouchard et al. 2006). Historically the term has been used most commonly in Europe, although the usage is now common across many countries (Bouchard 2009) to describe a variety of socio-economic initiatives addressing new opportunities and needs—initiatives clearly distinguished from those associated with the public or private sector.

Social-economy enterprises direct organizational and community resources to the pursuit of social and community goals, providing flexible and sustainable tools to assist communities to achieve their own objectives in the areas of job creation and skills development, the environment, social support networks, economic growth, and neighbourhood revitalization. Such enterprises exist across Canada built on the tradition of co-operatives and non-profit community enterprise as well as other innovative approaches (Quarter 1992; Lévesque and Malo 1992; Shragge and Fontan 2000; DeSantis et al. 2003).

24.2 Co-operative Context in Canada

Co-operatives have developed widely in Canada in numerous kinds of communities (MacPherson 1979; Fulton 1990; Fairbairn et al. 2000). They have proven to be a sustainable model for rural development (Fairbairn et al. 1991; Fulton and Hammond Ketilson 1992; Gertler 2004) and play an exceptional role in northern communities (Hammond Ketilson and MacPherson 2001). Newer types of co-operatives such as those involved in health, housing, childcare, alternative energy generation, and neighbourhood development, address the economic needs of low-income and other urban as well as rural groups (Macmurtry 2010). The distribution of co-operatives—their historical strength in rural communities and their new role in some indigenous and marginalized urban populations—is not accidental. It reflects the degree to which they developed by making use of social cohesion (DeSantis et al. 2003; Fairbairn and Russell 2014), both exploiting it and fostering it, as well as democratic structures and processes, in order to thrive in settings where other forms of enterprise could not succeed so well (Fulton and Hammond Ketilson 1992; Hammond Ketilson and MacPherson 2001; Fairbairn and Russell 2004).

Within Canada, co-operatives are typically grassroots in origin, emphasizing local innovation, understanding, and theory making. Democratic practice, citizen participation, and meaningful engagement are key. Social cohesion is about membership—citizenship in a state, residency in a geographic community, participation in a network or culture.

Co-operative enterprises are embedded in communities, often multiple communities of place and identities or interests, and these communities are themselves embedded within institutional contexts. Such enterprises, then, are continually negotiating boundaries that would circumscribe who they are and can be, whom they may represent and serve, what they can do and how, and with whom they can forge links. In this context, the growth and vigour of a co-operative depends on the innovation, improvization, and collective intelligence of its key players. Competitors for resources must become partners; providers of resources must reduce barriers; and all must maintain critical vigilance about their roles and responsibilities in a social economy that is plural and potentially transformative.

Co-operative enterprises are themselves innovative partnerships, and they readily partner with other organizations. Each partnership requires new approaches to collaboration, new ways of honouring identities and building relationships, new ways of inhabiting institutional and other spaces, new ways of engaging with the privileges and priorities of hinterland–homeland relations (Coates 2001; Davis 1971; Hammond Ketilson 2014). The work of effective partnering is never easy, but with vigilance, co-operative movements can make a place for new ways of doing things—and new forms of relationship connecting healthy people and vigorous, sustainable economies. They can help us move from principles of scarcity to celebrating our diversity and ending practices that waste, neglect, or discard rich resources of people and knowledge.

Well-functioning co-operative organizations pursue human and social development as part of their own success. In so doing, they contribute to wider policy goals.

But routine governance that is adequate for other purposes may not achieve these wider aims. For example, unless diversity among stakeholders is represented in governance, it is difficult for a co-operative organization to bridge between different categories of stakeholders and promote their effective collaboration. The roles and importance of leadership/representational diversity (de Clercy and Hammond Ketilson 2004) and of the functioning of multi-stakeholder boards (Leviten-Reid and Fairbairn 2011) are two significant themes of special importance.

24.3 MEASURING THE IMPACT OF CO-OPERATIVES ON COMMUNITIES

It is important to measure and report on such behaviours in a way consistent with what co-operatives are trying to achieve in keeping with co-operative principles. In addition to measures of business growth and stability, it is critical to measure the outcome of the relationship between the social and economic objectives of the co-operative (Brown et. al. 2015; Hammond Ketilson et al. 2015). The seventh co-operative principle, for instance, motivates co-operatives to demonstrate a commitment to community.

Within the Desjardins system of Quebec, this commitment is reflected in the goal to bring long-term prosperity to small business and society. The view is that a financial co-operative must be responsive to ordinary people, and support and contribute to the real economy. Within the credit union system in Canada, the easiest way to measure commitment is the amount invested through donations and sponsorships, scholarships and bursaries, charitable fundraising, and contributions to community economic development. In 2010 credit unions donated $37.6 million to support communities across Canada, an amount equal to 4 per cent of their pre-tax net income and almost four times the average pre-tax contribution of the big six banks of 1.1 per cent (CUCC 2011). In 2013, combined contributions of Credit Union Central of Canada affiliated credit unions and the Desjardins Financial Group returned $130 million to the community through sponsorships, donations, and bursaries (CUCC 2014: 1; Desjardins 2015).

24.4 WAYS IN WHICH CO-OPERATIVES CONTRIBUTE TO THE DEVELOPMENT OF COMMUNITIES

Previous studies examining the impact of co-operatives on communities (Hammond Ketilson et al. 1998) have identified particular benefits associated with the formation of co-operatives in the following three areas: building and strengthening physical infrastructure, personal infrastructure, and social infrastructure (social capital). An analysis of eleven case studies found similar benefits (Hammond Ketilson and MacPherson 2001).

24.4.1 Building and Strengthening Physical Infrastructure

Co-operatives contribute to the development of the physical infrastructure—roads, telecommunications, services—of a community through the construction of facilities and provision of services inadequately or not currently provided by government or the private sector. While it is more often in remote and rural communities that co-operatives play a major role in adding to and improving the physical infrastructure available to community residents, examples can also be found in large urban settings where market forces are not currently serving the needs of marginalized communities.

Within the remote north, co-operatives such as Ikaluktutiak offer retail services to provide food and housing essentials to the community, as well as other services—cable hook-up, for example. Through operating hotels and a craft-marketing co-operative, they provide employment as well, while facilitating the development of the tourism industry.

The Kahnawake First Nation had not been well served by the traditional banks, which often had little or no awareness of Aboriginal laws and culture, and had been reluctant to do business in the community. The criteria for granting loans—stable and permanent employment—was not consistent with the seasonal work force living on the reserve in winter, and working construction sites during the summer. The lending rules established by Caisse Populaire Kahnawake, located near Montreal, recognized the cultural realities of the First Nation, thereby providing a mechanism to support personal and business loans, assisting with economic development in the community.

24.4.2 Building and Strengthening Personal Infrastructure

The development of individual leadership within a community has been demonstrated to be one of three aspects critical for the development and maintenance of vibrant and entrepreneurial communities (Flora 1998). Education, training, and leadership development are central to principles of every co-operative, and examples within the Aboriginal co-operatives support the critical role leadership development plays in the success of the organizations.

Researchers identified enhanced self-esteem as a result of small and large accomplishments through involvement with a co-operative. This very positive aspect was echoed in comments by the members of Neechi Food Co-op, a worker co-operative located in an inner-city neighbourhood in Winnipeg. Neechi advocates the specific goal of ensuring that workplace stress does not disrupt co-operative relationships and adversely affect the healing process upon which indigenous members have embarked.

The Caisse Populaire Kahnawake has invested considerable effort in training its employees, with the assistance of the Fédération des caisses populaires Desjardins de Montreal et de l'Ouest-du-Québec. Most of the employees had never worked in a financial institution before, so the caisse offered them complete on-the-job training.

Participation in management training programmes is available through Arctic Co-operatives Limited, a member-owned wholesale serving the community co-ops of Nunavut and the North West Territories of Canada's Arctic. The opportunity to take part in leadership training and the democratic processes involved in running a co-operative, have contributed to the fundamental skills required to move on to positions of leadership in the recently formed Nunavut government. A large percentage of members participating in a human resource development initiative offered by Arctic Co-operatives Limited in the early 1980s went on to become hamlet managers, housing association managers, and members of parliament. At the time of the study, ten members of the Nunavut Legislature had had significant experience and training within the co-operatives (Hammond Ketilson and MacPherson 2001).

24.4.3 Building and Strengthening Social Infrastructure

A third necessary component that enables communities to exhibit entrepreneurial characteristics—social infrastructure or social capital—is the key ingredient that ties together the physical and human, allowing the community to develop. Unlike other forms of capital, social capital is not a single entity but a variety with elements in common, brought about through networks, social norms, and social trust. Community members develop social capital only through co-operation and mutual aid.

Co-operatives enhance the opportunities for the development of social capital within indigenous communities. For example, by working through Arctic Co-operatives Limited, remote communities have accessed, not only a broad network of suppliers for products and services, but they have also absorbed new ideas, training programmes, and managerial expertise that was not easily available in the north. Membership in Arctic Co-operatives means membership in Co-operatives and Mutuals Canada, and representation within the International Co-operative Alliance—and thereby access to ideas from across the world. On a local level, Arctic Co-operatives, in addition to the employment they have provided, have markedly increased the capacity of people to understand effective business practice, to assess economic activities, to reach consensus on complex issues, and to contribute to community economic and social development.

Caisse Populaire Kahnawake was the first banking institution to introduce a system of guarantees adapted specifically to the First Nation communities. Under this model, known as a 'trust agreement', trustees are used as third parties when loans are guaranteed. Because the trustees are members of the indigenous community, they may receive land as security and sell it to reimburse the caisse, in the event the borrower is unable to repay. The trustees are all volunteers and are politically independent—not appointed by a federal or provincial agency, or the band council. The Caisse Populaire Kahnawake has contributed to the development of social infrastructure by providing a mechanism to contain and recirculate financial resources within the community. With the support of the Desjardins federation, management training and technical support are made available, enhancing the ability of the community to access additional resources to further economic and social development.

24.5 CONTRIBUTIONS TO BUILDING COMMUNITY

Since the early 2000s, research carried out across Canada has demonstrated the essential role that co-operatives and credit unions have played within the social economy to improve the economic and social well-being of communities (Thompson and Emmanuel 2012). An analysis of the Northern Ontario, Manitoba, and Saskatchewan Social Economy Network projects provides evidence of four foundational elements central to this outcome: an engaged citizenry, entrepreneurial activity, sustainable approaches, and inclusive practices (Building Community 2011).

24.5.1 Engaged Citizenry

The engagement of citizens is critical to a healthy democratic society. Engagement is about connections and interactions, building relationships among people who work together for a common goal. It's about encouraging participation—determining local priorities and involving everyone in planning and making decisions. It's about acknowledging local expertise and acting on it. There are varying dynamics in community engagement, and a variety of strategies to ensure its success.

Co-operatives provide many opportunities to engage citizens through involvement in their co-ops. More than 100,000 Canadians are actively involved as volunteers on committees and boards of directors of their local co-operatives. Credit union and retail co-op employees collectively donate thousands of volunteer hours to events in their communities every year.

Participation on co-op boards at early stages in their careers has contributed significantly to the leadership skills of elected officials at all levels of government. Co-operative-sponsored education and training initiatives engage members, increasing their involvement in the organization and helping them develop the skills and confidence to take on additional leadership roles in their communities and beyond (Puchala and Heggie 2008).

In the early years of the Canadian west, however, co-operatives were a relatively unknown idea. Arriving from England in 1937, Watson Thomson believed that people would become emotionally connected if communities came together to discuss their personal and economic needs. Engaging thousands of people in his study-action groups, Thomson aimed to transform Saskatchewan and the other Prairie Provinces into an economically, socially, and culturally prosperous example of co-operative endeavour. Watson Thomson brought hundreds of thousands of Canadians to political conferences and 'coffee talks' via National Film Board documentaries (Chartier 2010). In 1944, he became director of Saskatchewan's Adult Education Division, charged with developing the 'biggest adult education program in the country'. Throughout early 1945, local communities and national leaders praised Thomson and his division for their community development and adult education work. They engaged citizens in discussions of controversial topics through the 'Living Newspaper' which combined a weekly paper with a live radio broadcast. Citizens across Saskatchewan provided Thomson and the division with their thoughts on local, national, and international issues.

The Adult Education Division was enormously successful, developing more than 1,500 study-action groups and nearly 100 co-operatives in a little over a year. The division continued to develop and distribute technical and informational brochures across Saskatchewan, leaving future generations to pursue Thomson's dream (Chartier 2010).

24.5.2 Entrepreneurial Activity

Economic development is often discussed in terms of stimulus packages, tax incentives, and cash injections. These methods rarely yield long-term stability and often result in temporary growth, large industry, or outside investment. Community economic development focuses on the needs of the whole community (CCEDNET 2015) and uses internal resources to create lasting results (Wuttunee et al. 2008).

Co-operative development utilizing a community economic approach focuses on local solutions to local problems, with communities using their own resources, skills, and abilities as the starting point for growth. Ideally this involves the entire community in creating a long-term plan that includes environmental, economic, and social outcomes. It promotes local ownership and local capacity building so the benefits of economic growth stay in the community (Birchall and Hammond Ketilson 2009)

PARO is a Latin term that means 'I am ready'. This is a fitting motto for the innovative organization that has enabled hundreds of women across Northern Ontario to build the skills and confidence, and acquire the funds, to become successful entrepreneurs. Although not a co-operative itself, PARO uses collaborative strategies to enable women to start their own small businesses, many of which are co-operatives. The organization offers training in important skills such as how to write business plans, apply for loans, and manage customer service. PARO also sets up peer networks that provide personal support and access to funding. PARO's goal is to give women the confidence to be independent and self-sufficient in both their business and personal lives. An added bonus is how this contributes to stronger families and communities.

Peer lending circles provide members with advice and support for their businesses, using a non-traditional lending model to access capital. Members review and approve one another's loan applications, give references for each other, and are collectively accountable for loan repayment. Capital comes from PARO's partners in the local financial community. Giving women access to financing for their micro-enterprises increases the entire community's capacity for economic self-reliance (PARO Centre for Women's Enterprise 2009).

24.5.3 Sustainable Approaches

Discussions about sustainability often address only environmental concerns, but when exploring community building it is also important to consider social, economic, and human issues. Healthy communities recognize the value of protecting significant social, cultural, and historical aspects of their heritage (Mayhew et al. 2008).

The Harvest Moon Society's Local Food Initiative is a Manitoba-based marketing collective that helps farmers market their products—beef, poultry, pork, fresh vegetables, and grains—directly to consumers in the area.

The Harvest Moon Society is about more than marketing. Education and celebration are important elements of their organization. They advocate for sustainable food systems through education about production methods and land use. They create linkages between rural and urban citizens through exchanges, retreats, and workshops. But the best part might be the pot-lucks, the annual Harvest Moon Festival, and other grassroots initiatives that unite and empower communities (Anderson and McLachlan 2012).

Producers across the country felt the financial burden of the BSE crisis. Co-operative marketing initiatives and community-supported agriculture are examples of how farmers use creativity and determination to change catastrophe into opportunity. With markets at an all-time low, some ranchers developed direct-marketing businesses to sell their beef. Consumers concerned about the safety of conventional beef turned to these local food sources, where trust-based relationships provided reassurance of safe, healthy food. Building on the momentum of the local food movement, these initiatives represent an important alternative to the traditional food system and are challenging the way we think about food (Novek and Nichols 2010).

24.5.4 Inclusive Practices

Co-operatives and other forms of social enterprise continue to play central roles in ensuring that all members of our communities feel welcome and have access to social and economic benefit (Fairbairn and Russell 2014; Hammond Ketilson 2014). They build their success on the strength of the group, whose pooled resources can achieve more than any one individual. The 'one member, one vote' principle ensures that each member has an equal say in how the co-op is run, setting policy, making decisions, and electing a board of directors. The democratic nature of co-ops empowers their members and facilitates inclusion. Co-operative organizations have assisted newcomers to Canada, and those long established who have not historically had equal opportunities.

The Northern Saskatchewan Trappers Association Co-operative (NSTAC) was formed to guide trapping development and advocate for northern trappers. As a co-operative, it is using its voice to secure support for trapping, preserve Aboriginal culture, protect the land, increase economic opportunities, practise sustainable food production, encourage young people to relearn their identities, and reconnect the generations for hope, healing, and health (Findlay et al. 2012; Pattison and Findlay 2010). Viewing young people as key actors in the co-op's future, NSTAC is working hard to include youth and renew their sense of cultural identity. Through school programming and trapper training, the NSTAC shares the knowledge, skills, and benefits of a traditional trapper lifestyle. The Justice Trapline is an initiative designed to engage young people. The pilot project paired young offenders with experienced trappers on the trapline. The youth learned to build cabins and canoes and prepare food and pelts, reconnecting with traditional Aboriginal culture and rebuilding their self-confidence. It also provided them with the knowledge and skills to face life challenges and see trapping as a way of life that can sustain them in their home communities (Findlay 2010).

24.6 Conclusions

Many years of research into the social economy across Canada has demonstrated that it is strong and diverse (Bouchard 2013; Thompson and Emmanuel 2012; Downing 2012; Macmurtry 2010). Co-operatives are the dominant organizational form; not-for-profit associations and social enterprises are significant players as well. Co-operatives and other forms of social economy organizations have built and strengthened rural and remote rural communities, and have contributed important services in urban centres. Sustainable food production, consumer-sponsored agriculture and alternative energy production are emerging growth areas which demonstrate a commitment to sustainable practices. Civic engagement and democratic decision-making are fundamental characteristics, empowering communities to direct social and economic initiatives in directions consistent with community needs. Traditionally marginalized communities have found inclusion through co-operatives focused on the disability community, newcomers, and others often disadvantaged in the employment market. Within indigenous communities, the social economy takes the form of band-owned enterprises and social service delivery associations. It is playing a growing role in resource-based economic development in forestry and non-timber forest products (Weinberg 2014a, 2014b). In Canada's northern indigenous communities, co-operatives play a central role.

Across Canada, the diversity of impacts from globalization and other internally and externally generated change, requires diverse approaches which may be more likely to pursue radical options. Today there tends to be more focus on the local, allowing for greater flexibility and innovation. These conditions contribute to an increased interest in co-operative organizations, whose strengths offer great potential for the future.

References

Anderson, C. and McLachlan, S. (2012), 'Community-Based Regional Food Distribution Initiatives'. Research Report prepared for the Northern Ontario, Manitoba, and Saskatchewan Regional Node of the Social Economy Suite. Saskatoon: Centre for the Study of Co-operatives, 2012.

Bauman, Z. (1988), *Globalization: The Human Consequences* (Cambridge: Polity Press).

Birchall, J. and Hammond Ketilson, L. (2009), *Resilience of the Co-operative Business Model in Times of Crisis* (Geneva: International Labour Organization).

Bouchard, M. J., ed. (2009), *The Worth of the Social Economy: An International Perspective* (Brussels: PIE Peter Lang, Ciriec collection Social Economy and Public Economy).

Bouchard, M. J. (2013), *Innovation in the Social Economy: The Quebec Experience* (Toronto: University of Toronto Press).

Bouchard, M. J., Ferraton, C., and Michaud, V. (2006), *Database on Social Economy organizations: The Qualification Criteria* (Montreal: Chaire de recherche du Canada en économie, Université du Québec a Montreal).

Brown, L., Carini, C., Gordon Nembhard, J., Hammond Ketilson, L., Hicks, E., Mcnamara, J., Novkovic, S., Rixon, D., and Simmons, R., eds (2015), *Co-operatives for Sustainable Communities: Tools to Measure Co-operative Impact and Performance* (Saskatoon and Ottawa: Centre for the Study of Co-operatives and Co-operatives and Mutuals Canada).

'Building Community: Creating Social and Economic Well-Being' (2011), An exhibit created by the Centre for the Study of Co-operatives in partnership with the Diefenbaker Canada Centre, University of Saskatchewan. http://usaskstudies.coop/news-and-events/building-community-virtual-exhibit.php (accessed 20 September 2016).

Canadian Community Economic Development Network. Available at https://ccednet-rcdec.ca/en/what_is_ced (accessed 20 September 2016).

Chartier, M. (2010), 'Adult Education and the Social Economy: The Communitarian Pedagogy of Watson Thomson'. MA thesis, College of Education, University of Saskatchewan.

de Clercy, C. and Hammond Ketilson, L. (2004), *Tapping the Talents of People: Board Diversity Research Report/Leadership and Diversity: A Study of Demographic and Attitudinal Homogeneity in Saskatchewan's Credit Union Governance Groups: Summary of Findings* (Saskatoon: Centre for the Study of Co-operatives, University of Saskatchewan).

Coates, K. (2001), 'Northland: The Past, Present, and Future of Northern BC in an Age of Globalization', in R. Epp and D. Whitson, eds, *Writing Off the Rural West: Globalization, Governments and the Transformation of Rural Communities* (Edmonton: The University of Alberta Press and Parkland Institute), 109–25.

Credit Union Central of Canada (CUCC). 'System Brief. December 2011'. Available at http://www.cucentral.ca/SitePages/CreditUnionIssues/Publications.aspx (accessed 20 September 2016).

Credit Union Central of Canada (CUCC) (2014). 'System Brief: National Credit Union Social Responsibility Forum Summary', December 2014. http://www.cucentral.ca/SitePages/CreditUnionIssues/Publications.aspx (accessed 20 September 2016).

Davis, A. K. (1971), 'Canadian Society and History as Hinterland Versus Metropolis', in R. J. Ossenberg, ed., *Canadian Society: Pluralism, Change, and Conflict* (Scarborough: Prentice-Hall), 6–35.

DeSantis, G., Gill, C., and Theriault, L. (2003), '"Social Economy" in Saskatchewan—An Historical Glance at Related Concepts, Meanings and Influences.' Document prepared for discussion. School of Social Work, University of Regina.

Desjardins. Website home page: http://www.desjardins.com/ca/about-us/desjardins/who-we-are/quick-facts/index.jsp (accessed 20 September 2016).

Downing, R., ed. (2012), *Canadian Public Policy and the Social Economy* (Victoria: University of Victoria).

Fairbairn, B., Bold, J., Fulton, M., Hammond Ketilson, L., and Ish, D. (1991), *Co-operatives and Community Development: Economics in Social Perspective* (Saskatoon: Centre for the Study of Co-operatives).

Fairbairn, B., MacPherson, I., and N., eds (2000), *Canadian Co-operatives in the Year 2000: Memory, Mutual Aid and the Millennium* (Saskatoon: Centre for the Study of Co-operatives).

Fairbairn, B. and Russell, N., eds (2004), *Co-operative Membership and Globalization: New Directions in Research and Practice* (Saskatoon: Centre for the Study of Co-operatives, University of Saskatchewan).

Fairbairn, B. and Russell, N., eds (2014), *Co-operative Canada: Empowering Communities and Sustainable Businesses* (Vancouver: University of British Columbia Press).

Findlay, I. M. (2010), 'Rebuilding Sustainable Livelihoods: Engaging Aboriginal Youth in the Northern Saskatchewan Trappers Association Co-operative', International Co-operative Alliance European Research Conference Co-operatives Contributions to a Plural Economy: Abstracts. Lyons, France: Université Lumière Lyon 2, 2–4 September.

Findlay, I. M., Ray, C., and Basualdo, M. (2012), 'Research as Engagement: Rebuilding the Knowledge Economy of the Northern Trappers Association Co-operative', in P. V. Hall and I. MacPherson, eds, *Community-University Partnerships: Reflections on the Canadian Social Economy Experience* (Victoria: University of Victoria).

Flora, J. L. (1998), Social Capital and Communities of Place, *Rural Sociology* 63(4), 481–506.

Fulton, M. E., ed. (1990), *Co-operative Organizations and Canadian Society: Popular Institutions and the Dilemmas of Change* (Toronto: University of Toronto Press).

Fulton, M. E. and Hammond Ketilson, L. (1992), 'The Role of Cooperatives in Communities: Examples from Saskatchewan, *Journal of Agricultural Cooperation* 7, 15–42.

Gertler, M. (2004), 'Synergy and Strategic Advantage: Cooperatives and Sustainable Development', *Journal of Cooperatives* 19, 32–46.

Hammond Ketilson, L. (2014), 'First Nations Co-operatives in Canada: (Re)inventing Appropriate Forms of Enterprise', in B. Fairbairn and N. Russell, eds, *Co-operative Canada: Empowering Communities and Sustainable Businesses* (Vancouver: University of British Columbia Press).

Hammond Ketilson, L., Gertler, M., Fulton, M., Dobson, R., and Polsom, L. (1998), *The Social and Economic Importance of the Co-operative Sector in Saskatchewan* (Saskatoon: Centre for the Study of Co-operatives).

Hammond Ketilson, L., Gordon Nembhard, J., and Hewitt, M. (2015), 'Assessing the Impact of Credit Unions on Their Communities: A Pre-Test of Possible Indicators', in L. Brown,

C. Carini, J. Gordon Nembhard, L. Hammond Ketilson, E. Hicks, J. McNamara, S. Novkovic, D. Rixon, and R. Simmons, eds, *Co-operatives for Sustainable Communities: Tools to Measure Co-operative Impact and Performance* (Saskatoon and Ottawa: Centre for the Study of Co-operatives and Co-operatives and Mutuals Canada).

Hammond Ketilson, L. and MacPherson, I. (2001), *A Report on Aboriginal Co-operatives in Canada: Current Situations and Potential for Growth* (Saskatoon: Centre for the Study of Co-operatives).

Lévesque, B. (1998), *The Social Economy in Québec* (Ottawa: Human Resources Development Canada).

Lévesque, B. and Malo, M.-C. (1992), 'The "Social Economy" in Quebec: A Misunderstood Concept, a Significant Economic Fact, in J. Defourny and J. L. Monzon Campos, eds, *Économie sociale: Entre économie capitaliste et économie publique/The Third Sector Cooperative, Mutual and Nonprofit Organizations* (Bruxelles: De Boeck-Université/CIRIEC,).

Leviten-Reid, C. and Fairbairn, B. (2011), 'Multi-stakeholder Governance in Cooperative Organizations: Toward a New Framework for Research?', *Canadian Journal of Nonprofit and Social Economy Research* 2(2), 25–36.

Macmurtry, J. J., ed. (2010), *Living Economics: Perspectives on Canada's Social Economy* (Toronto: Emond Montgomery Publications).

MacPherson, I. (1979), *Each for All: A History of the Co-operative Movement in English Canada, 1900-1945* (Toronto: Macmillan Co.).

Mayhew, M., Fernandez, C., and Chevrette, L. (2008), 'Community Supported Agriculture: Putting the "Culture" Back into Agriculture'. Research Report prepared for the Northern Ontario, Manitoba, and Saskatchewan Regional Node of the Social Economy Suite. Saskatoon: Centre for the Study of Co-operatives.

Novek, J. and Nichols, C. (2010), 'Eat Where You Live: Building a Social Economy of Local Food in Western Canada'. Research Report prepared for the Northern Ontario, Manitoba, and Saskatchewan Regional Node of the Social Economy Suite. Saskatoon: Centre for the Study of Co-operatives.

PARO Centre for Women's Enterprise, (2009), 'Northern Ontario Women's Economic Development Conference Report'. Research Report prepared for the Northern Ontario, Manitoba, and Saskatchewan Regional Node of the Social Economy Suite. Saskatoon: Centre for the Study of Co-operatives.

Pattison, D. and Findlay, I. M. (2010), 'Self-Determination in Action: The Entrepreneurship of the Northern Saskatchewan Trappers Association Co-operative'. Research Report prepared for the Northern Ontario, Manitoba, and Saskatchewan Regional Node of the Social Economy Suite. Saskatoon: Centre for the Study of Co-operatives.

Puchala, C. and Heggie, B. (2008), *Co-operative Youth Education in Saskatchewan: Co-op Schools and the Saskatchewan Co-operative Youth Program* (Saskatoon: Centre for the Study of Co-operatives).

Quarter, J. (1992), *Canada's Social Economy: Co-operatives, Non-Profits, and Other Community Enterprises* (Toronto: James Lorimer & Company).

Scholte, Jan Aart (2000), *Globalization: A Critical Introduction* (Basingstoke, UK: Macmillan).

Shragge, E. and Fontan, J. M. (2000), *Social Economy: International Debates and Perspectives* (Montreal/New York: Black Rose Books).

Thompson, M. and Emmanuel, J. (2012), *Assembling Understandings: Findings From the Canadian Social Economy Research Partnerships, 2005-2011* (Victoria: University of Victoria).

Weinberg, A. (2014a), 'The Reality of the Social Economy and Its Empowering Potential for Boreal Anishinaabek Communities in Eastern Manitoba'. Research Report prepared for the Northern Ontario, Manitoba, and Saskatchewan Regional Node of the Social Economy Suite. Saskatoon: Centre for the Study of Co-operatives.

Weinberg, A. (2014b), 'Relying on their Own Resources: Building an Anishinaabek-Run, Sustainable Economy in the East Side Boreal—Waabanong—of Lake Winnipeg'. Research Report prepared for the Northern Ontario, Manitoba, and Saskatchewan Regional Node of the Social Economy Suite. Saskatoon: Centre for the Study of Co-operatives.

Wuttunee, W., Chicilo, M., Rothney, R., and Gray, L. (2008), 'Financing Social Enterprise: An Enterprise Perspective'. Research Report prepared for the Northern Ontario, Manitoba, and Saskatchewan Regional Node of the Social Economy Suite. Saskatoon: Centre for the Study of Co-operatives.

CHAPTER 25

....

SHARED CAPITALISM
IN THE USA

evaluation and future policies

....

JOSEPH R. BLASI AND DOUGLAS L. KRUSE

25.1 INTRODUCTION

....

UNDERSTANDING policies to advance shared capitalism in the United States and the
world requires a current measurement of how much broad-based ownership at the
workplace currently exists in the USA, a brief overview of current policies, and some
far-reaching suggestions to expand these policies in a way that would meaningfully
expand worker ownership.

25.2 HOW MUCH BROAD-BASED
OWNERSHIP AT THE WORKPLACE
CURRENTLY EXISTS IN THE USA

....

To find out the extent of workplace-based profit-sharing and equity ownership, we
commissioned a special supplement to the General Social Survey (GSS) of the National
Opinion Research Center at the University of Chicago for 2002, 2006, 2010, and 2014.
The General Social Survey is a national random sample of the entire adult working population of the United States and is administered every two years. The General Social
Survey is supported by the US Government's National Science Foundation and is the
most widely used social survey for national data in the USA. The co-authors of this
chapter received support principally from the Employee Ownership Foundation with

additional support from other non-profit groups in order to commission this survey. The GSS is based on a national representative sample of all adult workers in the nation. The data are based on the 2006 and 2010 General Social Survey and will be updated when the 2014 survey data are available in 2016.

In light of the historical traditions mentioned in Chapter 8 *The Oxford Handbook of Mutual, Co-operative, and Co-owned Business* on broad-based property ownership and the wide experimentation in American industry on ways of distributing shares to workers in businesses, the United States is distinguished by a varied group of worker shares. Profit-sharing is most common and involves a formal or an informal commitment by the firm to share pre-tax profits with workers. There is no special legislation in the United States specifically encouraging cash profit-sharing as there is in some other countries (such as, for example, France). Rather, cash profit-sharing by a company is 100 per cent deductible as a business expense, just as wages are so deductible, from corporate income before federal corporate taxes are estimated for a company. Gain-sharing occurs when a company offers to share gains with workers. Gains are defined as any improvement in the firm's operations that can be measured in dollars that are not accounting profits and that are dependent on a group, team, department, or subdivision of the firm that is typically close in proximity to a specific employee group. For example, a gain could be an increase in sales or an improvement in quality, or on-time deliveries, and so forth.

Equity-sharing or employee ownership or employee stock ownership or worker ownership refers to ownership by workers of a individual ownership share in the firm where they work. This could either be structured as a stock market 'share' in a company listed on the stock exchange, or a share in a joint-stock company that is closely held (namely, not traded on a listed exchange), or a share in a worker co-operative structured as a classic worker co-operative or even as a limited partnership. Recently, in the United States, companies have granted restricted shares broadly to workers. Grants of restricted stock shares vest (namely, become legally available to workers) typically if the worker stays with the firm for a specific period of time. Firms are also granting 'performance shares' to workers broadly. These shares become legally available to workers typically dependent on certain performance goals being achieved by the firm or the business unit, such as a level of profit or share price increase, and so forth. In the United States, stock options are granted to workers in both listed stock market companies and in closely held businesses not traded on stock exchanges. A stock option is not a whole share of stock but the right of a worker to buy a share of stock for a specific period into the future, typically ten years in the USA, at the price the 'option' was granted. For example, Worker W receives one stock option on 1 January 2017 at $100 a share. The option is always granted at the price the share is trading on the day of the grant. This entitles Worker W to buy the stock for $100 for ten years. Thus, if in five years on 1 January 2022, the stock is trading at $150, Worker W can purchase a share of stock trading at $150 on 1 January 2022 for $100. Worker W then has the choice to sell the stock and take the $50 profit in cash or retain the stock and hope it goes up in price. In some sense, a stock option is similar to profit-sharing, since it shares the future upside on the equity value of the stock, which typically reflects the prospects of the firm's long-term profits.

Figure 25.1 shows that 47 per cent of adult workers in the United States have some form of profit/gain-sharing, or broad-based worker ownership, or broad-based stock options, or some combination of the these different forms. All of these forms of shares can be considered to be 'capital stakes in the firm'. About a third of all workers with shares have all three. The 2010 GSS shows that 17.4 per cent of adult workers had stock in their companies, and 8.7 per cent held stock options. More union workers proportionally than non-union workers have stock options and almost as many have employee stock ownership. Much of the worker ownership is because of Employee Stock Ownership Plans (ESOPs). The 2006 GSS established that about a third of US adult workers had profit-sharing and a fourth of US adult workers had gain-sharing. The reason for reporting all forms of shares initially is because in the USA, largely consistent with the historical tradition mentioned in Chapter 8 *The Oxford Handbook of Mutual, Co-operative, and Co-owned Business*, many firms will use combinations of profit/gain-sharing, different forms of worker ownership, and stock options. Even some pure worker co-operatives are known to practise cash profit-sharing.

Figure 25.2 shows the median and mean value of equity and profit shares. For profit shares and gain-sharing, the median share granted in the last year for which data were available was $2,000, which compares with $6,935 for the mean. Profit/gain-sharing have wide incidence but very low average annual dollar values in the USA. For worker ownership shares, the $10,000 median and $32,692 mean are the total value of all equity shares (forms of direct worker ownership) currently held at the time of the survey from all past years in which they were bought or granted. To underline this, the worker ownership measure reflects the dollar value of all worker ownership accumulated over the worker's tenure at the firm as of the day of the survey. Note that average worker ownership tends to be much higher than these national or median values in ESOPs which, as noted in Chapter 15 and Chapter 8, often have 30–50 per cent, majority, or 100 per cent ownership of the entire firm. For example, based on a study of 3,976 ESOPs for which all US Federal Government reporting information was

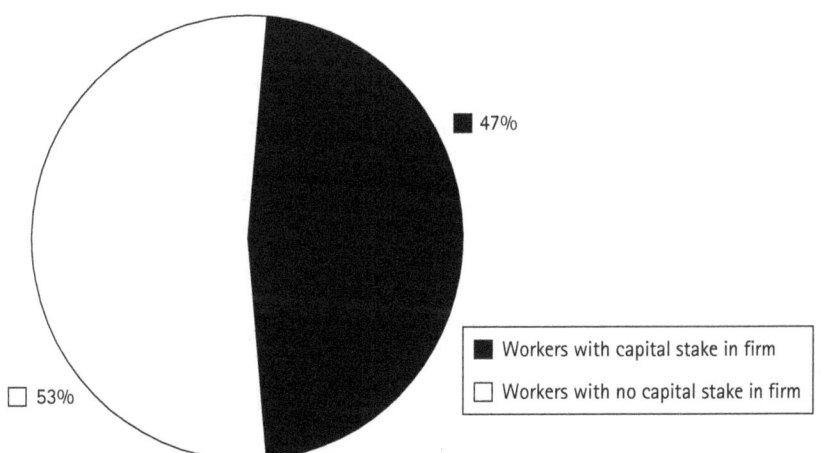

FIGURE 25.1 Citizens' shares in the United States.

Source: The Citizen's Share by Joseph Blasi, Richard Freeman, and Douglas Kruse (New Haven: Yale University Press, 2015), p. 112.

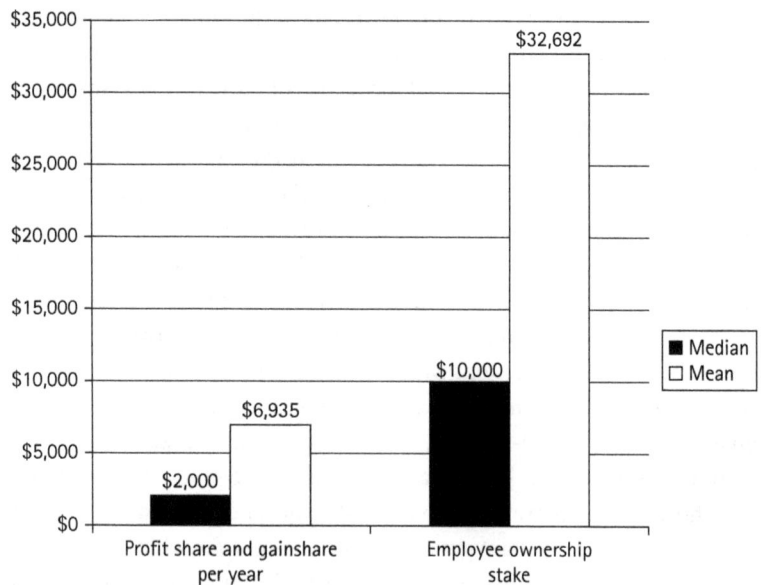

FIGURE 25.2 How much is the typical citizen's share?

Source: The Citizen's Share by Joseph Blasi, Richard Freeman, and Douglas Kruse
(New Haven: Yale University Press, 2015), p. 115.

available in 2006 and 2006 ESOPs (in other words, a population study), the average ESOP employee had an average account value of $55,836 (Rodgers 2010). Other data suggest that workers with stock options would have a median profit net of exercise of those stock options of $75,000 (mean of $249,900). Figure 25.2 illustrates that shares of profits and equity reach modest levels at the median. The rest of this discussion focuses only on worker ownership because that is the focus of this volume.

Figure 25.3 contrasts workers at different income levels in the national representative sample. The black bar shows typical or median employee ownership only for workers who reported to the GSS that they were paid at or above the market rate for their fixed wage, so those amounts net out possible substitution of wages for ownership. This is an important issue since, for policy purposes, the only worker ownership that is really meaningful is worker ownership on top of fair fixed wages. If worker ownership is in place of fair fixed wages then it is really what economists call 'wage substitution' and could result in lower wages for workers. The white bar represents workers in the top quarter of incomes. Workers making less than $50,000 have about $20,000 in worker ownership shares, but those with shares in the 25 per cent most generous plans accumulated about $40,000.

Figure 25.4 illustrates the incidence of worker owners in the United States by company size, industry, and occupation. The way to read this chart is that x per cent of all the adult workers in each category in the entire USA have worker ownership. For example, the figure shows that just over 40 per cent of all workers in companies of more than 10,000 employees own stock in the company where they work. Larger companies

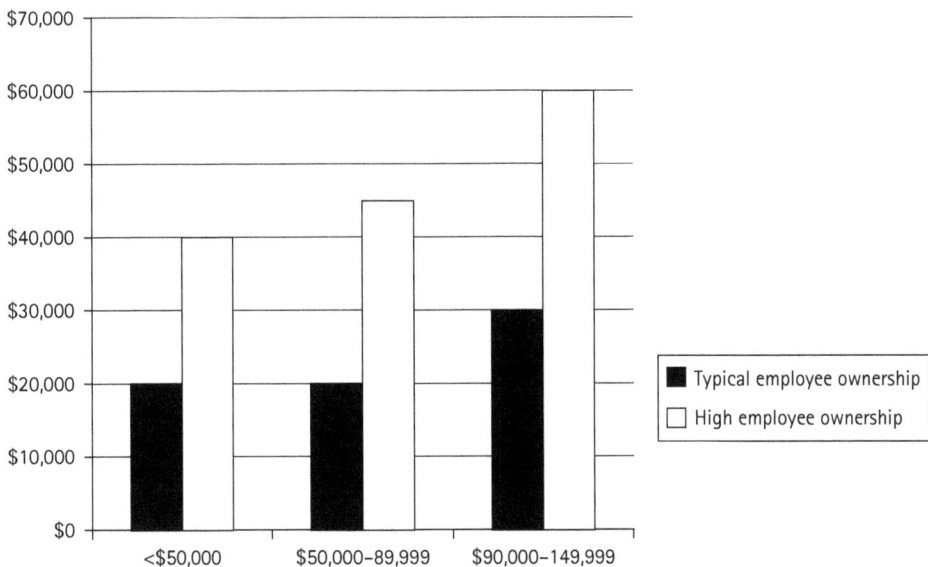

FIGURE 25.3 Employee ownership and income levels.

Source: The Citizen's Share by Joseph Blasi, Richard Freeman, and Douglas Kruse
(New Haven: Yale University Press, 2015), p. 120.

have more employee ownership plans. Worker shares are frequent in most industries except for the wholesale sector and are quite common in communications/utilities and nondurable manufacturing, representing more than 25 per cent of all the workers in the industry.

The figures on company size categories show that over 15 per cent of all workers in firms with 100 to 499 employees have equity shares, while over 30 per cent of workers in all firms with 500 to 999 workers have equity shares. These data largely reflect the importance of the ESOP sector in ownership in the United States. ESOPs are common, especially among closely held firms in these company size categories.

Because of specific reporting requirements for ESOPs in federal administrative data sets, we are able to look more closely at this form of employee ownership. Under US labour law, an ESOP qualifies as an employee benefit plan that gains certain tax benefits and must obey certain labour standards. As a result, every firm with an ESOP must file a Form 5500 with the U.S. Department of Labor and the U.S. Treasury's Internal Revenue Service (IRS), the federal tax collector. On the basis of U.S. Department of Labor data from the Form 5500s for the year 2011, which each ERISA (Employee Retirement Income Security Act) benefit plan, including ESOPs, must fill out annually, the National Center for Employee Ownership estimates there were about 7,000 ESOPs and ESOP-like plans with about 14 million employee participants and almost $1 trillion in market value in 2014. For comparative purposes, the value of the NYSE and NASDAQ were valued at approximately $25 trillion dollars at the end of October 2014 (National Center for Employee Ownership 2015). (A more detailed analysis of these data appears in Tables 1–3 of Chapter 29 by Corey Rosen.)

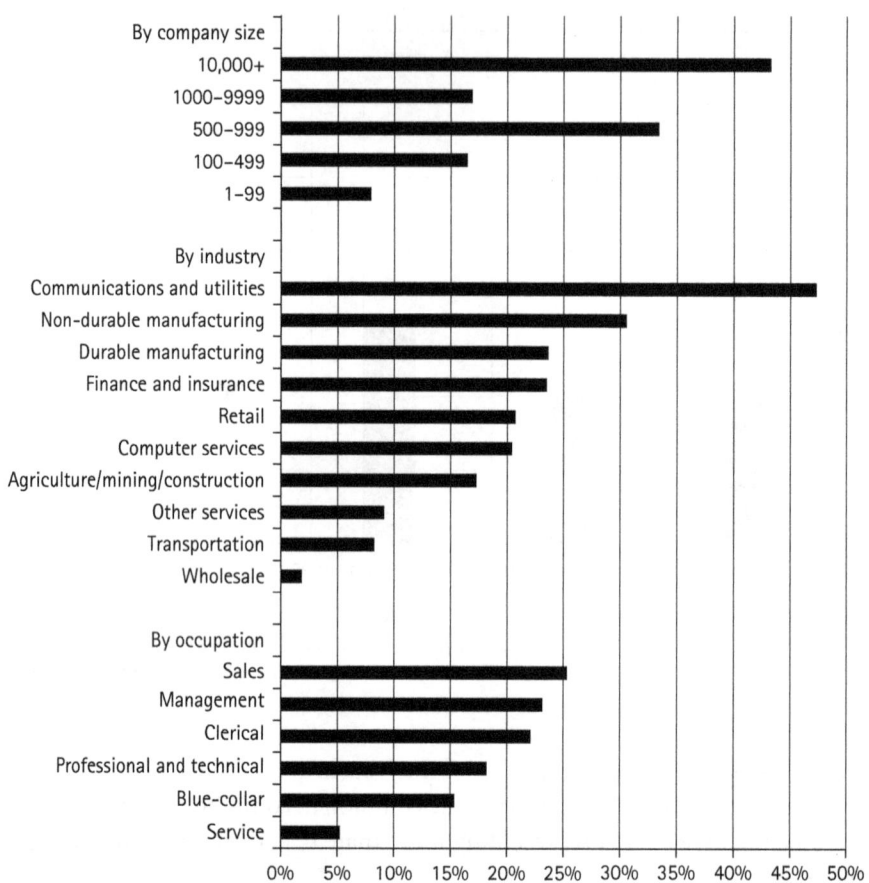

FIGURE 25.4 Employee ownership in different parts of the economy.

Source: The Citizen's Share by Joseph Blasi, Richard Freeman, and Douglas Kruse
(New Haven: Yale University Press, 2015), p. 117.

The National Center for Employee Ownership delves deeper into the data on ESOPs. Readers not familiar with corporate forms in the United States need to understand the difference between C corporations and S corporations. C corporations pay federal corporate taxes directly to the federal government, but S corporations pass their federal tax liability onto individual employee shareholders, who pay the taxes themselves directly to the Federal government. Sometimes observers of the US ESOP scene might be told or might say, 'S corporation ESOPs pay no Federal taxes.' That is in fact not accurate, rather, the tax liability is passed through to the individual employee owner/shareholders who actually pay the taxes. Almost half of ESOPs are in these S corporations. A few thousand ESOPs are majority worker owned with most of these being 100 per cent worker owned—which is substantially above the estimated 15 per cent to 20 per cent ESOPs that were all worker owned in 1988 and 1990. (National Center for Employee Ownership, 2016)

There are several singular and critical insights about the ESOP format. Unlike pure worker co-operatives, the ESOP uses financing, namely, it allows a worker trust (an ESOP trust) to borrow funds from a bank and use these funds to buy shares in a firm, with the firm not the workers putting up the collateral. The loan is paid back out of the operating revenues of the firm. Thus, ESOPs allow regular workers using a collective trust to use financing to acquire large chunks of capital. Additionally, many ESOPs today form when successful small and medium-sized business owners sell the business to the workers upon the retirement of the founding entrepreneurs. Business founders often make a schedule to sell the equity to the workers in stages until they are totally cashed out. The fact that ESOP workers generally buy already existing small businesses, that to some extent have already proven themselves, helps reduce the risk of failure of these ESOP firms. About 8 per cent of ESOPs are currently in publicly traded companies.

Looking at other data sets, some form of profit-sharing and equity-sharing is found in about 10 per cent of the Fortune 100, 20 per cent of the Fortune 500, and about half of the annual list of winners in Fortune magazine's 100 Best Companies to Work for in America competition. Profit- or equity-sharing in worker co-operatives has been relatively rare but is now on the rise and is currently estimated by the Democracy at Work Institute as involving about 300 worker co-operatives with about 6,000 members (Palmer 2014). These data and the survey of different industrial sectors and types of firms in the economy establish a fact useful in policy development: that broad-based employee ownership and profit-sharing have sufficient institutional presence as share mechanisms in the United States to be part of a national policy on shares (these data are adapted from Blasi et al. 2014: 57–108, 109–122).

25.3 POLICIES TO ENCOURAGE WORKER OWNERSHIP?

The Federal Government in the USA spends about a trillion dollars in tax incentives in the form of tax expenditures (namely, tax revenues not collected and given as deductions or credits to businesses) every five years (Blasi et al. 2014: 210 , 269). A complete and detailed legislative overview of the tax incentives for worker ownership in the USA is beyond the scope of this chapter. However, it will help international readers of the US experience to have a general context of what tax support the US Federal Government gives before we criticize these policies and discuss extensions to them. We will deal only with federal government tax incentives as there are 50 different states with varied tax treatments and general trends. (Specific information on each worker ownership plan can be found in publications by the National Center for Employee Ownership at http://www.nceo.org/main/publications.php or http://www.nceo.org/GPS-ESPP-Employee-Stock-Purchase-Plans/pub.php/id/474/.

Let's do this by very briefly reviewing the various forms of shared capitalism one by one as done in the foregoing brief census. We include tax incentives on all forms of shares in order to show the overall superstructure of tax support in the USA for the share idea.

Profit-Sharing and Gain-Sharing: These cash payments are tax deductible in figuring corporate taxes for the business offering them to workers and the principle behind this tax deduction is that all business expenses (such as profit/gain-sharing which are a form of worker compensation) are tax deductible.

There are a varied set of tax implications for the different forms of worker ownership:

Employee Stock Ownership Plans: As noted elsewhere in this volume, corporations receive tax deductions for principal payments and interest payments on loans to worker trusts (ESOP trusts) which buy stock in companies for workers. Remember, in the USA an ESOP means that worker trusts typically borrow funds to buy the shares and grant them to workers. Workers do not have to buy the shares with their own savings or pledge their personal/family assets as collateral on the loan. The value of worker shares accumulates and appreciates tax free in the ESOP worker trust, which acts like a tax shelter until the worker leaves the firm or retires. At that point, the worker can roll over the value into an Individual Retirement Account (called an IRA in the USA) and maintain the tax shelter until the worker takes the funds. When the worker takes out the value of the shares, the worker pays regular income tax on the share value contributed by the company to the worker over the years, but pays capital gains tax on the capital appreciation of the shares over the years. If a worker takes out the value of their shares before retirement (age 65) there is a 10 per cent excise tax.

Employee Stock Purchase Plans: If a company wants to give workers the opportunity to buy its shares at a discount, there are no special tax deductions to the company in the USA. For the workers, the amount of the discount is taxed as regular income but under most conditions any capital appreciation in the shares is taxed at the capital gains rate.

Company Stock in a 401k Retirement Plan: A common way that companies grant stock to workers is by giving workers stock as a match when workers contribute to a savings retirement plan called a 401k plan. In this case, the entire value of the company stock match is deductible to the company and, like an ESOP retirement plan, the worker gets to use the retirement plan to tax shelter the grant of shares and any capital appreciation on the shares until the worker takes the value out of the retirement plan.

Stock Options: When a company grants a non-qualified stock option to the worker, the company receives no tax deduction. When the worker exercises the stock option in the future and makes money on the difference (called the spread) between the grant price and the market price at that time, that amount is tax deductible to the company. Any profit on the option is taxed as regular income to the worker.

Grants of Restricted Stock: When a worker is granted restricted stock in the USA the grant is taxed as regular income when it is vested, namely, when any waiting period has expired. The company receives a tax deduction for the grant which is taxed as regular income to the worker.

Worker Co-operatives: Worker co-operatives have two primary tax benefits at the federal level. All types of co-operatives that follow certain US Internal Revenue Service guidelines avoid entity-level taxation on surplus distributed to their worker owners. To elect this benefit under Subchapter T (the tax law governing worker co-ops), companies must 'operate on a co-operative basis', which means that surplus in the co-operative is distributed to members based on patronage, and in a worker co-operative this means hours worked, comparative salary, or another formula that reflects the employees' contribution to the company through their labour. Also, return on capital is limited. Moreover, business owners who wish to sell their company to a worker co-operative can defer payment of capital gains tax on the proceeds of the sale, if the proceeds are invested in domestic stock, at least 30 per cent of the company is owned by employees at the close of the transaction, and the company qualifies as an Eligible Worker-Owned Co-operative, meaning a majority of the members are employees, a majority of company stock is owned by members, a majority of the board is elected by members on a one-person-one-vote basis, and a majority of earnings and losses are allocated to members on the basis of their labour, capital contributions, or a combination of the two.

An analysis of these major current policies shows that the USA has a varied approach to encouraging worker ownership. ESOPs and worker co-operatives appeal mainly to privately held companies and stock options are used in privately held entrepreneurial start-ups. Grants of stock options, restricted stock, and grants of stock matches in 401k plans are used mainly in listed stock market companies. The most intensive sector of worker ownership in the USA, namely ESOPs, functions because the USA has a legal mechanism of a worker trust (the ESOP trust) that can serve as a format to collect and hold worker shares over time and give stability to worker ownership, that can serve as a tax shelter for grants of shares of stock to workers and their capital appreciation until workers retire or need the funds, and that can serve as an entity that can borrow funds to buy more stock for workers; in other words, it can use leverage or debt to finance worker ownership. It is this use of leverage or debt to finance worker purchase of a large amount of capital assets that distinguishes US worker ownership. This is the abiding contribution of ESOP pioneer and creator, Louis O. Kelso, and is contained in the Employee Retirement Income Security Act of 1974 and related legislation (1955, 2014).

25.4 Policies to Significantly Increase US Worker Ownership

The first step to increasing the citizen's share is for the United States to make increasing the property ownership and capital income of citizens a national goal. Given the 'bully pulpit' of the White House, a president who declared that increasing the citizen's share was a priority for his or her administration would put broad-based capitalism front and centre in the national economic discourse. To make such a commitment real, the President could also establish a White House Office of Broad-Based Capitalism to co-ordinate federal policies dealing with broad-based capitalism, including worker co-ops, and to work with the private sector to publicize and encourage best practices (lack of co-ordination of policies has led to a number of policy errors and disasters, which we review in Blasi et al. 2014: 214–23).

The second step would be to reform the Section 162(m) deduction in the tax code. What is 162(m) and why should reforming it be part of a commitment to broad-based ownership? In 1993, seeking to rein in executive pay in a weak economy, the Clinton administration proposed to allow firms to deduct as a cost of business the fixed salary for the top five executives only up to a million dollars. Corporations could pay higher amounts of fixed pay, but they could not claim that against the corporate profits tax. As this initial proposal wound its way through bipartisan passage in the US Congress, Congress enacted the limitation of one million dollars of salary as deductible from corporate profits but added in Section 162(m), a provision that allowed firms to deduct unlimited 'performance-based pay' as a cost of business. This performance-related pay included various employee stock ownership and profit-sharing plans for the top five executives of all public corporations—namely, stock options, grants of stock, or bonuses paid for nonequity incentive plans—without requiring any evidence that the performance pay had any actual effect on performance.

The result was an unintended tax system that subsidized 'unshared capitalism', in which firms achieve tax savings by paying the top five executives with worker ownership stakes and profit shares in the firm for the top 1 per cent. We estimate that the exemption may have cost taxpayers $5 to $10 billion per year since 1993. In addition to this tax subsidy for unshared capitalism, many publicly traded corporations offer various narrow employee stock ownership or profit-sharing plans to the top 5 per cent of their employees that cost taxpayers from 2001 to 2007 many more billions per year. Our proposal is simple: if a corporation traded on a stock market offers any type of profit-sharing, gain-sharing, employee stock ownership, restricted stock, stock option, or equity plan to its top five executives, the business can deduct this equity and profit-sharing beyond the $1 million dollar limit only if it offers the same plan to all workers.

Our third suggestion is to link federal tax subsidies to businesses that offer some form of broad-based ownership. US corporate tax contains numerous provisions that enable firms to decrease their tax liability and improve their bottom line. By a recent estimate, businesses received about a trillion dollars in tax relief from 2008 through to 2014 from the three largest federal tax subsidy programmes: accelerated depreciation, deductions for US production and manufacturing activities, and research and experimentation tax credits. Without assessing the virtue or vice of particular provisions that reduce firms' tax liabilities, our proposal is that these tax deductions go only to businesses that offer a broad-based cash or deferred profit-sharing plan or a broad-based employee stock ownership plan not financed by worker savings or that is organized as a worker co-operative.

Our fourth proposal recognizes that employee stock ownership will never be a meaningful part of the economy if it is not adopted by a large number of the 5,000 public corporations traded on the NYSE and NASDAQ. Grants of stock to workers (i.e. that workers do not purchase either directly or indirectly through lower wages) are the low-risk way to do this. We propose a plan to encourage stock market companies to make grants of stock to all of their employees in a way that will be easy, favourable to the employees, favourable to the company, and free of bureaucratic red tape. Our idea is to facilitate small increments in employee stock ownership year after year to move most publicly traded corporations to the point where they have employee ownership in the 5 to 25 per cent range, as is done in a number of corporations that integrate employee ownership into their business model. Legislation has been introduced to the House of Representatives that seeks to accomplish this goal.

A publicly traded, listed stock market company would make grants of stock to all of its employees within some simple 'safe harbour,' straightforward limit of fairness that Congress would determine. For example, it could be according to salary or basically similar grants. The company would receive an immediate deduction based on the market value of the stock in the year it was granted. To give corporations the ability to promote these grants to their employees widely, the grants would be excluded from regular income taxes and other employment taxes and subject to capital gains taxes and dividend taxes depending on the amount of time the stock has been held. Because the goal is to create a positive environment for company-wide grants of stock to workers, any such proposal should include a provision to make the accounting for such grants favourable to the corporations and transparent to workers, shareholders, and the public.

The fifth proposal is to create tax incentives for corporations to make grants of stock to workers if the grants are equal for all workers, and adopt these tax incentives to encourage patronage distributions by worker co-operatives. Currently, corporations that wish to simply make grants of stock or ownership to the workers because they believe this will encourage greater private incentive and motivation and firm performance face a lot of regulatory barriers. The idea is to support the proposed legislation of conservative Congressman Dana Rohrabacher (Republican-CA) that allows corporations to make equal grants of stock to their workers, with the workers excluded from certain taxes the longer that they hold the ownership interest. This legislation would give every privately held and stock market company an incentive to consider ownership grants. It would be mostly used by stock market companies. It was H.R. 4089 of the 113th Congress and will be introduced soon into the current Congress. The extension of comparable tax incentives for individuals to members of worker co-operatives should also be explored.

The sixth idea is to remove the barriers for small business people to sell their business to an ESOP or a worker co-op when the founder/entrepreneur wishes to retire and does not have a relative to take over the business. One of the principal risks of a small businesses is finding a buyer so that the entrepreneur can cash out and retire if there is no sibling to take over the company. Currently, owners of a small business seeking to retire and cash out their equity in the business can receive deferral from capital gains taxes under Internal Revenue Code Section 1042 if they sell 30 per cent or more of the firm to the managers and workers in an ESOP in a C corporation. This has created many of the thousands of majority and 100 per cent owned ESOPs in counties throughout the country, although most counties (political subdivisions larger than cities in the USA, similar to districts) do not have even one ESOP. The growth of these sales has slowed in recent years because most small businesses are incorporated as S corporations.

This initiative would involve members of Congress endorsing S. 1212, the Promotion of Expansion of Private Employee Ownership Act in order to allow small business owners to receive the capital gains deferral for a sale to an S corporation, with the suggestion that the proposed legislation also allow the capital gains deferral for the sale to a EWOC (Eligible Worker-Owned Co-operative) as earlier specified in Internal Revenue Code Section 1042 and a Subchapter T worker co-operative and other worker co-operative corporations. A Subchapter T corporation is where the worker owners are the only voting owners. This bill now has bipartisan support. The impact will be a removal of the barriers to and an increase of sales of small businesses to workers and managers who helped build them in local communities so that the founding entrepreneur can retire and enjoy the benefit of having originally built the business. Similar bills, such as related model legislation, making its way through the New Jersey Legislations should be introduced into all the state legislatures.

The seventh idea is to provide incentives for the $2 trillion in size private equity sector of the economy to promote capital ownership by workers by allowing the owners of private equity industry to retain their preferential capital gains treatment on their profits from private equity operations and transactions only if these deals create broad-based capital ownership and profit-sharing.

These policies are discussed in our book with our colleague Richard Freeman (Blasi et al., 2014: 195–227).

ACKNOWLEDGEMENTS

The authors would like to thank Camille Kerr of the Democracy at Work Institute for her assistance on worker co-operatives.

REFERENCES

Blasi, Joseph R., Freeman, Richard B., and Kruse, Douglas L. (2014), *The Citizen's Share: Reducing Inequality in the 21st Century* (New Haven and London: Yale University Press).
Blasi, Joseph R., Freeman, Richard B., and Kruse, Douglas L. (2017), 'Evidence: What the US Research Shows about Worker Ownership', in J. Michie, J. R. Blasi, and C. Borzaga, eds, *The Oxford Handbook of Mutual, Co-operative and Co-owned Business* (Oxford: Oxford University Press), 211–226.

Kelso, Louis O. and Adler, Mortimer (1955), *The Capitalist Manifesto* (New York: Random House).

National Center for Employee Ownership, Statistical Profile

Palmer, Tim (2014), *Democratic Workplaces after the Great Recession: An Economic Overview of US Worker Cooperatives in 2013* (San Francisco: Democracy at Work Institute).

Rodgers, Loren (2010), 'Are ESOPs Good for Employees?' *Pension & Benefits Daily*, Volume 100, 1 November, 1–5.

Rosen, Corey (2017), 'Statutory Employee Stock Ownership Plans in the USA', in J. Michie, J. R. Blasi, and C. Borzaga, eds, *The Oxford Handbook of Mutual, Co-operative and Co-owned Business* (Oxford: Oxford University Press),

CHAPTER 26

....

WORKERS—AND CONSUMERS—OF THE WORLD UNITE! OPPORTUNITIES FOR HYBRID CO-OPERATIVISM

....

MAURIE J. COHEN

26.1 INTRODUCTION

....

A key point of many of the chapters in this handbook is that co-operative forms of busi-ness organization can effectively buffer economic insecurity, offset some of the vagar-ies of market capitalism, and enhance social solidarity.[1] An interesting—and in many respects peculiar—facet in the history of co-operativism is how worker (or producer) co-operatives and consumer co-operatives have evolved along completely separate tra-jectories. Yet a casual glance around makes clear that production and consumption are inextricably bound up in tight configurations. Moreover, no one is exclusively a pro-ducer or consumer and we repeatedly and iteratively change roles, often numerous times during the course of a single day.

We seem, for better or worse, to be at an auspicious moment to rectify this anomalous situation. In coming decades, large parts of the world are likely to experience increas-ing social and economic precariousness due to the stagnation of wages, the increase of contingent labour, and the dissolution of entire occupational categories (Standing 2011; Ford 2015; Putnam 2015). These conditions will make it necessary for households to develop alternative means with which to procure goods and services. While there has been in recent years growing attention devoted to recommendations to provide households with a reliable form of non-labour income, they are unlikely anytime soon

---

[1] This chapter draws significantly on Chapter 6 of Cohen (2017).

to receive sufficient political support outside of a handful of front-runner countries like Sweden, Finland, and the Netherlands. Elsewhere, it is probable that a considerable amount of time will need to pass before such propositions are enacted as policy and, in the meantime, there will be a need for more immediately implementable strategies. This chapter describes the notion of multi-stakeholder co-operatives—mutual associations that span both production and consumption—which could help to ensure satisfaction of basic needs during this turbulent period.

26.2 CURRENT POLICY DEBATES ON ECONOMIC PRECARITY

A future with less customary work—jobs that compensate employees on a salaried or hourly basis and provide modest health and retirement benefits—will unquestionably have sweeping impacts. Signs of these developments are already beginning to unfold in a number of countries as income becomes increasingly concentrated, the middle class haemorrhages, and working-class lives come under increasing strain. Rather than rely on full-time employment for their income requirements, households are finding it neces-sary to develop more diversified portfolios of gainful activities comprising waged work, freelancing, and home-scale and community-based production. It also seems probable that to avoid protracted economic insecurity on a mass scale, governments will need to create durable programmes of income supplementation.[2] A number of different ways to achieve this objective have been proposed, with most recommendations premised on devising sources of non-labour income. Three of the most notable alternatives are the provision of a universal basic income (UBI), the distribution of a 'citizen's dividend', and the implementation of broad-based stock ownership (BBSO) in corporate businesses.[3]

First, a UBI that is made without the need to work, entails payment of a modest stipend to members of a political community (Sheahen 2012).[4] Economists like Friedrich Hayek and Milton Friedman championed the idea during the 1970s, but by the early 1980s it had largely disappeared from the political agenda until it was resurrected in the 1990s by

[2] It is important not to lose sight of already institutionalized ways to augment incomes, most notably through partial or fully subsidized provision of public goods and services such as education, transportation, and healthcare.

[3] The concepts discussed in this chapter are all traceable to the foundational insights of former law professor, political economist, and investment banker Louis Kelso who advocated giving workers greater opportunity to accumulate wealth derived from the improving productivity of technology. See Kelso and Adler 1958.

[4] A variety of terms is used to describe the same idea, including unconditional basic income, guaranteed basic income, guaranteed minimum income, and citizen's wage. The notion of a negative income tax is a similar strategy, but does not entail a direct cash payment. At the international level, the leading campaign organization is the Basic Income Earth Network (formerly the Basic Income European Network).

Belgian philosopher Philippe van Parijs (1992) (see also Steensland 2007). More recently, champions of UBI have emerged across the political spectrum. Progressives embrace the idea because it provides a more secure safety net, while the prospect of a less bureau-cratically cumbersome way to address extreme poverty is appealing to reform-minded conservatives. Finland embarked in 2016 on an expansive experiment to test the feasi-bility of a national programme, and the concept is currently receiving consideration in Switzerland, Germany, France, the Netherlands, the United Kingdom, and elsewhere. There are, to be sure, numerous unresolved issues about how UBI would work in prac-tice, with vigorous debates around the use of means testing, the periodicity of payments, the eligibility of children and non-citizens, and numerous other policy-design features. Additionally, some detractors dismiss the concept out of concern that unconditional payments would reduce the incentive to work and generate an overabundance of idle and unproductive people. This criticism is probably overwrought because under most designs UBI would not substitute for wages but rather offer a modest supplement. All but the most frugal recipients would have an extremely hard time surviving on UBI alone and even if a handful of people developed lifestyles concordant with the disbursements, it is hard to see why, on a societal level, it would be an altogether adverse outcome.

Second, the idea of a citizen's dividend begins with recognition that there is a wealth of property in democratic societies that is effectively held in common (Barnes 2014). Such assets include the broadcast spectrum, the natural resources accessible on public lands, and the atmosphere. These jointly owned properties are typically appropriated either for a rela-tively nominal fee paid to a government agency (as is the case for rights to harvest timber in national forests) or for no cost at all (as pertains to the emission of greenhouse gases). A citi-zen's dividend is predicated on the principle that exploitation of these assets should be set at a fair market price, with the proceeds being outwardly distributed to all eligible recipients of the relevant jurisdiction (generally a state/province or a country, but under some formula-tions the world is envisaged as the relevant geographic territory) on an equal basis.

The most celebrated application of this idea is the Alaska Permanent Fund (APF), established in 1980 and financed by a tax on oil production in the state. A portion of the revenue is retained for investment (presently valued at approximately $50 billion) and the remaining share is dispensed as an annual dividend (generally between $1,000 and $2,000 per person in a given year) to all residents living in Alaska for at least twelve prior months. Households receive their distributions as an electronic transfer into a bank account and the money can be used on an entirely unrestricted basis. Because disburse-ments are made to every qualified adult and child, the sum received by a household can be sizeable.[5]

The same essential concept has been promoted in recent years at the national level—thus far without success—to curtail greenhouse-gas emissions in the United States

---

[5] The concept of the citizen's dividend was initially formulated over a half a century ago by the aforementioned Louis Kelso who developed a plan for a general stock ownership trust in the 1980s for Alaska that nearly became the model used instead of the APF. See Kelso and Adler (1958) for the general theory and Kelso and Kelso (1986) for the details of the plan.

(Riddle 2012). The proposal entails implementing a so-called cap-and-dividend pro-gramme whereby the money generated by auctioning the carbon permits would be used to capitalize a trust fund to pay an annuity to compensate consumers for higher energy costs, to invest in climate-mitigation measures, and to fund research on social and tech-nological innovations (Barnes et al. 2008). A slightly modified version of the concept, termed a common asset trust, has been under review in the state of Vermont as a way to generate a citizen's dividend as compensation for the devaluation or appropriation of common-property assets like the climate or groundwater aquifers (Farley et al. 2015).[6]

Finally, the notion of BBSO originates from recognition that productivity gains in many countries have in recent decades accrued disproportionately to the owners of capital. By contrast, working-and middle-class households have struggled to make ends meet. To rectify—or at least begin to mitigate—the problem of increasing inequality, BBSO advocates propose increasing the ability of workers-to benefit from the proceeds of capital. This objective can be realized by allocating, preferably through options and grants, company shares that could enable modest earners to supplement their wages with capital ownership and capital income comprising dividend distributions and asset appreciation. Moreover, evidence suggests that more democratic ownership of capital catalyses a positive feedback loop whereby firms that give employees a financial stake through profit-sharing are more productive and profitable than counterparts that rely on standardized organizational structures.[7]

While these three concepts warrant consideration, we need to acknowledge the polit-ical obstacles in many countries that are likely to preclude far-reaching and substan-tive action in the near to medium term. Strategies premised on mutualism and shared ownership—with a solid dose of creative financing—could prove to be, at least for the foreseeable future, more practicable ways with which to respond to the contraction of conventional job opportunities and the breakdown of established provisioning systems.

26.3 Towards Multi-Stakeholder Co-operativism

Economic insecurity in the United States, Europe, and other countries has been compounded in recent years by a politics of austerity, forcing households to make sharp reductions in consumption. Looming is a further contraction of working- and

---

[6] Barnes (2014) explains how a cap-and-trade initiative in California for reducing greenhouse-gas emissions has effectively evolved into a 'climate dividend' programme. He also describes several other schemes that achieve similar ends.

[7] The United States, for example, has approximately 10,000 companies with meaningful BBSO arrangements amounting to a trillion dollars and involving 15 million workers through employee stock ownership plans (ESOPs). As described by Blasi et al. (2013), the ESOP was another idea originally developed by Louis Kelso.

middle-class livelihoods due to the advent of new digital technologies that are likely to eliminate large numbers of jobs. Calls for social mobilization in the face of such challenges are important and well meaning, but it is difficult to see them coming to fruition and, even under the most fortuitous circumstances, they will take a long time to have meaningful effect (Geoghegan 2014; Phillips-Fein 2015). While it would be shortsighted to completely discount new possibilities further down the road, there is a need for workable alternatives that leverage currently available institutional capabilities and opportunity structures.

A concrete response to current circumstances has been to call for platform co-operativism to shift control of new modes of temporary labour (a key aspect of the regrettably and mistakenly termed 'sharing economy') away from venture capital-financed platforms such as Uber and towards the workers providing the service (Schneider 2014; Scholtz 2014, 2016; Gorenflo 2015). This idea calls for using the Internet in the same way as the Silicon Valley mediators, but to redirect customers to worker-owned companies. As a business model, platform co-operativism enables workers to earn more than casual wages, to own shares in the company, and to acquire an additional non-labour income stream.

There is little question that platform co-operativism is a laudable concept and it should be pursued where there is a critical mass of prospective participants. There is, though, an opportunity to push this scheme a bit further. Why limit co-operation only to workers while implicitly treating consumers as little more than a mass of aggregate demand? Why elevate workers over their customers when the distinction is artificial and rarely static? As Swedish political scientist Victor Pestoff (1995) observed more than twenty years ago:

> Most co-operatives are defined around one, and only one of its possible membership bases. In effect, they are single stakeholder organizations. Accordingly, there are consumer co-operatives, worker co-operatives, or primary producer co-operatives. The effect of each model is to include one, and only one group—and to exclude others, which nevertheless have a significant interest and stake in them ... Thus, a single exclusive interest is often dominant.

More ambitious application of platform co-operativism would not just create new Internet sites to support worker co-operatives. It would embrace workers and consumers as co-equals and seek to demonstrate the viability of novel business models that combine production and consumption under a single organizational umbrella.[8] The uniting of these two domains into a multi-stakeholder framework could help to

---

[8] Pestoff (1995) traces this polarization within the co-operative movement to the conference of the International Cooperative Alliance held in 1895. He describes how the French delegation argued at the conclave for the practice of 'co-partnership' between producers and consumers as a requirement for membership in the alliance. However, the so-called 'Anglo-Saxon view' of single-stakeholder co-operativism prevailed and continues to be dominant today.

overcome enduring fractures in the co-operative movement and give rise to new pre-dispositions that treat buyers and sellers as allies rather than rivals, prioritize community solidarity over return on investment, and emphasize collective enhancement instead of value appropriation.[9] Moreover, the fomented antagonism between producers and consumers that is inherent in prevailing systems of exchange, and the relentless pursuit of narrow conceptions of profitability tend to amplify consumption in excess of genuine needs—often through the use of tempting volume discounts and the manufacture of goods that become prematurely obsolete. By stressing their continuously shifting, and oftentimes reciprocal, relationships, worker–consumer co-operatives could bring the logics of production and consumption into closer alignment.

Fortunately, there are contemporary examples of multi-stakeholder co-operatives to which efforts to foster worker–consumer collaboration can turn for guidance. The paragon case is Eroski, a subsidiary of the venerable Mondragón Corporation head-quartered in the Basque Region, which operates a chain of 800 supermarkets and hyper-markets and a variety of other businesses, including petrol stations, travel agencies, liquor stores, and perfume shops in Spain (and a small number of additional establishments in France) (Manetti and Toccafondi 2012; Storey et al. 2014; Vézina and Girard 2014; Arando et al. 2015). Launched in 1969 as a joint venture involving ten small grocers, Eroski grew steadily during the following years by opening new stores and absorbing a number of other co-operatives. In the 1970s, in response to a series of economic crises, the group implemented an ownership structure premised on a hybrid worker–consumer model. After further expansion and acquisition involving several smaller regional retail food companies in Spain during the 1990s and 2000s (including a strategic partnership with France's Intermarche and Italy's Co-op Italia), the co-operative has become the second largest retail group in Spain (only Carrefour is bigger) and one of the 50 most sizeable retailers in Europe.

At the other end of the continuum is the Weaver Street Market, a modestly sized worker–consumer co-operative in North Carolina that operates three retail stores specializing in organic produce and fair-trade products. The flagship in Carrboro, a community of approximately 21,000 residents bordering Chapel Hill and part of the larger Research Triangle Park area comprising the rapidly growing cities of Raleigh and Durham, opened in 1988. Initial funding came from a local credit union with a commitment to community and locally owned businesses, the Carrboro municipal government, and a combination of individual loans and shareholder equity. Success over several years prompted the opening of new outlets in the nearby town of Hillsborough and the Southern Village neighbourhood of Chapel Hill. The expansion, however, was

---

[9] Multi-stakeholder co-operatives have management structures that allow for the direct participation of more than one category of stakeholder, and the specific model referred to here is sometimes known as a 'worker–consumer hybrid'. Other types could include some or all of the following that contribute to the co-production of the organization: suppliers, professional managers, investors, local community members, and government representatives. Some commentators also conceive of the full range of stakeholders as also comprising society at large and both past and future generations. See Levi (1998, 2006) and Martine Vézina and Jean-Pierre Girard (2014).

not without controversy, as some owners became concerned that the co-operative was growing too large. At present, the Weaver Street Market is owned by 200 workers and 18,000 customer-households.

Scaling up this model would entail establishment of worker–consumer co-operatives across a much wider range of activities (see Lund 2011). For instance, a co-operative taxi service could provide reliable local transportation on a similar basis, circumventing providers like Uber as well as conventional car services. By joining up with other worker–consumer co-operatives across the country, or indeed around the world, the business could become part of a wider Internet-facilitated consortium. Such collaboration would open up additional opportunities, for instance providing co-operators from afar with short-term travel accommodations as an alternative to ordinary hotels or Airbnb. By bridging the divide between production and consumption, and recognizing that we all produce and consume, the worker–consumer co-operative could facilitate seamless shifts between roles.

Realization of this vision could break the dependency of the new economy on Silicon Valley investors and contribute to bringing into view a more socially equitable future. An emergent line of investigation suggests that co-operativism has the potential to orient people towards more solidaristic and other-regarding dispositions (see, for example, Mittone and Ploner 2015). If correct, participation in firms of the kind described here could be a useful way to enhance social cohesion while more adequately meeting essential needs. None of this is to suggest that bringing worker–consumer co-operatives into wider existence will be easy. At this preliminary stage, three obstacles in particular pose major challenges: the prospect of organizational degeneration, the impediments on access to capital, and the composition of institutional sponsorship.

First, arrangements would need to be made to guard against one of the more common problems to which many co-operatives fall victim—passive engagement by co-operators leads either to organizational degeneration or the supplanting of democratic processes by professional managers (Storey et al. 2014; Whyman 2012; Bakaikoa et al. 2004; see also Olsen 2013). To address this situation, recent research has focused on wider deployment of several participatory models that have been applied across industries where worker ownership is relatively widespread (Shipper 2014). These studies suggest that decision-making in worker–consumer co-operatives could usefully range over a spectrum, depending on the circumstances and the level of collective commitment. For example, some enterprises might operate on the basis of direct participation by all worker–consumers while others would delegate most responsibilities to an elected board of directors.[10] Another variant has been successfully operationalized in the United States by the thousands of employee stock ownership plans (ESOPs) that

---

[10] An instance of the direct decision-making model applied to a worker co-operative is Isthmus Engineering & Manufacturing, a Wisconsin-based company with several hundred worker–owners that designs and builds custom automation equipment. See Billeaux et al. (2011) for further details. Some worker co-operatives actively encourage extensive participation with all worker–owners voting on the admission of new members because democratic socialization is deemed essential to ensure a high level of expected performance. An example is Equal Exchange, a worker-owned co-operative that specializes

currently exist in the country. In these businesses it is increasingly common for worker–owners to participate in governance through so-called high-performance systems that provide opportunities for input through cross-functional teams (including teams that work with the board of directors and with customers).

Second, co-operative businesses—both worker-owned and consumer-owned—tend to suffer from undercapitalization because the founding sponsors, as well as the subsequent shareholders, of these initiatives lack substantial savings or assets and are thus attracted to commercial niches with low requirements for start-up capital. Firms are then typically required to rely on debt, secured on relatively unfavourable terms, to underwrite the cost of operations and to grow the enterprise.[11]

A potential way for worker–consumer co-operatives to overcome weakness due to undercapitalization might be to structure their operations as an ESOP. This mode of organization would make it possible to partially compensate worker–consumer co-operators by contributing shares to a trust maintained on their behalf. This organizational structure would allow the enterprise to retain more cash for investment while at the same time accessing available tax benefits. Perhaps most importantly, the trust could borrow money from private lending institutions to purchase stock and use the proceeds to finance capital investments and even acquisitions. As is the case for conventional ESOPs in the United States, the stock could then be distributed to member–owners as the loan is paid off (Blasi et al. 2013). Combining democratic participation with access to credit afforded by an American-style ESOP could enhance the viability of worker–consumer co-operatives while demonstrating the effectiveness of this approach as an alternative business model.

Finally, relatively more prosperous communities with ample social capital should in many instances be able to raise the necessary resources to get modestly sized worker–consumer co-operatives off the ground. However, less affluent locales would probably need to rely on philanthropic foundations or other outside assistance to get started. Such circumstances raise significant risks because these sources of capital tend to evince vacillating and continuously evolving priorities and engender outcomes that fly in the face of intentions (Stroh 2015). In the absence of reliable organizational and financial support, worker–consumer co-operatives are liable to replicate (or even amplify) many of the inequities that are apparent in the more mainstream economy.

Two possible candidates for sponsorship of worker–consumer co-operatives are trade unions and municipal governments. Trade unions have been, at best ambivalent partners of the co-operative movement in most countries, but there are now indications that

---

in the sourcing and distribution of fair-trade products (see Harris et al. 2015). The representative democracy model is exemplified by Amsted Industries, a Chicago-headquartered federation of worker-owned companies that manufactures railway and vehicular equipment and construction and industrial products.

[11] The Mondragón Corporation was able to overcome the credit problem by establishing its own co-operative bank at an early point in its development, and in the United States the National Cooperative Bank has historically played an important role.

this long-standing chasm may be starting to narrow. For instance, at the height of the Great Recession in 2009, the United Steelworkers, the largest industrial union in North America, entered into an agreement with the Mondragón Corporation to encourage the establishment of worker co-operatives (Witherell 2013; Hanson Schlachter 2016). One of the more salient developments to emerge out of this accord has been the Cincinnati Union Co-op Initiative (CUCI) which has incubated two worker co-operatives and one worker–consumer co-operative.

In Cincinnati, the worker–consumer co-operative is a retail grocery called Apple Street Market that is a partnership with the local branch of the United Food and Commercial Workers Union. To date, it has recruited more than 1,000 consumer–owners. Initial experience demonstrates that trade unions can constructively enable the development of co-operatives, with especially valued services being the provision of technical assistance, financing, and access to healthcare and retirement planning. These experiments also highlight the important role that organized labour can play in education and training, as well as in mobilizing political support and conferring legitimacy.[12]

In projecting the future of union co-operatives it merits observing that the size of the businesses established thus far remains extremely small, but it does seem possible to successfully manage the conflicts. The real challenge will be how the relationship matures as the number and scale of the enterprises grow over time, and more bureaucratic organizational structures come to be established. Despite the practical inseparability of production and consumption, it nevertheless remains to be demonstrated whether a single organization can effectively harmonize the interests of the different—and potentially conflicting—constituencies.

Municipal governments provide a second source of potential institutional sponsorship of worker–consumer co-operatives. For instance, New York City established the Worker Co-operative Business Development Initiative in 2014 with considerable fanfare and has thus far allocated $3.3 million to this effort (Nzinga Ifateyo 2014). A broad coalition of economic justice and anti-poverty organizations, working under the leadership of the Federation of Protestant Welfare Agencies, spearheaded the effort to win municipal support. Momentum was jumpstarted with a widely circulated policy report highlighting the potential of co-operatives as a strategy for reducing income inequality (Jones Austin 2014). The document attracted the support of key political figures, including the then newly elected mayor, Bill de Blasio, who had campaigned on a platform of social inclusion. The public funding received to date has been allocated to an array of activities, including a legal assistance centre and an incubator for development of co-operatively owned environmental businesses.

While New York City's steps are pacesetting, it is not the only municipality currently working along these lines (Kerr 2015). Elsewhere in the United States, Madison (Wisconsin) has created a loan fund to provide low- and no-interest loans to co-operative

---

[12] Hanson Schlachter (2016) identifies ongoing union-co-operative projects in 11 cities in the United States, including Chicago, Denver, Los Angeles, Pittsburgh, and San Francisco.

businesses, Minneapolis (Minnesota) has—with public support—developed the highest density of retail food co-operatives of any city in the country, and Oakland (California) is drafting model legislation (Stearn 2015; Kerr 2015). While these undertakings are evidence of support among at least some municipal governments in the country, there is still much to learn about how best to develop this business model, and the fusion of workers and consumers into a single co-operative organization remains an unexplored option. It is, though, useful to keep in mind that recent action on the part of mayors and city councils has been in response to the growing scarcity of working- and middle-class jobs. Among policy makers and the general public, the ongoing period of upheaval continues to be framed in terms of scarce employment opportunities, inadequate incomes, and inequality, rather than inequitable consumption, but this could change. As the breakdown of customary provisioning practices becomes more conspicuous, the notion of municipal sponsorship of worker–consumer co-operatives is likely to acquire more relevance.

26.4 CONCLUSION

Persistent and protracted economic turmoil is taking its toll and a new wave of digital technologies is primed to dislocate large numbers of people from jobs that were, just a few short years ago, thought to provide a degree of economic security. There is a need to develop new and creative responses that are rooted in political realities. While there is no blueprint for how to approach this challenge, planning must proceed simultaneously for both the short and long terms. One strategy that may provide some relief is to dissolve the conceptual divisions within the co-operative movement that drive an artificial wedge between workers and consumers. Worker, consumer, and worker–consumer co-operatives are not panaceas, but the future will require the establishment of new institutions to meet the provisioning needs of households. These organizations can also inculcate democratic values and solidaristic social relations that will be essential for easing the overall process of innovating a new system of social organization.

REFERENCES

Arando, Saioa, Gago, Monica, Jones, Derek, and Kato, Takao (2015), 'Efficiency in Employee-Owned Enterprises: An Econometric Case Study of Mondragón', *Industrial and Labor Relations Review*, 68(2), 398–425.

Bakaikoa, Baleren, Errasti, Anjel, and Begiristain, Agurtzane (2004), 'Governance of the Mondragón Corporación Co-operativa', *Annals of Public and Co-operative Economics*, 75(1), 61-87.

Barnes, Peter (2014), *With Liberty and Dividends for All: How to Save Our Middle Class When Jobs Don't Pay Enough* (San Francisco: Berrett-Koehler).

Barnes, Peter, Costanza, Robert, Hawken, Paul, Orr, David, Ostrom, Elinor, Umaña, Alvaro, and Young, Oran (2008), 'Creating an Earth Atmospheric Trust', *Science* 319(5864), 724.

Billeaux, Michael, Reynolds, Anne, Young-Hyman, Trevor, and Zayim, Ayca (2011), *Worker Co-operative Case Study: Isthmus Engineering & Manufacturing* (Madison, WI: University of Wisconsin Center for Co-operatives).

Blasi, Joseph, Freeman, Richard, and Kruse, Douglas (2013), *The Citizen's Share: Reducing Inequality in the 21st Century* (New Haven, CT: Yale University Press).

Cohen, Maurie (2017), *The Future of Consumer Society: Prospects for Sustainability in the New Economy* (Oxford: Oxford University Press).

Farley, Joshua, Costanza, Robert, Flomenhoft, Gary, and Kirk, Daniel (2015), 'The Vermont Common Assets Trust: An Institution for Sustainable, Just and Efficient Resource Allocation', *Ecological Economics*, 109, 71–9.

Ford, Martin (2015), *Rise of the Robots: Technology and the Threat of a Jobless Future* (New York: Basic Books).

Geoghegan, Thomas (2014), *Only One Thing Can Save Us: Why America Needs a New Kind of Labor Movement* (New York: New Press).

Gorenflo, Neal, (2015), 'How Platform Co-Ops Can Beat Death Stars', *Shareable*, 3 November. Available at http://www.shareable.net/blog/how-platform-co-ops-can-beat-death-stars-like-uber-to-create-a-real-sharing-economy (accessed 16 October 2016).

Hanson Schlachter, Laura (2016), 'Stronger Together? The USW-Mondragón Union Co-op Model'. Paper presented at the Mid-Year Fellows Workshop in Honor of Louis O. Kelso, New Brunswick, NJ: Rutgers University, School of Management and Labor Relations.

Harris, Benita, Shipper, Frank, Manz, Karen, and Manz, Charles (2015), 'Equal Exchange: Doing Well by Doing Good', in Michael Hitt, R. Duane Ireland, and Robert Hoskisson, eds, *Strategic Management: Competitiveness and Globalization (Concepts and Cases)*, 11th ed., Stamford, CT: Cengage Learning), 119–32.

Jones Austin, Jennifer (2014), *Worker Co-operatives for New York City: A Vision for Addressing Income Inequality* (New York: Federation of Protestant Welfare Agencies). Available at http://community-wealth.org/sites/clone.community-wealth.org/files/downloads/202859367-Worker-CooperativeWorker-Cooperatives-for-New-York-City-A-Vision-for-Addressing-Income-Inequality.pdf (accessed 16 October 2016).

Kelso, Louis and Adler, Mortimer (1958), *The Capitalist Manifesto* (New York: Random House).

Kelso, Louis and Kelso, Patricia Hetter (1986), *Democracy and Economic Power* (Cambridge, MA: Ballinger).

Kerr, Camille (2015), *Local Government Support for Co-operatives* (Oakland, CA: Democracy at Work Institute). Available at http://www.uwcc.wisc.edu/pdf/local%20govt%20support.pdf (accessed 21 September 2016).

Levi, Yair (1998), 'Beyond Traditional Models: Multi-stakeholder Co-operatives and Their Differential Roles', *Journal of Rural Co-operation*, 26(1–2), 49–64.

Lund, Margaret (2011), *Solidarity as a Business Model: A Multi-Stakeholder Co-operatives Manual* (Kent, OH: Kent State University, Co-operative Development Center).

Manetti, Giamcomo and Toccafondi, Simone (2012), 'The Contribution of Network Governance to Preventing Opportunistic Behaviour by Managers and to Increasing Stakeholder Involvement: The Eroski Case', *International Journal of Business Governance and Ethics*, 7(3), 252–78.

Mittone, Luigi and Ploner, Matteo (2015), 'Co-operative Attitudes among Workers in Social Co-operatives: Evidence from an Artefactual Field Experiment', *Voluntas* 26(2), 510–30.

Nzinga Ifateyo, Ajowa (2014), 'A Co-Op State of Mind', *In These Times*, 18 August. Available at http://inthesetimes.com/article/17061/a_co_op_state_of_mind (accessed 21 September 2015).

Olsen, Erik (2013), 'The Relative Survival of Worker Co-Operatives and Barriers to their Creation', *Advances in the Economic Analysis of Participatory & Labor-Managed Firms*, 14, 84–107.

Pestoff, Victor (1995), 'Local Economic Democracy and Multi-Stakeholder Co-operatives. *Journal of Rural Co-operation*, 23(2), 151–67.

Phillips-Fein, Kim (2015), 'Why Workers Won't Unite', *The Atlantic*, April.

Putnam, Robert (2015), *Our Kids: The American Dream in Crisis* (New York: Simon and Schuster).

Riddle, Matthew (2012), 'Cap and Dividend: Carbon Revenue as Common Wealth', in James Boyce, ed., *Economics, the Environment, and Our Common Wealth* (Northampton, MA: Edward Elgar), 73–91.

Schneider, Nathan (2014), 'Owning is the New Sharing', *Shareable*, 21 December. Available at http://www.shareable.net/blog/owning-is-the-new-sharing (accessed 22 September 2016).

Scholtz, Trebor (2014), 'Platform Co-operativism vs. the Sharing Economy', *Medium*, 5 December. Available at https://medium.com/@trebors/platform-cooperativism-vs-the-sharing-economy-2ea737f1b5ad#.5r8m4nvf8 (accessed 16 October 2016).

Scholtz, Trebor (2016), *Platform Co-operativism: Challenging the Corporate Sharing Economy* (New York: Rosa Luxemburg Stiftung–New York Office). Available at http://www.rosalux-nyc.org/platform-cooperativism-2/ (accessed 16 October 2016).

Sheahen, Allan (2012), *Basic Income Guarantee: Your Right to Economic Security* (New York: Palgrave Macmillan).

Shipper, Frank (2014), *Shared Entrepreneurship: A Path to Engaged Employee* (New York: Palgrave Macmillan).

Standing, Guy (2011), *The Precariat: The New Dangerous Class* (New York: Bloomsbury).

Stearn, Michelle (2015), *From New York to Oakland, CA, City Governments Support Worker Co-ops* (Cleveland: Democracy Collaborative). Available at http://community-wealth.org/content/new-york-oakland-ca-city-governments-support-worker-coops (accessed 16 October 2016).

Steensland, Brian (2007), *The Failed Welfare Revolution: America's Struggle over Guaranteed Income Policy* (Princeton, NJ: Princeton University Press).

Storey, John, Basterretxea, Imanol, and Salaman, Graeme (2014), 'Managing the Resisting "Degeneration" in Employee-Owned Businesses: A Comparative Study of Two Large Retailers in Spain and the United Kingdom', *Organization* 21(5), 626–44.

Stroh, David (2015), *Systems Thinking for Social Change: A Practical Guide to Solving Complex Problems, Avoiding Unintended Consequences, and Achieving Lasting Results* (White River Junction, VT: Chelsea Green).

Van Parijs, Philippe (1992), *Arguing for Basic Income: Ethical Foundations for a Radical Reform* (New York: Verso).

Vézina, Martine and Jean-Pierre Girard (2014), 'Multi-Stakeholder Co-Operative Model as a Flexible Sustainable Framework for Collective Entrepreneurship: An International Perspective', in Caroline Guselinckx, Li Zhao, and Sonja Novkovic, eds, *Co-operative Innovations in China and the West* (New York: Palgrave Macmillan), 64–78.

Whyman, Philip (2012), 'Co-operative Principles and the Evolution of the "Dismal Science": The Historical Interaction between Co-operative and Mainstream Economics', *Business History* 54(6), 833–54.

Witherell, Rob (2013), 'An Emerging Solidarity: Worker Co-operatives, Unions, and the New Union Co-Operative Model in the United States', *International Journal of Labour Research* 5(2), 251–68.

CHAPTER 27

....

THE WORKER CO-OPERATIVE FORM IN THE HOME CARE INDUSTRY IN THE USA

....

DAPHNE BERRY

27.1 INTRODUCTION

....

> One in seven low-wage women workers is a home care aide—and overall, home care will add more new jobs than any other occupation over the decade from 2012 to 2022. Thus, the stability and growth of home care jobs have a significant impact on the nation's economy and on the quality of life in low-income communities.
>
> (PHI, 2015a)[1]

HOME care aides are people who work helping clients in their homes with the activities of daily living. Elderly people and those with disabilities often prefer home care because they can remain at home rather than live in a multi-person facility. Care by home health aides has also become the method of choice for governments, medical insurers, and others responsible for provisioning the care or paying for it because of the relative cost-effectiveness of home care. For various reasons, the home care industry is plagued by a growing shortage of workers. One factor in the shortage is the rate of ageing of the US population relative to the availability of working-age women in the population. By 2022, the demand for direct care workers (home care, home health, nursing, and personal care aides) overall is expected to increase by 37 per cent, while the number of women in the primary labour pool from which caregivers are drawn will increase by less than 1 per cent. Most of this growth in demand will be in the area of home- and community-based care

---

[1] Paraprofessional Healthcare Institute (PHI), a direct care research, policy, and training development organization.

(PHI 2014). This shortage of home health aides is exacerbated by the unfortunate poverty-level or near poverty-level wages for most home care jobs. Research has shown that quality jobs for home care workers could not only improve their economic situations, but also improve their attitudes toward their work and have an impact on their intention-to-turnover and the quality of care that they provide to clients (Eaton 2000).

In the midst of this high-turnover, low-wage industry, Co-operative Home Care Associates (CHCA)—a worker co-operative—stands as a model for high-road work practices that claim to be good for employees, customers, and the business, by extension, at a minimum. CHCA was started in 1985 as part of a sectoral strategy to create jobs for low-income women and address the low wages and generally poor quality of health aide jobs. The intention was to lead change by being a model for others in the industry. CHCA hoped to demonstrate how providing quality jobs for these front-line caregivers could facilitate providing quality care to clients—an oft-stated goal of home care businesses (Inserra et al. 2002). Fulfilling a dual mission, CHCA has grown to become the largest worker co-operative in the United States. The business reports consistently lower turnover than most home care businesses in the industry. Since CHCA is one of only a few worker co-operatives in the industry, which all have lower turnover than other types of home care businesses, this raises the question of whether the form of organization is important to this outcome.

In this study, I investigated the home health aide work-related attitudes across three home care businesses under different types of governance: a nonprofit, a 'conventional' for-profit, and a worker co-operative business. Using multiple methods of data collection, the researcher examined the work environments of the workers and their perspectives on their work. This chapter describes this research and its comparative results.[2]

27.2 The Home Care Environment

27.2.1 Industry Factors

In the home health aide industry, the Federal government as payer and as regulator of most home care services forces homogeneity across agencies related to caregiver wages, training, and reporting requirements, at a minimum. In their study of the interface between changes in the elderly population and in home health agencies' organization type, Swan and Estes (1990) studied isomorphism in the industry. They attributed an increase in privately owned and chain-affiliated agencies within a certain period to Medicare policy, deregulation, competition, and cost containment efforts. Swan and

---

[2] This chapter is based on the researcher's dissertation thesis 'Organizational Form and Quality of Care in the Home Health Aide Industry', 2011.

Estes also suggested that the once-dominant nonprofit organizations, in seeking continued legitimacy, sometimes organized and behaved like for-profit organizations. Another government-driven factor in home care is the October 2015 rule for inclusion of the home health aide workforce in coverage by the Fair Labor Standards Act. Arguing that coverage of home health workers would force a reduction in the jobs that they could offer, the home care industry has, for decades, fought the inclusion of this workforce under the country's fair labour laws. As of 1 January 2016, home care workers must now be paid the federal minimum wage, time-and-a-half for overtime, and pay for time travelling between clients.

27.2.2 The Workplace

For the largest number of client-facing workers in the home care industry—home care or home health aides—the work environment is not ideal, at its best. The Bureau of Labor Statistics (BLS) describes home care jobs as requiring the ability to assist clients with activities of daily living. These include bathing and dressing, taking vital signs, administering medication, performing light housekeeping chores, scheduling appointments, arranging transportation, accompanying clients to appointments, shopping for groceries, preparing meals, and keeping clients engaged with their communities. Home health aides are responsible for monitoring client health conditions and reporting complications. In some circumstances they help with prescribed exercises, with braces or artificial limbs, and with medical equipment such as ventilators. Sometimes home health aides work for multiple clients in one day and may be required to work evening and weekend hours depending upon the clients' needs. The BLS admits that the work is often physically and emotionally demanding with back injury to the worker being a particular risk. Aides may work with clients who have mental health issues and who display violent behaviours and, in addition, they may be exposed to infections and communicable diseases (BLS 2015). Add low pay and few benefits to the aforementioned features of this work, and the many challenges in this type of work seem insurmountable.

Almost 89 per cent of home care workers are women. Of these 47 per cent are (non-Hispanic) white, 30 per cent are African American, and 16 per cent are Spanish, Hispanic, or Latino. Approximately 55 per cent have high school diplomas or lesser qualifications, and 45 per cent have attended at least some college; 20 per cent are unmarried and living with children, and at least 25 per cent are foreign-born; 52 per cent are employed full-time year round. While the median annual earnings for home health aides is $19,000, 37 per cent of those working as aides in home health care services are uninsured. Finally, 16 per cent are 100 per cent under the federal poverty line while 46 per cent live in households that rely on public benefits (PHI 2015b). A number of studies indicate that extremely low wages and benefits are central among the reasons that direct care workers give for leaving their jobs. Scala (2008) has pointed out the incongruence of seeking a high quality and stable workforce to provide vital services under system-level conditions such as these.

Researchers have suggested that the rapid growth of for-profit agencies in the United States in the 1990s can be linked to the increased potential for profit that came with the rapidly growing need for home care and government reimbursement for client care (Harris 2005; Scala 2008; Swan and Estes 1990). In the United States, by 2008 the number of for-profit home care agencies was greater than three times that of nonprofit agencies and seven times greater than the number of government agencies. Overall, for-profits represented 70 per cent of the field. In the state of New York, nonprofit agencies predominated as the proprietary agencies made up only 20 per cent of the total. Worker co-operatives are technically for-profit organizations so they would fall under the proprietary category. Co-operative Home Care Associates is the only co-operative in the home care industry in the state.

27.3 STUDY OF WORKER ATTITUDES ACROSS THREE HOME CARE ENVIRONMENTS

27.3.1 The Agencies

The three home health aide agencies in this study were located in New York City. They were of similar size and drew from similar populations of workers and of clients. However, their governance and ownership structures were different. One agency was a non-profit; another, a conventionally owned for-profit business; and the third, a worker co-operative. Data for this study are from a survey, participant observation, semi-structured interviews, and archival documents. The mission and focus of each organization; its processes and practices related to training, compensation, levels of participation in decision-making by home health aides; and agency and caregiver interfaces with their union, were the focus of the researcher's inquiries. The survey instrument was based on one developed by Kruse et al. (2010) in their shared capitalism research project at the National Bureau for Economic Research in Cambridge, Massachusetts. The survey asked about home health aide levels of participation and inclusion in decisions made at work, relationships with peers and supervisors, intention to leave the firm, feelings about pay and compensation, and other measures related to High Performance Work Systems (HPWS) and positive outcomes to workers and workplaces. All three organizations operated as Licensed Home Care Services Agencies[3] and contracted through one or more Certified Home Health Agencies to provide home health aide services to

---

[3] CHHAs are authorized to bill Medicaid for the semi-skilled services (in support of some unstable or acute medical conditions) of home health aides who are supervised by a nurse. LHCSAs—also called Licensed Home Health Agencies (LHHAs)—may subcontract to provide services through a CHHA and cannot bill Medicaid directly. There are many more LHCSAs than CHHAs (see reference http://wnylc.com/health/entry/76/, accessed 22 September 2016).

clients. Home care workers had different titles, training, and different levels of compensation depending on the funding sources from which they were paid.

The websites of the home health care agencies were an important guide and source of information for agency stakeholders. Here, clients are introduced to the company mission and focus and they learn about the array of services the company offers and the education, training, and experience levels of the workforce. The websites assured potential clients of the agency's focus on clients' personal needs being met in their own homes. The co-operative website also displayed an explicit focus on the caregiver's well-being. The co-operative's site outlined goals of providing the highest possible salaries and benefits while building a profitable worker-owned company, providing workers the opportunities to grow as members of a health care team, and providing reliable, high-quality home health care services. Through prominently displayed leaflets, all of the agencies provided information to home care workers about community resources that could help bridge gaps left by low pay and benefits. This information included contact information for health care centres in the area, emergency services, and nonprofit treatment or research organizations. Also available was information on how to access no- or low-cost health screenings, how to get coverage and healthcare services through the N.Y. state-sponsored healthcare plan, or the union-sponsored plan; and how to file for workers' compensation or disability claims. Finally, pay-related information and notices related to union activity were usually placed in visible locations near training class areas or posted on bulletin boards.

The ownership profiles of home health aides at the three agencies were different. In the case of the worker co-operative, worker–owners owned one share each of company stock and had access to company profits via monetary disbursements to their 401(k) plans or cash. Workers at the nonprofit were not owners nor did they participate in profit-sharing. Workers at the conventional for-profit organization had access to a profit-sharing retirement account, but did not participate in a significant way.

27.3.2 The Caregivers

I conducted interviews with staff from all agencies and home care workers at two of the three agencies. All interview participants from the nonprofit, all but one at the conventional for-profit, and all but two at the worker co-operative were women. Of the 628 usable surveys collected—available in English and Spanish—over 99 per cent of the respondents were women. Surveys were administered after training sessions and similar group gatherings. Nearly everyone in attendance agreed to complete a survey. Comparable racial and ethnic demographics were collected from the conventional for-profit and nonprofit; however, the worker co-operative preferred that less specific demographic data be gathered. Therefore, the only demographic data used in this study was related to age and time at the agency.

An important question regarding caregivers across the agencies is whether self-selection into the different types of agencies might have been a factor in the study results.

Might participatory practices or ownership factor in a worker's choice of where to work? Aside from a single question on the survey of whether it is important to work for a company that provides ownership, in which caregivers at the worker co-operative provided different responses from home health aides at the other organizations, there are no data to address the question more specifically. However, observation and interviews revealed a common problem related to attracting and identifying quality workers. Therefore, relatively broad initial search processes followed by screening of applicants was performed by all three agencies. While turnover was reported to be noticeably lower at the worker co-operative, there appeared to be no advantage in the attraction and selection process at the worker co-operative. The quantitative analysis did indicate modest differences in age ranges of caregivers between the organizations.

27.3.3 Home Health Aide Routines and Daily Environments

At home care agencies, co-ordinators are people who assign caregivers to client cases; troubleshoot client–caregiver missed connections; help resolve conflict between caregiver and client or client families; handle emergencies; and are the first line in caregiver disciplinary action. When an aide has a problem, the co-ordinator is the first point of contact. Mornings at the agencies were often stressful for co-ordinators and caregivers in the field.

I engaged in observation in several venues that varied by organization. These included training classes, meetings with agency staff, and, for the worker co-operative, organization, work-group meetings, and company information sessions. Classes usually were held during a three-hour period during the evenings. Lessons covered how to recognize symptoms and various illnesses, and how to respond to and care for patients with these illnesses. Instructors covered topics such as stroke, diabetes, Alzheimer's, various cancers, dementia, and heart disease. In addition, home health aides learned which medications are prescribed for which illnesses, and they learned the clinical names for medical conditions. Caregivers were tested on differences between Types 1 and 2 diabetes, what a diabetic client can consume and when, which foods affect blood glucose levels, and how to get the most information from food labels. Aides were also responsible for detailed reporting of a client's condition so they had to be very familiar with client illnesses and report on client conditions and medication. Home health aides followed closely prescribed procedures regarding when they could arrive and leave work (within ten-minute periods) and for detailing task completion based on the client's individual care plans. There were procedures to follow if, after the aide has arrived for work, a client does not open the door. Procedures were different if the aide believed the client might be ill than if she guessed her denied entry was for some other reason. Aides had begun using an electronic sign in and sign out process via a telephone-based application designed for home care use.

27.3.4 The Union

Home care workers at all three of the agencies in this study were unionized with Local 1199 SEIU United Healthcare Workers East, the largest healthcare union in the country. The union had advocated for higher wages and improved working conditions and encouraged members to acquire greater knowledge in the healthcare sector. Home care workers' opinions about the union varied. A number of workers across the three agencies did not feel that the union had helped with the quality of their jobs. A specific disappointment was that initially, the union had promised to help get wages to ten dollars an hour across the board, but did not achieve this. A number of caregivers at all three agencies expressed disillusionment that part of their hard-earned wages were going to union dues to no effect. Others expressed appreciation of the union advocacy on behalf of educational benefits and paid sick time. To an open-ended request for comments at the end of the survey, the caregivers overwhelmingly cited the need for higher pay. In a specific reference to the union drive for across-the-board $10 an hour pay, one aide summed up a common refrain, 'Taking care of patients is a hard job. I believe we should make $10 an hour for the work we have to do in patients' homes. We aides go through a lot with these patients!'

27.3.5 The Conventional For-Profit Organization

The for-profit organization had been in business more than 25 years, was privately owned, and employed more than 1,500 home care workers and home attendants. In total, 170 home health aides at the for-profit agency completed the survey. Caregivers here indicated, on average, lower levels of job satisfaction, lower levels of inclusion and information sharing, lower involvement in decision-making related to their jobs or other problems at work, and less belief that the company's stated mission and goals were aligned with their practices, than at the nonprofit or the worker co-operative. However, it is important to also note that responses in these areas of caregivers at the non-profit and for-profit home healthcare agency were not significantly different from each other but that both were significantly different from responses from caregivers at the worker co-operative. Interview participants at the for-profit included co-ordinators—the first line of management to the home health aides in the field. One staffer (a former co-ordinator) described quality care as being efficient and effective care that takes account of a client's specific needs. She elaborated on two important points saying that quality means arriving on time and scheduling the tasks to be done around what is convenient for the client. If a client has a previously unscheduled doctor's appointment, knowing enough to be able to work around that is important. She explained 'knowing enough' as having the training and experience and knowledge about the patient's needs. She stated that clients were happy when they could trust a caregiver, when the caregiver knows the right questions to ask, and when she expresses genuine concern for a client: 'Good communication between the two would be needed ... I think a lot of people don't understand what care is—a lot of people think helping somebody with their meds, or getting them to the doctor, they don't see that as providing care. They see it as being a housekeeper or a babysitter. They don't use the term "care" or understand how important that is for a patient's well-being.' On what makes it hard to do the job, she said: 'If patients are not compliant or are resistant, it makes it hard for the aide. And families can be unco-operative.' In the for-profit, caregivers did not formally participate in decision-making although informally, they could offer their opinions. This staffer believed that a caregiver perspective is important for the agency to have explicitly 'because the face and the voice of the agency to that patient is mainly the home health aide'. The co-ordinators' educational backgrounds and experience varied but none had previously worked as home health aides. Nor was aide-to-supervisor or co-ordinator a possible career path for aides at the for-profit. However, the aide to trainer career path, depending upon the course content, and whether and what type of degree was involved, was possible. Co-ordinator–caregiver relationships appeared to be a bit tense in the for-profit agency. Caregivers at the for-profit agency earned average wages compared to others in the industry, and benefits were average. Union-affiliated healthcare coverage was individual only and it restricted coverage to those who worked a certain number of hours over a period—for many a hard-to-maintain minimum.

27.3.6 The Nonprofit Organization

The non-profit organization had been in business more than 30 years and employed more than 1,500 home attendants and home health aides. Two hundred caregivers from the non-profit completed the survey. Caregivers at the nonprofit indicated, on average, lower levels of job satisfaction, lower levels of inclusion and information sharing, less involvement in decision-making related to their jobs, and less belief that the company's stated mission and goals were aligned with their practices than at the worker co-operative, but more in these areas than at the for-profit business. However, responses from the nonprofit were not significantly different from those at the for-profit. Interview participants at the nonprofit agency included several managers in the organization. One manager said of home health aides, 'Nurses, therapists, and a host of professionals are providing services to a client. The person the client remembers is the aide—whether that aide was good for the client or not.' Another referenced the difficulties of getting a job done well because sometimes clients are abusive. Because there are all kinds of personalities involved, an ideal home health aide is assertive, patient, professional, knowledgeable, and very importantly, in possession of '*good judgement*' (emphasis on the part of the speaker): 'When you enter a client's home, you have to negotiate with the client, the neighbour, the granddaughter, the dog. And you have to balance all of these.' One administrator said that nurses visit periodically to say what additional care is needed and to develop a new care plan that involves the client. Therefore, the care plan includes the nurse, the client (or sometimes the family if the client has dementia), but not the aide. Aides usually have initial input via the nurses. Nevertheless, 'The aide is the eyes and ears for the organization because they are there ... sometimes a hospital will discharge a patient in very poor condition and we don't know that until the aide goes in.' Caregivers at the nonprofit agency earned slightly better than average wages compared to others in the industry and benefits were average. As for the for-profit agency, union-affiliated healthcare coverage was for the employee only and required that a minimum number of working hours be maintained.

27.3.7 The Worker Co-operative

At the worker co-operative, only workers in the enterprise may be owners and after three months, all home care workers are eligible to purchase a single share in the co-operative. Note, though, that at the worker co-operative, not all workers are home care aides as some administrative staff are also owners. Participation as an owner is highly recommended but voluntary. Ownership by home care workers varied between 75 and 90 per cent of the 1,700 workers there at the time, and each owner had one vote in the organization's affairs.

At the worker co-operative, 258 home health aides completed the survey.[4] Caregivers at the worker co-operative indicated, on average, statistically significant higher levels of job satisfaction, higher levels of inclusion and information sharing than at the nonprofit agency or the for-profit agency, and higher involvement in decision-making related to their jobs or other problems at work. During an interview, an administrator emphasized the importance of a quality job for caregivers to be able to provide quality care. A quality job means a living wage with comparable benefits, good classroom and on-the-job training, ongoing support once a caregiver is in the field, and opportunities for growth and self-improvement. The worker co-operative stressed its goals towards poverty-alleviation and asset building for the agency's worker–owners in its mission. An administrator also explained how the agency actively sought better paying contracts for the benefits of the workers, and that when the latest government reimbursement increase occurred, the worker co-operative was one of very few who passed the increase on to the home health aides. One home health aide discussed her role on the board of directors and the feeling of responsibility for the organization and the welfare of her fellow workers. When prompted about the power dynamics, she provided an example of when home health aides on the board had directed the use of surplus funds in a different direction than senior management, and said that while the aides listened carefully to other management input, they felt that their opinions were valued. Another home health aide mentioned the lack of respect aides received from some clients and their families. The caregivers at the worker co-operative earned average wages compared to others in the industry, but their benefits were above average. Although union-affiliated healthcare coverage was the same as at the other agencies, the worker co-operative

---

[4] The source of the data and findings for this chapter is Berry (2011).

subsidized caregiver hours to help them maintain coverage across lapses in working hours. Specifically, the worker co-operative paid additional money to a health insurance plan to help home care workers with just under the number of hours needed in two consecutive months to maintain their coverage. The company matched home health aide savings by a fixed percentage and also when voted by the board of directors, made additional deposits at the end of the year based on decisions of what to do with profits.

27.4 DIFFERENT OUTCOMES

Differences between the worker co-operative, the conventional for-profit agency, and the nonprofit organization that are linked to High Performance Work System-type practices or statistical analyses of factors in worker attitudes are summarized in Table 27.1.

In previous research, when findings showed that worker attitudes differed in organizations with different structural characteristics, the differences were often attributed to different human resource management systems or high performance work-related processes and practices within the organizations (Benz 2005; Borzaga and Tortia 2006; Friedman et al. 1999). The external environment in the home care industry, particularly the Federal government as regulator and payer, constrains and directs many internal processes within the three organizations. This includes those related to monitoring, reporting, training, and wages for caregivers. The outcomes of the current study indicate that caregivers who work at the worker co-operative provided notably different responses to not only most of the individual survey items, but also the constructs for worker attitudes such as job satisfaction and organizational commitment. In addition, results from the statistical analyses also showed that, even when various types of participation were accounted for, home health aides at the worker co-operative still indicated statistically significant higher levels of commitment, satisfaction, and lowered intent-to-turnover. While workers at all of the agencies in this study indicated that low wages and poor benefits were meaningful problems that needed attention, an in-depth pay satisfaction analysis was not part of this study. Since this sector involves mainly 'caring labour' for which standard economic theory related to self-interest does not apply well (Folbre and Nelson 2000), this may be a factor in the low-wage dimension of this sector of the economy.

Findings related to the worker-owned organization can provide new information on how ownership and participatory programmes can be important, particularly in an environment with multiple structural and process constraints, and generally adverse working environments. This study has highlighted positive outcomes from the worker co-operative organizational form in the home health aide industry in comparison to the nonprofit and conventional for-profit organizations. The growing shortage of home health aide workers, combined with the low wages and poor prospects in this occupation, do not bode well for an ageing society nor for its many front-line home care workers. Besides being a growth industry, the direct care industry is a large employer of poor,

Table 27.1 Worker Attitudes/Outcomes by Type of Organization

		Conventional for-profit	Nonprofit	Worker co-operative
Distinguishing Characteristics	Supervisors provide helpful feedback [5]	Lowest	Lower (significantly different from the for-profit and from the worker co-operative)	Highest
	Aides feel respected by supervisor	Lowest (significantly different from the worker co-operative but not from the nonprofit)	Lower	Highest
	Aides participate significantly in decision-making[6]	Lowest (significantly different from the worker co-operative but not from the nonprofit)	Lower	Highest
	Aides indicate job satisfaction	Lowest (significantly different from the worker co-operative but not from the nonprofit)	Lower	Highest
	Aides indicate organizational commitment	Lowest (significantly different from the worker co-operative but not from the nonprofit)	Lower	Highest
	Aides indicate intention to leave	Highest (significantly different from the worker co-operative but not from the nonprofit)	Higher	Lowest

Source: Berry 2011.

historically disenfranchized women in the United States who will probably continue to provide home healthcare services to many US families. In order to benefit caregivers and those for whom they provide care, the conditions of the work need meaningful improvement. If participative democratic workplaces (e.g. worker co-operatives) provide better outcomes for caregivers, and by extension to those for whom they care, these workplaces should receive more research and policy attention.

[5] Responses from home health aides at each organization are significantly different from the other organization with responses from the worker co-operative being highest and those from the for-profit firm being lowest.

[6] Decision-making can refer to a firm's overall strategy, policy, finances as well as day-to-day operational practices such as staffing, incentives, wage and benefit plans, disciplinary procedures.

References

Benz, M. (2005), 'Not for the Profit, but for the Satisfaction? Evidence on Worker Well-Being in Nonprofit Firms', *Kyklos*, 58(2), 155–76.

Berry, D. P. (2011), 'Organizational Form and Quality of Care in the Home Health Aide Industry', Retrieved from ProQuest Dissertations Publishing.

Borzaga, C. and Tortia, E. (2006), 'Worker Motivations, Job Satisfaction, and Loyalty in Public and Nonprofit Social Services', *Nonprofit and Voluntary Sector Quarterly*, 35(2), 225–48.

Bureau of Labor Statistics, U.S. Department of Labor (2015), 'Home Health Aides', *Occupational Outlook Handbook, 2016-17 Edition*. December. Available at http://www.bls.gov/ooh/health-care/home-health-aides.htm#tab-3 (accessed 22 September 2016).

Eaton, S. C. (2000), 'Beyond 'Unloving Care': Linking Human Resource Management and Patient Care Quality in Nursing Homes, *International Journal of Human Resource Management*, 11(3), 591–616.

Folbre, N. and Nelson, J. A. (2000), 'For Love or Money - or Both?', *Journal of Economic Perspectives*, 14(4), 123–40.

Friedman, S. M., Daub, C., Cresci, K., and Keyser, R. (1999), 'A Comparison of Job Satisfaction among Nursing Assistants in Nursing Homes and the Program of All-Inclusive Care for the Elderly (PACE), *The Gerontologist*, 39(4), 434–9.

Harris, M. D. (2005), *Handbook of Home Health Care Administration*, 4th ed. (Boston: Jones and Bartlett Publishers, Inc.).

Inserra, A., Conway, M., and Rodat, J. (2002), *The Co-operative Home Care Associates: A Case Study of a Sectoral Employment Development Approach* (Queenstown, MD: The Aspen Institute).

Kruse, D. L., Freeman, R. B., and Blasi, J. R. (2010), eds, *Shared Capitalism at Work: Employee Ownership, Profit and Gain Sharing, and Broad-based Stock Options* (Chicago: University of Chicago Press).

PHI (2014), 'Occupational Projections for Direct Care Workers, 2012-2022'. Available at http://phinational.org/sites/phinational.org/files/phi-factsheet14update-12052014.pdf (accessed 22 September 2016).

PHI (2015a), 'Paying the Price: How Poverty Wages Undermine Home Care in America'. Available at http://phinational.org/sites/phinational.org/files/research-report/paying-the-price.pdf (accessed 22 September 2016).

PHI (2015b), 'Direct Care Workers at A Glance'. Available at http://phinational.org/direct-care-workers-glance (accessed 22 September 2016).

Scala, E. (2008), 'Home-and-Community-Based Services: Workforce and Quality Outcomes', in E. Scala, L. Hendrickson, and C. Regan, eds, *A Compendium of Three Discussion Papers: Strategies for Promoting and Improving the Direct-Service Workforce: Applications to Home-and-Community-Based Services* (New Brunswick, NJ: Rutgers Center for State Health Policy).

Swan, J. H. and Estes, C. L. (1990), 'Changes in Aged Populations Served by Home Health Agencies', *Journal of Aging and Health*, 2(3), 373–94.

CHAPTER 28

....

RAIFFEISENBANKS AND VOLKSBANKS FOR EUROPE

the case for co-operative banking in Germany

....

HOLGER BLISSE AND DETLEV HUMMEL

28.1 INTRODUCTION

....

THIS chapter highlights the role that co-operative banking could play in the German banking system in the future. The creation and evolution of national banking systems with member-based and socially responsible institutions seem to be essential.

The basic idea of the co-operative concept—to share responsibility for each other and to promote members—has been a feature of local co-operative banks since they began emerging in the nineteenth century. Credit co-operatives were intended to also provide protection against the excesses of the free market.

Co-operative banks in Europe started on a local level and gradually evolved over the 150 years of their existence into universal banks. In most European countries they now operate very successfully with central and specialized institutions, and compete with other banks in complex federal structures. Co-operative banks originated in the German-speaking countries. The first banks of this type are closely associated with the names of their initiators, Hermann Schulze-Delitzsch (1808–83) and Friedrich Wilhelm Raiffeisen (1818–88).

This chapter will therefore focus on the German example. The history, structure, and operation of the co-operative banking network are central in order to position this private form of organization, which is supported by its members, in the market as a responsible, local institution. Indeed, the costs and earnings analysis shows that this type of institution has been able to successfully contribute to economic and social development in its region.

28.2 ECONOMIC AND LEGAL BACKGROUND

The very first modern co-operatives were created in Germany at around 1850 in order to respond to a serious economic problem faced by small- and medium-sized enterprises: artisans and small traders in the cities and farmers in the countryside were unable to easily cover their financial needs by loans from existing banks (for the history, see e.g. Faust 1977; Hummel and Blisse 2005).

The previous option, namely a private lender ('merchant') offering funds, was very expensive. In the individual contract design and monitoring of credit relationships with its clients, the lender incurred additional costs in obtaining information and there was also the uncertainty of an increased default risk. The lender was neither familiar with the economic conditions of his borrowers nor could he obtain additional collateral security from them. Furthermore, he could certainly take advantage of his clients' lack of financing alternatives. On the other hand, whether the private lenders would fail as partners remained uncertain for the borrower who nonetheless had no alternative but to use them. Co-operation between borrowers in local credit co-operatives offered an economical alternative. Compared to what other banks offered, credit co-operatives had an advantage in terms of quality since their members were able to take out the loans they would not have been able to access otherwise. They therefore became 'bank-worthy' and, in comparison with other options, this was an advantage because no collateral security was required apart from creditworthiness, that is the personal security of the borrower.

Compared to a loan with a private lender a credit co-operative was considerably cheaper since, thanks to the voluntary work of the members, it worked with lower overhead costs. A credit co-operative was also able to reduce risk premium, because all members were personally liable for the obligations of their co-operative. Furthermore, it was safer, because the members of a credit co-operative knew each other personally, and managed the co-operative directly, and therefore trust could grow in their community.

The organization rules on which these co-operatives were based are called co-operative principles. These include, first and foremost, the principles of identity, promotion, and democracy. The principle of identity, according to which members as owners are at the same time the customers, can be described more concretely with the Schulze-Delitzsch principles of self-help, self-management, and self-responsibility. The relationship between these principles can also be described as follows: self-help—the principle of promotion—addresses the economic orientation of the co-operative operations. Members establish a co-operative with the sole aim of economic promotion and raising capital. They are the most important customers, and in the ideal case of the traditional co-operative, members are the *only* customers. In order to guarantee the principle of democracy, the members' decisions in the General Assembly are made on the basis of equal voting rights, regardless of their amount of liability and raised capital. Self-management means that only members hold positions on the executive and supervisory boards. Members manage and control the co-operative independently. Ultimately, self-responsibility means that members not only provide capital, but also commit themselves to adhering to a framework for their co-operative and to making additional payments for the debts in case of economic difficulties, which initially, in the nineteenth century, covered the 'credit base' of the co-operative with respect to a third party (Bonus 1986).

As the number of co-operative start-ups rapidly increased, a fully fledged legal form appeared to be more useful than by-laws. This was fulfilled with the (Prussian) Co-operatives Act (GenG) of 1867, which was mainly designed by Schulze-Delitzsch and included the co-operative principles. The Austrian Co-operative Act came into force in 1873. This act allowed a greater legal leeway in transactions with members and third parties than the German Act.

In this period, the legal form proved to be an important condition for the creation and development of credit co-operatives.

28.3 Co-operative Banks in the German Banking System

28.3.1 Structure

Together with the private banks and the institutions of the savings bank sector, the 1,023 institutions of the co-operative sector (end of 2015, Deutsche Bundesbank 2016b) form the 'third pillar' in the German banking system. They are organized in a three-level structure: WGZ-Bank AG acts as the regional central bank for 182 co-operative banks in Rhineland and Westphalia (WGZ-Bank 2015: 90); DZ Bank AG, which emerged from DG Bank AG and GZ-Bank AG 2001, functions as a regional central bank for the other co-operative banks and as the central bank for all co-operative banks, further sector institutions, and the WGZ-Bank. The three-level structure also characterizes the public savings bank sector formed by 409 savings banks, 8 Landesbanken (Girozentralen), and the DekaBank Deutsche Girozentrale. Finally, the group of commercial banks, formed by four big banks, 160 regional banks and other private banks, and 107 branches of foreign banks, includes 271 institutes (end of 2015, Deutsche Bundesbank 2016b).

The primary services offered by co-operative banks are usually complemented by integrated financial services and corporate finance products. With respect to the services offered by each of the three groups, no significant differences appear, for example, in private or corporate loans, factoring, funds, mortgages, lease, or insurance business, but differences can probably be found in the target groups and in regional and international services. While the major banks provide these services within corporate structures, integrated subsidiaries (concerns), savings banks, and co-operative banks rely on specialized institutions within their network, which can now be denoted as bancassurance groups (e.g. BVR 2003: 66–90; Breuer and Mark 2004; Götzl and Gros 2010).[1]

In 2001, with the idea of 'joining forces', co-operative banks envisioned 'highly independent Volksbanks and Raiffeisen banks' (Anon. 2001: 2), with a lower number of banks (expected for 2008: 800 to 1,000 banks). Contrary to some formulations (Mußler 2001) and fears (Wanner 2004; Fehl and Kuhn 2005: 209), this model of a co-operative federal system should not amount to a concern (Anon 2001: 3.). As an economic goal, it applies less to increasing market share per se, but 'even better to exploiting the market potential of the co-operative financial services network, to improving the cost structure for securing and strengthening profitability and to creating a unified and efficient risk management.' (Anon. 2001a: 3).

28.3.2 Position in the Market

With the help of balance sheet- and income statement-oriented indicators, the market position is mapped in terms of the liquidity–financial sphere. The number of employees and branches reflects the market position in the technical–organizational sphere. Since the big international banks are included in the commercial bank sector, the savings bank and co-operative bank sectors include their central banks (Tables 28.1–28.3). Their share in total assets of the banking group in the sector of public institutions is, with 45.3 per cent, significantly higher than in the co-operative sector with 25.6 per cent (end of 2015) (see Table 28.1).[2]

Given the increasingly significant off-balance-sheet activities of banks, the current market situation can hardly be determined based on the balance sheet positions. Assuming that the interest rate and commission incomes are appropriate expense items, the profitability of the banking groups can be represented as shown in Table 28.2.

Employees (see Table 28.3) and the presence in the region with branches (see Table 28.4) describe quality and direct local supply in banking services for private and corporate customers. This is in spite of the fact that the number of employees has been decreasing in all banking groups since the year 2000. The weight of credit co-operatives emerges also when we look at the number of branches: credit co-operatives own over 33 per cent of all branches, a figure which is comparable to that of savings banks and higher than that of commercial banks. With respect to their number, credit co-operatives reach by far the highest rate: nearly 60 per cent of all institutes are credit co-operatives.

---

[1] As specialized institutions, mortgage banks, building societies, and banks with special functions have not been included in the data contained in Tables 28.1–28.3.

[2] Most recent data available (2014 or 2015).

Table 28.1 Assets–Based Market Share (in per cent)

Year Categories of banks	Balance sheet total assets	Lending of non-banks (non-MFIs)	Deposits and borrowing from non-banks (non-MFIs)	Savings deposits and bank savings bonds
2000				
CB	36.7	35.9	31.4	14.8
SB	46.9	47.2	46.9	55.7
CC	16.4	16.9	21.7	29.5
2005				
CB	37.7	36.7	34.4	15.7
SB	46.4	46.4	44.7	55.2
CC	15.9	16.9	20.9	29.1
2010				
CB	46.2	34.9	38.5	20.9
SB	39.0	47.6	41.7	51.1
CC	14.8	17.5	19.8	28.0
2015				
CB	48.3	35.0	41.7	19.5
SB	33.9	44.2	37.6	50.9
CC	17.8	20.8	20.7	29.6

CB: Commercial banks, SB: Landesbanken and savings banks, CC: Regional institutions of credit co-operatives and credit co-operatives.

Source: Deutsche Bundesbank.

28.4 INSIDE THE CO-OPERATIVE BANKING GROUP

The German co-operative banking group could be further described by means of sub-groups, which are part of the banking statistics. The Deutsche Bundesbank differed further in:

- 1,009 banks in the legal form of a registered co-operative (eG) (Kreditgenossenschaften) and
- 12 other banks in the co-operative sector (end of 2015, Deutsche Bundesbank 2016b: 4).

Table 28.2 Cost–Earnings–Based Market Shares (in per cent)

Year Categories of banks	Net interest received	Net commissions received	General administrative spending	Operating result before the valuation of assets
2000				
CB	36.6	60.2	48.7	45.9
SB	42.5	25.1	32.9	42.7
CC	20.9	14.7	18.4	11.4
2005				
CB	40.3	56.6	46.4	61.4
SB	40.8	27.8	34.7	28.1
CC	18.9	15.6	18.9	10.5
2010				
CB	38.8	57.2	48.8	36.6
SB	40.3	26.6	32.9	40.1
CC	20.9	16.2	18.3	23.3
2015				
CB	42.0	57.7	48.6	22.5
SB	36.5	25.8	32.6	47.1
CC	21.5	16.5	18.8	30.4

CB: Commercial banks; SB: Landesbanken and savings banks; CC: Regional institutions of credit co-operatives and credit co-operatives.
Source: Deutsche Bundesbank.

Table 28.3 Employees (absolute and in per cent)

Categories of banks	2000	2005	2010	2015
CB*)	252,750 (32.6)	205,350 (29.6)	189,700 (28.8)	178,600 (28.5)
SB	341,400 (44.1)	319,400 (46.1)	304,050 (46.3)	286,750 (45.7)
CC	180,400 (23.3)	168,300 (24.3)	163,350 (24.9)	161,800 (25.8)
Employees (total)	774,550 (100.0)	693,050 (100.0)	657,100 (100.0)	627,150 (100.0)

*) with private building societies.
Source: AGV Banken 2016.

Table 28.4 Number of Credit Institutions and their Branches (2015, in per cent)

2015 Categories of banks	(1) Credit institutions	(2) Branches in Germany	(3) Bank offices in Germany, total	Share of total (in per cent)		
				(1)	(2)	(3)
CB	288	9,698	9,986	16.6	30.0	29.3
BB	4	7,240	7,244	0.2	22.4	21.2
Rb/ocb	172	2,313	2,485	9.9	7.1	7.3
Bfb	112	145	257	6.5	0.5	0.8
SB	422	11,861	12,283	24.3	36.6	36.0
CC	1,027	10,833	11,860	59.1	33.4	34.7
Total	1,737	32,392	34,129	100.0	100.0	100.0

CB: Commercial banks with BB: Big banks, Rb/ocb: Regional banks and other commercial banks, and Bfb: Branches of foreign banks; SB: Landesbanken and Savings banks; CC: Regional institutions of credit co-operatives and credit co-operatives.

Source: Deutsche Bundesbank 2016a (9): 104.

The largest subgroup (Kreditgenossenschaften, credit co-operatives) consists mostly of Volksbanks and Raiffeisenbanks. In the case of mergers there is the question of the new name, which is supposed to usher in a new beginning in terms of a turning away from the precursor institutions and opening up of greater market opportunities. This, however, is not unproblematic in terms of customer loyalty. For example, the abbreviations RV- or VR-Bank have lately been chosen by mergers of Volksbanks and Raiffeisenbanks. The co-operative roots remain visible in the new name with a reference to the two preceding institutions (Volksbank and/or Raiffeisenbank).

The PSD banks emerged as a self-help organization of the postal workers in 1872, and the Sparda banks for railway employees from 1896 onwards (Aschhoff and Henningsen 1995: 62). As postal savings and loan associations, the PSD banks were, up to 1998, organized in the legal form of an economic association (wirtschaftlicher Verein) with the exception of the postal savings and loan co-operative in Saarbrücken (now PSD Bank Saarbrücken eG) (Lamsfuß 1992; Anon. 2002a). Currently, all PSDs operate in the legal form of a co-operative, which is seen as the 'contemporary legal form' (PSD Bank Karlsruhe 1998: 10). As a result of this transformation, PSDs changed their company name to PSD Bank. The Sparda banks form a distinct group (Hahn 1988; Anon. 2002b). The DZ BANK operates as the central bank for both the PSD and the Sparda banks.

Both groups concentrate on retail banking and implement the co-operative principle of members' promotion, inter alia, by offering a free-of-charge current account for their members. Both groups have a relatively high proportion of members (Table 28.5).

PSD banks and Sparda banks belong to their own auditing associations—the Verband der PSD Banken e.V., Bonn and the Verband der Sparda-Banken e.V., Frankfurt

Table 28.5 PSD Banks and Sparda Banks (end of 2015)

	Number of institutions	Balance sheet total (in bill. €)	Members	Share of total (in per cent)	
Credit co-operatives* with	1,018	806.211	18,283,324	Balance sheet total	Members
PSD Banks	15	24.374	660,957	3.0	3.6
Sparda Banks	12	67.984	3,602,040	8.4	19.7

* without VR Diskontbank, Edekabank, and Teambank.
Source: BVR (2015a): 77, 79.

am Main—and are also members of the national Bundesverband der Deutschen Volksbanken und Raiffeisenbanken (BVR).

Among other professional group banks there are also the church co-operative banks, the Deutsche Apotheker- und Ärztebank (pharmacists and doctors) (Heister 1990; Machauer and Schiereck 1999), and the BBBank (public officers) (on the emergence, see Loesch 1974: 15–24). These belong to the larger co-operative banks since they operate, not only on the local level, but also on the regional, and in some cases even national level. With approximately €36.4 billion (end of 2015) of total assets, the Deutsche Apotheker- und Ärztebank, Düsseldorf, is the largest German co-operative bank. It is owned by 107,768 members (397,000 customers) (end of 2015).

In the early 1990s, four banks for public officers (Beamtenbanken) merged to form the BBBank eG, Karlsruhe, which, with approximately €9.1 billion (end of 2015) in total assets and 436,465 members (end of 2015), is now one of the ten largest co-operative banks in Germany (see Table 28.6).

The twelve institutions of the subgroup of other banks in the co-operative sector play a special role. These banks don't operate in the legal form of a co-operative company (eG), but ten of them work as a corporation and two banks as KG (limited partnership). Several of these other banks belong to a co-operative non-banking group.

28.4.1 Local Co-operative Banks

On average, the total assets of all co-operative banks amount to approximately €790 million. This figure is significantly lower than that of the savings bank sector, which averages about €2.8 billion, or the commercial bank sector with over €5.5 billion (each end of 2015, only: Regional banks and other commercial banks, calculated by Deutsche Bundesbank, also see Table 28.7).

The average total assets for the co-operative bank sector have shown a fivefold increase since the end of 1993, when they amounted to €140 million (BVR 2003: 56). In the face

Table 28.6 Overview of German Co-operative Banks (2015)

Rank	Name	Location	Total assets (mill. €)
1	Deutsche Apotheker- und Ärztebank eG	Düsseldorf	36,617.7
2	Sparda-Bank Baden-Württemberg eG	Stuttgart	14,036.2
3	Berliner Volksbank eG	Berlin	11,850.7
	...		
507	Volks- und Raiffeisenbank Saale-Unstrut eG	Merseburg	380.1
508	Spreewaldbank eG	Lübben (Spreewald)	379.3
509	Volksbank Weschnitztal eG	Rimbach	378.0
510	Raiffeisenbank Parsberg-Velburg eG	Parsberg	377.0
	...		
1.017	Raiffeisenbank Maitis eG, Göppingen	Göppingen	22.0
1.018	Spar- und Darlehnskasse Stockhausen eG	Herbstein	19.2
1.019	Raiffeisenbank eG	Struvenhütten	15.6

Source: BVR.

Table 28.7 (1) Number of Institutes and (2) Balance Sheet Average for Each (in bill. €)

Year	2000		2005		2010		2015	
Categories of banks	(1)	(2)	(1)	(2)	(1)	(2)	(1)	(2)
CB	200	3.07	158	3.82	168	4.38	159	5.58
SB	562	1.70	463	2.19	429	2.52	414	2.77
CC	1,792	0.30	1,294	0.46	1,138	0.62	1,023	0.79

CB: Commercial banks only: Regional banks and other commercial banks, SB: Savings banks, CC: Credit co-operatives.
Source: Deutsche Bundesbank.

of relatively stable market shares of the co-operative banking group, this growth can be attributed to mergers. The proportion of mergers slowly rose from the very low level of 1995 (2.6 per cent), doubled between 1997 and 1998 (from 3.5 per cent to 7.0 per cent), and in 2000—with 240 mergers—it reached its highest value (11.3 per cent). However, it has fallen ever since, and the rate of change was 2.5 per cent for 2014 (26 mergers)

(BVR 2015a: 76). Mergers do not only mean larger units are formed; indeed, at the same time, they also mean market overlap and competition among co-operative banks in a specific area are avoided.

The decreasing number of co-operative banks has also affected the structure of associations, data centres, network institutions, and central banks. At the central bank level a merger to a single institution was agreed in August 2016, as had already been attempted in 2001.

Considering that in many federal systems of co-operative banks in other European countries, the functions of associations and central banks have been merged into a single entity, the question would be whether this could be seen as desirable by all parties, or rather create concerns regarding the role of co-operative banks and whether their independence could be undermined (Anon. 2004; Wanner 2004).

In the case of a single co-operative central bank, the former project of a (partial) IPO (initial public offering) of DZ Bank could be renewed. This would weaken the co-operative ownership structure from bottom-up to top-down. However, the question arises as to whether the then likely involvement of external investors would increase their weight of interest. The management of DZ Bank therefore suggested addressing members of co-operative banks as shareholders. In order to offer members another investment incentive, without competing for members' capital from two sides of the network—that is, from both the co-operative banks (members' shares) and the federal institutions, such as the the central bank (see the proposal of a network-based participation share offered by each co-operative bank in Hummel and Blisse 2004; Blisse 2006)—other options might be more feasible.

There have been no mergers among the different banking groups so far (Blisse and Hanisch 2011). In the savings bank sector, the savings bank of Stralsund showed ambitions, but for a while it was unclear whether the share of the city at the Frankfurter Sparkasse, a free savings bank, would be sold to an interested investor outside of the savings banks' finance group. Mergers of co-operative banks with savings banks were evaluated rather sceptically (see Pleister in Eigendorf and Schwaldt 2004). Nevertheless, academic research has examined the transformation of savings banks into registered co-operatives (see e.g. Klein 2003; Scheike 2004; Dagott 2005), which would facilitate mergers in individual cases. On the other hand, models with a foundation for municipal savings banks have also been discussed and, in some cases, implemented, for example in Austria and Italy (see Blisse 2016). This, in the event of a change in the public legal form, could mean the identity of savings banks rather than the emergence of new private legal forms. Indeed, a foundation could easily preserve the orientation of savings banks which support the public weal.

The co-operative system is managing to preserve institutes and protect the trust in the co-operative credit institutions (Art. 1 paragraph 1 of the Statute of the protection scheme, BVR 2015b). The statute of the protection scheme came into force on 1 January 2004. The financial contributions to the protection fund provided for securing means are, among other things, based on the quality of the risk management instruments in the co-operative bank (Kollbach 2002; Stappel 2015). In many cases, BAG Bankaktiengesellschaft plays a key role in the rehabilitation of performance. The bank with a full banking licence is nearly a 100 per cent subsidiary of the BVR: the 'bank acquires problematic exposures of the Volksbanks and Raiffeisenbanks' (BVR 2002: 78). Direct mergers among co-operative banks have also been initiated as a restructuring measure.

For over 20 years, there has been an intensive discussion between banking supervision, science, and co-operative practice about how big co-operative banks should actually be, so that they can economically fulfil their mission of serving members, in the economic structures, and as part of a banking system. Already in 2000, experts of the Banking Supervision (BaFin) had warned about the decentralization of the co-operative banking group in Germany (Beckmann 2000). The co-operative banks were seen as becoming the clear loser in Germany in an even tougher fight for survival. Large retail banks were considered to be in a much better position (Thiesler 2000). A more recent study (Gischer and Richter 2011) reports on the ongoing consolidation process in the banking industry throughout Europe, which has led to a higher concentration and intense competition. However, empirical studies do not clearly prove the relationship between the concentration in the banking sector and reduction of systemic risk for the banking systems (Gischer and Richter 2011: 187). On the contrary, the authors state that decentralized banking structures can actually reduce the systemic risk to a banking system, as the German example shows when compared to other EU countries. Nevertheless, this relationship needs to be further explored empirically in order to make a valid statement about the optimal size of a bank, even of a co-operative bank.

28.5 CONCLUSIONS

The creation of credit co-operatives and the customer demand in recent years reflect a renaissance of this proven institution and offer further potential towards customer-supported banks. For this reason, co-operatives should be able to turn customers into members. This opens up new sources of capital, which will become a requirement as a result of the Basel III regulation. In this respect, the regulatory requirements raise the question as to what extent capital can really be better allocated in larger units, since larger units tend to become more systemically important and have to check and cover higher loans. Smaller units, on the other hand, can very quickly become overwhelmed by additional regulatory requirements in the area of compliance or regulatory reporting. Consequently, serious existential questions arise, in particular for smaller local co-operative banks, which are part of the co-operative financial group in Germany with strong prevention and control elements, equipped with a highly developed, very special corporate governance.

The tendencies of the banking union in Europe should, therefore, be pursued very critically and implemented prudently (Anon. 2014). Banking regulation necessarily means a restriction of freedom in carrying out banking and financial market operations. This is undoubtedly necessary if a free financial market functions against the interests of economy and society. The German case shows that further developing a varied co-operative banking culture can be very positive for the stability and resilience of a banking system. We would suggest not only keeping the current diversity but opening up opportunities for new co-operative start-ups as the decentralized banking structure in Germany cushioned the full impact of the banking crisis of 2008 on the banking system.

REFERENCES

AGV Banken (2016), 'Beschäftigte im Kreditgewerbe'. Available online at http://www.agvbanken.de/AGVBanken/Statistik/_Beschaeftigung/2016_Statistik_Besch%C3%A4ftigte.pdf (last accessed 2 October 2016).

Anon., 'BVR-Verbandstag 2001 'Bündelung der Kräfte': Die Umsetzung der Strategie beginnt', *Bankinformation und Genossenschaftsforum*, 28(7), 2–4.

Anon. (2001a), 'PSD Banken: "Sonder-Genossen" auf dem Weg der Öffnung—Redaktionsgespräch mit dem Vorstandsvorsitzenden des Verbandes Wolf-D. Rosenthal', *Bank und Markt*, 31(7) (2002a), 10–12.

Anon. (2002b), 'Sparda-Banken: Verbundtreu mit Sonderwegen—Redaktionsgespräch mit dem Verbandsvorsitzenden Dr. Peter Scharpf', *Bank und Markt*, 31(3), 12–15.

Anon. (2004), 'DZ Bank macht den Weg für Fusion frei'. *Handelsblatt* (187), 27 September, 17.

Anon. (2014), 'Viele Tendenzen der Bankenunion beobachten wir aus ordnungspolitischer Sicht skeptisch (Redaktionsgespräch mit Uwe Fröhlich)', *Zeitschrift für das gesamte Kreditwesen*, 67(20), 984–7.

Aschhoff, G. and Henningsen, E. (1995), *Das deutsche Genossenschaftswesen*, 2nd edn., Veröffentlichungen der DG Bank Deutsche Genossenschaftsbank 15 (Frankfurt am Main: Fritz Knapp).

Beckmann, K. (2000), 'Die Dezentralität im genossenschaftlichen Bankensektor', *Zeitschrift für das gesamte Kreditwesen*, 53, 119–22.

Blisse, H. (2006), *Stärkung der Kreditgenossenschaften durch verbundbezogenes Eigenkapital der Mitglieder—Ein Beitrag zur Corporate Governance-Diskussion*, Schriftenreihe Finanzierung und Banken, Bd. 10 (Sternenfels: Verlag Wissenschaft und Praxis).

Blisse, H. (2016), 'Die Stiftung als Eigentümerin einer Sparkasse oder Bank – Erhalt institutioneller Vielfalt im Bankensystem?' *Zeitschrift für Stiftungs- und Vereinswesen*, 14 (1), 1–8.

Blisse, H. and Hanisch, M. (2011), 'Bankengruppen übergreifende Tendenzen im deutschen Bankensystem? Bankhistorisches Archiv', *Banking and Finance in Historical Perspective*, 37(1), 62–78.

Bonus, H. (1986), 'The Co-operative Association as a Business Enterprise: A Study in the Economics of Transactions', *Journal of Institutional and Theoretical Economics*, 142, 310–39.

Breuer, W. and Mark, K. (2004), *Perspektiven der Verbundkooperation am Beispiel der Sparkassen-Finanzgruppe. Untersuchungen über das Spar-, Giro- und Kreditwesen* (Berlin: Duncker and Humblot).

BVR (2002), *Wir bündeln Kräfte: Wege* (Berlin: BVR).

BVR (2003), *Wir bündeln Kräfte: Jahresbericht* (Berlin: BVR).

BVR (2015a), 'Stabil für Europa: Jahresbericht 2015'. Available online: https://www.bvr.de/p.nsf/0/D2CE61DB16DA4E4DC1257FBD004D551C/%24FILE/BVR_Jahresbericht_durck-optimiert.pdf (accessed 2 October 2016).

BVR (2015b), 'Statut der Sicherungseinrichtung (Statute of the Protection Scheme)'. Available online: https://www.bvr.de/p.nsf/0/9F246F0DFD10AE8FC1257CE6003E91EB/$file/SE-St_2015-05-06.pdf (last accessed 2 October 2016).

Dagott, M.-P. (2005), *Kommt die Volks- und Raiffeisensparkasse? Status quo und Perspektiven der Zusammenarbeit von Sparkassen und Genossenschaftsbanken* (Wiesbaden: DG Verlag).

Deutsche Bundesbank (2016a), 'Bankenstatistik. Statistisches Beiheft 1 zum Monatsbericht', Various numbers.

Deutsche Bundesbank (2016b), *Verzeichnis der Kreditinstitute und ihrer Verbände sowie der Treuhänder für Kreditinstitute in der Bundesrepublik Deutschland. Bankgeschäftliche Informationen 2* (Frankfurt am Main: Deutsche Bundesbank).

Eigendorf, J. and Schwaldt, N. (2004), 'Kein Kauf der Berliner Bank—BVR-Chef Christopher Pleister ist gegen Fusionen mit Sparkassen: ' "Wir brauchen keinen Champion" ' (Gespräch mit Christopher Pleister)', *Berliner Morgenpost*, 28 June: 6.

Faust, H. (1977), *Geschichte der Genossenschaftsbewegung: Ursprung und Aufbruch der Genossenschaftsbewegung in England, Frankreich und Deutschland sowie ihre weitere Entwicklung im deutschen Sprachraum* (3rd edn). Frankfurt am Main: Fritz Knapp.

Fehl, U. and Kuhn (2005), 'Kreditgenossenschaften im Spannungsfeld von Wettbewerb und Regulierung', *Zeitschrift für das gesamte Genossenschaftswesen*, 55, 190–209.

Gischer, H. and Richter, T. (2011), 'Konsolidierung, Effizienz und Stabilität: Sind große Banken leistungsfähiger als kleine?' *Jahrbuch für Wirtschaftswissenschaften*, 62(2), 172–95.

Götzl, S. and Gros, J. (2010), *Regional Banks for 160 Years: Co-operative Banks in Germany—Characteristics, Structures, Benefits* (Wiesbaden: DG Verlag).

Hahn, O. (1988), ' "Die Position der Sparda-Banken"—Kritische Betrachtung eines Bankentyps (überarbeiteter Text eines Vortrages)', *Zeitschrift für das gesamte Genossenschaftswesen*, 38, 176–88.

Heister, W. (1990), 'Die wirtschaftliche Genossenschaft im kirchlichen Bereich', *Zeitschrift für öffentliche und gemeinwirtschaftliche Unternehmen*, 13, 327–36.

Hummel, D. and Blisse, H. (2004), 'Zum Eigenkapitalbedarf im Verbund der deutschen Kreditgenossenschaften—Der Vorschlag eines Verbundbeteiligungsanteils', *Die gewerbliche Genossenschaft*, 132(5–6), 22–30.

Hummel, D. and Blisse, H. (2005), 'Zur weiteren Entwicklung deutscher Kreditgenossenschaften', in H. Blisse and M. Hanisch, eds, *Finanzierung und genossenschaftlicher Finanzverbund im Wandel* (Berlin: Institut für Genossenschaftswesen an der Humboldt-Universität zu Berlin), 105–26.

Klein, J. (2003), *Das Sparkassenwesen in Deutschland und Frankreich—Entwicklung, aktuelle Rechtsstrukturen und Möglichkeiten einer Annäherung: Untersuchungen über das Spar-, Giro- und Kreditwesen* (Berlin: Duncker und Humblot).

Kollbach, W. (2002), 'Objektiv und zuverlässig—Die Entwicklung des Klassifizierungsverfahrens', *Bankinformation und Genossenschaftsforum*, 29(11), 10–12, 14–17.

Lamsfuß, W. (1992), 'Post-Spar- und Darlehnsvereine', in E. Mändle and W. Swoboda, eds, *Genossenschaftslexikon* (Wiesbaden: DG Verlag), 505–6.

Loesch, A. v. (1974), *Die deutschen Arbeitnehmerbanken in den zwanziger Jahren* (Frankfurt am Main, Köln: Europäische Verlagsanstalt).

Machauer, A. and Schiereck, D. (1999), 'Geschäftsstruktur und Geschäftserfolg kirchlicher Kreditgenossenschaften', *Zeitschrift für das gesamte Genossenschaftswesen*, 49, 195–211.

Mußler, H. (2001), 'Bankgenossen auf dem Weg zum Konzern', *Frankfurter Allgemeine Zeitung* (133), 11.06., 17.

PSD Bank Karlsruhe (1998), *Geschäftsbericht 1998* (Karlsruhe: PSD Bank Karlsruhe).

Scheike, A. (2004), *Rechtliche Voraussetzungen für die materielle Privatisierung kommunaler Sparkassen—Eine Untersuchung unter besonderer Berücksichtigung der Rechtsform der eingetragenen Genossenschaft* (Frankfurt am Main u.a.: Peter Lang).

Stappel, M. (2015), 'Einlagensicherung in Deutschland nach der Reform', Konjunktur und Kapitalmarkt – Eine Research-Publikation der DZ BANK AG, Volkswirtschaft, Special, July, 21.

Thiesler, E. (2000), 'Wie groß müssen Kreditgenossenschaften sein? Die Zukunft für die Volksbanken und Raiffeisenbanken liegt im Information Brokerage', *Bank-Archiv*, 48(9), 743–53.

Wanner, C. (2004), 'Genossen müssen sich zusammenraufen', *Handelsblatt*, 188(28), September, 23.

WGZ-Bank, *Geschäftsbericht 2015*. Düsseldorf. Available online: https://www.dzbank.de/content/dzbank_de/de/home/unser_profil/investorrelations/berichte/2015.html (accessed 2 October 2016).

CHAPTER 29

....

STATUTORY EMPLOYEE STOCK OWNERSHIP PLANS IN THE USA

....

COREY ROSEN

29.1 INTRODUCTION

THE term 'employee stock ownership plan', as well as its acronym, ESOP, is widely used in a variety of countries to describe a variety of kinds of plans. In the USA, however, an ESOP is a very specific, statutory plan, which means it is based on federal legal statutes with significant tax benefits and a long list of regulations and requirements.

An ESOP is a qualified, defined contribution employee benefit plan that invests primarily in the stock of the employer company. ESOPs are 'qualified' (i.e. tax-qualified) in that in return for meeting certain rules designed to protect the interests of the employee plan participants, ESOP sponsors, namely companies that set ESOPs up, receive various tax benefits. ESOPs are 'defined contribution plans', which are a particular type of employee benefit plan in the USA. The employer makes yearly discretionary contributions that accumulate to produce a benefit that is not defined in advance. In contrast, under defined benefit plans (mostly traditional pension plans similar to pension plans given by many governments and many companies worldwide), employees are guaranteed a specified benefit, funded by the company through required periodic corporate contributions, that covers a percentage of past wages during retirement.

An ESOP is designed to invest primarily in employer stock. An ESOP is the only type of qualified employee benefit plan that can also borrow money from or on the credit of the employer, provided the ESOP uses the money to buy employer stock. That is called a leveraged ESOP. To set up an ESOP, a company creates an employee stock ownership trust (ESOT, also referred to as the ESOP trust) and funds it by one or a combination of the following methods: contributing company shares; contributing cash to buy company shares; or having the plan borrow money to buy shares and then making payments to the ESOP trust to repay the loan.

Note that company contributions, not the employee-participants themselves, fund the plan. While in some cases there may be changes in other compensation when an ESOP is set up, employees only rarely buy stock directly for their ESOP accounts or rarely make concessions. In short, ESOPs use financing to help worker collective trusts buy company stock, with the company, not the workers' assets, serving as collateral.

The ESOP may acquire treasury shares, newly issued shares, or shares of existing shareholders. Employees do not directly buy or hold shares through the plan. Instead, the plan trustee buys, holds, and sells the shares in the trust's name for the benefit of the employees. References in this analysis to stock held by the ESOP are thus to stock held by the ESOP trust. The ESOP trust may own any percentage of the company's stock. In recent years, the average percentage of shares owned by an ESOP has increased, and the typical ESOP now owns or will eventually own most of the sponsoring company's shares.

Normally, all full-time employees aged 21 and older participate. The plan's shares are allocated to individual participant accounts, subject to vesting requirements. Participants normally receive the stock, or cash equal in value to the stock, after they leave the company.

ESOPs are used for many purposes, including to:

- Use tax-deductible corporate earnings to buy shares from owners of closely held companies who wish to sell to the workers while deferring taxation on capital gains from the sale.
- Create a market for inside or outside shareholders in closely held companies.
- Allow shareholders with founders or entrepreneurs or management in closely held companies to sell gradually and ease out of the business over a period of years.
- Finance corporate acquisitions through the loan that buys stock for a leveraged ESOP.
- Enhance corporate performance and job satisfaction by creating a corporate 'ownership' culture.
- Reward employees with a benefit tied to corporate performance while affording the company substantial tax benefits.

Employees participating in an ESOP are not taxed on stock allocated to their accounts until they receive distributions. Additionally, ESOPs have five significant tax advantages for corporations, employees, and selling shareholders:

- The employer can, within limits, deduct contributions to the ESOP, including both principal and interest on loans the ESOP uses to buy company stock. Companies can contribute their own shares to the ESOP and take a tax deduction for them.
- The employer, if a C corporation (a US corporate form in which corporations pay income tax and owners pay taxes on any dividends they receive), generally can

deduct reasonable cash dividends paid on ESOP-held stock and used to repay an ESOP loan, passed through to participants, or reinvested in company stock at the direction of participants. This is the only form of tax-deductible dividend under US law. Only ESOP companies can take a tax deduction for their dividends.

- The owner of a closely held C corporation can defer taxation on his or her capital gains from the sale of company stock to the ESOP by reinvesting the sale proceeds in stocks, bonds, or other securities of US operating companies, provided the ESOP owns 30% or more of the company's shares after the sale.
- S corporation ESOPs are not taxed on their share of corporate income (S corporations do not pay tax but their owners pay personal income taxes on their pro-rata share of earnings). Furthermore, an ESOP's share of S corporation shareholder distributions (i.e. dividends) is retained by the ESOP and may be used to repay an ESOP loan, fund ESOP benefits, or pay ESOP administration expenses.
- Employees participating in an ESOP are not taxed on the stock allocated to their accounts until they receive a distribution (generally upon retirement, death, disability, or termination of employment).

Aside from the above tax incentives, ESOPs have other powerful advantages for companies:

- Unlike other qualified retirement plans, ESOPs can borrow money on employer credit to acquire company stock, thus providing a market (funded with pretax dollars) for shareholders in closely held companies who want to sell.
- Funds borrowed by an ESOP also can be used to repurchase shares with pretax dollars in public companies, although sellers may not defer capital gains from the sale, or can be used to buy newly issued or treasury shares in any company.
- Proceeds from a sale of the company's stock to its ESOP can be used for purchasing new equipment, buying another business, refinancing debt, or any other business purpose.
- The company funds the ESOP's repayment of the loan with pretax dollars.

ESOP contributions can also be used to match employee 401(k) contributions, including under a safe harbour matching formula, encouraging greater participation in a 401(k) plan and making it easier to meet federal requirements that attempt to ensure that most employees participate. A 401k plan is a benefit plan in which the employer typically matches employee contributions to a retirement trust that is invested in mutual funds to yield a retirement account for the employee over time.

Research shows that when an ESOP is combined with programmes that provide opportunities for employees to share ideas and information about their work, it can result in higher productivity, corporate growth, and employee satisfaction and retention. When an ESOP is implemented, participating employees now have an additional benefit, one that is not taxed until they receive distributions (which for the most part is only after they leave the company)—and not even then if it is rolled over into an individual retirement plan (a tax-sheltered trust that holds benefits for employees until retirement age) or a successor plan in another company. Owning stock through the ESOP allows participants to share in the growth of their company, just as the company's original owners have.

An ESOP account can be a valuable component in a worker's retirement plan. Like any undiversified investment, however, it should be seen by employees as part of a larger retirement planning process.

29.2 GROWTH OF ESOPS AND EQUIVALENT PLANS

ESOP formation grew steadily until the early 1980s, when many public companies set up ESOPs. Stock market companies grew less interested in ESOPs, however, as some tax benefits specifically for them were removed, and accounting rules made ESOPs appear less favourable to their income statements.

Meanwhile, ESOPs in closely held companies were growing, both in numbers and size. The number of plans shows a slight decline in recent years, but the number of participants has grown much larger. We believe that this is due to three factors:

- ESOP companies grow employment about 2.5% per year faster than they would have absent an ESOP
- ESOPs are being set up in larger companies than in the past
- ESOPs are doing a lot of acquisitions, something that did not start until the early 2000s.

Students of ESOPs believe the number of plans may soon accelerate as baby boomers look to retire and choose ESOPs as a logical and tax-favoured exit vehicle (at least twice as many companies will be for sale in the next decade as the last). Table 29.1 presents a breakdown of ESOPs in terms of plans, participants (this term includes both current employees and former employees still in the plan awaiting payout), and assets by both company size and public/private status. Because there is a lag time in when data become available, 2011 data are the latest usable numbers.

Note that while large stock market companies make up a tiny percentage of all ESOPs, they account for a much larger percentage of participants and assets. One company with a few hundred thousand employees has as many participants as a few thousand companies with 100 each, although the asset size per participant is higher in closely held companies.

Table 29.2 presents data on ESOP growth since 2002, the first year for which we have reliable data.

The decline in the number of plans between 2002 and 2004 is accounted for by changes in laws for S corporation ESOPs. When these laws were first passed, some practitioners promoted schemes that would channel all the tax benefits of these plans to a small number of owners while leaving employees broadly with either no shares or worthless shares. The ESOP community, along with the US Internal Revenue Service (IRS), the tax authorities,

Table 29.1 Estimated Number of ESOP Plans, Number of Participants, and Plan
            Asset Value, 2013

Type	Number of plans	Total participants	Employer securities	Total assets
Standalone ESOPs	5,489	1.66 million	$102.9 billion	$115 billion
KSOPs	1,306	12.26 million	$159.4 billion	$1.12 trillion
Total for all literal ESOPs	6,795	13.9 million	$262 billion	$1.23 trillion
ESOP-like plans	2,528	1.18 million	$22.2 billion	$64 billion
Total for ESOP and ESOP-like plans	9,323	15 million	$284.6 billion	$1.3 trillion

National Center for Employee Ownership website, A Statistical Profile of Employee Ownership,
December 2015.

Table 29.2 Estimated Growth of ESOPs, 2002–2013

Year	Number of plans	Number of plan participants	Number of actively employed plan participants	Assets
2002	8,874	10,230,00	7,946,00	$490 million
2003	7,934	10,049,000	7,570,000	$620 million
2004	7,348	10,243,000	7,826,000	$669 million
2005	7,198	11,998,000	9,448,000	$709 million
2006	7,384	12,584,000	9,850,000	$794 million
2007	7,326	13,219,000	10,174,000	$877 million
2008	7,305	13,038,000	10,055,000	$665 million
2009	6,690	12,997,000	10,015,000	$773 million
2010	7,138	13,477,000	10,307,000	$916 million
2011	6,941	13,463,000	10,288,000	$943 million
2012	6,908	13,823,595	10,603,334	$1.1 trillion
2013	6,795	13,927,535	10,578,114	$1.3 trillion

National Center for Employee Ownership website, A Statistcial Profile of Employee Ownership,
December 2015.

and Congress, strongly objected to these scam arrangements. The IRS determined they were 'listed' transactions, meaning they had no business purpose other than avoiding taxes. As such, they were illegal and subject to severe penalties. Congress went a step further, creating S corporation ESOP anti-abuse rules that provided draconian taxes for any plans that are set up only to avoid taxes. As a result, probably a couple of thousand plans, few of which ever actually got launched but had started making filings, were terminated.

The data do not allow us to estimate the percentage of the company that ESOPs typically hold, but, based on NCEO surveys, we believe 45 per cent to 55 per cent of all US ESOPs are majority-owned by ESOPs, and most of these are 100 per cent ESOP-owned. Both percentages continue to grow. The emergence of 100 per cent ESOPs is a result of changes in the tax law in the late 1990s allowing S corporations to have ESOPs and then to exclude from taxation any profits attributable to the ESOP's ownership. That made 100 per cent ESOPs nontaxable at the federal level and usually the state level as well. The result was that more ESOP companies wanted to get to 100 per cent and continue to be ESOPs for the long term (which is why ESOP terminations started to drop as well). The extra cash reserve then fuelled the boom in ESOP companies acquiring other companies.

The median number of active employee participants in US ESOPs is about 60, but there are about 700 plans with more than 1,000 active participants, and over 3,000 with more than 100. The largest 100 majority-owned ESOPs employ over 600,000 people, a number that has grown steadily since the NCEO started compiling this list. Companies now must have at least 1,250 employees to be on the largest hundred ESOP list, up from 750 a decade ago. ESOPs are represented in all industries, as Table 29.3 shows.

The data show that the only significant variations between ESOP companies and the general universe of companies are in finance and in healthcare and social assistance. In finance, many community banks have ESOPs because they provide a good liquidity mechanism when there are dozens or more owners in firms that are still closely held or thinly traded. ESOPs also help companies increase capital reserves. In healthcare and social assistance, by contrast, ESOPs are rare because the workforce in such companies tends to be much more transient, which is not a good fit for ESOPs, and a high percentage of the employers are nonprofits, which cannot have ESOPs. The National Center for Employee Ownership maintains a list of the hundred largest majority-owned companies in the US at https://www.nceo.org/articles/employee-ownership-100/.

29.3 THE EFFECT OF ESOPS ON CORPORATE PERFORMANCE

There is now considerable research on how ESOPs affect corporate performance. In the discussion that follows, we break out the most important studies on ESOPs. For studies looking at the impact of ESOPs on corporate performance, we focus primarily on those that evaluate the before-and-after effect of the plans.

Table 29.3 Distribution of Plans by Industry

NAICS code	Description	ESOPs	non-ESOPs
11	Agriculture, Forestry, Fishing, and Hunting	1%	1%
21	Mining, Quarrying, and Oil and Gas Extraction	1%	1%
22	Utilities	1%	0%
23	Construction	11%	7%
31–33	Manufacturing	22%	11%
42	Wholesale Trade	9%	5%
44–45	Retail Trade	6%	5%
48–49	Transportation and Warehousing	2%	2%
51	Information	2%	2%
52	Finance and Insurance	17%	9%
53	Real Estate and Rental and Leasing	1%	3%
54	Professional, Scientific, and Technical Services	18%	20%
55	Management of Companies and Enterprises	3%	0%
56	Administrative and Support and Waste Management and Remediation Services	2%	2%
61	Educational Services	0%	2%
62	Healthcare and Social Assistance	2%	22%
71	Arts, Entertainment, and Recreation	0%	1%
72	Accommodation and Food Services	1%	1%
81	Other Services (except Public Administration)	2%	6%
92	Public Administration	N/A	N/A

Source: NCEO analysis of the Private Pension Plan Research File made available by the Department of Labor. The file includes all company sponsors of private pension plan filers that file a Form 5500. Direct Filing Entities (DFEs), welfare plans, one-participant plans, public retirement plans, and duplicate filings of other retirement plans are excluded from the research file.

29.3.1 The Impact of ESOPs on Performance in Closely Held Companies

In the largest and most significant study to date of ESOPs in closely held companies, in 2000, Douglas L. Kruse and Joseph Blasi of Rutgers University found that ESOPs increase sales, employment, and sales per employee by about 2.3 per cent to 2.4 per cent per year over what would have been expected absent an ESOP (the data are available on the NCEO's website at http://www.nceo.org/main/article.php/id/25, accessed 23 September 2016). ESOP companies are also somewhat more likely than their competitors to still be in business several years later. ESOP companies are also substantially more likely than comparable companies to offer other retirement benefit plans along with their ESOPs.

Kruse and Blasi obtained files from Dun and Bradstreet on companies that had adopted ESOPs between 1988 and 1994. They matched these companies to non-ESOP companies that were comparable in size, industry, and region. Then they looked for which of these companies had sales and employment data available for a period three years before the plan's start and three years after. The sales and employment growth data were then compared for each year for each paired company. They also checked the companies' filings with the U.S. Department of Labor to determine which of the companies had other retirement-oriented benefit plans. Finally, they looked to see what percentage of the companies remained in business from 1995 through to 1997.

The process yielded 343 ESOP companies and 343 pairs for the overall sample. However, missing data meant that employment data were available for only 254 ESOP companies and 234 pairs, sales data for 138 ESOP companies and 77 pairs, and sales/employee data for 115 ESOP companies and 65 pairs (some non-ESOP companies could be paired with more than one ESOP company).

The results showed that ESOP companies perform better in the post-ESOP period than their pre-ESOP performance would have predicted. Table 29.4 shows the difference in the pre-ESOP to post-ESOP period for ESOP companies' sales growth, employment growth, and growth in sales per employee.

The first study to show a specific causal link between employee ownership and corporate performance was by Michael Quarrey and Corey Rosen of the National Center for Employee Ownership (Rosen and Quarrey 1987). The study looked at the performance of employee ownership companies for five years before and after they set up their ESOPs. It factored out market effects by looking at how well employee ownership companies did relative to competitors in the pre- and post-ESOP periods, then subtracted the difference. For example, if a company were growing 3 per cent per year faster than its competitors in the pre-ESOP period, and 6 per cent per year faster in the post-ESOP period, a +3 per cent difference would be attributable to the ESOP, other things being equal.

Table 29.4 Difference in Post–ESOP to Pre–ESOP Performance, ESOP vs. Comparable Non–ESOP Companies

Annual sales growth	2.4%
Annual employment growth	2.3%
Annual growth in sales per employee	2.3%

National Center for Employee Ownership website, Research on Employee Ownership, Corporate Performance, and Employee Compensation.

The study found that ESOP companies had sales growth rates of 3.4 per cent per year higher and employment growth rates 3.8% per cent per year higher in the post-ESOP period than would have been expected based on pre-ESOP performance. When the companies were divided into three groups based on their levels of participative management, however, only the most participative companies showed gains. These companies grew 8 per cent to 11 per cent per year faster than they would have been expected to, while the middle group did about the same, and the bottom group showed a decline in performance.

Participation alone, however, is not enough to improve performance. A number of studies show that the impact of participation absent ownership is short lived or ambiguous. Ownership seems to provide the cultural glue to keep participation going.

An intriguing analysis of 328 majority ESOP-owned companies by Brent Kramer (Kramer 2008) in 2008 found that majority ESOP-owned companies had sales per employee that were 8.8 per cent greater than comparable non-ESOP companies. Although the study does not quite meet the standards for a quasi-scientific study, its results are striking enough to merit inclusion here. Kramer found 100 per cent ESOP-owned companies did better than those that were over 50 per cent owned but not 100 per cent. Smaller companies and companies with greater ESOP account value per employee also did better. Employee influence on new products, work design, and marketing were also all strongly related to performance outcomes, with each one-point increase in worker influence on the combined measure of these three factors (on a five-point scale) leading to a $19,000 increase in the ESOP company sale per employee advantage.

The study does not demonstrate that having an ESOP per se causes these performance benefits because it is not a before-and-after study. Its design cannot preclude the possibility that better-performing companies are more likely to have ESOPs in the first place. The correlates of performance, however, are less subject to this chicken-and-egg problem and provide useful insight into what makes an ESOP work, particularly in their very strong confirmation of the importance of employee involvement.

29.3.2 Research on Public Company Performance and ESOPs

A 2008 study (Kim and Ouimet 2008) by E. Han Kim and Paige Ouimet of the University of North Carolina found that listed stock market ESOPs have a positive effect on company value. Using Tobin's Q, a ratio of the company's stock value to its book equity value), they found that ESOPs led to an 8.12 per cent increase in company valuation relative to the industry median. Companies with ESOPs with less than 5 per cent ownership showed a valuation increase of 16 per cent relative to the industry median; companies with larger ESOPs showed neither an increase nor a decrease. The impact of company value is positively correlated with greater leverage, perhaps because companies are keeping overall compensation costs more neutral.

To conduct their study, Kim and Ouimet studied public listed companies with ESOPs between 1980 and 2004 for which they could determine an adoption date and for which there was sufficient before-and-after data to conduct analysis over a significant time period. They found 756 public ESOPs during this time, but had the needed data for 418.

For the first time in ESOP studies, the researchers used the Standard Statistical Establishment List from the U.S. Bureau of the Census. The list provides detailed data on all forms of compensation, including ages, benefits, leave policy, severance pay, etc. From this, the researchers computed a measure of total compensation and benefits. These data were then paired with Compustat data on company performance. They analysed performance for five years before and ten years after the ESOP was set up, excluding the year of adoption, with a shorter timeline for some of the sample companies for a minority of the companies.

In the 2006 study, The ESOP Performance Puzzle in Public Companies (Stretcher et al. 2006), which was published in the fall 2006 issue of the *Journal of Employee Ownership Law and Finance*, 196 publicly traded US ESOP companies during the years 1998 through 2004 were examined. Each ESOP company was matched to a comparable non-ESOP company. This is one of the few public company studies to use the more methodologically rigorous matched-pair technique. The ESOP companies had returns on assets that were higher than the matched non-ESOP companies in all seven years, net profit margins that were higher in all of the five years where comparable data were available, and better operating cash flows in three of the five years where data were available. The authors present the data for each year, rather than as a single summary measure. Below, we show our own calculated mean of the difference for the years in question:

Return on assets: +5.5%
Net profit margin: +10.3%
Operating cash flow to assets: +0.1%

On several other measures, the differences achieved statistical significance but in less than a majority of the measured years. Keeping in mind, then, that the differences reported may be the result of chance, we can calculate the means of the differences year-by-year for each of these measures:

Return on equity: +5.6%
Sales growth rate: −0.8%
Market-to-book ratio: +0.8%
Debt ratio: −2.9%
Operating cash flow to sales: +0.4%
Operating cash flow per employee: +5.7%

29.4 EMPLOYEE OWNERSHIP AND EMPLOYEE FINANCIAL WELL-BEING

In the wake of Enron, WorldCom, United Airlines, the dot-com implosion, and other employee ownership train wrecks, it seems legitimate to question whether employee ownership is actually good for employees or bad for them. There are three key questions here:

- To what extent is employees' ownership a trade-off for wages or other compensation?
- Does employee ownership impose excessive retirement risk on employees?
- Aside from whether there are trade-offs or risks, how much wealth does employee ownership actually deliver to employees?

The conventional view of economic theory is that employee ownership has to be a trade-off for wages or other compensation, but theory and practice don't always mesh. If employee ownership companies are, as suggested above, more productive, they may be better able to both share ownership and pay as well as, or better than, comparable companies, because they make the economic pie larger.

On the ESOP front, the groundbreaking study was a 1998 analysis by Peter Kardas and Jim Keogh of the Washington Department of Community, Trade, and Economic Development, and Adria Scharf of the University of Washington (Kardas et al. 1998), which shows that, in fact, employees are significantly better compensated in ESOP companies than are employees in comparable non-ESOP companies. Using 1995 employment and wage data from the Washington State Employment Security Department, and 1995 data on retirement benefits from a survey of companies and from Form 5500, the study matched up 102 Washington State ESOP companies with 499 comparison companies in terms of industrial classification and employment size. In terms of wages, the median hourly wage in the ESOP firms was 5 to 12 per cent higher than the median hourly wage in the comparison companies, depending on the wage level of those being compared. The study found the average value of all retirement benefits in ESOP companies was equal to $32,213, with an average value in the comparison companies of about $12,735. Looking only at retirement plan assets other than ESOPs, the ESOP companies had an average value of $7,952, compared to $12,735 for non-ESOP companies. Given that the typical ESOP is actually about 20 per cent invested in diversified assets other than company stock, employees in ESOP companies would have had about as much in diversified assets as employees would have in all assets in non-ESOP companies. In ESOP companies, the average corporate contribution per employee per year was between 9.6 and 10.8 per cent of pay per year, depending on how it is measured. In non-ESOP companies, it was between 2.8 and 3 per cent.

In a 2010 project funded by the Employee Ownership Foundation, the National Center for Employee Ownership did an extensive analysis of ESOP companies using data from the U.S. Department of Labor Form 5500 reports. This provides the most comprehensive analysis of the issue of the impact of ESOPs on employee financial well-being to date. Unlike prior research, the study carefully compiled data from multiple plans within a single company. It was also not a sample. It looked at every ESOP company for which data are available compared to all retirement plans.

The study found that ESOP companies are more likely to offer a second defined contribution (DC) plan than non-ESOP companies are to offer any DC plan at all (56% compared to 47%). This is an important finding because a common critique of ESOPs is that they replace more diverse retirement plans. Clearly, that is not the case. Considering only DC assets originally contributed by the company, ESOP participants have approximately 2.2 times as much in their accounts as participants in comparable non-ESOP companies with DC plans, and 20 per cent more assets overall. The average ESOP company contributed $4,443 per active participant to its ESOP in the most recently available year. In comparison, the average non-ESOP company with a DC plan contributed $2,533 per active participant to its primary plan that year. In other words, on average, ESOP companies contributed 75 per cent more to their ESOPs than other companies contributed to their primary DC plan. Controlling for plan age, number of employees, and type of business increases, the ESOP advantage is 90 to 110 per cent above the non-ESOP companies in our sample. But the most important finding of this study, as noted in Chapter 15 of this handbook by Blasi, Freeman, and Kruse, is that the ESOP company benefits were entirely financed and contributed by the company, whereas, in the comparison group of companies, with other defined contribution plans (typically 401k plans), the workers contributed most of the dollars to the savings plan themselves. ESOPs thus have bigger amounts saved over time and these amounts come from the company rather than the employee's personal assets.

The study followed up on a 2007 NCEO analysis of participant ESOP account balances in 401(k) plans. Among the companies studied, the average value of plan assets per participant was approximately $46,000. That number is hard to interpret, however, because plan age varies widely (new plans have very low account balances) and averages can be distorted by extremes at the high end. One way to compare this is to note that data for the same year on 401(k) plans from the Employee Benefit Research Institute showed an average account balance of $58,000. However, about two-thirds of that comes from participant contributions, whereas the ESOP contributions are almost entirely from the company.

Also on the issue of whether ESOPs are a trade-off for other retirement plans, Blasi and Kruse, as part of their comprehensive analysis of closely held ESOP companies in 2002 reported on the National Center for Employee Ownership website, found that ESOP companies were considerably more likely than comparable non-ESOP companies to offer diversified retirement plans. In other words, an employee working for an ESOP company is considerably *more* likely to have a diversified retirement plan than an employee working at a non-ESOP company, as Table 29.5 indicates. Note that this study

Table 29.5 Percentage of Companies Having Other Retirement Plans

	ESOP	Non-ESOP
Plan type		
Defined benefit	20.1%	4.9%
401(k)	33.3%	6.2%
Non-401(k) profit-sharing	35.7%	8.0%
Other defined contribution	14.7%	2.3%

National Center for Employee Ownership website, Research on Employee Ownership, Corporate Performance, and Employee Compensation.

was not based on a sample: it included all closely held ESOP companies during the study period for which data were available.

The article by E. Han Kim and Paige Ouimet referred to in the previous section, Employee Capitalism or Corporate Socialism? Broad-Based Employee Stock Ownership, found that ESOPs owning less than 5 per cent of company shares have a small but positive 0.8 per cent effect on total compensation, while in companies in which the ESOP owns more than 5 per cent, total compensation is 5.2 per cent higher. The more leverage associated with the ESOP, the lower the increase in employee compensation, perhaps because companies exercise restraint on total compensation in the face of greater debt. By contrast, the subsample of companies in which the ESOP was established in conjunction with declining sales had lower total compensation (2.8% for small ESOPs and 6.3% for large ESOPs).

ESOP and broad-based equity plan companies are also less likely to lay people off. The 2010 General Social Survey found that 3 per cent of employees with employee stock ownership were laid off in 2009–2010 compared to a 12 per cent rate for employees without employee stock ownership. In 2006, the numbers were 2.3 per cent compared to 8.6 per cent, and in 2002, 12.1 per cent and 2.6 per cent. The estimated cost in saved unemployment benefits and foregone taxes to the federal government varied between $8 billion in non-recession years to $13 billion in recession years.

29.5 ESOPs and Default Rates

Based on a National Center for Employee Ownership analysis of 1,232 leveraged ESOP transactions at three large banks, between 2009 and 2013, 1.3 per cent of ESOP companies defaulted on their loans in a way that imposed losses on their creditors (or an annual rate of 0.2%). The defaults accounted for 1.5 per cent of the total value of the ESOP loan portfolio for these companies during this period. The bank data were only available for defaults imposing losses; the data do not include defaults that resulted in loan restructuring where the loans were ultimately repaid or were being paid on the new schedule.

In a parallel analysis, the National Center for Employee Ownership also asked ESOP appraisal firms to provide us with data on defaults among the ESOP companies they appraised between 2009 and 2013. Eighteen firms responded out of the 40 ESOP appraisal firms we asked to provide data. The firms were selected because they were members of the National Center for Employee Ownership's directory of service providers. Previous data indicated that directory members account for about half of all the ESOP appraisals. The 18 responding firms were able to report data on 845 companies over the study period. Of these, 9 (1.1%, or an annual rate of 0.2%) defaulted in a way that imposed losses on their creditors, while 26 (3.1%, or an annual rate of 0.6%) had to restructure their loans but had repaid or were repaying their loans currently.

Both the bank data and the data from the appraisal firms came from a wide variety of companies. The loan sizes ranged from less than $1 million to well over $50 million, and companies were in a variety of industries, including especially manufacturing, wholesale, and construction. The number of people employed at the businesses ranged from under 50 to several thousand.

In conclusion, in the USA, the ESOP has significant federal tax advantages, it allows workers to use financing and leverage to build large worker ownership stakes, and the positive outcomes of this phenomenon on average are supported by decades of research.

References

Blasi, J. R., Freeman, R. B., and Kruse, D. L. (2017), 'Evidence: What the US Research Shows about Worker Ownership', in J. Michie, J. R. Blasi, and C. Borzaga, *The Oxford Handbook of Mutual, Co-operative and Co-owned Business* (Oxford: Oxford University Press).

Kardas, P., Keogh, J., and Sharf, A. (1998), 'Wealth and Income Consequences of Employee Ownership', *Journal of Employee Ownership Law and Finance*, 3(4) (Fall), 449–76.

Kim, E. and Ouimet, P. (2008), 'Employee Capitalism or Corporate Socialism? Broad-Based Employee Stock Ownership', *Journal of Finance*, 69(3), 975–1413.

Kramer, B. (2008), 'Employee Ownership and Participation Effects on Firm Outcomes', PhD thesis, City University of New York.

Rosen, Corey and Quarrey, Michael (1987), 'How Well Is Employee Ownership Working?' *Harvard Business Review*, 65(5), 126–32.

Stretcher, R., Henry, S., and Kavanaugh, J. (2006), 'The ESOP Performance Puzzle in Public', *Journal of Employee Ownership Law and Finance* (Fall), 3–18.

CHAPTER 30

....

EMPLOYEE OWNERSHIP IN BRITAIN TODAY

....

ANDREW PENDLETON AND ANDREW ROBINSON

30.1 INTRODUCTION

....

EMPLOYEE ownership is becoming an increasingly important form of business owner-ship and organization in Britain. Employee-owned firms are found in a range of sectors, including retail, wholesale, ancillary health services, social care, business consultancy, and manufacturing. Although some firms have been employee owned for many years—the most well-known employee-owned firm (the John Lewis Partnership) has had employee ownership since the late 1920s—employee ownership started to become more prevalent from the mid 1980s. There was a wave of conversions to employee ownership in the late 1980s and early 1990s, often using an ESOP-type structure, though employee ownership was short lived in many cases. After a lull in conversion activity in the late 1990s, conversions to employee ownership picked up in the 2000s, with the pace accel-erating from around 2010. In this chapter we consider the influences on the develop-ment of modern forms of employee ownership, and highlight the factors contributing to the current rise in employee ownership conversions. Political support for employee ownership is found to be the strongest, but not the only influence on levels of employee ownership activity.

There is considerable heterogeneity across the employee-owned sector in Britain. Traditionally, workers' co-operatives have been the most widespread form of employee ownership, but since the late 1980s a variety of new ownership forms and structures have developed. Some firms are entirely employee owned, whilst in others minority employee ownership is the norm. Some firms have indirect employee ownership, with shares held collectively in an Employee Benefits or Employee Ownership Trust, whilst others have direct employee ownership whereby individual employees own shares. It is common for ownership to take a hybrid form, combining direct and indirect ownership. Governance arrangements are equally diverse: in some cases employees elect workers onto the company board to be non-executive directors; in others, employee participation takes a more direct form.

It will be argued in the chapter that the diversity of ownership and governance arrangements reflects the interaction of choices and interests of those involved in the transition to employee ownership and the circumstances of the conversion (see Pendleton 2001). Initially, the chapter will outline the features of the main ownership forms. It will then consider the influences upon the development of employee ownership. Then, it will identify and discuss groupings of employee-owned firms, based on the circumstances of their conversion. Four main groups are identified: ownership conversions arising from privatization, business succession, sharing ownership, and business start-ups. The discussion draws on interim findings of a major research project conducted by the White Rose Employee Ownership Centre during 2014–15 in collaboration with the Employee Ownership Association.[1]

30.2 Forms of Employee Ownership in Britain

There is no universally accepted definition of non-co-operative forms of employee ownership, with the result that identifying employee-owned firms is not straightforward. Kruse and Blasi (1997) highlight four main dimensions of employee ownership: the proportion of company shares owned by employees, the proportion of employees owning shares, the distribution of ownership amongst employees, and the nature and extent of rights associated with ownership. Whilst this identifies key dimensions of employee ownership, identifying the divide between employee-owned firms and those said not to be employee-owned is not straightforward. For instance, a firm might be 100 per cent owned by its employees but most of the ownership held by a small group of senior employees. Should this firm be said to be employee owned? Our working definition here is that employee ownership refers to firms where 25 per cent or more of the ownership of the company is broadly held by all or most employees (or on their behalf by a trust), taking into account that in nearly all cases the remainder of the ownership will be held by a smaller group of employees. The reason that 25 per cent is chosen as a cut-off is that ownership of a 25 per cent stake is viewed in some company legislation as a 'material stake'. In practice, levels of employee ownership are much higher in most cases: the average in our sample is 83 per cent (median = 100).

The largest and most well-known employee-owned firm in Britain is the John Lewis Partnership, operator of John Lewis department stores and Waitrose supermarkets,

---

[1] The White Rose Employee Ownership Centre is a collaboration between employee ownership academics at the universities of Leeds, Sheffield, and York. For details go to http://lubswww.leeds.ac.uk/wreoc/home/ (accessed 23 September 2016).

with 91,000 employees in 2014. John Lewis has been a beacon for employee ownership in Britain, especially in recent years when it has been far more overt in advertising its ownership to customers, lobbying governments, and supporting the development of the employee ownership sector. John Lewis exemplifies one form of employee ownership—the indirect or trust-based model. The Partnership was initially established in 1929 to provide profit-sharing to the employees, with the firm being passed to the Trust in 1950. The trust deed requires that the trust benefit employees past, present, and future. Although employees do not directly own John Lewis (technically, it can be argued that John Lewis is not employee owned as such), they receive a substantial portion of the profits each year in the form of a profit share. This has been as much as 17 per cent of annual salary in recent years. Employees also have a substantial role in governance, with elected institutions at store, region, divisional, and head office level.

The opposite of the indirect, trust-based model is direct ownership of shares by employees, which they acquire either by gift, or purchase, or a combination of the two. An exemplar of the direct model is Sheffield-based Gripple, manufacturers of a wire joining and tensioning device used in fencing and construction known as a Gripple. Currently, all of Gripple's 460 strong workforce directly own shares in the company, with new employees since 2004 required to purchase £1,000 of shares within a year of joining the company, assisted by a loan from the company (EOA 2014; Silcox 2009). Somewhat earlier, the privatization of the National Freight Corporation in 1982 was brought about by individual subscriptions to shares by employees: 35 per cent of the company's 24,500-strong work force chose to buy into ownership of the new company with an average shareholding of around £700 (Bradley and Nejad 1989). A key advantage claimed by adherents of this model is that it provides a highly tangible and direct form of ownership, with employees benefiting directly from company growth (EOA 2013). Against this, achieving successful conversions to employee ownership may be more dependent on the wealth and liquidity of employees. Since individual circumstances and preferences determine participation in ownership, it is common for ownership to be less widespread amongst the workforce and for shareholdings to be unequal in the direct form of employee ownership.

A variant of the direct share ownership model is the membership model. In this, employees can become a member of the company by purchasing a nominal share (often £1). The roots of this form of ownership can be found in the worker co-operative and friendly society tradition, and it is common for firms using this model to register as a membership society under the Co-operative and Community Benefit Societies Act 2014 and its predecessors. As in worker co-operatives, ownership rights are equally distributed amongst eligible and participating employees. Clearly, this model is not suitable for raising capital to bring about an ownership conversion but can be appropriate where conversion does not involve a substantial purchase price. Examples include transfers of employees to newly formed organizations with no prior trading history or where there are few physical assets. This form of ownership is common in the public service spin-outs from central and local government and the National Health Service which have been taking place since the late 2000s. A notable feature of many of these public service 'mutuals' is that service users can also become members. For instance, Explore—the spin-out of library services from the City of York Council—will become two-thirds owned by members of the local community and one-third owned by its staff.

A hybrid model of employee ownership comprises elements of both direct and indirect models by combining trust ownership with share distributions to individual employees. This form of employee ownership first developed in the mid 1980s based on the ESOP form that had developed in the United States after the passage of the 1974 ERISA pension legislation. In this model, ownership is initially held collectively in an employee trust, but over time all or some of this ownership is transferred to individual employees. This model emerged in Britain when advocates of employee ownership developed structures that linked trust vehicles to the share-based profit-sharing legislation introduced by the Labour Government in 1978. Typically, the initial ownership conversion is achieved using an Employee Benefits Trust (EBT), with shares held in this trust then being passed to an Approved Profit Sharing Trust (since replaced by the Share Incentive Plan) for distribution to employees (see the technical discussions in Wilson 1992). The benefit of this arrangement is it sidesteps the liquidity constraints and co-ordination costs that arise if capital contributions are sought from individual employees. Shares are passed to employees after the profit-sharing scheme acquires shares from the EBT using company profits. The profits passed to the EBT are then used to repay the loan typically incurred by the EBT to acquire the shares in the first place

The first ESOP to be formed in Britain is said to be the motorway services organization Roadchef in 1986. In this case, an EBT initially acquired a 12.5 per cent stake, later rising to 34 per cent, in the company from the estate of the recently deceased finance director (See Pendleton 2001: 19).[2] The ESOP structure was then widely imitated during the wave of bus company privatizations in the late 1980s/early 1990s (ibid; 87–94). More recent ESOPs have used the Share Incentive Plan (SIP) to distribute shares (this plan replaced Approved Profit Sharing from 2000). SIPs can be used to distribute shares at no cost to employees ('Free Shares') or to provide a means for employees to purchase shares ('Partnership Shares') on highly advantageous terms (tax concessions and the potential award of 'Matching Shares'). Some firms using an ESOP-type model require employees to purchase shares, some award free shares, and some use a combination of the two.

Table 30.1 provides details of the distribution of the main ownership types in our sample.

The choice of the most appropriate structure for employee ownership has been the subject of continuing debate within the employee ownership community for many years. Some prefer the trust-based model because ownership conversion is less reliant

---

[2] Roadchef ceased to be employee owned in 1998 when the business was sold. A long-standing issue has been a transfer of shares from the main EBT to a trust controlled by the CEO to the benefit of the latter. This was taken to court in 2014, with the court deciding that the transfer was null and void. For a good recent review of the history, see http://www.thisismoney.co.uk/money/markets/article-2339152/CITY-FOCUS-Tim-Ingram-Hill-make-court-appearance-accused-cheating-RoadChef-staff-millions-pounds.html (accessed 23 September 2016).

Table 30.1 The Main Structures of Employee Ownership *Percentages of sample*

	Employee benefit trust only	Direct ownership only	Hybrid of trust ownership and direct ownership
Proportion of total sample (%)	23	40	37
Average level of employee ownership (median) %	84 (100)	89 (100)	76 (89)

N = 57

Source: The White Rose Employee Ownership Survery.

on employee wealth and liquidity. Once trust ownership has been achieved, the level of risk-bearing by individual employees is clearly lower than where employees have purchased shares. Finally, trust-based employee ownership appears to offer greater ownership sustainability because ownership is less susceptible to individual preferences. It is notable that John Lewis has been trust-owned for over 50 years, during which time other well-established employee-owned firms have converted out of employee ownership. For instance, the individual owners of the National Freight Corporation sold their shares on the open market once the company had listed, and a very rapid dilution of employees' shareholding in the company took place. This is not to say that the trust-based form of employee ownership is immune from re-conversion to 'conventional' ownership: if trustees have clear grounds for believing that the employee beneficiaries want to liquidate the share-holding in the company, their fiduciary duty is to implement these wishes. This is what happened with the bus company ESOPs during the latter half of the 1990s, to the extent that substantial employee ownership has disappeared from the bus industry.

The primary argument advanced by advocates of the direct form of employee ownership is that individual shareholdings promote responsible ownership. Employees more clearly perceive links between their own actions and company outcomes, and are more likely to be motivated by them because they have a direct and immediate stake in these outcomes. This argument receives some support from the literature on ownership and employee attitudes which suggests that employees need to receive a direct financial benefit from ownership to feel like owners (French 1987; Buchko 1992).

The hybrid model combines benefits of both the trust and direct models of ownership by enabling conversions at low up-front cost to employees whilst facilitating direct participation in ownership. A further benefit of the hybrid model is that the trust can be used to re-purchase shares from departing employees, thereby limiting the potential for dilution of employee ownership when employees want or are required to sell their shares. However, a potential problem with such arrangements is that the trust may require resources for repurchases, with the company being the most likely source of these. This has led to severe cash-flow problems in firms with large proportions of employees approaching retirement.

30.3 THE DEVELOPMENT
OF EMPLOYEE OWNERSHIP

Employee ownership is clearly not a common form of business ownership. Currently, we estimate that there are somewhere between 300 and 400 firms with significant employee ownership in Britain. The forms of employee ownership described earlier have mainly developed since the early 1980s, with an intensification of interest and acceleration of ownership conversions in the last five years. Employee ownership was by no means new in the early 1980s—there had been an upsurge in the number of worker co-operatives in the 1970s—but the ownership structures and forms of conversion in the mid 1980s were relatively novel. Why did these new forms develop, and what explains the subsequent patterns of growth in employee ownership conversions?

Previous analyses of employee ownership have proposed two types of explanation for the development of employee ownership and related forms of employee involvement and reward. In industrial relations, the 'cycles of control' perspective developed by Ramsay (1977) suggested that the strength of labour was a strong explanatory factor: firms adopted profit-sharing or employee ownership when organized labour was strong. A problem for this explanation, however, is that the growth in employee ownership, and indeed in employee share ownership more widely, since the 1980s has coincided with a long phase of trade union weakness (see Pendleton 2005). An alternative explanation, put forward by Poole (1989), draws attention to 'favourable conjunctures': the coming together of sets of factors that work together to encourage employee ownership. In the ensuing analysis, two main sets of factors can be identified: developments at the micro-level and government policy initiatives, both set within a broader economic context favouring new forms of corporate organization.

Several long-run developments provide a favourable context for the development of employee ownership. One is the shift from manufacturing to services in advanced industrial economies. This has favoured the development of firms that are rich in human capital and less dependent on physical assets for the generation of value. Firms that are dependent on human capital clearly need to attract, retain, and develop high quality human resources to achieve competitive advantage (Rousseau and Shperling 2003). As value generation by the firm resides in employee skills and knowledge, it seems appropriate to provide employees with rights to control and to the returns to human capital. It is notable that employee ownership is spreading fast amongst 'human capital' firms providing business consultancy, architecture, and engineering design services, with some world-leading firms such as Arup owned by or on behalf of their employees. A second development is increasing economic and employment insecurity. Globalization, competition, and deregulation have made it increasingly difficult for firms to offer the implicit guarantees of long-term employment, career progression, and social benefits that became common in large firms post Second World War. But how can firms achieve employee commitment, more important than ever given the growing dependence on human capital, when less can be committed in return? Margaret Blair (1995) has argued that employee ownership provides a means to break out of this 'hold-up' situation by giving employees control and return rights commensurate with those of other shareholders (see Pendleton and Robinson 2011). The adoption of employee ownership in the American airline industry and the British bus industry can be viewed as a way of securing employee support for changes to traditional wage and employment structures in response to increased competition, deregulation, and new entry (Gordon 2000). Finally, the financial crisis of 2007–8 and its aftermath have heightened interest in alternative forms of corporate organization (Ownership Commission 2012).

Within this broader context, micro-level developments and policy initiatives explain the development of employee ownership. At the micro level, an important factor is the emergence of an employee ownership 'expert community' as a body able to develop forms of employee ownership, and penetrate and influence the policy-making process. The initial ESOP form in the 1980s was developed by a small number of professional services providers, primarily lawyers, who were able to weld together various legal instruments such as EBTs and profit-sharing schemes to create feasible means for converting conventional firms. Their role model was the ESOP form of ownership that had developed in the United States after the 1974 ERISA legislation, and their interest in this stemmed in part from the perceived failure of the hitherto main form of employee ownership—the worker co-operative. There had been considerable growth of workers' co-operatives in the 1970s, but the perceived failure of the 'Benn Co-operatives' in the late 1970s left a legacy of disillusion with this form of worker ownership. One of the appeals of the emergent ESOP form of employee ownership was that worker ownership could be combined with conventional forms of company management.

The role of employee ownership 'champions', with a deep personal commitment to employee ownership, cannot be underestimated. Through relationships with key lobbyists they have been able to exert influence on policy-makers, leading to a series of legislative and policy changes. The articulation of interests within the employee ownership community (employee-owned firms and their advisers) has developed as the sector has grown, assisted by the development of an employee ownership trade association (the Employee Ownership Association) and the decision of key employee-owned firms, John Lewis Partnership especially, to act as champions for the employee ownership cause. Waitrose, for instance, now highlights employee ownership in its mass consumer advertising. This lobby group has been able to exploit the opportunities provided by a favourable political context: the sometimes uneasy governing coalition between Liberals and Conservatives, with both interested in developing employee ownership, though for different motives. In addition to lobbying, the active diffusion of information through a variety of networks has enhanced mimetic processes of ownership conversion. We can now observe clusters of employee-owned firms in various sectors such as social care, architecture, design and advertising, and retail/wholesale. In short, because of these factors, employee ownership appears to be growing in legitimacy within business.

The focus on influencing the policy process highlights the importance of the second factor: government action. There are two elements to this: regulatory initiatives and privatization. Regulatory initiatives comprise the establishment of share plan legal identities and the provision of tax concessions. Since the late 1970s, successive UK governments have initiated several employee share schemes, including Approved Profit Sharing (1978) and the SIP (2000). Although these schemes were not designed with substantial employee ownership as a primary objective, they have nevertheless provided mechanisms for employee-owned firms to distribute equity to employees.[3] There have also been several initiatives targeted more specifically at promoting employee ownership. In 1989 the Conservative Government introduced the Qualifying Employee Share Trust (QUEST), commonly referred to as a Statutory ESOP to distinguish it from the 'case law' ESOP developed from the amalgam of trust and profit-sharing instruments described earlier. This was designed to simplify ESOP creation by enabling the use of one rather than two trusts, and by making expenses incurred in establishing a trust tax deductible by statute (rather than case law). Most notably, however, it provided an incentive for owners to establish QUESTs by allowing CGT (Capital Gains Tax) rollover relief if at least 10 per cent of the company's equity was sold to the QUEST. The QUEST form was not widely used, however, because the conditions for securing tax concessions were seen as inflexible (e.g. a requirement, later relaxed, that a majority of trustees should be elected by the entire work force). It was sunk, however, by its use in some large listed companies to secure a corporation tax concession when operating SAYE (Save as you Earn) schemes (see Pendleton 2001: 68–71).

Recently, there has been a series of initiatives by the Conservative–Liberal coalition that have enhanced the position of employee ownership. In 2012 the Government initiated a major review (known as the 'Nuttall Review') of employee ownership by employee ownership expert Graeme Nuttall to consider the barriers to employee ownership (Nuttall 2012). The Coalition Government undertook to implement most of the proposals put forward in the review, most of which focused on overcoming barriers to employee ownership, such as inadequate information and financial support. In the Finance Act 2014 a series of measures were implemented to encourage trust-based employee ownership. Owners selling 50 per cent or more of their company to an Employee Ownership Trust were exempted from capital gains tax on the growth in value, whilst firms with at least 50 per cent ownership by a trust became able to award profit shares to employees that are exempt from income tax up to a value of £3,600 each year. This was designed to mirror the tax reliefs available in the SIP scheme for distributions of shares in direct ownership schemes. At the time of writing these legislative changes are new so it is difficult to evaluate their effectiveness. However, they appear to have stimulated a great deal of interest in employee ownership.

---

[3] However, a limitation of SIP is the limit on the length of time shares may be held in trust before distribution to employees.

These kinds of initiatives provide incentives for firms and their owners to consider conversion to employee ownership. Their justification is that they counter-balance obstacles to employee ownership, such as the expense of establishing trust structures (where used), a lack of awareness and knowledge of employee ownership amongst professional advisors such as lawyers and accountants, as well as amongst business owners, and a perceived unwillingness of financial institutions to provide support for employee ownership conversions (see All Party Parliamentary Group on Employee Ownership 2008).

Privatization is the other main government activity that has stimulated employee ownership. Waves of employee ownership conversions correspond with privatization programmes in Britain. Two main phases can be discerned: the first is the privatization programme of the Thatcher–Major Governments in the 1980s and first half of the 1990s; and the second is the current privatization programme, mainly implemented by the Conservative–Liberal Coalition Government from 2010, but initiated by the Labour Government preceding it. In the first phase of privatization notable conversions to employee ownership included the National Freight Consortium, and state and local authority owned bus passenger companies in England and Scotland. At its peak, most of the major bus operators in most of the largest English and Scottish cities were employee owned. Privatization into employee ownership was encouraged by governmental offers of preferential pricing. Whilst many local authorities were ideologically opposed to privatization, they viewed employee ownership as preferable to acquisition by companies based elsewhere, with consequent loss of local control of bus services. Although national trade unions were generally hostile to privatization, local union organizations often preferred employee ownership to acquisition by new entrants to the bus industry with reputations for changing wage and employment structures. However, none of these bus companies survive as employee-owned entities, and employee ownership appears to have been a transitional stage in the re-concentration of the industry (see Pendleton 2001: 193–5).

The second phase of privatization has involved the divestment of local authority, national government, and National Health Service activities into 'public service mutuals'. This is a continuation of contracting-out measures initiated in the first phase of privatization. Divestments from the Health Service were introduced by the 2005–10 Labour Government whereby primary care trust staff were given the 'right to request' the formation of social enterprises to deliver community health services (see Ellins and Ham 2009). The Coalition Government has continued this policy with its 'right to provide' policy for NHS trusts and adult social care. Support has also been given for the creation of public service 'spin-outs' from national and local government services by the Mutuals Support Programme. By mid 2014, 100 'mutuals' had been spun-out. Examples include children's social care, youth services, and libraries, as well as healthcare. The Coalition Government is also keen to extend the mutual model to the fire and probation services. Some members of the government have been ardent advocates of the mutual form as a way of empowering work forces and improving services, but others have probably viewed employee ownership as a relatively less contentious means of privatizing services, especially in the politically sensitive health service.

A deeper question concerns the origins and rationales for the policies of the political parties in Britain. As argued elsewhere (Pendleton 2001), all political parties have found employee ownership attractive, though some policy-makers have seen employee ownership as a means of achieving objectives other than an extension of economic and industrial democracy. The main exception to this is the Liberal Party. Over the years, the Liberal Party has perhaps been most committed to employee ownership as a desirable end in itself, emanating from its philosophy of bridging the gap between capital and labour (see Brione and Nicholson 2012). Some of the most significant policy initiatives have taken place because of Liberal Party activity, such as the recent measures to stimulate employee ownership conversions using employee benefit trusts. The Conservative Party has also provided practical support for the extension of employee ownership, with a series of policy initiatives over the years. Employee ownership has formed an element of broader policies to encourage 'shareholding democracy' and entrepreneurialism. Some Conservatives have seen employee ownership as an alternative to trade unions and employment regulation, as exemplified by the Shares for Rights legislation passed in 2013. It has also been viewed as a way of 'shrinking the state' and privatizing public services.

The Labour Party has also supported ESOPs and employee ownership over a long period of time. Employee ownership formed a part of the discourse surrounding efforts to move the party's philosophy away from nationalization as a key means to achieve social ownership and towards the notion of a 'social market economy'. However, in government (1997–2010), its record was somewhat mixed. Its efforts mainly focused on promoting share schemes to achieve corporate growth, rather than encouraging employee ownership to bring about economic democracy. The SIP and Enterprise Management Incentives were important innovations, with the former acting as a useful instrument for employee-owned firms to distribute equity to employees. However, shortly after the introduction of the SIP, the government withdrew the corporation tax deduction for contributions to case-law employee trusts, resulting in fewer transfers to employee ownership (Mason 2009). Nevertheless, Labour initiated employee ownership amongst NHS spin-outs with its Right to Request programme.

The current high levels of activity to support employee ownership by the Conservative–Liberal Coalition is unprecedented in Britain. It is perhaps best explained by competition between the two government parties (cf. Carter and Jacobs 2013), with the Liberal Party in particular keen to introduce policies that give it a distinct identity within a government in which it is a minority member. Policies to support employee ownership during privatization have been emanating from the Treasury and Cabinet Office, primarily controlled by the Conservatives, whilst policies that encourage employee ownership conversions during business succession have been introduced by the Department of Business, Innovation, and Skills, headed by a Liberal Democrat. Policy experts, lobbyists, and 'flagship' employee-owned firms, aided by 'policy entrepreneurs' in the employee ownership community, have been able to exploit this competition to push employee ownership further onto the political agenda (cf. Kingdon 1995).

30.4 THE NATURE OF THE EMPLOYEE OWNERSHIP SECTOR

The employee-owned sector in Britain is heterogeneous in character. Clusters of employee ownership can be found in a variety of sectors such as social care, health services, retail, business consultancy, and manufacturing, to name but a few. In an earlier discussion, based on employee ownership in the late 1990s, several main forms of employee ownership were identified according to the circumstances in which they were created: privatization, paternalist divestments, and 'forced divestments' (i.e. worker responses to shut-downs) (Pendleton 2001). Nearly 20 years on, with the further development of the sector, the balance of activity within the sector has changed: business succession has become much more important and there are more employee-owned start-ups. There are also more firms where groups of owner–managers are choosing to share substantial ownership with a wider body of employees. Nevertheless, a key structuring variable remains the circumstances in which employee ownership is created. Superimposed on top of this is the range of actors involved in the ownership conversion. The interests and objectives of these actors influence the structures of ownership and governance adopted, taking into account the circumstances in which employee ownership is created.

Based on early stage findings of a major survey of employee ownership in Britain, we identify four main contexts in which employee ownership is typically created: business succession, privatization, sharing ownership, and start-ups. The proportions of each type are as shown in Table 30.2.

As can be seen, the distribution of cases between the privatization, sharing ownership, and start-ups is similar, with business succession cases being somewhat more prevalent than each of these. Although the sample currently comprises a minority of employee-owned firms in Britain, we believe it to be broadly representative of the employee-owned sector.

30.4.1 Business Succession

Employee ownership of this sort arises when business owners want to exit the business but do not want to sell the company to a competitor or to pass the company to a family member (often because family members do not wish to take over the business). It can include cases where the owner wishes to retire or to share part of the ownership as a stage in the process of withdrawing from ownership. Employee ownership is a way of

Table 30.2 Employee Ownership: Ownership and Governance Characteristics of Employee Ownership Groups *Percentage of firms in each category*

	Business succession	Privatization	Sharing ownership	Start-ups
Proportion in the total sample (%)	31	22	26	21
Average level of employee ownership (%)	85	85	76	88
Proportion using a trust (%)	93	23	67	42
Proportion with worker directors (%)	40	69	27	50
Proportion with employee shareholder council (%)	67	62	33	8
Median employees (n)	76	650	350	29

N = 58

Source: The White Rose Employee Ownership Survey.

protecting the company and the interests of the company's work force as the owner exits. There has been a steady expansion of these cases in recent years: whereas they accounted for 16 per cent of the population of employee-owned firms in the late 1990s they are now nearly one-third of the sample.

Ownership conversion in these cases is nearly always instigated by the business owner, and the design of the ownership and governance structures typically reflects this. Employees often have little direct involvement in the conversion, and sometimes only become more deeply involved once the ownership conversion has taken place. The level of employee ownership is typically fairly high (average employee ownership is 85 per cent) to provide protection against acquisition by other firms. There is widespread use of employee trusts amongst these firms (93 per cent of cases) tempered by the view of some owners that direct ownership is more likely to lead to 'responsible' ownership. In most cases the owner sells the ownership share to the trust but there are cases where owners gift the company, and in some instances owners either defer the payment or provide a loan to the EBT to purchase the shares from them. In others, the EBT secures an external loan to purchase shares from the owner, backed by future income streams. The advantage of an EBT in these circumstances is that lack of worker expertise, and employee wealth and liquidity constraints, do not prevent the conversion from taking place. Owner instigation of the conversion also sidesteps the co-ordination problem that would arise if workers themselves were to organize the conversion.

The predominance of the business ownership in the initiation and design of employee ownership affects governance as well as ownership structures. Whilst these companies are often highly participative, employee representation on the company board of directors itself is less widespread than the use of employee councils to represent the views of employee shareholders to the board.

30.4.2 Privatization

Privatization was an important backdrop to many conversions to employee owner-ship in the late 1980s/early 1990s, accounting for over 50 per cent of conversions at the time. It then declined in importance until very recently. The Conservative–Liberal Coalition Government of 2010–15 reinvigorated privatization, primarily by spinning-off parts of public services out of the private sector. This has focused especially on the National Health Service and central government. Local government spin-outs have been less common, in part because of ideological objections amongst local authori-ties, but are likely to become more common given severe constraints on local author-ity finance.

Although the mean level of employee ownership is very similar, public service 'spin-outs' differ from business succession conversions in several ways. Firstly, because many of these organizations provide public services, they have typically registered as either Community Benefit Societies, Industrial and Provident Societies (until 2014) or Community Interest Companies (CICs). Secondly, because of lower capital require-ments than in business succession companies, there has been less perceived need to vest equity in EBTs (found in just 23 per cent of cases). In the health service spin-outs, own-ership is usually offered directly to the work forces, typically in the form of £1 shares. Subscription by employees, along with users, gives them membership rights. The typical subscription level within these organizations is around 80 per cent of the work force. There is greater use of employee benefit trusts in local authority spin-outs, but own-ership is nevertheless mainly vested in direct, individual ownership. Unlike business succession and sharing ownership conversions, these conversions are typically insti-gated by managers and employees, often with substantial trade-union involvement. As a result, there tends to be extensive employee involvement in governance. There are worker directors in 69 per cent of cases, and employee councils in 62 per cent (some companies clearly have both).

30.4.3 Sharing Ownership

The sharing ownership group comprises cases where, prior to employee ownership, the company was typically owned by a group of owner–managers serving as company direc-tors. Whereas in business succession cases conversion is typically instigated by family owners, in these cases a group of directors is more likely to be responsible. Often these companies are human-capital-rich firms providing business and professional services (see Pendleton 2011). They devote more resources to training and development than the other groups of companies in our sample, and experience greater difficulty in recruiting employees with specialist skills. Employee ownership serves to extend ownership to a wider group of employees than hitherto. Unlike most business succession cases, owner–managers typically continue to work in the firm though the conversion may form part of a longer-term succession plan.

The average level of employee ownership tends to be somewhat lower than in business succession firms because of continuing ownership by directors. The use of an employee trust is also somewhat less widespread than in business succession firms, and a third of these firms require employees to subscribe to shares to become owners. Employee directors are relatively uncommon (found in just over a quarter of cases), reflecting a concern to maintain existing management approaches and practices. The use of employee shareholder councils is also less widespread than the business succession and privatization companies.

30.4.4 Start-ups

In the past, employee ownership does not seem to have been that well suited to business start-ups. There have been significant barriers to the supply of capital and the assumption of risk by employees, except in the case of the smallest companies. For this reason, there were no business start-ups in our survey of employee-owned companies in the late 1990s. However, with the continuing shift to services, and the importance of human capital in some service industries (such as business consulting) these barriers to employee ownership are much less significant. Employee ownership can be a form of 'glue' that links together members of an otherwise fairly loose network of consultants or creative employees. Of the current sample, 21 per cent are start-ups. As in business succession and privatization conversions, the average level of employee ownership is high (88 per cent).

Several features flow from these circumstances of employee ownership creation. One, ownership tends to take the form of direct ownership: employees may be required to subscribe to shares to supply working capital and to show their commitment to the emergent organization. There is a trust in 42 per cent of cases, but these hold on average lower levels of equity than business succession and sharing conversions. Two, as most are relatively recent start-ups they are typically considerably smaller than companies in the other ownership categories, with median employment of 29 employees at the time of the survey. Three, perhaps reflecting the small size of these organizations, formal institutions of employee governance are in some respects less in evidence than the other groups, with just 8 per cent of these companies holding employee shareholder councils. The proportion with employee directors is, however, relatively high at 50 per cent of cases.

30.4.5 Rescues?

It might be anticipated that the financial crisis of 2007–8 would have led to employee ownership conversions involving firms in economic distress. It has been argued that co-op formation will increase during downturns of the business cycle because the opportunity costs for risk-averse workers of forming co-ops will be lower than during better economic times (Ben-Ner 1988). In practice, however, ownership conversions of this type are rare in Britain, though there have been some well-known examples such as the rescue of Tower Colliery in South Wales in the 1990s (where miners contributed £8,000 of their redundancy money from British Coal to acquire the colliery). In our sample so far there are no cases of rescue conversions.

The reason that they are so rare in Britain is that they are fraught with difficulty. Raising cash from financial institutions to effect a buy-out is extremely difficult for obvious reasons. Meanwhile, many workers may be reluctant to risk investing any money they are due from redundancy payments. To the problems of raising capital, have to be added those of a lack of expertise amongst those organizing the rescue. Finally, compared with some other European countries, there is little support from government and local agencies in Britain to find innovative ways to prevent failing companies from going into receivership or administration.

30.5 Conclusions

The chapter has endeavoured to review the development of non-co-operative forms of employee ownership over a 30-year period, and draws on research conducted over much of this period. The role of political support for employee ownership emerges as critical to the development of employee ownership, with the extent of conversion activity broadly correlating with levels of policy activity and innovation. The current level of support for employee ownership is unprecedented, and this is reflected in a vibrant and growing employee ownership sector. This review has also highlighted the variety of ownership forms and contexts within the employee ownership sector. This makes it difficult to generalize about the sector, and highlights the imperative that policy prescriptions should be sensitive to the various contexts in which employee ownership is created. Nevertheless, our current research suggests there are distinct constellations of employee-owned firms, created in distinct sets of circumstances. As yet, this research draws on a modest number of firms, but the patterns observed are not dissimilar from those generated by earlier research and we believe our findings to be representative of the broader population of employee-owned firms. Our interim findings provide a detailed portrait of the growing employee-owned sector: as the research develops further we hope to portray in greater depth the richness of employee ownership in Britain today.

References

All Party Parliamentary Group on Employee Ownership (2008), *Share Value: How Employee Ownership is Changing the Face of Business* (Elstree: All Party Parliamentary Group on Employee Ownership).

Ben-Ner, A. (1988), 'The Life Cycle of Worker-Owned Firms in Market Economies', *Journal of Economic Behaviour and Organisation*, 10, 287–313.

Blair, M. (1995), *Ownership and Control* (Washington DC: Brookings Institution).

Bradley, K. and Nejad, A. (1989), *Managing Owners: The National Freight Consortium Buy-out in Perspective* (Cambridge: Cambridge University Press).

Brione, P. and Nicholson, C. (2012), *Employee Ownership: Unlocking Growth in the UK Economy* (London: CentreForum).

Buchko, A. (1992), 'Effects of Employee Ownership on Employee Attitudes: A Test of Three Theoretical Perspectives', *Work and Occupations* 19(1), 59–78.

Carter, N. and Jacobs, M. (2013), 'Explaining Radical Policy Change: The Case of Climate Change and Energy Policy under the British Labour Government 2006-2010', *Public Administration*, 92(1), 125–41. doi: 10.1111.

Ellins, J. and Ham, C. (2009), *NHS Mutual: Engaging Staff and Aligning Incentives to Achieve Higher Levels of Performance* (London: The Nuffield Trust).

EOA (Employee Ownership Association) (2013), *Employee Ownership: How to Get Started.* London: Employee Ownership Association).

French, L. (1987), 'Employee Perspectives on Stock Ownership: Financial Investment or Mechanism of Control?' *Academy of Management Journal* 27(4), 861–9.

Gordon, J. (2000), 'Employee Stock Ownership in Economic Transitions: The Case of United and the Airline Industry', in M. Blair and M. Roe, eds, *Employees and Corporate Governance* (Washington DC: Brookings Institution).

Kingdon, J. (1995), *Agendas, Alternatives, and Public Policies*, 2nd edition (New York: Harper Collins).

Kruse, D. and Blasi, J. (1997), 'Employee Ownership, Employee Attitudes, and Firm Performance: A Review of the Evidence', in D. Lewin, D. Mitchell, and M. Zaidi, eds, *The Human Resource Management Handbook* (London: JAI Press).

Mason, N. (2009), *A Matter of Trust: How to Create more Employee-owned Businesses* (London: Employee Ownership Association).

Nuttall, G. (2012), *Sharing Success: The Nuttall Review of Employee Ownership* (London: Department of Business, Innovation, and Skills).

Ownership Commission (2012), *Plurality, Stewardship, and Engagement: the Report of the Ownership Commission* (Borehamwood: Mutuo).

Pendleton, A. (2001), *Employee Ownership, Participation, and Governance: A Study of ESOPs in the UK* (London: Routledge).

Pendleton, A. (2005), 'Employee Share Ownership, Governance, and Industrial Relations', in B. Harley, J. Hyman, and P. Thompson, eds, *Participation and Democracy at Work: Essays in Honour of Harvie Ramsay* (London: Palgrave Macmillan).

Pendleton, A. (2011), 'Employee Ownership in Britain: Diverse Forms, Diverse Antecedents', in E. Carberry, ed., *Employee Ownership and Shared Capitalism: New Directions in Research* (Champaign, IL: Labor and Employment Relations Association).

Pendleton, A. and Robinson, A. (2011), 'Employee Share Ownership and Human Capital Development: Complementarity in Theory and Practice', *Economic and Industrial Democracy*, 32(3), 439–58.

Poole, M. (1989), *The Origins of Economic Democracy: Profit-Sharing and Employee-Shareholding Schemes* (London: Routledge).

Ramsay, H (1977), 'Cycles of Control: Workers' Participation in Sociological and Historical Perspective', *Sociology* 11, 481–506.

Rousseau, D. and Shperling, Z. (2003), 'Pieces of the Action: Ownership and the Changing Employment Relationship', *Academy of Management Review*, 28(4), 553–70.

Silcox, S. (2009), *Making Employee Ownership Work: A Benchmark Guide* (London: Employee Ownership Association).

Wilson, N. (1992), *ESOPS: Their Role in Corporate Finance and Performance*, (Basingstoke: Macmillan).

PART VII

CORPORATE AND
SECTOR CASE
STUDIES

CHAPTER 31

....

CORPORATE GOVERNANCE BEYOND NEOLIBERALISM

agency, democracy, and co-operation

....

WILLIAM DAVIES

31.1 INTRODUCTION

WRITING in 1961, Raymond Williams, one of the founders of what became known as 'cultural studies', argued that liberal democracies suffered from a peculiar blind spot, with respect to some of their central political values. While values of freedom and democracy are asserted as essential at the level of national constitutions, they are rarely translated into institutional norms and templates at smaller scales of governance. Williams argued: 'This is the real power of institutions that they actively teach particular ways of feeling, and it is at once evident that we have not nearly enough institutions which practically teach democracy' (Williams 2010: 358). Williams suggested that people need to be trained in the skills and art of responsible dialogue, such that they are able to engage in participatory governance structures. 'Conventions of discussion', such as the ability to disagree with someone without attacking them personally, or to bring a complaint which is not simply a private grievance, do not come naturally to people, but are a feature of culture and education. And yet these have rarely been recognized as teachable skills, leading them into a state of neglect which then reinforces a pessimistic view of possibilities for democratization more broadly.

The experience of many co-operatives and mutuals confirms precisely Williams' insight. These organizations routinely discover that their greatest challenge—greater even than access to capital—is to identify supportive professional advice and models with regard to governance and member engagement (see, for example, Davies and Yeoman, 2013). When member engagement doesn't work (either through inadequate participation, or the wrong sort of participation) confidence in the governance model can deteriorate. And yet, member-owned organizations which persevere will often discover that members learn the types of 'conventions of discussion' that are suitable for constructive, critical, socially oriented participation in governance. The governance of mutuals needs to be seen, not only in terms of its formal legal template (although that is of course fundamentally important), but in terms of how such a template becomes normalized, understood, and embedded as a set of day-to-day practices, or what Williams terms 'structures of feeling'. Achieving this more tacit aspect of governance, however, takes patience and learning.

In the wake of the global financial crisis of 2007–9, various questions have been raised about the ethics and economic sustainability of orthodox models of corporate governance, not only in financial services but elsewhere (Davies 2009; Haldane 2011; Engelen et al. 2011; Williamson et al. 2014). Listed companies and privately owned companies have been entangled in a number of high-profile scandals, while these ownership models seem also to now funnel all the proceeds of growth into the hands of senior executives and financial intermediaries (Dorling 2014). Firms have become increasingly 'financialized', in the sense that they privilege financial performance measures, even while many listed companies have no need to raise capital externally (Lapavitsas 2013). In these respects, orthodox corporate governance models are instruments which benefit the '1 per cent', while generating no increases in income or wealth for their employees or society at large.

The apparent legitimacy crisis of orthodox corporate forms would seem to offer an opportunity for alternative institutional models. And yet, in common with other dimensions of neoliberalism, the financial crisis has not ushered in the degree of change or paradigm shift that was expected when it reached its gravest moment in the autumn of 2008. As various scholars have noted, the neoliberal model that emerged in the late 1970s seems to have been unexpectedly strengthened by the financial crisis and the political responses to it (Crouch 2011; Mirowski 2013; Streeck 2014). In the UK, the case for alternative models of governance was not helped by the governance problems that swept the Co-operative Bank and Co-operative Group during 2014. This results in the unfortunate situation in which dominant models of governance have lost credibility, but seem virtually impossible to challenge or replace.

Drawing from disciplines of economic sociology and cultural economy, this chapter reflects on the apparent crisis of neoliberal corporate governance, and asks how we might take up Raymond Williams' challenge of developing democratic alternatives, in a way that is attuned to the difficulty of getting participation to work effectively. A key reason why it proves difficult to shift the paradigm of governance is that the status quo is held in place by infrastructures of expertise, professional advice, normative rituals, and the 'particular ways of feeling' described by Williams. The idea that institutions are there to be exploited by financial interests has become a common sense in its own right, which survives partly because it has a wide-ranging set of theories and world views (or what some might term 'ideology') to accompany it. This remains the case, even when such exploitation seems devoid of any broader public legitimacy. Challenging this, and supporting the development of member-owned organizations, requires attacking this common sense and offering a different one.

The rest of the chapter is in three parts. In the next section, I describe the distinctive neoliberal claims about human agency, co-operation, and governance; emphasizing the failure to adequately capture the nature of institutions or trust in this paradigm. The chapter then turns to the elements of a democratic alternative, which emphasizes a different notion of collective action and the life of organizations. The conclusion then asks what would be involved in offering an alternative template which actively encouraged people to participate in the exercise of shared power.

31.2 NEOLIBERAL GOVERNANCE

The term 'neoliberalism' refers to the intellectual, political, and technical efforts to reinvent market liberalism in the age of large corporations and the welfare state. Intellectually, it emerged during the middle decades of the twentieth century as a critical response to socialism and Keynesianism (Mirowski and Plehwe 2009), and then became increasingly influential over policy-makers in advanced capitalist economies from the late 1970s onwards. While the term has frequently been associated with 'market fundamentalism', a more nuanced understanding of neoliberalism is that it seeks to modernize non-market institutions (such as firms and governments) in ways that inject a *market-like ethos*, rather than necessarily expanding the reach of markets per se (Davies 2014a). Not *all* public services are privatized under neoliberalism, and not all monopolies are broken up (indeed, on the latter point, neoliberal reforms have been very sympathetic to monopolies), but managerial and regulatory innovations are developed which view hierarchies and social relations as normatively and culturally similar to markets. It is this, I suggest, that is responsible for legitimacy crises of governance, and where mutual models have an obvious advantage.

What is the market ethos which is being promoted in non-market situations, such as firms? Two characteristics are worth highlighting in particular, both of which are complicit with the gradual financialization of firms. To repeat, neither is necessarily about increasing the power of markets as such, but about seeking to re-model social relations upon qualities ostensibly found in markets. The core assumption is that markets have in-built sources of transparency which need replicating elsewhere.

Firstly, there is a belief that progress (be it economic, scientific, or social) can only be achieved on the basis of competitive relations. Competition holds a privileged place in the neoliberal imaginary, as it is thanks to competition that entrepreneurs and consumers can discover new products, services, ideas, and so on. Competition, as Friedrich Hayek described it, is a 'discovery process', meaning that markets (as sites of competition) perform an important role in the circulation of knowledge, quite aside from the maximization of output (Hayek 2002). Competition is how human beings in complex societies manage their differences of perspective, and gradually build up a shared view of reality. The alternative is for the perspective of centralized experts to be imposed upon everyone, at the expense of pluralism. This is why markets are deemed valuable, from the neoliberal perspective: they offer an alternative to planning by expert dictat.

When it comes to institutions such as firms (or, for that matter, government bureaucracies and public services), neoliberal governance reforms insist on injecting competition by artificial means. In the public sector, this may involve the construction of rankings, audit, and quasi-markets, to make 'winners' and 'losers' distinguishable from each other. In the private sector, it means elevating the power of 'exit' over 'voice' (Hirschman 1970). Turnover of senior managers increases, staff are valued to the extent that they might leave for a better job elsewhere (what McKinsey consultants have referred to as the 'war for talent'), investors become more prone to withdraw in search of greater returns elsewhere. From a neoliberal perspective, these are positive cultural and normative behaviours, as they suggest that firms are imbued with competitive dynamics, in which failure is quickly identified and eliminated from the game. There is no other way of identifying where value lies, than to encourage an ethos of exiting in search of higher value, from one moment to the next.

Secondly, there is a belief that trust can only be established on the basis of the most explicit information, which typically means quantification. Markets have the great advantage of quantifying value automatically, through the price mechanism. This means that, potentially, human interaction can occur without any form of qualitative, moral, or discursively expressed judgement at all. For neoliberals such as Milton Friedman, who held very pessimistic views of democratic processes, this represented a major political advantage of markets. Hence, non-market institutions would benefit from having equally explicit forms of valuation and judgement: performance metrics, audits, risk models, targets, and indicators would strip out the ambiguity of social relations and dialogue.

The rise of 'shareholder value' as a central principle of corporate governance during the 1980s was the most prominent example of this neoliberal commitment to explicitness of valuation. While only a few management scholars have ever expressly promoted 'shareholder value' as a basis on which to run a firm (e.g. Rappaport 1986), the broader culture and ethos of senior management, business media and, above all, the financial sector, has transformed the company share price into an iconic representation of how that firm is performing over all. And while many top executives may distance themselves from the idea, expressing a commitment to their customers, reputation, or employees as their abiding concern, this does little to avert a broader epistemology which seeks to reduce value to a single metric and, as Theodor Porter puts it, place 'trust in numbers' (Porter 1995). In the financial sector itself, this same ethos sees the construction of ever more complex instruments of risk distribution, which too often forget the limits of mathematical models to approximate the realities they seek to describe (MacKenzie 2006). Or, to put that another way, they forget the crucial distinction between 'risk' (mathematically calculable) and 'uncertainty' (the underlying one-off nature of events) (Knight 1957). What is described as 'financialization', that is, the gradual ascendency of financial logic, firms, profits, and products over all others, is partly about assuming that non-market activity (for instance, higher education or households) is as amenable to calculative analysis as market activity.

Once the emphasis on competition and on explicit quantification are taken together, the resulting neoliberal theory of the firm is one which is primarily concerned with problems of 'agency', that is, the perpetual threat of individuals reneging on their commitments to each other. Managers promise to act on behalf of shareholders, but may actually act in their own interests (the dominant 'principal–agency' problem of corporate governance). Employees are viewed with suspicion, in that they may hoard knowledge and 'human capital'. Those in critical positions of agency, such as professional intermediaries (such as lawyers or financiers) must be extremely highly remunerated, to guard against them abusing their positions of power. The premise of all this is a paranoid and pessimistic one.

Critiques of neoliberalism, which view it (not unfairly) as a project for the privatization of gain and the socialization of risk, tend to overlook the accompanying philosophy through which it seeks to establish legitimacy and authority of governance. For those thinking about alternatives to the orthodox model of corporate governance, it is important to understand something of the philosophy that needs to be challenged, even if that philosophy appears to be failing. Moreover, given that the epistemology and ethics of neoliberalism assumes that all relations can be re-modelled according to the example of markets (specifically their competitive and explicitly calculative nature), there are good reasons to believe that legitimacy crises are constantly lurking in the neoliberal model, given that it rests on a fundamental misrepresentation of the social and political relations on which it is imposed, such as those within the firm. The problem is that such crises are usually met with a call for a more thorough dose of the medicine: failure means that things *still* haven't got competitive or explicit (usually referred to as 'transparent') enough. Only rarely do questions get posed about the adequacy of competition and calculation to deal with the ambiguous cultural and moral reality which is governance of complex institutions.

In Williams' terms, institutions that are constructed and governed according to these principles will inevitably produce certain 'structures of feeling'. This will include the sense that everyone is expendable, and prioritizing their own calculated interests from one moment to the next. The need to combat such feelings, using reputational and brand management with respect to customers, and 'soft' human resource management with respect to employees, becomes all the greater, where the foundational structures of business assume that social relations are constantly threatened by competition and calculation. Recent efforts to reform the 'culture' of banks indicate the nature of the problem. Arguably, the 'culture' which sanctions fraud, greed, the chasing of fees regardless of the quality of service, extreme competitiveness, and fetishization of money is an honest reflection of the formal mechanisms on which the neoliberal theory of governance is based. Where 'free-riding' and 'agency' problems are treated as endemic, and in need of constant audit to solve, it is scarcely surprising if 'culture' develops in a similarly pessimistic way.

31.3 Beyond Neoliberal Governance

Businesses which are not formally owned by outside equity investors have a tremendous opportunity to develop new models of governance, with different forms of accountability and organizational purpose. Alternative ways of balancing the interests of different stakeholders become possible, which in turn can improve relationships with employees, customers, and suppliers. However, if such businesses are viewed as slightly deformed versions of shareholder-owned companies, then governance and accountability (in addition to finance) can become much harder to establish, rather than easier. If businesses are expected to still be regulated and audited like more orthodox companies, as if their central problem is one of 'agency' (as per the neoliberal model), then not only will their value be misunderstood, but their day-to-day activities may become substantially more difficult.

In order to fully appreciate the virtues of participatory governance models, and member-owned organizations more generally, it is helpful to contrast these with the neoliberal model just outlined. For the reasons discussed, the neoliberal model, which stresses agency problems as the basic challenge for effective governance, rests on a fundamental misrepresentation of how productive, co-operative institutions work. Rather than analyse production, service, and co-operation on their own terms, the neoliberal approach views them via the template of market relations, and asks how they can be improved by injecting a more competitive, calculative ethos. An alternative to this premise, which is potentially offered by co-operatives and mutuals, is to view the social relations of firms on their own terms, and to ask how governance might work best in order to maximize the potential of those relations. This means thinking beyond competition and calculation. But how to conceive of relations within the firm differently? Let's consider this question with respect to both competition and explicitness of value, the key virtues that the neoliberal sees in markets.

First of all, how can we conceive of the search for economic value, without seeking to introduce mechanisms of competition? As we have seen, neoliberalism presupposes that only the power of exit, that is, to abandon one investment in search of a better one, is what will hasten the discovery of valuable activities. But the alternative to exit is *voice*. As many managers can testify, organizations which develop a culture of rapid employee turnover can enter a vicious circle in which nobody is willing to trust others, or to share ideas or discretionary effort. The agenda for 'employee engagement' is partly an effort to counter this ethos (McLeod and Clarke 2010). To put this another way, where it becomes normal to exercise one's power through exit, it can become harder to encourage individuals to exercise it through voice. What is needed are instruments which facilitate and enforce commitment, and not simply a set of incentives to co-operate in the short term. Mechanisms which actually prevent individuals from exiting or acting competitively have the positive effect of forcing people to seek alternative forms of expression and discovery. This is what Streeck has termed the 'beneficial constraints on rational voluntarism' (Streeck 1997).

One of the advantages of mutual-style governance is the level of commitment that it both requires and facilitates amongst managers and members. In the British context, one of the most common reasons for establishing a company as an employee mutual, or converting it to one through a leveraged buy-out, is that the founder or family owners have witnessed firms being destroyed or dissolved due to excessive influence of finance, or excessive pursuit of financial return (Davies 2009, 2012). The inability of investors to exit (such as where equity is held in a trust) allows for greater long-term decision-making. Staff turnover tends to fall in such firms, and a culture can develop in which there is a collective purpose which goes beyond the pursuit of profit.

The neoliberal rejoinder to this would be: what is there to avoid a form of stasis, whereby the firm becomes closed to new ideas, new people, or the 'creative destruc-tion' through which capitalism advances? What will be the 'discovery process', if it is not the constant trial and error of competition? The answer is that democracy—even if in the minimal sense of consultation—can offer the alternative way of discovering new ideas, products, and services. Through higher levels of dialogue within the firm, based upon higher levels of presupposed commitment, things can be discovered on the basis of social relations, rather than an attempt to replicate market relations, as per the neo-liberal model. What competition is to neoliberalism (a means of drawing on multiple perspectives, testing them out, seeing which one is best), democratic dialogue is to the post-neoliberal alternative offered by member-owned governance models. Clearly, this involves greater optimism about the capacity of participatory, dialogical structures to function effectively, although this also assumes that training, expertise, and practice are required before such functioning is possible.

Secondly, how can we understand the performance of organizations, if not in terms of a single metric of value? How to think beyond the neoliberal emphasis on explicitness and quantification of value, as dominant principles of management and governance? This is another major challenge for co-operatives and mutuals, who often struggle to ascertain how well they are doing, in the absence of orthodox metrics of performance. Developing benchmarking tools and indicators that can work in the absence of profit-maximization and shareholder value is something that the sector undoubtedly needs, and could start doing more of (Michie and Davies 2012).

However, it is worth also appreciating what is gained from an absence of explicit indi-cators of performance or value. Where performance and value remain ambiguous, this avoids the risk of placing excessive trust in risk models, indicators, and targets. It has been recognized for some time in the public sector that the introduction of targets pro-duces the phenomenon of 'gaming', in which people alter their behaviour to reach a tar-get, thereby allowing themselves to become blameless when things go wrong (Bevan and Hood 2006; Hood 2011). In the financial sector, the excessive trust that was placed in risk models produced more catastrophic consequences. The mutual alternative to this is that the question of value and performance is never easily answered with a single num-ber. While this may be less satisfying in certain respects, it has the virtue of ensuring that a broader diversity of perspectives and notions of value (beyond monetary value) are at play in the organization. The economic sociologist David Stark argues that the capacity to keep multiple notions of value in play in a single social unit represents the quintessential entrepreneurial function, or what he terms 'heterarchy' (Stark 2009). By that standard, the neoliberal commitment to render all activities explicit in terms of their numerical value is actually contrary to the spirit of entrepreneurship, which embraces ambiguity of valuation.

The great limitation of the neoliberal governance model is that it obscures the basic difference between market relations and non-market relations, believing that the latter can become re-modelled along the lines of the former. When this doesn't work, the argument can be made that the re-modelling needs to go further—more agency problems need ironing out, more transparency needs injecting. This helps explain the durability of the model: it can always be claimed that more needs to be done to perfect it. By contrast, member-owned organizations have an underlying recognition that co-operative relations in the firm are a product of rules and norms, many of which necessarily remain tacit. 'Agency' does not appear as a significant problem once rules and norms are in place which reflect the collective, social nature of successful business ventures.

The critique of the status quo, and the advocacy for alternative models of the firm and governance, needs to be rooted in this fundamental difference. It is not enough for scandals, greed, and asset-stripping to be presented as 'cultural' aberrations which can be solved with greater 'transparency' and codification of procedures. It is more honest to paint these as the cultural reflection of the neoliberal premise that agency problems are endemic everywhere other than the market, where they are dealt with thanks to competition and the price mechanism. The appeal of co-operatives, mutuals, and employee-owned models of governance, given the present juncture, is that they develop non-market relationships using suitably non-market instruments, culture, and ethics. The governance of the firm is treated as a social and political problem, requiring constitutions, participation, forms of authority, and processes of dialogue in order to be solved. It is not solved by being modelled upon something it is not, namely the market.

Yet the abiding problem, confronting these alternative forms of governance, is—as the quote from Williams at the outset indicated—that individuals have rarely had the chance to develop their capacities as participatory, empowered members of organizations, beyond the limited forms of voice that are offered via 'soft' human resource management. The 'structures of feeling' that accompany contemporary work, management, and investment are those that have developed in response to the neoliberal governance model. Chief amongst these are forms of ironic detachment (Sennett 1998), which can make the transition to mutualism harder still. One initial response of many employees or customers to participatory governance models will be either suspicion ('what do they want from me?') or opportunism ('how can I exploit this to my advantage?'). This reinforces a negative view of these organizational forms. And yet viewed from the perspective of cultural sociology, there is nothing inevitable or permanent about this orientation. The question is how to develop research, training, and education with respect to democratic processes and member-owned governance, as they operate at the level of firms and service-providers.

31.4 Conclusion: A New Approach to Risk

All organizations have the capacity to fail, and with some—as with most private businesses—failure may be expected to result in the disappearance of the organization altogether. However, organizations that strive to escape a political orthodoxy face an additional challenge: their failure will be interpreted as a failure of their very 'ideology' or 'paradigm'. Despite shareholder-owned banks creating costs to the public of hundreds of billions of pounds, only the failure of the Co-operative Bank—described by its chief executive as 'ungovernable'—was represented as a product of its underlying template of organization. The endurance of neoliberalism is partly down to the fact that it accommodates failure, is able to explain it, and can recommend solutions, all of which involve more competition and more explicitness of evaluation.

What is needed at the present moment is a careful building up of both theory and practice, of a new vision of normality, that can cope with occasional failures, through trial and error, without being condemned as idealistic. This needs to start from the premise that work, production, service, and co-operation are not human activities that are reducible to questions of competitive strategy or calculation. Instead, they are rooted in human needs and capabilities. The Centre for Research on Socio-cultural Change at Manchester University has developed a theory of what it terms the 'foundational economy', which are those aspects of economic life which cannot be easily off-shored, opened up to competition, or supplied via quasi-markets, because they are needed for economic life to persist (Bowman et al. 2014). The social sciences, including economics, need to build on this sort of example, to rediscover the heterogeneity of economic institutions, so as to provide forms and templates that are suitable for different types of socio-economic activities and needs.

With respect to alternative models of governance, what this would also involve is a more nuanced account of entrepreneurship, which recognizes the urge of some entrepreneurs to come up with new forms of ownership, work, governance, and participation. Entrepreneurship is recognized as a transformative activity, but typically *within* the terms of finance-led capitalism. Other than in the form of 'social entrepreneurship' (which is often equated with not-for-profit), there has been relatively little attention paid to the capacity of entrepreneurs to alter the very building blocks of capitalism, or even to move beyond capitalism altogether. While some socialist thinkers (e.g. Wright 2010) have offered typologies of what alternative forms of economic power look like, the question of who might pursue these, with what spirit, what forms of professional support, and what obstacles they face, has been less studied. We live in a society that purports to celebrate 'risk-takers' and 'innovators', but which says very little about how entrepreneurs might alter the very terms on which risks and innovation occur, such that they become more collective ventures.

A further ingredient of a paradigm shift, away from the neoliberal orthodoxy, is the presence of lawyers and other professional advisers, willing to help develop the templates and formal processes on which businesses depend. All businesses are in some sense fictions, inscribed into being thanks to the accounts and legal paper work which render them tangible and recognizable to regulators, banks, and the public. Without sympathetic professional advisors to help draft these 'fictions', it can be almost impossible for co-operative and mutual businesses to get off the ground or to grow. They remain mired in a state of legal and financial ambiguity, which is counter-productive, and renders them even more dependent on the strength of personality of their founders and senior managers. It is arguable that lawyers have the greatest responsibility of all in facilitating a paradigm shift in governance, seeing as they are the means by which institutions become imbued with a ritualized, codified, and sovereign identity (Davies 2014b).

Finally, what of the 'institutions which practically teach democracy', as Williams put it in 1961? Given that all manner of personal skills are now deemed teachable in school, from 'happiness', to 'resilience', to 'character', it does not seem unreasonable that schools might also teach children how to participate in collectively accountable governance institutions. If that sounds a little far-fetched, then a more plausible possibility is that lessons of governance successes and failures be collected and circulated more, much as the Co-operative College, the Foundation Trust Network, and various trade organizations already do very effectively. In many ways, this is what is most crucial. The vicious circle of neoliberalism, which traps us in a paradigm which we no longer have any belief in, is that wherever individuals are found to be self-serving, calculating, and revelling in competition with each other, it reinforces the need to build institutions with a culture of paranoia and ever-expanding audit. Amongst the various risks run by co-operatives and mutuals is that that same culture of opportunism undermines their ethos and culture, and they appear naive. Somehow the vicious circle, which insists that people can only be motivated by incentives, that value must be capturable in a single metric, that only competition can deliver innovation, needs to be broken.

References

Bevan, G. and Hood, C. (2006), 'What's Measured Is What Matters: Targets and Gaming in the English Public Health Care System', *Public Administration*, 84, 517–38.

Bowman, A., Froud, J., Johal, S., Law, J., Leaver, A., Moran, M., and Williams, K. (2014), *The End of the Experiment? From Competition to the Foundational Economy* (Manchester: Manchester University Press).

Crouch, C. (2011), *The Strange Non-Death of Neoliberalism* (Cambridge: Polity).

Davies, W. (2009), *Reinventing the Firm* (London: Demos).

Davies, W. (2012), *All of our Business: Why Britain Needs More Private Sector Employee Ownership* (London: Employee Ownership Association).

Davies, W. (2014a), *The Limits of Neoliberalism: Authority, Sovereignty and the Logic of Competition* (London: SAGE).

Davies, W. (2014b), 'Recovering the Future: The Reinvention of "Social Law"', *Juncture*, 20(3), 216–22.

Davies, W. and Yeoman, R. (2013), *Becoming a Public Service Mutual: Understanding Transition and Change* (Oxford: Centre for Mutual and Employee-Owned Business).

Dorling, D. (2014), *Inequality and the 1%* (London: Verso Books).

Engelen, E., Ertürk, I., Froud, J., Johal, S., Leaver, A., Moran, M., Nilsson, A., and Williams, K. (2011), *After the Great Complacence: Financial Crisis and the Politics of Reform* (Oxford: Oxford University Press).

Haldane, A. (2011), 'Control Rights (and Wrongs)', Bank of England. Available at https://www.scribd.com/document/114894981/Haldane-Control-Rights-and-Wrongs (accessed 24 September 2016).

Hayek, F. A. von. (2002), 'Competition as a Discovery Process', *The Quarterly Journal of Austrian Economics*, 5(2), 9–23.

Hirschman, A. O. (1970), *Exit, Voice, and Loyalty: Responses to Decline in Firms, Organizations, and States* (Cambridge, Mass: Harvard University Press).

Hood, C. (2011), *The Blame Game: Spin, Bureaucracy, and Self-Preservation in Government* (Princeton, NJ: Princeton University Press).

Knight, F. H. (1957), *Risk, Uncertainty and Profit* (8th impression) (New York: Houghton Miffin Co.).

Lapavitsas, C. (2013), *Profiting Without Producing: How Finance Exploits Us All* (London and New York: Verso).

MacKenzie, D. A. (2006), *An Engine, Not a Camera: How Financial Models Shape Markets* (Cambridge, Mass: MIT).

McLeod, D. and Clarke, N. (2010), *Engaging for Success: Enhancing Performance through Employee Engagement* (London: Department for Business, Innovation and Skills).

Michie, J. and Davies, W. (2012), *Measuring Mutuality: Indicators for Financial Mutuals* (Oxford: Centre for Mutual and Employee-owned Business).

Mirowski, P. (2013), *Never Let a Serious Crisis Go to Waste: How Neoliberalism Survived the Financial Meltdown* (London: Verso Books).

Mirowski, P. and Plehwe, D., eds, (2009), *The Road from Mont Pèlerin: The Making of the Neoliberal Thought Collective* (Cambridge, Mass: Harvard University Press).

Porter, T. M. (1995), *Trust in Numbers: The Pursuit of Objectivity in Science and Public Life*, (Princeton, NJ: Princeton University Press).

Rappaport, A. (1986), *Creating Shareholder Value: The New Standard for Business Performance* (New York: Free Press).

Sennett, R. (1998), *The Corrosion of Character: The Personal Consequences of Work in the New Capitalism* (New York: W. W. Norton & Company).

Stark, D. (2009), *The Sense of Dissonance: Accounts of Worth in Economic Life* (Princeton, NJ: Princeton University Press).

Streeck, W. (1997), 'Beneficial Constraints: On the Economic Limits Of Rational Voluntarism', in J. R. Hollingsworth and R. Boyer, eds, *Contemporary Capitalism: The Embededness of Institutions* (Cambridge: Cambridge University Press), 197–219.

Streeck, W. (2014), *Buying Time: The Delayed Crisis of Democratic Capitalism* (London: Verso Books).

Williams, R. (2001), *The Long Revolution* (Peterborough, ON: Broadview Press).

Williamson, J., Driver, C., and Kenway, P., eds (2014), *Beyond Shareholder Value: The Reasons and Choices for Corporate Governance Reform* (London: TUC).

Wright, E. O. (2010), *Envisioning Real Utopias* (London: Verso).

CHAPTER 32

CO-OPERATIVES:
A DEVELOPMENT STRATEGY?

*an analysis of argan oil co-operatives
in south-west Morocco*

ZAHIR DOSSA

32.1 CONTEXT AND HISTORY

'I realized argan forests are going to disappear so I wanted to study how to commercialize argan [in order to provide an incentive to communities to protect the forests],' remarks Zoubida Charrouf about the impetus behind the argan oil industry. The constantly expanding cosmetic product lines and luxury culinary brands surrounding 'liquid gold' therefore stemmed from the goal to improve the status of the argan tree. The 80-million-year-old tree species, once spanned all of North Africa, preventing desertification and providing numerous benefits to the people cultivating it (Charrouf and Guillame 2009). Steadily declining over the ice age, argan trees can now only be found in the Sous Valley—a region in south-west Morocco. Charrouf and Guillame estimate that the argan forests further diminished by 50 per cent during the twentieth century due to a heightened demand for fuel, over-grazing, and conversion to exportable crops. As a result, the argan forest was declared a UNESCO Biosphere Reserve in 1998.

Charrouf aimed to incentivize local populations to protect the argan forests by commercializing argan oil. Moreover, she recognized that an increased demand for argan oil would raise the price of argan—financially motivating local communities to disengage from harmful practices to the forests. By using scientific processes to affirm local Berber knowledge of argan oil's medicinal and beautification properties, Charrouf was able to draw global attention to argan oil. Despite this, the process to produce argan oil was too arduous at the time to develop a significant supply. Mobilizing the mechanization of this process, Charrouf addressed another important issue central to rural Morocco: the socio-economic status of women.

The majority of women in south-west Morocco are uneducated and illiterate. The lack of education and inability to speak Arabic make it difficult for Berber women to leave the countryside. In addition, as is customary in traditional Islamic societies, the socially conservative and tightly woven family units often discourage employment opportunities for women. Families are therefore dependent on a single source of income, contributing to an approximate rural GDP per capita of 1,325 EUR[1]—60 per cent less than the overall GDP per capita.

To ameliorate this situation, Charrouf developed the first argan oil enterprise and structured it as a female co-operative. The Amal co-operative was equipped with a mechanized system for the pressing and filtration of argan oil, procedures originally performed by hand. The efficient production process alongside the growing awareness of argan oil spurred an international market concentrated in Europe. This market growth led to the birth of other argan oil companies, which were primarily privately owned. Due to their superior managerial resources and technical skills, private enterprises outperformed co-operatives. An early study conducted by Lybbert et al. (2002, 2004) found that under this market mix, the argan forests did not improve nor did local communities benefit from the growth of the argan oil industry. In fact many communities were negatively affected by the rising cost of argan oil sold locally, while trees were over-harvested due to the rising prices of argan fruit (Lybbert et al. 2002; Lybbert et al. 2004). Although co-operatives benefited local communities considerably in comparison to private enterprises, these effects were negligible due to the minimal number of co-operatives and their capacities. If rural development was to occur, a strategy to promote the creation of new co-operatives and enable them to compete would be necessary.

32.2 Life Cycle

The life cycle of co-operatives has significantly improved through two interventions—donor funding and the development of associations. Initially, women earned less than 1 EUR per day and had to also supply the co-operative with raw materials. Due to the poor quality of argan oil produced from hand-presses, co-operatives were forced to sell argan kernels, a semi-processed product that captured little of the value chain. Co-operatives with the ability to purchase machines did not fare much better because of their inability to brand and market oil. Co-operatives therefore resorted to selling oil in local markets, earning marginal profits.

By petitioning the European Union and the Agence de Developpement Social (Social Development Agency) in Morocco for funds, government officials and community

---

[1] Triangulated from data in CIA World Factbook: GDP = $105 billion EUR; Agricultural Composition of GDP = 17.1 per cent; Population = 32 million; Rural Population = 42 per cent.

development leaders were able to establish Projet Arganier (PA)—a government agency responsible for the financing and expansion of co-operatives. The injection of donor funding into argan oil co-operatives attracted managers with strong business competencies to the countryside, where they organized groups of women into co-operatives. Managers then submitted funding proposals to PA in order to mechanize their oil production process while completing the legal steps necessary to export oil. The success of PA is evident from the number of requests received, which far exceeded expectations. As a result, PA added the caveat that a co-operative had to be in existence for at least two years before it could be financed.

While donor funding surged the number of co-operatives, the birth of co-operative associations enabled their expansion. Internally, co-operatives lacked the technical knowledge and scale necessary to effectively brand and market their products. Consequently, nearly all co-operatives are grouped under associations soon after being formalized. Associations provide co-operatives with the sales, marketing, and branding capacities necessary to compete with private enterprises and therefore expand. Under this scheme, a co-operative effectively sells argan oil to its association, which resells it on the global market. Alongside donor financing, associations are responsible for the surge of co-operatives from 15 in 2003 to 154 in 2004 (Boussaid 2011).

32.3 CORE VALUE CHAIN AND THE ROLE OF CO-OPS

The value chain for argan oil co-operatives, shown in Figure 30.1, begins with procuring argan fruit. Initially purchased from local harvesters for 15 cents per kilogram, argan fruit can be priced as high as 35 cents per kilogram after factoring in distance, transportation, and demand. The price of this fruit has risen significantly. Ten years ago, argan could be purchased for a tenth of its present-day price. As the argan oil market expands and the availability of argan becomes more constrained, co-operatives will have a significant competitive advantage in the market. Furthermore, the high level of social capital that co-operatives share with suppliers often enables them to be more competitive than private or foreign-owned enterprises in markets with limited or volatile supply (Ghorpade 1973; Attwood and Baviskar 1987; Nunez-Nickel and Moyano-Fuentes 2004).

After being purchased from harvesters, argan fruit is set to dry over the course of at least four weeks to facilitate members in removing the pulp. As briefly illustrated in Figure 32.1, members tear off the flesh and crack open the nut, obtaining anywhere from one to three kernels. These kernels are collected to be pressed into argan oil, while the pulp is fed to animals and the nuts are used as fuel. Obtaining the kernels is the most painstaking process in the value chain, requiring 30 kilograms of fruit and a full day of work to obtain 1 kilogram of oil. The female producers of argan are therefore vital in the value chain of argan oil. Members are compensated for each kilogram of kernels they

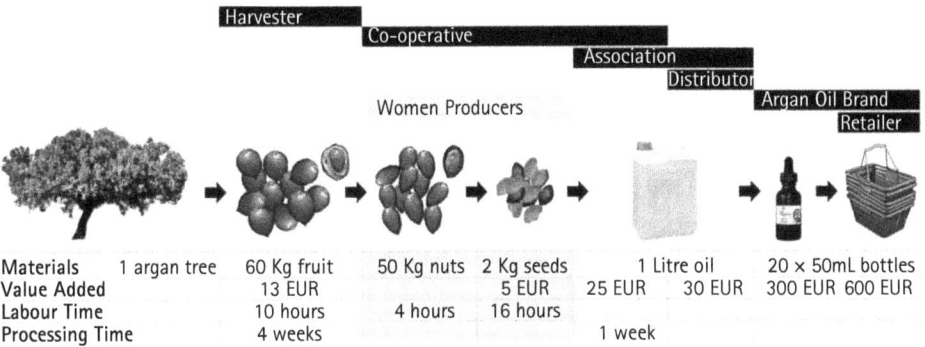

FIGURE 32.1 Value chain of argan oil co-operatives.

Author's diagram based on interviews.

yield. Aside from offering higher salaries than private enterprises, co-operatives provide Arabic classes, vacation days, and by-products of the production process to their
members.

The remaining process after the kernels are obtained is usually mechanized, altering
slightly depending on the type of argan oil. While both cosmetic and culinary argan
oil are dry-pressed, culinary argan oil is derived from roasting the kernels beforehand.
Both oils are filtered separately for approximately one week. Some co-operatives still use
traditional tools instead of machines but the oil resulting from the process is of poorer
quality and has a shorter shelf-life. Consequently, many associations will charge member co-operatives lacking machines a small fee to use theirs, highlighting yet another
benefit offered by associations.

Co-operatives sell the filtered argan oil in bulk to their associations. While co-
operatives are able to sell their oil directly to purchasers as well, their outreach ability is
limited and the vast majority of oil is sold to the association. An association then uses its
brand, or the co-operative's, to sell the oil to a variety of partners in the global market.
As demonstrated by the amounts in Figure 32.1, associations and retailers add the most
substantial value in the value chain: 71 per cent. The failure of co-operatives to create
and capture more value in the chain reveals their lack of vertical market integration—a
significant setback that is not unique to the argan oil industry (Ghorpade 1973; Attwood
and Baviskar 1987; Haller 1992; Peterson and Bruce 1996; Kyriakopoulos 1998; Katz and
Boland 2002; Nunez-Nickel and Moyano-Fuentes 2004; Taylor 2005).

32.4 INSTITUTIONAL STRUCTURE
AND GOVERNANCE

There are over 150 argan oil co-operatives in south-west Morocco. As mentioned earlier, nearly all co-operatives belong to an association, which ranges in size from five

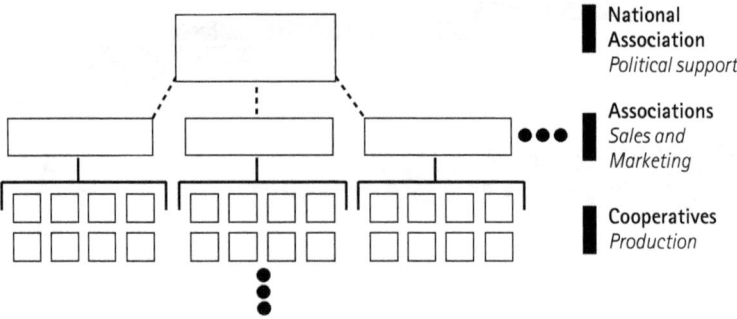

National
Association
Political support

Associations
*Sales and
Marketing*

Cooperatives
Production

FIGURE 32.2 Institutional hierarchy (Projet Arganier 2008).

Author's diagram based on information gathered from Projet Arganier, 2008.

co-operatives to 22 (Projet Arganier 2008). Associations have been pivotal in promoting the co-operative movement, as was discussed earlier. All associations are advocated by the national association, 'Association Nationale des Coopératives Arganières'. The hierarchy described, along with the roles of each institution, is illustrated in Figure 32.2.

Although the co-operatives studied vary in size from 18 to 60 women, the average co-operative has 46 female members (Projet Arganier 2008). Six of these members compose the leadership board of the co-operative, which includes the president, vice-president, secretary, and treasurer. In addition to the members, each co-operative employs staff to operate the machinery, an employee to run the retail store, and a manager to oversee co-operative operations. Even though the organizational structure and proceedings of co-operatives are formalized under Moroccan law, their governance starkly contrasts with that of an ideal co-operative because of internal and external pressures.

Though heralded for the democratic decision-making they foster, co-operatives among marginalized communities are frequently managed and controlled by local elites (Tendler 1984; Tendler et al. 1988; Hudson and Hudson 2004; Philpott et al. 2007). Consistent with the case literature, co-operative managers dominate the decision-making and cash flow of the co-operative. This unilateral governance prevalent among co-operatives is largely shaped by internal pressures and external pressures. The primary internal pressure applied within co-operatives is meant to emanate from the membership. In addition, there are three external pressures that affect organizations as identified by DiMaggio and Powell (2000): coercive (regulatory pressures), normative (community/donor pressures), and mimetic (isomorphic pressures). These internal and external forces are summarized in Table 32.1.

Gender dynamics and information asymmetry largely dictate the marginal internal pressure applied by the member base within the co-operative scheme. As stated above, the patriarchal society makes it difficult for women to actively participate in co-operative decision-making. In fact, while every co-operative is intended to be female-founded and run, co-operative managers are males who conduct business in the names of their wives and make unilateral decisions. Significant co-operative

Table 32.1 Framework of Internal and External Pressures Affecting Governance

		Indicators
Internal Pressure	Membership	Profit distribution; level of power/control the manager has; voting rights and exercising of these rights by participants; amount of complaints/requests made by participants and responded to by management
External Pressures	Mimetic	How closely co-operative resembles other co-operatives in terms of salary, benefits offered, etc.
	Normative	Response to community/donor demands
	Coercive	How closely the co-operative follows the law, among other rules and regulations mandated by donor/government agencies

Author's data.

procedures such as elections, which are meant to keep leadership in check, are reduced to ceremonies—a common trend in the bureaucratization of domestic enterprises within developing countries (Meyer and Rowan 1991). When asked about the co-operative leadership, a common response was: 'I don't understand all that … Every year we do elections. They ask, do you want to keep them [the managers and the leadership board]? We all say yes.' Intended to hold co-operative leadership accountable, male-run elections are transformed into quick, white-ballot procedures that reaffirm the status quo. As a result, neither the manager nor the board (which solely exists on paper) changes from the onset.

The dynamic of internal pressure is further exacerbated by the lack of member awareness about the co-operative structure. Not a single member interviewed could describe what a co-operative was or their role in it. Members simply viewed their duty as they would any normal job, albeit being extremely appreciated for the rewards reaped. Although included in the formal by-laws of a co-operative, member education, meant to improve member knowledge of the co-operative structure, has been replaced with Arabic-language classes. Therefore, the lack of member awareness alongside gender inequities severely hinders the internal pressures that can affect co-operative behaviour.

The unbalanced combination of external pressures outlined in Table 32.1 also contributes to the poor governance structure of co-operatives. Mimetic pressures overpower normative and coercive pressures—reinforcing the power dynamics described. Isomorphism, a term into which mimetic pressures can be bundled, is the concept that powerful forces act upon organizations operating in similar fields causing them to be similar to each other (DiMaggio and Powell 2000). Alternatively stated, 'If you look at the competition long enough, you become them'. Argan oil co-operatives, through the role of associations and PA, exemplify this phenomenon and, consequently, are barely distinguishable from one another. All the co-operatives that were studied are governed by an identical management structure and offer the same sets of benefits to their members in terms of salary, Arabic classes, etc. This universality is encouraged by PA and the associations, which 'streamline' co-operatives by imposing various practices upon them while implicitly condoning others—particularly the power dynamics.

Although there are cases identified by Tendler (1984, 1988) where local communities were able to affect the governance of co-operatives, the same was not evident in Morocco. Interviews with local community members not involved in the co-operative industry revealed concern towards the 'European political movement meant to disrupt the local traditions' in the countryside. The promotion of social equity and democratic processes, which are indeed foreign to the region, alienate local communities from the co-operative movement rather than encouraging them to influence co-operative behaviour. Because donor financing was primarily focused on expanding co-operatives and increasing employment, no further normative pressures affecting governance were placed on co-operatives. Consequently, the weak normative and coercive pressures (discussed in Sections 32.5 and 32.6) did not counter the strong mimetic pressures that dictated co-operative governance.

32.5 External Relations

Co-operatives primarily engage with donors and public authorities. While co-operatives share a competitive yet distant relationship with their private counterparts, associations often look to private enterprises as role models. Observing best practices from the private argan oil sector, associations replicate and disseminate strategies to their system of co-operatives. Although co-operatives often default on their principles by adopting these practices, public authorities and donor organizations informally permit them to do so due to the resulting community development outcomes.

Public authorities strongly support co-operatives from both a national and local standpoint. Viewing the co-operative movement as a strategy to encourage rural development, the national government created a political environment and attracted donor funding to enable co-operatives to flourish. At the local level, officials assist co-operative efforts based on the community development benefits co-operatives deliver to their locales. These officials conduct a balancing act of sorts by promoting co-operatives yet tolerating their faulty governance dynamics described in Section 32.4. To demonstrate this, local officials are the personnel in charge of overseeing the 'white-ballot' elections held by co-operatives every year. These officials confirm that there are no major issues members have towards the manager and the board before renewing the leadership through a quick, informal vote.

Donor organizations also share a similar relationship with argan oil co-operatives. Although in a position to levy wide-ranging controls over the co-operatives they provide grants to, donors such as the EU and the Social Development Agency focus on a few metrics while otherwise allowing co-operatives to operate in the way they wish.

Moreover, PA was founded on the imperative to improve the environment and create employment opportunities for women in rural regions of Morocco. Subsequently, the primary performance indicators PA aims to improve are the number of trees planted (performed through a government ministry) and the number of women employed. To ensure funds are used efficiently and the co-operative is economically solvent, a representative from PA makes monthly visits to each co-operative that receives financing. Understanding that women's employment and education is dependent on the profitability of the co-operative, PA advises co-operatives in poor financial standing to join an association and adopt other known best practices. As has been demonstrated, it is not due to a lack of resources but rather a different set of priorities that causes donors and officials not to adopt a regulatory stance towards co-operative behaviour.

32.6 POLICY ENVIRONMENT

Rural poverty is a significant problem in Morocco: 44 per cent live in rural areas with an estimated GDP per capita of 877 EUR. The government has developed policies to tackle this problem by improving the services delivered to rural areas and by adopting industrial policies that benefit these regions. However, improving services such as rural electrification, education, and social welfare has been limited in scope and impact. Moreover, such an approach relies on one of two fundamental assumptions: 1) jobs exist or 2) jobs will be created through the improvement of human capital (otherwise referred to as Say's Law). Instead, the government's industrial policies in these regions have been a much more effective approach to spurring local development. The industrial policies pertaining to co-operatives in the argan oil sector exemplify this.

Co-operatives, which were once completely foreign to Morocco, had been introduced by Europeans for the local development outcomes they often foster. In support of this movement, the government legalized the co-operative form of organization along with its by-laws, practices, and regulations in 1984, and further revised it in 1993 (Lamrani et al. 1984). As a result of the protection, co-operatives were guaranteed under Moroccan law, the government of Morocco and development leaders were awarded a grant from the EU to establish and finance a government entity, PA, responsible for the creation and expansion of argan oil co-operatives. The government's aim was to counter the dominance of private and foreign-owned enterprises in the argan oil sector, which did little in furthering rural development as has been discussed.

Occurring in reverse order from usual, the government supported argan oil co-operatives *before* being able to regulate them. Co-operatives have not been regulated due to a disconnection between the practices championed by political offices and their execution among rural societies. As previously discussed, rural communities lack the adequate skill sets to effectively implement co-operatives with their principles intact. Therefore co-operatives are melded into the only form of organization that is understood, accepted, and feasible: a private enterprise, albeit a socially responsible one. Local officials responsible for 'regulating' co-operatives overlook these shortcomings due to the positive impacts co-operatives achieve. Thus, officials will legalize women argan oil co-operatives, which are actually run by males, and host annual elections, which are mere white-ballot ceremonies. It can therefore be argued that it is not the lack of support for co-operatives but the lack of regulation that is preventing argan oil co-operatives reaching their highest potential in contributing to local development. This argument is assessed in the following sections.

32.7 IMPACT ANALYSIS

32.7.1 Impact of Co-operative Successes on Sustainable Development

Co-operatives in the Argan oil sector, despite their setbacks, have contributed signifi-cantly to local economic development, social equity, and environmental preservation outcomes. As of 2009, roughly 150 co-operatives were directly employing 7,000 women with a market cap of over 26-million EUR, as extrapolated in Table 32.2. Based on the interviews conducted, the average member earns an annual income of 617 EUR from her enrolment in a co-operative. While 617 EUR is slightly lower than the rural GDP

Table 32.2 Economic Data by Co-operative, by Member, and by Sector (numbers are in EUR)

		Agadir Co-op	Per member[1]	Argan Co-op Sector[2]
Revenues	Argan oil sales	224,000	3,733	26,133,333
	Membership fees	–	–	–
Costs	Materials	(60,600)	(1,010)	(7,070,000)
	Member wages	(37,000)	(617)	(4,316,667)
	Salaries (excluding director)[3]	(2,600)	(43)	(303,333)
Profits		126,400	2,107	14,746,667

[1] Economic data per co-operative member is derived from Agadir co-operative figures and can be assumed to remain consistent across co-operatives as most if not all co-operatives are in a steady state (i.e. are mechanized or have access to mechanization) and sell through an association.

[2] Economic data for the entire sector was extrapolated based on 'per member' data and total estimated membership (7,000 women).

[3] The assessment did not obtain the salary for the director, although background interviews suggest it is a significant portion of the profits.

per capita of 877 EUR, it is important to note that women only work 30 hours per week. Therefore, the average earnings per day in a co-operative are nearly twice the daily average rural GDP per capita. Thus, the average rural GDP per capita in villages where a co-operative is present has risen dramatically.

Through employing women, the co-operative movement has also improved the social status of women and strengthened social capital. Although initially averse to the co-operative movement, many community members when interviewed a year later were appreciative of the secondary source of income co-operative membership provides to households. Due to the better lifestyles women are able to provide for their families, each member interviewed was extremely thankful (to God) for having the opportunity to work in a co-operative. Not a single complaint or further desire was expressed. This level of contentment also stems from member cohesion among a co-operative. Although women do not exercise their voice in election matters or salary increases, they speak up as a group on matters such as increasing supply of raw materials or increasing membership. When concerned about limited supplies affecting their wages, women jointly press the co-operative to purchase more argan and prevent new women from joining. Described as a 'union', the female membership is capable of having a voice that is rarely heard in traditional Muslim societies.

Having discussed the economic and social development outcomes of argan oil co-operatives, it is important to mention the positive environmental conservation behaviour that has resulted. The increasing value of argan fruit provides locals with a strong monetary incentive to conserve the forests and exercise responsible grazing practices. Conservation practices are also enforced by co-operatives, which are directly impacted by waning supplies of argan. Accordingly, co-operative members, who are often responsible for endangering the argan forests, are educated on proper conservation schemes through PA's member curriculum. Extending beyond conservation, the government has begun a replanting effort of argan trees through the assistance of the foreign aid funds received from the EU. As of 2007, 212,033 had been planted from these efforts—33 times the amount planted in 2000 (Projet Arganier 2008; Charrouf and Guillaume 2009).

32.7.2 Impact of Co-operative Setbacks on Sustainable Development

Despite the positive development outcomes argan oil co-operatives afforded, they strayed from four basic co-operative tenets: 1) democratic decision-making; 2) equitable profit distribution; 3) open membership; and 4) member education on co-operatives (Holyoake 1879; Fairbairn 1994; Ortmann and King 2007). Interviews with pioneers of the argan oil co-operative movement revealed that co-operative behaviour can be attributed to the initial set of stakeholder priorities and local circumstances. Appeasing donors and the Moroccan government, the focus on argan oil co-operatives was placed on creating employment opportunities for women. Democratic processes to govern co-operatives were ignored and not re-emphasized by other stakeholders due to the lack of member knowledge and adverse community dispositions. This context in which initial co-operatives were established shaped the co-operative movement and was reinforced through isomorphic processes.

As referenced throughout this chapter, the setbacks uncovered are not unique to co-operatives in the argan oil sector. Although often ignored, the same is true about the successes. It is therefore important to challenge our assumptions on how co-operatives should behave and whether these characteristics should indeed be considered setbacks of the co-operative movement, or if instead they should be considered prerequisites for its success in certain contexts. That is, if co-operatives behaved ideally, would the same level of community development occur?

The author argues that the success of argan oil co-operatives is attributed to their abandonment of basic co-operative principles. Moreover, the inequitable profit distribution and unilateral rule was necessary to attract managers with business expertise to the co-operative movement and enable them to dictate co-operative decisions instead of the membership, which lacked basic business competencies. Similarly, closing new memberships after a certain point was necessary to protect the livelihoods of current members. As a result of these 'failings', the growth of the co-operative movement far exceeded the most aggressive expectations by donors. Should this expansion not be encouraged unless co-operatives provide better community development outcomes than other forms of enterprises as has been demonstrated?

A discussion about the appropriateness for democracies is re-emerging, with many critics arguing that democracy is not fitting for all countries. Taking this strain of argument deeper, are democracies appropriate in all contexts and organizations? Even if appropriate, are the democratic ideals upheld by co-operatives *feasible* in all contexts? In order to answer, we need to first understand the enabling conditions that make co-operatives feasible and effective in particular environments. From there, we can begin to understand how co-operatives, or employee-centric firms, can be adapted to their environments or vice versa.

32.8 PROSPECTS OF EVOLUTION

Returning to the challenge of developing successful co-operatives that behave ideally, even in developing contexts, the author has developed a new co-operative model that incorporates Internet-based strategies.

The Argan Tree is a co-operative of 18 women that produces argan oil and is directly connected to consumers in North America through http://theargantree.com. This action research engagement has the potential to overcome setbacks that plague many co-operative models, including: inequitable profit distribution to members, a lack of member awareness and participation in decision-making processes, and excessive profit margins captured by retailers. In other words, Internet-based strategies that enforce

equitable value chains through transparency and the elimination of market intermediaries can circumvent these obstacles to potentially strengthen co-operative organizational forms towards achieving real sustainable development.

The value chain transparency espoused by the Internet-based co-operative model
serves to increase the accountability within co-operatives and to positively influence
consumer buying behaviour. By publishing the cost breakdown and revenue distribution, the model increases member awareness and inhibits managers from misallocating
finances. Alongside improving co-operative accountability, this level of transparency
improves consumer purchasing behaviour by informing customers where their money
goes. To foster a deeper relationship with consumers and drive purchasing behaviour
further, biographical data with statements specific to each of the members are published.
A brief exploration reveals that one widow uses the money to pay for electricity and
send her children to school, while another woman is replacing the broken door to her
home as her husband is unemployed. Highlighting this rich, social impact through the
medium of the Internet offers an advantage to Fair Trade and other certification labels
due to the avoidance of expensive, lengthy procedures and the depth of information
conveyed. Even further, consumers get a tangible understanding of the social impacts
from their purchases. A pilot study performed in 2010 demonstrates the potential of this
new model in improving consumer purchasing behaviour. In this limited study, consumers who visited the 'Meet the Women' page purchased over twice the amount than
consumers who did not.

Extending beyond impacting consumer behaviour and improving accountability, the
co-operative model makes important strides to improve profitability through reducing
market intermediaries. In the argan oil sector, associations and retailers retain a significant share of the profits by commercializing products for co-operatives (see Figure
32.1). Under the Internet-based model, marketing through the online medium does not
require extensive administration. As a result, the women of the co-operative earn 60 per
cent of the revenues—20 times more than they would earn in a traditional co-operative
scheme. Even further, consumers are able to purchase products at lower prices. Argan
oil sold at The Argan Tree is priced 55 per cent and 32 per cent lower than the retail average for cosmetic and culinary oil, respectively.[2]

Despite balancing social and economic outcomes, co-operatives that employ
Internet-based strategies require considerable technical assistance at the outset. Due
to the limited expertise available at affordable prices, expanding the co-operative and
scaling the model will be challenging. While a system that automates various technical
procedures can partially overcome this hurdle, the model may, ironically, require the
creation of an association—albeit a socially responsible one that serves more as an ena-
bler rather than a middleman.

Contrasting the two co-operative models in their current state, we can observe
a trade-off between maintaining co-operative ideals and scaling; by forgoing one, we

---

[2] A sample size of 16 was used to determine the retail average prices of cosmetic and culinary
argan oil.

are awarded the other. The streamlining of Internet-based models has the potential to achieve rapid expansion while upholding co-operative principles, but further research needs to be conducted. In the meantime, development practitioners championing co-operatives will often be faced with the difficult decision of either promoting ideal co-operatives that have a difficult time succeeding, or relaxing certain principles in order to let them thrive.

REFERENCES

Attwood, D. M. and B. S. Baviskar (1987), 'Why Do Some Cooperatives Work But Not Others: A Comparative Analysis of Sugar Cooperatives in India', *Economic and Political Weekly,* 22(26), A38–A56.

Boussaid, M., ed. (2011), *Arganeraie Biosphere Reserve, Morocco, and the Role of Women's Cooperatives: Biosphere Reserves in the Mountains of the World: Excellence in the Clouds?* (Vienna, Austrian Academy of Sciences Press).

Charrouf, Z. and Guillaume, D. (2009), 'Sustainable Development in Northern Africa: The Argan Forest Case', *Sustainability,* 1(4), 1012–22.

DiMaggio, P. J. and Powell, W. W. (2000), 'The Iron Cage Revisited: Institutional Isomorphism and Collective Rationality in Organizational Fields' (Reprinted from the *American Sociological Association,* 48, 147–60, 1983), *Advances in Strategic Management,* 17, 143–66.

Fairbarn, B. (1994), *The Meaning of Rochdale: The Rochdale Pioneers and the Co-operative Principles* (Centre for the Study of Co-operatives: University of Saskatchewan).

Ghorpade, J. (1973), 'Organizational Ownership Patterns and Efficiency: Case Study of Private and Cooperative Sugar Factories in South India', *Academy of Management Journal,* 16(1), 138–48.

Haller, L. E. (1992), *Branded Product Marketing Strategies in the Cottage Cheese Market: Cooperatives versus Proprietary Firms* (Food Marketing Policy Center: University of Connecticut).

Holyoake, G. J. (1879). *The History of Co-operation in England: Its Literature and Its Advocates* (Philadelphia: J. B. Lippincott & Co).

Hudson, M. and Hudson, I. (2004), 'Justice, Sustainability, and the Fair Trade Movement: A Case Study of Coffee Production in Chiapas', *Social Justice,* 31(3), 130–46.

Katz, J. P. and Boland, M. A. (2002). 'One For All and All For One? A New Generation of Co-Operatives Emerges', *Long Range Planning,* 35(1), 73–89.

Kyriakopoulos, K. (1998), 'Agricultural Cooperatives: Organizing for Market-Orientation. Building Relationships to Feed the World: Firms, Chains, Blocs', IAMA World Congress, VIII, Punta Del Este, Uruguay.

Lamrani, M. K., Berrada, M. et al. (1984), 'Fixant le statut général des coopératives et les missions de l'Office de développement de la coopération'. (Fixing the general status of cooperatives and the missions of the Office for the development of cooperatives), Rabat.

Lybbert, T. J., Barrett, C. B. et al. (2002), 'Market-Based Conservation and Local Benefits: The Case of Argan Oil in Morocco', *Ecological Economics,* 41(1), 125–44.

Lybbert, T., Barrett, C. B. et al. (2004), 'Does Resource Commercialization Induce Local Conservation? A Cautionary Tale from Southwestern Morocco', *Society & Natural Resources: An International Journal,* 17(5), 413–30.

Meyer, J. and Rowan, B. (1991), 'Institutionalized Organizations: Formal Structure as Myth and Ceremony', in W. W. Powell and P. J. DiMaggio, eds, *The New Institutionalism in Organizational Analysis* (Chicago: University of Chicago Press), 340–63.

Nunez-Nickel, M. and Moyano-Fuentes, J. (2004), 'Ownership Structure of Cooperatives as an Environmental Buffer', *Journal of Management Studies*, 41(7), 1131–52.

Ortmann, G. F. and King, R. P. (2007), 'Agricultural Cooperatives I: History, Theory and Problems', *Agrekon*, 46(1): 18–46.

Peterson, H. C. and Bruce, L. A. (1996), 'Cooperative Strategy: Theory and Practice', *Agribusiness*, 12(4), 371–83.

Philpott, S. M., Bichier, P. et al. (2007), 'Field-Testing Ecological and Economic Benefits of Coffee Certification Programs'. *Conservation Biology*, 21(4), 975–85.

Projet Arganier (2008), 'Appui a l'amelioration de la situation de l'emploi de la femme rurale et gestion durable de l'arganeraie dans le Sud-Ouest du Maroc' (Support for Improving the Employment Situation of Rural Women and Sustainable Management of the Argan Tree in South-Western Morocco) (Agadir: P. Arganier).

Taylor, P. L. (2005), 'In the Market but Not of it: Fair Trade Coffee and Forest Stewardship Council Certification as Market-Based Social Change', *World Development*, 33/1), 129–47.

Tendler, J. (1984), 'The Well-Tempered Capitalist: Profiles From Some Bolivian Coops', *Grassroots Development*, 82), 37–47.

Tendler, J., Healy, K. et al. (1988), 'What To Think About Cooperatives: A Guide from Bolivia', in A. Sheldon and P. Hakim, eds, *Direct to the Poor: Grassroots Development in Latin America* (Boulder, Colorado 80302: Lynne Rienner Publishers, Inc,).

CHAPTER 33

FAIR TRADE AND CO-OPERATIVES

ALEX NICHOLLS AND BENJAMIN HUYBRECHTS

33.1 INTRODUCTION

THE Fair Trade and co-operative movements have much in common. This chapter aims to examine the convergences and divergences between the two notions, highlighting what they can learn from each other and how practitioners and researchers in the two areas can better collaborate.

Fair trade is an innovative avenue to economic development that uses a market-driven approach to exploit the growing trend in ethical, or cause-based, consumption (Nicholls and Opal 2005). Fair Trade organizations aim to re-engineer the value chains between poor producers and artisans—typically in developing countries—and their wholesale buyers, such that a greater proportion of the overall rents accrue to those who provide the inputs. Put simply, Fair Trade aims to ensure that the poorest actors in a supply chain benefit from more of the overall financial value creation as a development tool. Moreover, Fair Trade reconnects producers and consumers at the point of purchase, such that consumption becomes a political—or, at least, lifestyle—choice.

The definition developed by international Fair Trade networks and most commonly used in the academic literature (e.g. Moore 2004) is the following:

> Fair Trade is a trading partnership, based on dialogue, transparency and respect, that seeks greater equity in international trade. It contributes to sustainable development by offering better trading conditions to, and securing the rights of, marginalised producers and workers—especially in the South. Fair Trade organizations (backed by consumers) are engaged actively in supporting producers, awareness raising and in campaigning for changes in the rules and practice of conventional international trade.

To do this Fair Trade follows several key principles:

- A minimum price paid to producers determined by local economic conditions. This should be above the cost of production and will hold should world market prices drop below it. When market prices are above the minimum price, Fair Trade organizations will honour the higher price
- An additional development premium (typically 10% of the overall contract) for community projects
- Long-term contracts that allow producers to plan their investment and spending over several years
- Pre-payment of a part of each contract to ensure that producers can smooth their income flow and invest in improving their crops or products before sale
- Technical support and capacity building to enable producers to maximize the value of their outputs
- Minimum labour standards, including no child labour
- Capacity building and technical assistance, for example to move towards higher value organic production
- Minimum sustainability and environmental standards

Starting in the Netherlands in 1988, these principles were formalized into a set of audited standards that are certified to consumers by a product mark or brand. Initially created on a country-by-country basis, in 1997 the Fair Trade Labelling Organizations ('FLO', now 'Fairtrade International') brought together national labelling initiatives, producer networks, and associate members within an umbrella organization that agreed common standards and, in 2002, established a common Fair Trade mark. However, there are also a large number of Fair Trade products for which labelling standards do not yet exist. Producer organizations in this category are often members of the second key coalition network in the sector: the World Fair Trade Organization. The latter established a Fair Trade Organization, peer-reviewed, label.

In 2013, global *certified* Fair Trade sales amounted to £4.4bn (+15% on 2012). The UK market—the largest in the world—accounted for over 40 per cent of the total. As well as the development benefits of the guaranteed minimum price, an additional €52 million was distributed to communities via the Fair Trade premium in 2013. In the same year, there were 30,000 certified Fair Trade products in 125 countries worldwide coming from more than 800 producer organizations in 74 countries. It has been estimated that Fair Trade benefits more than six million poor people across the globe.

In addition to direct action reconfiguring existing supply chains both to empower producers and to increase economic development, Fair Trade also campaigns for political change and trade justice. Indeed, these wider impacts of Fair Trade may well have had a greater overall impact than its direct economic benefits. As a consequence of consumer support for Fair Trade standards, many major multinational organizations have reviewed their supply chain practices, often acknowledging the need to integrate producers and artisans more fairly in their overall value chains. This has increasingly become known as creating shared value (Porter and Kramer 2011).

This chapter is structured as follows. After this introduction, the second section describes the development of Fair Trade from its historical roots to the current organizational landscape and market organization. Next there is a discussion of several key issues and challenges that have emerged as Fair Trade has become increasingly institutionalized. Then, the fourth section explores the relationship between Fair Trade and the co-operative and mutual movements. Finally, conclusions serve to sum up the chapter.

33.2 THE DEVELOPMENT OF FAIR TRADE
AND THE ROLE OF CO-OPERATIVES

The origins of the Fair Trade movement are located just after the Second World War, with various initiatives focused on the import and distribution of handicrafts into the UK to relieve poverty. These were led by development NGOs and charitable organizations, often with a religious background (e.g. Diaz Pedregal 2007; Moore 2004; Nicholls and Opal 2005; Raynolds et al. 2007). Later, handicrafts, and then food products (mainly coffee), were typically sourced from producer (farmer or artisan) co-operatives, initially in Latin America. One emblematic example was the Union of Indigenous Communities of the Isthmus Region (UCIRI) in Chiapas, Mexico, where coffee growers were looking for new export opportunities in the 1980s. With the help of Dutch priest Frans van der Hoff, who worked in their co-operative, the producers managed to sell their coffee to Dutch supermarkets, paving the way for the first Fair Trade label, *Max Havelaar Netherlands* (Roozen and van der Hoff Boersma 2001). In the handicraft sector, producer co-operatives joined together with European Fair Trade importers to launch the first international Fair Trade network (the International Federation for Alternative Trade [IFAT], later renamed World Fair Trade Organization or WFTO).

These two examples illustrate the central role of co-operatives in the emergence of Fair Trade and paved the way for the two main Fair Trade models. On the one hand, product certification has been developed by national labelling initiatives and later internationally by Fairtrade International to enable the retail of Fair Trade products (mainly food) in mainstream markets (see next section). On the other hand, organizational membership has been developed by the WFTO as another avenue to guarantee the ethical quality of committed fair trade organizations (FTOs), especially for more complex products such as handicrafts for which product certification is more difficult to implement. Over time, these two complementary approaches to Fair Trade have diverged from each other (see next section), with product certification developing massive sales volumes through mainstream markets as compared with a 'niche' positioning of specialized FTOs.

Whilst supplying producer co-operatives in developing countries have remained present in both approaches, co-operatives in the North are of different types depending on each model. In the first, mainstream market approach, the presence of co-operatives can be found at the retail level through co-operative supermarket chains such as The Co-Op in the UK or Migros and Coop in Switzerland. These supermarkets have been instrumental in mainstreaming fair trade in their respective countries, but they of course also offer other, non-fair trade products. On the contrary, co-operatives participating in the second approach are specialized FTOs that exclusively import or retail fairly traded products. In both cases, Fair Trade offered an effective model via which to implement the principle of co-operation *between* co-operatives (Crowell and Reed 2009).

In Europe and in the USA, some of the organizations that were created specifically for the import and retail of Fair Trade products also chose to adopt the co-operative form, for example CTM Altromercato in Italy or Equal Exchange in the UK. In a study on specialized Fair Trade importers and retailers in four European countries (Belgium, France, Italy, and the UK), Huybrechts (2010a; 2012) found that 22 per cent of the FTOs had adopted a single co-operative or related form (such as the Community Interest Company in the UK) and that an additional 12 per cent were group structures comprising one co-operative entity (besides a second, non-co-operative or business entity). This proportion varies greatly depending on each country. In Italy, where the legislation on co-operatives, and more particularly social co-operatives, has been very dynamic (Borzaga and Santuari 2001), the vast majority of 'worldshops' (specialized Fair Trade shops) and Fair Trade importers have adopted the co-operative form (Viganò et al. 2008). The co-operative as well as the purely non-profit form are seen as the most adequate organizational avenues to develop a Fair Trade activity and are even required for membership of the national Fair Trade network 'Equo Garantito'. This means that Fair Trade initiatives that start up have incentives to choose the co-operative form as opposed to small business or self-employed statuses (Huybrechts 2012). Alternatively, most other countries offer a broader range of legitimate organizational forms, from non-profit to for-profit, including different types of 'social enterprise' models. Interestingly, the co-operative form was favoured, for example in Belgium, by the pioneer FTOs that sought to reinforce their commercial profile to be able to compete (and also collaborate) with mainstream supermarkets and brands.

When examining the types of co-operatives created to develop a Fair Trade import or retail activity, besides a few purely consumer or worker co-operatives, most organizations have clearly developed a 'multi-stakeholder' model in which different stakeholder groups interact: paid workers, volunteers, consumers, partner FTOs or NGOs, local public representatives, and even in some cases producers (Huybrechts 2010b). The involvement of producers as organizational members represented in the General Assembly and in the Board of Directors is a trend that has been launched by British FTOs (Cafédirect and Divine in particular) and adopted elsewhere, despite the practical difficulties of selecting producer representatives and having them regularly travel to Europe. The involvement of, and interactions between, different stakeholder groups through the governance of multi-stakeholder FTOs has been highlighted as a way to advance the multiple dimensions of Fair Trade (Mason and Doherty 2016) and social enterprise in general (Huybrechts et al. 2014), and has been eased by specific legal forms such as the 'social co-operative' in Italy or the 'SCIC' (sociétés coopératives d'intérêt collectif), in France.

On the supply side of the Fair Trade model, the co-operative form has been advocated as the optimal structure to ensure integrated and effective producer ownership, although other forms of legal incorporation are permitted depending on the local context. Co-operative ownership ensures the right to participate in the decision-making and to receive part of any profit as a dividend. As a consequence, it is typically recommended that any producers who enter the Fair Trade system form a producer co-operative or mutual and, then, either become a member of the WFTO or request being listed as a registered producer organization in the context of the 'Fairtrade International' Fair Trade certification and audit scheme. The first avenue provides access to specialized Fair Trade importers and retailers, likely to offer a dedicated and long-term partnership to producers. WFTO producers are also typically in the handicraft or textiles sectors and, generally, operate at small volumes. The second avenue provides access to a much broader array of import and retail companies generally not focused solely on Fair Trade, including large food multinationals and supermarket chains. Certified Fair Trade products are typically food commodities such as tea, coffee, cocoa, or sugar.

33.3 CONTESTED ISSUES IN FAIR TRADE

The increased distribution of Fair Trade products in mainstream supermarkets has resulted in a huge increase in the overall volume of sales—leading to annual double-digit sales growth for more than ten years. This process has been described as *mainstreaming*. The conditions and the extent of this mainstreaming, however, have also raised concerns among practitioners and stakeholders about the possible dilution or co-option of the Fair Trade movement (Jaffee 2010; Moore et al. 2006; Nicholls and Opal 2005; Raynolds and Wilkinson 2007). This has been particularly focused on the actions of Fairtrade International—the prime advocate of the mainstreaming strategy.

An example of the type of decisions made by Fairtrade International that have been contested by the WFTO and other Fair Trade supporters was the inclusion of plantations as registered producer organizations. Plantations are not typically owned by producers, who are, instead, usually employed only as salaried workers who do not take part in organizational decision-making (they are not part of the General Assembly) nor enjoy any of the main economic benefits (dividends) of the company beyond their salaries. Fairtrade International decided to admit plantations to the Fair Trade certification scheme for some commodities that were traditionally produced through the plantation system, rather than (such as tea) via producer-owned organizations. However, the inclusion of plantations for any type of commodity was widely criticized for discouraging producer mutual ownership and for introducing unfair competition for other cooperatives. Indeed, whereas Fair Trade initially aimed to offer the latter a sheltered space for economic development, the new system put them on an equal footing with large plantations that had the volumes and capacities potentially to squeeze the co-operatives out of the Fair Trade system entirely.

Following criticisms from producer organizations and specialized Fair Trade importers and retailers regarding this type of decision, the Fair Trade movement has become increasingly fragmented. This has also been reflected in the certification systems, which have diversified away from the historical monopoly of the FLO label. While the latter still accounts for the majority of Fair Trade sales, other (often organic) certifiers have launched competing labels, including Ecocert and IMO. The WFTO, historically focused on accrediting its members at the organizational (rather than product) level has accelerated the development of its own product labelling system. Finally, producer co-operatives in Latin America have joined together to create a producer-led Fair Trade label called *Simbolo de Pequenos Productores* (SPP). These last two examples show a willingness of some Fair Trade pioneers, including numerous co-operatives in the North and South, to reclaim grass-roots control over an initiative that they had helped to launch years earlier.

The integrity of the Fairtrade International certification and label system is also under increasing stress as some important organizations have disengaged due to divergences on the vision for the future of Fair Trade. In 2011, Fairtrade USA decided to reverse the trend that saw country-level Fair Trade initiatives coming together to form FLO, and left the common certification system to focus on a more market-oriented approach. At the other side of the spectrum, specialized FTOs such as CTM Altromercato, GEPA and Oxfam Fair Trade have decided to remove the 'Fairtrade' certification from their food products and focus on their own organizational reputation as committed Fair Trade pioneers to convince consumers and supporters. Since the integrity and universality of a single Fair Trade commodity brand has been widely seen as central to the exponential growth of sales in food commodities, these changes represent a significant challenge going forward.

A further critical issue has emerged concerning the overall impact of the Fair Trade model. In particular, in 2014, a research team based at the School of Oriental and African Studies (SOAS) at the University of London produced research funded by the UK government Department for Foreign and International Development (DFID) suggesting that:

> This research was unable to find any evidence that Fairtrade has made a positive difference to the wages and working conditions of those employed in the production of the commodities produced for Fairtrade certified export in the areas where the research has been conducted. This is the case for 'smallholder' crops like coffee—where Fairtrade standards have been based on the erroneous assumption that the vast majority of production is based on family labour—and for 'hired labour organization' commodities like the cut flowers produced in factory-style greenhouse conditions in Ethiopia. In some cases, indeed, the data suggest that those employed in areas where there are Fairtrade producer organisations are significantly worse paid, and treated, than those employed for wages in the production of the same commodities in areas without any Fairtrade certified institutions (including in areas

characterised by smallholder production). At the very least, this research suggests that Fairtrade organizations need to pay far more attention to the conditions of those extremely poor rural people—especially women and girls—employed in the production of commodities labelled and sold to 'ethical consumers' who expect their purchases to improve the lives of the poor.

(Cramer et al. 2014: 15–16)

Whilst the findings of the SOAS study were questioned by both the Fairtrade Foundation (in the UK) and Fairtrade International it, nevertheless, highlighted the difficulties in demonstrating the impact of the model with robust evidence. The research also revealed the relative paucity of data concerning Fair Trade's effect on the lives of poor producers beyond sales figures alone. The controversy around the SOAS report also emphasized the danger of having an organizational, rather than individual, focus in terms of stated impact. Perhaps somewhat ironically, the centrality of co-operatives in the Fair Trade model may have contributed to this loss of focus on the individual producer or farm labourer.

A final challenge to Fair Trade emerged in 2014, when UK year-on-year sales fell for the first time since the FLO label was established in 1997. The fall was only 4 per cent, but was nevertheless seen as a blow to the future development and growth of the Fair Trade sector, since it occurred in the largest single market. The cause was generally felt to be the rapid growth of discounters such as Lidl and Aldi in the UK supermarket sector—retailers that were, generally, less sympathetic to Fair Trade. However, only time will tell how significant this drop may or may not prove to be.

33.4 Fair Trade and Co-operatives: Convergences and Divergences

Several key principles of Fair Trade—for example, its focus on community development, a *fair* price, economic democracy, and the exclusion of intermediates—have been directly inspired by the co-operative movement (Gendron et al. 2009). Interestingly, the term *fair trade* was even used to describe the trading relationships among co-operatives in the nineteenth century (Anderson 2009; Develtere and Pollet 2005). From this perspective, the contemporary Fair Trade movement can be seen as a model for international co-operation among co-operatives (Crowell and Reed 2009). Moreover, Develtere and Pollet (2005) identified a number of other, specific, convergences between the Fair Trade and co-operative movements, which are summarized here:

- Both movements were initially conceived as alternatives to the dominant capitalist model, while at the same time being integrated in the market
- Equitable income is central to both initiatives

- In both cases, the economic activity serves—or, at least, coexists with—social and political purposes
- Both co-operatives and Fair Trade actors try to balance ethical standards, on the one hand, and survival in a competitive market environment, on the other

However, several key differences can also be observed between the Fair Trade and co-operative movements. Fair Trade, by definition, applies to international supply chains between the North and the South (and, increasingly, between the South and the South); co-operatives, on the other hand, may be active at the local and/or at the international level. Moreover, Fair Trade mainly locates the notion of *fairness* at the level of individual producers rather than at the level of the organization itself, especially given the recent evolutions in certification that no longer require co-operative ownership. Also, unlike Fair Trade, co-operative principles do not operate at the level of the supply chain per se, but rather are located and expressed within organizations.

In many contexts, co-operatives have become sustainable over time by evolving an increasingly strong business focus that has, at times, threatened to dilute some of the field's central political dynamics (e.g. Monaci and Caselli 2005). Some co-operatives have evolved to appear very similar to normal businesses, while others have been subject to buy-outs by mainstream corporations, particularly in the retail and banking sectors. This trend led to the scandal concerning the UK based Co-operative Bank that almost destroyed it in 2014. Nevertheless, some authors have suggested that, even in such cases, the co-operative form still constitutes an alternative to the dominant capitalist model (Reed and McMurtry 2009), especially when the business is backed by a citizen movement or strong community engagement (Vienney 1997). The commercial evolution of Fair Trade over the past decade could be seen as following a similar path to that which many co-operatives followed, in that the challenges of maintaining the original features of the concept under conditions of mainstreaming (Nicholls and Huybrechts 2016) lead to debates that opposed radical and pragmatist actors within the movements (Fridell 2009).

33.5 Conclusion

This chapter has set out the principles and practices that define Fair Trade and also considered some of the movement's most urgent challenges and issues. It has also considered how Fair Trade and the co-operative movement relate to each other in terms of guiding *ethos* as well as activities on the ground. This discussion suggests, in conclusion, that the Fair Trade and co-operative movements have much in common, both conceptually and in practice. Nevertheless, Fair Trade is more than just a re-actualization of the co-operative idea. It has integrated itself in, and was inspired by, other movements seeking to ally economic activity and social and/or societal goals without necessarily focusing on a particular organizational or legal form exclusively. Its roots in disaster relief, poverty alleviation, and development via international trade also differentiate it from the co-operative movement's origins in community empowerment and local *fair-trading*. These two models of *capitalism with a conscience, doing well by doing good* or *creating shared value* have, however, signposted larger changes in global markets that they have both helped inspire—and can, in future, strongly benefit from.

References

Anderson, M. (2009), 'Cost of Cup of Tea: Fair Trade and the British Co-operative Movement, c. 1960-2000', in L. Black and N. Robertson, eds, *Consumerism and the Co-operative Movement in Modern British History* (Manchester: Manchester University Press), 240–60.

Borzaga, C. and Santuari, A. (2001), 'Italy: from Traditional Co-operatives to Innovative Social Enterprises', in C. Borzaga and J. Defourny, eds, *The Emergence of Social Enterprise* (London: Routledge), 166–81.

Cramer, C., Johnston, D., Oya, C., and Sender, J. (2014), *Fairtrade, Employment and Poverty Reduction in Ethiopia and Uganda* (London: SOAS, University of London, for the Department for International Development).

Crowell, E. and Reed, D. (2009), 'Fair Trade: A Model for International Co-operation Among Co-operatives?' in D. Reed and J. J. McMurtry, eds, *Co-operatives in a Global Economy: The Challenges of Co-operation Across Borders* (Newcastle upon Tyne: Cambridge Scholars Publishing), 141–77.

Develtere, P. and Pollet, I. (2005), *Co-operatives and Fair Trade* (Berlin: COPAC Open Forum on Fair Trade and Cooperatives).

Diaz Pedregal, V. (2007), *Le commerce équitable dans la France contemporaine: Idéologies et pratiques* (Paris: L'Harmattan).

Fridell, G. (2009), 'The Co-Operative and the Corporation: Competing Visions of the Future of Fair Trade', *Journal of Business Ethics,* 86(0), 81–95.

Gendron, C., Bisaillon, V., and Rance, A. (2009), 'The Institutionalization of Fair Trade: More Than Just a Degraded Form of Social Action', *Journal of Business Ethics,* 86(0), 63–79.

Huybrechts, B. (2010a), 'Explaining Organisational Diversity in Fair Trade Social Enterprises', Université de Liège, HEC Management School, Thèse de Doctorat en Sciences Economiques et de Gestion, 469.

Huybrechts, B. (2010b), 'The Governance of Fair Trade Social Enterprises in Belgium', *Social Enterprise Journal,* 6(2), 110–24.

Huybrechts, B. (2012), *Fair Trade Organizations and Social Enterprise: Social Innovation through Hybrid Organization Models* (New York: Routledge).

Huybrechts, B., Mertens, S., and Rijpens, J. (2014), 'Explaining Stakeholder Involvement in Social Enterprise Governance through Resources and Legitimacy', in J. Defourny, L. Hulgard, and V. Pestoff, eds, *Social Enterprise and the Third Sector: Changing European Landscapes in a Comparative Perspective* (London and New York: Routledge), 157–75

Jaffee, D. (2010), 'Fair Trade Standards, Corporate Participation, and Social Movement Responses in the United States', *Journal of Business Ethics,* 92(0), 267–85.

Mason, C. and Doherty, B. (2016), 'A Fair Trade-off? Paradoxes in the Governance of Fair-Trade Social Enterprises', *Journal of Business Ethics,* 136(3): 451–69.

Monaci, M. and Caselli, M. (2005), 'Blurred Discourses: How Market Isomorphism Constrains and Enables Collective Action in Civil Society', *Global Networks*, 5(1), 49–69.

Moore, G. (2004), 'The Fair Trade Movement: Parameters, Issues and Future Research', *Journal of Business Ethics*, 53(1), 73–86.

Moore, G., Gibbon, J., and Slack, R. (2006), 'The Mainstreaming of Fair Trade: A Macromarketing Perspective', *Journal of Strategic Marketing*, 14(4), 329–52.

Porter, M. and Kramer, M. (2011), 'Creating Shared Value', *Harvard Business Review*, 89(1/2): 62–77.

Nicholls, A., and Huybrechts, B. (2016), 'Sustaining Inter-Organizational Relationships across Institutional Logics and Power Asymmetries: The Case of Fair Trade', *Journal of Business Ethics*, 135(4), 699–714.

Nicholls, A. and Opal, C. (2005), *Fair Trade: Market-Driven Ethical Consumption* (London, SAGE Publications).

Raynolds, L. T., Murray, D. L., and Wilkinson, J. (2007), *Fair Trade: The Challenges of Transforming Globalization* (London: Routledge).

Raynolds, L. T. and Wilkinson, J. (2007), 'Fair Trade in the Agriculture and Food Sector, in L. T. Raynolds, D. L. Murray, and J. Wilkinson, eds, *Fair Trade: The Challenges of Transforming Globalization* (London: Routledge), 38–48.

Reed, D. and McMurtry, J. J. eds, (2009), *Co-operatives in a Global Economy: The Challenges of Co-operation Across Borders* (Newcastle upon Tyne: Cambridge Scholars Publishing).

Roozen, N. and van der Hoff Boersma, F. (2001), *L'aventure du commerce équitable: Une alternative à la mondialisation* (Paris: JC Lattès).

Vienney, C. (1997), 'Le maintien et le renforcement de la réciprocité entre l'entreprise et le mouvement', in B. Lévesque, ed., *Desjardins: Une entreprise et un mouvement?* (Montreal: Presses Universitaires de Québec).

Viganò, E., Glorio, M., and Villa, A. (2008), *Tutti i numeri dell'equo: Il commercio equo e solidale in Italia* (Rome: Edizioni dell'Asino).

CHAPTER 34

....

FROM TRADITIONAL TO INNOVATIVE MULTI-STAKEHOLDER MUTUALS

the case of rochdale boroughwide housing

....

RUTH YEOMAN

34.1 INTRODUCTION: CONTEMPORARY MUTUALISM IN UK PUBLIC SERVICES

....

IN contemporary public administration, the competitive principle is in the ascendency (Myers and Cato 2011). Privatization and 'spinning out' have generated new organizational forms which compete to deliver essential services in a public-service economy reconceived along neoliberal lines. In this emergent political economy, mutualization—that is, transferring public services to co-ownership by staff and/or service users—has been re-presented as a desirable pathway for creating independent organizations which are free to innovate and generate efficiencies. However, proponents of the philosophy and practice of mutuality claim that mutual organization is not just one competing option amongst others which are equally good, but is a normatively and instrumentally superior model for public-service delivery.

On 24 July 2014, Francis Maude, Minister for the Cabinet Office, speaking at a Downing Street reception, declared: 'A hundred new British businesses have spun out from the public sector and are delivering nearly £1.5 billion of public services.' He went on to say 'mutuals now employ 35,000 people and have generated over 3,000 additional jobs in the last 3 years alone' (Cabinet Office 2014). Despite this welcome diversification, the official face of contemporary mutualism in the UK public sector interprets mutual ownership narrowly as the creation of 'staff mutuals'. In particular, rhetoric evoking a 'John Lewis-style economy' conflates mutual organization with employee-ownership, with the consequence that the rich learning and motives for collective action arising from user/consumer ownership are marginalized. Yet user/consumer ownership is a valuable resource when organizations must tap into the tacit knowledge and commitment of all those affected by its activities in order to create economic, social, and environmental value. Indeed, the potentially novel contribution of contemporary mutualism lies in uniting user ownership to staff ownership in dual or even triple constituency mutuals, and furthermore, in extending the values and principles of mutuality beyond the level of individual organizations to sector and regional governance of public services.

34.2 UNDERSTANDING MUTUALITY

Mutuality is a philosophy which describes how we are to live with one another. As such, mutuality is concerned with the values, principles, and practices which specify the conditions under which we are prepared to join our effort to those of others in order to secure together what one cannot secure alone. Mutuality is therefore fundamentally relational, where mutual inter-relations possess the normative features of mutual respect, mutual esteem, dignity, equality, fairness, and care. At an organizational level, Birchall (2010: 4) defines a mutual as a member-owned business that is 'owned and controlled by members who are drawn from one (or more) of two types of stakeholder—consumer and producer—and whose benefits go mainly to these members'. The objective of mutual organization is to distribute among all affected stakeholders a fair share of the benefits and burdens arising from that organization's activities. A mutual organization is sustained over time by the sense of legitimacy which accumulates when stakeholders and members judge the procedures and outcomes of distribution to be fair and mutually advantageous.

34.3 ORGANIZATIONAL CHANGE GROUNDED IN THE VALUES AND PRINCIPLES OF MUTUALITY

The micro- and meso-level practices needed to become a public-service mutual are under-researched. This means that institutional entrepreneurs and public policy makers do not fully appreciate the time and investment required for successful organizational change. The desire of politicians to lay claim to early success is unhelpful in this regard, leading to a tendency for government to declare a mutual organization to be in operation at the moment of its legal establishment. However, *de jure* mutuality does not equal *de facto* mutuality. Moreover, managing the transition to mutuality is challenging because the new organization is often being created at the same time that other major changes are taking place. Specifically, managers struggle with the democratic elements of the new governance arrangements, cultural adaptation depends upon existing mutual assets such as a public-service ethos which employees and service users feel is threatened by the new emphasis upon commerciality, new leadership capabilities based upon communicative action need to be developed, and the whole organization must adopt norms, assumptions, and behaviours consistent with the self-identity of being a co-owner (Davis and Yeoman 2013).

Although the moment of constitutional founding is critical, this simply signals the beginning of substantive change work, including behavioural and cultural shifts, new forms of governance and leadership, differently configured power relations, and operational retooling for effective supply chain management, information systems, and service delivery models. This is the work, not of a few weeks or even months, but of years. Simmons (2008) points out that 'it can take time for the grounding in everyday working practices of such characteristics as self-organization ('doing it for ourselves'), dialogic forms of regulation, and a concern for both social and economic outcomes' (ibid: 281). This chapter will explore the dynamics of transitioning to a public-service mutual, using the example of Rochdale Boroughwide Housing (RBH), a multi-constituency provider of affordable housing which is jointly owned by its tenants and employees.

34.4 THE RESEARCH

Semi-structured interviews were conducted with managers, staff, and tenant representatives of Rochdale Boroughwide Housing. This data was supplemented by information acquired during a leadership programme which included the specification of an organizational template for mutualization (see Figure 34.1 for the generic model and Figure 34.2 for the RBH interpretation).

34.5 PLURALISM IN MULTI-CONSTITUENCY MUTUALS

In institutional terms, dual-purpose organizations such as public-service mutuals are constituted by hybridity or a 'pluralistic environment where multiple institutional logics coexist' which 'entails unique challenges that require actors to negotiate conflict and carry out integrative and adaptive work' (Yu 2013: 105; cf. Kraatz 2009). Yu argues that because the 'pluralistic organization does not automatically hold itself together' (Kraatz

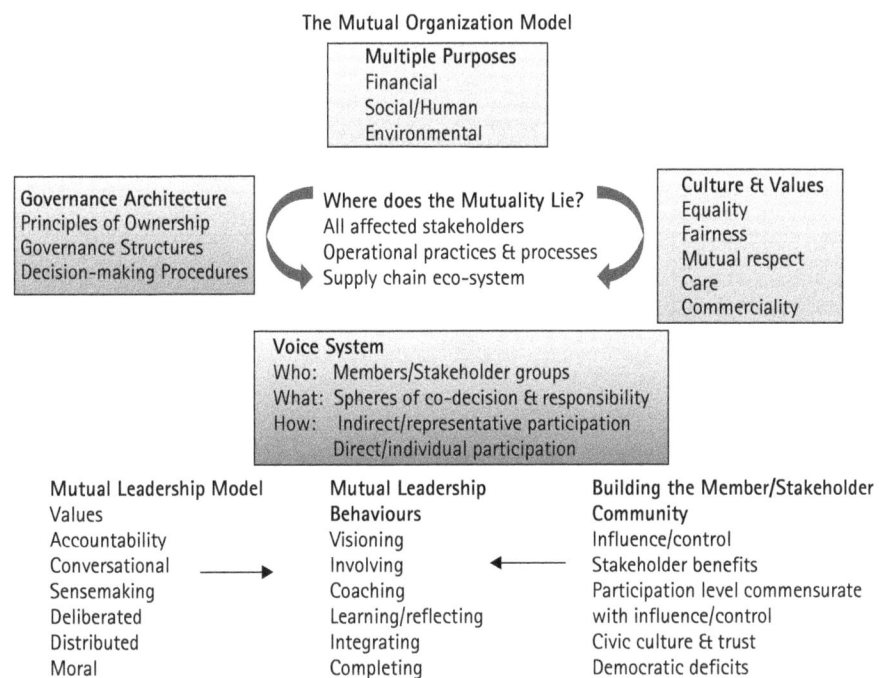

FIGURE 34.1 The Mutual Organization Model.

Derived from research.

and Block 2008: 263), then 'crafting integrative processes out of contentious processes is essential' (Yu 2013: 107). Actors must exercise choice and creativity in generating novel scripts which are consistent with the new organizational template. Yu proposes that the key task that actors must undertake is the achievement of an 'integrated organizational identity' (ibid.), where organizational identity 'represents members' shared beliefs and perceptions regarding their sense of who they are as an organization and what they do that is central, distinctive, and enduring' (Barge et al. 2008: 366; cf. Hatch and Schultz 2002).

Organizational change is successful when members manage to reconcile their 'conflicting needs to create continuity and discontinuity between existing and future organizational identities' (Barge et al. 2008: 366). In a public-service mutual, distinctive organizational identity is achieved when the old identity of public service is reconciled with the values, norms, and beliefs associated with the new identity of co-ownership. However, this is not an unproblematic integration in which the new identity replaces or harmonizes with the old one. Instead, member representation based upon different communities of interest means that members must hold their new self-identity of being a co-owner in tension with their existing identities as service users or as employees if they are to cohere their opposing interests for mutual benefit. Thus, multi-constituency ownership brings the outside into the organization (and turns the inside out) by hardwiring a permanent tension into both the organizational template and the psychology of

The RBH Mutual Organization Model

Purpose: Financial and Social
Vision: *To use our exceptional position as a mutual to help to create inspiring communities which enhance the lives of the people who live and work in them.*
Mission: *Meet the aspirations of our communities by providing inclusive opportunities and quality homes in safe, secure and friendly neighbourhoods where people want to live and work.*
Corporate Objectives: 1. provide high quality homes; 2. deliver safe & attractive neighbourhoods; 3. support friendly & inclusive communities; 4. make membership matter; 5. obtain best value services

Governance
Principles (values into action)
Representative body & board.
15 elected tenants
8 elected employees
Decision-making procedures

 Robust and Sustainable Mutual Performance

Values & Culture
Responsibility
Equity
Democracy
Pioneering
Openness & honesty
Caring
Championing

The Voice System
Who: Member and non-member employees; tenant members
What: Business decisions; setting strategy (depending on member status)
How: Influencing through getting involved in member activities
        Neighbourhood planning and participatory budgeting
        Voting and standing to be an elected representative

Empowerment
Engagement
Champions
⇦

Mutual Leadership
Behaviours
Visioning
Involving
Coaching
Learning/reflecting
Integrating
Completing

Building the Member
Community
Create affinity
Encourage positive behaviours
(commitment, respect, mutual ⇨
support)
Member activities/rewards
Democratic responsibilities
Recruitment/communication

2000 members
Aims
1. Grow membership to
   reflect tenants/employees
2. Provide opportunities
   to influence
3. Build engagement,
   affinity, & loyalty

FIGURE 34.2 The RBH Mutual Organization Model.

Derived from RBH leadership workshops.

its members. The need to conciliate differences arising from institutionalized mobilization of interest-group representation stimulates a polyvocal conversation between co-owners (Hazen 1993). The virtue of doing so lies in the potential for making difference productive, when diverse perspectives are incorporated into the co-production of service delivery by means of the shared purpose, obligations, and commitments generated by co-ownership.

This suggests that 'integrating' in the sense of merging or dissolving tensions into a new organizational identification is not only unrealistic but also undesirable. Rather, what is to be preferred is the creation of a relational or intersectional organizational identity which combines the particularist identifications of being a service user or employee with the universalist identifications of being a co-owner. This is because, when participants are permitted to bring their distinctiveness and difference into the deliberative space, interactive processes to conciliate opposing interests for mutual advantage are potentially generative of collective action and unexpected innovations. However, to make productive the conflicts arising from the divergent identifications of an intersectional or relational identity requires a constantly adjusting balance of values, meanings, and differences which is always in the process of becoming (Tsoukas and Chia 2002). This means actors must acquire capabilities in thinking, feeling, and acting:

> To define oneself intersectionally, one must activate competencies that mesh intellect and feeling in order to seek out and assimilate nonstandard interpretive frameworks. One must be introspectively vigilant, attuned to signs of frustration and dissatisfaction, attentive to baffling subjective anomalies, and willing to puzzle out gaps in one's self-understanding. (Meyers 2000: 167)

An intersectional self makes progress in self-knowledge and self-definition through the interplay between plural and opposing elements. In a multi-constituency mutual, this interplay is experienced when the particularist concerns with being a service user or public-service professional/employee influence, and is influenced by, the universalist demands of being a co-owner during institutionalized deliberative procedures aimed at the common good.

34.6 ACHIEVING A CO-OWNERSHIP INTERSECTIONAL IDENTITY

An intersectional identity is achieved interactively through structures and processes of communicative action which have been consciously designed to influence change (see Barbour et al. 2013). In a power-sharing mutual, processes of communicative action for making difference productive are guaranteed by the status of formal co-ownership which makes a stable or 'structurally anchored' voice system (Weber et al. 2008) an entitlement which managers are obliged to provide. However, formal status, although necessary, is insufficient for efficacy in communicative action—this requires additionally psychological engagement with being a co-owner, through which members grow in confidence in the ability to speak and to act as co-authorities in decision-making. Kaarsemaker and Poutsma (2006) identify the features of an organizational system based on employee ownership which combines management commitment to an appropriate philosophy of work with a specific bundle of HRM practices. They suggest that the appropriate philosophy of work is one where 'the relative role and value of employees relates to their co-ownership', such that 'employees are seen as worthy of their co-ownership of the company and they are taken seriously as owners' (ibid: 678; cf. Young 1991). And they identify the relevant core HR practices needed to become participants in decision-making, profit-sharing, information-sharing, training for business literacy, and mediation (Kaarsemaker and Poutsma 2006: 680).

Developing confidence in being a co-authority is vital for participating in the meaning-making upon which the creation of a new organizational identity depends

(Weick 1995). Successful negotiation of an intersectional identity requires deep engagement by the individual with the organizing philosophy governing change—a process which is enabled, facilitated, and supported by high levels of discursive interaction, including having an influence over the rules which frame the context of change, and sharing in the co-production of new organizational practices which enact the organizing philosophy. In the pluralistic environment of a multi-constituency mutual, this means that co-owners must grapple with the dilemmas, tensions, and paradoxes which emerge from conflicting institutional logics. In other words, co-owners must engage in dualistic thinking in order to work with oppositional (but not exclusive) tendencies emerging from diverse perspectives, behaviours, and actions (Seo et al. 2003). The micro-processes of dualistic thinking are developed during organizational change which encourages dualities to emerge, proliferate, and then be captured for productive use.

34.7 Dualistic Thinking in Mutual Change

Conventionally, organizational change is understood against Lewin's (1951) model of unfreezing, moving, and refreezing. However, this model does not capture the complex movements involved in pluralistic organizations such as multi-constituency mutuals. Instead, change management needs to be understood as 'paradox management' (Smith and Graetz 2011: 197), or the management of the dilemmas, paradoxes, and tensions which arise in hybrid organizations characterized by:

- Rational planning with adaptive strategic thinking
- Cultural renewal with structural change
- Empowerment with strong leadership
- Continual incremental adaptation with radical transformation
- Social goals with economic goals (Smith and Graetz 2011: 184)

Dualities thinking is both/and rather than either/or. Smith and Graetz (2011) argue that applying duality theory to organizational change requires organizations to hold in tension or 'dynamic synthesis' (ibid: 185) the contradictions of change and stability. They identify five duality characteristics that managers can use to develop a 'dualities aware perspective' (ibid: 188) in the conduct of organizational change. These help managers to avoid seeing dualities as alternatives and focusing on one or other pole thus 'making it difficult to enact both ends of the continuum simultaneously' (ibid.). The five characteristics are: simultaneity, relational, minimal threshold, dynamism, and improvization.

Graetz and Smith (2008: 271) describe these characteristics as 'escalating': that is, dualities become increasingly mature and available for productive use as the organization cycles through phases of continuity/change. At the foundational level, simultaneity describes dualities as existing in a latent or *dormant* condition unless stimulated through organizational change. At subsequent levels of escalation, dualities emerge (relational), proliferate (minimal threshold), stabilize (dynamism), and embed (improvization): *emerging* through the formation of relational connections between one pole and the other; *proliferating* through the creation of minimal levels at each pole of the duality; *stabilizing* through the dynamic feedback from new habits and practices; and *embedding* through improvization which fosters evolution of and interaction between dualities (ibid):

> simultaneity is the most basic property. But the simultaneous presence of traditional and new forms of organizing is a necessary but not sufficient condition for dualities to emerge. Because organizing forms are inter-dependent and relational, minimal levels of new and traditional forms are needed to create a benefit and ensure that organizations can enjoy the advantages afforded through the complementary forces of continuity and change. However, thresholds change with contextual pressure, so for dualities to endure, they must also possess a dynamic property. Ultimately, dualities are characterized by improvisation because the previous conditions do not arise without some form of intervention and management. (ibid: 271)

34.8 CREATING A NEW ORGANIZATIONAL IDENTITY GROUNDED IN CO-OWNERSHIP USING DUALITIES

Organizational change in RBH can be analysed using the process of escalating dualities to describe the achievement of an intersectional, organizational identity based upon co-ownership. Prior to mutualization, RBH had moved from being a traditional council-run housing association to an ALMO—an arms-length management organization. However, the executive management team (EMT) realized that being an ALMO would not secure the organization's long-term future. They envisioned an organization which would integrate, and make co-operative use of, the interests, ambitions, and diverse perspectives of its key stakeholder groups. In 2011, RBH began its mutualization journey by establishing a constitution commission to co-create the constitution together with key stakeholders. This was followed by stock transfer in March 2012 into a community benefit society, and the formation of a shadow representative body and shadow board. Formally, RBH became a mutual in June 2013. The crux of the challenge for RBH was to create a power-sharing model which would transform the organizational system from hierarchical command and control to values-leadership, polyvocality, and co-production, held together by multi-stakeholder governance. In this endeavour, the shift to an organizational identity based upon co-ownership was vital to ensuring that interactions between represented groups would be governed by the characteristics of mutual inter-relations (fairness, equality, mutual respect, dignity, and care)—characteristics which are the necessary preconditions for deliberative encounter.

34.8.1 Simultaneity: Latent Dualities

> Simultaneity is the 'simultaneous presence of contradictory forces' (Smith and Graetz, 2011). However, although they are contradictory, they are not mutually exclusive (ibid.), and work through 'mutual specification' (Ford and Backoff 1988: 102) in order to foster 'a complementary interplay'. (Smith and Graetz 2011)

In RBH, historical experiments with independence, the collaborative development of the constitution, and the collection of values (drawn from the International Cooperative Alliance's values and RBH's own public-service ethos)[1] established a number of potentially productive, but still latent, dualities: public-service ethos/commerciality, particularist/universalist identifications, and member decision-making/ management control. The movement towards instituting the new mutual organization template was rooted in the fundamental continuity/change duality where continuity was represented by traditional public-service values and change by new commercial imperatives. Already existing participatory practices, such as tenant involvement through tenants' associations and community groupings, informed the appointment of a constitution commission and the design of the engagement process. However, since tenants were often suspicious of housing transfers and tenants' associations, RBH needed to find a way of communicating how the mutual would be different. In January 2012, a membership strategy was launched to reach out to tenants and employees. Member champions were recruited and events and communications organized, including requiring employees to do volunteer days in the community. Through this process, the organization secured some early tenant members with 40 signing up immediately, and employees were mobilized to communicate the model and win support. Also, RBH made some connections between the organization, its employees, and its tenants, which built social capital and established the basis for trust-building. However, these did not yet constitute the common bond and shared sense of identification through co-ownership which would make the link between membership and governance productive for collective decision-making and co-production. Although formal representation at the meso-level created the voice structures for the communicative action necessary for shifting organizational identity, this would be insufficient

---

[1] Rochdale Boroughwide Housing drew consciously upon Rochdale's co-operative roots. The Rochdale Pioneers remain a potent cultural and historical symbol for a socially and economically deprived town which has not benefited to an equal extent from the economic regeneration of the Manchester City region.

without individual members gaining confidence in and starting to engage with direct participatory practices at the micro-level.

34.8.2 Relational: Emerging Dualities

> Dualities are relational and inter-dependent (Smith and Graetz, 2011: 190). They exhibit a 'bi-directional, interdependent relationship between opposite poles' (ibid: 194) and generate 'mutual feedback' (ibid.) in interactions between the poles of a duality and in interactions with other dualities.

By the end of 2012, RBH had specified its purpose, constitution, and governance arrangements. Mutual values had been identified (responsibility, equity, democracy, pioneering, openness and honesty, caring, championing), although these were not yet fully disseminated or adopted into organizational practices. At this stage, prospective members did not fully appreciate how tenants would need to learn to speak up and how employees would have to make their own decisions. In particular, the organization began to understand that a major area of transformation would be the self-identity and capabilities of leaders. One manager reported, 'My job doesn't feel as different as it should, and that concerns me.' At the same time, in response to funder requirements for cost reductions, work restructuring began. Employees had to reapply for their roles, resulting in the movement of people between roles, as well as the recruitment of individuals from outside the organization, including from the private sector. At this stage, management emphasis upon the pole of commerciality in the emerging public-service/commerciality duality made the idea of the mutual remote for the majority of tenants and employees who were not involved in the shadow governance structures.

Nonetheless, the emergence of a public-service/commerciality duality began to stimulate an attitudinal and cultural shift towards 'having a more commercial mindset' (manager). People became increasingly aware of the importance of economic viability if RBH was to be in a position to fulfil the broader social ambitions required by its mutual values and principles. Despite not yet having a full understanding of what mutuality meant, members became more sensitive to their new status as co-owners, as they started to think of how co-ownership not only bound them together, but could become the means to improving organizational efficiencies and generating income.

34.8.3 Minimal Threshold: Proliferating Dualities

> Smith and Graetz (2011: 191) specify that 'dualities need a minimal threshold' or 'a certain level at each pole [which] creates the tension necessary to stimulate a duality'. If the duality is to contribute productively to organizational development, then members and managers must then work with each pole simultaneously through 'maintaining a balance between enabling and constraining forces' (ibid: 194), rather than privileging one and ignoring the other.

In this phase of escalation, dualities started to proliferate, building presence at each pole, rather than strengthening one pole to the exclusion of the other. In a case study of a government project to create an inter-agency information system, Stoltzfus et al. (2011) identified three interdependent dualities associated with the tensions arising from multiple stakeholder groups with unequal power. These were 'stakeholder self-interest/collective good, stakeholder inclusion/exclusion, and emergent stakeholder consensus/leader-driven decision making' (ibid: 358). Stoltzfus et al. (2011) showed how the tensions arising from these dualities had to be managed interactively (ibid: 360). Barge et al. (2008) described the importance of *connection* which 'recognizes that both poles are crucial and that they must be related in such a way that the contributions of each pole are maintained. The difference between the two poles is preserved but the two poles are connected to each other in a synergistic manner where they become mutually beneficial' (Barge at al., 2008: 368). In RBH, the tensions arising from dualities were discursively managed using values-talk as the means for connecting one pole to the other. By using values through discursive encounter to relate the oppositional poles in emerging dualities, members reinforced the shift towards organizational identification based upon co-ownership.

Stoltzfus et al.'s (2011) three stakeholder-related dualities are relevant for understanding the organizational transformation of RBH. In RBH, stakeholder inclusion/exclusion is formally managed through the shared status of co-ownership in the two-tier governance system with tenant and employee representatives on the representative body. When tensions arise from the duality of stakeholder self-interest/collective good, this structure provides a basis for deliberation. Expressing this duality through formal representation aids decision-making when conventional assumptions that each member group will automatically pursue its own interests at the expense of the other are challenged. For example, during an intense phase of cost reductions, the representative body discussed changes to employee working practices based upon agile working. Tenant representatives were anxious to know what the potential impact upon employee well-being would be. Such shared concerns meant that, as groups began to interact through their common status as co-owners, the structure of discourse shifted. One manager described how he now uses his participatory leadership style to have different conversations with his staff and tenants. For example, with tenants, there are fewer 'adversarial performance discussions' where tenants ask 'Why aren't you getting this right?' and more conversations related to how staff and tenants can work together, or 'How can you help us get this right?' However, in order to develop the potential of values-talk in managing dualities discursively through interactive deliberation and negotiation, co-owners needed to acquire facility and confidence in using communicative tactics and tools.

In RBH, raising the communicative capabilities of co-owners was one objective of a leadership programme which supported managers, staff, and tenants in having new kinds of conversations which were attentive to values tensions. The programme introduced thinking tools, including a 'values, principles, activities, outputs, outcomes, and value' chain, to help participants convert mutual values into activities consistent with institutionalizing the new organizational template.[2] Values-talk spread rapidly among staff members based at Sandbrook Park (headquarters), but dispersed more slowly in services located on the housing estates. Despite the different rates of dispersal, at the time of interviewing, nearly every part of the organization had taken at least some first steps towards mutual organizing through 'everyday framing' (Alvesson 2002). In a late micro-level example, one supervisor whose front-line service team had suffered a fall in service standards as a consequence of externally imposed cost cutting said: 'I need to give you more ownership of what you're doing at the properties ... I want you to be your own person. I want you to work in there and do what you think is necessary.' His staff were startled, with one saying: 'that's the best meeting I've ever been to. You've told me more today than anyone's ever told me'. In a single exchange, this supervisor signalled the beginnings of a new way of thinking and acting.

An early micro-level example was recorded in the caretaking section where the new caretaking manager fostered a co-ownership identification amongst his team by increasing their communicative capabilities.[3] This manager took charge of six caretaking sections who 'felt they had... no power, no influence ... they just felt whatever people said they had to do, they had to do it'. Despite many years of service, some caretaking staff had never met one another, so there was an urgent need to develop social capital and shared purpose. The resource available to the section was being reduced, so the manager began working with the senior caretakers to develop minimum service standards through a set of public promises which described 'what we are capable of, based upon the strength of our section'. Values-talk, using language drawn from the values and principles of mutuality, enabled an occupational group with low status and a low sense of self-worth 'to have really good conversations ... not just what we need to do, but how we felt we need to do that, and how feeling the way we need to do things does actually change the quality of what we are doing'. The manager asked the caretaking supervisors to write down statements describing each of the values and to bring those into discussions about how mutual values ought to shape offer promises. They came back with 'fantastic but practical sentences', such as 'we should aim to be the best caretaking section in the North-West as defined by Houseman'. They talked about mutuality expressed in the value of care as 'easy for us' because 'we are caretakers we take care of things'. This lively connection of a mutual value to the experience of the work was a key moment in the supervisors' self-understandings and their identification as co-owners of the new mutual.

[2] In 2013, the Centre for Mutual and Employee-owned Business, University of Oxford, was commissioned to develop a leadership and cultural change programme. The aim was to develop the self-identity and skills for enacting mutual leadership in an organization. Rather than prescribing how managers ought to adopt and model the habits and practices of mutual leadership, the programme sought to educate managers in the philosophy of mutuality, train for a broad range of techniques, and develop thinking and feeling by addressing challenges in the participants' own specific contexts.

[3] In turn, this manager was supported by one of the heads of service (the line of management below the EMT).

The supervisors subsequently used these interpretive conversations to make sense of mutual values with their own caretaking staff: 'They've taken that down to the caretakers, asked them to be part of the decisions and pilot programmes.' Consequently, supervisors and caretakers experienced an increasing confidence and ability to negotiate with other parts of the organization—'now say to people, you need to know about what is going on here, this is not the caretakers' job. We will help where we can but there are some issues where you cannot expect us to do that because we have responsibilities of our own. We have to look to those responsibilities.' This ability to be able say what they would or would not do was secured by a greater understanding of the importance of their work to tenants, and therefore to the success of the new mutual. Indeed, the caretakers began to lay claim to their work being intrinsically mutual by arguing that what they did was already, by its nature as an activity of care, laden with mutual values. Their capacity to make these claims grew as their identification with being co-owners increased—they now had more confidence that they had the right to speak up about the importance of what they did, and therefore of what they needed to do a good job.

34.8.4 Dynamic Property: Stabilizing Dualities

> Lively dualities create energy through interaction and feedback. According to Smith and Graetz (2011: 194) 'dynamic interaction between duality poles [ensures] ongoing flexibility, creativity and adaptability'. In the escalation of dualities from simultaneity, relational, minimal threshold to dynamic property, dynamism stabilises 'a constructive tension' (ibid: 192) or 'a state where there is sufficient tension to mobilize change and action, but not so much as to engender politicisation or perverse, unintended consequences. (Evans 1999: 330)

The leadership programme was supported by intensive mentoring (ten hours per participating manager and selected tenant representatives), and produced a series of action learning groups which included both participating and non-participating managers in addressing an issue of common concern. This learning-in-action generated feedback mechanisms at both an individual and a collective level for managing the connections between poles, thereby enabling RBH to stabilize dualities, making them productive for decision-making and innovation.

During this phase of escalating dualities, the representative body and the board started to gain a clearer sense of their respective roles and responsibilities. In particular, tenant members of the representative body gained an increased understanding of mutual organization, and improved their ability to ask relevant questions when holding management to account. Even so, the duality of public-service/commerciality generated tensions in how board members understood mutuality, and the distinctive contribution mutuality had to make to organizational performance. This led the board to emphasize the pole of commerciality by concentrating upon financial performance to the exclusion of mutual performance. As a consequence, the board's ability to assess key aspects of the mutual organization template, such as the quality of member engagement, the development of the mutual culture, and the resilience of the voice system, was inhibited. This resulted in disconnections in the governance system between the representative body, the board, heads of services/EMT, and the variety of formal and informal groupings. One manager said: 'I'm doing that [the mutuality]… [my team are doing activities] to align themselves with a mutual ethos, but I'm not communicating these, there isn't a forum for me to communicate these'. In other words, even though the 'mutuality work' of managers and teams was generating new norms, novel practices, and behaviour shifts, the means for evaluating and disseminating the fruits of this labour were still embryonic and not yet fully integrated into the strategic decision-making processes of the organization, particularly at the level of governance.

Despite this, the move towards a more commercial mindset, embodied through tensions in the public-service/commerciality duality, continued to be played out, particularly in changes to operational processes. At first, the mutuality pulled away from initiatives to improve operational procedures.[4] Mutuality was interpreted as belonging to the realm of culture and values—one separate and distinct from operations which were governed by the commercial imperative of cost reduction and process improvement. No connection was established between the two poles of public service/commerciality. However, this began to be remedied as values-talk took hold in several parts of the organization. Staff members started to use mutual values to settle conflicts and differences in designing new operational processes. Increasingly, values became the flexible and adaptive connection between the poles of public service/commerciality. A particularly important device was a project board set up in 2012 by the EMT to invite proposals from staff and tenant members to promote innovation. This generated initiatives such as an employee engagement steering group. However, this also exposed tensions in the empowerment/control duality when some proposals were rejected by senior management decision without clear explanation, except that commercial need trumped other considerations. Co-owners found it difficult to understand this reversion to one pole of the duality by management fiat, and these incidents have, in turn, stimulated new dualities; in particular: inclusion/exclusion and stakeholder consensus/management control in decision-making, accompanied by an increased awareness of the need for new organizational practices, such as information disclosure.

34.8.5 Improvization: Embedding Dualities

> Smith and Graetz (2011: 194) describe improvization as 'ongoing, iterative action, a fusion of intended and emergent action drawing on simultaneity, interrelation, minimal threshold and dynamism to mediate between constantly contradictory goals'. At this level of escalation, embedded dualities can be routinely evoked in decision-making using devices such as 'boundary heuristics. (ibid: 195)

---

[4] I am indebted to Jan O'Hara, an Oxford Associate and management consultant, for this observation.

Dualities are embedded when new communicative scripts consistent with the target organizational template start to guide thinking and acting. Successful achievement of a new organizational identity is evidenced by expressions of affective commitment to the philosophy and purpose of the new organization and by attentiveness to maintaining the objective conditions of the organization such as the voice system. Importantly, to underpin affective commitment, voice systems have to be stable and reliable, so that their existence is not vulnerable to the arbitrary will of powerful stakeholders: 'In the past [voice] had been at the whim of management ... that can't exist any more' (supervisor).

> 'We've always had our voice but it fell on deaf ears, no matter what we said. It's oh that's a good idea that, but it never went any further. [We've] actually come up with ideas ... we can actually see them working now.' (supervisor)

With respect to conversations, one supervisor said:

> 'consultation in the old days, we're telling you what we're gonna do so you've been consulted. Not like that now. People sit down with a piece of paper with some ideas. We'll all get together and chat. Those ideas will be scratched and rewritten, scratched and rewritten ... argued ... argued.' (supervisor) [*laughter*]

Managers in the front line of change had to grapple with the control/empowerment duality. This duality is a permanent feature of a power-sharing mutual, requiring managers to develop a raft of competences in communicating, coaching, visioning, enabling, and advocating. In the case of the caretaking section, the aim of the caretaking manager was to 'turn the seniors into a very effective and confident team (never been a team before but needed to be)'. To achieve this, he knew he needed to increase their capabilities and confidence to the extent where 'they know they are capable of running the service. Got the backing from me to run the service'. In this example of the control/empowerment duality, the manager used, not only empowerment to increase individual capabilities and a sense of self-worth, but also control to provide cover and advocacy during transition.

In RBH, the move to mutualization generated very high levels of expectation, ranging from hope for how becoming a mutual would change the lives of tenants, through volunteering and becoming involved in governance, to expectations for how it would enable people to undertake new entrepreneurial projects. One staff member said: 'In my head, I can see how we could be excellent'. One manager said that each day he was struck by the 'sheer commitment people have, day after day committed to making it right, committed to delivering the service'. Employees expressed desire for interesting and skilled work such as building kitchens or planting gardens: 'they like doing a kitchen and want to do bigger work' (supervisor). They also described the positive contribution RBH could make to the capability development of disadvantaged communities through initiatives such as volunteer programmes. Such attitudes are evidence of high levels of normative commitment, which is known to aid staff retention through strong obligations to stay (Meyer et al. 2002). They are also evidence of the shift towards an identity of being a co-owner as people begin to perceive the connections between co-ownership, innovation, community development, and commercial viability:

> 'This used to be a job where you got paid for coming to work but now we are more actually out there. The more we get the tenants on our side the better for us because the company belongs to the tenants and the staff now. So you're not just coming in and working for somebody, you're basically working for yourself, or that's how it seems now … people starting to take a bit more pride in what they're doing or that's the message that's coming back from the lads.' (supervisor)

One route for embedding the public-service/commerciality duality in RBH was the use of co-production to create operational efficiencies by eliciting the tacit knowledge, skill, and craft of staff members and tenant members. One member commented that he had been suspicious of a detailed interview with an external consultant because he believed his knowledge would be exploited to remove him from his job. In a mutual, however, he believed that his knowledge was 'safe' because his co-ownership status protected his position and would ensure that he would benefit through increased job security within a viable organization. Interviewees demonstrated an increased understanding of their permanent and unavoidable interdependence with their colleagues and with their customers. This extended to an awareness of the need to include the suppliers and contractors as sources of potential new ideas and practice.

Using values-talk to connect the poles of dualities generated the need to increase communicative capabilities. Increasingly, managers and supervisors had to cascade clear positive values-based messages through the organization, where those messages needed to retain their integrity and content by the time they reached front-line staff. One manager said that he now asked: 'How we communicate that down to managers, and when it gets to the middle managers, do you think that conversation will still be intact?' Managers needed to monitor the uptake of mutuality in their teams. This work was not fully captured by existing performance-assessment mechanisms and a development system (training packages, assessment tools, mentoring programmes) was in the process of being created for inculcating mutual leadership.

34.9 Cognitive and Emotional Work in Organizational Identity Formation

Creating an intersectional organizational identity which holds particularist member identifications—being an employee, public-service professional, or service user—in tension with the universalist identifications of co-ownership is vital for pluralist institutions such as multi-constituency mutuals. Such mutuals are engines for generating the interactions needed for information-rich, multi-voiced, and difference-proliferating conversations. However, even where there is an organizational template designed for dualistic thinking, the cognitive and emotional labour necessary for establishing new, stable self-identities remains demanding and time consuming:

> '[…] times when we are talking, it's like it really is they've got it … he's got it. He's not got it yet, we need to … see what we can do to bring him into the culture and philosophy we want to work at … there can be times when we [can think] I've lost it. It's strange, you can be talking and you can be thinking and feeling, do you know I've cracked this … and then you can think about things … even half an hour later, its fuzzy … [I say] don't worry, don't get upset about it, don't panic, we're on our ten year road here, make sure we are moving on our road to get to it, … one of the things helps us all.' (manager, RBH)

When enabled by dualities thinking, this vital labour unlocks the human, social, and economic potential of public-service mutualization. It also distinguishes mutualization from other forms of public-service ownership because in a co-owned organization all those who contribute knowledge, skill, and craft, whether employees or service users, will share in the benefits through meaningful work, service improvements, reinvestments into the community, and the satisfactions of collective action for the common good.

ACKNOWLEDGEMENTS

The leadership programme was designed and facilitated by the author, Oliver Nyumbu, and Jan O'Hara—both Associates of the Oxford Centre for Mutual and Employee-Owned Business. My sincere thanks to them for their professionalism, creativity, and commitment. I am also extremely grateful to Cliff Mills of Anthony Collins Solicitors and Senior Associate of the Oxford Centre who designed the governance and legal framework for RBH, and advised the Constitution Commission.

Above all, I am indebted to the co-owners of Rochdale Boroughwide Housing for providing generous access to their organization. None of this research would have been possible without their bravery and vision.

REFERENCES

Alvesson, M. (2002), *Understanding Organizational Culture* (London: Sage).
Barbour, J. B., Jacocks, C. W., and Wesner, K. J. (2013), 'The Message Design Logics of Organizational Change', *Communication Monographs*, 80(3), 354–78.
Barge, K. J. et al. (2008), 'Managing Dualities in Planned Change Initiatives', *Journal of Applied Communication Research*, 36(4), 364–90.
Birchall, J. (2010), *People-Centred Businesses: Co-Operatives, Mutuals and the Idea of Membership* (London: Palgrave Macmillan).

Cabinet Office (2014), 'Cabinet Office Mutuals Reach Century Success. Press release. Available at https://www.gov.uk/government/news/cabinet-office-mutuals-reach-century-success (accessed 28 September 2016).

Davis, W. and Yeoman, R. (2013), *Becoming a Public Service Mutual: Understanding Transition and Change* (Kellogg College, University of Oxford). Available at : http://www.kellogg.ox.ac.uk/wp-content/uploads/2015/11/Becoming-a-public-service-mutual.pdf (accessed 21 October 2016).

Evans, Paul, A. L. (1999), 'HRM on the Edge: A Duality Perspective', *Organization*, 6(2), 325–38.

Ford, J. D. and Backoff, R. W. (1988), 'Organizational Change in and out of Dualities and Paradox', in Quinn and Cameron, eds, *Paradox and Transformation: Toward a Theory of Change in Organization and Management* (Cambridge, MA: Ballinger), 81–121.

Graetz, F. and Smith, A. C. T. (2008), 'The Role of Dualities in Arbitrating Continuity and Change in Forms of Organizing', *International Journal of Management Reviews*, 10(3), 265–80.

Hatch, M. J. and Schultz, M. S. (2002), 'The Dynamics of Organizational Identity', *Human Relations*, 55(8), 989–1018.

Hazen, M. A. (1993), 'Towards Polyphonic Organization', *Journal of Organizational Change Management*, 6(5), 15–26.

Kaarsemaker, E. C. and Poutsma, E. (2006), 'The Fit of Employee Ownership with Other Human Resource Management Practices: Theoretical and Empirical Suggestions Regarding the Existence of an Ownership High-Performance Work System', *Economic and Industrial Democracy*, 27(4), 669–85.

Kraatz, M. S. (2009), 'Leadership as Institutional Work: A Bridge to the Other Side', in T. B. Lawrence, R. Suddaby, and B. Leca, eds, *Institutional Work: Actors and Agency in Institutional Studies of Organizations* (Cambridge: Cambridge University Press), 59–91.

Kraatz, M. S. and Block, E. S. (2008), 'Organizational Implications of Institutional Pluralism', in R. Greenwood, C. Oliver, K. Sahlin-Andersson, and R. Suddaby, eds, *The Sage Handbook of Organizational Institutionalism* (Los Angeles: SAGE Publications), 243–75.

Lewin, K. (1951), *Field Theory in Social Science*, New York: Harper.

Meyer, J. P., Stanley, D. J., Herscovitch, L., and Topolnytsky, L. (2002), 'Affective, Continuance, and Normative Commitment to the Organization: A Meta-Analysis of Antecedents, Correlates, and Consequences', *Journal of Vocational Behavior*, 61(1), 20–52.

Meyers, D. T. (2000), 'Intersectional Identity and the Authentic Self? Opposites Attract!' in Mackenzie and Stoljar, eds, *Relational Autonomy: Feminist Perspectives on Autonomy, Agency and the Social Self* (New York and Oxford: Oxford University Press), 151–80.

Myers, J. and Cato, M. S. (2011), 'From 'Personal' to 'Mutual': Exploring the Opportunities for Co-operative and Mutual Forms of Ownership and Governance in the Design and Delivery of Social and Public Services', in Hill et al., eds, *Dialogues in Critical Management Studies Vol. I: The Third Sector* (Bingley, UK: Emerald Group Publisher Ltd), 33–51.

Seo, M., Putnam, L. L., and Bartunek, J. M. (2003), 'Dualities and Tensions of Planned Organizational Change', in M. S. Poole and A. Van de Ven, eds, *Handbook of Organizational Change and Innovation*, Thousand Oaks, CA: SAGE, 73–107.

Simmons, R. (2008), 'Harnessing Social Enterprise for Local Public Services: The Case of New Leisure Trusts', *Public Policy and Administration*, 23: 278–301.

Smith, C. T. and Graetz, F. M. (2011), *Philosophies of Organizational Change* (Cheltenham, UK and Northampton, MA, USA: Edward Elgar).

Stoltzfus, K., Stohl, C., and Seibold, D. R. (2011), 'Managing Organizational Change: Paradoxical Problems, Solutions, and Consequences', *Journal of Organizational Change Management*, 24(3), 349–67.

Tsoukas, H. and Chia, R. (2002), 'On Organizational Becoming: Rethinking Organizational Change', *Organization Science*, 13(5), 567–82.

Weber W. G., Unterrainer, C., and Höge, T. (2008), 'Sociomoral Atmosphere and Prosocial and Democratic Value Orientations in Enterprises with Different Levels of Structurally Anchored Participation', *German Journal of Research in Human Resource Management*, 22: 171–94.

Weick, K. E. (1995), *Sensemaking in Organizations* (Thousand Oaks, CA: SAGE).

Young, K. M. (1991), 'Theory O: The Ownership Theory of Management', in C. Rosen and K. M. Young, eds, *Understanding Employee Ownership* (Ithaca, NY: ILR Press), 108–35.

Yu, K.-H. (2013), 'Institutionalization in the Context of Institutional Pluralism: Politics as a Generative Process', *Organization Studies*, 34(1), 105–31.

CHAPTER 35

THE EMERGENCE OF MULTI-STAKEHOLDER CO-OPERATIVES IN THE MOVEMENT OF FARM MACHINERY CO-OPERATIVES (CUMAS) IN FRANCE

FRANCK THOMAS

35.1 INTRODUCTION

RURAL territories are no longer just agricultural. Managing landscapes, preserving the environment, creating local jobs, maintaining local services … the issues farmers have to deal with concern questions that are new to them. Responding to these issues gives rise to brand new forms of collaboration and makes the traditional actors in these territories question their assumptions: in France, for example, local farmers' co-operatives are wondering how to extend their membership base to new stakeholders.

35.2 A DENSE NETWORK OF FARM MACHINERY CO-OPERATIVES

There are 11,260 of them in France: the farm machinery co-operatives (CUMAs)[1] represent a dense network of small groups (almost 50 per cent of French farmers, 25 farmers

---

[1] CUMA stands for *Coopératives d'Utilisation de Matériel Agricole* [Co-operatives for the Use of Agricultural Equipment].

per co-operative for €49,000 turnover on average) who mutualize the necessary equipment (ploughs, trucks, tractors, combine harvesters, etc.) for the activities of the member farms. They function mainly on a volunteer basis, even if 1,580 of them employ a total of 4,560 employees (drivers and mechanics). Since CUMAs do not just provide equipment but are also organized to work together and develop good neighbour relationships, they also take part in local development initiatives such as countryside management, landscape development, sharing jobs, and waste treatment.

CUMAs are federated in a national network. They therefore benefit from the activities and the advisory services for agro-equipment, organization, financing, accounting, and legal matters that 25 local federations, five inter-regional resource centres, and a national federation provide. Even though CUMAs can also be found in Spain, Belgium, Quebec, and Benin, they remain a French peculiarity, whose history can be traced back over more than 70 years of agricultural development.

35.3 Farm Machinery Co-operatives: Seventy Years of History

CUMAs were born after the Second World War as a result of the state's firm intention to mechanize agriculture so as to once again reach self-sufficient food capacity in the country. From their outset, CUMAs have been intimately associated with agriculture's transformations: the arrival of the first tractors, the set-up of development organizations, the fodder revolution, Common Agricultural Policy reform, etc.

The history of the network of CUMAs in France was initially rooted in farming's mutual-aid traditions. In the 1920s, in particular, wheat threshing became mechanized and *locomobiles* entered the scene.[2] *Locomobiles* operate large threshers at a fixed site. But the cost of this piece of equipment, which is only used for a few weeks in the summer, led farms to form syndicates or co-operatives to buy one and use it. This system worked right up to the 1960s. Threshing sites brought several dozens of neighbouring farmers together and became an important gathering point of rural life.

On 12 October 1945, the decree giving the CUMAs their official status was issued. At the end of the Second World War, French agriculture needed rebuilding. Mechanization was only taking its first steps. 'Our impoverished country has to increase the productivity of its rural workers with modern equipment while seeking to reduce its production costs. This cannot be done equipping too large a number of excessively small farms on an individual basis,'[3] René Dumont wrote in 1946, when he was given the task of drafting an orientation and equipment plan for agriculture. The Marshall Plan (1948–52) organized the arrival of

---

[2] *Locomobile*: steam engine machine with wheels used to work threshers (Larousse).
[3] R. Dumont (1946). *Le problème agricole français*, Paris: Les éditions nouvelles.

American equipment in French farms, thereby supporting their mechanization, especially through introduction of the first tractors. CUMAs were one of the instruments of this plan, designed to facilitate shared investment in agricultural equipment. The number of CUMAs exploded to 8,000, even if many would disappear shortly afterwards.

Some 15 years later (in the 1960s), agricultural development promoted collective organizations once again. The Jeunesse Agricole Catholique (JAC) structured a powerful youth movement that aspired to free agricultural holdings from the family setting in which they were traditionally enclosed. 'You criticise the government and you complain about your deputies; so start by trying to help your neighbour and make the necessary effort—by associating yourself with him you'll be helping yourself'[4] wrote René Colson, general secretary of the JAC from 1941 to 1948. In the year 1960, the orientation laws proposed by Edgar Pisani, Minister of Agriculture at the time, created the GAEC, the *groupements agricoles d'exploitation en commun* (farmers' associative groups). The so-called 'group' agriculture had the wind in its favour and CUMAs consolidated their position.

The agricultural sector developed strongly, even if at the same time the number of farms dropped. New practices connected to the equipment's progress became necessary. From the 1970s, stock-rearing regions started to be transformed by the fodder revolution. Maize-growing became standardized, and all operations from sowing to distribution, including silage and storage, became mechanized. Just as for threshing in the past, neighbouring farmers had to be mobilized to form teams in order to harvest silage, each one being in charge of one of the farm machines needed. A whole section of the CUMAs' network was structured around this development dynamic.

At the beginning of the 1980s, CUMAs had the support of a federative network that progressively consolidated and institutionalized itself. This network launched its own journal (Entraid') and in June of 1980, it organized its first agricultural fairs (the Salon des Fourrages [Fodder Fair]). CUMAs standardized and computerized their management with standard software; consolidating the data on mechanization and compiling statistics directly from the users (publishing 'cost price' guides). In 1982, the Minister of Agriculture, Édith Cresson, encouraged collective action by making state-subsidized loans to CUMAs to acquire equipment. The minister also instituted the recognition of CUMA agriculture representative bodies (i.e. mixed commissions and chambers of agriculture). CUMA federations strengthened their official position. New activities then developed in CUMAs (such as drainage, irrigation, collective small-scale workshops processing agricultural products, and maintenance of rural areas), and this development highlighted the need for a reform of CUMAs' statutes. Nonetheless, successive governments refused to change the legal rules, thereby restricting CUMAs' activities and their membership base.

Improving their living and working conditions became an important concern for farmers. Whereas CUMAs depended on volunteers for their activities, the number of jobs shared in CUMA increased (drivers, mechanics, and secretaries). The 2006 agricultural orientation law even allowed CUMAs to carry on activities as a group of employers: besides equipment, the co-operative could now share agricultural employees.

---

[4] Quoted in M. Godreau (2014). *Bruits de moteur sur les champs de Vendée*, Bourneau: Durand-Peyroles.

Today—despite a continuous decline in the number of farmers—CUMAs are as active as ever, even if reorganization (such as inter-co-operative mutualization and the merging of CUMAs) is necessary.

35.4 CASE STUDY 1: THE CUMA OF FONT DEL PRAT

The CUMA of Font del Prat, located in the Department of Aude, in southern France, was created in 1980. It provides equipment and labour for agricultural production and its legal status is that of a CUMA. The CUMA of Font del Prat has eleven member farmers and one employee, and it has a €55,000 turnover.

The CUMA's registered office is located in the small village of Saint Martin Lalande, in the South of France. Farming has left a strong mark on this territory, where, in the past, cereal crops such as hard wheat were predominant. Farms are generally medium-sized family farms. Mechanized equipment—especially that needed for harvesting cereals—is a heavy overhead for such farms. Therefore, in 1980, four neighbouring farmers agreed to mutualize the purchase and use of this harvest equipment by creating a CUMA.

Over the years, new needs for mechanization have emerged on the farms, and other members have joined the founding group. In 2014, the co-operative counted eleven member farms with sizes ranging from 10 hectares (market gardens) to more than 150 hectares. The CUMA provides equipment and a driver for harvesting large crops and diversified plantings (sowing beetroot, onions, beans, etc.).

The CUMA of Font del Prat works by involving its members as volunteers. A managing committee and a chairman are elected and a general meeting is held every year. The group has defined its working rules (invoicing terms, organization for booking equipment, etc.) in its articles. The CUMA's managers are themselves advised by the technicians of the local CUMA federation, who help manage and develop the co-operative project.

Over the years, the co-operative has developed in line with its members' needs. In the 2000s, for example, the traditional bean production was relaunched locally. This bean is part of the recipe for the 'cassoulet', a traditional local dish. The farmers of the CUMA, joined by new members, invested in a bean harvester—specialized and expensive machinery—so as to handle this new and quite tricky crop. Relaunching this traditional crop benefited the whole local economy since it represents an important attraction for local tourism. A position for a shared driver was created in order to shorten the time that farmer members had to work. The mechanical skills of this driver also made maintenance operations, standards updating, and complex settings of the bean harvester easier.

The CUMA has also made it easier for three young male farmers and one young female farmer to start their market gardening or specialized crop projects. Moreover, it has made limitation of financial risk possible and has allowed farmers to take full advantage of contacts with other members. Finally, the CUMA has recently been endowed with a sprayer washing area so that the farms can comply with environmental standards in this field.

35.5 From the Agricultural Issue to the Question of the Multi-Stakeholder Co-operative

35.5.1 The Agricultural 'Double Quality'

One of the bases of co-operatives is the 'double quality' principle: the social actors who are the beneficiaries of the enterprise action are also the members of the enterprise.[5] Thus, in a CUMA a farmer is at the same time both a 'contributor of capital' in the enterprise and a 'user of the service' it produces. This 'double quality' places the power of the enterprise in the hands of both the contributors of capital (as in every private company) and the users of the service (specificity of a co-operative). Thanks to this design, the enterprise's strategic choices really integrate the expectations both of the capital contributors and of the users.

CUMAs are agricultural co-operatives. In French legislation this results in two strong orientations. First of all, a CUMA must only work for its members (principle of exclusivity) and it is not possible to mutualize agricultural equipment with persons other than members of the co-operative. Furthermore, only farmers (or persons deemed to be such) may be members of a co-operative. The sharing of resources with other actors in the territory (such as artisans and local authorities) is extremely limited. All this at a time when mutualizing resources between farmers and other actors in the countryside has become increasingly urgent due to recent developments in agriculture.

35.5.2 Agricultural Issues Involve Rural Areas in Their Whole

Rural areas have changed substantially over the last 40 years. Historically devoted to farming, today these areas are also utilized for new purposes: residential, leisure, and environmental protection. The coexistence of these functions involves a growing diversity of actors and can generate conflicts.

For example, the degradation of water quality in a certain area often highlights the incompatibility of certain agricultural practices with supplying neighbouring towns with drinking water. Reopening public footpaths raises the question of the paths for agricultural circulation and the partnerships to be invented for maintaining them. Managing the green waste collected by local authorities and taking care of hedges requires new partnerships with farmers. Agricultural issues therefore no longer belong just to farmers, and the necessary solutions are being developed around a new and more open set of actors.

---

[5] J.-F. Draperi (2007). *Comprendre l'économie sociale*, Paris: Edition Dunod.

35.5.3 Working With and For Local Authorities

CUMAs are well aware of the fact it is necessary to work with and for local authorities. As early as the 1990s, a few CUMAs promoted initiatives of a new kind by forming partnerships with local authorities or countryside enterprises to produce wood for energy, compost waste, or maintain a smith's workshop. The CUMA fair, historically baptized 'le Salon des Fourrages' (the Fodder Fair) even changed its name at this time to become 'le Salon des Fourrages et des Initiatives Rurales' (the Forage and Rural Initiatives Fair) to mark its openness to new actors in the countryside.

Quite quickly, however, these initiatives came up against the legal limit imposed by the legal status of agricultural co-operatives, which only allows farmers to be members and benefit from CUMA's services. Therefore, alternative legal solutions—most of the time non-co-operative in nature—were found (alongside CUMAs, '*sociétés anonymes*' [limited companies] and '*groupements d'intérêt économique*' [joint ventures] were created). For these reasons—and as early as the 1970s—the national federation of CUMAs asked the Ministry of Agriculture—but to no avail—to allow local authorities to become members of CUMAs as well: farmers in the CUMAs wished to include other actors in the countryside inside their co-operative practices. This wish was all the stronger as it was clear for some of the CUMAs and agricultural co-operatives that the developments in agriculture (direct selling, production of renewable energy, shared management of the environment, etc.) made closer working relationships with those active in the territory more and more necessary. Although this intuition was not shared by all members, it still led the CUMA movement to meet other co-operative and associative networks who were also looking to widen their membership to new partners.

35.6 With Worker-Owned Co-operatives—Envisaging Multi-Stakeholder Co-operatives

In France, people started thinking about a new form of co-operative as early as the 1990s, encouraged by the building of two groundswells.[6]

On the one hand, the worker-owned co-operatives movement ('Mouvement des Scop') was looking for answers in the face of the changes that were occurring within the society and the differing expectations in entrepreneurship. In November 1997, in

---

[6] H. Sibille (2012), 'Contexte et genèse de la création des sociétés coopératives d'intérêt collectif (SCIC)', *Recma*, 324: 110–17.

Lille, the Scop National Conference affirmed its wish to become more open and appear as a network of enterprises with innovative solutions in the fields of employment and economic development. The 'Action Charter' that followed the Conference affirmed 'the imperative for the movement of starting a new stage of development and openness and consequently entering into a dynamic process of modernising its organisation and reforming its articles'; it committed itself to fomenting the understanding of new forms of co-operatives that could offer a legal framework compatible with a changing society and new entrepreneurial methods.

On the other hand, the government of the time created an important programme to encourage youth employment ('*Nouveaux services, emplois jeunes*': 'New services, jobs for young people') and promoted Alain Lipietz's report on new forms of enterprises, particularly those with social objectives.[7] In the light of this job-creation policy, the scheme '*Nouveaux services, emplois jeunes*'—that aimed both at reabsorbing youth unemployment and at developing new activities in order to meet emerging or unsatisfied needs— raised the question of how the activities it supported could be perpetuated when, five years later, public aid would stop. Offering perspectives for development, in particular thanks to articles of association capable of making competing and non-competing sectors work together, represented an important issue.

In this context, in 1998, the worker-owned co-operative movement launched an action-research to assess the feasibility of a new version of the co-operative law of 1947 that would allow and regulate multi-stakeholder co-operatives. The movement also took part in the European research project 'Digestus' that aimed at harmonizing the criteria and ways of working of 'enterprises with social goals' (it should be noted that the Italian law on social co-operatives dates back to 1991). In 1999, the French worker-owned co-operative confederation (Confédération générale des Scop: CGSCOP) initiated a 'collective innovation approach' with an inter-networks reflection group, which, in 2001, was to contribute to forming the legal framework for the Sociétés coopératives d'intérêt collectif (SCIC: collective interest co-operative enterprise), the first form of multi-stakeholder co-operative in France.

The SCIC is a co-operative enterprise with the object of producing goods or services that meet the collective needs of a territory by making the best possible use of its economic and social resources. It has the status of a commercial company and as such functions like any enterprise subject to the imperatives of good management and innovation.[8]

SCICs enable multiple actors to be associated around the same project, necessarily grouped in three categories of stakeholders, that is, employees, beneficiaries, and a third

---

[7] A. Lipietz (2000), 'L'opportunité d'un nouveau type de société à vocation sociale'. Report relating to the mission letter of 17 September 1998 addressed by Mrs Aubry, Minister of Employment and Solidarity.

[8] M. Daupleix (2002), 'La Scic: Entre démarche d'utilité sociale et construction de l'intérêt collectif. De l'organisation au territoire'. Master's dissertation. Toulouse: Université Toulouse Le Mirail

left to be decided by the project's initiators. In this way employees, volunteers, users, local authorities, businesses, associations, private individuals ... and all kinds of persons and corporations interested for various reasons may be associated with SCICs.[9] They respect the rules for co-operatives: sharing power on the basis of the principle 'one person = one vote', involvement of all the members in the life of the enterprise and in the main management decisions, and maintaining the enterprise's profits in the form of locked-up reserves that ensure its autonomy and perpetuation. In 2016, there were more than 550 SCICs in France.[10]

Quite quickly the national CUMA federation (Fédération Nationale des CUMA: FNCUMA) saw in this new form of co-operative—the SCIC—an opportunity to resume the debate on making local authorities members of co-operatives.[11] Even if collaborations between different forms of co-operatives scarcely existed—if at all—the FNCUMA started the first exchanges with the CGSCOP. It discovered new facets of co-operative development and took part in the beginning of the 'collective innovation approach'. FNCUMA promoted the idea that several of the issues farmers and, more widely, rural areas faced could find solutions in the quite new form of the SCIC co-operative, as it allows all the actors interested in the co-operative's activity to join it. For the first time in French law, multi-stakeholder co-operatives were proposed and it became possible to transcend the limits of the articles of agricultural co-operatives, which were too narrow to allow the involvement of elected officials or the heads of the areas' enterprises.

The multi-stakeholder co-operative remains the hallmark of the SCIC. It dares to contradict the founding experience of the 28 weavers of Rochdale in England who, in creating their co-operative in 1844, announced the founding principles of the co-operative movement: 'one person = one vote', discounts, political and religious neutrality, etc. The Rochdale pioneers reached the bitter conclusion that it was impossible to serve the interests of consumers and employees at the same time and in 1862, the general meeting adopted by 502 votes for and 162 against (out of 1,500 members) the abolition of membership for employees. The divorce between consumers and employees had occurred and was to mark the history of the co-operative movement for a long time. For nearly a century and a half, this orientation—which Charles Gide would call 'the heartrending revision'—ratified the idea that a single co-operative enterprise could not durably benefit both consumers and producers simultaneously.[12]

---

[9] A. Margado (2004), 'A New Co-Operative Form in France: Société Coopérative d'Intérêt Collectif (SCIC)', in C. Borzaga and R. Spear, eds, *Trends and Challenges for Co-operatives and Social Enterprises in Developed and Transition Countries* (Trento: Edizioni 31), 147–63.

[10] http://www.les-scic.coop

[11] Pionneau, F. (2007), 'Scic et Cuma: La Scic, une nouvelle coopérative agricole?' FNCUMA internal report. Paris: FNCUMA.

[12] Quoted in J.-F. Draperi (2005), *L'économie sociale—Utopies, pratiques, principes*. Paris: Presses de l'économie sociale.

35.7 New Multi-Actor Co-operatives in Rural Territories

On 17 January 2001, the law creating the SCIC was enacted. Since then, project initiators have progressively made this new co-operative their own. In rural areas several multi-stakeholder organizations appeared in the fields of direct sales, environment preservation, or neighbourhood services supply. In all of these sectors the involvement of a large set of actors represents the keystone of the project's viability.

Multi-stakeholder co-operatives manage short production chains for fuel wood. Using wood from hedges and coppices, they organize the production and delivery of woodchips for the boilers of ordinary consumers or local communities. The implementation of this type of project involves mobilizing farmers, local authorities, and enterprises.

Short food supply chains seek to reduce the distance between consumers and producers. Project initiators use the SCIC to organize this convergence within the governance of their project: market-gardeners, stock-raisers, consumers, and employees sit together on the same administrative board, deliberate together on the price to charge, and choose the suppliers who respect the project's value.

Short food supply chains also require the conservation of local slaughterhouses in order to remain economically viable despite small volumes and the necessity of working with several species of animals. Local initiatives have shown that this viability depends on a new commitment by the various actors present in rural areas, from slaughterhouse employees and stock-raisers, to local authorities, butchers, and restaurant owners.

The disappearance of the last café or grocer's in certain villages has led their inhabitants to take action to preserve their local shops. Nonetheless, maintaining these services involves combining various activities at the same time (grocers, services to the population, cultural activities, etc.) and the commitment of several actors (such as farmers, inhabitants, local authorities, and managers). The SCIC provides a legal framework that suits a constructive co-ordination of actors and activities.

The farming profession is not transmitted exclusively from father to son. New forms for setting up a farm have emerged in the form of project incubators and nurseries; a system of support service coupled with an availability of land is offered to young people who wish to test themselves on a form of agricultural production without having to start by investing in costly installations. In France, the RENETA network (Réseau National des Espaces Tests Agricoles: National Network of Agricultural Test Areas) brings these initiatives together. One of them opted for the SCIC system; others are considering it carefully. In order to succeed, these 'incubators' need to be supported by wide partnerships built around young entrepreneurs: local authorities, banks, professional agricultural organizations, farmers already in business, etc.

Environment management activities (such as water distribution, landscape management, and waste collection) are on the cusp of various activities. Several of them also combine activities involving populations that have difficulties. The SCIC's legal status makes the fitting of suitable multi-partner governance within the aims of the project possible.

All these new ways of co-operating open interesting paths for development for the actors in rural areas and their networks. Nonetheless, they also raise critical questions: how is it possible to go beyond a homogeneous membership base and treat an employee, a customer, or a supplier as a peer? How can various co-operative institutions—often founded for the defence of a particular legal status—collaborate to develop a form of multi-stakeholder co-operative that, by nature, has to rise above the actors' approaches and tactics?[13]

35.8 Case Study 2: Progressive Installation in Farming

The 'Coopérative d'installation en agriculture paysanne' (CIAP—Installation in Farming Co-operative) operates in Loire Atlantique, Pays de la Loire. It was created in 2013 and has 171 project promoters, 2 employees and 50 associates (agricultural, social economy, and solidarity organizations, local authorities, citizens, and employees). Its legal status is Société coopérative d'intérêt collectif (SCIC). The CIAP's key function is that of offering services and assisting would-be farmers, in order to respond to the current challenges farmers have to face.

The agricultural sector is in fact undergoing profound mutations. Its demography is characterized by an ageing population, a reduction in the number of working persons (−200,000 working persons between 2000 and 2010), and a phenomenon of agricultural disengagement, as demonstrated by an increase in the size of farms at the expense of a more local agriculture.

At the same time, consumers' demands are evolving towards a request for quality and local produce beyond what the current offer can satisfy. People who do not come from an agricultural environment (i.e. urban, with no farming skills, real estate, or experience) are turning towards farming; in fact 30 per cent of installations by under-40s are termed 'outside family context'.

Lastly, new forms of co-operation are being developed. They respond to globalization of the economy, the dismantling of previous regulations, and the increasingly shorter production cycles that all lead to a diversification of agricultural job realities (starting with the food, energy, and environmental fields).

All these phenomena have resulted in rethinking on how to accompany installation projects of new farmers. The CIAP was created to support new farmers and place their

[13] Thomas, F. (2008), 'Scic et agriculture: Le temps des défricheurs', *Recma*, 310, 17–30.

installation on a more solid basis by providing professional training, a legal, administrative, and accounting address, financing for the farm's assets, and areas for testing their activities.

The CIAP offers three types of services:

- organic agriculture testing areas, mainly for market-gardening, but also for stock raising;
- 'creative farming' courses in which the project initiators benefit from the training and the tutoring of a referring farmer (200 hours of training and 1,620 of course) when they get their farming site;
- temporary project support and validation of the economic project before the actual installation on the site (legal, administrative, and accounting address).

The CIAP is part of an 'eco-system' that responds to the expectations of the stakeholders: co-operative organizations and agricultural unions, local communities, local associations, etc. The SCIC CAP 44 was created in 2008, with the ambition of developing smallholding farming (helping project initiators and existing farms, conducting collective projects, training, advising local authorities, etc.). Broadly speaking, the SCIC CAP 44 originated the CIAP, by designing its engineering and set-up.

In the same way, the SCIC Nord Nantes, a civil agriculture production company created in 2013, assures the recovery of agricultural land by restoring its condition and bringing it back under cultivation. It also manages the land on a temporary basis and makes it available to the project initiators that the CIAP helps.

Two project initiators are accommodated by the CIAP, 55 trainees—looking for an installation—are looked after and five project initiators benefit from temporary business support. In order to accompany these installations, an investment of €80,000 is planned for 2014.

Half way through 2014, about 55 'agricultural testing areas' existed in France. Most of these areas have an associative status and for them becoming a SCIC, and therefore gaining the security of the legal framework of a commercial but co-operative company, is increasingly on the agenda.

35.9 Case Study 3: Bois Bocage Energie

Since 2006, the Bois Bocage Energie (Hedge Fuel Wood) has produced and distributed fuel wood chips in Normandy, Central France, and Pays de la Loire. From a legal point of view Bois Bocage Energie is a SCIC. It has 190 members (including 26 local authorities, one employee, and 116 producers) and a €466,500 turnover.

Bois Bocage Energie recycles wood from hedges by transforming it into woodchips for fuel. It creates a win–win relationship between all the actors who take part in its multi-stakeholder governance. This renewable energy recycling project emerged in the context of local protest against the installation of a nuclear waste disposal site, as well as a project for reparcelling the land that would endanger the *bocage* (a particular landscape characterized by small and irregularly shaped fields separated by hedges and ditches).

In economic terms, the main aim of Bois Bocage Energie is to produce and sell fuel wood chips and pellets to supply about 50 local boilers. To consolidate its economic viability, the SCIC also sells consultancy services on hedge management and, in the context of recycling, fuel wood projects. In terms of social utility, the aim is to create a 'local development tool to the benefit of the actors in the territory' that simultaneously provides a correct remuneration for the producers and a just price for the clients, as well as an action in favour of the environment, and the development of the local economy.

This SCIC project arises from an idea shared by several local actors: elected officials concerned about environmental issues and inclined to develop clean energies on their territory and their institutions, farmers in favour of sustainable management of the *bocages*, inhabitants concerned about their well-being and sustainable development, and potential entrepreneurs, as well as customers for fuel wood.

The status of SCIC offers the possibility of establishing a multi-stakeholder co-operative. Within Bois Bocage Energie the governance includes five categories of members: employees, clients, producers, local authorities, and other persons or corporations. In practice, the 190 members are grouped in voting colleges with producers and clients having the heaviest weighting—given that within each college one person has one vote independently from the held capital. On a daily basis, a full-time employee provides the information service and co-ordinates the management of the co-operative.

The SCIC has allowed satisfaction of the co-operative members' expectations: the promotion of renewable energy in the territory as a political project, economic development of the *bocage* in order to maintain the landscape, local renewable energy production accessible to small installations, and shared management of the activities in the rural area. Beside the benefits to its members, the SCIC demonstrates it is possible to produce renewable energies while respecting the environment, with significant involvement of the local actors—a factor towards social cohesion in the community. From an economic point of view, this configuration contributes to structuring a new sector, and creating a relationship of co-operation rather than one of competition between the actors—given that prices are fixed by the producers and the clients every year.

Since 2006, the SCIC Bois Bocage Energie has had its emulators: its founders have significantly contributed to hiving off this experiment to other regions; so much so that 22 local fuel wood enterprises and co-operatives are currently active in France and federation projects are developing.

Acknowledgements

This chapter was written thanks to the kind collaboration of Catherine Friedrich and Adelphe de Taxis du Poët (Confédération générale des SCOP) and of Christine Ferrier (FNCUMA).

References

Daupleix, M. (2002), 'La Scic: Entre démarche d'utilité sociale et construction de l'intérêt collectif. De l'organisation au territoire'. Master's dissertation. Toulouse: Université Toulouse Le Mirail.

Draperi, J.-F. (2005), *L'économie sociale—Utopies, pratiques, principes* (France: Presses de l'économie sociale).

Draperi, J.-F. (2007), *Comprendre l'économie sociale* (Paris: Edition Dunod).

Dumont, R. (1946), *Le problème agricole français: Esquisse d'un plan d'orientation et d'équipement* (Paris: Les éditions nouvelles).

Godreau, M. (2014), *Bruits de moteur sur les champs de Vendée* (Bourneau: Durand-Peyroles).

Lipietz, A. (2000), 'Sur l'opportunité d'un nouveau type de société à vocation sociale'. Official report for the Ministry of Employment and Solidarity.

Margado, A. (2004), 'A New Co-Operative Form in France: Société Coopérative d'Intérêt Collectif (SCIC)', in C. Borzaga and R. Spear, eds, *Trends and Challenges for Co-operatives and Social Enterprises in Developed and Transition Countries* (Trento: Edizioni 31), 147–63.

Pionneau, F. (2007), 'Scic et Cuma: La Scic, une nouvelle coopérative agricole?'. FNCUMA internal report. Paris: FNCUMA.

Sibille, H. (2012), 'Contexte et genèse de la création des sociétés coopératives d'intérêt collectif (SCIC)', *Recma*, 324, 110–17.

Thomas, F. (2008), 'Scic et agriculture: Le temps des défricheurs', *Recma*, 310, 17–30.

CHAPTER 36

....

AGRICULTURAL
CO-OPERATIVES IN CHINA

....

LI ZHAO

36.1 INTRODUCTION

....

AGRICULTURE is of vital importance in China. It is an important industry for ensuring food security, rural employment, farmers' livelihoods, and conservation of the agricultural ecological environment. Starting from the institutional transition of 1978 from a planned agricultural economy to the household contract responsibility system (HCRS), the Chinese rural economy has undergone substantial structural change, and the share of agriculture in GDP has been declining. But the significance of agriculture as the basis of China's national economy has never changed. Nowadays, almost one-third of the population in China still depends on agriculture.

The importance of producers' organizations in agriculture is widely acknowledged. In a country such as China where agriculture is dominated by smallholders, the importance of such organizations is even more evident. The ongoing transition has witnessed the development of agricultural co-operatives and the emergence of new organizational types in China. Since the late 1990s, agricultural co-operatives in China have grown rapidly. Particularly after the promulgation of the Law of the People's Republic of China on Farmers' Specialized Co-operatives (FSCs) in 2007, rural China has been experiencing a rising tide in co-operative development. Recent statistics showed that at the end of 2014, there were 1.29 million registered FSCs nationwide, an increase of 31.18 per cent in one year. The total shares accounted for 2.73 trillion Yuan, an increase of 44.15 per cent during the same period.[1]

According to the 2007 law, an FSC is a 'mutual-aid economic organization which is voluntarily formed by production and business operators of similar agricultural

---

[1] The website of SAIC (State Administration for Industry and Commerce in China): http://www.saic.gov.cn/zwgk/tjzl/zhtj/xxzx/201501/t20150123_151591.html (accessed 29 September 2016).

products, or by providers or users of similar agricultural production and business services on the basis of rural household contractual management and which is subject to democratic management' (Article 2). Although the 2007 law on FSCs introduces the term 'farmers' specialized co-operative', agricultural co-operatives in China also exist in other forms, such as farmers' specialized associations, land-based co-operatives, and rural community co-operatives. Besides, agriculture-based co-operation is also found in the form of some experiments of co-operative federations and regional co-operative associations. They can be regarded as new types of co-operation. Another new co-operative model concerns the shareholding co-operative system as an innovative adaptation to new socio-economic challenges in rural China. Furthermore, a division can be made between capital-led co-operation, characterized by specialized agricultural production with vertical market integration, and community-based co-operation, typified by diversified production with horizontal market integration.

Since the concept of a co-operative is still relatively new in China, it needs to be widely diffused in society and correctly understood. At present, as noted by Zhao and Yuan (2014: 33), the creation of agricultural co-operatives can 'result from different motivations, driven by various promoters, presenting diverse organizational forms, and pursuing distinct missions'. As a consequence, the nature of co-operatives is highly controversial, raising abundant debates. It is questioned, for example, whether they are truly benefiting the majority of smallholders when the organizations are dominated by big producers or the commercial enterprises who initiate the co-operatives. At times they are considered as false co-operatives and denounced. Sometimes it seems difficult to differentiate real co-operatives from pseudo ones. Being characterized as heterogeneous and diverse, agricultural co-operatives in China demonstrate 'signs of diversity, with variations in their quality' (Zhang 2013: 19).

The aim of this chapter is to examine the evolution, diversity, and dynamics of Chinese agricultural co-operatives and the institutional environments in which the development of these organizations took place. The chapter proceeds as follows. Section 36.2 looks at the emergence and development of agricultural co-operatives in China since the 1980s. Sections 36.3 and 36.4 provide an analysis of the diversity and dynamics of Chinese agricultural co-operatives, with a particular focus on diverse operational patterns and initiating forces, respectively. Finally, the chapter concludes with an assessment of recent developments in Chinese agricultural co-operatives and proposals for institutional improvements.

36.2 The Evolution of Chinese Agricultural Co-operatives

Although the development of agricultural co-operatives has a decennia-long history in China, this chapter focuses on the economic transitional background since 1978, when the economic reform was triggered in China's rural areas. Since then, three main periods can be broadly delineated to examine the emergence and development process of rural co-operatives in China.

The transition started with the implementation of the HCRS and the abolition of communes in rural China, when farmer households began to contract land and became responsible for their own purchasing, production, and marketing decisions. On the one hand, traditional agricultural co-operation firstly re-appeared in the form of technical associations, providing services such as market information and technical training. These technical associations were mostly registered as social entities and were therefore not allowed to participate in profit-generating activities. As agricultural productivity increased, farmers were progressively concerned about selling their products and earning money. With the gradual emergence of specialized farmer households, the specialization of agricultural production and the diversification of economic co-operation became popular, although there were relatively few markets at that time. Later on, technical associations also took on additional roles, such as transportation, storage, joint marketing, and purchasing of inputs (Fock and Zachernuk 2006: 12). On the other hand, a new type of co-operation, typified by the shareholding co-operative system, was invented by local villagers out of spontaneous actions as an experiment to solve the problems created by the dismantling of collective properties (Zhao and Develtere 2010). This system created a new organizational ownership form and governance model in rural enterprises. It also paved the way for multi-stakeholder co-operation between local governments, collective enterprises, and community residents (Christiansen and Zhang 1998). In the 1980s, in response to those local initiatives, institutional support from the central government came into being for the development of farmers' organizations. Such support was manifest in particular during 1982 and 1986 in the five Number One Documents.[2]

The second period of the mid transition in the 1990s was accompanied by a process of marketization, industrialization, and capitalization. Whereas the market economy had fully gained its official status in the national economy, the 'promotion of capitalism relegates co-operative development to a tertiary role behind the state and large corporate entities' (Melnyk 2009: 7). A survey reported by Shen et al. (2004: 13) on the development of farmer associations noted that up until the mid 1990s, there were very few farmers' associations and there was no systematic activity to promote them. As the state's interest in local rural development faded and shifted to the promotion of urbanization, an increasing income gap between rural and urban residents was witnessed throughout the 1990s. In the agricultural sector, a number of serious problems were also emerging, such as the diminishing size of the arable land, agriculture's ecological sustainability

---

[2] The Number One Document refers to the first central document of the year, issued jointly by the Central Committee of the Communist Party of China and the State Council. During the period 1982–86 and the years since 2004, there were Number One Documents that focused on agricultural and rural development. This illustrated the absolute priority granted to these areas.

crisis, and land pollution. Besides these problems, the rural area of China was plagued by vulnerable employment opportunities as well as the dissolution of rural communities and local ties. Furthermore, China's entry into the World Trade Organization (WTO) also posed new challenges to its agriculture. Institutional arrangements, such as tax and fiscal reforms, financial reforms, and public policies concerning agricultural industrialization and modernization, further influenced the sustainability of agricultural production and rural livelihood in a negative manner. This rural crisis caused the central government to suffer from a legitimacy crisis, which required a state reorientation in rural policy (see Zhao 2013).

In response to the rural crisis, in the third period, which started with the new millennium, the state has made rural development once again a top priority. It was in this context that agricultural co-operatives started to boom. Since 2003, the government has been giving greater importance to agriculture, with a series of supports under the summarized guideline of 'giving more, taking less, and liberalization'. In 2004, to 'give more' to farmers, the central government launched a major scheme of direct subsidies, particularly to grain producers. The other elements of the comprehensive subsidy system included seed subsidies and input subsidies, as well as machinery purchase subsidies. Concerning 'taking less', the abolition of agricultural taxes in 2006 has been widely regarded as a political decision with historical significance. Finally, with a range of rural reforms, the Chinese government was determined to 'liberalize' its rural economy. That included liberalizing its domestic grain market (and thus liberalizing all agricultural product markets except for tobacco), facilitating the circulation of agricultural products, encouraging labour mobility between rural and urban areas, and implementing a new round of land reform that included adjustments of land use rights and clarifications on the rights to transfer and exchange contracted land. Finally, from 2004 up to the present time, the central government started again to draft 12 Number One Documents concerning agricultural and rural issues. These policies all indicated momentous changes in the agricultural policy of present-day China.

In this context, agricultural co-operatives in China have grown rapidly. On the one hand, thanks to the improvement in markets, producers have started to specialize, thus becoming more efficient in production. Local regions were encouraged to become specialized in planting crops for which they have already established a good reputation, which is known as 'one county, one industry' and 'one village, one product'. Statistics show that the number of villages that became specialized producers of one single product grew from 20 per cent in 1995 to 40 per cent in 2004 (see Huang and Rozelle 2009: 18). Besides, as the agricultural markets developed, producers started to shift into higher-value crops (such as fruit and vegetables, sugar, and tobacco), making planting and marketing decisions increasingly on market-oriented principles (Huang and Rozelle 2006). Along with the development of product markets to foster specialization, on the other hand, changes in the land market also promoted agricultural co-operative development in rural China. As non-agricultural employment opportunities increased, millions of farmers started to seek off-farm jobs. Heterogeneity in households in terms of their on-farm productivities and their ability to access off-farm opportunities triggered their willingness to transfer land-use rights. After recent renewal of land-use contracts for an additional 30 years and the adoption of the Rural Land Contracting Law in 2002, farmers' long-term land use rights were guaranteed, which further stimulated the voluntary land transfer among farmers. As pointed out by a recent OECD report, 'at the centre of this rural adjustment process are agricultural producers who either wish to continue to farm or who realise their skills could yield a higher marginal product if employed elsewhere' (OECD 2015: 101). Land transfers allowed producers to gain access to additional arable land and therefore to scale up their operations, which enhanced their competitiveness. In view of small-scale land holdings per household owing to historical land assignment, transfers in and out of land use rights are considered to be important in enhancing efficiency in resource allocation (Riedinger and Yadav 2009). By the end of June 2014, the total land area being transferred had reached 380 million Mu (equivalent to 25.3 million hectares), accounting for 29 per cent of total arable land in China. There were 60 million households transferring out their partial or total land use rights, accounting for 26 per cent of the total households in rural China.[3]

36.3 Chinese Agricultural Co-operatives: A Diverse Landscape

With enactment of the 2007 law on FSCs, Chinese agricultural co-operatives have become highly institutionalized organizations. But ever since their emergence in the late 1980s, they have been deeply rooted in the local community to satisfy the unmet needs of farmers and other disadvantaged groups. With the development of the market economy during the past 30 years, their evolution has been constantly embedded in the specific historical context. Local traditions, the markets, and institutional pressure from public agencies have all shaped the behaviour and organizational model of these enterprises. Particularly during the past decade, innovative forms of agricultural co-operatives have been emerging, driven by multiple forces and playing varied roles. Meanwhile, many traditional agricultural co-operatives in China have been looking for new ways to raise equity, improve competitiveness, and conform to the new legal norms. In the process of this co-evolution of organizations and institutions in the field of Chinese agricultural co-operatives, the generation and development paths of these enterprises have become highly diversified.

In order to describe the diverse operational patterns of Chinese agricultural co-operatives, we can divide them into four categories, namely, traditional co-operatives, specialized associations, shareholding co-operatives, and co-operative federations

---

[3] See http://news.xinhuanet.com/fortune/2015-03/06/c_1114552428.htm (accessed 29 September 2016).

(see Zhao and Yuan 2014). In numerous previous studies, similar classifications exist (e.g. Huang et al. 2006; Xu and Wu 2014). Generally speaking, traditional agricultural co-operatives represent the very classic model of co-operation by following the ICA principles in a strict way, such as voluntary and open membership, member equal economic participation, limited capital compensation, and democratic member control by 'one member one vote'. Although internationally they are regarded as a majority type (Nilsson et al. 2009), based on an estimation in Xu and Wu (2014), this type accounted for only 10 per cent of the total number of agricultural co-operatives in China. As another traditional type of co-operation, specialized associations are mainly characterized by co-operation based on service provision, such as technical and market information services. Unlike traditional co-operatives that operate on the basis of common property rights, specialized associations tend to have relatively loose contact with their members. Currently, about 30 per cent of the total number of Chinese agricultural co-operatives belong to this type (Xu and Wu 2014).

Shareholding co-operatives and co-operative federations exemplify innovative co-operative forms in the face of a changing environment with increasing market competition. Shareholding co-operative structure is regarded as a hybrid form of co-operation, combining orthodox co-operative principles and an alternative shareholding system (Zhao 2012; Zhao and Develtere 2010). The emergence of shareholding co-operatives had already shown their hybridity: in some cases they emerged when the shareholding system was introduced into collective organizations (e.g. the formation of land shareholding co-operatives); in some cases they were formed when traditional co-operatives transformed their organizational structure and diversified their membership with the purpose of mobilizing additional resources (e.g. a process of organizational change driven by new registration after enactment of the 2007 law on FSCs; see Zhao 2012), and in other cases they were created at the outset (e.g. the establishment of FSCs featured in shareholding systems). So, ever since their development from the mid 1980s, different models of shareholding co-operatives have started to emerge.

The hybridity feature of shareholding co-operatives has certain advantages and is regarded by many as appropriate for China's rural society, which is both labour-abundant and capital-scarce. For example, the study prepared by Fock and Zachernuk (2006: 35) described it as 'common' for Chinese agricultural co-operatives to adopt this form in order to 'raise start-up capital'. This was regarded as 'a major cause of [their] deviations from international co-operative principles' (ibid.). In short, shareholding co-operatives are characterized by the heterogeneity of their membership base and a mixed profit distribution system based on shared capital and patronage. With respect to their membership base, shareholding co-operatives are typified by the co-existence of a small number of big producers and a big number of smallholders. Also, in many cases, they have both individual (farmers or non-farmers) and institutional members (e.g. commercial entities, local supply and marketing co-operatives, village collectives, local public utilities, etc.) (see Zhao 2012: 10). Concerning their profit-distribution system, empirical observation showed the tendency for 'capital control' (Zhang 2004), in that big shareholders as core members and large investors were able to control the organizations and receive much higher dividends than smallholders or common members. According to Xu and Wu (2014), this type accounted for 40 per cent of the total number of Chinese agricultural co-operatives, thus already becoming the dominant form of co-operation in China.[4]

Recently, the imbalance in supply and demand of agricultural products has triggered the emergence of agricultural co-operative federations in China. Although theoretical understanding of co-operative federations in China is still lacking, in practice this phenomenon is widespread. Based on a recent study (RDCF 2014), there are more than 6,000 co-operative federations nationwide, linking 84,000 individual co-operatives and 5.6 million farmer households. These associational organizations can be classified into four types: (1) those based on production, (2) those based on marketing, (3) those based on industrial chains, and (4) regional co-operative federations. Co-operative federations have basically played four roles. First of all, they help increase the negotiating power of individual co-operatives and help strengthen their voice in articulating their interests during price negotiations with input suppliers and processing industries, thus functioning as a competitive yardstick. Secondly, they function to achieve scale economies, and reduce uncertainty and transaction costs. This typically happens in the process of building a farm–supermarket direct supply chain for agricultural products. These inter-organizational networks can bring the scattered co-operatives together to meet supermarkets' requirements for a wide variety of products, large quantities, and continuous supplies. Sometimes supply chain networks may be established when co-operatives enter the processing and storage industries and create their own product brands. These networks also enhance co-operatives' competitiveness through pooling capital for investment. As a third role, co-operative federations help avoid vicious competition among co-operatives having the same or similar products by, for instance, setting up a common price scale (Zhao and Yuan 2014: 49–50). Finally, particularly for regional co-operative federations, they are formed by agricultural co-operatives that have various kinds of products (and non-co-operative types of actors such as commercial enterprises and quasi-public agencies) to provide research and development support and other forms of support for community development (e.g. by facilitating land transfers between member organizations and village communities).

36.4 AGENT-DRIVEN DEVELOPMENT OF CHINESE AGRICULTURAL CO-OPERATIVES

The 2007 law on FSCs particularly encourages producers of similar agricultural products to establish co-operatives. In this type of co-operation, members are relatively

---

[4] This section draws upon Zhao and Yuan (2014: 47–49).

homogeneous and share similar benefits. In reality, however, only a small number of co-operatives are formed by ordinary producers. For Chinese agricultural co-operatives, the multiplicity of their organizational forms has a great bearing on organizational agents, found either in the market, in the (quasi-) public sector, or in civil society.

Concerning the actors driven by the market force, investor-owned commercial companies and business dealers are the two main initiators of agricultural co-operative in China. Previous observations indicate the broad presence of agricultural co-operation led by commercial enterprise in China. In the wake of industrialization and agricultural marketization in the 1990s, large commercial agro-food companies started to build co-operation with upstream and downstream trading partners in order to reduce market uncertainty and risks. Product market competition has led them to establish co-operatives and draw up long-term contracts with farmers. Thanks to the long-term commitment by farmers as product suppliers, these companies were able to reduce transaction costs. The recent changes in institutional environments have provided additional motivations for these profit-seeking companies to found a co-operative, that is, to take advantage of public support in terms of subsidies, grants, and tax exemptions. Furthermore, policy changes in the land market have encouraged them to utilize the organizational form of co-operative to rent more land and expand their scale of operation. In this type of co-operation, however, local governments, as major stakeholders, are very likely to be present and play a co-ordination role.

Public agencies consider the involvement of large commercial companies important in order to achieve agricultural modernization in China and thus encourage it. However, this model is neither farmer-independent nor farmer-determined. As stated by Zhang (2013: 20), '[...] allowing leading enterprises to be members of co-operatives essentially transfers the external relations of leading enterprises, co-operatives and farming households into a co-operative. In other words, it internalizes the relations and conflicts between the different stakeholders'. By internalizing contractual relations, the companies tend to control the co-operatives' decision rights and income rights. Due to the for-profit feature of these corporate entities, they are very likely to prefer the shareholding co-operative structure in working with local producers, and are therefore likely to have the effect of 'capital control'. Besides, in the case of a need for business expansion and development, companies might also be willing to participate in the establishment of co-operative federations, which may in turn facilitate co-operation with other local stakeholders (e.g. producers, co-operatives, village collectives, or public agencies).

Business dealers are mostly local elites that are able to take advantage of new market opportunities. In rural China, they can be large-scale specialized farmers 'who are often part of a disadvantaged group (struggling amid market competition) and have certain economies of scale and relatively highly commercialized agricultural products' (Zhang 2013: 19). The initial motivation for such people to create a co-operative seems to have been an economic one, that is, enlargement of the sales market or achievement of a brand product. In other words, they foresaw the advantage of a co-operative in capturing external economies of scale by linking individual producers with the agro-food supply chain. In the wake of large commercial enterprise stepping into the rural markets in the 1990s, these big specialized growers started to become aware of the importance of building countervailing market power by forming alliances with small local producers. Later on, along with an increase in public subsidies in rural areas, the eagerness to win government projects also became a motivation for them to form co-operatives.

Compared to large commercial enterprises, the rural elites were embedded in local community structures and were able to identify local economic, social, cultural, and value needs. This implanting pushed rural elites to treat co-operatives in a different manner from the way in which large commercial enterprises normally were. That happened particularly at times when there was a drifting away from co-operatives' original goals due to changes in their role identities and behaviours. For example, co-operatives might be empowered by normative systems through accreditation, certification, and awards received from the authorities, and thus start to consciously take up social responsibilities (Zhao 2012). In this case, co-operatives were expected to keep the local agricultural economy alive and to lead social change by creating and managing a project or venture. By using co-operative entrepreneurial principles and the market economy, they were able to solve the region's most pressing social problems and to promote rural development. When motivated by local social, economic, and cultural needs, they could simply follow the legal norms in a strict way, and adopt the principle 'limited capital compensation' to benefit smallholder members, rather than 'capital control'. This model of co-operation has the potential for representing a true partner relationship between the organization and ordinary producer members. However, for the moment, a majority of business dealers, as core members, are found to control the decision rights and income rights of their co-operatives (see Zhao and Yuan 2014: 41). For those driven in large part by pragmatic motivations, or at least in cases in which such motivations outweigh value-based ones, business dealers are likely to choose the shareholding co-operative structure. In this case the outcome is similar to that of for-profit companies as co-operative initiators.

Besides market forces, the (quasi-) public agencies could take the initiative to create an agricultural co-operative. In reality, however, after enactment of the 2007 law on FSCs and since co-operatives are supposed to be self-help organizations, these agencies can no longer be legitimate co-operative initiators. Therefore, as shown in numerous cases, government personnel have been requested to provide personal shares as individual members, to substitute for the government shares provided at the initial stage of co-operative development when there were still no judicial requirements. Field observations have demonstrated that the objectives of public agencies' initiating efforts were multifaceted, combining economic objectives (e.g. building a brand for the local flagship product and raising incomes for farmers), social ones (e.g. job security and local development), and political ones (e.g. keeping local society stable and achieving political performance objectives) (see Zhao and Yuan 2014: 42).

In general and in spite of multiple motivations, public agencies' main concern seems to be the promotion of inclusive local development. For this reason these facilitators are likely to choose the traditional forms of co-operation. Furthermore, with the aim of co-ordinating local public goods provision or supply chain activities, they might also play an important role in promoting the establishment of co-operative federations. Finally, note that owing to the vast geographical area of rural China and its diverse local context, one can observe a different degree of government intervention in the Chinese co-operative field, from a higher degree of intervention in less developed regions to a lower degree of intervention in developed areas. In particular, in less developed regions, when government intervention happens in an intensive manner, co-operatives run the risk of losing their autonomy and decision-making power.

Along with market and public forces, an increasing number of co-operatives are led by civil society actors, including, for example, village communities, non-governmental organizations (NGOs), and international agencies. When co-operative founders are village cadres, they are more likely to be concerned about the role a co-operative can play in community development and how it can enhance villagers' welfare. When local rural elites provide benefits to local citizens by creating a co-operative enterprise, they gain new opportunities to participate in village resource management decisions and thus to receive more political capital. This might pose a potential threat to village leaders in times of village committee elections. For the sake of winning political votes, many village cadres are willing to run a co-operative and help the organization develop in many ways (i.e. by providing infrastructure services, village accountants for co-operatives' book-keeping, and local social networks). Besides, in some of the most developed coastal areas and in peri-urban rural areas characterized by rapid urbanization and industrialization, village leaders tend to use the co-operative form to manage land as collective assets. They are likely to lead the co-operative and represent community interests in the decision-making processes. When village leaders form a co-operative and consider the village collective as an institutional member (such as in the case of land-based co-operatives), the shareholding co-operative structure tends to be adopted. But all organizational forms seem possible in other cases, depending greatly on the motivations of village cadres.

Recently, NGO participation in promoting co-operatives has also been on the rise. Many NGOs supported agricultural co-operatives in China because they foresaw the potential roles a co-operative could play in poverty reduction, work integration, and community development in rural areas. Inspired by the social enterprise model, many Chinese NGOs turned to the co-operative model and started to conduct entrepreneurial and economic risk-taking activities. By carrying out pro-poor businesses, NGOs can overcome the financial constraints and meanwhile fulfil their social mission. In this case, NGOs chose to co-found or provide aid and credits to agricultural co-operatives whose mission appeared to be in accordance with their values. For example, a local federation of the disabled is willing to support an initiative that helps households with people with disabilities plant and sell products, or support those who provide employment opportunities to people with disabilities. A local women's federation may participate in producer co-operatives organized by middle-aged or elderly women. A fair-trade organization can take the lead in organizing local producers to work together for agro-ecological products (e.g. Song et al. 2014; Zachernuk and Liu 2014). In this type of co-operation, co-operative leaders are also willing to co-operate with NGOs for the sake of capital, technical, and social support. Therefore, many NGOs have also played a role in co-operative capital acquisition (see Zhao and Yuan 2014: 44–45).

Somewhat similar to NGOs, international agencies have long been interested in facilitating agricultural co-operative development in China and in designing and carrying out their projects on poverty reduction and community-driven development. International agencies tend to push for a development model with smallholders' participation or a bottom-up approach, autonomy, and democratic member control (Zachernuk and Liu 2014). These aspects are nevertheless different from the other initiators that we have discussed. Driven by their commitment to the values of equity and inclusion, NGOs and international agencies are very likely to prefer the traditional model of co-operation, thus facilitating co-operatives in providing support, such as technical assistance and training, and valuing participative decision-making on the basis of 'one member one vote'.

36.5 CONCLUSIONS

Although the development of Chinese agricultural co-operatives is still at the early stage, these member-based organizations have already explored and developed their own character strengths within the context of rural China. This chapter has presented an analysis of the evolution, the diversity, and the dynamics of agricultural co-operatives and the co-evolution of these organizations and institutions in China. It has also highlighted the contextual influences on the preferences of different actors and their willingness to engage in co-operation. Moreover, this chapter has underlined the rationale of different promoters in the co-operative field by explaining organizational flexibility. In other words, the ownership and control structures formed by different types of stakeholders, together with their choices as regards specific organizational arrangements, have allowed for diversity in Chinese agricultural co-operatives. Triggered by the recently adopted legislative framework, some traditional co-operatives have undergone organizational changes which demonstrate their need to find a new approach in order to engage with the external environment. Meanwhile, the spontaneous emergence of the shareholding co-operative system and co-operative federation structure fully reflect how Chinese agricultural co-operatives take their own initiatives in order to survive, adapt to the external environment, and develop.

Moreover, the discussion on the nature of co-operatives and on non-standard institutional arrangements found in the Chinese co-operative field has indicated the existence of two basic models of co-operation. In the first model, the co-operation is basically formed by owner members and user members (e.g. those formed by ordinary producers and smallholders, or those promoted by NGOs and international agencies). This model represents a standard mechanism of co-operation. In the second model, the co-operation is mainly stimulated by members providing business operation services together with owner members and user members (e.g. those led by investor-owned commercial companies, business dealers, public agencies, village cadres, and other rural elites). When business operators are largely motivated by considerations of self-interest, they seem to share few common interests with smallholders and tend to remain as the main beneficiaries of co-operatives. Consequently, one can observe 'a growing tension between the priorities and values emphasized by different partners and the co-operative sector per se', which 'has raised a number of critical issues influencing rural co-operative development in China', as pointed out by Zhao and Yuan (2014: 55). In this sense, it becomes important for Chinese policy makers to evaluate the impact of the current legislative framework on the development of agricultural co-operatives. Given the rapid increase in co-operative economic activities and the co-evolution of organizations and institutions examined in the previous sections, this chapter envisages the possibility of building a set of legal institutions that can enable, motivate, and guide those business operators as definitive stakeholders to create both private and social wealth. Such institutional developments would further improve the role of the co-operative model in China's agricultural economy and rural development in the near future.

References

Christiansen, F. and Zhang, J., eds, (1998), *Village Inc.: Chinese Rural Society in the 1990s* (Richmond, Surrey: Curzon Press).

Fock, A. and Zachernuk, T. (2006), 'China: Farmers Professional Associations: Review and Policy Recommendations'. Departmental Working Paper Report No. 37430. Washington, DC: World Bank.

Huang, J. and Rozelle, S. (2006), 'The Emergence of Agricultural Commodity Markets in China', *China Economic Review*, 17: 266–80.

Huang, J. and Rozelle, S. (2009), 'Agricultural Development and Nutrition: the Policies behind China's Success', World Food Programme Occasional Paper. No. 19. Beijing: World Food Programme China Office.

Huang, Z., Xu, X., and Song, Y. (2006), 'On the Institutional Arrangements of Farmer Co-operatives in China', in S. Song and A. Chen, eds, *China's Rural Economy after WTO: Problems and Strategies* (Aldershot, England: Ashgate): 325–35.

Melnyk, G. (2009), *Walking Backwards into the Future* (Saskatchewan, Canada: Centre for the Study of Co-operatives, University of Saskatchewan).

Nilsson, J., Kihlén, A., and Norell, L. (2009), 'Are Traditional Co-Operatives an Endangered Species? About Shrinking Satisfaction, Involvement and Trust, *International Food and Agribusiness Management Review*, 12(4): 101–22.

OECD (Organization for Economic Co-operation and Development) (2015). *OECD Economic Surveys: China*. Paris: OECD Publishing. http://dx.doi.org/10.1787/eco_surveys-chn-2015-en/ (accessed 29 September 2016).

RDCF (Research Team on Development of Co-operative Federations) (2014), 'Survey Report on Development of Farmers' Specialized Co-operative Federations', *China Farmers' Co-operatives*, 4: 59–63.

Riedinger, J. M. and Yadav, V. (2009), 'The Impact of Legal Changes on Land Market Activity in China. Mimeo'. Available at http://siteresources.worldbank.org/INTIE/Resources/Riedinger_Yadav_paperRev.docx (accessed on 29 September 2016).

Shen, M., Rozelle, S., and Zhang, L. (2004), 'Farmers' Professional Associations in Rural China: State Dominated or New State-Society Partnerships?' Draft report for the World Bank. http://web.cenet.org.cn/upfile/65141.pdf (accessed on 29 September 2016).

Song, Y., Qi, G., Zhang, Y., and Vernooy, R. (2014), 'Farmer Co-operatives in China: Diverse Pathways to Sustainable Rural Development', *International Journal of Agricultural Sustainability*, 12(2): 95–108.

Xu, X. and Wu, B. (2014), 'The Development of Chinese Co-operatives in Rural Areas', in C. Gijselinckx, L. Zhao, and S. Novkovic, eds, *Co-operative Innovations in China and the West* (Basingstoke: Palgrave MacMillan), 163–178.

Zachernuk, T. and Liu, G. (2014), 'Co-operatives and Poverty Reduction in China', in C. Gijselinckx, L. Zhao, and S. Novkovic, eds, *Co-operative Innovations in China and the West* (Basingstoke: Palgrave MacMillan), 179–97.

Zhang, X. (2004), 'Promoting the Co-Operative Development Led by Agricultural Product Producers: Cases from Farmers' Specialized Co-operatives in Zhejiang', *Chinese Rural Economy*, 11: 4–23.

Zhang, X. (2013), 'Challenges Facing the Development of Farmers' Specialized Co-operatives in China', in Bruno Roelants, ed., *Co-operative Growth for the 21st Century* (Brussels: CICOPA), 19–21.

Zhao, L. (2012), 'New Co-operative Development in China: An Institutional Approach', Doctoral dissertation, Leuven: Institute for International and European Policy, Catholic University of Leuven.

Zhao, L. (2013), 'Conceptualizing the Social Economy in China', *Modern Asian Studies*, 47(3): 1083–123.

Zhao, L. and P. Develtere (2010), 'New Co-operatives in China: Why They Break Away from Orthodox Co-Operatives?', *Social Enterprise Journal*, 6(1): 35–48.

Zhao, L. and P. Yuan (2014), 'Rural Co-operatives in China: Diversity and Dynamics', *The Chinese Economy*, 47(4): 32–62.

PART VIII

....

THE FUTURE
OF CO-OPERATIVES

....

CHAPTER 37

US WORKER CO-OPERATIVES

MARK J. KASWAN

37.1 INTRODUCTION

THE United States has a long and proud tradition of co-operative labour arrangements. However, worker co-operatives today make up a very small portion of the US economy. This chapter will discuss the history and current extent of worker co-operatives in the USA, as well as the particular challenges and opportunities for growth and change in the worker co-operative sector. It will also consider the character of the sector in terms of its principal objectives and orientation.

37.2 HISTORY

The practice of co-operative and collective labour in the United States began long before the country existed. To begin with, most indigenous nations in what is now the USA have emphasized communal values and practised economic co-operation for centuries (Curl 2012). While the modern history of the USA generally excludes these indigenous practices, among the European settlers use of these practices stretches back to the first colonies established by the Pilgrims. All of the early settlements were based on collective labour, including the sharing of the produce of their harvests, at least initially. Curl notes, 'New settlements tended to be collective or communal at first, like Plymouth. While each family staked a separate plot, they still retained their co-operative way of life' (2012).

The advent of industrial production brought with it conflict between workers and the owners of capital. It was not uncommon in the late eighteenth and early nineteenth centuries for striking workers in the USA to set up co-operative workshops to enable them to engage in productive labour while on strike, in some cases competing directly with their employers. However, as these workshops were meant principally as a means of engaging in productive labour while on strike and placing pressure on the employer, they were disbanded as soon as the strike ended (Curl 2012). This kind of organizing had ended by 1815 when a series of court cases involving striking shoemakers found that any collective action for the purpose of raising wages was illegal because it constituted a 'conspiracy in constraint of trade' (Curl 2012).

A different direction for organizing arose in the 1820s, as workers and their advocates turned toward the work of Robert Owen, a Welsh reformer and factory owner, and Charles Fourier, a French social philosopher, who argued for the organization of productive labour into co-operative communities where people would both live and work. Owen came to the USA in 1824 to start a co-operative community called New Harmony. Although the community failed after three years, the idea proved attractive to many. However, co-operative communities were quite different from both the co-operative workshops just mentioned and worker co-operatives today. The notion of shared labour was certainly an element of these communities, but the Owenite model, in particular, called for internal exchange among the members of the community, not the production of goods or provision of services for exchange with non-members.

Once a more favourable legal environment for organizing unions was established in the 1830s, early trades unions often sought to support co-operatives, primarily as a means for developing employment for members who were otherwise unemployed. Economic instability was often an impetus for the development of worker co-operatives in the middle part of the nineteenth century, often with the support of unions (Curl 2012). However, while a crisis could lead to a flourishing of co-operatives, a crash would wipe them out (Curl 2012). Jones finds evidence of over eighty worker co-operatives forming from the 1840s through to the 1870s, with lifespans ranging up to over 20 years (Jones 1979). Aldrich and Stern put the number at about 130 between 1835 and 1874, mostly concentrated in the north-east and upper Midwestern parts of the country. Whether one uses Jones's or Aldrich and Stern's figures, though, as a portion of the US economy the number is, as Aldrich and Stern put it, 'infintesimally small' (Aldrich and Stern 1983). Generally speaking, Aldrich and Stern pin the limited development of worker co-operatives in this period on their inability to overcome the 'emerging individualistic incentives of monopoly capitalism', despite the resources offered by populists and trade unionists (Aldrich and Stern 1983).

The first great wave of worker co-operatives in the USA came with the establishment of the Knights of Labor in 1869. The establishment of 'co-operative institutions such as will tend to supersede the wage-system' was an integral part of their goals (Curl 2012). The Knights were the largest part of a movement referred to as 'labor republicanism' that offered a kind of 'social democratic vision' that asserted 'a direct link between civic virtue, political democracy, and the economic welfare of the laboring classes' (Fink 1988). Estimates vary, but hundreds of co-operatives were established by the Knights between 1880 and 1888 (Curl 2012). At its peak there were between 750,000 and a million members of Knights of Labor locals (Curl 2012). However, the Knights and the co-operatives were attacked by established business interests who undertook concerted action to make it difficult for the co-operatives to do business, and, not long after their peak, they collapsed. Most of the co-operatives were gone by 1888 (Curl 2012).[1]

During the Great Depression of the 1930s, hundreds of thousands of unemployed workers organized themselves on the principle of mutual aid into labour exchanges in which they would exchange labour for goods, or 'surplus labor for surplus products' (Taylor and Kerr 1934). In fact, those who were engaged in these were still considered 'unemployed', and the organizations they formed often served a dual purpose, organizing both productive labour and political action to demand support and aid for the people. Many of them were quite informal in structure and may be better understood as barter systems than what might be recognized today as worker co-operatives. They were quite popular and extensive. By the end of 1932 some 300,000 people were members in 37 states, and by the end of 1934 a survey found 310 different organizations with a total membership of over 500,000 members (Curl 2012). One of the first acts in the New Deal was the establishment of a Division of Self-Help Co-operatives to provide technical assistance and grants to support co-operatives and barter associations (Curl 2012). Although in some cases they were supported by state and federal grants, the co-operatives and their supporting organizations largely died out with the formal establishment of works programmes by the federal government (Taylor and Kerr 1934; Curl 2012).

The rise of the Cold War and suspicion of worker co-operatives as excessively socialistic led to a decline in organizing activity in the 1950s, but the radical politics of the 1960s and 1970s led to a new, very active, and highly ideological period of worker co-operative development. The vast majority of these were small collectives that sought to function outside of the capitalist system. These were particularly oriented around the food distribution system, with between 5,000 and 10,000 small food co-operatives (including worker-owned, consumer-owned, and hybrid structures) being formed in the 1970s, with several thousand still in existence and doing some $500 million in annual business in 1979. However, these faced both internal and external pressures. The internal pressures included ideological conflict; the external pressures included the increasing adoption of organic and natural foods—a co-op innovation—by mainstream grocery stores (Curl 2012).

The 1980s, dominated by the conservative politics and aggressive capitalism of the Reagan era, was a period of retrenchment. Curl estimates that, at its peak, 'There were probably some 750 to 1,000 small worker and producer co-operatives and collectives in 1979, most of them averaging fewer than fifteen members.... In total, there were probably some 17,000 members.... Only a small fraction remained by 1989' (2012). A new

---

[1] Opposition by the established business community strengthened as they grew. However, their collapse was especially rapid as a consequence of events that led up to and followed from the 1886 bombing and subsequent police action at Haymarket Square in Chicago. The media of the time blamed the Knights for the unrest. As Curl puts it, 'railroads refused to haul their products; manufacturers refused to sell them needed machinery; wholesalers refused them raw materials and supplies; banks wouldn't lend' (Curl 2012).

phase began in the 1990s with the establishment of regional organizations in the four primary centres of worker co-operative activity in the USA: the San Francisco Bay Area, the Pacific Northwest, the upper Midwest (principally Minnesota and Wisconsin), and New England (particularly Massachusetts). Increasing organizational capacity in these regions, and increasing communication between the regions, led to the first national conference of worker co-operatives and the establishment of the US Federation of Worker Co-operatives (USFWC) in 2004. The Great Recession of 2008–9 and the Occupy Wall Street movement in 2011 provided new impetus and interest in worker co-operatives as alternative forms of economic organization that would help to address problems of economic inequality as well as promote social democratization.

37.3 CURRENT SIZE AND EXTENT

An exact accounting of worker co-operatives in the USA is difficult because there is no standard manner by which they are established (Deller et al. 2009). The incorporation of businesses is generally a state matter, and there is substantial variation among the 50 states with respect to their statutes and the degree to which they recognize co-operatives as a distinct form of business. Certain ambiguities as to what constitutes a worker co-operative adds to the difficulty, for example where, for legal reasons, enterprises that function as a worker co-operative may technically be organized as marketing co-operatives.[2]

The effect of all this is that there does not exist a conclusive accounting of the number of worker co-operatives in the USA, their economic impacts, or the number of people they employ. In 2014 the Democracy at Work Institute (DAWI) conducted a survey of members of the US Federation of Worker Co-operatives and other firms they could identify as worker co-operatives. They found 256 co-operatives in the USA and Puerto Rico employing an estimated 6,300 workers, with annual revenue of $367 million. The cities of San Francisco and New York account for 30 per cent of all worker co-operatives in the USA. Most of the rest can be found in the Pacific Northwest, Massachusetts, and Madison, Wisconsin (Palmer 2014).

The Democracy at Work Institute study shows that worker co-operatives in the US are fairly young, with 80 of the 256 co-operatives having been formed since 2010 and over half founded since 2000. Palmer suggests that this may reflect a surge in interest in worker ownership in the wake of the Great Recession, although he notes that without the advantage of longitudinal data, it is impossible to determine whether this is a

---

[2] For immigrant communities in which significant numbers of workers are undocumented, the worker co-operative model enables workers to remain technically self-employed. Although they are blocked by law from becoming formally employed, there are no statutory prohibitions against their being self-employed and from forming what are, in effect, marketing and support co-operatives that assist the self-employed workers and enable them to engage in mutual support.

normal pace for co-operative creation or whether it reflects a short lifespan for this type of business (Palmer 2014). Of further note is that 42 per cent of all worker co-operatives were conversions from conventional businesses, volunteer organizations, or non-profits (Palmer 2014). They also tend to be small, with a median size of ten employees, but because this does not take into account whether they are full- or part-time employees, the number of full-time equivalents is almost certainly smaller.

The demographics of the worker co-operative work force are significantly different from those of the economy as a whole. Over 70 per cent of workers in co-operatives are women (versus 47 per cent in the general work force), and over 65 per cent are Latina/ Latino or African American (versus 34% for US workers generally). Much of the difference comes from the fact that 52 per cent of employees in worker co-operatives are in the home care industry, which is dominated by Latina or African American women. As it happens, the largest co-operative in the USA, Co-operative Home Care Associates (CHCA), has about 2,400 employees (including both members and non-members), which alone accounts for at least one-third of all employees of US worker co-operatives, so any discussion of the work force must take this into account. CHCA's dominance may also help explain why compensation was found to be somewhat lower—and in some cases substantially lower—than that found in their respective industrial sectors. According to Palmer, worker co-operatives, including CHCA, are concentrated in 'the lower-paying portions of their industrial sectors … (e.g. home care presence in the overall health sector, bike taxis in the transportation sector, etc.)' (Palmer 2014). The rate of worker-ownership for the firms reporting, however, is quite high, at 84 per cent, so to the extent that the co-operatives are profitable, patronage dividends may help boost their compensation.

After home care, retail is the second largest industrial sector for worker co-operatives in terms of number of workers. In terms of the number of firms, the largest sectors are manufacturing (16%), retail trade (15%), and accommodation and food services (12%). In terms of revenue, the largest sectors are manufacturing, retail trade, and healthcare in that order (Palmer 2014).

On average, worker co-operatives report higher rates of profit than the US average (6.4% vs. 5.9%). The average profit in manufacturing co-operatives is double, and nearly triple in the retail trades. However, these results must be tempered by the fact that the estimates of total revenue and profitability suffer from low levels of reporting (97 co-operatives reported total revenue, and only 67 reported profit data). The small size could reflect self-selection, as one might imagine that those that are more established and are doing well would be more likely to report than others (Palmer 2014).

The Democracy at Work Institute report provides a reasonable estimate, and at least provides a sense of the magnitude of the size of the worker co-operative sector in the USA. Even if the census only captures half of the existing co-operatives, it does not change the assessment that worker co-operatives make up a very small portion of the US economy. Nonetheless, more needs to be done to get an accurate picture of their size and extent. That said, the variety of organizational/corporate forms and the lack of a national standard present significant challenges for researchers.

37.4 GROWTH AND CHANGE

Given the advantages of the worker co-operative model, researchers and advocates have long asked why there aren't more of them in the USA. Abell (2014) identifies several factors that combine to constrain their growth. The first is a cultural barrier, as individualism and self-reliance are written deeply into the American narrative. Further, the relative rarity of worker co-operatives means that most Americans are simply unfamiliar with them. Given that elites have engaged in a decades-long ideological campaign against anything that contains hints of socialism—such as workers owning the means of production—worker co-operatives are viewed with suspicion. So, while worker co-operatives have vocal supporters on both the right and left of the political spectrum, public policy is, generally speaking, not supportive.

A general lack of business acumen among co-operative entrepreneurs is a second problem identified by Abell (2014). Worker co-operatives tend to attract people who have less interest in the traditional measures of success and little appreciation for the skills associated with business success. In addition, a preference for the collective form, which requires high levels of engagement by all members of the co-operative, suppresses growth because the members of such organizations generally want to maintain a small size. As a result, while they may be quite successful, they have little or no incentive to grow.

The problems of culture and business skills are significant, although addressable through outreach, education, and training. A third major difficulty, more deeply embedded in the structure of the US economic system, is the problem of financing. There are two sides to this. First, worker co-operatives are particularly attractive for low-income communities as a means of building wealth. But people who are poor have few assets—either of their own or that they can get from friends or family—that they can use to start a business. Even if they have some assets they may run into a second problem: the reluctance of traditional lenders to finance something unfamiliar to them. 'Investors', notes a co-operative developer, 'are skeptical of the co-op structure'. In traditional banking circles, the co-operative model 'is not well understood, and accountability is perceived as too diffuse' (Abell 2014). The exclusion of investors from any role in governance only adds to the discomfort of traditional lenders, even if the terms are favourable. A final challenge for finding funding, particularly for low-income individuals who wish to establish a co-operative in a low-margin industry, is that they require what Abell calls 'patient capital' that is willing to allow longer than normal terms (2014).

A further challenge Abell identifies for worker co-operative development and growth is what some consider its greatest strength: the democratic nature of the enterprise. But while the democratic process can be highly efficient, it often requires a substantial amount of training and commitment. In a society that values social independence but paradoxically expects that labour relations will be hierarchical, most people do not have well-developed skills when it comes to participation in democratic procedures. By the same token, those who form worker co-operatives precisely because they are attracted to their democratic character may react strongly against the attempts of individuals to take on the kinds of leadership roles that may be crucial for success. As one worker co-operative developer puts it, 'Leadership is a bad word in our movement' (Abell 2014).

A further constraint is that worker co-operatives in the USA have been developed and have operated in an autonomous fashion with little or no attention to the need for a supportive infrastructure that would help them address the challenges already discussed. While some regional associations have been established over the years, these were generally quite weak, and their ability to provide technical or other kinds of mutual support has been limited. This has begun to change somewhat, as will be discussed, but the US Federation of Worker Co-operatives is still primarily a membership organization that serves to promote the interests of its members, in contrast to an organization dedicated to providing direct support for either existing or developing co-operatives.

Despite all these barriers, there are reasons to believe that the worker co-operative sector may see significant growth over the next five to ten years. It has received renewed attention in the aftermath of the Great Recession and Occupy Wall Street as an economic model that can address problems of inequality of wealth and income as well as a means of revitalizing local economies, building local wealth, and anchoring jobs in communities.[3]

Many of these new initiatives are led by non-profit organizations with a broader social mission. Because of the fiscal and organizational challenges involved, including the need for start-up capital as well as a lack of business expertise, Ji and Robinson (2012) note that in low-income immigrant communities in particular, most worker co-operatives are developed by mission-driven non-profit organizations whose staff do much of the work of creating and supporting the businesses.

A significant feature of some of these development efforts—for example, the Arizmendi bakery co-operatives in the San Francisco Bay Area and the Evergreen co-operatives in Cleveland, Ohio—is that they are modelled on the successful Mondragón co-operatives based in Spain. In particular, they establish a central organization, similar in some respects to Mondragón's Caja Laboral, that acts as the developer of the co-operatives that will be associated with that organization. The organization provides education and training, as well as administrative and other support services to the co-operatives in return for a percentage of either the gross revenue or net proceeds of the business. The non-profit organization may also establish a development fund as the depository for asset (capital) accounts established by the co-operatives they develop, providing assets that can be leveraged in the development of new co-operatives. By centralizing technical support and establishing a development fund, these organizations are able to address some of the key barriers that have been discussed.

---

[3] In fact, this renewed interest predates the Great Recession. See, for example, the work of Gar Alperovitz 2005.

The Evergreen co-operatives, developed with the assistance of the Democracy Collaborative based at the University of Maryland, are also an example of the use of worker co-operatives as a strategy for community and economic development. In particular, Evergreen is an example of development through partnering with so-called anchor institutions, or large-scale public institutions that are anchored in their community—in other words, they are extremely unlikely to relocate. The goal is to capture a portion of these institutions' annual expenditures and redirect it to locally owned worker co-operatives in order to alleviate significant problems of poverty in the surrounding community. In contrast to the traditional grass-roots model of organizing a co-operative, however, this is a top-down development. All of the preparatory work necessary to establish the business is completed by the developer, and the workers—who would become the owners—are only brought in once the preliminary steps have been completed.

A more grass-roots approach to developing worker co-operatives to alleviate poverty is found in the suite of co-operatives developed by the Center for Family Life (CFL) in Brooklyn, NY. A Catholic social service agency that for many years engaged in workforce development, helping local low-income residents prepare résumés and improve their job skills, staff at the Center for Family Life found that their efforts were not bearing fruit because of a lack of job opportunities. In 2006 Center for Family Life staff decided that the co-operative model could address this problem, and invited graduates of the training programme to work with them to develop a co-operative. Their first co-operative, Sí Se Puede! (Yes We Can!) is a residential house-cleaning company; an additional five co-operatives, all service based (including babysitting, elder care, and dog walking), have since been developed.[4]

In addition, the Democracy at Work Institute is taking an active role in promoting worker co-operative development. One important project involves reaching out to single proprietors of established businesses who are nearing retirement but lack a plan for succession; conversion to a worker co-operative may be the only option to save the business and employees' jobs, which is an especially important issue in rural areas where there are few employers (Institute 2014). In addition to conducting and supporting research into worker co-operatives, the Democracy at Work Institute is the home to the Democracy at Work Network (DAWN), a peer-advice network made up of experienced developers and members of worker co-operatives who have completed a training and certification process in order to be able to provide other co-operatives with technical support. This does not address the crucial issue of financing, but the provision of technical support that can help to ensure the success of worker co-operatives and promote their growth will make it easier for new co-operatives to obtain financing. Other initiatives, such as a national credit union specifically organized for worker co-operatives, are being developed to help address the fiscal issues.

---

[4] Interview with Vanessa Bransburg, Center for Family Life co-operative programme director, 1/8/2015.

37.5 Economic and Ideological Motives

The worker co-operative movement in the USA can be characterized in terms of a set of four principal motivations or orientations that fall under two categories (see Table 37.1). The first category is primarily economic in nature. The main motive for the first type is self-interest: the workers want to be able to capture the surplus value of their labour, less for ideological reasons than for the greater material gain they can realize. Where the main motivation is simply to prevent the workplace from closing, the idea of democratizing it may be a secondary or even an undesirable consequence. A second type is socially oriented, for example the Evergreen or CFL co-operatives, which are developed to address serious problems of poverty in low-income communities.

In the second category are found the third group, made up of those co-operatives that form for ideological reasons, either because the workers feel that they have a right to the full produce of their labour, or because of an interest in workplace democracy and an antipathy toward the traditional hierarchical structure of the workplace. The individuals involved in these co-operatives may or may not see themselves as part of a broader movement. The fourth and final group, then, consists of those who are attracted to worker co-operatives as part of a broad-based movement for fundamental social change.

Because the first group's principal orientation is employees' self-interest, they may be difficult to spot. These are most likely to want to maintain a high level of autonomy and

Table 37.1 Categories of Worker Co-operatives in the United States Based on Principal Motivation

Category	Orientation	Description	Examples
Economic	Micro	Employees seek to retain their jobs, capture the full produce of their labour	Conversions from traditional businesses
	Social	Poverty alleviation, community asset-building	Evergreen, Center for Family Life, Prospera, Project Equity
Ideological	Micro	Emphasis on workplace democracy in management and governance, workers' right to the full produce of their labour	Individual co-operatives
	Social	Worker co-operatives as a vehicle for social change to a more egalitarian and democratic society; empowerment of low-income communities	Democracy at Work Institute; Association of Arizmendi Co-operatives

Source: Author's analysis.

have less interest in participating in national meetings or responding to surveys, and they are unlikely to see themselves as part of a larger movement for social and economic change.[5]

The area of poverty alleviation is where the most development activity is currently taking place. The Evergreen and the Center for Family Life co-operatives are intended as models for worker co-operative development targeting an impoverished community. In addition to paying above-average wages for typically low-wage work, the co-operatives enable people who have historically had great difficulty acquiring meaningful assets to gain equity and ownership of businesses that will help them work their way out of poverty. Cities in the USA have begun to notice these efforts and support them. Evergreen, for example, received crucial support from city agencies in Cleveland. In 2010, the city of Richmond, California, established an office specifically to promote the development of worker co-operatives. In 2014 a coalition of worker co-operatives and advocates for low-income communities succeeded in getting the New York City Council to agree to establish a $1.2 million fund to assist the development of worker co-operatives, and in January, 2015, the city of Madison, Wisconsin, committed five million dollars over five years to support worker co-operatives in that city.

For organizations developing worker co-operatives to address endemic poverty, the ideas of worker control and the development of democratic businesses are seen as important and valuable, but they are not their primary motivating factors. It is also significant to note that the development of these worker co-operatives is not initiated by the workers themselves, although, as has been discussed, Evergreen and the Center for Family Life approach the development process differently.

The second general category includes co-operatives that are primarily organized for ideological reasons, particularly with respect to the rights of workers to work in a fully democratic workplace and to control the surplus value of their labour. Oftentimes these are established explicitly as an alternative to the traditional capitalist model, although in contrast to the co-operatives in the 1960s and 1970s, they often pay greater attention to the need to remain viable as businesses.

The fourth group is primarily made up of developers of worker co-operatives who see them as an essential element for broad-based social change. The Arizmendi bakeries in the San Francisco Bay Area are a good example of this type. Two of the founders, Tim Huet and Jaques Kaswan, are long-time activists in the co-operative movement who wanted to set up worker co-operatives as a viable element of an alternative economic system based on democratic principles.[6] The US Federation of Worker Co-operatives itself makes quite clear that they have a strong social-change agenda, although not all its members necessarily consider that their first priority.

---

[5] A consequence of this is that a census of worker co-operatives such as the Democracy at Work Institute's will be unlikely to find them, resulting in an undercounting of worker co-operatives.

[6] Huet articulates the social change agenda in his *Cooperative Manifesto* (2004), as does Kaswan in an unpublished 1988 manuscript entitled *Cooperative Democracy*.

These different motivations are not mutually exclusive. Workers who form a co-operative or take over an existing business primarily for economic reasons may also like the idea of democratic governance by the workers and believe that forming as a co-operative will help build a more just and democratic society. Those who are mostly interested in developing worker co-operatives as a community and economic development strategy often do so precisely because of their concerns about inequality and their interest in broad social change. In some cases, where the primary motivation is to create decent-paying, stable jobs for low-income workers, a longer-term objective is to empower the workers more broadly.[7]

37.6 CONCLUSION

The US economy is very large, and worker co-operatives make up only a very small part of it. Despite their long history, as a sector of the economy they face substantial challenges to attaining significant scale. New initiatives, such as the San Francisco Bay-based Project Equity, are developing creative approaches to address those challenges.[8] The Democracy at Work Institute and the US Federation of Worker Co-operatives are actively working to expand the sector. Worker co-operatives may be expected to remain a fairly small part of the US economy for some time, but they may be able to make a significant difference in the lives of people in the communities where they do have a presence.

REFERENCES

Abell, Hilary (2014), *Worker Co-operatives: Pathways to Scale* (Takoma Park, MD: The Democracy Collaborative).

Aldrich, Howard and Stern, Robert N. (1983), 'Resource Mobilization and the Creation of US Producers' Co-Operatives, 1835-1935', *Economic and Industrial Democracy* 4(3), 371–406.

Alperovitz, Gar (2005), *America Beyond Capitalism: Reclaiming our Wealth, our Liberty, and our Democracy* (Hoboken, NJ: John Wiley & Sons).

Curl, John (2012), *For All the People: Uncovering the Hidden History of Co-operation, Co-operative Movements, and Communalism in America*, 2nd ed. (Oakland, CA: PM Press).

Deller, Steven, Hoyt, Ann, Hueth, Brent, and Sundaram-Stukel, Reka (2009), *Research on the Economic Impact of Co-operatives* (Madison: University of Wisconsin Center for Co-operatives).

Fink, Leon (1988), 'The New Labor History and the Powers of Historical Pessimism: Consensus, Hegemony, and the Case of the Knights of Labor', *The Journal of American History* 75(1), 115–36.

---

[7] This is the case, for example, with the non-profit co-operative incubator Prospera. See http://prosperacoops.org/ (accessed 30 September 2016).

[8] http://www.project-equity.org/our-solution/ (accessed 30 September 2016).

Huet, Tim (2004), 'A Co-operative Manifesto', *Grassroots Economic Organizing* (61) (March–April), 10–12.

Institute, Democracy at Work (2014), *The Rural Succession Dilemma and the Co-operative Solution, Research Publication Series* (San Francisco, CA: Democracy at Work Institute).

Ji, Minsun and Robinson, Tony (2012), *Immigrant Worker Owned Co-operatives: A User's Manual* (Middleton, WI: The Co-operative Foundation).

Jones, Derek, (1979), 'U.S. Producer Co-operatives: The Record to Date, *Industrial Relations* 18(3), 342–57.

Kaswan, Jaques (1988), 'Cooperative Democracy', unpublished ms.

Palmer, Timothy C. (2014), *Democratic Workplace Ownership After the Great Recession* (San Francisco, CA: Democracy at Work Institute).

Taylor, Paul S. and Kerr, Clark (1934), 'Putting the Unemployed at Productive Labor', *Annals of the American Academy of Political and Social Science* 176, 104–10.

CHAPTER 38

....

THE ESSENTIAL ROLE
OF CO-OPERATIVE LAW
AND SOME RELATED ISSUES

....

ANTONIO FICI

38.1 THE ESSENTIAL ROLE
OF CO-OPERATIVE LAW

....

CO-OPERATIVE law falls within organizational law, thus sharing, in principle, its general objectives. The real question, therefore, is whether co-operative law performs any specific function in relation to organizational law in general or to the organizational law of other entities, notably company law.

Professors Hansmann and Kraakman assign to organizational law the essential role of providing a form of 'asset partitioning' that could not be established otherwise.[1] In the same article, they also address the issue of whether the 'formal separation of control rights from distribution rights whereby those who control the firm are barred from appropriating the firm's net earnings'—a defining feature of non-profit entities—is an attribute that these entities may enjoy without the benefit of specially designed organizational law. They conclude that it would not be feasible and, consequently, that the provision of the non-distribution constraint constitutes an essential function of the law of non-profit organizations.[2]

Although the previous argument regards non-profit entities, it is also relevant to co-operative law to the extent that co-operatives, like non-profit entities, are characterized

---

[1] Hansmann and Kraakman (2000), 386 ff. As the authors explain, 'essential' means that for aspects of organizational law other than asset partitioning, workable substitutes could be found elsewhere in the law (ivi, p. 437).

[2] Hansmann and Kraakman (2000), 435 ff. and see ivi fn. 77 for explanation.

by a specific purpose, which co-operative law, like the law of non-profit entities, should recognize and protect. Indeed, when a legal entity, or category of legal entities, has a defining feature that relates to the objective it pursued—whether negative (the profit non-distribution constraint that qualifies non-profit entities) or positive (the mutual purpose that qualifies co-operatives)—the organizational law of that entity, or category of entities, defines the entity's particular identity in light of its objective.

This applies to a greater extent to co-operatives, since their identity is complex and consists of several, at times interrelated, aspects, which do not only pertain to their purpose.[3] Stipulating the co-operative identity and preserving its distinguishing features should therefore be considered the primary objective of co-operative law. Indeed, the rigidity of the co-operative form, which results from its identity being defined by law, enhances a founder's or member's 'ability to signal, via their choice of form, the terms that the firm offers to other contracting parties, and to make credible [their] commitment not to change those forms'.[4] Therefore, by establishing and mandating a precise co-operative identity, co-operative law does not perform a prescriptive function but an enabling function.[5]

This seems evident also with respect to the relationship between the organizational law of co-operatives and other bodies of law that deal with co-operatives, notably tax law and competition law. Indeed, if organizational law carefully defines the co-operative legal identity, it is possible to justify a particular treatment of co-operatives under tax law. This treatment would not be preferential but simply specific to the subject matter that it regulates and would therefore be perfectly compatible with competition law.[6]

38.2 THE CO-OPERATIVE PURPOSE

In principle, there are three general purposes among which a legal entity may elect its ultimate objective. The for-profit purpose entails doing business with the aim of making profits and distributing them to the owners of the legal entity. The not-for-profit purpose entails conducting an activity without the aim of distributing profits to the owners of the legal entity.[7] The mutual purpose, which characterizes co-operatives and constitutes the focus of the following analysis, must be distinguished by both the for-profit and the not-for-profit purpose, although it shares some traits of both.

---

[3] An analysis of the aspects of the co-operative identity other than the mutual purpose would exceed the scope of this chapter; see however Fici (2013a) and Fici (2013b).

[4] In these terms, see Kraakman et al. (2009), 22.

[5] On the possible enabling function performed by mandatory rules, in a similar way to default rules and in a context of plurality of legal forms and freedom of choice among these forms, see ibid.

[6] For this kind of effectiveness of co-operative organization law, with specific regard to the regulation of the European Cooperative Society, see the judgment by the Court of Justice of the European Union of 8 September 2011 (C-78/08 to C-80/08), and Fici (2013c).

[7] What therefore qualifies non-profits is the 'non-distribution constraint' and not the fact that they are barred from earning profits from an economic activity: see Hansmann (1996), 17 ff.

The famous Rochdale Society of Equitable Pioneers began its operations by selling basic foodstuff to, and in the interest of, its members. As stated in its objects, the Society acted 'for the pecuniary benefit, and improvement of the social and domestic condition of its members' by performing several economic activities, including 'the establishment of a store for the sale of provisions', the manufacturing of articles for the employment of unemployed or underemployed members, and the purchase or rent of estates of land to be cultivated by the members.

The Rochdale Society's objectives substantially coincide with those that existing co-operative law attributes to co-operatives. Indeed, although differences of various extent and nature may be found across jurisdictions,[8] co-operatives are legal entities that conduct an enterprise in the interest of their members as consumers, providers, or workers of that enterprise. This organizational objective may be referred to as 'mutual purpose', although only in some countries is this exact formula employed by legislatures and/or legal scholarship to identify the co-operative objective and distinguish it from that of other legal entities.[9]

More precisely, the co-operative objective comprises two elements: the ultimate purpose of benefiting members and the conduct of a particular activity to fulfil this purpose, namely, an enterprise with the members as consumers of the goods or services provided by the co-operative ('consumer co-operatives'), as providers of the goods or services employed by the co-operative for running its business ('producer co-operatives'), or as workers of the co-operative enterprise ('worker co-operatives').

Since benefiting members is a purpose that is common to all the legal entities that pursue an 'internal' goal, the specificity of the mutual purpose (and of co-operatives pursuing it) lies in the particular activity that is essential for both the co-operative to achieve its ultimate goal and for its members to satisfy their individual interests.

The development of this particular activity with the members (or 'co-operative enterprise') is a characteristic of co-operatives that significantly contributes to their distinction from companies. In companies, like in any other for-profit entity, the economic activity is simply an instrument for pursuing the entity's final objectives, and it is irrelevant whether this activity is conducted with the members. By contrast, co-operatives are formed and exist to run an enterprise that may directly satisfy the interests of their consumer-, provider-, or worker-members.[10]

The nature of the co-operative purpose affects the nature of co-operative membership. In principle, members of a co-operative may only be those who are interested in and can make use of the particular service provided by the co-operative, and are therefore consumers, providers, or workers of the co-operative enterprise. Consequently, in

---

[8] See Cracogna et al. (2013), where this aspect is usually treated in the third section of the various chapters in part III. See also Fici (2013c), 56 ff.

[9] A 'mutual purpose' is explicitly referred to co-operatives, for example, by Italian law (see art. 2511, Italian civil code).

[10] This may also be expressed by the distinction between a 'profit undertaking' and a 'service undertaking' as conceptualized by Fauquet (1951), 88 ff.

co-operative theory it is usually stated that members of co-operatives possess a 'double quality' since they are at the same time members of the co-operative entity and users of the co-operative enterprise. Similarly, the 'identity principle' is invoked in order to point out the fact that, in a co-operative, members (of the organization) and users (of the enterprise performed by the organization) are identical, which is not necessarily the case in other business organizations.[11]

This aspect per se appears sufficient to successfully oppose the theory according to which co-operatives are not dissimilar from companies, or rather that companies are a particular type of producer co-operative, that is, 'lenders' co-operatives' or 'capital co-operatives'.

Professor Henry Hansmann—moving from the assumptions that the owners of a firm 'are those persons who share two formal rights: the right to control the firm and the right to appropriate the firm's profits, or residual earnings'; that a firm's patrons are 'all persons who transact with a firm either as purchasers of the firm's products or as sellers to the firm of supplies, labour, or other factors of production'; and that 'nearly all large firms that have owners are owned by persons who are also patrons'[12]—comes to the conclusion that 'the conventional investor-owned firm is nothing more than a special type of producer co-operative—a lenders' co-operative, or capital co-operative'.[13] Indeed—like in a typical producer co-operative, for example, a cheese co-operative owned by farmers who supply the factory with raw milk—in a capital co-operative, owners are those persons who supply a particular factor of production, that is, capital. In Hansmann's words, 'the members of the capital co-operative each lend the firm a given sum of money, which the firm uses to purchase the equipment and other assets it needs to operate'.[14]

Certainly, if one considers the firm's ownership structure alone and adopts general concepts of firm owners and patrons, one may correctly conclude that investor-owned companies cannot be distinguished from co-operatives, that the co-operative is the general conceptual category of patron-owned firms, and that companies conceptually pertain to the category of co-operatives and represent a particular species of producer co-operatives.[15] This reasoning, however, fails to consider the previously described double quality of co-operative members, which the participants of a company, that is, the shareholders, do not possess.

Shareholders, as such, do not make use of the company's enterprise and do not directly benefit from it. The relationship of shareholders with the company only takes place at the organizational level and does not involve a parallel transaction for the exchange of goods or services or the execution of work. In other words, shareholders are only owners of the company and are not also users of its enterprise. The provision of capital is the

[11] See Münkner (1974), 31 ff.
[12] Hansmann (1996), 11 ff.
[13] Hansmann (1996), p. 11.
[14] Ibid., 14.
[15] See Hansmann (2013).

'price' they pay to become owners and not the object of an additional transaction with their company.[16]

In contrast, the members of a co-operative (or 'co-operators') are the direct users and beneficiaries of the co-operative enterprise. The co-operative enterprise serves their needs directly and not only indirectly (by capital remuneration and/or share appreciation), as it occurs in companies with regard to shareholders.[17]

Co-operative members take on two types of relationship with the co-operative:[18] the organizational relationship which stems from their status of members (normally also as contributors of capital) and the transactional relationship which derives from the fact that they are providers, consumers, or workers of the co-operative enterprise. The two relationships are connected; in many jurisdictions they may even be subject to the same body of law (i.e. co-operative organizational law) and be hardly distinguishable one from the other, but they never entirely overlap.

In any event, co-operatives and companies—or, if one prefers, co-operatives and 'capital co-operatives'—differ in many other substantial aspects. Indeed, as previously stated, the legal identity of co-operatives is not limited to the functional aspect and the related ownership structure, but includes governance and financial aspects that are typical of co-operatives and cannot be found in other business organizations. The democratic principle 'one member, one vote', which ensures the democratic control of the organization by its members (and excludes the control by only one member or by a minority of members), and moreover precludes the external control of a co-operative; the partial 'outward' orientation, which makes meeting the members' needs the main but not the exclusive mission of a co-operative; as well as the variability of capital and the 'open-door' principle, which permits third parties to share the utility that a co-operative is able to produce, all definitely differentiate co-operatives from companies and determine, as we shall observe, their unique 'social function' compared to other business organizations, notably for-profit stock companies.

38.3 CO-OPERATIVE TRANSACTIONS AND THEIR REGULATION

Implementation of the mutual purpose involves transactions between the co-operative and its members for the exchange of goods or services or for the execution of work,

---

[16] By way of contrast, Hansmann (1996), 14, holds that members' contributions of capital are, in effect, loans, although the fact that the fixed interest rate paid on loans from lender-members is typically set at zero obscures this fact.

[17] The role of the enterprise is, therefore, diverse in co-operatives and in companies. As Charles Gide (1921), 12, puts it, 'it is only in co-operative association that production is organized solely with the view of satisfying needs', whereas in companies, production is a means for making profits.

[18] Or, if one wants to adopt a slightly different view shared by some jurisdictions, one must state, in a partially different way, that the relationship between the co-operative and its members comprises both an organizational relationship and an exchange relationship.

depending on the type of co-operative. Among all the transactions that are necessary for a co-operative to act as a firm in the market, these transactions play a distinctive role. They are the very transactions through which co-operatives fulfil their typical purpose and co-operative members satisfy their individual interests: the *raison d'être* of a co-operative for those who establish it. For this reason, in co-operative legal theory these transactions ('co-operative transactions') must be kept separate from all others, first of all by giving them a distinctive name, as some co-operative laws appropriately do, using formulas such as 'co-operative acts' (as in the Latin American legal environment) or 'mutual relationships' (as in Italian law).[19]

Due to their particular function, co-operative transactions require specific regulation. A matter that needs careful consideration is, for example, whether and to what extent a co-operative and its members are (or must be) obligated to transact with each other. Evidently, a co-operative that does not engage in transactions with its members does not fulfil its institutional purpose and does not satisfy the interests of its members. By the same token, a member that does not participate in co-operative transactions would prevent a co-operative from fulfilling its purpose (and indirectly, the other members from satisfying their interests). Therefore, freedom to transact is incompatible with the concept of co-operative, especially if the co-operative is given such a freedom.

On the other hand, the law can hardly state the exact extent of the obligation to transact. Consequently, in principle, a reasonable solution to this problem is to leave to co-operative by-laws the freedom to regulate the matter, by making it, however, compulsory for them to provide for the minimum extent to which co-operative members are obligated to transact with the co-operative, or at least for the manner in which it is to be determined. This corresponds approximately to the co-operative practice, especially in agricultural co-operatives where the problem of inactive members is probably perceived more than in other types of co-operatives (for example, large consumer co-operatives, such as co-operative banks), and to the solution adopted by some co-operative laws.[20] This issue may also be dealt with by awarding co-operatives the right to expel inactive members and members the right to withdraw from the co-operative if the co-operative refuses to transact with them without reasonable grounds.

The co-operative's obligation to treat members equally in the conclusion and execution of co-operative transactions, as for example in Italian co-operative law,[21] is a significant provision, not only in general terms, but also in dealing specifically with the preceding issue. Indeed, this obligation indirectly protects the right of a member to

---

[19] Also 'co-operative activity' (*actividad cooperativizada*) in Spanish law; and 'purpose transactions' (*Zweckgeschäfte*), as opposed to 'counter-transactions' (*Gegengeschäfte*), in the German legal doctrine: see Münkner (2013).

[20] See, for example, art. 15, par. 2, lit. b, of Spanish Law n. 27/1999. However, as Gide (1921), p. 63, warns, 'the loyalty of members is a matter of education, not of coercion'. Binding and uniform agreements between a farmer co-operative and its members, which award the co-operative the power to define quantity, quality, and other terms of the exchange relationships, are one of the attributes of the so-called new generation co-operative model (see Chaddad and Cook (2004), 355; Chaddad (2012), 456).

[21] See art. 2516 of the Italian civil code.

transact with their co-operative, since the co-operative could not be excused for not transacting with that member if the impossibility to transact was due to an excessive, and therefore unequal, amount of transactions with other members (or, which would be worse, with non-members).

Another fundamental legal issue raised by co-operative transactions is that of the potential application to them of bodies of law regulating those types of market transactions which they resemble and to which they would undoubtedly be subject had they been carried out outside a co-operative. Is contract law (notably, consumer contract law) applicable to the exchange of goods and services between a consumer or a producer co-operative and their members? And is labour law applicable to the relationship between a worker co-operative and its worker members? Or does co-operative organizational law regulate them exclusively? Obviously, the point is yet more delicate when mandatory rules of contract or labour law are considered, such as those protecting consumers against defective products or awarding workers the right to strike.

If, on the one hand, subjecting co-operative transactions to ordinary contract or labour law would imply ignoring their specificity as compared to market transactions, on the other hand, some rights of co-operative members may deserve protection in all cases. The matter is complex and is handled differently by jurisdictions and legal scholarships. Solutions should be in line with the concept of co-operative transactions that is adhered to. In principle, co-operative law and co-operative by-laws should be given precedence over other possible sources in the regulation of co-operative transactions, which therefore should only apply residually and additionally to fill the gaps left by co-operative law and co-operative by-laws. In any event, one must not forget that private autonomy (i.e. the power of self-regulation by by-laws) and co-operative law remain subject to sources of a higher ranking in the hierarchy of legal sources. Accordingly, the regulation of co-operative transactions, for example, cannot be such as to violate fundamental rights recognized by national constitutions or international treaties and conventions.

38.4 Co-operative Activity with Non-Members

Once precise concepts of 'co-operative enterprise' and 'co-operative transactions' are adopted and they are employed to distinguish co-operatives from other business organizations, the issue arises of whether a co-operative can engage in transactions with non-members for the provision of goods, services, or jobs of the same kind as those provided to members. It must be clear that this problem only exists with reference to 'co-operative transactions' as we have outlined and not to all the other transactions that are necessary for a co-operative to make co-operative transactions possible and to operate in the market as a firm, which by their very nature are transactions with non-members (even if they accidentally involve persons who are members of the co-operative). Hence, it must be enquired whether a consumer co-operative can sell goods or services (of the same kind as those provided to members) to non-members, a producer co-operative can buy goods and services (of the same kind as those supplied by members) from non-members, or a worker co-operative can employ non-members.

In principle, this co-operative activity with non-members (or non-member co-operative transactions) contradicts the essence of a co-operative as a user-owned and not as an investor-owned organization.[22] However, in practice, co-operatives have been acting in this way. Even the Rochdale Society would sell to the general public.[23] And in theory, prohibiting all transactions with non-members would hamper the expansion of the co-operative business, the capacity of the co-operative to face sudden contractions of the member demand or offer of goods, services or work, and its potential willingness to allow more people to enjoy the benefits (not only of an economic type) it is able to produce, that is, to attract new members. This is probably the reason why co-operative laws usually do not prohibit non-member co-operative activity, but subject it to specific limits and conditions, in order to prevent a co-operative from acting as an ordinary business organization on the market, which 'exploits' the general public by making profit out of them.[24] Usually, therefore, co-operatives are not required to be 'fully mutual' but only 'mainly mutual'.[25] In addition, in some co-operative laws, measures are taken to ensure that co-operative members do not, at least directly, benefit from the co-operative activity with non-members, which is what a company's shareholders (aim to) do. Such measures include the compulsory allocation of profits from non-member co-operative transactions to indivisible reserve funds,[26] the obligation to treat non-members on equal terms as members,[27] and the obligation to admit to membership those non-members involved in co-operative transactions (provided that they meet the requirements laid down by the co-operative by-laws), which, for example, is a general rule in French co-operative law.[28]

---

[22] See Gide (1921), 49 ff.

[23] See ibid, 50, which, however, explains that the Society adopted, as an ingenious rule, the method of giving the non-members a bonus or dividend at half the rate of that returned to members, placing the surplus in the reserve fund.

[24] See Cracogna et al. (2013), where this aspect is usually treated in the third or fourth section of the various chapters in part III.

[25] In some jurisdictions, this is an obligation only under tax law, which means that under organizational law, co-operatives may freely act with non-members. In other jurisdictions, where a minimum of mutuality is required for all co-operatives, the different degree of mutuality only affects the tax treatment of co-operatives.

[26] Which, however, is a solution that makes sense only if these reserves are indivisible also upon dissolution, because otherwise, members would equally profit from non-member transactions although at a later stage, i.e. at co-operative dissolution.

[27] Which, however, is a solution that does not transmit adequate incentives to non-members to become members, unless of course they are specifically interested in acquiring governance rights.

[28] See art. 3 of Law 47/1775. See also art. 23 of Mexican general cooperative law of 1994 and Gide (1921), p. 52.

38.5 The Social Function of Co-operatives and the General Interest Co-operatives

The co-operative purpose is 'internal', given that members benefit from a co-operative's activity and its results. In this specific aspect co-operatives are not different from for-profit companies. This puts the question of why some Constitutions around the world attribute a social function to co-operatives and obligate legislatures to promote co-operatives.[29]

The social function of co-operatives stems from a number of elements. First of all, it must be recalled that co-operatives are not for-profit investor-owned entities, but organizations whose aim is to satisfy member needs other than capital remuneration and appreciation (although the co-operators' needs may have an economic nature). Moreover, these needs may be fundamental needs related to human personality, such as work and housing, which are not attended to by the market and for-profit players therein.

Secondly, the intrinsic sociality of co-operatives derives from their governance structure, where, among other things, persons count more than capital and all count equally, given the democratic principle 'one member, one vote', which makes the control of a co-operative by a single member or a minority of members impossible and thus ensures that all the members may control the co-operative, thereby stimulating effective member participation in the management of the co-operative and consequently in the economic life of a country.[30] In addition, the 'open-door' principle, if effectively implemented, is a very important instrument of socialization of the economic results of an enterprise.[31]

Thirdly, co-operatives have a social function because their regulation—following the ICA principles—usually provides for certain 'external' destinations of their own resources in favour of non-members (or future members), other co-operatives, and the co-operative movement and the community at large.[32] This per se attenuates the 'internal' nature of the purpose that co-operatives have in common with companies.

---

[29] See, among others, the Constitutions of Greece, Italy, Malta, Spain, and Portugal and Fici (2015).

[30] In some co-operative laws, co-operative by-laws are empowered to award more than one vote to members. Plural voting may be considered still compatible with the co-operative identity as long as it does not lead to and allow the control of the co-operative by a sole member or a minority of members and is not based on their capital contribution but on other criteria, like the volume of a member's co-operative transactions with the co-operative (see Fici (2013b), 50 ff.).

[31] On this principle and its 'social' impact, see ibid, 55 ff.

[32] On these 'external allocations', which contribute to the social function of co-operatives, see ibid, 45 ff.

Only to the extent that co-operative law provides for these elements and protects them—which is to say, stipulates and preserves a distinct co-operative identity—is it possible to conclude that co-operatives have a social function as compared to other business organizations, in particular for-profit investor-owned companies. Otherwise, in this particular regard, the co-operative difference would almost dissolve and state promotion of co-operatives would become hardly justifiable.

Notwithstanding this, co-operatives remain entities oriented towards their members, whose interests they (mainly) aim to satisfy. Co-operative members are 'owners' in Hansmann's sense, since they hold both the right to control the firm and the right to appropriate the firm's benefits.[33] Therefore, co-operatives cannot be considered non-profit entities, given that the beneficiaries of the entity are the very people who control it.[34] Co-operatives have a social function, but are not (mainly) altruistic or solidaristic organizations. They are distinct from non-profit firms and in particular from 'social enterprises' as recently provided for in some jurisdictions.

This conclusion, however, holds true only for the traditional type of co-operative that corresponds to the Rochdale Society's norm and to the model contemplated by the ICA principles and has occupied these pages until now. In contrast, a different conclusion applies to a new (and additional) general type of co-operative, which legislatures around the world—beginning in Italy with Law n. 381/1991 on social co-operatives—are increasingly introducing into their legal systems.

Italian social co-operatives—like French collective interest co-operatives, Spanish social initiative co-operatives, and Portuguese social solidarity co-operatives, to mention but a few—'pursue the general interest of the community' (as explicitly stated by Law n. 381/1991) and not the interest of their members. They are not mutual co-operatives but general interest co-operatives (GICs).

The tendency to detach co-operatives from the pursuit of a pure internal purpose may also be found in the legislation on 'social enterprises', where it is generally admitted that (also) co-operatives may acquire the legal status of social enterprises, provided that they have a general interest objective and meet other general requirements.[35] Co-operatives, therefore, are no longer necessarily linked to a mutual purpose, and the law increasingly admits their pursuing the general interest. Co-operative legal theory has to recognize this fact and also start dealing with GICs, which relative to mutual co-operatives present different problems of regulation, due to their distinct objective.[36]

---

[33] In a co-operative, however, the firm's benefits are appropriated by members in a particular way, i.e. as 'co-operative returns' or 'patronage refunds': on this concept, which presupposes that of 'co-operative surplus', see Fici (2013b), 39 ff.

[34] See, in this sense, Hansmann (1996), p. 17.

[35] Examples include Finnish act n. 1351/2003, Italian act n. 155/2006, and the UK CIC regulation. See Fici (2016).

[36] For example, the governance structure of a GIC should be shaped by law consistently with its external purpose, e.g. by giving voice to beneficiaries who are not members, including representatives of the community in which the co-operative operates. See Fajardo et al. (2016).

REFERENCES

Chaddad, F. (2012), 'Advancing the Theory of the Cooperative Organization: The Cooperative as a True Hybrid', *Annals of Public and Cooperative Economy* 83(4), 445–61.

Chaddad, F. and Cook, M. (2004), 'Understanding New Cooperative Models: An Ownership-Control Rights Typology', *Review of Agricultural Economics* 26(3), 348–60.

Cracogna, D., Fici, A., and Henrÿ, H., eds, (2013), *International Handbook of Cooperative Law* (Heidelberg: Springer).

Fajardo, G., Fici, A., Henrÿ, H., Hiez, D., Meira, D., Münkner, H.- H., and Snaith, I. (2017), *Principles of European Cooperative Law. Principles Commentaries and National Reports* (Cambridge: ?????) forthcoming.

Fauquet, G. (1951), *The Co-operative Sector* [a translation of the fourth French edition published in 1942] (Manchester: Co-operative Union Limited).

Fici, A. (2013a), 'Cooperative Identity and the Law', *European Business Law Review*, 24(1), 37–64.

Fici, A. (2013b), 'An Introduction to Cooperative Law', in D. Cracogna, A. Fici, and H. Henrÿ, eds, *International Handbook of Cooperative Law* (Heidelberg: Springer), 3–62.

Fici, A. (2013c), 'The European Cooperative Society Regulation', in D. Cracogna, A. Fici, and H. Henrÿ, eds., *International Handbook of Cooperative Law* (Heidelberg: Springer), 115–51.

Fici, A. (2015), La Función social de las cooperativas: notas de derecho comparado, REVESCO – Revisita de estudios cooperativos, 1187, 77–98.

Fici, A. (2016), 'Recognition and Legal Forms of Social Enterprise in Europe: A Critical Analysis from a Comparative Law Perspective', *European Business Law Review*, 27(5), 639–67.

Gide, C. (1921) [a translation of the third French edition published in 1917], *Consumers' Co-operative Societies* (Co-operative Union Limited: Manchester).

Hansmann, H. (1996), *The Ownership of Enterprise* (Cambridge: Belknap HUP).

Hansmann, H. and Kraakman, R. (2000), 'The Essential Role of Organizational Law', *Yale Law Journal*, 110(3), 387–440.

Hansmann, H. (2013), 'All Firms Are Cooperatives – and So Are Governments, *Journal of Entrepreneurial and Organizational Diversity*, 2(2), 1–10.

Kraakman, R., Armour, J., Davies, P., Enriques, L., Hansmann, H., Hertig, G., Hopt, K., Kanda, H., and Rock, E. (2009), *The Anatomy of Corporate Law: A Comparative and Functional Approach*, 2nd ed. (New York: OUP).

Münkner, H.-H. (1974), *Co-operative Principles and Co-operative Law* (Bonn: Friedrich-Ebert-Stiftung [4th reprint 1981].

Münkner, H.-H. (2013), 'Germany', in D. Cracogna, A. Fici, and H. Henrÿ, eds, *International Handbook of Cooperative Law* (Heidelberg: Springer), 413–29.

CHAPTER 39

....

CONVERSION FROM STAKEHOLDER VALUE TO SHAREHOLDER VALUE BANKS
the case of UK building societies

....

DAVID T. LLEWELLYN

39.1 INTRODUCTION AND OUTLINE

....

THE focus of this chapter is on the changing fortunes of mutuality in the financial system of the UK. The experience of the UK is quite different from that of most other European countries due in large part to the conversion of a critical mass of mutual building societies and life assurance institutions from the mutual model to a Shareholder Value (SHV) status. The conversion of some of the largest building societies in the 1990s produced a major structural change in the British financial system, and in the process severely weakened the balance between mutuals and SHV institutions in the retail savings and mortgage markets, and also in the insurance market. Since the wave of de-mutualizations, most remaining mutual building societies have put in place various mechanisms (such as Charitable Assignments) to prevent current members having any claim on the economic value of a de-mutualized society.

A central theme of this chapter is that consumer interests through enhanced effective competition and systemic stability are boosted through diversity in the financial system, and that this has been eroded over the past two decades. This applies most especially with regard to contrasting business, capital, and ownership models and in particular the balance between SHV firms and mutuals—which, for purposes of comparison with other European countries can be defined as Stakeholder Value (STV) institutions.

In contrast to many other European countries, the degree of diversity in the British financial system is low and has been in decline for several years. This is especially marked in the balance between SHV and STV institutions. A major factor in this decline has been the conversion in the 1990s of ten of the largest mutual building societies (accounting for around 70 per cent of the combined assets of building societies at the time) to public limited company status. Many of the large mutual insurance companies also converted. This has substantially eroded the critical mass of the mutual sector in banking, insurance, and life assurance markets. As a result, the British financial system has come to be dominated by the SHV model which has created something of a mono-culture, and is in sharp contrast to virtually all other European countries.

Two central themes of what has come to be known in the UK as the *Civic Approach* to financial reform (see ResPublica 2014) are that the mutual model in finance remains a valuable and viable alternative to the dominance of the SHV model, and that there is a consumer and public policy interest in enhancing diversity, most especially with respect to ownership structures and business models. On the basis of both theoretical analysis and experience, there can be no presumption that the typical SHV model is best for all types of financial transactions. On the contrary, and as many analysts have demonstrated, many financial transactions (most especially those that are low risk, and where there is an ongoing customer relationship with the provider of financial services) are more suited to the mutual model. The position has been put well by John Kay:

> the special value of mutuality rests in its capacity to establish and sustain relational contract structures. These are exemplified in the most successful mutual organisa-tions which have built a culture and an ethos among their employees and their cus-tomers, which even the best of plc structures find difficult to emulate. (Kay 1991: 311)

There are strengths and weaknesses in all business models. However, and irrespective of these, there is a systemic advantage in having a mixed system and a strong critical mass of institutions (most especially mutuals and co-operatives) that are not dominated by the SHV model.

British building societies were originally established as mutual self-help organiza-tions as long ago as the nineteenth century. For a long time, mutual institutions domi-nated housing, finance, and life-assurance markets in the UK. For several decades, mutual building societies dominated the mortgage market, even after the intensifica-tion of competition which followed deregulation and the entry of banks and wholesale-funded lending institutions in the early 1980s. Not only have mutual institutions tended to dominate certain segments of the financial services market, they have also enjoyed a superior public image compared with their SHV counterparts and have compared favourably in terms of performance measures such as cost/income ratios.

39.2 SHV v. STV Models: Key Differences

Before considering the conversion movement in the UK, the context is set by consid-ering the nature of two contrasting business models. A generic distinction is made between Shareholder Value banks and financial firms and Stakeholder Value banks (see Ayadi et al. 2009 and 2010). The STV sector in the British financial system includes mutual building societies and insurance companies, Friendly Societies, Credit Unions, and Industrial and Provident Societies. The essential characteristic is that, unlike SHV banks, their primary purpose is not to maximize profits but to focus more explicitly on the interests of customers who are also their owners. This is a fundamentally different culture from that in SHV banks: mutuals are under no pressure to maximize profits so as to increase returns for external shareholders, many of whom (institutional shareholders) are themselves under pressure to maximize shareholder returns (often on the basis of short time horizons) for their own investors and stakeholders.

In contrast to the SHV model, in the STV model there are many stakeholders, including most importantly its members. A key difference between mutuals and SHV banks is that in the former the customers are themselves the 'owners' (members) whereas there is a separation of the two in the case of SHV institutions. The objective of a mutual is to look after the interests of its members who, in the main, are also its customers and owners. In the STV approach, while profitability is needed to finance future growth, it is not the exclusive, or even primary, objective.

As already noted, in many ways mutuality may be particularly suited to the provision of some financial services, and especially those relating to longer-term contractual relationships such as mortgages and life assurance. This may be due in part to the possibility that financial mutuals are able to address agency problems more efficiently. As a result, they also have a comparative advantage in establishing trust (Kay 2006), which is important in three cases in particular: consumer 'lock in' (transaction costs or penalties of exits are high); where there is asymmetric information between the firm and the customer; and in the case of longer-term contracts.

Several key characteristics encapsulate the essence of the mutual model in whatever sector of the financial system they are located:

- In contrast to SHV banks, maximizing the rate of return on capital is not the exclusive or even dominant business objective of mutual building societies. In practice, this means that a STV bank will not pursue profit maximization to the same degree, or with the same intensity, as will SHV banks (Llewellyn 2005). The position is described well in Christen et al. (2004) and in Ayadi et al. (2009) as 'Double Bottom Line' institutions, indicating that STV banks need to generate profit in order to survive and expand, but that profit is not the sole or even primary bottom-line objective.
- Mutuals are owned by their members, and although a building society may have customers who are not members, a key feature of building societies is that, in general, there is no separation of owners and customers. They therefore tend to be more customer-focused. The typical mutual seeks to maximize consumer surplus.
- Mutuals usually have an element of a 'social mission' often, though not exclusively, focused on the local community.
- While the cost of capital of an SHV bank is a claim on revenue (through, for instance, the payment of dividends to outside shareholders), mutuals are not required to service externally held capital. This gives them a potential 'margin

advantage' which can be used in terms of the pricing of deposits and loans for the benefit of members. The absence of external shareholders in mutuals is an inherent advantage in that, other things being equal, they should be able to operate with lower margins.

- Voting rights conferred by membership are based on the principle of One-Member-One-Vote (OMOV): i.e. they are not proportional to the size of a member's stake in the society. The implication is that ownership rights are widely dispersed, with no individual or group able to build up a controlling position.
- Most building societies in the UK are locally based and have a particular focus and expertise on the local community. This has the effect of mitigating the powerful centrifugal tendencies in the financial system.
- Unlike SHV banks, ownership stakes are not marketable and members cannot sell their ownership stakes in a secondary market. Because of this, there is no market in corporate control in that it is virtually impossible for hostile bids for ownership to take place: a mutual building society or Co-operative Bank cannot be bought by new owners through a hostile bid.
- The almost exclusive source of capital for a mutual is its retained profits. There are no external shareholders/owners who are not themselves members of the mutual, and no specialist outside risk-takers supplying equity capital which needs to be separately remunerated.
- In general, all profits are retained within the mutual and added to reserves (capital) and dividends are generally not paid.
- Mutuals, in general, tend to adopt a lower risk profile than the typical SHV bank partly because of their ownership structure. The May 2009 Report of the Treasury Select Committee of the House of Commons of the UK Parliament concluded that:

To date, building societies have generally been shown to have operated a safer business model. Certain features of the building society model, including the low reliance on wholesale funding and the focus on the protection of members rather than the service of shareholders, have left building societies better equipped to defend against the shockwaves of the current crisis.

- The evidence suggests that, across Europe, STV banks tend to be more stable than commercial banks with lower volatility of returns (Groeneveld and de Vries 2009; Ayadi et al. 2010). Furthermore, such banks came out well in the recent crisis compared with SHV banks.

Mutuals tend to be specialized and relatively low-risk institutions. There are several reasons why mutuals would tend to adopt a lower risk profile. Firstly, they are not under pressure to maximize profits which, at times, induces SHV banks into a higher risk profile. Secondly, mutuals are under less short-termist pressure and are more inclined to adopt a longer-term horizon in their business decisions. Thirdly, as it is less easy for mutuals to raise external capital, they tend to have a lower risk appetite than SHV banks, as capital that is destroyed cannot easily be replaced. Finally, the fact that mutuals are owned by their members (rather than large institutional investors) makes them less prone to the asset-substitution problem and hence less inclined towards risk-taking (Drake and Llewellyn 2001).

A key issue focuses on the incentives to take risk. SHV banks often face incentives to take on excessive risk as shareholders face capped losses but no cap on potential gains. In evidence to the UK's Parliamentary Commission on Banking Standards, some SHV banks suggested that management faced pressure from shareholders to increase leverage (and hence risk). The Royal Bank of Scotland suggested that 'in some instances investors pressed for what were arguably unsustainable levels of return, creating pressure to increase leverage and take on additional risk'. Compared to this, building societies, being owned by their members, face no immediate conflict of interest between customer and owner: as owners, members have the nominal status of equity holders but on the basis of a debt contract (deposits). Mutual members have no upside gain through risk-taking and, in general, are themselves risk averse. As a result of their ownership structure, the culture of mutuals tends to be different from that in SHV banks.

39.3 *WHY IT MATTERS*: BENEFITS OF THE MUTUAL MODEL

Several recent studies (for instance, two reports—Ayadi, et al. 2009 and 2010—issued by the Brussels-based Centre for European Policy Studies) demonstrate clear economic, systemic, and welfare benefits to be derived from a successful mutual or co-operative sector in the financial system. In 2009 and 2010, the Centre for European Policy Studies published the two studies of European Savings and Co-operative banks just referred to: the analysis—both theoretical and empirical—found that such STV banks enhance competition in the financial sector, enhance stability characteristics, contribute to alleviating social exclusion and, because of their local focus, contribute to regional development. In particular, a strong case is made in favour of diversity in the financial system with contrasting business models competing with each other.

A financial system populated by diversity of ownership and governance structures, and with contrasting business models, is likely to be more competitive and systemically less risky than one populated by a single dominant model, whatever that model might be. This is what should make the enhancement of diversity in finance a major public policy issue.

39.4 DIVERSITY OF BUSINESS MODELS

Our central theme is that there is a public policy interest in fostering diversity in the financial system, and yet diversity has declined steadily over the years. Furthermore, the degree of diversity is less in the UK than in many other European countries where there has been little, if any, decline. In general, STV banks are more prominent in continental European countries than in the UK.

A general case for diversity has been made well by Michie (2011):

> [diversity of ownership] creates a corresponding diversity in forms of corporate governance, risk appetite and management, incentive structures, policies and practices, and behaviours and outcomes. It also offers wider choice for consumers through enhanced competition that derives in part from the juxtaposition of different business models. (p. 309)

There are three particular aspects of a lack of diversity in the British financial system: the dominance of large SHV banks, the balance between SHV banks and mutuals, and the decline in the degree of diversity within the SHV bank sector. The large-scale conversion movement in the UK was, in part, a reflection of the free-market consensus that came to favour the SHV model.

Tracking the trend of diversity in the financial system has recently been made possible with the construction of a Diversity Index (Michie and Oughton 2013) incorporating four main components: the ownership model of financial firms, the degree of concentration and competitiveness, funding models of financial institutions, and geographical concentration of financial services. The profile of the overall Diversity Index (Figure 39.1) shows a clear downward trend in diversity since 2004. In terms of diversity of ownership structures (a proxy for SHV and mutual building societies), there has been a similar decline in terms of mortgages though not in terms of deposits (Figure 39.2). The decline

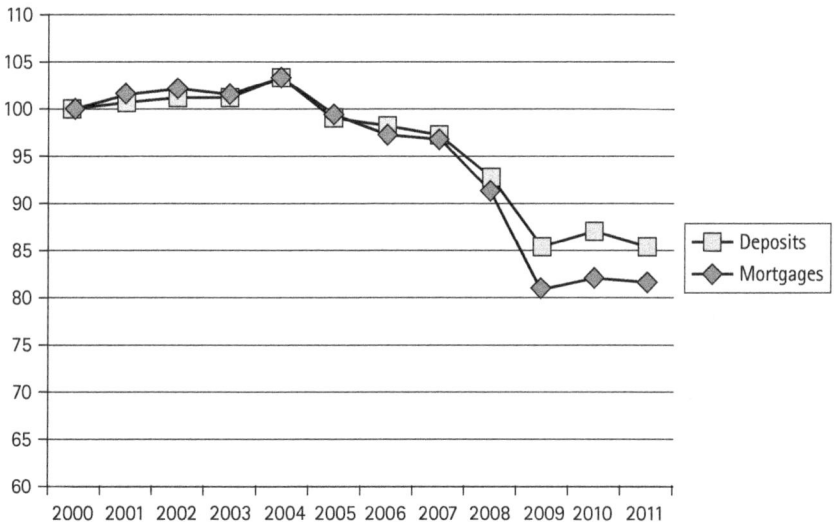

FIGURE 39.1 Diversity Index for financial service (D-Index): Ownership, competitiveness, resiliences, and geographic spread.

Source: Index developed by Jonathan Michie and Christine Oughton.

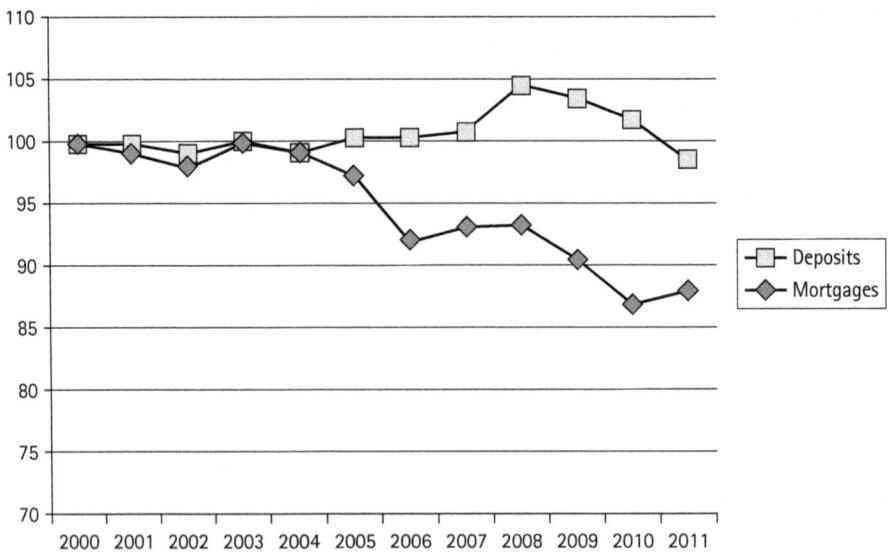

FIGURE 39.2 Ownership Index: Banks, mutuals, and NS&I.

Source: Index developed by Jonathan Michie and Christine Oughton.

in funding model diversity produced higher system risk (Figure 39.3). This is also discussed in Haldane (2009), Haldane and May (2011), and Goodhart and Wager (2012).

The general case for financial structure diversity has been made by official agencies and by published empirical research. Thus, the EU Commission published a report in 2007 on European retail banking, and the European Parliament subsequently issued a Resolution on 5 June 2008 which argued:

> the diversity of legal models and business objectives of the financial entities in the retail banking sector (banks, savings banks, co-operatives, etc.) is a fundamental asset to the EU's economy which enriches the sector, corresponds to the pluralist structure of the market and helps to increase competition in the internal market.

A study by the Centre for European Policy Studies finds that

> legal, political, and risk-related considerations serve to highlight the need for a European banking model based on diversity. (Ayadi et al. 2010:149)

The case for a financial system being populated by a diversity of organizational forms is as significant as the merits and drawbacks of each particular model. Cuevas and Fischer (2006), for example, argue that a financial system that presents a diversified institutional structure, including institutional types, will be more efficient in promoting economic growth and reducing poverty. It is in this respect that a significant public policy issue arises.

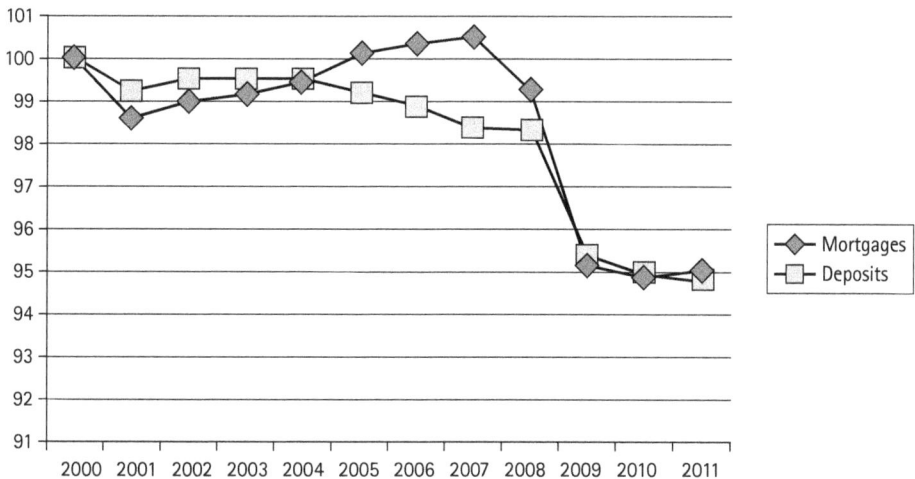

FIGURE 39.3 Competitiveness Index: Mortgage balances outstanding and UK deposits.

Source: Index developed by Jonathan Michie and Christine Oughton.

For these, and other, reasons much was lost to the British financial system by the demutualization of building societies, both in terms of the intrinsic merits of the mutual model, and in terms of systemic diversity and competition. A former non-executive director of the Halifax Building Society when it was a mutual has argued: 'With hindsight, [conversion] was a mistake that damaged a fine business' (Kay 2008). More generally, *The Times* has also questioned the wisdom of de-mutualization:

> Of itself, the move to [SHV] status was harmless. But it had two dangerous elements. It liberated those once cautious building society bosses to diversify into new activities, and provided them with the capital to do so. It also loaded them with remuneration packages so poorly structured that they encouraged short-term recklessness.

39.5 MUTUAL MODELS: UK v. EUROPEAN CONTEXT

In the context of the conversion movement in the UK which has had a major impact on the structure of the retail financial services industry, it is instructive to consider some of the key structural differences that exist between the UK and continental European financial systems, most especially with respect to the balance between STV and SHV financial institutions.

Co-operative banks and other financial mutuals play a substantial role in most European economies and, in contrast to the experience of mutual building societies and insurance companies in the UK, have increased their share of business over the past ten years. The UK is out of step, having travelled in the opposite direction since the demu-tualizations of the 1990s. Five EU member states (including France and Germany) have more than a 40 per cent share of co-operative or mutual banks in terms of branch net-works. An IMF study (Cihak and Hesse 2007) finds that the overall market share of co-operative and mutual banks in terms of total banking sector assets increased from about 9 per cent in the mid 1990s to about 14 per cent in 2004.

In contrast, the size of the mutual sector and the number of mutual building socie-ties in the UK has declined substantially. At one time, building societies accounted for 60 per cent of the mortgage market, though this has since declined to around 20 per cent. In 1910 there were 1,723, many of which had their historical origins deep in the nineteenth century. By 1992 the number had been reduced by mergers to 89 in 1990, and further to 52 by the end of 2013 through a process of mergers and several conversions to SHV bank status.

The experience of continental European countries in the balance between SHV and mutual (co-operative) banks is instructive. Although there are similarities between mutual building societies in the UK and co-operative banks elsewhere in Europe (most especially with regard to corporate objectives and the principle of one-member-one-vote), there are two central differences:

- Partly as a result of de-mutualizations in the 1990s, building societies generally have a lower market share of retail deposits, mortgages, and consumer loans than do many co-operative banks in continental Europe.
- The capital of a building society belongs to the members rather than, as with co-operative banks elsewhere in Europe, being held in perpetuity by the bank itself. The capital base of a co-operative bank (i.e. its net asset value) does not belong to the current cohort of members. Capital is essentially an inter-generational endowment held by the co-operative in perpetuity for the benefit of current *and future* members. Capital cannot, therefore, be appropriated by the current cohort of members as future generations are counted amongst the stakeholders. The concept of de-mutualization is alien (if not legally impossible) in most European countries. In the UK the owners are able to vote for conversion to SHV status and receive a share of the capital.

Because of this, de-mutualizations are generally not possible in other European coun-tries, where the law requires that the reserves of any de-mutualized bank must be trans-ferred to another co-operative bank or otherwise used for purposes of general interest. Above all, they cannot be appropriated by the current members.

39.6 UK Conversion Experience

The 1986 Building Societies Act conferred more business powers on building societies (though still within prescribed limits), but at the same time enabled members to vote for conversion to SHV bank status. In 1986 building societies were given the option of abandoning their mutual status and converting to proprietary banks and ten of the previous largest twelve societies did so. The conversion of some of the largest building societies represented a major structural change in the financial system, shifting the balance between mutuals and banks in the retail savings and mortgage markets.

Given the newly acquired option of converting to SHV status, a total of ten building societies (including eight of the largest ten that existed in 1992) subsequently converted (or in some other way abandoned their mutual status), and these accounted for 70 per cent of the total assets of building societies in 1992. In the second half of the 1990s, a powerful trend emerged towards de-mutualization: mutual building societies converting to SHV bank status. This could be done in one of two ways: on an independent stand-alone basis, or though conversion and immediate purchase by an existing bank.

A de-mutualization could only occur on the votes of existing members. Unlike in continental Europe, de-mutualization of building societies (and mutual life assurance offices) involved payments to current members as the concept of inter-generational legacy was not enshrined in British law. Although the reserves of building societies are built up over several generations of members, on a de-mutualization the current cohort of members have claim on the economic value of the mutual. In essence, de-mutualization involves the appropriation of the mutual's intergenerational endowment by the current cohort of members. This also implies that the current generation of members are able to deny future generations the benefits of membership of the mutual. This represented an inter-generational transfer of benefits and wealth and, under these circumstances, it is perhaps not surprising that the current cohort of members tended to vote in favour of de-mutualization.

In fact it was more stark than this as thousands of investors (who came to be known as carpet baggers), made deposits at several building societies with the clear and only intention of using the voting power that membership conferred in order to vote for conversion and thereby gain the windfall profits that were paid out on conversion. In other words, the profits (capital) that had been built up over very many decades (in some cases over a century) by previous generations of members could be appropriated by the current transitory generation of members.

Members voting for conversion were effectively voting to unlock the ownership value embodied in the reserves of their society. This picture is not quite accurate in one important respect which has implications for the structure of voting rights in the conversion process. The position as described presupposes that those who gain from the conversion (current members) are the same as those who, over many years, contributed to the reserves of the society, and who were forced to hold value in *locked* form. Neither of these is in fact the case when 'carpet-baggers' entered the scene because the current generation of members were able to appropriate for themselves the value that had been built up over many decades (sometimes over a century) by previous generations of members. In effect, there was an inter-generation financial transfer. The receipt of such 'subsidies' clearly biased the outcome of voting as it was almost inevitable that the current generation of owners would vote for such subsidies.

Overall, the bias would inevitably produce a sub-optimum outcome, because the voting involved cross-subsidies from those who could not vote (past and potential

future members) towards those who could; the longer-run and systemic consequences were not taken into account when voting as individual voters have no incentive to consider the systemic implications. In other words, the outcome was likely
to be costly, because not all the relevant externalities were taken into account in the
voting procedure. Given the 'margin advantage' of mutuals, members of a building
society when they vote for conversion may in practice be exchanging a short-run
gain (the one-off withdrawal of embedded value) at the cost of a higher cost of services in the long run.

The conversion movement was, in part, a reflection of the free-market consensus
that favoured the shareholder-value (SHV) model in banking where the almost exclusive objective of bank mangers is to maximize shareholder value, often based on a fairly
short time horizon. Non-SHV institutions (such as mutuals) were criticized for being
an exception to this rule, for being relatively inefficient, for not being subject to the discipline of the capital market and the market in corporate control, and for having weak
corporate governance arrangements. Above all, it was alleged that their objectives were
not clear because of the absence of a single focus. However, many of these oft-repeated
criticisms can be, and have been, challenged in an extensive research literature (see, for
instance, Drake and Llewellyn 2001).

These demutualizations were facilitated by badly drafted conversion provisions
inserted late into the Building Societies Act 1986—and then a failure to do anything
about the fact that the legislation had been badly drafted and did not deliver the intended
outcome: this enabled a 'get rich quick' option at board level and immediate cash bribes
to current members.

39.7 THE RATIONALE OF CONVERSION

The economic rationale for the demand for conversion could be regarded as a demand
by existing members of societies to unlock their supposed entitlement to *locked* value
(see Drake and Llewellyn 2001). In practice, however, it became opportunistic, in that
the motive was to secure windfall gains (sometimes amounting to several thousand
pounds for individual members) which could also be reaped by new members who
made nominal deposits at building societies with the sole purpose of pressing for conversion and expropriating a share of the reserves. However, the major *declared* motives
for conversion were different:

- *To secure greater access to capital*
  With the exception of the issuance of Permanent Interest Bearing Securities or
  some forms of subordinated debt, the only source of capital for building societies
  was the surplus earned on its operations.
- *To secure a stronger position to participate in structural change in the financial
  system*

Some converted building societies stated in their conversion documents that one motive for conversion was to be able to take a more pro-active part in the consolidation and re-structuring of the financial sector that many analysts at the time judged to be inevitable.

- *To gain more flexibility with respect to lending and funding*
  Building societies faced limits on the extent of their wholesale funding (which could not exceed 50 per cent) and on diversification away from residential mortgages (which by law had to represent a minimum of 75 per cent of their lending).

- *To diversify into areas where the nature of the risk is judged to be inappropriate for a mutual, such as financial trading*
  Because mutuals cannot readily increase their capital by fresh injections, they tend to adopt a lower risk profile. Thus, if a mutual planned to diversify into high-risk business, it would be appropriate for it to convert. For building societies this was also mandated by legislation because of certain prohibitions on riskier forms of financial trading.

- Clarity of objectives
  Some analysts (particularly those with an ideological bias towards the traditional SHV mode) argued at the time that, in contrast to the SHV model, mutuals have a somewhat ambiguous business objective which is difficult to define and, most especially, to measure. In which case, the argument asserted, there was too much scope for mutuals to become inefficient. On the other hand, maximizing shareholder value is clearly defined and on this criterion performance is easy to measure. This set of arguments has, however, been challenged (see, for instance, Ayadi et al. 2009 and 2010; Drake and Llewellyn 2001).

- Governance
  In a similar vein, the argument was put that, partly because of the diverse ownership structure, internal governance arrangements tend to be weak in mutuals and also that, given that there is no traded capital, they lack capital market discipline. This too has been challenged as already mentioned, and also in Groeneveld and Llewellyn (2012).

These were the stated arguments the management of building societies put to members as reasons for conversion and seeking their votes. For a more detailed discussion of the reasons for conversion, see Drake and Llewellyn (2001). The consensus that underlay much of the above rationale subsequently came under challenge as a result of the global financial crisis, particularly with respect to short-termist 'shareholder value' strategies and the assumption that efficient markets based on shareholder value models are self-correcting.

39.8 LOCKED V. UNLOCKED VALUE

Although both mutuals and SHVs create value for their owners, the nature and 'usability' of this value differs. This is where problems began to emerge in the UK—when the value of a mutual (as measured by reserves) became 'excessive'. As building socie-ties' reserves were built up, the implicit or embedded value to the owners was steadily increased. And yet this value could not be released to the owners except through a con-version to SHV status.

Curiously, in the UK, mutuals came to be potentially vulnerable not only when they had too little capital, but also if they had too much. The former was because it is more difficult for a mutual to augment its reserves other than through profits, and the lat-ter because it encouraged members to seek to unlock embedded value by changing the society's structure. Apparent 'success' (as measured by the build up of excess reserves) for a mutual can sow the seeds of its own destruction, and this is precisely what hap-pened in the UK.

A central feature of a SHV institution is that there is a continuous re-pricing of its value through changes in the stock market price of shares. Ownership rights are tradea-ble and shareholders can sell them and claim the full value of their stake in the company because the value of the company is reflected in the current share price. It also means that, if a new shareholder wishes to acquire a claim on the value of the company that has been built up over many years, it can do so but has to pay the market price for this value as reflected in the share price. However, this is not the case with mutuals as new shareholders can buy into the accumulated value of reserves simply by opening a share deposit.

This in turn leads to an important and crucial distinction between what might be termed *locked* versus *open* value for owners. In effect, the ownership stake in a mutual is *locked* within the firm as there is no way that owners can liquidate that value other than through conversion. On the other hand, the ownership stake that an equity holder has in a SHV firm can be immediately *unlocked* in the secondary market in shares. This is precisely where problems began to arise with building societies in the early 1990s because they had built up substantial reserves, and hence the value of ownership stakes of their members. The distinction between the creation of value for owners in SHVs and mutuals is given in Table 39.1, where a distinction is made between *locked* and *open* value-creation for owners.

It is when we come to retentions that the major distinction emerges. In the case of a mutual, when value is created it is in non-usable form. With a SHV company such

Table 39.1 Value Creation in SHV and STV Banks

Value created via	Mutual	SHV
(1) Margin advantage exploited in pricing	Open	n/a
(2) Distributions of profits	n/a	Open
(3) Retention of profits in reserves	Locked	Open

Source: The author.

retentions also create value but in a usable form. This is because the value created will normally be reflected in the share price and hence it can be liquidated by owners. In this way value can be extracted at very little cost.

In summary, therefore, the two key distinctions between the mutual and the SHV firm (as shown in the table) are that the mutual has the option of giving value to owners in the price structure of its products and services, whereas the SHV does not. While value is created in both cases when reserves are increased, it is *open* in the case of the SHV but *locked* with the mutual.

Problems emerged when the value of building societies (as measured by reserves) became 'excessive' because reserves represent locked value (LV). On the other hand, low mortgage rates and high deposit rates represent open value (OV). When the 'margin advantage' was used to increase reserves, the ratio of locked to open value (LV/OV) rose which resulted in members seeking to transform LV into OV by liquidating the reserves. This could be done via conversion.

39.9 THE POST CONVERSION SCENARIO

By 2008 all the converted societies had lost their independent status, either because they were purchased by other banks (e.g. Abbey National and Alliance & Leicester were purchased by Bank Santander), or because they failed and needed to be taken into public ownership (notably Northern Rock, and Bradford & Bingley). Demutualizations have weakened diversity and effective competition in the retail financial services sector. Much has been lost to the British financial system by the demutualization of building societies and insurance companies, both in terms of the intrinsic merits of the mutual model, and in terms of competition and systemic diversity. A former non-executive director of the Halifax when it was a mutual has argued:

> It is now apparent that the conversion of the mutual building societies to public limited companies did, in the end, inflict considerable damage on the UK financial services sector. All the large societies that converted either failed or were absorbed into larger financial conglomerates. This reduced competition, and the institutions that were eliminated had achieved significantly higher levels of customer satisfaction than their listed counterparts. (Kay 2008).

Andrew Bailey of the Bank of England, speaking at the 2011 Annual Building Societies Conference argued that:

> Demutualisation, as it developed, was a failed and very costly experiment.

The conversions that occurred in the 1990s amounted to a very substantial de-mutualization of the building society sector as, while it was only ten of the 89 societies that existed in 1992 that demutualized, because they were amongst the largest, they represented around 70 per cent of the sector's assets. The subsequent history of the demutualized building societies indicates that problems emerged on both sides of the balance sheet. Thus, Abbey National (the first of the societies to convert) encountered problems because of its diversification on the assets side of the balance sheet, particularly in the treasury area, while Northern Rock, Halifax (HBOS), and Bradford & Bingley initially failed because of diversification on the liabilities side of the balance sheet as they became excessively dependent upon securitization and wholesale funding. Later it emerged that asset quality at all three institutions was also poor.

39.10 THE ISSUE OF TRUST
AND CONFIDENCE

As a result of a series of high-profile scandals in banking in the UK (and to some extent elsewhere) consumer trust and confidence has been weakened in many parts of the British banking system (see Llewellyn 2014; Llewellyn et al. 2014; and ResPublica, 2014).

In many respects, mutuals should have an intrinsic advantage in securing consumer Trust and Confidence, not the least because they have 'members' rather than exclusively customers which is likely to create a different culture because consumers already have a firmer, more explicit, and higher level of relationship with the mutual than with other companies by virtue of 'membership'. This also means there is no conflict of interest between consumers and external shareholders. The corporate governance objective of a mutual is to behave in the interests of members rather than external shareholders. Although not all customers in a mutual are necessarily members, the distinction between owners and customers is less in a mutual than in other companies. An IMF study (Fonteyne 2007) suggests that as consumer-owned institutions, co-operative banks have a comparative advantage in gaining the trust of their customers.

Evidence from a variety of surveys suggests that consumers do in fact have more trust and confidence in building societies than in, for instance, SHV banks. Research conducted in July 2013 shows that customers of mutuals consider that their provider delivers on various aspects of service to a superior extent than do consumers at banks: being more trusted to act in their best interests, mutuals outscore banks by 17 pp; being open and honest, mutuals outscore banks by 11 pp; having high ethical standards mutuals have a superior score of 24 pp; in the area of treating customers fairly, the superior score is 10 pp, and in being valued as a customer mutuals outscore banks by 16 pp. In terms of overall satisfaction, mutuals have an excess score of 12 pp in mortgages and in the savings market it is 10 pp. In 2004, the Myners review into governance arrangements in life mutuals found that members of life mutuals had a very positive view of mutuality, with high levels of trust (Myners 2004).

Whilst no claim is made that mutual financial firms are necessarily paragons of virtue, their ownership model and basic business model suggests that the internal culture is likely to be less potentially hazardous for consumers than is the case with SHV institutions:

- they are not shareholder value driven with the incentive structures that often go with this model
- they are less likely to be prone to a short-termist ethos
- the merging of customers and owners which is a central feature of a mutual is itself likely to create a different culture and, in particular, a lower risk appetite
- many STV institutions have a 'social mission' in their core objectives.

Overall, survey evidence indicates that members/customers of mutuals do in fact have a higher degree of trust than exists with customers of SHV banks and financial firms.

39.11 REFORM PROGRAMME IN THE UK: THE CASE FOR DIVERSITY

There is a political commitment in the UK to enhance the diversity structure of the financial system. In the light of the analysis outlined above, several reform proposals have been made (e.g. ResPublica 2014) to enhance the mutual sector. There are several areas where public policy initiatives could enhance the position and role of mutuals in the interests of both competition and systemic stability:

- Removing or alleviating barriers to the creation of new mutuals.
- A further political commitment to recognizing the systemic benefits of diversity and, as an act of public policy, to monitor trends in the degree of diversity in the financial system over time.
- Consideration to be given to the possibility of a re-mutualization of some financial firms. This is discussed in detail in Michie and Llewellyn (2011).
- Consideration to be given to facilitating the creation of Central Network Institutions within the mutual sector (see Ayadi et al. 2010).
- Mutuals should not be disadvantaged by the legislative framework or by regulation. In particular, they should not undermine the ability of mutuals to compete on a fair basis with other providers.
- The removal of the Too-Big-To-Fail implicit subsidy to banks would contribute to levelling the competitive playing field between such banks and building societies.
- Allowing greater access to external capital in forms that do not undermine the mutual concept.

- Building societies and other mutuals should not be hindered by disproportionate barriers in (most especially prudential) regulation. For instance, few building societies could be regarded as being systemically significant and hence any additional capital requirements based on systemic significance should not be applied to the vast majority of building societies.
- The Building Societies and Cooperatives Acts need modernizing to reflect the evolution of competitive conditions.
- The wholesale funding limit should be removed from the Building Societies Act.
- The Building Societies Association also has concerns about the funding of deposit insurance and the implementation of the EU's Deposit Guarantee Scheme Directive. It argues that, if the cost of such insurance is based on the size of the deposit base, building societies, because they are predominantly retail-funded institutions, would be liable for a considerable share of the total costs even though, as they are low-risk institutions, they are unlikely to make as many calls on the scheme. In particular, funding the scheme without reference to the riskiness of the institutions would impose a disproportionate cost on the building society sector.

It remains to be seen how far the declared political commitment to enhancing diversity and mutuality is translated into positive action.

39.12 Re-mutualizations?

Northern Rock, which for over one hundred years was a mutual building society, was one of the large societies that converted to SHV status in the 1990s. It subsequently became one of the biggest banking failures in the UK during the 2007/8 banking crisis (Balling et al. 2009). It was taken into public ownership as part of its rescue plan. After a few years, the issue arose as to how it would be re-privatized, with one option considered being a re-mutualization of the state-owned bank (Michie and Llewellyn 2011).

Given the systemic (externality) advantage in enhancing the mutual sector (in effect, re-instating the *status quo ante* before Northern Rock was demutualized), the taxpayer had a legitimate interest in the project. The systemic and competitive benefits of remutualization (even if it meant some form of indirect tax-payer contribution) would outweigh any cash benefit to be derived from a quick sale of the Government's capital holding in Northern Rock. The case for remutualizing Northern Rock was made on the basis of the intrinsic merits of the mutual model, the systemic advantage of having a mixed system with a critical mass of mutuals along with other bank models, and the enhanced competition to which a remutualized Northern Rock would contribute.

In the event, the UK Government was tempted by a short-term 'dash for cash', selling the failed financial institution to the highest bidder. This was almost certainly a mistake and one likely to cost the UK economy in the long term. Firstly, paying off the public-sector debt that was incurred as a result of the failures of SHV banks, could not realistically happen overnight. Secondly, the timescale over which the performance of the once-failed financial institutions would need to be judged, and over which they could be expected to generate a return to the taxpayer, should not be too short. Thirdly, although the remutualization option would provide less cash up-front in the short term, it would create a more durable and sustainable business which would be in a position, not only to make repayments over time, but also to contribute positively to the UK economy in terms of enhanced competition in the financial system and tax revenues generated for the Treasury.

In addition to remutualized enterprises being able to make a long-term return to government, and contribute to a more resilient and less risky financial sector, a stronger mutual sector, reinforced by newly remutualized businesses, would also be better placed than would private banks to deliver on the broader social agenda. There are several key issues in this regard which point to the benefits that might flow from re-mutualizations:

- The effect that a strong mutual sector has in enhancing competition because mutuals adopt a different business model compared with SHV banks: for this to be an effective enhancement to competition a strong critical mass of mutuals is needed.
- Because mutuals are not owned by investment institutions, they are not subject to the short-termist pressure of the capital market.
- Most building societies (and many mutual and co-operative banks in other European countries) are locally or regionally based and have a particular focus and expertise on their communities.
- The systemic advantage through having a mix of institutions with different portfolio structures—with the potential to reduce overall systemic risk because institutions are not homogeneous. The more diversified is a financial system in terms of size, ownership, and structure of businesses, the better it is able to weather the strains produced by the normal business cycle, in particular avoiding the bandwagon effect, and the better it is able to adjust to changes in consumer preferences. As put in a *Financial Times* editorial (27 April 1999):

  a pluralist approach to ownership is conducive to greater financial stability. With their contrasting capital structures, banks and building societies balance their risks and loan portfolios differently. Systemic risk is therefore reduced. (p. 12)

- In an uncertain market environment, diversity has advantages as it cannot be predicted which form of corporate structure is best suited to all particular circumstances.
- The ownership structure, regulation, and traditional business model of mutuals (particularly the dominance of retail funding) makes them less prone to risky speculative activity than shareholder-owned banks.
- A mixed system of different corporate structures is likely to produce a more stable financial system.
- It would contribute to eroding the monoculture and dominant position of the SHV banks.

39.13 ASSESSMENT: WHAT HAS BEEN LOST?

There are compelling reasons in the UK for creating an enhanced role for mutual build-ing societies and other financial institutions such as credit unions, friendly societies, etc. Several studies demonstrate clear economic, systemic, and welfare benefits to be derived from a successful mutual or co-operative sector in the financial system. A financial sys-tem populated by diversity of ownership and governance structures, and with contrast-ing business models, is likely to be more competitive and systemically less risky than one populated by a single dominant model, whatever that model might be. This is what should make the enhancement of diversity a major public policy issue in finance.

Much has been lost to the financial system by the demutualization of building soci-eties, both in terms of the intrinsic characteristics of the mutual model, and in terms of systemic stability and effective competition. Various reform measures have recently been proposed in the UK with a view to enhancing the role of the mutual model in the financial system. It is emphasized, however, that the case being made is not in favour of any particular model but the public policy interest in having a higher degree of diversity in the financial system.

REFERENCES

Ayadi, R., Schmidt, R. H., and Carbo Verde, S. (2009), *Investigating Diversity in the Banking Sector in Europe: The Performance and Role of Savings Banks* (Brussels: Centre for European Policy Studies).

Ayadi, R., Schmidt, R. H., Llewellyn, D. T., Arbak, E., and De Groen, W. P. (2010), *Investigating Diversity in the Banking Sector in Europe: Key Developments, Performance and Role of Cooperative Banks* (Brussels: Centre for European Policy Studies).

Bailey, A. (2011), Keynote Speech at the Building Societies Association Annual Conference, May. Available on Bank of England website, www.bankofengland.co.uk (accessed 2 October 2016).

Balling, M., Llewellyn, D. T., and Bruni, F. (2009), *The Failure of Northern Rock: A Multi-Dimensional Case Study*, SUERF Study (Vienna: SUERF).

Christen, R., Rosenberg, R., and Jayadeva, V. (2004), 'Financial Institutions with a "Double Line Bottom Line"', CGAP Occasional Paper No. 8, CGAP, Washington, DC: GCAP.

Cihak, M. and Hesse, H. (2007), 'Cooperative Banks and Financial Stability', IMF Working Papers, No. WP/07/02, Washington, DC: International Monetary Fund.

Cuevas, E. and Fischer, P. (2006), 'Cooperative Financial Institutions, World Bank Working Paper, no. 82.

Drake, L. and Llewellyn, D. T. (2001), 'The Economics of Mutuality: A Perspective on UK Building Societies', in J. Birchall, ed., *The New Mutualism in Public Policy* (London: Routledge), 14–40.

European Parliament, (2008), European Parliament resolution: Competition: Sector Inquiry on retail banking (2007/2201(INI))

Fonteyne, W. (2007), 'Cooperative Banks in Europe: Policy Issues, IMF Working Paper 07/139, Washington DC: International Monetary Fund.

Goodhart, C. and Wagner, W. (2012), 'Regulators Should Encourage More Diversity in the Financial System', *Voxeu.org* (April), 1–2.

Groeneveld, H. and de Vries, B. (2009), 'European Cooperative Banks: First Lessons of the Sub-Prime Crisis', *International Journal of Co-operative Management*, 4(2), 1–22.

Groeneveld, H. and Llewellyn, D. T. (2012), 'Corporate Governance in Cooperative Banks', in J. Mooij and W. W. Boonstra, eds, *Raiffeisen's Footprint: The Cooperative Way of Banking* (Amsterdam: VU University Press).

Haldane, A. (2009), 'Credit is Trust'. Available on the Bank of England website, www.bankofengland.co.uk (accessed 2 October 2016).

Haldane, A. G. and May, R. M. (2011), 'Systemic Risk in Banking Ecosystems', *Nature*, 469(2), 187–98.

Kay, J. (1991), 'The Economics of Mutuality', *Annals of Public and Cooperative Economics*, 62(3), 309–18.

Kay, J. (2006), 'The Mutual Interest in Building Trust Still Remains', *Financial Times*, 26 April, p. 12.

Kay, J. (2008), 'The Titan's Inability to Say Sorry', *Financial Times*, December 16, p. 12.

Llewellyn, D. T. (2005), 'Trust and Confidence in Financial Services: A Strategic Challenge', *Journal of Financial Regulation and Compliance*, 13(5), 333–46.

Llewellyn, D. T. (2014), 'Reforming the Culture of Banking: Restoring Trust and Confidence in Banking', *Journal of Financial Management, Markets and Institutions*, 2 (2), 221–35.

Llewellyn, D. T., Steare, R., and Trevellick, J. (2014), *Virtuous Banking: Placing Ethos and Purpose at the Heart of Finance* (ResPublica: London).

Llewellyn, David T. and Wildman, Adam (2014), 'Markets for the Many: How Civic Finance Can Open up Markets and Widen Access', London: A Respublica Green Paper.

Michie, J. (2011), 'Promoting Corporate Diversity in the Financial Services Sector, *Policy Studies*, 32(4), 309–23.

Michie, J. and Llewellyn, D. T. (2011), 'Converting Failed Financial Institutions into Mutual Organisations', *Social Entrepreneurship*, 1(1), 309–23.

Michie, J. and Oughton, C. (2013), 'Measuring Diversity in Financial Services Markets: A Diversity Index', Centre for Financial and Management Studies Discussion Paper Series, No. 113, London: School of African Studies.

Myners, P. (2004), *Myners Review of the Governance of Life Mutuals* (London: HMSO).

CHAPTER 40

THE PERFORMANCE OF MEMBER-OWNED BUSINESSES SINCE THE FINANCIAL CRISIS OF 2008

JOHNSTON BIRCHALL

40.1 INTRODUCTION

IT used to be accepted by most economists that the investor-owned business was a superior form to any other, and that the 'triumph of capitalism' was the result of a natural process of evolution in which it had out-competed less efficient and effective ownership types. Since the financial crisis of 2008, and the subsequent downturn in the global economy, this assumption has increasingly been questioned. Investor-ownership is beginning to be seen as unstable and risky. Its managers are seen as being out of control, and demanding more and more incentives just to do their job. Government regulation is seen as being ineffective in preventing managerial greed and corruption (e.g. Mayer 2013; Stout 2012). In contrast, there is a growing interest in member-owned businesses that are based on a different set of incentives.

Social commentators are searching for an 'alternative to capitalism', and have become interested in the potential of member-owned businesses to provide that alternative (e.g. Harrison 2013). The protestors who 'occupied Wall Street' had a strong anti-narrative, but they lacked a counter-narrative that might persuade people that there was a different way of doing business (Birchall 2013a: Ch. 12). In particular, they needed some evidence that there is a different way of owning and controlling banks that, if it were supported, could prevent a similar crisis from occurring again. That evidence was provided by the European co-operative banks that have a 20 per cent market share of the banking sector, and by the worldwide credit union movement that is particularly strong in

North America (where it has a market penetration of 45 per cent).[1] Thus, a campaign to 'Move your Money' has been successful in persuading millions of people to switch their current accounts to a co-operative bank, building society, or credit union.

The argument for member-owned businesses (more usually defined as co-operatives or mutuals) has been made for more than just the financial services sector. A report for the International Labour Organization (ILO), written just after the crisis, provides this summary:

> Cooperative enterprises around the world are showing resilience to the crisis. Financial cooperatives remain financially sound; consumer cooperatives are reporting increased turnover; worker cooperatives are seeing growth as people choose the cooperative form of enterprise to respond to new economic realities. (Birchall and Hammond Ketilson 2009: 3)

The authors of the report argue, quite modestly, that co-operatives should be supported as a way of mitigating the economic crisis and providing what the ILO calls 'decent work'. However, other authors have been less cautious; Sanchez Bajo and Roelants (2011) extend the analysis of what went wrong in the banking crisis to a broader critique in which the argument for co-operatives becomes much more ambitious (Sanchez Bajo and Roelants 2011). As we shall see in this chapter, it also becomes more difficult to sustain. What the recent analyses of member-owned businesses agree on is that the business model provides evidence of a great deal of resilience, both during the financial crisis and in the subsequent economic downturn.

This chapter will try to measure just how resilient member-owned businesses (MOBs for short) have been in comparison with their investor-owned rivals (IOBs for short). The obvious way to do this is to measure their performance through standard indicators such as size of assets, profitability, turnover, changes in market share, and so on. Since MOBs are businesses, these measures are a good starting point. However, members often want more from MOBs than shareholders want from IOBs. They have a 'dual bottom line' that includes both the conventional financial indicators and other, more diverse measures of success. In consumer OBs, these include measures of quality, convenience, trust-worthiness, and sometimes of ethical acceptability in the product. In producer OBs, these include the ability of the business to help members to sustain their own businesses (as farmers, retailers, or service providers). In employee OBs these include the effectiveness of the business in providing them with secure, dependable, and satisfying employment. In order to meet the criteria of success in the second bottom-line, MOBs often put less emphasis on the first. If the purpose of the business is to provide a low-cost service to members rather than to maximize profits, then it is misleading to use profitability as a measure of performance.

---

[1] Market penetration is the percentage of economically active adults in a given population who are credit union members.

Surrounding every business there are other stakeholders who are also affected by its operations. It is possible for a business to perform well by the narrow criterion of increase in shareholder value, while imposing costs on these other stakeholders. There is an argument that all types of business should be managed on behalf of these stakeholders (Freeman et al. 2007). We do not have to go this far to recognize that the measure of performance should take into account the effects on non-member employees, local economies, the wider society, and so on.

40.2 The Performance of MOBs Since the Crisis

We now examine the evidence for the performance of the different types of MOBs since the financial crisis. The evidence is, of course, patchy and incomplete. Advocates of the member-owned alternative have sometimes been content to cite examples of a co-operative sector in one country, or cases of individual, high-performing co-operatives, that show MOBs performing well. These are suggestive, but they do not show the whole picture. Where possible, we should be looking for broader trends across whole industry sectors and world regions. Happily, the statistical trends for co-operative banking in Europe and for credit unions worldwide are available, and they can be used to show how the whole sector is performing. For other sectors such a global picture is not available. This is why the chapter will not be dealing with agricultural co-operatives (that, in any case, have not been as affected as other sectors), or with shared service co-ops (a category that is not well recognized and so for which there is little information on performance).

Here is a simple classification that will help us to structure the chapter. Apart from the investors of capital, there are three main stakeholders in a business: its consumers, the producers who supply inputs to or take the outputs from the business, and its employees. In a MOB, usually one of these other stakeholders is put at the centre of the business. This gives us three classes: consumer-owned, producer-owned, and employee-owned businesses.[2] Within these classes there are specific types classified by sector.[3] The types that will be discussed here include three types of consumer OB (financial co-operatives, retail consumer co-operatives, and insurance mutuals), one type of producer OB (retailer-owned wholesalers), and the employee OB (including worker co-operatives and employee-owned businesses).[4]

---

[2] It is also possible to subsume the third—employees—under producer ownership—see Birchall et al. (2011) for a discussion.

[3] For a full listing of these types, see Birchall (2011a), Ch. 1.

[4] The distinction between them is a fine one. Worker co-operatives are usually wholly worker owned, while employee-owned businesses are at least 50% employee owned and often have part of the equity held in a trust.

40.2.1 Financial Co-operatives

Financial co-operatives can be divided into three types: co-operative banks, credit unions, and building societies (Birchall 2013a).[5] Co-operative banks are the result of two social movements that began in Germany in the 1850s, under the tutelage of two founding 'fathers': Schulze-Delitsch founded an urban banking sector designed to meet the needs of small businesses and self-employed artisans, and Raiffeisen founded a rural banking sector designed to meet the needs of small farmers. The two movements spread rapidly throughout Europe, in some countries coalescing into one, but in others (notably Austria and Italy) still retaining two distinct groupings. Together they consist of 4,000 local banks with 56 million members and 217 million customers, organized in national level federations with powerful central banks such as Rabobank in the Netherlands, Credit Mutuel in France, and Raiffeisen Bank in Austria. Together, they have around 20 per cent of the market (EACB 2013).

When the co-operative banking movement reached Canada and then the USA in the early twentieth century, it underwent a change of name but the credit union movement developed along the same lines.[6] When it reached India at around the same time, it became the 'savings and credit co-operative' and began to be promoted all round the British Empire. Now it is a worldwide movement, with 57,000 credit unions in 103 countries, serving 208 million people and with a market penetration of just over 8 per cent (WOCCU, 2014).

The building society movement began in Britain in the eighteenth century with 'terminating' societies whose aim was to help a restricted group of members finance their own housing, after which point they were wound up. With the invention of the 'permanent' society in the 1850s, the movement grew quickly and became a more commercial—but still mutual—way of cycling small savings into residential mortgages. The idea was copied in the USA where societies were known as 'savings and loans' or 'thrifts'.[7] In the 1980s and 1990s, in both countries banking deregulation led to widespread demutualization, but there are still a significant number of societies. In the UK some of the larger societies have branched out and now offer full banking services, rivalling the investor-owned banks. There are 45 societies, with more than 20 million customers, and a similar share of the mortgage and savings market to the European co-operative banks; around 19 per cent (BSA 2015a). In the USA, the demutualization of the 1980s was followed by a serious banking crisis, and most of the 'S&L' sector disappeared. However, there are still 577 'mutual banks', an amalgamation of the S&L sector and a 'mutual' (really trustee)

---

[5] There is a fourth category of banks owned by other types of co-operative, such as the UK Co-operative Bank that was owned by the Co-operative Group (now only 20% owned). However, this is not an important category statistically.

[6] During the 1970s, the co-operative banks were given the right to offer services to non-members but the credit unions have always remained fully mutual.

[7] Small sectors emerged in several other countries, notably Australia and Germany, but these are not important enough to be considered here.

bank sector that, with assets of $209 billion is a useful supplement to the much larger credit union sector (America's Mutual Banks 2015).

How has this diverse sector been performing? Evidence summarized by this author from several reports shows that before the crisis the European co-operative banks were as efficient as their competitors. They were at least as profitable, and in several countries more profitable, but they were everywhere more stable than the investor-owned banks (Hesse and Cihak 2007). Between 2005 and 2007 in every country assets increased; for Europe as a whole they increased by over 23 per cent (Birchall 2013b). Co-operatives had comparable or slightly higher earnings than investor-owned banks, and achieved higher return on equity. In terms of earnings stability, in all countries other than Germany and Spain, co-operatives were significantly more stable than other banks (Ayadi et al. 2010). Clearly, the general trend just before the banking crisis of 2007 was upwards.

It was a similar picture for credit unions. Over the same two years, the amount of savings increased everywhere by an average of 29 per cent, while loans increased everywhere by 39 per cent. Reserves increased by 26 per cent and assets by 32 per cent. The number of members increased by 13 per cent. Market penetration increased almost everywhere from 6.65 per cent to 7.5 per cent. Again, it was a similar picture for the UK building societies. While the number of societies continued to fall due to mergers, all the indicators of performance—numbers of depositors and borrowers, total assets, and so on—were showing strong growth (Birchall 2013a: 101–2). In an enquiry by a parliamentary group, the only bank that outperformed the societies was Northern Rock, a demutualized society that was about to go bankrupt, triggering the banking crisis in the UK (All-Party Parliamentary Group 2006).

Co-operative banks entered the crisis with a stronger capital base than their competitors, which they subsequently strengthened; by 2009 they all received an A rating, while Rabobank was rated one of the safest banks in the world (Groeneveld and de Vries 2009). Some of them made losses (the Austrian banks in particular made losses in Eastern Europe), but those that remained true to their traditional business model came through the crisis much better. Co-operative banks accounted for 7 per cent of all the European Banking Industry write-downs and losses between the third quarter of 2007 and first quarter of 2011, even though they had 20 per cent of the market. This was because of their limited exposure to sub-prime mortgages, and fewer investment activities. Their assets grew by nearly 10 per cent between 2007 and 2010. Their market share of deposits and loans remained roughly the same, but the number of customers grew by 14 per cent. In general, they came out of the crisis very well. Seven of them were in the top 50 safest banks in the world, and across Europe they exceeded the minimum legal capital ratio requirement of 8 per cent, with an average ratio of about 9 per cent. This was reflected in very good credit ratings, which ranged between AA- and AAA for the largest co-operative banking groups (Ferri et al. 2014).

For credit unions, the worldwide picture was one of strong growth during the period from 2007 to 2010 (WOCCU 2011). Savings increased by only 1 per cent in 2008 but then by 15 per cent in 2009, and another 7.3 per cent in 2010. Loans decreased very slightly in 2008 then grew by 7.6 per cent and 5.3 per cent over the next two years, and reserves increased by over 14 per cent, indicating that the system was in good health and that risks were being kept low. The post-crisis downturn had begun to affect savings, but all the other indicators showed continued good health. However, in Canada, SaskCentral and Desjardins both had significant losses on their investments. For the US centrals, the situation was much worse. They had been investing heavily in the kinds of toxic assets that the American banking system had been so good at producing until the crisis broke. At the time the investments were rated as low-risk products, but the consequences were dire. Five corporate unions were put into conservatorship by their regulator. These held 70 per cent of the entire corporate system's assets and 98 per cent of the investment losses. As a result, member unions had to pay an increased insurance premium to a National Share Insurance Fund to help make up for the losses (Birchall 2013b).

During the crisis, UK building societies benefited from being seen as a safe haven for people's savings. In the first half of 2008, nearly £6.3 billion of customer money flowed into their savings accounts, compared to just £3.8 billion for the same period in 2007. However, as a result of the financial turmoil, building society profitability was significantly lower in 2008 than in previous years, and some building societies reported large losses for the first time in many years. Five societies sought refuge through mergers, and one (Kent Reliance) formed a new company with a venture capital group, with its members holding a majority share of the assets. None of this is surprising given the enormity of the crisis in the banking and financial system, the serious recession, declines in property prices, and a generally weak housing market. More seriously, one, the Dunfermline society failed and was taken over by the largest society, Nationwide, with the UK government providing £1.6 billion to fund the excess of deposits over assets being absorbed. The second largest society, Britannia, merged with the Co-operative Bank, but a few years later its losses brought down the bank; the Co-operative Group is now a minority owner with only a 20 per cent share. In both these cases, the societies grew by commercial lending that was much more risky than their traditional business, and they paid the price. A report from an Oxford University research centre sums up the lessons learned:

> the mutual building societies were generally less scathed by the financial crisis than were banks in general and demutualised building societies in particular. Indeed, converted building societies proved to be more vulnerable the further they moved away from their traditional model. (Oxford Centre 2009: 12)

After the crisis, and during the subsequent euro-crisis and several years of global economic recession, financial co-operatives have continued to grow. Between 2010 and 2012 the European co-operative banks recorded a 30 per cent increase in assets, and 19 per cent increase in members (EACB 2013). Credit unions recorded a 5 per cent increase in assets worldwide, but with not much change in the level of market penetration. Their performance varied somewhat in different world regions, going down slightly in Africa and increasing dramatically in Australia and New Zealand, where a combination of new government legislation and a desire on the part of credit unions to compete with the (largely discredited) investor-owned banks led to a massive increase in all growth indicators. Building societies have also continued to grow, despite difficult trading conditions. In 2014, their market share was 26 per cent, well above the sector's natural market share (given its size) of 19 per cent (BSA 2015b).

40.2.2 Retail Consumer Co-operatives

Consumer co-operatives trace their origins to the Rochdale Pioneers Society of 1844 in the North of England. This was not the first such society, nor was it even the first that had been tried in Rochdale, but it was the first that was really successful. The Pioneers established the principles of linking voting rights to persons rather than shares, of paying a 'dividend on purchases' (better described as a patronage refund) rather than on shares, and of remunerating capital only with fixed and limited interest. They also had the—then revolutionary—ideas of opening branch stores so the society could expand, and of channelling their purchases through their own wholesale society (Birchall 1994). These co-operative principles and business practices were then applied conscientiously by societies that sprang up all over Europe and beyond, in much the same way as the co-operative banks were growing; they were, in effect, parallel social movements.

The movement reached its peak in the 1950s, when the British co-operatives had 12 per cent of the market for food and more than 40 per cent of staples such as coal, bread, and milk. All over Europe they then lost ground to investor-owned multiple chains that were better managed, well integrated, and had huge buying power. To meet the competition the co-operatives had to merge into regional or national units, and accept the disciplines of the sort of group structure that the banks had always had. Their relative success in making this transition explains much of the difference we see today in national consumer co-operative sectors: in France, Germany, and Belgium they have virtually disappeared, in Italy, Finland, and Switzerland they have become the leading retail chain, while in the UK, Canada, and Sweden they are struggling to hold on to a modest market share. Newer sectors, such as in Spain, Japan, and Singapore, have their own dynamic (see Birchall 2011: Ch. 3 for a full description).

The financial crisis did not affect them directly, except in the case of the UK Co-operative Group which had its own bank. Even then, the effect was delayed; the Group was thrown into crisis in 2013 by losses made by its subsidiary bank after it had merged with a much larger building society that had a risky commercial loan portfolio (Birchall 2014a). It has started to recover by selling parts of the business and completely restructuring its governance. Indirectly, consumer co-operatives have been seriously affected. Throughout Europe and Scandinavia, all retailers have been under growing pressure to lower prices in response to the static or falling incomes of customers, and the only winners so far have been the discount chains.

There are three scenarios. First, where co-operatives are in a commanding market position we can expect them to absorb the threat. In Singapore, NTUC Fair Price has become the market leader with 57 per cent of the grocery market (Birchall

2013a: Ch. 11). In Switzerland, Migros and Co-op Swiss between them have around a 50 per cent market share, and Migros owns its own discount chain. Despite the effects of 'shopping tourism' (customers driving to France to take advantage of lower prices), Migros reported a growth in retail sales in 2013 of over 7 per cent (Migros 2013), while Co-op Suisse maintained its share with growth of 1.7 per cent (Co-op Suisse 2013). In Finland, the S-Group (with a 21 per cent market share) is also adapting to challenging market conditions: in the first half of 2014 in a stagnating market its retail sales declined by 1.1 per cent, though it still managed to return €178 millions in patronage refund to members (SOK 2014).

Second, in countries such as Japan (6% market share—see Kurimoto 2010) and Italy (18% share), where regional co-operatives have a strong presence in an unconsolidated market, we can expect serious competition from multiple chains and groups of independent retailers, but the competition is less intense. Third, in countries such as the UK (8% market share but dropping) and Spain, where co-operatives are strong but multiple chains are stronger, we can expect co-operatives to struggle to hold their share of the market. However, there is no 'quick fix'. In an attempt to grow quickly to gain market power, Co-operative Group (UK) and Eroski (Spain) both acquired another retailer. Suffering from a downturn in the property market and falling turnover caused by intense competition, they both made large losses on the deals and will take a long time to recover.

40.2.3 Insurance Mutuals

There are three types of insurance mutual. Friendly societies began in Britain in the seventeenth century (though in France there is an unbroken tradition going back to the medieval guilds). In return for a small weekly payment, they provided sickness and death benefits, and help with medical costs. From these origins, they have grown into very large and sophisticated societies. Their main competitor has been the state, and their size and functions vary with the extent of medical cover and benefits provided by government (for a typology, see Birchall 2011: Ch. 4). Mutual insurance companies also spread rapidly throughout the USA, providing general insurance (sometimes known as assurance) against the risk of fire, theft, death, illness, and so on, and then began to offer life insurance. Like the friendly societies, they began by filling a gap left in the market, building on the trust that members have in a mutual at a time when investor-owned equivalents were seen as too risky. Government regulation of the industry made it possible for IOBs to enter the market, and then in the 1980s there was a trend towards demutualization. Surprisingly, this has not reduced the mutuals as much as we might have expected and they are still serious competitors in the industry. Finally, there are insurers set up as secondary co-operatives to serve the needs of other types such as farmer and consumer co-operatives.

The sector can now be seen as one unified grouping, brought together by an International Cooperative and Mutual Insurance Federation (ICMIF). How has the sector been faring after the financial crisis? Since 2007, it has been the fastest growing part of the global insurance market, moving from a market share of 23.4 per cent in 2007 to 27.3 per cent in 2013. It wrote $1.26 trillion in insurance premiums compared to less than a trillion in 2007, and held almost $8 trillions in assets (ICMIF 2015). Its premium income grew by 28 per cent compared to 11 per cent for the global insurance market as a whole. Three of the top ten largest insurance companies in the world are mutuals: the National Mutual Insurance Federation of Agricultural Co-operatives (Zenkyoren) in Japan; State Farm mutual, the largest non-life insurance company in the USA; and the Kaiser Foundation Group of Health Plans, also in the USA.

How do we explain this success story? The CEO of the ICMIF says their growth is due to 'the greater levels of trust and satisfaction which they engender among customers', the disillusion with shareholder-owned companies since the financial crash, and their ability to take a longer-term view to protect the interests of customers (ICMIF 2015). It looks as if they have the same comparative advantages as the financial co-operatives. It is interesting to note that, while the non-life business grew modestly from 27.7 per cent in 2007 to 28.9 per cent in 2011, the life business grew much faster: from 20.8 per cent to 25.1 per cent. Mutual life insurance was invented because it was difficult to persuade potential policyholders to commit to a long-term relationship with uncertain returns. With the failure of government regulation of the financial services industry, this specific advantage seems to have become relevant again.

40.2.4 Retailer-Owned Wholesale Distribution Co-operatives

It is not surprising that, when faced with the concerted buying power of both consumer co-operatives and multiple chains, independent shopkeepers have banded together in a different kind of co-operation, but to achieve the same purposes. The sector can be traced back to the founding of Unified Grocers in 1922. The World Co-operative Monitor lists the largest co-operatives in the world, in all the different industry sectors; in the wholesale and retail sector the top three are all retailer-owned wholesalers—Rewe Group in Germany, followed by Leclerc in France, and Edeke Zentrale in Germany (Euricse, 2013).[8] There are seven more in the top 20, making four in Germany, three in France, two in the USA, and one in the Netherlands. They have large market shares: Kesko has 30 per cent of the market in Finland, Leclerc 18 per cent in France, Edeka 26 per cent in Germany, Conad in Italy 10 per cent, and so on (Birchall 2014b: Ch. 4). In fact, in Italy Conad is a serious competitor, with the consumer co-operatives federated in Co-op Italia, who have 18 per cent of the market. In 2012, Conad opened more than 100 new stores and posted a growth in turnover of 8 per cent, which in recession-hit Italy

---

[8] Though the largest in the world is Spar, with stores in 35 countries; it has a mixed ownership, sometimes being controlled by retailers, sometimes by wholesalers.

shows the power of this type of co-operation (Global Retail 2015). Similar success stories can be told about retailer-owned wholesalers in the USA and New Zealand, and about other sectors such as pharmacy (in Europe) and hardware (in the USA).

This type used to be seen as antagonistic towards consumer co-operatives (Birchall 1994), but no longer; where the threat from discounters and multiple chains is strong they are banding together in buying groups. For instance, in 2006, the UK Cooperative Group and Spar announced a joint buying venture, and in 2014 Colruyt Group, CONAD, COOP Suisse, and REWE Group entered into a strategic alliance; between them they have 20,000 stores in 18 European countries and a nearly 7 per cent market share in Europe (Retail Detail 2014). In Spain this trend towards partnership has been taken even further. Eroski (the Mondragón Corporation-linked retailer) is jointly owned by its consumers and employees, and has over 1,000 stores, but it also has 500 stores franchized to independent retailers.

40.2.5 Employee-Owned Businesses

Since the late nineteenth century, in countries where there are strong worker co-operatives, these have tended to increase in number during recessions, both as new start-ups and takeovers of ailing businesses. We can expect the same to happen in the current recession, as workers attempt to protect their own livelihoods. We can also expect that in sectors where the downturn is severe there will be some failures, though also some counter-cyclical behaviour in the form of employees voluntarily sharing out work and taking pay cuts in order to survive.

There is strong evidence of growth in the worker co-operative sector. In France, in 2013 more than 263 co-operatives were set up, which is an increase of 17 per cent since 2009, making a total of 2,252 new start-ups. They helped create or preserve more than 10,500 jobs (Confederatione Generale 2014). Their survival rate is better than that of conventional firms: 77 per cent as opposed to 65 per cent. There is similar evidence for Germany and Quebec (cited in Birchall and Hammond Ketilson 2009: 29–30). Evidence gathered by the industry body CICOPA for 2009 and 2010 showed that the economic situation had worsened, but that the level of indebtedness of worker co-ops was lower than that of comparable enterprises, and that those who were organized in group structures were surviving the best. In Spain there were job losses, but these were 6.4 per cent in co-operatives compared with 11.9 per cent in other types of enterprise (Sanchez Bajo and Roelants 2011).

In Italy, worker co-operatives demonstrated greater resilience to shocks, because unlike conventional firms they had built up their equity during the 'good' years and were able to adjust pay downwards to prevent the loss of jobs (Delbono and Reggiani 2013). In the industrial and services sector, between 2008 and 2009 their numbers decreased by 3.6 per cent, but this was due mainly to mergers rather than failures, and in 2010 their numbers began to increase again. Over the ten-year period from 2000, the number of employees rose by 15 per cent compared to a decline of 29 per cent in companies run as partnerships. The stability in their employment levels was remarkable; in 2010 the number of employees increased by nearly 10 per cent (Carini and Carpita 2014).

A report from the trade association for worker and social co-operatives, CICOPA, provides a broader view from a survey of co-operatives in 17 European countries (where there are 50,000 worker-owned enterprises employing around 1.3 million workers). Between 2008 and 2011 there was, unsurprisingly, a general downturn in production and sales among affiliated co-operatives. Then things improved, except in the construction sector. In the Nordic countries the crisis did not affect co-operatives so strongly; here the number of co-operatives was increasing. There was a more general recovery in Europe except in Spain, where in 2011 the number of worker co-ops decreased by 2.5 per cent (though conventional enterprises decreased by nearly 15 per cent). As in the financial co-operative sector, the stability of this ownership type is impressive. In Italy, for instance, in 2011 over 68 per cent of co-operatives kept the same level of employment, while in 18 per cent employment grew, and only in 13 per cent did it contract (Roelants et al. 2012). The reasons are clear. They used short-term, emergency measures such as reductions in costs and wages, use of reserves, and changes in production. Then in the longer term they invested more in training, technological innovation, and further changes in the product. The worker-owned governance model, far from being a hindrance to these measures, allowed them to take bold decisions, sometimes very quickly.

Unfortunately, the bankruptcy of one of the most famous worker co-operatives, Fagor, came as a shock. Part of the Mondragón group, it should have been protected by the group structure from failure; traditionally, the group has imposed financial disciplines on its member co-operatives, and job losses have been prevented by reassigning redundant workers to other co-operatives. However, Fagor was a manufacturer of domestic electrical goods, and as such was particularly hard hit by the recession in Spain. Its losses could not be made up by the other co-operatives, particularly since Eroski was also struggling to make up losses made in its takeover of another retail chain. The fate of Fagor reminds us that worker ownership does not always guarantee success.

40.3 THE BENEFITS OF HAVING A SUCCESSFUL CO-OPERATIVE BUSINESS SECTOR

The performance of co-operatives is not the only bottom line. What has been their contribution to the 'other bottom line' that measures the wider benefits of co-operation? Financial co-operatives have demonstrated some wider benefits (summarized in Birchall 2013a: Ch. 7). Low-income countries prevent market failure by providing an alternative to moneylenders who charge exorbitant rates of interest on loans. This helps people to avoid one of the most serious of poverty traps—that of chronic indebtedness. High-income countries provide competition that lowers the cost of banking to the customer. Where they have strong federal structures and central banks, they spread the risks around the group and thus cut down on the systemic risks. They foster long-term, high-trust relationships between the bank and its customers. The surpluses they make are ploughed back into the business for the benefit of their customers, and because they keep high levels of reserves they are well capitalized and so more stable than the investor-owned banks (Groeneveld 2015). Because customers are also members, there is a strong informational advantage and, in general, a lower level of losses from bad debts. Customers also benefit from the commitment of financial co-operatives to remaining locally based, keeping an extensive branch network (when their competitors are cutting theirs), and maintaining a high level of lending to local small and medium-sized businesses (see Birchall 2013a: Ch. 6 for a summary of the evidence).

There should be an ethical advantage in trading as a member-owned business, but this is not always maintained. The UK Co-operative Bank used to win awards for its ethical policy, and yet it has been implicated in mis-selling scandals. Rabobank has a strong ethical stance, and yet some of its top executives have been implicated in the LIBOR rate-rigging scandal. The financial crisis and subsequent scandals have exposed serious ethical failure in the banking profession, from which the member-owned sector has not been immune. However, in general the presence of a large member-owned sector has advantages for the banking system as a whole, providing diversity and an alternative business model (Ayadi et al. 2010). There are wider benefits still, as member-owned banks (along with savings banks) provide a means by which savings can be cycled into loans at the level of the local economy, resulting in a significant pro-growth impact within regions where they are strong.

The benefits from consumer co-operatives are less obvious. Like the banks, where they are strong they have a commitment to keeping open local outlets (small village and suburban stores) that put service before profit. Their commitment to an equal price policy between small and large stores benefits less mobile customers, but makes it difficult for them to compete with more footloose competitors. Where they have the only store in a village (as is often the case in the UK) they still have the ability to prevent monopoly pricing. However, the slowdown in the world economy has made it difficult for them to pass on surpluses as rewards to members. In Finland, the S-Group, with its powerful central, SOK, is able to do this: in 2012 it passed back €420 million in patronage refunds from its retail and banking arms (Birchall 2014b). In the UK, though, the Co-operative Group has failed to give any real benefits to members, weakening member commitment and making it difficult to demonstrate the 'co-operative difference'. In Japan, there is a different set of challenges: the rise in women's paid work threatens the 'han' system of joint buying that has been at the centre of the co-operative business strategy (Kurimoto, 2010)

The benefits from mutual insurance are becoming more evident, particularly in the life insurance sector where contracts require a high level of trust over long timescales.

The benefits from worker co-operatives are also illustrated by the financial crisis. They have the ability to create new job opportunities and to protect existing jobs, though sometimes at the expense of living standards.

40.4 PREDICTING THE FUTURE OF MEMBER-OWNED BUSINESSES

It is difficult to predict the future of co-operatives in general. If they are going to be an alternative to investor-owned businesses, then that alternative will have to be competed for in each industry sector, and the results will vary depending on the extent to which they can realize the 'co-operative advantage'. However, in general they have proved their resilience to both the financial crisis and a longer-term recession. The occasional failures show that they should remain true to their original model: stay member-centred, grow organically rather than through risky acquisitions, keep to a conservative and low-risk management style, build up reserves in the good times, and above all work together in group structures that provide mutual support.

REFERENCES

All-Party Parliamentary Group for Building Societies and Financial Mutuals (2006), *Windfalls or Shortfalls: the True Cost of Demutualisation* (London: All-Party Parliamentary Group for Building Societies and Financial Mutuals).

America's Mutual Banks (2015), See americasmutualbanks.com (accessed 4 October 2016).

Ayadi, R., Llewellyn, D., Schmidt, R. H., Arbak, E., and de Groen, W. P. (2010), *Investigating Diversity in the Banking Sector in Europe: Key Developments, Performance and the Role of Co-operative Banks* (Brussels: Centre for European Policy Studies).

Birchall, J. (1994), *Co-op: the People's Business* (Manchester: Manchester University Press).

Birchall, J. (2011), *People-Centred Businesses: Co-operatives, Mutuals and the Idea of Membership* (London: Palgrave Macmillan).

Birchall, J. (2013a), *Finance in an Age of Austerity: The Power of Customer-Owned Banks* (Cheltenham: Edward Elgar).

Birchall, J. (2013b). *Resilience in a Downturn: The Power of Financial Co-operatives* (Geneva: International Labour Office).

Birchall, J. (2014a), 'Innovation in the Governance of Large Co-Operative Businesses: The Alarming Case of UK Co-operative Group', *International Journal of Co-operative Management* 7(1), August, 22–8.

Birchall, J. (2014b), *The Governance of Large Co-operative Businesses* (Manchester: Co-operatives UK).

Birchall, J. and Hammond Ketilson, L. (2009), *Resilience of the Co-operative Business Model in Times of Crisis* (Geneva: International Labour Organization).

Birchall, J., Mayo, E., and Simon, G. (2011), *Practical Tools for Defining Co-operatives* (Manchester: Co-operatives UK).

BSA (Building Societies Association) (2015a), See bsa.org.uk (accessed 4 October 2016).

BSA (Building Societies Association) (2015b), 'Building Societies Continue to Perform in Highly Competitive Market'. Press Release, London: BSA.

Carini, C. and Carpita, M. (2014), 'The Impact of the Economic Crisis on Italian Co-operatives in the Industrial Sector', *Journal of Co-operative Organisation and Management*, 2, 14–23.

Confédération Générale des SCOP (2014), Annual Report, France.

Co-op Suisse (2013), Annual Report.

Delbono, F. and Reggiani, C. (2013), Cooperative firms and the crisis: Evidence from some Italian mixed oligopolies', *Annals of Public and Co-operative Economics* 84(4), 383–97.

EACB (European Association of Co-operative Banks) (2013), Annual Report for 2013. Brussels: EACB.

Euricse (2013), World Co-operative Monitor, University of Trento.

Ferri, G., Kalmi, P., and Kerola, E. (2014), 'Organizational Structure and Exposure to Crisis among European Banks: Evidence from Rating Changes', *Journal of Entrepreneurial and Organizational Diversity*, 3(1), 35–55.

Freeman, R., Harrison, J., and Wicks, A. (2007). *Managing for Stakeholders* (New Haven: Yale University Press).

Global Retail Magazine (2015), See globalretailmag.com (accessed 4 October 2014).

Groeneveld, H. (2015), 'Member-Based Enterprises: The Spotlight on Financial Services Co-Operatives'. Inaugural address at Tilburg University. Available at https://www.tias.edu/docs/default-source/Kennisartikelen/20150213-hg-webversion-inaugural-publication.pdf?sfvrsn=0

Groeneveld, H. and de Vries, B. (2009), 'European Co-Operative Banks: First Lessons of the Subprime Crisis', *International Journal of Co-operative Management*, 4(2), 8–21.

Harrison, R. (ed.) (2013), *People Over Capital: The Co-operative Alternative to Capitalism* (Oxford: New Internationalist Publications).

Hesse, H. and Cihak, M. (2007), 'Co-operative Banks and Financial Stability', IMF Working Paper WP/07/02, Washington DC: IMF.

ICMIF (International Co-operative and Mutual Insurance Federation) (2015), See icmif.org (accessed 4 October 2016).

Kurimoto, A. (2010), *Toward Contemporary Co-operative Studies: Perspectives from Japan's Consumer Co-ops* (Tokyo: Consumer Co-operative Institute of Japan).

Mayer, C. (2013), *Firm Commitment: Why the Corporation is Failing Us* (Oxford: Oxford University Press).

Migros (2013), Annual Report for 2013. See migros.ch (accessed 4 October 2016).

Oxford Centre for Mutual and Employee-owned Businesses (2009), *Converting Failed Financial Institutions into Mutual Organisations* (Oxford: Kellogg College).

Retail Detail (2014), See retaildetail.eu (accessed 4 October 2016).

Roelants, B., Dovgan, D., Eum, H., and Terrasi, E. (2012), *The Resilience of the Cooperative Model* (Brussels: Cecop/Cicopa Europe (European Confederation of Workers' Cooperatives, Social Cooperatives and Social and Participative Enterprises).

Sanchez Bajo, C. and Roelants, B. (2011), *Capital and the Debt Crisis? Learning from Cooperatives in the Global Crisis* (Basingstoke: Palgrave Macmillan).

SOK Corporation (2014), Interim Report, 1 Jan–30 June 2014.

SOK Corporation (2015), 'The Greatest Change in a Decade', (CEO of SOK). Available at https://www.s-kanava.fi/web/s/en/asiasana (accessed 22 October 2016).

Stout, L. (2012), *The Shareholder Value Myth* (San Francisco: Barrett Koehler).

WOCCU (World Council of Credit Unions) (2011), 2011 Statistical Report, Madison: WOCCU.

WOCCU (World Council of Credit Unions) (2014). 2013 Statistical Report, Madison: WOCCU.

CHAPTER 41

....

CREATING SOCIALLY
SUSTAINABLE ENTERPRISE

....

DAVID ERDAL

41.1 THEORIES OF ECONOMIC SUSTAINABILITY

....

WHEN it comes to the sustainability of the economy, whose ideas should we trust? Today we are asked by those making the big political decisions to trust the market. In recent years the gradual move in China from a state-run to an increasingly market-based approach has provided spectacular reinforcement for the argument in favour of doing so.

Faith that the market will create both a wealthy and a socially sustainable economy takes its confidence empirically from the global economic experience of the last two centuries up to 2008, and as a theory from Adam Smith's famous observation that— 'frequently' (implying 'not always')—butchers and bakers acting selfishly in the market are led as if by an invisible hand to achieve socially beneficial outcomes; moreover, they do this more effectually than if they had these outcomes in view. The elaboration of the theory into econometric models has been boundless, and some of the models do seem to work reasonably for some of the time.

Experiments in the real world tend to be more messy. The experience of Russia, where the economy was plunged into the deep end of the market approach, was rather different from that of China. Without the control by government institutions powerful enough to regulate the activity of the players in the economy it rapidly descended into banditry. Powerful people acting selfishly do not come remotely near fitting the econometric models.

Even the normal small imbalances of power created by differences in information available to different players—which is true of every market in the real world—is enough to render the models false. Joe Stiglitz, who was awarded his Nobel Prize for work on information in real-world markets, concluded that the reason Adam Smith's invisible hand is invisible is that it is not there (Stiglitz 2008).

If we needed further data to encourage questioning the social sustainability of an economy based on the current market orthodoxy, 2008 provided more evidence than anyone could have wished. Keeping the enormously powerful financial institutions afloat cost the world's present and future taxpayers undreamt of sums. The regulation of these institutions had been relaxed over decades on the grounds that this market-liberation would allow them to be more creative. They did indeed act creatively—discovering and inventing a multitude of ways to remove cash in vast quantities from the clients they were supposed to be serving, with no social benefit whatsoever. It also allowed them to become enormously powerful. When the house of cards collapsed they used that power to pass on the costs.

In other words the market, liberated on the grounds of a theory that still holds ideological sway today, created a grotesquely unsustainable situation (Kay 2009).

41.2 THE CONCEPT OF SUSTAINABILITY

This chapter focuses on the sustainability of business as a social institution—the level of micro- rather than macro-economics—and does not deal with issues of environmental or ecological sustainability. The concept of sustainability is used in a dual sense: it includes the neutral description of the ability to maintain a system over a long period of time, and in addition the value-oriented notion that it is worthwhile to do so.

The feudal system provides an example of a set of social institutions which meets the first criterion, but not the second. It proved sustainable over some six centuries in Europe, but as one of the great modern historians of the period remarked, 'even among the sovereigns whose power is most vaunted by the chroniclers, it would be impossible to find one who did not have to spend long years in suppressing rebellions' (Bloch 1961: vol. 2: 409). If a system evinces rebellion on that scale, with consequent persistent destruction of human lives and wealth, then no matter how long it lasts it fails the 'worthwhile' criterion, and cannot be described or promoted as a sustainable system. Clearly, feudalism required large numbers of people to live and behave in ways that they simply could not accept. The military superiority of the feudal aristocracy was backed up by an intensive ideology—including the notions of noble blood, God-given social position, the propriety of serfdom, and eternal damnation for those who protested. But all these were in vain: the people rebelled against gross domination and exploitation.

41.3 HUMAN NATURE

A developing strand of anthropology argues that the sharing and co-operation essential to human evolution itself was sustained only due to this tendency to counter attempts by strong individuals to impose their dominance. For the last several million years our primate ancestors have always lived a highly social existence—as members of a developing species we have always made a living *together*. After the split from the chimpanzees some nine million years ago, the social environment in which we made our living during a formative stages of our species' development was the hunter–gatherer band. The counter-dominance evident universally in modern hunter–gatherers was key to ensuring that meat was shared with everyone, a factor vital in human evolution (Boehm 1999; Whiten and Erdal 2012). When seeking to design sustainable institutions we are trying to suit the human nature shaped by and in that social environment, a nature with a strong tendency to resist domination and so to preserve autonomy, and in addition to respond positively to perceived fairness.

41.4 Sustainability in Human Systems

If any institution is to be sustainable over the long term, it must go with the grain of human nature. The keys to the most sustainable *political* system so far developed—democracy—include factors that respond exactly to these aspects of human nature. Thus the system gives all its members together the right to appoint and dismiss their leaders, which embodies pure counter-dominance; this requires that they are able to obtain all the information they wish (with a small number of publicly agreed exceptions); to organize to campaign for any purpose they decide (as long as the purpose is not expressly illegal); and to share in all the benefits of the particular society in which they live (Keane 2009). These characteristics of democracy are not arbitrary: at root they acknowledge the need to gain each person's voluntary acceptance. To achieve such acceptance it is necessary to respect each person's autonomy and other rights, in order to avoid triggering the reactions that sooner or later follow when people are treated disrespectfully, repressed, or exploited—reactions that we have seen so bedevilled even the best of the feudal leaders.

41.5 Socially Sustainable Businesses

Just as sustainable political systems depend on the co-operation of all the people in them, so the success of *any* business depends on the voluntary co-operation of all the people working in it; enterprises, however they are constituted, are superb examples of voluntary co-operation. In almost all of them there is a defined hierarchy of decision-making authority, but in all without exception the decisions made are carried out by people working together, co-operating to ensure the success of the operation. It is sometimes not clearly seen that in all cases this is the voluntary co-operation of autonomous individuals; they are not controlled by the hierarchy but voluntarily co-operating with it to execute the decisions taken. It is physically impossible for a human being to pass over control to another person: obedience is always voluntary co-operation (Ellerman 1992).

This distinction is highlighted when employees decide instead to 'work to rule'. This involves obeying to the letter the contractual rules by which the hierarchy and business processes are officially constituted—the official 'control' mechanism—but doing so without displaying the normal voluntary co-operation. Everything quickly grinds to a crawl. A vivid example was provided by the dock workers in Antwerp in 1965. They showed a great deal of initiative and creativity—human capacities which it is the dream of entrepreneurs and managers to harness positively in the interests of their enterprise—in implementing their protest in the very process of meeting technically the requirements of their contracts. As reported at the time in the UK newspaper, *The Daily Telegraph*:

> Every conceivable safety precaution is being applied, some of them dating back well into the last century and made obsolete by port improvements. Locks have never been filled so slowly. It is many years since the levels were so minutely checked with a plumbline, or swingbridges so carefully examined lest a belated reveller be sleeping off a hangover on the turntable beneath. (*Daily Telegraph* 1965)

In normal times, when there was no protest, the dock workers, like the employees in any corporation, would identify with the purpose of their employer and co-operate voluntarily to ensure that that purpose was achieved; exercising insight and common sense, they would constantly adjust their behaviour to help complete the port operations efficiently.

In the normal capitalist corporation this dependence on voluntary co-operation has always been assumed, but seldom overtly recognized. An assumption in traditional economics is that the degree of application by well-supervised employees is more or less fixed and remains unaffected by social factors such as power relations (Altman 2014). It is as if the people involved are viewed as 'hired hands', not under voluntary self-control but under the control of the managers in the hierarchy—the fiction of 'purchased labour' rather than the reality of co-operating people, who are autonomous, responsible individuals and whose enthusiasm is modulated in response to incentives that include social factors. For example, people respond with greater application and enthusiasm when they are given respect, treated fairly in their own judgement, and have the opportunity to contribute all they can, including ideas for improvement. Today, with the growing importance of creativity and self-motivation—crucial, for example, in the software and creative industries—the importance of employee involvement has been increasingly recognized, and a variety of management techniques has been developed to encourage individual commitment to the enterprise (e.g. McCoy 1996). In many cases this involves allowing greater freedom and self-control to the people involved, and a fuller openness of communication. But in terms of actual power, these techniques only rarely allow any but the most local influence. Outside the worker co-operative movement (e.g. Luviene et al. 2010) the idea that democracy, the *sine qua non* of our political life, should be extended into the world of work is not shared widely.

So it is that democratic rights are accessible only during those hours when people are not at work. At work the corporation, the standard institutional design, is a top-down hierarchy in which information, influence, and voting decision-making are not available by right to the vast majority of people. Instead, they are the exclusive preserve of the 'owners' of the business.

41.6 THE OWNERSHIP METAPHOR

The word 'ownership' applied to corporations is a metaphor: concretely, a business is in its essence a group of people working together to make a living, using assets that need not be owned—they can be leased or borrowed. So the rights of 'ownership' are in fact political rights: the right to govern the people in the business, including the right to control all the information and decision-making, and the right to appropriate any wealth created. The securitization of these rights together as 'equity' allows these political rights to be bought and sold; a conventional corporation may justly be described as a tyranny in which the position of tyrant is bought and sold. To an extent that varies widely in different countries, the autocratic aspects of this rule have been constrained by employment legislation, without changing their essentially autocratic nature, and without bestowing on the employees the key rights to information, expression of views, voting, and sharing in any wealth created. The essence of the conventional capitalist corporation as a social institution is thus that it is controlled by the owners of equity capital—not by the state, but also not by the people who do the work and make it successful.

41.7 COMPANY LAW

This top-down constitution of the capitalist enterprise, with the outside financiers controlling information, influence, and all the wealth created, misses an important trick in marshalling human motivation.

The problem has long been recognized, but that insight has not been absorbed into the mainstream. In 1944, the eminent British statesman Lord Eustace Percy put it like this:

> Here is the most important challenge to political invention ever offered to the jurist or the statesman. The human association which in fact produces and distributes wealth, the association of workmen, managers, technicians, and directors is not an association recognised by the law. The association which the law does recognise—the association of shareholders, creditors and directors—is incapable of producing and distributing and is not expected to perform these functions. We have to give law to the real association and withdraw meaningless privilege from the imaginary one. (Percy, 1944; cited in Goyder 1987)

Percy clearly had in mind the reconstitution of company law. David Ellerman (1992) has argued that this can be achieved by a relatively simple process, converting equity to purely contractual financial instruments, and allowing all employees the rights to information and decision-making, as personal untradeable rights. These rights are currently bundled only as tradeable equity rights.

There is thus a mismatch between what it takes to make an enterprise successful—the voluntary co-operation of skilled and knowledgeable individuals—and the structure of the corporation, which gives to the employees no rights at all to information, to influence, or to share in the wealth created. Those rights are given in their entirety to the owners of the shares, whose role in helping make the company successful is limited to the points at which new equity is injected into the company, something that happens only very rarely. By contrast, the trading of a company's shares on a stock exchange is of no benefit to the business enterprise, and tends to lead to pressure to extract cash from the business (Appelbaum and Batt 2014).

41.8 CONVENTIONAL PREDICTIONS FOR MEMBER-OWNED ENTERPRISE

The predictions made for member-owned enterprise have tended to have their source in the assumptions embodied in traditional econometric modelling: of 'rationally self-interested' people as monothematically driven by self-interest, rather than responding also to social and ethical factors; of people as units of labour rather than autonomous individuals; of supervision as vital to ensure consistent application.

These ideas have frequently included a clearly ideological element. Jensen and Meckling (1979) forecast dire results for employee-ownership, all of which predictions have been disproved empirically since then. For example, they predicted that member-owned businesses would not be permitted by their members to invest unless the investments produced a higher cash-flow per member, and in any case had no longer a life than the members' retirement dates. These predictions, stemming from the 'rational self-interest' view of human nature, show that view to be far too unidimensional. For example, in the experimental ultimatum game, the question of fairness has been shown cross-culturally to drive economic behaviour to a significant extent—in every culture, people are prepared to reject significant personal gains if the bargain offered is seen as unfair (Güth et al. 1982; Altman 2014). Most dramatically, Jensen and Meckling included the forecast that even simple consultation with employees, as required in the German *Mitbestimmung* system, would produce 'a significant reduction in the country's capital stock, increased unemployment, reduced labor income and an overall reduction in output and welfare … The final outcome will be fairly complete, if not total, state ownership of the productive assets in the economy' (1979: 504). As it turned out it was the 'creativity' of the deregulated banks that had that effect; the actual effects of employee ownership have proved to be thoroughly constructive.

41.9 EMPIRICAL SUSTAINABILITY IN MEMBER-OWNED ENTERPRISE

Turning to the experience of member-owned enterprises, the oldest existing worker co-op in Italy, La Ceramica d'Imola, was handed to its employees by its owner in 1874; the shares in the German optics manufacturer Zeiss were transferred to a Stiftung, the German equivalent of a trust, in 1891; those of the leading UK retailer today, the John Lewis Partnership, were sold to a trust for the employees in 1929 (Oakeshott 2000; Cox 2010; Erdal 2011). Inspired by the local priest, the first worker co-operative in Mondragón in the Basque region of Spain began in 1956, a seed that has since grown to a network of some 120 businesses and a bank (Oakeshott 1990 and 2000; Whyte and Whyte 1988). In the same year, in America, the first leveraged employee buyout of a corporation was implemented by the owners of Peninsula Newspapers in Palo Alto, acting on the advice of their lawyer, Louis Kelso. By then the owners of Publix, today the top-rated retailer in the USA, were also developing a system of employee ownership. Since all but Peninsula Newspapers and just one of the Mondragón co-operatives continue successfully in member-ownership, the potential sustainability of member-owned enterprises is not in doubt (e.g. Bradley and Taylor 1992; Cox 2010; *Economist* 2000; Whyte and Whyte 1988).

The long-lasting European enterprises we have listed all share one feature: to a substantial or complete extent they are owned *collectively*, by all who work in them together. While in the worker co-ops individuals have personal stakes, the businesses build substantial reserves which are held collectively; the employee-owned companies are owned collectively by trusts or their equivalent. By contrast, in the American ESOP (Employee share Ownership Plan) system, the original trust ownership is transferred over time into personal retirement accounts, so that it is necessary for each generation to fund the employee purchase of the business anew if the employee ownership is to be sustained for more than a generation; this requirement, while it enables an advantageous tax regime, proves over the long term a substantial financial burden. The same is true when the ownership is in the form of stakes held directly by the members as individuals. In spite of this, Peninsula stayed in employee ownership for 25 years before selling out to a large newspaper group.

Constitutionally, the worker co-op form is more rational—in the sense of more closely reflecting the reality—than the employee-owned company; it steps outside the 'ownership' metaphor, and recognizes the essentially social nature of the business as a human institution. So the members as persons, in their role as the members of the co-operative, are allocated the political rights: to be informed, to vote, and to participate in wealth or losses created. A more accurate designation than 'member-owned' would be 'member-controlled'. By contrast, the employee-owned form sustains the metaphor of property ownership, with the rights to information, vote, and wealth still bundled in the form of shares, hence still ostensibly tradeable. Thus while it would be illogical for a member of a co-operative to believe that he or she could sell the rights (to information, influence, and participation in results) to anyone else, since they belong to the role of current membership, it seems to make sense to employee-owners of shares that they can sell those rights to others, because they are still bundled as tradeable equity rights. In the longer term, the development of sustainable businesses may find more viable the worker co-operative allocation of rights to persons because of their role in the business, that is, the recognition that autonomous human beings co-operating have rights per se, and not because of a notion of tradeable ownership. Ellerman's argument is persuasive that the concept of tradeable ownership of companies is fraudulent, in that it purports to buy and sell control over people, when each person has control over himself or herself, such control being physically inalienable. No matter how hard we try, we cannot pass over control into the hands of anyone else. The most we can do is co-operate with others, retaining our autonomy and responsibility. This invalidates the employment contract's passing to 'owners' the right to appropriate the wealth created by the autonomous, responsible employees (Ellerman 1992).

41.10 HUMAN EFFECTS

If we consider sustainability in terms of the broader effects on the people involved, multiple strands of research point to the likelihood that member-owned enterprise will have better effects on health and well-being than the current system. In an enormous study over some 17 years, Marmot, after controlling for all known lifestyle and medical influences, showed that a strong hierarchy at work shortens the lives of all but those at the very top (e.g. 1991). Member-owned enterprises tend to place significantly less stress on hierarchy. Erdal produced suggestive evidence that the effect on whole communities may be positive on a number of social measures when there is a relatively large proportion of member-owned enterprises (2014). Wilkinson and Pickett demonstrated that greater equality of wealth is associated with significantly better outcomes on a number of social measures (2009); the tendency of member-owned enterprises is to pay those in senior positions less than they would be paid in conventional businesses, and since the members have the right to share in profit, it follows that relative to the employees of their conventional competitors, the distribution of wealth in member-owned enterprise will be less unequal (Kruse et al. 2010).

There are thus multiple factors pointing towards the conclusion that member-owned enterprise will be sustainably constructive in human terms.

41.11 Economic Sustainability

Clearly, to be a sustainable enterprise it is necessary to achieve economic success—a basic requirement of any sustainable economic system is that it should create wealth. If it needs to be subsidized substantially or for more than a short period then it is not in the long term sustainable—this is one of the indications that the current financial system is not sustainable in its present form, with the banks having been provided with truly vast sums of capital simply to avoid systemic collapse.

Productivity is a key measure if any business system is going to be sustainable. In the four decades since the ESOP legislation was passed, there have been dozens of studies of the economic performance of companies that are at least partly owned by their employees. Overwhelmingly, these studies (by far the most numerous being in America) have concluded that employee ownership stimulates faster productivity growth. For a good review and confirmation, see Blasi et al. (2010).

There is an important qualification: simply transferring ownership will *not* reliably produce an increased productivity effect—the management style must at the same time be or become participative, sharing information with all employees and engaging them in contributing ideas and initiatives in shaping the way business is conducted.

The performance of worker co-ops has been less thoroughly studied, but the results are confirmatory, at the very least showing that member ownership does not detract from performance. For example, Fakhfakh et al. (2012), comparing large representative samples of conventional businesses and worker co-ops across a range of industries in France, found the co-ops to be no different in size and if anything more productive, as well as lasting longer, creating more jobs, and sustaining them better through economic downturns.

Whichever of the two systems of member-owned enterprises is used, the resulting performance effects are similar: their productivity is higher (Doucouliagos 1995); they last longer (Blair et al. 2000); they create more jobs (Quarrey and Rosen 1993); they sustain them better through downturns (Fakhfakh et al. 2012); their distribution of wealth is less skewed (Kruse et al. 2010); they are less plagued by free riders (Freeman et al. 2010). This last study refutes one of the key forecasts of the conventional model. Its empirical research shows that the process of supervision by one's fellow owners tends to be more thorough, supportive, and effective than conventional top-down supervision. But it is this latter that is key to the conventional model.

41.12 Economic Multiplier

One subject that has not yet been studied is the local-economy economic multipliers of member-owned enterprises. Logically, the multipliers must be greater than those of conventionally owned corporations. For example, the employee-owned John Lewis Partnership pays an annual bonus of the same per cent of salary to each of its 81 thousand employee 'partners'. In 2013 the sum totalled some 210 million pounds. Distributed among 81 thousand largely low-paid families, the money, spent on things that low-paid families normally buy, will have had a significant economic multiplier. By contrast the 270 million pound dividend distributed by similarly sized Marks and Spencer went overwhelmingly to financial institutions. It is reasonable to surmise that, to the extent that this was subsequently distributed in fees, it will have made already wealthy individuals wealthier, which will among other effects have fed the less than healthy bubble in London property prices; but much will have been invested in financial instruments, including derivatives, which have in recent years tended to have dubious effects on the economy as a whole. The multiplier effect on local economies, as also on aggregate demand in the overall economy, must be significantly greater in the case of John Lewis (John Lewis 2014; Marks and Spencer 2014).

41.13 FINANCE

So far, we have reviewed multiple indications that an economy dominated by member-owned enterprise would be better for the people in it and thoroughly effective in creating and distributing wealth.

However, one aspect of enterprise that needs to be efficiently and effectively solved if an economic system is to prosper has not yet been demonstrated to be as good in the case of member-owned enterprise as the current system. That aspect is the provision of finance for new ideas and new start-ups. Currently, without the sale of equity, many new ventures would simply not obtain the capital needed to start. The start of any new venture is a risky business, and without the ability to exercise considerable influence, many venture capitalists would not provide capital.

There is a positive pointer, however, in the experience of Mondragón. As has been mentioned, in 1959, in response to a relatively hostile attitude from the existing conventional banks, the four existing worker co-operatives jointly supported the start-up of the Caja Laboral Popular, a savings bank in the form of a credit co-operative. That bank grew rapidly and funded the start-up of over one hundred new worker-co-operative businesses, with never a failure until one caused by the deep global recession due to the irresponsible behaviour of the banks. During the 1990s, as the supervision of banks tightened to the extent of disallowing the investment of significant capital in loans to the co-operatives, the function of financing new ventures and new growth was passed to a venture fund supported at arm's length by the bank and by annual contributions from the co-operatives. The system includes the subsidy of multiple research institutes which feed their results to existing and new co-operatives (Erdal 2011).

A similar venture fund is maintained by the eight thousand worker co-ops in the Lega network in the Italian region of Emilia Romagna (e.g. Caselli 2013).

The key discovered in this way is that when a financial system is developed which is aimed, not at making the maximum profit possible—an aim which perverted the global financial institutions to the point of mass recklessness and criminality—but whose purpose is to support member-owned enterprise, then it is possible to solve the problem. The Caja Laboral Popular has long been high on the list of most securely financed banks in the world, and was barely touched by the threatened global collapse, having invested in none of the dubious derivative instruments, although it did hold a relatively small quantity of Lehman Brothers bonds, and was taken to task for doing so.

In summary, the question of financing new member-owned enterprises has been solved in ways that suggest a fundamentally different form of financial institution is required, one that is directed towards fulfilling that financial role, rather than simply towards maximizing its own profit.

41.14 CONCLUSION

Member-owned enterprises have proved their social sustainability; their sustainability in human, economic, and financial terms. They should form a significant part of any way forward as we seek to improve the existing unbalanced and precarious system. The conventional model has such a strong hold on those running the global economy, however, that the empirical results have not been appreciated nor their lessons learned. It is time for that learning to take place, and for those lessons to be given due recognition in any discussion of business and the economy.

REFERENCES

Altman, M. (2014), 'Are Co-operatives a Viable Business Form? Lessons from Behavioural Economics', in S. Novkovic and T. Webb, eds, *Co-operatives in a Post-Growth Era* (London: Zed Books), 176–93.

Appelbaum, E. and Batt, R. (2014), *Private Equity at Work: When Wall Street Manages Main Street* (New York: Russell Sage).

Blair, M., Kruse, D., and Blasi, J. (2000), 'Is Employee Ownership an Unstable Form? Or a Stabilizing Force?' in T. Kochan and M. Blair, eds, *The New Relationship: Human Capital and the American Corporation* (Washington, DC: The Brookings Institution), 241–98.

Blasi, J. R., Freeman, R. B., Mackin, C., and Kruse, D. L. (2010), 'Creating a Bigger Pie? The Effects of Employee Ownership, Profit Sharing and Stock Options on Workplace Performance', in D. L. Kruse, R. B. Freeman, and J. R. Blasi, eds, *Shared Capitalism at Work: Employee Ownership, Profit and Gain Sharing and Broad Based Stock Options* (Chicago: University of Chicago Press), 139–65.

Bloch, M. (1961), *Feudal Society* (London: Routledge & Kegan Paul).

Boehm, C. (1999), *Hierarchy in the Forest: The Evolution of Egalitarian Behavior* (Cambridge, MA: Harvard University Press).

Bradley, K. and Taylor, S. (1992), *Business Performance in the Retail Sector* (Oxford: Oxford University Press).

Caselli, S. (2013), Presentation to International Cooperative Alliance, Cape Town. http://www.slideshare.net/cooperatives/d-simona-caselli-ica-cape-town (accessed 4 November 2016).

Cox, P. (2010), *Spedan's Partnership: The Story of John Lewis and Waitrose* (Cambridge: Labatie Books).

Daily Telegraph (1965), 8 January. http://www.telegraph.co.uk

Doucouliagos, C. (1995), 'Worker Participation and Productivity in Labor-Managed and Participatory Capitalist Firms: A Meta-Analysis', *Industrial and Labor Relations Review* 49, 58–77.

Economist (2000), 'Zeissmic Shift', *Economist.* 11 November.

Ellerman, D. (1992), *Property and Contract in Economics: The Case for Economic Democracy* (Cambridge MA: Blackwell).

Erdal, D. (2011), *Beyond the Corporation: Humanity Working* (London: Bodley Head).

Erdal, D. (2014), 'Employee Ownership and Health: An Initial Study', in S. Novkovic and T. Webb, eds, *Co-operatives in a Post-Growth Era* (London: Zed Books) 43–66.

Fakhfakh, F., Pérotin, V., and Gago, M. (2012), 'Productivity, Capital and Labor in Labor-Managed and Conventional Firms: An Investigation on French Data', *Industrial and Labour Relations Review*, 65(4), 847–9. Also at HAL Id: halshs-00838518 https://halshs.archives-ouvertes.fr/halshs-00838518

Freeman, R. B., Kruse, D. L., and Blasi, J. R. (2010), 'Worker Responses to Shirking under Shared Capitalism', in D. L. Kruse, R. B. Freeman, and J. R. Blasi, eds, *Shared Capitalism at Work: Employee Ownership, Profit and Gain Sharing and Broad Based Stock Options* (Chicago: University of Chicago Press), 77–103.

Goyder, G. (1987), *The Just Enterprise* (London: André Deutsch).

Güth W., Schmittberger, R., and Schwarze, B. (1982), 'An Experimental Analysis of Ultimatum Bargaining', *Journal of Economic Behavior and Organization* 3(4), 367–88.

Jensen, M. C. and Meckling, W. H. (1979), 'Rights and Production Functions: An Application to Labor Managed Firms and Codetermination', *Journal of Business*, 52, 469–506.

The John Lewis Partnership (2014), *Annual Report*.

Kay, J. (2009), 'Narrow Banking'. http://www.johnkay.com/wp-content/uploads/2009/12/JK-Narrow-Banking.pdf (accessed 4 October 2016).

Keane, J. (2009), *The Life and Death of Democracy* (London: Simon and Schuster).

Kruse, D. L., Freeman, R. B., and Blasi, J. R. (2010), 'Do Workers Gain by Sharing? Employee Outcomes under Employee Ownership, Profit Sharing, and Broad Based Stock Options', in D. L. Kruse, R. B. Freeman, and J. R. Blasi, eds, *Shared Capitalism at Work: Employee Ownership, Profit and Gain Sharing and Broad Based Stock Options* (Chicago: University of Chicago Press), 257–89.

Luviene, N., Stitely, A., and Hoyt, L. (2010), *Sustainable Economic Democracy: Worker Cooperatives for the 21st Century*, Boston: MIT CoLab http://web.mit.edu/colab/pdf/papers/Sustainable_Economic_Democracy.pdf (accessed 4 October 2016).

McCoy, T. J. (1996), *Creating an Open Book Organization: Where Employees Think and Act Like Business Partners* (New York: Amacom).

Marks and Spencer (2014). Annual Report and Financial Statements.

Marmot, M. G. (1991), 'Health Inequalities among British Civil Servants: The Whitehall II Study', *Lancet* 337, 1387–93.

Oakeshott, R. (1990 [1978]), *The Case for Workers' Co-ops* (London: Macmillan).

Oakeshott, R. (2000), *Jobs and Fairness: The Logic and Experience of Employee Ownership* (Norwich: Michael Russell).

Percy, E. (1944), *Riddell Memorial Lecture: The Unknown State: A Plea for the Study of Government* (Oxford: Oxford University Press).

Quarrey, M. and Rosen, C. (1993), *Employee Ownership and Corporate Performance* (Oakland, CA: National Center for Employee Ownership).

Stiglitz, J. (2008), Presentation to the Congreso Internacional CIRIEC, Seville. Available at http://www.congresociriec.es/en (accessed 4 October 2016).

Whiten, A. and Erdal, D. (2012), 'The Human Socio-Cognitive Niche and its Evolutionary Origins', *Philosophical Transactions of the Royal Society B*, 367, 2119–29.

Whyte, W. F. and Whyte, K. K. (1988), *Making Mondragón: The Growth and Dynamics of the Worker Cooperative Complex* (New York: ILR Press).

Wilkinson, R. and Pickett, K. (2009), *The Spirit Level: Why More Equal Societies Almost Always Do Better* (London: Allen Lane).

....

CHAPTER 42

THE CO-OPERATIVE
BUSINESS MODEL

the shape of things to come

....

CHARLES GOULD

42.1 INTRODUCTION

....

PREDICTING the future is a pleasant parlour game, but one fraught with risk. The temptation is strong to over-emphasize events one personally favours and to treat as aberrations those events one hopes will fall by the wayside. And the Black Swan we do not anticipate, that changes everything, is always circling.

It is nonetheless useful to ponder the future and note trajectories that seem to be emerging, and this short chapter will do a bit of that. Equally, however, it will point out some of the environmental conditions that are driving these trajectories and address whether these seem to be sustainable and persistent, and the implications if they shift.

42.1.1 Core Identity

It will be important in the future that co-operatives assert their identity if they are to avoid misuse of the form, and risk undermining its reputation and credibility. History is replete with examples where the co-operative form has been co-opted by governments or development agencies seduced by its ability to stimulate growth. In attempting to form co-operatives, however, they have too often under-appreciated the critical component of self-help. Businesses that are not democratically controlled and independent from government will not fully capture the commitment of their members and, whatever they are, they are not co-operatives.

The co-operative business model is defined by its Principles. The Statement of Co-operative Identity, where these Principles are embedded, is stewarded by the

International Co-operative Alliance (Alliance 1995). Its members in one hundred countries have agreed that these seven Principles define what it means to be a co-operative. Securing and maintaining this consensus is no mean feat in itself.

The co-operative business model embraces certain social principles: open membership, democratic control, economic access, and equity. Today these concepts, which have long had broader lip service even outside of the co-operative movement, are receiving heightened attention. Co-operatives are well positioned to speak with an authentic voice on these principles of core co-operative identity.

The Principles have been enshrined in key documents of intergovernmental organizations and in the legislation of some countries. Consequently, there is a reluctance to tinker with them. Recognizing, however, that the business and political environment is continually changing, and that the Principles must be refreshed from time to time if they are to be 'of our time', the Alliance has committed to drafting a series of guidance notes to interpret and apply the Principles. The notes are intended to discuss new situations and reflect on how co-operatives are dealing with them, consistent with the Principles.

In addition to defining the co-operative identity, co-operatives must assert that identity. The Alliance launched a global co-operative marque in 2013 to encourage co-operatives around the globe to graphically project their co-operative identity. Together with the continued extension of the co-op top-level domain on the Internet, co-operatives have readily available tools to signal their inclusion in the co-operative community.

42.2 WHAT DIFFERENTIATES THE CO-OPERATIVE BUSINESS MODEL?

In its *Blueprint for a Co-operative Decade*, the International Co-operative Alliance has identified two areas of competitive advantage for co-operatives. The *Blueprint* is a document adopted by the members of the Alliance at the close of the United Nations International Year of Co-operatives 2012, to increase the impact of co-operatives in the global economy by 2020 (Alliance 2012).

42.2.1 Participation

The first differentiator of the co-operative model that the *Blueprint* identifies is participation. The *Blueprint* asserts that the co-operative is the most participatory model of business. In a co-operative, members are guaranteed a voice, which is a compelling message at a time in history when so many people express such discontentment, even outrage, at the dominant social and economic models that shape and control their lives and yet from which they feel so disconnected.

To maintain the legitimacy of this argument in the future, however, co-operatives must ensure that members are, in fact, participating. If they are not engaged in the business of the co-operative and its governance, the co-operative's distinctiveness will be undermined. At its heart, this means that the members must believe that they are, in fact, the owners, and they must find this member-ownership useful to them.

A steady stream of social unrest—the Occupy movement, the Arab Spring, civil wars, street riots in Western capitals—have ensured that the desire for voice and impact is more than academic. The dissatisfaction that these situations reflect is impetus for change. What actual change comes about will be influenced by prevailing social thought, and co-operatives can help to shape that thought.

Among the dominant themes amid this social unrest is a concern about growing inequality. Thomas Piketty's elegant work on capital has presented the data that shows that inequality is the natural course of the economic systems that have been dominant in recent times (Piketty 2014). The Organization for Economic Co-operation and Development reports that global income inequality has been at its highest level in the last 50 years (OECD 2011). Further work in this area will reinforce the opportunity that co-operatives have to demonstrate the responsiveness of their model to such conditions.

Further shaping prevailing social thought, especially for younger generations, are the intriguing new possibilities that technology has opened. The Internet, in particular, has evolved in directions that demonstrate the benefits of collaboration. The many 'wiki' sites are based on the premise that all of us together are more knowledgeable and creative than any of us singularly, and that this shared wisdom is a viable alternative to a strictly competitive approach that holds information and knowledge closely and 'selfishly'. Jeremy Rifkin has written compellingly of what he terms a 'collaborative commons' and speaks in that regard of 'a co-operative renaissance' (Rifkin 2014).

There is no guarantee that this embrace of collaboration will rebound to the benefit of co-operatives especially, but it seems likely that young people weaned on collaboration will find the co-operative model more naturally agreeable than a generation bred on strict competitive values. It is helpful to co-operative growth that younger generations seem to be adapting to an emerging techno-social environment that is aligned with co-operative values.

In fact, it is easy to see how the very platform that has facilitated this collaboration—the Internet—would lend itself to application of the co-operative model. Various groups are today engaged in designing co-operative vehicles that would allow individuals to control use of their private information by the websites they frequent.

Similarly, the Internet has also facilitated global conversations, access, and action. Crowd funding for business start-up or for growth capital is just one example of global conversations moving to the important stage of action. Again, there is no assurance that this will be of greater benefit to co-operatives, although the opportunity is present. It will be necessary to convert a stark investment opportunity, in the case of crowd funding, to a democratically controlled activity with equal economic participation.

Not every social trend is a harbinger of success for co-operatives, of course. There has for some years been evidence of growing mistrust of institutions in many countries.

While co-operatives can capitalize on this, to the extent they distinguish themselves from other institutions, this mistrust has sometimes been identified as accompanied by a 'reluctance to join'. If this hardens, it will become more difficult for co-operatives to convert collaborative individuals into the active, engaged, participating members the model requires.

42.2.2 Sustainability

The other of the two differentiators in the *Blueprint*, and perhaps the leading co-operative social message today, is sustainability—environmental, social, and economic. Co-operatives believe that they are by design inclined towards greater sustainability than other business models. This inclination is a result of the community regard that is inherent in co-operatives and that is explicit in the Seventh Principle in the Statement of Co-operative Identity.

Forged in the Industrial Revolution, co-operatives have long seen themselves as the antidote to the excesses of a monolithic capital-based system, to a system that places capital at its centre, rather than people. Co-operatives are about need, not greed, the saying goes. With such an ideological core, it was natural to align in the early days with the labour movement, with garden cities, with Robert Owen. Later, co-operatives stood firmly with the peace movement. Today there is close affinity with the environmental movement and sustainability.

Co-operative members make decisions based not solely on economic benefit, but also taking into account the impact on their community, their families, and their neighbours. The generally local nature of co-operatives ties them willingly and intentionally to their community. Because the member-owners are engaged in the co-operative for the purpose of their own livelihood, co-operatives are not typically subject to the relocation of plants and factories to places where labour is less expensive or environmental regulations less protective.

This bucolic picture is more than aspirational: it is a design element. That does not mean, of course, that it is universally true for all co-operatives, nor that it is always practised to its fullest. The sustainability work that the Alliance has undertaken in pursuit of this strategic area is in part testing the alignment between promise and practice, with the intent of setting a clear standard for practice.

It will be essential for the future that co-operatives do not fall behind in this critical area. The public alarm at environmental degradation is not lost on corporations that are intent on positioning themselves to their consumers and workforce as responsible corporate citizens.

There is solid evidence that the co-operative form is proving useful to those wanting to lead in sustainability, especially in energy. Electric power has long been provided, especially in rural areas, through co-operatives. Eighty per cent of the land mass of the United States receives its electricity through a co-operative, for example. More recently, there has been a surge of new green co-operatives in a number of countries—Germany, in particular, as the country recommits with renewed vigour to a non-nuclear energy infrastructure. From 2006 to 2011, Germany averaged one hundred new energy co-operatives formed each year (Bilek 2012). It is not at all fanciful that co-operatives could become a dominant form for energy delivery in many parts of the world.

42.3 CHALLENGES

While the co-operative business model can be the beneficiary of the current conver-gence of political and economic events that are of the magnitude that resets expecta-tions, it faces challenges in capturing that potential.

42.3.1 Ideology

The co-operative is a business model with specific business attributes defined by domes-tic business legislation, which itself is generally devoid of any particular ideological bias and not necessarily inclusive of the Co-operative Principles. Some who adopt a co-operative business form are most definitely not driven by a commitment to the ideo-logical roots of the co-operative movement: it is the appeal of the business structure that is alluring. For example, Swift (the Society for Worldwide Interbank Financial Telecommunication), the primary global platform for financial messages, is a co-operative owned by its financial institutions. Without impugning those owners, there is no indication that they have a collective ideological platform. It probably would not be going far out on a limb to suggest that a number of the principles one would expect to find among these global financial institutions would be poster children for holding capi-talist positions that would mortify the more ideologically pure among the co-operators.

There is no particular benefit to the co-operative movement, as a movement, if the business model is co-opted by institutions that admire the functionality of its financial attributes without aspiring to its social agenda. The best that can be said is that such adoptions might signal the credibility of the model in important policy circles that have traditionally been inordinately corporate.

With a commitment to the Co-operative Principles, these secondary co-operatives with business owners (co-operative businesses or others) could have a substantial role in shaping the future profile of co-operatives. Purchasing, marketing, and service co-operatives—like Ace Hardware and Best Western Hotels—employ Co-operative Principles to benefit small, community-based businesses. Lesser known, but substan-tial, co-operative purchasing and management groups are behind carpeting outlets, mechanical contractors, and similar businesses central to people's everyday lives. The co-operative story need not be only of individuals lifting themselves out of poverty. A model that allows small local businesses to survive and thrive has a politically palat-able message and resonant social value.

42.3.2 Scale

The second of the fundamental challenges facing co-operatives in achieving the promise that lies before them is dealing with the tricky nature of 'scale'. Co-operatives are generally community based, but business is globally connected and influenced. Most co-operatives find it necessary to aggregate beyond the purchasing power or market access of their single local co-operative. Co-operatives are developed to grant access, but access is needed to larger and more aggregated forums.

Dairy farmers have been a particular area of co-operative success, due to the vulnerability that the perishable nature of their product imposes. Amul Dairy in India, with three million farmer members, is the largest dairy co-operative in the world, made up classically of small dairy farmers supplying on average a few litres of milk a day. The 'food co-ops' in the United States, while quintessentially of their neighbourhood, access organic products through a nationwide purchasing group, the National Cooperative Grocers Association.

The last decades of the past century and the start of this one saw a drive for scale among co-operatives. There is nothing about scale that is at odds with the co-operative model. Its magic is in allowing individuals to band together to improve their access to goods or services or markets or to improve their position.

The movement towards scale, however, has been beyond the coming together of individuals in a single co-operative: it has been the combination of co-operatives into formal co-operative groups or into single larger co-operatives. This drive for scale was driven largely by the need to compete with the pricing and purchasing advantages that massive scale brought to other business models and, in particular, to the corporate model.

The difficulty is in achieving scale and its benefits without so elongating the thread that runs between members and decision-making that it becomes thin and bare. Scale tends to lead towards 'professional managers' and more of them. Member control of key decisions can be arrogated by management with increasing member acquiescence. Members' emotional ties to the co-operative as a community benefit to be stewarded for subsequent generations grows into a quaint and distant concept. Eventually, someone tumbles to the insight that equity is locked up in the business and ought to be released through demutualization, and thereby ends the story of a sustainable community benefit and a way of life.

Some of the world's larger co-operatives have stumbled in recent years: a co-operative bank caught up in the LIBOR scandal; a worker co-operative defaulting in a global white goods division; an icon of co-operative history divesting of key assets to disentangle complex business enterprises years in the making. The most widely heralded explanation for what are perceived as failings is 'co-operative governance'. Co-operatives can at least take comfort in knowing that this is always the assessment in corporate circles, too, when companies flounder. It is always much easier to believe that the wrong people were at the helm than to actually look beyond that in an attempt to understand the specific complex business reasons for the problem.

The present mantra is to disparage the co-operative board structure by impugning the judgement of the people in ordinary walks of life who serve on the board because of the nature of their professions: 'housewives', ministers, etc. It is essential for the future of the co-operative model that co-operatives not be bullied into unfounded concessions that educated middle-class individuals are incapable of contributing to a business strategy. There is much more evidence that incestuous board relationships comprised of 'professionals' in an industry are harmful to the business, although seldom to the interests of those professionals themselves.

42.3.3 Differentiation

Today there is a robust field of business forms. Co-operatives are not the only alternative to a corporate form. Communist actors embrace aspects of capitalism. Partnerships are growing for the first time since the Victorian age, when they defined the landscape. Government-owned enterprises are an important part of many economies. Family-owned businesses are on the rise, and limited liability companies are more popular among entrepreneurs than are corporations. At the same time, corporations sound like charities in their marketing, with only 'our interests' at heart.

Perhaps more importantly, there is a new creativity in the so-called social enterprise or solidarity economy space—those creatures designed to conduct business in a socially responsible way with social outcomes in mind. B-corps and benefit corporations create a legally binding fiduciary obligation to pursue stated social or environmental missions, in addition to their financial objectives. Low-profit limited liability companies (LC3) allow for investors in companies established for a social purpose. These forms allow their principals to access funds without being subject to the same degree of fiduciary responsibility for a financial return as a regular corporation would have to pay regard to on behalf of its shareholders, or a foundation would need in order to qualify for tax-favoured investment treatment.

Co-operatives have not universally agreed their categorization in the social economy. While there is little opposition to aligning with those in that space, there is at best ambivalence in many regions about the benefit of being categorized as such. In part, that may reflect a fear of marginalization, of not being taken seriously as an important and potentially critical component of the global economy.

For the most part, the alternative models within the social enterprise space have aligned objectives with which co-operatives would find themselves in solidarity, but they do not necessarily subscribe to the principles that co-operatives have found to be essential over time, such as open access, democratic control, and equal economic participation of the members. This combination has allowed millions to lift themselves from poverty, to improve and sustain their economic condition, and to benefit their communities. As a proven model with a century and a half of experience, the co-operative should be an assertive voice in this space.

In the coming years, co-operatives may find that the expansion of the model will require two levels of differentiation. As in the past, they may need to explain why a non-capital-based model is preferable. If those who argue that we have entered a post-capitalism period are correct, when the creation of a 'better life' involves more than maximizing profit, this part of the equation may be made easier for co-operatives. They may then, however, face increasing challenges, and marketplace confusion, in differentiating themselves from a panoply of social enterprises, trying to convince these entrepreneurs to become 'co-opreneurs'.

42.4 Creating the Conditions for Co-operative Growth

42.4.1 Legal Framework

The essential social objectives of the co-operative model notwithstanding, it is nonetheless a business model. Like every business model, it requires recognition in the controlling legislative regime. Individuals seeking to establish a business will be influenced in their choice of business form by the ease of, or obstacles to, establishment, and by such factors as the applicable tax regime. Today the relevant legislative and regulatory regimes do not universally acknowledge the factors instrumental to co-operative growth or creation.

Too many countries have outmoded or protectionist provisions that prevent co-operatives from operating in the banking or insurance sectors in particular. There are countries that fail to distinguish publicly traded enterprises from member-owned co-operatives and so do not appreciate why public policy considerations that justify anti-monopolistic legislation, for example, ought not to be applied to limit co-operatives from extending benefits to their members. Ideally, legislation is adopted that is specifically designed to allow co-operatives to engage in activities that they are good at and that are of benefit to the overall economy.

The public policy arguments for a co-operative friendly legal framework are strong. Co-operatives are nicely positioned today to show that they bridge the space between value-devoid businesses and the social economy. One way to highlight this is by the impact co-operatives have in driving the 'real economy', in the creation of local jobs. Job creation is a high priority for most governments. Corporations have been quick to shed jobs in an economic downturn, slow to add them when business picks up, and eager to relocate them where costs are lowest. Co-operatives have become an engine of job creation in local economies. The International Labour Organization estimates that co-operatives provide one hundred million jobs, at least 20 per cent more than multinational corporations (ILO 2007). These jobs have 'liveable' attributes, typically providing wages and benefits consistent with the underlying values the co-operative espouses. This again is a reflection of a community-based, member-owned enterprise.

Co-operatives sometimes find ways to 'work around' these restrictions, such as a co-operative owning a bank rather than establishing a truly co-operative bank, but these distorted creatures have distinct disadvantages and often ticking time bombs embedded. In addition, the juxtaposition of a co-operative structure and a non-co-operative structure inside a common enterprise is likely to confuse and erode management commitment to co-operative principles.

A particular area of opportunity is in a sector of relative recency for co-operatives: social co-operatives. With the contraction of direct government services in many industrial countries, caregivers have found the co-operative form a helpful way to organize to provide their services, and an antidote to the chronic quality failures that have plagued this sector.

The Italian experience is the best known example, developing in the last quarter of the last century, and now the dominant form of social enterprise in Italy. Typically, these co-operatives involve about two dozen worker-members. Japanese co-operatives, too, have added extensive social services for their members, The social co-operative model is being adapted in countries around the world. Those countries where government has not historically provided such services, but which now experience pressing demands from their citizens, may find care co-operatives a useful alternative to the wind-up and wind-down that Western governments have undergone in the provision of social benefits. In addition, co-operatives can be more accessible than other business forms to individuals in the informal economy, where caregivers are well represented.

At the intergovernmental organization level, in particular the United Nations and its specialized agencies, there has long been recognition of the value of the co-operative model. The support these organizations bring to the model gives important guidance to domestic policymakers. For the co-operative to have appropriate relevance in the future, the newer global governance hubs must also acknowledge the rightful place co-operatives can fill. An example of this new recognition is the inclusion, at long last, of a co-operative in the B20, the business advisory group to the G20. That representation has led to greater awareness of the co-operative model and acknowledgement in the B20 policy statements that mutualization is an approach that should be considered to develop the infrastructure needed to stimulate global economic growth. Modest, but a promising start.

42.4.2 Capital

In addition to a supportive legal environment, co-operatives require capital. They require capital for start-up, typically from members, but that source is not always adequate for every business sector. They require capital to grow, again not always available at the levels needed from members.

Some of the emerging hybrid models of business that are appearing in the social enterprise space have been designed with access to capital in mind. To compete against these models, co-operatives must have access to a reliable stream of financial capital, and this capital must be accessible without compromise to the Co-operative Principles.

The *World Co-operative Monitor* that the International Co-operative Alliance and its scientific partner, Euricse, publish annually ranks the largest co-operatives in the world. The 300 largest have an annual turnover in excess of USD two trillion. These co-operatives have been able to achieve growth, but how they have done so and how applicable their lessons are for other co-operatives today have not been adequately studied.

The Alliance has undertaken a preliminary review of how co-operatives are financing start-up and growth which should shed some important light on such questions as debt versus equity; co-operative financial institutions' contribution to sector growth versus that from other financial institutions; and the role of public capital. This is envisioned as an annual or periodic review complementary to the *Monitor*, which is steadily being expanded to analyse the co-operative sector beyond the world's largest co-operatives.

Inherent in this last discussion is the assumption that growth is desirable, and on this point co-operatives are not unanimous. There is a considerable co-operative cohort that believes growth is the wrong rubric, that it buys into corporate rhetoric, that it is unsustainable. This position is aligned with a broader post-growth or de-growth conversation occurring among economists and social scientists.

We can at least commit here to desiring that, to the extent goods and services are to be produced, it would be better that they be produced through co-operatives, and that we can at least seek growth of co-operatives in preference to growth through other economic models.

At least co-operatives are inclined toward sustainability, are committed to jobs with liveable wages and benefits, and to principled development. Growth and sustainability can be reconciled, and the future of co-operatives depends in part on their being able to make the case that it is the co-operative model that best achieves this reconciliation.

42.4.3 Development

Co-operatives in Europe and North America have a long history, are generally well established in mature sectors, and are showing growth in emerging areas such as renewable energy and technology. In Latin America, agricultural and credit co-operatives are well established and other sectors are growing steadily. The Asia & the Pacific Region's co-operative sector is showing substantial growth, reflective of the overall economic growth in that part of the world.

The African story is still being written. There is a history of co-operative development on the continent, but with uneven successes. The national apex organizations are generally weak, and so primary co-operatives rely on government support, which is not always conducive to the autonomy the co-operative model requires to foster local decision-making that in turn ensures economic participation. And yet the African continent is experiencing record economic growth.

The agricultural sector is dominated by smallholders, with 500 million smallholders producing 80 per cent of the food consumed in Asia and sub-Saharan Africa (IFAD 2013). These farms are certain to see improvements in productivity. The world's food demands will ensure this. What is not certain is to whose benefit the improvements will accrue. Governments around the world whose nations are experiencing growth eye Africa with strategic interest. Multinational corporations are determined not to miss out on the profit potential that is clear to see.

The co-operative model, properly employed, could help ensure that the benefits of investment in the continent accrue to the African people and their communities.

While Africa is the focus of attention, it is not the only part of the world showing promise of significant co-operative development. Similar trends to improve the productivity realized from smallholder farms are underway in areas such as Central Asia, as well.

Achieving the potential in these developing areas will require a commitment from the intergovernmental organizations, such as the United Nations and its Food and Agriculture Organization (FAO) and the International Labour Organization (ILO) in particular. All indications at present are that they are prepared for this task. The ILO has published on the African co-operative renaissance (ILO 2009). The FAO has been helping smallholders participate more equitably in value chains. The international Co-operative Alliance, representing the co-operative movement across the world, is fully committed, adopting an African Plan that its members in Africa have developed and the co-operative ministers in a number of countries on the continent have endorsed.

The success or failure of individual co-operatives in the future will vary by sector, competitive environment, and cultural affinity to the values and principles of the co-operative model, in addition of course to their operating efficiency and strategic vision. The success or failure of the model itself, however, relative to capitalism and other competing models, is likely to be largely determined by the factors identified here: providing a channel for meaningful participation; demonstrating a commitment to sustainability; displaying the ability to shape a supportive legal framework; and gaining access to capital. Co-operatives will need to make the case for their model in contrast to a capital-based model, while increasingly showing their advantages over robust social enterprises. They must do all of this while achieving a level of scale that allows them to meet their members' needs without compromising their principles. In spite of the daunting nature of this list, the social and technological environment to achieve this is present, and co-operatives have the authenticity of proven success over almost two centuries to support them in these efforts. It is an exciting time.

References

Alliance (1995), *Statement of Co-operative Identity* (Geneva: Switzerland: International Co-operative Alliance).

Alliance (2012), *Blueprint for a Co-operative Decade* (Brussels, Belgium: International Co-operative Alliance).

Bilek, A. (2012), *Revitalizing Rural Communities through the Renewable Energy Cooperative* (Washington, DC: Heinrich Böll Stiftung).

IFAD (2013), *Smallholders, Food Security, and the Environment* (Rome, Italy: International Fund for Agricultural Development).

ILO (2007), *100 Million Jobs: The Contribution of Cooperatives to Employment* (Geneva, Switzerland: International Labour Organization).

ILO (2009), *Cooperating out of Poverty: The Renaissance of the African Cooperative* (Geneva, Switzerland: International Labour Organization).

OECD (2011), *Divided We Stand: Why Inequality Keeps Rising* (Paris: OECD Publishing).

Piketty, T. (2014), *Capital in the Twenty-First Century* (Cambridge, MA: The Belknap Press of Harvard University Press).

Rifkin, J. (2014), *The Zero Marginal Cost Society* (New York, NY: Palgrave Macmillan).

Index

Note: see individual main entries for topics referring to that country/area

Abbey National 105
Abell, Hilary 532
accountability
  collective accountability 355
  enterprise form xxix, 228–31, 236, 242
  governance 228, 450, 454
  mutuals 232, 236, 242
  neoliberal governance 450
  value chains 467
Adams, John 116
Adler, Mortimer 124
Africa 607–8
  African Plan (ICA) 608
  agricultural co-operatives 608
  credit unions and co-operatives banks 575
  development 607–8
  growth 607–8
  ICA 48, 608
  ILO 608
  multinationals 608
  South Africa 195
  turnover 269–70, 273
agency
  agricultural co-operatives 167
  authority/hierarchy 64
  governance xxxiii, 153, 447, 449–50, 452
  neoliberalism 449, 450, 452
agricultural co-operatives 158–70 see also
      China, agricultural co-operatives
      in; France, multi-stakeholder co-
      operatives in Movement of Farm
      Machinery Co-operatives (CUMAs)
      in; Morocco, argan oil co-operatives
      in South West
  agency 167
  Better Farming, Better Business, Better
      Living (Three Betters) 256–7

capitalism 158–9, 162
centralized decision-making 164
challenges 159–60
characteristics of agricultural sector 161
coalition approach 167
collective bargaining 158, 164–5
competition 158, 162, 165
consumer co-operatives 161
co-ordination mechanism, co-operation
      as a 56, 58, 68
democracy 87, 166
developing countries xxviii, 161
development 607–8
economic rationale 161–2
efficiency gains 68
entrepreneurship as collective
      action 164–5
European Union 159
family farms 161–2
financial crisis of 2008 572
financial stability 158
firms, co-operatives as 163–5
governance 160, 166–7, 256–7
health care service 187
historical perspective 102–3
horizon problem 165–6
identity xxviii, 159–62, 163, 167
inequalities, collective action against 160
incentive structures 166
insurance 68
job security 158
large co-operatives xxviii, 166
long-term perspective 159
managers 163–4, 166
members 163–4, 166
multi-stakeholder co-operatives 87
new co-operatives models 165–6

agricultural co-operatives (*Cont.*)
  nexus of contracts approach 167
  non-firms, as 162, 163, 165–6
  non-traditional models 165–6
  non-profit distribution constraints 167
  opportunistic behaviour 161, 164–5
  ownership costs 161
  participatory model of
      decision-making 158
  Plunkett approach 256–7
  portfolio problem 165–6
  poverty alleviation 158
  productive processes 161–2
  property rights/incentive problems 165
  reasons for emergence 161–2
  rural development xxviii, 158
  scale of businesses 603
  size of co-operatives 166, 268
  social and solidarity co-operatives 172,
      176, 179
  social objectives 83, 87, 158, 167
  stakeholders 163–5
  trade unions 159
  user-benefits principle 166
  user-control principle 166
  user-owner principle 166
  vertical integration concept 163, 164, 167
Aldrich, Howard 528
Allen, F 22
Allende, Salvador 337
American Economic Association
      (AEA) 118–19
American Federation of Labor (AFL) 120
Anthony, Joseph 114
Arando, Saioa 134
Arctic Co-operatives Ltd 352
argan oil *see* Morocco, argan oil co-
      operatives in South West
Argentina xxxi, 335–6, 338–40, 345
  agricultural co-operatives 339
  colonialism 338
  consumer co-operatives 339
  credit unions 339
  dependency 340
  electricity 188
  financial crisis of 2008 336
  historical perspective 338

  legislative framework 339
  military dictatorship 339
  National Institute of the Social Economy
      (INAES) 339
  neoliberalism 339–40
  networks 339
  social and solidarity economy
      sector 338–9, 345
  social containment 339
  utilities 188, 339
  water 188
  worker co-operatives 338–40
  worker-recuperated enterprises 339–40
Arizmendiarrieta, José Maria 108, 280–2
Asia
  Central Asia 608
  growth 607
  large co-operatives 268
  turnover 269–70, 273
asset locks 69, 231–2, 310
Astrachan, JH 18
Atwater, Lyman 120–1
Australia
  building societies 105
  credit unions and co-operative banks 575
  employee ownership 206
  small-sized enterprises 270
  tax 202
Austria
  credit unions and co-operative
      banks xxviii, 105, 152, 573–4
  financial crisis of 2008 152
  renewable energy 187
  water services 188
authoritarian regimes, spread of 103–4
Ayadi, R 552
Azkarraga, J 291–2
B20 (business advisory group to G20) 606
BAG Bank Aktiengesellschaft
      (Germany) 407–8
Bailey, Andrew 563–4
Bakaikoa, B 287
Banco Santander 105
banking and financial services *see also* **credit**
      unions and co-operative banks
  design of institutions xxxvi, 587, 589
  diversity 6–8, 10

Europe, reports on banking in 7–8
exclusion of co-operatives 605
financial crisis of 2008 6–9, 150–2, 409,
    446, 570–6, 581, 585–6
legal framework 605
ownership 6–9
regulation 23, 149, 154, 155, 586
socially sustainable enterprises xxxvi,
    585–6, 595–6
speculation 6
TITF (too important to fail)/TBTF (too big
    to fail) 7

Barge, KJ 490
Barnes, WS 43–4
Barrett, CB 457
Barth, JR 23
Basel II 154
Basel III 154, 408
Basque Country, Spain 107–8, 134, 279–80,
    286–8, 291, 379, 591
Bauwens, Michele 258
BBBank (Germany) 405
Becker, S 325
Begiristain, A 287
behavioural economics 62–3
Belgium 106, 473, 576, 588
Benton, Thomas Hart 118
Bergengren, Roy 148
best practices xxix, 196, 203–6
Big Data 47
biogas 326
biomass 321, 323
Birchall, Johnston 152, 249, 481
Blair, Margaret 432
Blanc, Louis 102
Blasi, Joseph 213, 389, 418–19, 423, 427
Bolshevik Revolution 121
bonus culture 6
Bonus, H 162
Böök, Sven-Åke 257
Borzaga, C 76–7
Bowles, Samuel 58
Brazil 336, 345
Bretton Woods 4, 10
British Journal of Industrial
    Relations 220, 222

broad-based stock ownership (BBSO) xxxii,
    115–21, 125, 361–7, 370, 375, 377
Bryson, Alex 212
building societies xxxvi, 234–5, 573–5 see
    also United Kingdom, conversion of
    building societies in
Burdín, Gabriel 134, 137, 140
Burlton, Bob 248
Bush, George W xxxii
business literacy/skills
    directors 250
    employee ownership 205
    growth 354, 532
    intersectional identity 485
    leadership 352–3
    Plunkett approach 256–7
    private enterprises 457
    rural communities 463

Cambodia, employee ownership in 195
Cameron, David 206, 251
Canada 348–60 see also Quebec, Canada
    agricultural co-operatives 110 161, 355
    consumer co-operatives 110, 576
    context 349–50
    contributions to building community 353–5
    credit unions and co-operative banks 110,
        147, 155, 350, 351–3, 573, 575
    culture 355, 356
    democracy 353, 356
    Desjardins Group 350, 352–3, 575
    development of communities xxxi, 348–60
    diversity 349, 350, 356–7
    education and training 351–6
    engaged citizenry 353–4, 356
    entrepreneurial activities 351–2, 354–5
    globalization xxxi, 348, 357
    governance 350
    grass-roots initiatives 349, 355
    historical perspective 110
    ICA 352
    inclusive practices 355–6
    indigenous areas xxxi, 348, 349, 351–3, 356
    institutional contexts 349
    insurance 109
    Kahnawake First Nation 351, 352–3
    large co-operatives 268–9

Canada (*Cont.*)
  management training 352–3
  marginalized urban areas 348, 349, 351
  marketing 110, 355
  measurement of impact on
      communities 350
  micro-enterprises 355
  multi-stakeholder governance 350
  networks 353–5
  one member one vote principle 356
  partnerships 349
  peer lending circles 354–5
  personal infrastructure, building and
      strengthening 351–2
  physical infrastructure, 352
  remote areas xxxi, 348, 351, 356
  retail co-operatives 110, 351, 353, 356
  role of co-operatives xxxi, 348–60
  rural areas xxxi, 348, 349, 351, 355
  social and solidarity
      co-operatives 175, 178–9
  social capital 352
  social cohesion 349
  social economy xxxi, 348–9, 353–6
  social infrastructure, building and
      strengthening 352–3
  stakeholders 350
  sustainability of communities xxxi, 348–60
  trappers 356
  types of co-operatives 349
  urban areas xxxi, 348, 349, 351, 355, 356
  utilities 188–9
  women 354–5
  worker co-operatives 351–2, 579
capital/capitalization
  access to capital, impediments on 380
  broad-based stock ownership (BBSO) in
      corporate businesses 377
  capital co-operatives 233
  company capital model 145
  credit unions and co-operative banks 146,
      154, 155
  crowd funding 600
  growth 606–8
  hybrids 606–7
  ICA 607
  identity 48

  principles and values 48, 607
  private ownership 29
  recapitalization 154
  share capital, companies limited by 228–30,
      232–3, 237, 239–42
  start-ups 606
  sustainability 594, 601, 607
  under-capitalization 261
  worker co-operatives 131–2, 134–7, 141
capitalism *see also* **United States, shared
      capitalism in**
  agricultural co-operatives 158–9, 162
  alternatives 3–10, 570–1
  democracy 34–5, 37
  development 608
  economic growth 9
  enterprise form 604
  entrepreneurial activities 23, 453
  fair trade 477–8
  financial crisis of 2008 570–1
  golden age 4, 9–10
  historical perspective xxvii, 97–101, 111–12
  inequalities 30, 600
  laissez-faire 4, 7
  neoclassical economics 4
  ownership xxv, 3–10
  post-capitalism 605
  rights violations 30
  social and solidarity
      co-operatives 175, 178–9
  socially sustainable enterprises 594
  unleashed capitalism 4, 6–7, 9–10
  varieties of capitalism 23
  voluntary co-operatives 588
  welfare state 34
  worker co-operatives 137
care industry *see* **United States, home care
      industry in**
Carey Shanker, M 18
Castro, Fidel 343
centrally planned economies 3–4
**Centre for European Policy Studies
      (CEPS)** 7–9, 554, 556
Chaddad, F 165
Charrouf, Zoubida 456–7
Cheney, G 282
Chernobyl disaster 321

childcare providers 77, 86, 87–9, 90, 176
Childs, M 83
Chile xxxi, 336–8, 345
　agricultural co-operatives 336
　Catholic Church 336–7
　civil society, breakdown of 337
　Department of Mutuals and
　　Co-operatives 337
　economic crisis of 1980s 337
　general interest services 337–8
　independence 337
　legal recognition 337
　military coup 337
　mutuals 337
　neoliberalism 337
　non-profit sector 336–7
　social and solidarity economy sector 336,
　　337, 345
　social economy sector 336
　trade unions 337
　waste recycling 338
　water 337–8
　welfare model 337
China, agricultural co-operatives in 512–24
　agent-driven development 518–20
　business dealers 519–20
　capital-led co-operation 513
　capitalization 514
　challenges and opportunities xxxv, 514–15
　civil society 519, 521
　commercial companies 519–20, 522–3
　communes, abolition of 514
　community-based co-operation 513
　co-operative federations 516–17, 518,
　　521, 522
　democracy 517, 522
　diversification 513, 514
　diversity xxxv, 513, 516–18
　elites 519–21
　entrepreneurial activities 520–1
　evolution 513–16
　false co-operatives 513
　Farmers' Specialized Co-operatives,
　　definition of 512–13
　governance 514
　growth 512, 515, 523
　historical perspective 516

horizontal co-operation 513
household contract responsibility system
　(HCRS) 512, 514
hybrids 517
ICA principles 517
industrialization 514, 519, 521
initiators 519, 522
innovation 513, 516
institutional arrangements 514, 515, 522–3`
internalization of contractual relations 519
international agencies 522
Law on Farmers' Specialized Co-operatives
　(FSCs) 2007 xxxiv, 512–13, 516, 518–20
legitimacy 515
marketization 514
multi-stakeholder co-operation 514
new models 513, 514
NGOs 521–2
Number One Documents 514, 515
one member one vote principle 517, 522
poverty reduction xxxv, 521–2
producers' organizations 512, 518–19, 521
regional federations 518
rural crisis 515
rural economy 512–23
Rural Land Contracting Law 516
self-interest 523
shareholder co-operative system 513, 514,
　516, 517–18, 522
socio-economic challenges 513
specialization 515, 516, 517, 520
structural changes 512
sustainability 515
tax 515, 519
traditional co-operatives 516–17, 522
transfer of land-use rights 515–16
transition 512, 513–14
urbanization 514, 521
vertical integration 513
women 521
World Trade Organization 515
Christen, R 552
Churchill, Winston 6
citizen's dividend, distribution of 375, 376–7
City of London 6
civil and political rights 33, 589, 591–2
Clark, John Bates 118, 120

Clinton, Bill 370
Coase, Ronald 55
Cogeca (General Committee for Agricultural
    Co-operation in the EU) 159
collective bargaining 158, 164–5
Colson, René 501
commitment
    agricultural co-operatives 519
    associationism 292
    business efficiency 81
    citizen's share 370
    credit unions and co-operatives banks 146,
        379, 581
    employee ownership 431–2, 439, 485
    governance 250, 448–52
    ideology 602
    long-term commitments 258
    neoliberalism 448–52
    NGOs 522
    organizational democracy 81
    pay 138, 284
    political commitment 565–6
    principles and values 290–1, 350, 606
    profit-sharing 362
    rural areas 507
    social commitment 171–5, 236, 282, 588
    solidarity 285, 289
    stakeholders 232, 316, 481, 484–5, 494
    sustainability 356, 608
    worker-consumer co-operatives 380
    worker co-operatives 380, 395–6, 532
common good xxv, xxxvi, 21–2, 33, 36
communications and standards for
    communications 202–3, 253–6
community co-operatives xxviii–xxix, 184–7
community interest companies (CICs)
    (UK) 228, 236–7, 239–40
companies see for-profit enterprises
competition/competitiveness
    agricultural co-operatives 158, 162, 165
    co-operative law xxvi, xxxvi, 45, 540
    co-ordination mechanism, cooperation as
        a 64, 66
    credit unions and co-operative banks 145,
        149, 150
    efficient competition, logic of 79–80
    exit 450

financial crisis of 2008 6
historical perspective 99, 104
imperfect competition 15
neoliberal governance 447–51, 454
ownership 10
principles and values xxvi, 45
private sector 448
public sector 448
scale of business 603
social and political dimensions 78, 89, 91
sustainable development xxvi, 45
welfare systems 89
Confederation of Finnish Co-operatives 103
constitutions 39
consumer co-operatives
    access to capital, impediments on 380
    agricultural co-operatives 161
    co-operative law, role of 541
    democracy xxxii, 87–8, 383
    financial crisis of 2008 xxxvi, 571–2, 581–2
    governance 246, 381
    health care services 176
    institutional sponsorship 380, 382–3
    Internet 380
    multi-stakeholder co-operatives 87–8
    municipal governments, sponsorship
        by 382–3
    mutuals xxv, 15–16, 234–5, 237, 238–9
    organizational degeneration 380
    participatory models 380
    retail consumer co-operatives xxxvi, 379–
        80, 572, 576–9, 581
    social and political dimensions 81,
        82, 86, 87
    social and solidarity
        co-operatives 171–2, 176
    solidarity xxxii, 383
    taxi services 380
    trade unions 381–2
    travel accommodation 380
    utilities 184, 192
    worker co-operatives xxxii, 379–82
consumption and production, association
    between xxxii, 374, 379, 382
control
    agricultural co-operatives 166
    community co-operatives 186–7

co-operative law 48, 539, 542–3, 547–8
  enterprise form xxix, 242
  external control 543
  governance 63
  user-control principle 166
  utilities 185
  worker co-operatives 131, 138–9, 141
conventional enterprises *see* **for-profit
    enterprises**
Cook, M 165, 167
co-operation
  co-ordination mechanism, as xxvi, 55–75
  governance xxxiii, 447, 450, 453
  international economic co-operation 9
  social and political dimensions 81
co-operative advantage xxxvi, 252, 582
Co-operative College 102
co-operative, definition of xxxvi, 46–7, 77,
    184–5, 263–4, 599
Co-operative Group 4, 246–53
  Co-operative Bank 246
  Co-operative Wholesale Society
    (CWS) 105
  directors, quality of 250–1
  economic and social competencies 257
  education 247–9
  engagement, model of 256
  fair trade 477
  financial crisis of 2008 152, 575–7, 581
  governance 246–53, 256–7, 446, 453
  losses 246
  mis-selling scandal 581
co-operative law 539–49
  challenges for legislators 48–50
  characteristics of
    co-operatives xxxv, 539–43
  company law 589–90
  comparative studies 43
  competition law xxvi, xxxvi, 45, 540
  constitutions 39
  consumer co-operatives 541
  contract law 545
  control 48, 539, 542–3, 547–8
  co-operative purpose 540–3
  co-operative transactions and their
    regulation xxxv, 543–6
  democracy 543, 547

design 201, 231
differentiation between for-profit
    enterprises and co-operatives 40–1,
    542–3, 545, 547
distribution 539–40
diversity 263
equally, duty to treat members 544–6
EU law, harmonization of 48–9
flexibilization 44
for-profit companies xxxv, 40–1, 540,
    542–3, 545, 547
foreign ownership laws 202
general interest co-operatives 547–8
global law 50
globalization xxvi, 41, 46, 49
governance 543, 547
growth, legal framework for 605–6
harmonization 48–9
historical perspective 39
human rights 44, 46–7, 545
hybridization 49
ICA principles 547–8
identity xxxv, 540, 542, 548
ILO
  harmonization 48–9
  Recommendation No 193 42, 45, 47
institutions, building 44
internal nature of purpose 541, 547–8
labour law 201–2, 545
law-making in open, egalitarian and
    contestable way 33
legal arguments 41–3
legal structure of co-operatives xxvi, 49
measuring co-operative law xxvi, 46
membership, nature of 541–5
  double quality 542–3
  equally, duty to treat members 544–6
  users, members as 542–3
mutual purpose xxxv, 540–1, 543–4
mutuals 546, 548
non-members, co-operative activities
    with xxxv, 543, 545–6
non-profit companies xxxv, 539–40, 547–8
objectives/purpose xxxv, 540–4, 547–8
organizational law 539–40
ownership structure 542–3
pedagogical purpose of legislation 44

co-operative law (*Cont.*)
  political arguments 43–8
  politics/law nexus 44
  prescriptive function 540
  producer co-operatives 541–2
  regulation xxxv, 543–6, 548
  Rochdale Society of Equitable Pioneers 541,
      546, 548
  role xxxv, 539–49
  rule of law 44
  small-sized enterprises 263
  social economy 41
  social enterprises, legislation on 548
  social function xxxv, 547–8
  social justice 46–7
  socio-psychological dimension 49
  tax law 540
  technical aspects 44
  third parties 44
  transactions and their
      regulation, xxxv, 543–6
  UN GA Guidelines 42
  worker co-operatives 541
co-operative principles *see* **principles**
      and values
Co-operative Party 102
co-operative transactions and their
      regulation xxxv, 543–6
Co-operative Union of Danish Dairy
      Producers 102
co-ordination mechanism,
      cooperation as a 55–75
  application of new framework 67–70
  authority/hierarchy 56, 64, 70
  economic theory xxvi, 55–8, 70
  economics of co-operatives xxvi, 55, 61–7
  evolutionary economics 62
  fair procedures 57
  features and objectives of co-operative
      forms 62–4
  governance 64, 66–7, 70
  institutional theory 66
  intergenerational solidarity 65
  interpretation 55–6
  investor-owned firms
      (IOFs) 56, 69
  isomorphism 68, 70

limitations of co-operative
      enterprises 65–7, 70
market exchanges 64, 70
market failure 55–6, 64, 68
perverse reactions to market stimuli 65
profit maximization xxvi, 55, 57, 63, 68
reciprocity xxvi, 66
self-seeking individuals 55, 57
size of co-operatives 66
social capital 62, 66, 69
social welfare 63–4, 66
specific kind of co-operation mechanism,
      co-operation as 58–61
theoretical developments xxvi, 55–6
COPA (Committee of Professional
      Agricultural Organisations) 159
co-opreneurs 605
corporate governance xxx, 246,
      248–9, 445–55
  accountability 454
  agency xxxiii, 447, 449–50, 452
  ambiguity of valuation xxxiii, 451–2
  challenges xxx, 246, 248–9
  co-operation xxxiii, 447, 450, 453
  corporate governance approach xxx,
      246, 248–9
  credit unions and co-operative
      banks 152–3
  culture xxxiii, 445, 446
  democracy xxxiii, 446, 454
  dialogue xxxiii, 446, 448
  diversity 23
  entrepreneurial activities 453
  enterprise form xxix, 227, 239, 242
  failure of organizations 453
  financial crisis of 2008 446
  financialization 446
  foundational economy 453
  innovation xxxiii, 447, 453–4
  legitimacy crisis 446
  mutuals 446
  neoliberalism xxxiii, 446, 447–54
  ownership 9–10
  participatory governance xxxiii, 446
  scandals 446
  stakeholder versus shareholder theory
      debate 23

theories xxv, 19, 21, 23
trust xxxiii, 447–8, 450–1
corporate social responsibility (CSR) 23, 89
Cox proportional hazards models 134
Coxe, Tench 114
Craig, B 137
Creative Commons 60
Crédit Agricole 102, 106
credit rating agencies 149, 574
Credit Union Extension Bureau 148
Credit Union National Association
        (CUNA) 148
credit unions and co-operative banks 145–57
        see also banking; building societies;
        Germany, co-operative banking in
    audit function 149
    business model of financial
        co-operatives 146
    capitalization 146, 154, 155
    challenges 154–5
    company capital model 145
    competition 145, 149, 150
    consumption 147
    co-ordination mechanism, cooperation
        as a 64
    core values 146
    credit ratings 574
    democratic governance 145
    descending business model 145
    developing countries 69
    diversity in financial markets 156
    economic growth 154
    entrepreneurial activities 145
    entry and exit 155
    ethical behaviour 146
    EU banking union, introduction of 154
    financial crisis of 2008 151–3, 154,
        572, 573–6
    financial exclusion, countering 241–2
    gentrification 155
    governance 145, 149–50, 152–3
    growth of banks 153
    historical perspective 102
    innovation 145, 151, 153
    integration in financial
        co-operatives 148–50
    large investment projects 149

    liquidity 149
    local identity 146
    mergers 150, 151, 154, 155
    middle-class 147, 155
    mortgages 574
    mutuals 145, 573
    national laws xxviii, 145
    network structure 148–50
    new co-operatives, establishing 155–6
    one member one vote principle 145, 146
    open door principle 145
    ownership rights 145–6
    performance 151–2
    production 147
    profit maximization 146, 151
    proportionality 154
    prudence 146
    Raiffeisen model 146–7, 149, 155
    rating agencies 149
    rationing in developing countries 69
    recapitalization 154
    regulators 149, 154, 155
    relationship-based retail banking 69, 146
    religion 147
    responsiveness 146
    retail banking 150
    return on equity (ROE) 151
    rural society 147
    self-help 146–7, 155
    small size 145, 149–50
    social and solidarity co-operatives 172
    social cohesion 150
    social co-living 147
    solidarity 146, 150
    specialization 146
    stress tests by ECB 154
    takeovers 145
    technological challenges 155
    transparency 146
    universalism 147
    usury in developing countries 69
    voting 145, 146, 153
    well-being of members 146
    worker co-operatives 594
Cresson, Édith 501
Croatia 175, 177–8
crowd funding 600

Cuba xxxi, 342–5
    agricultural co-operatives 342–4
    Agricultural Development Bank 342
    Agricultural Production
        Co-operatives 343
    autonomy and independence 342
    Basic Units of Co-operative Production
        (UBPC) 343–4
    campesinos 343
    Credit and Services Co-operatives 343
    ICA 342
    land 343
    legislative framework 344
    Los Lineamientos 344
    National Association of Small Farmers
        (ANAP) 343
    producer co-operatives 343
    Revolution 342–3
    size of co-operatives 342–3
    state, links to 342–4
    urban-based co-operatives 344–5
    worker co-operatives 343–4
Cuevas, E 556
culture
    banking 449
    bonus culture 6
    changes 9
    development 608
    employee ownership 200
    enterprise form 227
    governance xxxiii, 252–3, 445, 446–52, 454
    neoliberalism 447–52, 454
    ownership 5, 9
    principles and values 40
    social and political dimensions 81
    stakeholder versus shareholder theory
        debate 23
    trust 450
    turnover of staff 451
CUMAs *see* France, multi-stakeholder
        co-operatives in Movement of
        Farm Machinery Co-operatives
        (CUMAs) in
Curl, John 527, 529
currency exchange 202
customer-owned co-operatives xxix, 184–7,
        189, 191–2, 229, 234–5

Cyprus, financial crisis of 2008 in 152
Czech Republic 177, 178, 181

data privacy laws 203
Davies-Coates, Josef 258
de Blasio, Bill 382
de Tocqueville, Alexis 83
de Vries, B 152
Dean, A 137
democracy *see also* one person one vote
        principle; voting
    agricultural co-operatives 87, 166
    broad-based stock ownership (BBSO) in
        corporate businesses 377
    capitalism 34–5, 37
    common goods xxvi, 33, 36
    community co-operatives 185–6
    consumer co-operatives xxxii, 87–8, 383
    co-operative law, role of 543, 547
    co-operatives, formation of 35–6, 37
    co-ordination mechanism, cooperation
        as a 58
    credit unions and co-operative banks 145
    crowd funding 600
    deliberative democracy 32–3, 35, 47
    democratic deficit xxvii, 76
    democratic pioneers xxvii, 90
    democratic school 80–1, 83–4
    distribution of wealth 37
    economics xxvii–xxviii, 139–41
    enterprise form xxix, 230, 240
    governance xxxiii, 248, 255, 446, 448,
        451–2, 454
    grass-roots democracy 90
    internal decision-making 87–8, 90–2
    inequality of income and wealth 34–6
    justice, principles of 33
    liberal socialism 36
    liberalism xxvi, 32–7
    logic of democratic membership 79
    market 86, 92
    multi-stakeholder co-operatives 87–8
    mutuals 35–6, 37, 482
    neoliberalism 448, 451–2
    one member one vote principle 87
    political participation 33, 35
    private property in productive resources 34

property-owning democracy 34–5, 36
relational goods, provision of 85
representative democracy 166
self-ownership 34
social and political dimensions 76–8, 81, 82
social and solidarity co-operatives 177, 179
social democracy xxv, 4
social justice xxvi, 36
socially sustainable enterprises 587, 589
societal changes 90
tax 34–5
theory of justice 33–4
utilities 185–6, 192
voluntary associations 90, 589
welfare services 47, 87, 90
worker co-operatives xxvii–xxviii, xxxii, 35, 139–41, 383
Denmark
agricultural co-operatives 83, 102, 159
consumer co-operatives 83
credit unions and co-operative banks 150
dairy producers 102–3
historical perspective 102–3
renewable energy 187
social and political dimensions 83
strategic networks 150
utilities 188
wind farms 188
Desjardins, Alphonse 110
Desjardins Group 147, 150, 350, 352–3, 575
Desrochers, M 150
developing countries 16, 69, 159, 161, 461, 470, 472–3
development 607–8
agricultural co-operatives 607–8
capitalism 608
culture 608
dynamic model of co-operative development xxvii, 78–80
ILO 608
local endogenous development 262
organizational development 78
renewable energy 607
rural areas xxviii, 158, 179–80
small-sized enterprises 262
sustainability 608
technology 607

Develtere, P 476–7
differentiation between for-profit enterprises and co-operatives
categorization of co-operatives 604–5
co-operative law 40–1, 542–3, 545, 547
co-opreneurs 605
enterprise forms 604
future of co-operative business model 604–5
marginalization 604
post-capitalism 605
principles and values xxvi, 43–4, 47
profit-maximization 605
social and solidarity co-operatives 173
social economy space 604
solidarity 604
disadvantaged workers 85, 176–9, 309–11, 314, 316–18, 356
diversity
banking in Europe, reports on 7–8
business models xxv, 7–9
co-operative law xxvi, 44, 45, 49, 50, 263
credit unions and co-operative banks 156
economic growth 556–7
enterprise form 233, 237
financial crisis of 2008 7
financial services sector 6–8, 10
ownership xxv, 5–6, 7–10
Doidge, C 23
domain names 59
Donati, P 84–5
Doucouliagos, Christopher 211–12
Dumont, René 500
Dunn, JR 166
Duttweiler, Gottlieb 108

Eastman, George 121
economics
agricultural co-operatives 161–2
behavioural economics 62–3
community co-operatives xxix, 185
co-ordination mechanism, cooperation as a xxvi, 55–8, 61–7, 70
democracy xxvii–xxviii, 139–41
evolutionary economics 62
growth 9, 11, 154, 354, 556–7, 606–7
importance of co-operatives 97

economics (*Cont.*)
  inequalities 30
  international economic co-operation 9
  justice 30
  neoclassical economics 10–11, 55, 57
  ownership 5
  precarity, policy debates on 375–8
  security 46–7, 171
  social and political dimensions 81
  social and solidarity co-operatives 171–3
  social economy xxxvi, 41, 604–7
  sustainability 585–6, 593, 596, 601
  systems, contribution to
       functionality of 262
  theory xxvi, 55–8, 70, 131–2
  utilities xxix, 185, 187
  worker co-operatives xxvii–xxviii,
       131–2, 139–41
electricity 188–90, 321, 323–4, 327–8, 330–1
electronic communications 203
Ellerman, David 590, 592
Emelianoff, IV 163, 167
employee ownership 195–207 *see also* **United
       Kingdom, employee ownership in;
       United States, employee ownership in**
  acquired rights 201
  age discrimination 201
  best practices xxix, 196, 203–6
  business literacy 205
  communications and standards for
       communications 202–5
  cultural norms 200
  currency exchange 202
  data privacy laws 203
  design of ownership plans xxix, 196–204
  discrimination 201
  electronic communications 203
  European Commission pilot project 206
  foreign ownership laws 202
  foundational issues 196–7
  future of companies 197
  global employee ownership xxix, 195–207
  incentives 205, 206
  joint stock corporations 195–8
  labour law 201–2
  legal requirements xxix, 195, 198, 201–3
  matrix unification 200–1
  multi-country employers xxix, 198–201
  organized labour rights 202
  ownership metaphor 591–2
  participation 205
  pay/equity compensation xxix, 196–205
  phantom stock 198
  private ownership 30
  profitability, formula for 206
  public face of company 197
  recent developments 206
  regulation 195, 201–3
  restricted stock 198
  risk allocation 196–7
  role of employee-owners 197
  securities 202
  single-country employers 196–7
  stock purchase plans 201
  strategy 200
  taxation 202, 206
  voice of employees 197
  worker co-operatives 591–2
employees *see* **employee ownership; worker
       co-operatives**
energy *see also* **Germany, co-operatives and
       transformation of energy sector in**
  biogas 326
  biomass 321, 323
  climate change xxxi, 321
  electricity 188–90, 321, 323–4, 327–8, 330–1
  hydro energy 321
  natural gas 189
  photovoltaics 321, 323, 331
  renewable energy 187, 321, 323–4, 326, 331
  solar energy 324
  sustainability 601–2
  utilities 184, 187–8
  wind energy 188, 321, 323–4
Enke, Stephen 163
enlightened shareholder value 231
entrepreneurial activities 14–26
  affirmative action 15
  agricultural co-operatives 56, 164–5
  archetypical form of enterprise,
       presumption of xxv, 14
  capitalism 453
  common good theories xxv, 21–2
  co-operatives xxv, 15, 16–17, 19

co-opreneurs 605
co-ordination mechanism, cooperation as
    a xxvi, 56
corporate social responsibility 23
credit unions and co-operative
    banks 56, 145
economic growth 354
externalities 21–2
family firms xxv, 15–16, 17, 19
governance xxv, 19, 21, 23, 453
imperfect competition 15
industrial organization theories xxv, 19
labour market 14–15
market failure 14–15
mutual producer/consumer
    associations xxv, 15–16
non-archetype enterprises xxv, 14–19, 23–4
non-profit sector 16–18, 23
normative approach 19–23
pluralism xxv, 14–26
positive approach 15–19
private limited companies, archetype
    enterprise as xxv, 14
privatization 21–2
productive sector 15
profit maximization 14–16, 19–23
public limited companies (PLCs) xxv, 14–15
Shareholder Value (SHV) theory 19–23
single enterprise model 14, 15–19
size of sector in Europe 16–17
social enterprises xxv, 15–16, 49
stakeholder inclusion theories xxv, 19–20
stakeholder theory xxv, 19–23
Stakeholder Value theory (STV) 19–23
stakeholder versus shareholder theory
    debate 15, 19–23
turnover 19
workforce, extent of 17, 18
enterprise form *see also* **particular forms (eg
    worker co-operatives)**
accountability xxix, 228–31, 236, 242
archetypical form of enterprise,
    presumption of xxv, 14
balance of power 228
capital co-operatives 233
capitalism 604
context 227

control rights xxix, 242
co-operative law, design of 231
co-ordination mechanism, cooperation
    as a 61–2
credit unions and co-operative
    banks 241–2
culture 227
democracy xxix, 230, 240
distribution 227
diversity of interests 233, 237
empirical evidence 237–42
enlightened shareholder value 231
financial crisis of 2008 234, 237–9
financial exclusion, countering 241–2
financing 228, 229–31, 234–6, 239
governance xxix, 227, 228–33,
    235–6, 239–42
hybrid forms 235–6
income xxix, 229, 233
investor mutuals 233
legal structures xxix, 227, 228–37, 242
literature, theoretical and
    empirical xxix, 227–45
managers, role of 229–30
multiple outputs 229
multi-stakeholder governance 232, 242
new legal forms of social enterprise 235–7
non-archetype enterprises xxv, 14–19, 23–4
ownership xxv, xxix, 4–5, 10, 228–31, 242
participation xxix, 227–31, 234, 237–42
performance xxix, 227–8, 237–42
property rights 228–9, 242
risks, division of 228, 230, 231–2, 234
shareholders 228–32, 234, 236, 239
small-sized enterprises 263–5
social impacts 241–2
stakeholders 227–33, 240–2
state ownership forms xxv, 3–5, 9–10
sustainability xxix, 232–3
voice rights xxix, 229, 231, 233, 242
welfare services 241
wider social impacts 241–2
environment
cap-and-dividend programme 377
climate change 377
common asset trusts 377
energy xxxi, 321, 323, 326

enterprise form (*Cont.*)
  Green New Deal 9
  greenhouse gases 321, 376–7
  social and solidarity co-operatives 173
  sustainable development 601–2
equality *see* inequalities
Erdal, David E 140, 592
Eroski 108, 259, 281, 287, 379, 579–80
Errasti, A 287
ESOPs (Employee Stock Ownership Plans)
    (United States) 295–307
  100% employee ownership xxvii–xviii,
      xxxiii, 127, 295, 296, 298–9, 420
  account values 364
  add-on transactions 300–5, 306
  advantages 414
  anti-abuse rules 417
  C corporations 296, 297, 372, 413–14
  closely held companies 415, 418–19
  concepts of ESOPs xxx
  contributions of stock and cash by
      companies xxxiii, 412–13, 423
  consumer co-operatives 380–1
  debt-financed ESOPs 295, 298–9, 305–6
  default rules 424–5
  defined benefit plans 412
  defined contribution plans, as 412, 423
  directors 296, 301–2
  diversification 415, 422–3
  effect on corporate performance 417–21
  employee ownership xxvii, 196, 201, 416–17
    default rules 424–5
    financial well-being 422–4
    historical perspective 120, 122–7
    performance, causal link with 419
    research 421–2
  employer stock, investment in 412–13
  equivalent plans 415–16
  ERISA 126
  expert advice 306
  external buy-outs xxxi
  external considerations 303–5
  fair value calculations 303
  Federal Law xxxiii, 412
  financial transactions to create ESOPs 295
  financing 297–9, 305, 367
  floor price protection (FPP) 302

governance 296, 301
General Social Survey 424
Great Depression 123–4, 126
growth 415–16
historical perspective xxvii, 110,
    120, 122–7
Individual Retirement Account (IRA) 368
internal considerations 301–3
labour standards 365
large companies 417, 420–1
leveraged ESOPs (LE) 296, 297,
    298–300, 412–13
loans 412–14, 424–5
majority-ownership by ESOPs 297
monitoring corporate management 296
multi-stage ESOPs xxx–xxxi, 296, 300
newly issued shares, acquisition of 413
non-leveraged ESOPs (NLE) 296, 297–300
participatory management 297
pay 422, 424
performance, effect on 417–21
personal retirement plans 591
plans, participants and assets 415–16
public companies 415, 420–1
purpose and background 296–9, 413
quasi-retirement plans 297
repurchase of shares 414
S corporations 296, 297, 356, 414, 415–17
scams 415, 417
sectors 417, 418
shared capitalism xxxii, 362–72
shares of existing shareholders,
    acquisition of 413
size of companies 417, 420–1
small enterprises 367, 371–2
socially sustainable enterprises 591, 593
statistics 295
statutory ESOPs xxxiii, 412–25
tax xxxii, 126–7, 365, 368, 412–17
  loans 425
  small enterprises 371–2
  sustainability 591
  transfer of ownership 296, 297–8
  trust structure 296, 298
trade-off or risks 422, 423–4
transfer of ownership 296, 297–301, 305–6
treasury shares, acquisition of 413

trust structure xxxiii, 296, 298, 301–2, 367, 369, 413, 591
typical series of transactions 300–1
well-being, employee ownership and employee financial 422–3
worker co-operatives 380–1
Estes, CL 387–8
Estrin, S 135
Euricse 19, 262–3, 312–13, 607 *see also World Co-operative Monitor* (ICA/Euricse)
European Central Bank (ECB) 154
European co-operative banks xxv–xxxvi, 148, 151–2, 272–3, 570–1, 573–5
European Federation of Employee Share Ownership (EFES) 206
European Union
    agricultural co-operatives 159
    banking union 154
    Cogeca 159
    Commission
        Communication on promotion of co-operatives xxiv
        pilot project on employee ownership 206
        Social Business Initiative xxiv
    data privacy laws 203
    Deposit Guarantee Scheme Directive 566
    diversity 556
    Europe 2020 xxiv
    European Central Bank (ECB) 154
    European ParliamentReport on Social Economy xxiv
    harmonization 48–9
    Mondragón movement 286
    Morocco, argan oil co-operatives in 457–8, 462–3, 465
    Social Business Initiative xxiv
experimental economics 62

Fagor Electrodomésticos 281, 286, 288–90, 580
fair trade 10, 470–9
    audits 471, 474
    capitalism 477–8
    consumption 470
    contested issues 474–6
    co-operatives, comparison with xxxiv, 470, 476–7
    definition 470
    developing countries 470
    development of fair trade 472–4
    economic development xxxiv, 470, 474–5
    Fairtrade Foundation 476
    Fairtrade International 471, 476
    fragmentation 475
    impact 475–6
    labelling 471–2, 475–6
    lifestyle choice 470
    mainstreaming 474, 477
    market approach 470
    multinationals 471–2, 474
    multi-stakeholder models 473–4
    mutuals xxxiv, 472
    networks 470
    political change, campaigns for 471
    poverty 472, 478
    principles and values 471, 476–7
    producer groups xxxiv, 470, 472–3
    product certification 472, 474–7
    product marks or brands 471
    role of co-operatives 472–4
    sales, amount of 471
    shared value 472, 478
    SOAS report 475–6
    supermarket chains 473, 474, 476–7
    supply chains 471–2, 477
    value chains 470
    World Fair Trade Organization 471–2, 474–5
Fakhfakh, Fathi 134, 135–6, 140, 593
family firms xxv, 3, 15–16, 17, 19
farms *see* agricultural co-operatives
Federation of Danish Dairy Producers 102–3
Ferri, Giovanni 18, 152
feudal system 586
Fici, Antonio 43–4
fiduciary duties 11, 21
Filene, Edward 148
Filippini, Giuseppe 104
financial co-operatives *see also* credit unions and co-operative banks
    financial crisis of 2008 xxxv–xxxvi, 572, 573–6, 580–1
    interest rates 580–1
    local communities 581
    poverty traps 581
    self-interest 150

financial crisis of 2008
  agricultural co-operatives 572
  banking 6–9, 150–2, 409, 446, 570–6,
    581, 585–6
  benefits of successful business sector 580–2
  bonus culture 6
  building societies xxxvi, 238–9, 573–5
  business models 6
  capitalism, alternatives to 570–1
  consumer co-operatives xxxvi, 571–2, 581–2
  co-operative advantage xxxvi, 582
  credit unions and co-operative banks 151–
    3, 154, 572, 573–6, 581
  diversity 7
  enterprise form 234, 237–9
  ethics 571, 581
  European co-operative banks xxxv–xxxvi,
    570–1, 573–5
  evidence 572–80
  financial co-operatives xxxv–xxxvi, 572,
    573–6, 580–1
  future 582
  governance 446
  ILO 571
  indicators 571
  inequalities 6
  insurance mutuals xxxvi, 577–8, 581
  investor-owned businesses, comparison
    with 570, 571–84
  market approach 585–6
  ownership xxv, 4, 6–7
  performance of member-owned businesses
    since crisis xxxvi, 570–84
  producer co-operatives 571
  profit maximization 571
  resilience xxxvi, 571, 579–80, 582
  retail consumer co-operatives 572,
    576–7, 581
  retailer-owned wholesale distribution
    co-operatives xxxvi, 578–9
  risk xxxvi, 570, 582
  sectors 572
  shared service co-operatives 572
  shareholder value 22–3, 572
  socially sustainable enterprises xxxvi,
    585–6, 590–1
  stakeholders 572

trust 571
  utilitarianism 22–3
  worker co-operatives xxxvi, 571–2,
    579–80, 582
  worldwide credit union sector xxxvi, 570–1
financial services sector *see* **banking and**
    financial services; credit unions and
    co-operative banks
financing
  enterprise form 228, 229–31, 234–6, 239
  financialization 446–7, 448–9
  ICA 607
  neoliberal governance 447, 448–9
  socially sustainable enterprises xxxvi,
    594–5, 596
  worker co-operatives 132
Finland
  agricultural co-operatives 159
  consumer co-operatives 103, 576–7, 581
  credit unions and co-operative
    banks xxviii, 150
  forestry industry co-operatives 103
  historical perspective 103
  mutual insurance co-operatives 103
  non-labour income 375
  social and solidarity co-operatives 174
  universal basic income (UBI) 376
  utilities 188
  water companies 188
Fischer, KP 150
Fischer, P 556
Fock, A 517
Foerster, Robert 122
for-profit enterprises *see also* **differentiation**
    between for-profit enterprises and
    co-operatives
  archetypical form of enterprise,
    presumption of xxv, 14
  autocracy 5889
  broad-based stock ownership (BBSO) in
    corporate businesses 375, 377
  company capital model 145
  company law 589–90
  co-operative law xxxv, 40–1, 540, 543, 547
  co-ordination mechanism, cooperation as
    a 56, 69
  corporate social identity 49

failures of current model 5–9
financial crisis of 2008 570, 571–84
future of enterprises xxxvi, 197, 599–602
information asymmetries 590
motivation 589
participation 599–601
principles and values xxvi, 43–4, 47
public limited companies (PLCs) 14–15
Shareholder Value (SHV) theory 19–23
sustainability 589–90, 601–2
trust 89, 600–1
utilities xxviii–xxix, 184–7
worker co-operatives, conversion of 102
Ford, Gerald 126
Fordism 98–9, 111
foreign ownership laws 202
form of organizations *see* enterprise form
Fortune Magazine 220
Fourier, Charles 528
France *see also* France, multi-stakeholder
    co-operatives in Movement of
    Farm Machinery Co-operatives
    (CUMAs) in
agricultural co-operatives 179
agro-industry 106
alliances 106
collective interest co-operatives 548
construction sector 133
consumer co-operatives 106, 576
credit unions and co-operative
    banks xxviii, 106, 156, 573
democracy 179
electricity 188
employee ownership 201
entrepreneurialism 179
historical perspective 106
insurance 106, 109
Intermarche 379
local development 178, 179, 180
manufacturing sector 133
multi-stakeholders 179, 181
non-members, co-operative activities
    with 546
number of co-operatives 132–3
number of employees 133
pay 138
personalist thinkers 280

profit buy-back rule, compulsory 135–7
retail co-operatives 106, 379
rural development 178, 179, 180
SCICs 179, 181
sectors 133, 261
SICAEs 188
small-sized enterprises 261, 272
social and solidarity co-operatives 174–5,
    178, 179, 180–1
under-investment 135–7
universal basic income (UBI) 376
utilities 188
worker co-operatives 102, 132–7, 579
France, multi-stakeholder co-operatives in
    Movement of Farm Machinery Co-
    operatives (CUMAs) in 499–511
Bois Bocage Energie (Hedge Fuel
    Wood) 509–10
case studies 502, 508–10
CIAP 508–9
collective innovation 506
collective organizations 501
consumers/employees, divorce
    between 506
demographics 508
double quality principle 503
economic needs xxxiv
entrepreneurial activities xxxiv, 504–5
environmental management 507–8, 509–10
FNCUMA 506
fodder revolution 501
Font del Prat, CUMA of 502
GAEC, creation of 501
globalization 508
historical perspective 500–2, 503
incubators and nurseries 507
Jeunesse Agricole Catholique (JAC) 501
legal status of agricultural
    co-operatives 504
living conditions 501
local authorities, working with and for 504
local development initiatives 500
local shops 507
Marshall Plan 500–1
mechanization 500–2
multi-stakeholder co-operatives 503–10
mutuals 499–500

France, multi-stakeholder co-operatives in
    Movement of Farm Machinery
    Co-operatives (CUMAs) in (Cont.)
  national network 500
  new forms of co-operation 508
  new multi-actor co-operatives in rural
      territories 507–8
  number of co-operatives 499–500
  progressive installation in farming 508–9
  RENETA network 507
  representative bodies, recognition of 501
  rural areas xxxiv, 499–500, 503, 506–8
  SCICs (collective interest co-operative
      enterprise) 505–10
  Scop National Conference 505
  state-subsidized loans 501
  worker co-operatives 504–6
  working conditions 501
  youth 501, 505, 507, 508
Franco, Francisco 107–8, 280
Fraunhofer Institutes 11
free and equal personhood 27
free riders 218–20, 593
Freeman, Edward 20
Freeman, Richard 212, 389, 423
Frei Montalva, Eduardo 337
Friedman, Milton 20, 22, 375, 448
friendly societies 234, 241, 428, 552, 568, 577
Fukushima disaster 321
Fulton, M 251
fundamental rights 30, 33, 44, 46–7, 545,
    589, 591–2
Furubotn, EG 57, 65, 134–5
future of co-operative business
        model 598–609
  Blueprint for a Co-operative Decade.
      ICA xxxvi, 599–602
  challenges 602–5
    differentiation 604–5
    ideology 602
    scale 603–4
  conventional corporations, co-operatives
      distinguished from xxxvi, 599–602
  co-operative, definition of xxxvi, 599
  core identity xxxvi, 598–9
  differentiation 604–5
  financial crisis of 2008 582

growth, creating the conditions for 605–8
ICA
  Blueprint for a Co-operative Decade.
      ICA xxxvi, 599–602
  global marque, launch of 599
ICA Statement on Co-operative Identity,
        Principles under xxxvi, 598–9, 601
  co-operative, definition of xxxvi, 599
  guidance notes 599
  ideology 602
  intergovernmental organizations 599
  interpretation 599
  sustainability 601
ideology 602
inequalities 600
Internet 599, 600
participation 599–601
scale 603–4
social economy options, co-operatives
        distinguished from xxxvi
social principles 599
sustainability xxxvi, 601–2
trust 600–1

game theory 66
Gebhard, Hannes 103
Gebhard, Hedvig 103
gender see women
general interest services 76–7, 84, 173–5,
    180–1, 186, 547–8
Germany see also Germany, co-operative
        banking in; Germany, co-operatives
        and transformation of energy
        sector in
apprenticeships 11
central management organization 107
consumer co-operatives 107, 576, 578
credit unions and co-operative banks 107
democracy, decentralization in name of 107
entrepreneurship 180
family firms 17
Fraunhofer Institutes 11
historical perspective 107
insurance 109
Mittelstand 5
mutuals 102
Nazi regime 107

regionalization 107
retail co-operatives 107
size 11, 107, 272
small and medium-sized enterprises 11
social and political dimensions 86
social and solidarity
    co-operatives 174–5, 180–1
sustainability 601–2
trusts 591
universal basic income (UBI) 376
wholesale distribution co-operatives 578
worker co-operatives 579
worker participation 107–8
Germany, co-operative banking in 398–411
    assets-based market share 402, 405–6
    auditing associations 404–5
    bancassurance groups 401
    BAG Bank Aktiengesellschaft 407–8
    BBBank 405
    church co-operative banks 405
    consultation 590
    co-operative principle 399, 404
    costs-earnings-based market shares 403
    decentralized networks xxviii, 154
    default risk 399
    democracy 399–400
    diversity 156
    DZ Bank AG 400, 407
    economic and legal background 399–400
    economic development 398
    financial crisis of 2008 409, 573–4
    German banking system 400–2
    GZ-Bank AG 400
    historical perspective 105
    identity, principle of 399
    legal form 400
    local co-operative banks 405–8
    mergers 406–7
    number of credit institutions and
        branches 404, 406
    off-balance sheet activities 401
    pharmacists and doctors 405
    position in the market 401–2
    primary services 400–1
    private lenders 399
    promotion 399
    PSD banks 404–5

public officers 405
Raiffeisen model xxxii–xxxiii, 146–7, 149,
    401, 404–5, 408
retail banking 404
savings banks 406–7
Schultze-Delitzch model 102, 146–7
    self-help 399, 404
self-management 399–400
self-responsibility 399–400
size of banks 408
small and medium-sized enterprises 399
social development 398
Sparda banks 404–5
structure 400–1
sub-groups 402–3, 405
supervision 408
Volksbank xxxii–xxxiii, 146–7, 401,
    404–5, 408
voting rights, equality of 399–400
WGZ-Bank AG 400
Germany, co-operatives and transformation
    of energy sector in 187, 321–34
    barriers to entry 323, 331
    biogas 326
    biomass 321, 323
    Capital Investment Law 332
    citizen participation 322, 326, 330–1
    climate change xxxi, 321
    competitive advantage 330
    conflicts xxxi, 323, 325–6
    costs of ownership, typology of factors with
        impact on 330
    decentralization 322, 332
    democratization 322, 332
    direct marketing 323, 331
    distribution 323
    diversification 327, 331
    electricity sector 321, 323–4, 327–8, 330–1
    emission targets 321
    exporter of energy 322
    feed-in tariffs 323–4, 326, 331
    financial crisis of 2008 332
    financial incentives 323–4
    financial regulation mechanism 331
    food crops, use of 326
    future 331–2
    governance 330

Germany, co-operatives and transformation of energy sector in (*Cont.*)
  greenhouse gases 321
  grids 325, 327
  hydro energy 321
  identity, conflicts over 326
  investment per member 328
  job creation 322
  land use, conflicts over 325–6
  liberalization of energy sector 323
  local co-operatives 322
  market premium 323
  newly registered co-operatives 328, 331
  nuclear opt-out 321–2
  number of members 327–8
  oligopolistic character of energy
      market 323
  photovoltaics 321, 323, 331
  price premiums 330, 331
  procedure, conflicts over 323, 325
  regional development 322, 327
  regulations, overview of consequences of
      important 329
  Renewable Energy Sources Act xxxi,
      323–5, 331
  share of renewables 321–2
  solar energy 324
  sustainable energy 321, 323
  technology
      conflicts over 326
      progress 332
  theoretical perspectives 329–31
  value chains 327
  wind energy 321, 323–4
Gilead Sciences xxvii
Gladden, Washington 121
Glyn, Andrew xxv
global employee ownership *see* **employee
      ownership**
**Global Impact Investing Network
      (GIIN)** 265
global law 50
globalization xxvi, 41, 46, 49
Goodpaster, KE 21
Google xxvii
governance 246–60 *see also* **voting**
  accountability 228, 450, 454

agricultural co-operatives 160,
      166–7, 256–7
authority/hierarchy 64
Better Farming, Better Business, Better
      Living (Three Betters) 256–7
challenges xxix–xxx, 246–60
communications/marketing
  governance, aligning with 253
  members, with 254–6
Competence based approach xxx, 246,
      249–50, 256–7
complexity 246
comply or explain approach 248
consumer co-operatives 246, 381
control rights 63
co-operative law, role of 543, 547
co-ordination mechanism, cooperation as
      a 64, 66–7, 70
credit unions and co-operative banks 145,
      149–50, 152–3
culture 252–3
definition 152–3
democracy 248, 255
education of co-operators 255
election of members 255–6
engagement structures 248
enterprise form xxix, 227, 228–33,
      235–6, 239–42
historical perspective 104, 247
incentives 248
innovation xxxiii, 228, 447, 453–4
interactions with co-operatives are part
      of being a co-operatives, ensuring
      all 253–6
large co-operatives 251–2, 253
managers, role of 252–3
meetings 255
members
  becoming a member 254
  communication 254–6
  elections 255–6
  engaging the member 255
  meetings 255
  role of 252–3
  W approach to Board consultation 256
multi-stakeholder co-operatives 69–70,
      232, 242

neoliberalism xxxiii, 446, 447–54
Open co-operatives approach xxx,
    246, 258–9
outside, approaching the 253
participation 600
Plunkett approach 256–7
purpose of co-operatives 251–2
scale of businesses 603
self-interest 240, 253
shopfloor, form of 253–4
size of co-operatives 251–2, 265–6
small co-operatives, purpose
    of 251–2, 253–6
social and solidarity co-operatives 179, 181
solidarity 179, 181, 247–8
staff, connection with the 253
sustainability 252
technical, economic and social
    competencies 256–7
Trust based approach xxx, 246, 247–8
utilities 192
Values based approach xxx, 246, 251–6
W approach to Board consultation 256
worker co-operatives xxxii, 383, 580
Graetz, F xxxiv, 486–7
Grameen Bank 77
Gray, John H 119
Great Depression 123–4, 126
    credit unions and co-operative banks 148
    labour exchanges 529
    ownership xxv, 4, 6–7
    trade unions 382
Great Place to Work Institute 220–1
Greece
    financial crisis of 2008 152
    local development 178, 180
    social and solidarity co-operatives 175,
        178, 180
    welfare services 180
    work integration 178
Green New Deal 9
Greenspan, Alan 7
Grillo, Michele 66
Gripple 428
Groenveld, JM 152, 561
Groupement national de la cooperation
    (GNC) 106

Grow, Galusha 118
growth 605–8
    banking sector, exclusion of 605
    capital 606–7
    conditions 605–8
    creating the conditions 605–8
    development 607–8
    economic growth 9, 11, 154, 354,
        556–7, 606–7
    insurance sector 578, 605
    legal framework 605–6
    protectionism 605
    publicly traded companies, failure to
        distinguish 605
Gründtvigts, Nicolas Friedrich 102
guilds 97
Guillame, D 456

Haas, Jérôme 44
Haas, Wilhelm 147
Haldane, Andy 7, 556
Hamilton, Alexander 114
Han Kim, E 420–1, 424
Hansmann, Henry 43–4, 67, 92, 162, 230–1,
    237, 539, 542, 548
harmonization of law 48–9
Harrington, James 116
Harvest Moon Society 355
Hasdell, Iain 206
Hayek, Friedrich 375, 447
health and psychiatric disorders 140–1
health services
    agricultural co-operatives 187
    consumer co-operatives 176
    economic precarity 375
    employee ownership 234, 436, 438
    historical co-operatives 110–11
    hybrids 382
    insurance 109
    multi-stakeholder co-operatives 88
    size of co-operatives 268
    social and political dimensions 77, 81, 88, 90
    social and solidarity co-operatives 173–4,
        176, 178–9, 316, 356
    sustainability 349
    utilities 190–1
    worker co-operatives 140–1

Heath, Joseph 59
Helmberger, P 164
Heras-Saizarbitoria, I 282
Hicks, Clarence 122
historical perspective 97–113 *see also* United
    States, historical perspective on
    employee ownership in
    50 years, developments in 104–11
    1850–1899 97–8
    19th century xxvii, 101, 107–8, 111
    1950–1999, novelties emerging in late xxvii
    agricultural co-operatives 102–3
    authoritarian regimes, spread of 103–4
    birth and early evolution 99–104
    capitalist corporations, differentiation
        from xxvii, 97–101, 111–12
    chambers of merchants 97
    community co-operatives 186
    competitive advantage 99, 104
    co-operative law 39
    credit unions and co-operative banks 102
    diffusion of 19th century co-operatives
        across world xxvii
    economic importance of co-operatives 97
    Europe xxvii, 98, 100–1
    feudalism 586
    Fordism 98–9, 111
    governance 104, 247
    guilds 97
    ICA
        authoritarian regimes, spread of 103–4
        creation 103
        identity 103
        largest co-operatives, statistics on 99
        Paris Congress 104
        principles of co-operatives 104
        state-controlled enterprises as
            members 103–4
    insurance co-operatives 106, 109
    Internet 111
    largest co-operatives, list of 300 100
    limitations xxvii
    models of co-operatives 99, 101–2
    multi-stakeholder model 104
    mutuals 104, 109
    producers 99
    renaissance of co-operatives xxvii

service industry 98–9
social and political dimensions xxvii, 82,
    83–4, 90
socially sustainable enterprises 586
stakeholders 104
theories of co-operatives 99
users 99
utilities 184, 187, 189–90
worker co-operatives 99, 102
Holstenkamp, L 326–7
Holyoake, George 98
home care industry *see* United States, home
    care industry in
Hong Kong, employee ownership in 201
Honoré, Anthony 29–30, 36
Hoos, S 164
housing *see* Rochdale Boroughwide
    Housing (RBH)
Howart, Charles 101
Huber, Victor 171
Huet, Tim 536
human effects 592, 596
human nature xxxvi, 586–7, 589, 590
human rights 30, 33, 44, 46–7, 545, 589, 591–2
human systems, sustainability in 587
Humphrey, Hubert 125
Hungary 175, 177
hybrid co-operatives *see also* multi-
    stakeholder co-operatives
    co-operative law 49
    enterprise form 235–6
    innovation 242, 377, 383
    social and political dimensions 77–81,
        85–7, 91–2
    social and solidarity co-operatives 172
    social economy 606–7
hydro energy 321

ICA *see* International Co-operative
    Alliance (ICA)
identity
    agricultural co-operatives xxviii, 159–62,
        163, 167
    capitalization 48
    co-operative law xxxv, 41, 540, 542, 548
    core identity xxxvi, 598–9
    corporate social identity 49

credit unions and co-operative banks 149
domain names 599
future of co-operative business
	model xxxvi, 598–9
government, independence from 598
ICA 109
local identity 149
principles and values 39, 41–8
protection, rationale for 41–8
self-help 47, 598
Iliopoulos, C 165
Impact Reporting and Investment Standards
	(IRIS) 265
India 573
indigenous people xxxi, 348, 349, 351–3, 356,
	472, 527
individualism 20, 528, 532
industrial organization theories xxv, 19
Industrial Revolution 101, 171, 601
industrialization 82–3, 117–18, 160, 514–15,
	519, 521
inequalities
	agricultural co-operatives 160
	broad-based stock ownership (BBSO) in
		corporate businesses 377
	capitalism 34, 36, 600
	collective action 160
	discrimination 176–7, 201
	duty to treat members equally 544–6
	equal treatment principle 41
	financial crisis of 2008 6
	future of co-operative business model 600
	income and wealth 34–6
	ownership xxv, 3–4, 6, 9, 11
	progressive taxation 9
	redistribution of income and
		wealth 28, 30–1
	theories of justice 34
	universal basic income (UBI) 375–6
	welfare state capitalism 34
	worst-off group, maximum benefit of 34, 36
information asymmetries
	entrepreneurial activities 14–15
	gender dynamics 460
	labour market 14–15
	market approach 585
	socially sustainable enterprises 590

utilities 184, 190–1
welfare services 88
worker co-operatives 139
innovation
	credit unions and co-operative banks 145,
		151, 153
	disadvantaged workers 309
	employee ownership 214, 217, 222, 435, 440
	fair trade 484
	governance xxxiii, 228, 447, 453–4
	historical perspective 104, 108–9
	hybrids 242, 377, 383
	indigenous people 342
	local innovation 349
	ownership 5, 11, 214, 217, 222
	participation 205
	research and development 66
	social and political dimensions 81, 86
	social and solidarity co-operatives 175, 179,
		181, 314–18
	social innovation 70
institutions
	co-operative law 44
	co-ordination mechanism, cooperation
		as a 66
	municipal governments, sponsorship
		by 69–70
	new institutionalism 65–8
	social aims, institutionalization of 69–70
	social co-operatives 69–70
	sponsorship 382–3
	theory 66
insurance
	agricultural co-operatives 68
	AMICE 109
	comparative advantage 578
	co-ordination mechanism, co-operation
		as a 68
	exclusion of co-operatives 605
	financial crisis of 2008 xxxvi, 577–8, 581
	friendly societies 577
	growth 578, 605
	historical perspective 106, 109
	ICA 109
	International Co-operative and Mutual
		Insurance Federation (ICMIF) 109,
		265, 267, 577–8

insurance (*Cont.*)
    life insurance 578, 581
    legal framework 605
    mutuals xxxvi, 109, 265, 267–8, 577–8, 581
    size of sector 265, 267–8
    small-sized enterprises 265, 267–8
intergenerational solidarity 65
intergovernmental organizations
        (INGOs) 599, 606, 608
International Co-operative Alliance
        (ICA) *see also World Co-operative
        Monitor* (ICA/Euricse)
    authoritarian regimes, spread of 103–4
    Blueprint xxxvi, 41–2, 44–5, 48, 599–602
    capital 607
    Centennial Meeting of World Congress 91
    co-operative, definition of xxxvi, 77, 599
    Co-operative Law Committee 48
    co-operative law, role of 547–8
    creation 103
    Euricse 19, 262–3, 312–13, 607
    financing, review of 607
    global marque, launch of 599
    Guidance Notes 48, 599
    historical perspective 103–4
    identity 103
    ideology 602
    ILO Recommendation No 193 42
    infrastructure 352
    insurance 109
    intergovernmental organizations 599
    interpretation 599
    largest co-operatives, statistics on 99
    Paris Congress 104
    principles and values 104, 517
        Blueprint 41–2, 44–5, 48
        Co-operative Law Committee 48
        co-operative law, role of 547–8
        Guidance Notes 48
        ILO Recommendation No 193 42
        re-interpretation of principle 48
        Statement 39–40, 42, 47, 173–4,
            598–9, 601
    re-interpretation of principle 48
    social and political dimensions 76–7, 87, 91
    state-controlled enterprises as
        members 103–4

    Statement xxxvi, 39–40, 42, 47, 173–4,
        598–9, 601
    sustainability 601
International Court of Justice (ICJ) 45
International Covenant on Civil and Political
        Rights (ICCPR) 46–7
International Labour Organization (ILO)
    development 608
    financial crisis of 2008 571
    harmonization 48–9
    job creation, statistics on 605
    principles and values 42, 45, 47–9
    Recommendations No 193 xxiv, 42, 45, 47
international law 45
Internet
    Big Data 47
    crowd funding 600
    domain names 599
    economic precarity, policy debates on 378
    electronic communications 203
    future of co-operative business
            model 599, 600
    global conversations, access, and
            action 600
    historical perspective 111
    multi-stakeholder co-operatives 378
    social networking 49
Ireland 17, 105, 256–7
Israel, credit unions and co-operative
        banks in 155
Italy *see also* Italy, social co-operatives in
    city-states 97
    communities, role in 142
    community co-operatives 185
    consensual networks 150
    consumer co-operatives 576, 578–9
    Co-op Italia 379
    credit unions and co-operative
            banks xxviii, 150, 154
    employee ownership 195
    fair trade 473–4
    family firms 17–18
    historical perspective 105–6
    market leaders 106
    membership 103
    multi-sector approach 105
    mutuals 185

networking 106
number of co-operatives 132
pay 138
perverse supply response 137
profit buy-back rule, compulsory 135–7
relational goods 85
renewable energy 187
retail co-operatives 379
sectors 261
size of firms 133
small-sized enterprises 261, 272
social and political dimensions 77, 83, 90–1
social and solidarity co-operatives 85, 90,
    104, 106, 174–7, 181, 606
under-investment 135–7
welfare services 77, 175
wholesale distribution co-operatives 578–9
worker co-operatives 132–4, 177, 579–80,
    591, 594
  failure rates 134
  number of co-operatives 132
  under-investment 135–7
workforce, extent of 17, 18
Italy, social co-operatives in 308–20
  added value xxxi, 313, 317–18
  asset lock 310
  challenges 313–15
  community interest co-operatives 316
  culture 308–9, 314
  democracy 310
  demographic changes 309
  distributive function 318
  diversity 310, 318
  economic changes 308
  emergence and evolution xxxi, 308–11, 315
  endogenous dynamics 313–14, 318
  entrepreneurial activities 309–11, 317
  exogenous dynamics 313
  financing 310, 312, 313, 316
  future 315–17
  general interest services 308, 310, 312, 317
  governance 314–16, 318
  grass-roots initiatives 308
  growth 311–12
  health care 312
  institutionalization 311

Law 381/1991 xxxi, 85, 104, 175–6, 308,
    310–11, 548
  legal recognition xxxi, 85, 104,
    175–6, 308–11
  local authorities, contracts with 311
  multi-stakeholders 310, 314–16
  networks 314–16
  non-profit distribution constraints 310–11
  number of co-operatives 308
  public bodies, ties with 311, 312–14
  public resources 312, 313
  resources 312–13, 315–18
  size of co-operatives 308, 314
  social changes 308
  socio-economic context xxxi, 317–18
  sovereign debt crisis 313
  stakeholders 310, 314–17
  structure 310
  sustainability 315
  types of services 312
  unemployment 315, 317
  welfare services xxxi, 308–12, 315–18
  work integration 309–10, 312, 317–18

Jacoby, Sanford 123
James, DC 166
Japan
  agricultural co-operatives 111, 176
  authoritarianism 111
  banking 111
  consumer co-operatives 111, 576–7, 581
  elder care 90
  employee ownership 206
  Fukushima disaster 321
  health care 77, 88, 176
  historical perspective 110–11
  insurance 109
  large co-operatives 268–9
  legislation 40
  multi-stakeholder co-operatives 88
  post-war resurgence 111
  social and solidarity co-operatives 174,
    176, 606
  welfare services 77, 91
  women 581
Jefferson, Thomas 114–17
Jensen, MC 590

Ji, Minsun 533
job security 138–41, 158, 218–19, 291, 431, 495
John Bates Prize in Economics 118
John Lewis Partnership 133, 197, 426, 427–8,
    430, 432, 591, 594
joint assets, exploitation of 376–7
joint ownership of the world 30–1
joint stock corporations 135, 195–8
Jones, Derek 135, 528
Jowell, Tessa 5
justice
    basic structure 33–4
    civil and political rights 33–4
    equal basic liberties 33
    fair equality of opportunity 34
    fairness, justice as 33–4
    self-ownership 34
    social and economic inequalities,
        conditions for 34
    social justice xxxvi, 36, 46–7

Kaarlehto, P 164
Kaarsemaker, EC 485
Kalmi, P 152, 166
Kardas, Peter 422
Kaswan, Jaques 536
Kay, John 551
Keen, George 250
Kelso Institute 124–5
Kelso, Louis O 124–5, 369, 591
Kelso, Patricia Hetter 124–5
Kennedy, John F 126
Keogh, Jim 422
Kerola, E 152
Ketley, Richard 105
Keynesianism xxv, 4, 6, 9, 447
King, William 247
King, William Lyon Mackenzie 121
Kirchner, Cristina 340
Kirchner, Néstor 340
Kodak 121
Kraakman, Reinier 43–4, 539
Kramer, Brent 420
Kruse, Douglas 213, 297, 389, 418–19, 423, 427

La Porta, R 23
labour law 201–2, 545

labour market 14–15, 200
Laidlaw, AF 76–7, 173
laissez-faire 4, 7
Lane, Todd 101
large co-operatives
    agricultural co-operatives xxviii, 166
    governance 251–2, 253
    historical perspective 100
    list of largest co-operatives 100
    quantification of socio-economic impact
        of large co-operatives xxx, 261–3,
        265–6, 273–4
    small-sized enterprises xxx, 261, 266–73
    statistics 99–100
    ten largest family firms 19
Larson, K 251
Latin America 335–45 see also individual
    countries
    agricultural co-operatives 607
    anarchist schools 335
    Catholic Church 335, 336–7
    civil society 335
    colonialism 335
    consumer co-operatives 345
    credit co-operatives 607
    development 607
    evolutionary trends xxxi
    financial crisis of 2008 335
    historical perspective xxxi, 335
    ICA 335, 336
    ILO 335
    indigenous co-operatives xxxi, 336, 345
    inequality 335
    legal frameworks, lack of xxxi, 337
    neoliberalism xxxi, 335, 337, 345
    number of organizations 335
    potential for further development xxxi
    producer co-operatives 345
    rural co-operatives 345
    social and solidarity economy sector 172,
        336, 345
    social marginalization 335
    socialist schools 335
    state, ties with the 345
    unemployment 335
    urban co-operatives 345
    utopian schools 335

work-for-welfare co-operatives xxxi
worker co-operatives 345
worker-recuperated co-operatives xxxi, 345
law *see* co-operative law
left libertarianism xxvi, 31–2, 36
legislation *see* co-operative law
legitimacy
    crisis 446–7, 449, 515
    governance 446
    mutuals 447, 449, 481
    neoliberal governance 447, 449
    private property xxvi
Leo XIII, Pope 280
Lewin, K 486
liberal philosophies of ownership 27–38
    democratic liberalism xxvi, 32–7
    free and equal personhood 27
    left libertarianism xxvi, 31–2, 36
    right libertarianism xxvi, 27–31, 36
liberalism xxvi, 32–7 *see also* liberal
        philosophies of ownership
libertarianism *see* left libertarianism; right
        libertarianism
LIBOR scandal 603
limited liability 3, 228, 234, 236, 604
Lincoln, Abraham 118
Lipietz, Alain 505
Llewellyn, DT 561, 565
local communities
    endogenous development 262
    financial co-operatives 581
    identity 146
    job creation 605–6
    municipal governments, sponsorship
        by 69–70
    social and solidarity co-operatives 178–80
Locke, John 28–9
London, UK 6
Long, Russell 126
Ludlow Massacre 121
Luzzatti, Luigi 98
Lybbert, TJ 457

Madison, James 116–18, 122
Major, John 434
management
    agricultural co-operatives 163–4, 166

building societies 105
enterprise form 229–30
governance 252–3
limits 70
New Public Management (NPM) 84–5
personnel management, logic of 79–80
private ownership 29
social and political dimensions 79–80
supply chain management 482
Mandl, I 17
market
    agricultural co-operatives 159, 161
    co-ordination mechanism, co-operation as
        a 55–6, 64, 68, 70
    democracy 86, 92
    exchange 56, 64, 70
    failure 14–15, 55–6, 64, 68, 131, 138
    fair trade 470
    financial crisis of 2008 585–6
    imbalances of power 585
    information asymmetries 585
    invisible hand 585
    labour market 14–15, 200
    liberalization 188–9
    pay 196
    perfect markets 56
    perverse reactions to market stimuli 65
    relations 447, 449–50, 452
    social and political
        dimensions 79, 86, 92
    socially sustainable enterprises 585–6
    worker co-operatives 131, 134, 138
marketing 253–6
Marks and Spencer 594
Marmot, MG 592
Marshall, Alfred 98
Marshall Plan 500–1
Marxism xxv, 3–4
Massachusetts Association of Credit
        Unions 148
Maude, Francis 480
May, RM 556
Mazzini, Giuseppe 98
Meade, James 36
Meckling, WH 590
members *see also under* individual main
        entries

Mexico xxxi, 335, 340–2, 345
  agricultural sector 341, 342
  Catholic Church 341
  Constitution 341
  credit institutions 341
  fair trade 472
  indigenous people 341, 342
  large co-operatives 342
  legal framework 341–2
  National Institute of Social Economy 342
  non-profit sector 16
  number of co-operatives 341
  reciprocity 341, 342
  social and solidarity economy
    sector 340–2, 345
Michie, J 555, 565
Microsoft xxvii
Miliband, Ed 12
Mill, John Stuart 35, 98
Milne, Seumas 4
models
  agricultural co-operatives 165–6
  credit unions and co-operative
    banks 145–6
  diversity of business models xxv, 7–9
  failures of current model 5–9
  financial crisis of 2008 6
  future of co-operative business
    model xxxvi, 599–602
  historical perspective 99, 101–2
  new models 165–6
  participatory model of
    decision-making 158
  single enterprise model 14, 15–19
Mondragón movement 135, 137–8, 279–94
  automotive sector 286
  banking 595–6
  Basque Country 107–8, 134, 279–80, 286–8,
    291, 379, 591
  Caja Laboral Popular 284
  capitalism 279, 287
  Catholic Church 280
  civil war 280
  communitarianism 280
  Co-operative Congress 284–5, 289
  Corporate Management Model
    (MGC) 284, 288

credit unions and co-operative banks 281
culture 280, 284
diversification 281, 287
Divisional Councils 284
dual or coopitalist model 287–8
economic liberalization 291
educational institutions xxx, 279, 280–1
entrepreneurial activities 280
EU, admission into 286
expansion 279, 283, 287
financial crisis of 2008 279–80, 288–90
foundation xxx, 280–2
future goals 290
General Assemblies 283
General Council 284–6, 288–9
general managers 283
generational dimension 282
geographical groupings 284–5
governance 283–8, 290
Governing Council 283–5
historical perspective xxx, 279–82
home care industry 533
industrial firms 279
internationalization 279, 286–90
Management Council 283
Mondragón Corporation (MCC) 284, 379
Monitoring Commission 283
multi-stakeholder co-operatives 379
network governance 285
number of firms 279
open co-operatives approach 259
pay 138, 284, 289, 291
principles and values 279, 280–2, 287–92
  internationalization 287
  ten guiding 281–2
profit buy-back rule, compulsory 135–7
re-founding 290–2
representative bodies 283
repression 280
rural areas 280
severance of ties 285
size of members 279, 281, 286
Social Council 283, 285
social provision 281
socially sustainable enterprises 591, 594–5
solidarity 279–81, 285, 290
Standing Committee 284

structure of organizations 282–5
subsidiaries, workers in local and
    foreign 287–9
trade unions 280, 283, 382
vocational training 279–81
welfare system 285
wholesale distribution co-operatives 579
worker co-operatives xxx, 133, 135–7, 279,
    282–91, 382, 580
moral hazard 139, 190
**Morocco, argan oil co-operatives in South
    West** 456–69
accountability 467
associations 459–62, 467
Berbers 456–7
Biosphere Reserve, Sous Valley as a 456
competitive advantage 458
conservation 465
context and history 456–7
core value chain 458–9
custom 457
democratic decision-making xxxiv, 460,
    462, 465–6
development of associations 457
donor funding 457–8, 462
economic development xxxiv, 465
education on co-operatives for
    members xxxiv, 465
elites, control by 460
European Union 457–8, 462–3, 465
evolution, prospects of 466–8
external relations 462–3
governance 459–62
impact analysis 464–6
information asymmetries 460–1
institutional structure 459–61
internal and external pressures 460–1
Internet 466–8
Islam 457
life-cycle of co-operatives 457–8
mechanization 456–7, 459
number of co-operatives 458, 459–60
open membership xxxiv, 465–6
patriarchy 460–1
pay 457, 458–9, 464–5
policy xxxiii–xxxiv, 463–4
poverty 463

price 457, 467
principles, abandonment of
    co-operative xxxiv, 466
private enterprises 457
profit distribution 465–6
Projet Arganier (PA) 458–65
regulation 463–4
retailers 459
role of co-operatives 458–9
rural areas xxxiv, 457, 463–5
setbacks 465–6
social capital 458, 465
social development xxxiv, 465
Social Development Agency 457–8, 462–3
stakeholders 465–6
sustainable development 464–7
value chains 458–9, 467
vertical market integration 459
women 456–61, 463–7
    gender dynamics 460–1
    social capital 465
    socio-economic status 456–7
mortgages 573–4
Müller, JR 329
multi-country employers xxix, 198–201
multinationals
fair trade 471–2, 474
historical perspective 99
job creation in local economies 605–6
jobs, number of 605
protectionism 338
shared capitalism 214
multi-stakeholder co-operatives 374–85
    see also **France, multi-stakeholder
    co-operatives in Movement of
    Farm Machinery Co-operatives
    (CUMAs) in**
agricultural co-operatives 87
consumer co-operatives 87–8
economic precarity, policy debates
    on 375–8
fair trade xxxiv, 472
governance 69–70, 232, 242
historical perspective 104
income supplementation 375–7
Internet 378
non-labour income 375–7

multi-stakeholder co-operatives (*Cont.*)
  broad-based stock ownership (BBSO) in
    corporate businesses 375, 377
  citizen's dividend, distribution
    of 375, 376–7
  universal basic income (UBI) 375–6
  open co-operatives 259
  platform co-operativism 378
  production and consumption, association
    between xxxii, 374, 379, 382
  retail co-operatives 379
  self-interest 490
  social and political dimensions 85,
    87–9, 91–2
  voluntary associations 89
  welfare services 87
  worker-consumer
    co-operatives xxxii, 379–83
Murray, Robin 258
mutuals
  accountability 232, 236, 242
  building societies 573
  community co-operatives 185
  compulsory health insurance 109
  concept of mutuality 481
  consumer co-operatives xxv, 15–16, 234–5,
    237, 238–9
  co-operative law, role of 546, 548
  co-ordination mechanism, cooperation as
    a 69–70
  credit unions and co-operative
    banks 145, 573
  definition 264–5, 481
  democracy 35–6, 37, 482
  demutualization 265
  economic growth 606
  governance 446–7, 451–2, 454
  historical perspective 104, 109
  institutionalization of social aims 69–70
  insurance xxxvi, 109, 265, 267–8, 577–8, 581
  investor mutuals 233
  left libertarianism 32
  mutuality principle 172, 175
  neoliberalism 447, 451–2, 454
  organizational change 481–2
  ownership xxv, 4–5, 10
  principles and values 481–2

  producer co-operatives xxv, 15–16, 229,
    234, 237
  public services 480–1
  purpose 481
  small-sized enterprises 264–5,
    267–70, 272–3
  social and solidarity co-operatives 172, 175
  supply chain management 482
  transitions 482
Myners, Paul (Lord Myners) 249–50, 253, 564
Myners Review 564

**National Bureau for Economic Research
    (NBER)** 213–20, 389
**National Centre for Employee Ownership
    (NCEO)** 356, 417, 423–5
National Freight Corporation (NFC) 428,
    430, 434
National Health Service (NHS) 240, 428,
    434–5, 438
nationalization 3–4
natural gas 189
neoclassical economics 10–11, 55, 57
neoliberal governance xxxiii, 446, 447–54
  accountability 450
  agency 449, 450, 452
  audits 449, 450
  competition 447–51, 454
  culture 447–52, 454
  democracy 448, 451–2
  failure 453
  financialization 447, 448–9
  free riders 449
  legitimacy 447, 449
  market relations 447, 449–50, 452
  mutuals 447, 451–2, 454
  neoliberal, definition of 447
  participatory governance 450–1
  performance indicators 451
  privatization 447, 449
  quantification 448–9
  securitization of risk 449
  shareholder value 448
  socialism 447
  stakeholders 450
  transparency 447
  trust 448–50

Netherlands
  agricultural co-operatives 159
  credit unions and co-operative
      banks xxviii, 159, 573–4, 581
  fair trade 471
  non-labour income 375
  non-profit sector 16–17
  small-sized enterprises 272
  universal basic income (UBI) 376
  wholesale distribution co-operatives 578
New Institutional Economics (NIE) 161
New Public Management (NPM) 84–5
New Zealand
  building societies 105
  credit unions and co-operative banks 575
  small-sized enterprises 270
  wholesale distribution co-operatives 579
nexus of contracts approach 167
Nixon, Richard 126
non-governmental organizations
      (NGOs) 42, 80, 338, 472–3, 521–2
non-labour income 375–7
  broad-based stock ownership (BBSO) in
      corporate businesses 375, 377
  citizen's dividend, distribution
      of 375, 376–7
  universal basic income (UBI) 375–6
non-members, co-operative activities
      with xxxv, 543, 545–7
Northern Rock 105, 238, 563–4, 566, 574
Northern Saskatchewan Trappers
      Association Co- operative
      (NSTAC) 356
Nourse, EG 161–2
Nova González, A 343
Nozick, Robert 27–31
Nuttall Review 433

Occupy Wall Street 530, 533, 570, 600
Okobank 103
one person one vote principle
  community co-operatives 185
  co-operative law, role of 543, 547
  co-ordination mechanism, cooperation
      as a 64
  credit unions and co-operative
      banks 145, 146

social and political dimensions 87
  utilities 185
open co-operatives approach xxx, 246, 258–9
open door principle 145, 543, 547
opportunistic behaviour xxvi, 56, 59, 66, 153,
      161–5, 238, 569
organizational challenges xxix–xxx, 246–60
organizational law 539–40
organizational theory 164
organized labour rights 202
original entitlements, theory of 28
Ostrom, Elinor 58–9, 67, 164–5, 167
Otsuka, Michael 32
Ouimet, Paige 420–1, 424
Owen, Robert 3, 101, 117, 247, 528, 601
ownership 3–12 see also employee
      ownership; liberal philosophies of
      ownership
  absentee shareholders 5
  agricultural co-operatives 161
  banking in Europe, reports on 7–8
  broad-based stock ownership (BBSO) in
      corporate businesses 375, 377
  business models, diversity of xxv, 7–9
  capital ownership 377
  capitalism xxv, 3–10
    alternatives 3–10
    golden age 4, 9–10
    laissez-faire 4, 7
    neoclassical economics 4
    unleashed 4, 6–7, 9–10
  centrally planned economies 3–4
  collective ownership 591
  competition 10
  co-operative law, role of 542–3
  co-operative ownership forms xxv, 4–5, 10
  corporate governance 9–10
  corporate pluralism 11
  costs 161
  credit unions and co-operative
      banks 145–6
  culture 5, 9
  definition xxix, 228–31, 242
  democracy 34–5, 36
  diversity of ownership forms xxv, 5–6, 7–10
  economic conditions 5
  employee engagement 11

ownership (*Cont.*)
    employee-owned model 10
    environmental sustainability 9–10, 11
    excessive corporate pay xxv, 5
    failures of current model 5–9
    family ownership xxv, 3
    financial crisis of 2008 xxv, 4, 6–7
    financial services sector 6–9
    foreign ownership laws 202
    Great Depression xxv, 4, 6–7
    Green New Deal 9
    importance 3–12
    income and wealth inequality xxv, 3–4,
        6, 9, 11
    international economic co-operation 9
    joint ownership of the world 30–1
    Keynesianism xxv, 4, 6, 9
    limited liability 3
    long-termism 5, 9, 10–12
    Marxism xxv, 3–4
    metaphor 589, 591–2
    mutual ownership forms xxv, 4–5, 10
    nationalization 3–4
    neoclassical economics 10–11
    Ownership
        Commission (UK) 5–6, 11–12
    participation of owners 5, 11
    policy reforms 9–11
    political rights 589, 591–2
    private ownership xxv, 3–5, 9–10,
        28–31, 36, 85
    privatization 4, 5
    property-owning democracy 34–5, 36
    public policy 10–11
    Second World War, reconstruction after 9
    securitization 589
    self-ownership 28–9, 32, 34
    shared responsibilities 11
    shareholders 3, 5, 10, 228–31
    short-termism 5, 6, 11
    small-sized enterprises 265–6
    social democracy in Western Europe xxv, 4
    socially sustainable enterprises 589, 591–2
    state ownership xxv, 3–5, 9–10
    stewardship 5, 11
    user-owner principle 166
    worker co-operatives 591–2

Oxford Centre for Mutual and Employee-
    Owned Business 10

Palmer, Timothy C 530–1
Parliamentary Commission on Banking
    Standards (UK) 554
Parnell, Edgar 252, 259
PARO Centre for Women's Enterprise 354–5
participation and voice rights
    agricultural co-operatives 158
    decision-making 158
    employee ownership 197, 205
    enterprise form xxix, 227–31, 233–4, 237–42
    for-profit enterprises and co-operatives,
        differences between 599–601
    future of co-operative business
        model 599–601
    governance 446, 450–1, 600
    innovation 205
    ownership 5, 11
    pay 197
    political participation 33, 35, 171
    principles and values 41, 45, 46–7
    public-private partnerships 47
    social and political dimensions 76, 86
    sustainability 45
    voting rights 47
    worker-consumer co-operatives 380
pay/equity compensation
    benefit levels 203–4
    bonus culture 6
    components 196
    design of ownership plans 196–8, 201–4
    determination 131–2, 138–9
    employee ownership xxix, 196–205
    excessive corporate pay xxv, 5
    job creation in local economies 606
    participation 197
    predictability 205
    relative to market 196
    risk allocation 196–7
    socially sustainable enterprises 592, 594
    universal basic income (UBI) 375–6
    worker co-operatives 68–9, 131–2, 138–9
Pejovich, S 57, 65, 134–5
Pellervo 103
Pencavel, J 133–4, 136–7, 139

Pendleton, Andrew 239
Peña Nieto, Enrique 341–2
Percy, Eustace 589–90
performance
  credit unions and co-operative banks 151–2
  enterprise form xxix, 227–8, 237–42
  financial crisis of 2008 xxxvi, 570–84
  financial performance, equal
      conditions for 46
  neoliberal governance 451
  small-sized enterprises 265
Perón, Juan 339
Pestoff, Victor 378
Philippines, utilities in the 189
Phillips, R 163
photovoltaics 321, 323, 331
Pickett, K 592
Piketty, Thomas 9, 600
Pillsbury, Charles S 120–1
Pisani, Edgar 501
platform co-operativism 378
Plunkett Foundation for Co-operative
      Studies 102, 252–6
Plunkett, Horace 256–7
Poland 175, 177–8
politics see also social and political
      dimensions of co-operatives
  change, campaigns for 471
  civil and political rights 33, 589, 591–2
  co-operative law, arguments for 43–8
  participation 33, 35, 171
Pollet, I 476–7
Poole, M 431
Porter, Theodor 448
Portugal
  CSS (social solidarity co-operative) 177
  family firms 17
  legislation 40
  social and solidarity co-operatives 174, 177,
      181, 548
  work integration 177
Poutsma, E 485
poverty
  agricultural co-operatives 158
  fair trade 472, 478
  financial co-operatives 581
  right libertarianism 30

social and solidarity co-operatives 171–2
traps 581
universal basic income (UBI) 376
Princeton University, Rockefeller
    programme at 122–3
principles and values
  capital 607
  competitiveness xxvi, 45
  constitutions 39
  consumer co-operatives 576
  co-operative, definition of 46–7
  co-operative identity 41
  corporate social identity 49
  credit unions and co-operative banks 146
  culture 40
  deliberative democracy 47
  distinguishing co-operatives from other
      enterprises xxvi, 40–1, 43–4, 47
  diversity of enterprise types xxvi, 44,
      45, 49, 50
  economic security 47
  entrepreneurial activities 49
  epistemological connections 44–5
  equal conditions for financial
      performance 46
  equal treatment principle 41
  fair trade 471, 476–7
  governance xxx, 246, 251–6
  human rights 44, 46–7
  ICA xxxvi, 104, 598–9, 601
    Blueprint 41–2, 44–5, 48
    Co-operative Law Committee 48
    Guidance Notes 48
    ILO Recommendation No 193 42
    legal frameworks for co-operatives,
        evaluation of 40
    re-interpretation of principle 48
    Statement 39–40, 42, 47
  identity 39, 41–8
  ILO 42
  international organizations 42, 45
  internationally recognised
      principles xxvi, 43
  mutuals 481–2
  national differences 40
  NGOs 42
  participation 41, 45, 46–7

principles and values (*Cont.*)
political arguments 43–8
principle, definition of 39
public international law, as concept of 45
public policy 44
regional organizations 45
self-help 47
sustainability 41, 45, 46–7
sustainable development xxvi, 45–7
private enterprises *see* **for-profit enterprises**
private property xxv, xxvi, 3–5, 9–10, 28–31,
34, 36, 85
privatization
enterprise form 234, 239–41
entrepreneurial activities 21–2
external resources xxvi
neoliberal governance 447, 449
public services 82, 84–5
utilities 189–92
worker co-operatives 135, 136
Proctor & Gamble 120–1, 124
Proctor, William Cooper 120–1, 124
producer co-operatives
capital co-operatives 542
co-operative law, role of 541–2
co-ordination mechanism, co-operation as
a 58, 63, 68
fair trade xxxiv, 470, 472–3
financial crisis of 2008 571
historical perspective 99
lender co-operatives 542
mutuals xxv, 15–16, 229, 234, 237
new institutionalism 68
professional partnerships 234
**production and consumption, association
between** xxxii, 374, 379, 382
professional partnerships 229, 234
**profit buy-back rule,
compulsory** 135–7, 139–41
profit maximization
co-ordination mechanism, co-operation as
a xxvi, 55, 57, 63, 68
credit unions and co-operative
banks 146, 151
entrepreneurial activities 14–16, 19–23
family firms 17
financial crisis of 2008 571

for-profit enterprises and co-operatives,
difference between 605
Shareholder Value (SHV) theory 19–23
social and political dimensions 77
socially sustainable enterprises 592, 595–6
stakeholder versus shareholder theory
debate 19–23
tragedy of the commons 22
value-added maximization 63
worker co-operatives 68, 137, 139
profit-sharing
broad-based stock ownership (BBSO) in
corporate businesses 377
capitalism 362–3, 367, 370
employee ownership 212–24, 428–33
historical perspective 115, 118, 120–3
hybrids 377
multi-stakeholder mutuals 485
property
private property xxv, xxvi, 3–5, 9–10, 29–31,
34, 36, 85
property-owning democracy 34–5, 36
property rights 228–9, 242
protectionism 605
psychiatric disorders 140–1
public benefit co-operatives 185–6
public international law 45
public limited companies 14–15, 605
public policy
co-operative law 44
co-ordination mechanism,
co-operation as 56
legal framework 605
ownership 10–11
welfare services 175
public-private partnerships 47
**public utilities, co-operatives
providing** 184–92
aims 185, 191
consumer co-operatives 184, 192
control rights 185
co-operative, definition of 184–5
customer-owned public utilities xxix,
184–7, 189, 191–2
democracy 185–6, 192
economic function 185, 187
electricity 188–90

energy 184, 187–8
Europe 187–9
feed-in tariff (FIT) agreements 187
functional principle 185
governance 192
historical perspective 184, 187, 189–90
information asymmetries 184, 190–1
market liberalization 188–9
moral hazard 190
natural gas 189
new co-operatives xxviii–xxix, 184, 188–9
one person one vote principle 185
price regulation 190–1
privatization 189–92
public benefit co-operatives 185
public finance crisis 191
regulation 184, 190–1
renewable energy 187
residual, appropriation of the 185
service quality 184, 190–1
supplier-owned co-operatives 186–7
traditional co-operatives xxviii–xxix, 184–7
water 184, 188–90
Putnam, Robert 83

Qualcomm xxvii
Quarrey, Michael 419
Quebec, Canada
ambulance transport services 178–9
credit unions and co-operative
    banks 147, 350
homecare services to elderly 179
local development 179–80
social and solidarity
    co-operatives 175, 178–9
worker co-operatives 579

Raiffeisen Bank xxxii–xxxiii, 102, 146–7, 149,
    171, 398, 401, 404–5, 408, 573
Raiffeisen, Friedrich Wilhelm 147, 171,
    398, 573
Ramsay, H 431
rating agencies 149, 574
Rauschenbusch, Walter 121
Rawls, John 20, 33–6
Reagan, Ronald 6, 125
rectification principle 29

Reeves, Joe 248
regulation
    banking 23, 149, 154, 155, 586
    co-operative law, role of xxxv, 543–6, 548
    co-operative transactions xxxv, 543–6
    co-ordination mechanism,
        co-operation as 55
    credit unions and co-operative banks 149,
        154, 155
    employee ownership 197
    social and solidarity co-operatives 172,
        176, 179–81
    utilities 184, 190–1
relational goods, provision of xxvii, 85
relational sociology 85
remuneration see pay/equity compensation
retail consumer co-operatives xxxvi, 379–80,
    572, 576–9, 581
return on equity (ROE) 151
Ridley-Duff, R 239–40
right libertarianism xxvi, 27–31, 36
risk
    division of risks 228, 230, 231–2, 234
    enterprise form 228, 230, 231–2, 234
    financial crisis of 2008 xxxvi, 570, 582
    pay 197
    securitization 449
Robinson, A 239
Robinson, Tony 533
Robotka, F 163
Rochdale Boroughwide Housing
    (RBH) 480–98
    ALMO (arm's-length management
        organization) 487
    caretakers 491–2
    cognitive and emotional work
        in organizational identity
        formation 495–6
    communicative capabilities 490–2, 495
    confidence, development of 485–6
    constitution 487–8
    continuity/change duality 483, 487–8
    creation of new organizational
        identity 487–95
    culture 493
    dualistic thinking xxxiv, 482–3, 486–96
    dynamic property 492–3

Rochdale Boroughwide Housing
      (RBH) (*Cont.*)
   embedding dualities 493–5
   emerging dualities 489
   empowerment/control duality 493–4
   governance 487, 489–90, 493
   improvization 493–5
   innovative multi-stakeholder mutuals
   integration 484
   intersectional identity 485–7
   latent dualities 488–9
   leadership programme 490–2
   minimal threshold 489–92
   multi-constituency providers 482,
      485–6, 495–6
   multi-stakeholder governance 487, 490
   Mutual Organisation Model 484
   mutuals xxxiv, 483, 486–96
   organizational change 483, 486–7
   organizational identity 484–95
   paradox management, concept
      of xxxiv, 486
   principles and values 491–3, 495
   proliferating dualities 489–92
   public service/commercial duality 489,
      492–3, 495
   relational dualities 489
   self-identity xxxiv, 483, 494–6
   simultaneity 488–9
   social capital 488, 491
   stabilizing dualities 492–3
   staff and tenants, ownership by xxxiv, 481
   supervisors 491–2, 495
   traditional multi-stakeholder mutuals
   transition experience xxxiv, 487–8
   trust 488
Rochdale Society of Equitable Pioneers 39,
      42, 171, 247, 259, 506
   consumer sovereignty 101
   co-operative law, role of 541, 546, 548
   credit unions and co-operative banks 146
   historical perspective 101–2
   non-members, co-operative activities
      with 546
   objectives 548
   principles and values 576
Rockefeller, John D Jr 121–5

Roelands, B 571
Rohrabacher, Dana 371
Rommel, L 329
Roosevelt, Theodore 257
Rosen, Corey 201, 295, 419
Royal Arsenal Co-operative Society 248
Royal Bank of Scotland (RBS) 554
Rozelle, S 514
rural areas
   agricultural co-operatives xxviii, 158
   credit unions and co-operative banks 147
   development xxviii, 158, 179–80
   poverty 171
Russia
   banditry 585
   Soviet Union 4, 83, 103–4

Saitama Medical Co-op 88
Salamon, LM 16–17
salaries *see* pay/equity compensation
Sanchez Bajo, C 571
Scala, E 388
   scale of sector 603–4
scandals 446, 452, 477, 564, 581, 603
Scandinavia 77, 83–4, 90 *see also* individual
      countries
Scharf, Adria 422
Schnedier, C 201
Schulze-Delitzsch, Hermann 102, 146–7,
      171–3, 398, 400, 573
Schulze-Delitzsch model 146–7
SCICs (collective interest co-operative
      enterprise) 505–10
Scotland 141, 255
Second World War,
      reconstruction after 9
security of employment 138–41, 158, 218–19,
      291, 431, 495
self-help 47, 146–7, 155, 171, 598
self-interest
   agricultural co-operatives 523
   behavioural economics 62
   financial co-operatives 150
   governance 240, 253
   home-care in US 395
   multi-stakeholder mutuals 490
   rational self-interest 590

socially sustainable enterprises 590
worker co-operatives in US 535
share capital, companies limited by 228–30,
    232–3, 237, 239–42
shared capitalism see United States, shared
    capitalism in
Shared Capitalism Research Project,
    National Bureau of Economic
    Research 213, 219
shared service co-operatives 572
shareholders
    absentee shareholders 5
    enlightened shareholder value 231
    enterprise form 228–32, 234, 236, 239
    ownership 3, 5, 10, 542–3
    shareholder value xxxv, 19–23, 448,
        550–69, 572
    stakeholder versus shareholder theory
        debate 15, 19–23
    stock purchase plans 123, 127, 198–9, 201,
        212, 368
Shen, M 514
Simmons, R 482
Singapore 576–7
single enterprise model 14, 15–19
size of enterprises see also large
        co-operatives; small-sized enterprises
    agricultural co-operatives 166
    co-ordination mechanism,
        co-operation as 66
    critical mass 66
    governance 251–2
    purpose of co-operatives 251–2
    social and political dimensions 90–1
    worker co-operatives 131, 133, 134–5
    World Co-operative Monitor xxx, 262–74,
        578, 607
small-sized enterprises 261–75
    agricultural co-operatives 268
    comparative studies xxx, 261–75
    co-operative, definition of 263–4
    credit unions and co-operative
        banks 145, 149–50
    description of organizations 265
    economic performance 265
    economic systems, contribution to
        functionality of 262

empirical evidence xxx, 261–74
enterprise form 263–5
European co-operatives 272–3
financial performance 265
governance 251–2, 253–6, 265–6
insurance
    mutuals 265, 267–8
    size of sector 268–70
International Co-operative &
    Mutual Insurance Federation
    (ICMIF) 265, 267
large co-operatives xxx, 261, 266–73
local endogenous development 262
measurement of dimensions xxx, 262
mutuals 264–5, 267–70, 272–3
ownership structures 265–6
quantification of socio-economic impact
    of large co-operatives xxx, 261–3,
    265–6, 273–4
sectors 261
SMART indicators 265
statistical data 261–74
under-capitalization 261
worker co-operatives 131, 133, 134–5
World Co-operative Monitor xxx, 262–74
    2014 Report 266–71
    Alliance with the Global 300 263, 266
    Euricse xxx, 262–74
    European co-operatives 272–3
    ICA xxx, 262–74
    methodological issues 263–6, 273–4
    Metrics Framework Structure 265
    types of organizations 264
Smith, ACT xxxiv, 486–7
Smith, Adam 585
social and political dimensions of
        co-operatives 76–93
    20th century, major social change in
        82–3, 90
    agricultural co-operatives 83, 87, 158, 167
    amalgamations 80, 83, 92
    associational school 80–1
    audits 89–90, 92
    building communities 76
    business school 80–1
    childcare providers 86, 87–8
    civil society 85

social and political dimensions of co-operatives (*Cont.*)

commercial dimension 80

competitive advantage 78, 89, 91

consumer co-operatives 81, 82, 86, 87

co-operation 81

co-operative, definition of 77

co-ordination mechanism, co-operation as xxvi, 63–4, 66

culture 81

democracy xxvii, 76–84, 87–8, 90–2

distribution of goods and services 84–5

dynamic model of co-operative development xxvii, 78–80

economic and financial aspects 81

efficient competition, logic of 79–80

employees 79

external environment 79–80

food safety and security 76

general interest services 76–7, 84

governance 86

government, relations with 76

historical perspective xxvii, 82, 83–4, 90

hybrid nature of co-operatives 77–81, 85–7, 91–2

ICA 76–7, 87, 91

   Centennial Meeting of World Congress 91

   co-operative, definition of 77

industrialization 82–3

internal decision-making 87–8, 90–2

managers, limits on 79

market 79, 86, 92

members 79–81, 87, 91

multiple goals xxvii, 77–81, 91–2

multi-stakeholder co-operatives 85, 87–9, 91–2

non-profit organizations, relations with 81

organizational development 78

participation 76, 86

personnel management, logic of 79–80

political changes, adapting to major 82–5, 90

private ownership 85

profit maximization 77

public authorities 79

public services, privatization of 82, 84–5

relational goods, provision of xxvii, 85

roadmap for 21st century 85–90

size of co-operatives 90–1

social accounting and audit 89–90, 92

social and solidarity co-operatives 171–3

social capital 85

social changes, adapting to major 82–5, 90–1

social goals 77–8, 89–90

social service providers xxvi, 77, 83, 84–91

socially sustainable enterprises 590

stability 78, 92

staff and clients, promotion of dialogue between 88–9

stakeholders 78–81, 87–8, 91–2

standard of living 82–3, 86

trade unions 83

trust, creation of 89

urbanization 82–3

voluntary associations 81, 89–90

welfare systems 76–7, 82–7, 89–91

women 81

worker co-operatives 76, 88–9

social and solidarity co-operatives xxviii, 171–83 *see also* **Italy, social co-operatives in**

agricultural co-operatives 172, 176, 179, 187

capitalism 171

companization 172

consumer co-operatives 171–2, 176

credit co-operatives 172

democracy 177, 179

diversification 172, 176

economic functions 171–3

economic security 171

entrepreneurialism xxv, 15–16, 49

environment 173

former Communist countries 175, 178

governance 179, 181

health services 173, 176

hybrids 172

ICA

   Conference 173

   Statement 173–4

Industrial Revolution 171

innovation 175, 179, 181, 314–18

international context 174–80

legal framework 606
local development 178–80
mutuals 172, 175
mutuality principle 172, 175
new forms, development of 174–5, 180
new role 173–4
political participation 171
poverty alleviation 171–2
private sector, distinctiveness from 173
public interest 172
regulation 172, 176, 179–81
rural development 179, 181
rural poverty 171
self-help 171
services of general interest 173–5, 180–1
social aims 173–4
social dimension 171–3
social freedom 171
social inclusion 176–8
solidarity 177, 179, 180
stakeholders 173, 179, 181
unmet needs 171, 175
welfare services 175–7, 179–81
worker co-operatives 172, 176–9, 181
social capital
co-ordination mechanism, co-operation
as 62, 66, 69
entrepreneurial activities 352
hybrids 381
multi-stakeholder mutuals 488, 491
social and political dimensions 85
trust, reciprocity and fairness 62, 488
value chains 458
women 465
worker-consumer co-operatives 381
social co-living 147
social co-operatives
asset locks 69
co-operative law, role of xxxv, 547–8
co-ordination mechanism, co-operation
as 69–70
entrepreneurial activities xxv, 15–16
institutional devices 69–70
multi-stakeholder governance, formal
introduction of 69–70
rules, social goals made explicit in 69
social economy xxxvi, 41, 604–7

social justice xxxvi, 36, 46–7
social networking 50
social services *see* **welfare services**
socialism 36, 447
socially sustainable enterprises, creation
of 585–97, 601
capital 594
capitalism 589
collective ownership 591
company law 589–90
concept of sustainability 586
conventional capitalist
corporations 589–90
democracy 587, 589
design of sustainable institutions xxxvi,
587, 589
economic multiplier 593–4
economic sustainability 585–6, 593, 596
empirical sustainability 591–2
ESOPs 591, 593
feudal system 586
financial crisis of 2008 xxxvi, 585–6, 590–1
financial institutions xxxvi, 585–6
financing xxxvi, 594–5, 596
free riders 593
historical perspective 586
human effects 592, 596
human nature xxxvi, 586–7, 589, 590
human systems, sustainability in 587
ideology 590
information asymmetries 590
market approach 585–6
ownership metaphor 589, 591–2
pay 592, 594
predictions 590–1
productivity 593
profit maximization 592, 595–6
rational self-interest 590
social and ethical factors 590
voluntary co-operation xxxvi, 587–9, 590
worker co-operatives 591–2, 594
socio-psychological changes 49
solar energy 324
solidarity *see also* **social and solidarity**
co-operatives
credit unions and co-operative
banks 146, 150

solidarity (*Cont.*)
  for-profit enterprises and co-operatives,
      difference between 604
  governance 247–8
  intergenerational solidarity 65
  worker-consumer co-operatives xxxii, 383
South Africa 195
South Korea 175
Soviet Union
  collapse 4, 83
  state-controlled enterprises as
      members 103–4
  state ownership 4
Spain *see also* **Mondragón movement**
  19th century 107–8
  consumer co-operatives 108
  credit unions and co-operative
      banks 150, 574
  consumer co-operatives 579, 586–7
  employee ownership 195
  globalization 108
  historical perspective 107–8
  pay 138
  regional organizations 107–8
  retail co-operatives 379
  sectors 261
  size of firms 133–4
  small-sized enterprises 261
  social and solidarity co-operatives 174, 177
  social initiative co-operatives 548
  wholesale distribution co-operatives 579
  work integration 177
  worker co-operatives 108, 132–7,
      142, 579–80
Sparda Bank (Germany) 404–5
Special Conference Committee (US) 121–3
sponsorship by municipal
      governments 69–70
Staark, David 451–2
Staatz, JM 162, 167
stakeholders *see also* **multi-stakeholder
      co-operatives**
  agricultural co-operatives 163–5
  commitment 232, 316, 481, 484–5, 494
  co-ordination mechanism,
      co-operation as 64
  enterprise form 227–33, 240–2

fiduciary duties 21
financial crisis of 2008 572
historical perspective 104
inclusion theories xxv, 19–20
neoliberal governance 450
social and political dimensions 78–81,
      87–8, 91–2
social and solidarity co-operatives 173,
      179, 181
stakeholder versus shareholder theory
      debate 15, 19–23
theory xxv, 19–23
  descriptive part 20
  instrumental part 20
  interdisciplinary, as 20
  normative part 20
  organization theory, as 20
  Stakeholder Value theory (STV) 19–23
  worker co-operatives 131
Standard Oil 123
state ownership forms xxv, 3–5, 9–10
Stern, Robert N 528
stewardship 5, 11
Stiglitz, Joe 16, 585
Stiglitz-Sen-Fitoussi Report 16
stock ownership,
      broad-based (BBSO) xxxii, 115–21,
      125, 361–7, 370, 375, 377
stock purchase plans 123, 127, 198–9, 201,
      212, 368
Stoltzfus, K 490
Streeck, W 450
supplier-owned co-operatives 186–7
sustainability *see also* **socially sustainable
      enterprises, creation of; sustainable
      development**
  capital 601, 607
  community impact 601
  competitiveness xxvi, 45
  co-ordination mechanism,
      co-operation as 55
  development 608
  economic sustainability 601
  energy 601–2
  enterprise form xxix, 232–3
  for-profit enterprises and co-operatives,
      differences between 601–2

future of co-operative business
    model 601–2
governance 252
ICA Statement 601
participation 45
regional organizations 45
worker co-operatives xxvii, 131, 139–41
sustainable development
future of co-operative business
    model 601–2
ICJ 45
ownership 9–10, 11
principles and values xxvi, 45–7
public international law, as concept of 45
Swan, JH 387–8
Sweden
agricultural co-operatives 83, 103
amalgamations 80, 83
childcare providers 86, 88–9, 90, 176
    co-producers 86
    Ostersund 86
    parent participation 86
    staff and clients, promotion of dialogue
        between 88–9
    Stockholm 86
    worker co-operatives 88–9
consumer co-operatives 79–80, 82–3,
    88–91, 576
Co-op Norden 77, 80
co-producers 86
historical perspective 103
KF 77, 83
Konsum 83
membership, move from active to
    passive 84
non-labour income 375
school of democracy, as no longer
    being 83–4
social and political dimensions 79–80,
    82–3, 88–91
social and solidarity co-operatives 174–6
trade unions 83
voting 83
wage-earner funds 10
worker co-operatives 88–9
Swift 602
Switzerland

consumer co-operatives 576–7
credit unions and co-operative banks 108
fair trade 473
historical perspective 108
retail co-operatives 108
size of co-operatives 108
supermarket chains 473
Swiss Union of Consumer
    Co-operatives 108
universal basic income (UBI) 376

tax
democracy 34–5
employee ownership 202, 206
left libertarianism 31–2
progressive taxation 9
self-ownership 34
tax law 540
technology *see also* **Internet**
co-operative law 44
credit unions and co-operative banks 155
development 607
singularization of production 49
Tendler, J 462
Thatcher, Margaret 4, 6, 434
third parties
co-operative activities with xxxv,
    543, 545–6
co-operative law 44
Thomson, Watson 354
Toniolo, Giuseppe 98
trade unions
agricultural co-operatives 159
consumer co-operatives 381–2
Great Depression 382
social and political dimensions 83
worker co-operatives 381–2
traditional enterprises *see* **for-profit
    organizations**
tragedy of the commons 22, 67, 165
trust and confidence
corporate social responsibility 89
financial crisis of 2008 571
for-profit enterprises and co-operatives,
    differences between 600–1
future of co-operative business
    model 600–1

trust and confidence (*Cont.*)
  governance xxx, xxxiii, 246, 247–8,
      447–8, 450–1
  neoliberal governance 448, 450
  private companies 89
  quantification 448–9
  social and political dimensions 89
  social capital 62
  turnover of staff 450
  voluntary associations 89
  welfare systems 89
  worker co-operatives 89
Turnbull, S 285

under-investment 131–2, 134–7, 141
Unión Cerrajera 280–1
**Union of Indigenous Communities of the
    Isthmus Region (UCIRI)** 472
United Kingdom *see also* **Co-operative
    Group; Rochdale Boroughwide
    Housing (RBH);**
**United Kingdom, conversion of building
    societies in; United Kingdom,
    employee ownership in**
  agricultural co-operatives 161
  Bank of England as lender of last resort 7
  banking sector 6–7, 10, 554
  Big Society 234
  capitalism 101
  City of London 10
  Coalition Agreement xxiv
  Community Benefit Societies
      (Bencoms) 185–6
  community co-operatives 185–6
  community finance societies 187
  community interest companies (CICs) 188,
      228, 236–7, 239–40
  competition 480
  consumer co-operatives 105, 246, 576–7
  consumption models 105
  credit unions and co-operatives
      banks 241–2
  decline of co-operatives 105
  diversity, lack of 5, 550–1, 554–5, 563
  economic stagnation 6
  employee ownership 195, 197, 206
  English model 101–2

  enterprise form 228, 234, 236–7, 239–42
  essential services, delivery of 480
  excessive executive pay unrelated to
      performance 5
  fair trade 473, 476
  financial crisis of 2008 4, 6–7
  German Mittelstand 5
  governance 246–53, 256–7
  health and psychiatric disorders 140–1
  hostile bids 11–12
  Hunt Review 206
  innovation 480
  joint stock corporations 135
  large co-operatives 133
  long-termism 5, 11–12
  manufacturing 5
  market contagion 6
  mission drift 237
  mutuals 480–1
  neoliberalism 480
  NHS 240, 428, 434–5, 438
  ownership 3–7, 11–12
  Ownership Commission 5–6, 11–12
      preconditions for good ownership 5–6, 11
      Report 2012 xxiv
  privatization 189, 234, 239–41, 480
  public limited companies (PLCs) 5–7, 11–12
  public-sector spin-outs 240
  public services, mutualism in 480–1
  renewable energy 187
  Rochdale Society of Equitable Pioneers 39,
      42, 101–2, 171, 247, 259, 506
  Scotland 141, 255
  short-termism 5, 6
  small and medium-sized enterprises 5, 272
  spinning out 480–1
  staff mutuals 481
  stakeholders 6–7, 240–1
  supermarket chains 473, 476
  tax 206
  TITF (too important to fail) 7
  under-investment 135
  universal basic income (UBI) 376
  utilities 187–9
  village shops 251–2
  worker co-operatives 133–5, 140–1,
      234, 239–40

United Kingdom, conversion of building societies in 550–69

agency problems 552

asymmetric information 552

Birmingham, 18th century in 105

bogus arguments for conversion xxxv, 560

Building Societies Act 1986 558–9, 566

capital 553, 558, 560–2, 565

Civic Approach to financial reform 551

clarity of objectives 561

competition 551, 554, 563, 565

conflicts of interest 554

consumer interests 550–1, 564

consumer lock-in 552

culture 554, 564–5

demutualization 105, 238–9, 241–2, 550, 557–9, 563–4, 568

Deposit Guarantee Scheme Directive 566

deregulation 551

diversification 238, 561, 564

diversity

  balance between SHVs and STVs 555

  competiveness 554, 565

  decline 550–1, 554–5, 563

  Diversity Index 555–6

  dominance of large SHV banks 555

  economic growth 556

  European Union 556

  governance 554

  ownership structures and business models xxxv, 550–1, 554–7

  political commitment 565–6

  poverty 556

  public policy 554–5, 556, 568

  reform 565–6

  risk 554, 556, 561, 567

Europe, comparison with xxxv, 550–1, 554–5, 557–8

experience of conversion 558–60

failures of banks 566–7

financial crisis of 2008 238–9

flexibility, gaining 561

general interest, purposes of 558

governance 235, 554, 560–1, 564

historical perspective 105

hostile bids for STVs, impossibility of 553

insurance companies xxxv, 550–1, 557–8, 563

intergenerational transfers of wealth xxxv, 559

key differences between SHV and STV models 551–3, 557–8, 561–3

local communities 553

locked value versus unlocked (open) value 561–3

longer-term contracts 552

management 105

mergers 558

mortgage market 551, 552, 555, 557–9

objectives 552, 558, 561

ownership structure 552–3, 567

perpetuity, reserves held in xxxv

post-conversion scenario 563–4

profit maximization 552–3

public image of mutuals 551

public policy interests 551, 554–5, 556, 565, 568

rationale for conversion 560–1

reform 565–6

regional development 553, 554

re-mutualization 566–7

retail savings 559

retained profits as source of capital 553

risk 553–4, 556, 561, 567

shareholder value (SHV) banks, conversion to xxxv, 550–69

Stakeholder Value (STV) institutions (mutuals) xxxv, 550–69

  advantages 554, 564, 566, 568

  characteristics 552–3

  culture 554

  customers as members 552

  demutualization 550, 557–9, 563–4, 568

  diversity xxxv, 550–1, 554–7

  Europe, comparison with xxxv, 550–1, 554–5, 557–8

  key differences between SHV and STV models 551–3, 557–8, 561–3

  objectives 552

  one member one vote principle 553

  re-mutualization 566–7

  risk 553–4

structural change, dealing with 560–1

United Kingdom, conversion of building societies in (*Cont.*)
systemic stability 550, 565
Too Big to Fail subsidy 565
trust and confidence 552, 564–5
United States, savings and loans
associations in 105
value creation 561–3
voting rights 553, 559–60
wholesale funding 561
windfall profits xxxv, 559, 560
United Kingdom, employee ownership in 426–41
Approved Profit Sharing 433
bus services 434
business start-ups 427, 436, 439
business succession 427, 436–7, 438–9
'champions' of employee ownership 432
circumstances in which ownership is
created xxxiii
competition 431–2
conversions xxxiii, 426, 428, 429–31,
434, 436–40
cycle of control perspective 431
definition of employee ownership 427
democracy 435
deregulation 431–2
development of employee
ownership xxxiii, 426, 431–6
direct forms xxxiii, 426–7, 428, 430, 439
diversity 427
employee participation 427–8
entrepreneurial activities 435–6
enterprise form xxxiii, 426–32
Enterprise Management Incentives 435
ESOPs 429–30, 432, 435
financial crisis of 2008 432, 439–40
fire and probation services 434–5
friendly societies 428
globalization 431
governance xxxiii, 426–7, 428, 437, 438
heterogeneity 426–7, 436
historical perspective 426
human capital 431–2, 438–9
hybrids xxxiii, 426–7, 429–30
indirect ownership 426–7, 428
influences on development xxxiii, 426

lobbying 432
main structures 430
membership model 428
micro-level developments 432
minority ownership 426
mutuals 428–9, 434–5
nature of employee ownership
sector 436–40
new forms of employee ownership xxxiii
NHS 428, 434, 438
nominal shares, purchase of 428
non-executive directors 427
number of firms 431
pay 432
policy initiatives 432–5
political parties, policies of 435–6
political support 426, 440
privatization 427, 434–6, 438–9
profit-sharing 428, 433
public service spin-outs 428–9, 434, 438
QUEST (Qualifying Employee Share Trust)
(statutory ESOP) 433
registration 428
rescues 439–40
sectors 426, 436
sharing ownership 427, 436, 438–9
SIP 433, 435
social market economy 435
tax 433
trust-based ownership xxxiii, 426, 428–30,
433–4, 437, 438–9, 591
White Rose Employee Ownership Centre/
Employee Ownership Association
project 427
worker co-operatives 426–7, 428, 431
United Nations (UN)
development 608
GA Guidelines 42
specialized agencies 606
Year of the Co-operative xxiv
United States *see also* **ESOPs (Employee
Stock Ownership Plans) (United
States)**; United States, employee
ownership in; **United States, home
care industry in**; United States,
shared capitalism in; **United States,
worker co-operatives in**

1980s recession 148
agricultural co-operatives 109, 158–9, 161
Alaska Permanent Fund 376
benefit corporations 228, 236
collective labour 527
colonialism 527
communal values of indigenous
     nations 527
consensual networks 150
consumer co-operatives 110
consumer lending 148
Cooperative League of the USA 110
credit unions and co-operative
     banks 109–10
decentralization of banking sector 148
EBITDA 206
economic co-operation of indigenous
     nations 527
electric co-operatives 188
employers, defined by 148
energy 601
enterprise form 228, 236
European co-operative banks, differences
     from 148, 151–2
fair trade 473
financial co-operatives 575
food co-operatives 249, 603
governance 249
Great Depression 148
greenhouse gases 376–7
historical perspective 109–10
ICA 109
indigenous nations 527
insurance 109–10, 577
large corporations, model of 107
large co-operatives 268–9
low-profit limited liability companies
     (L ₃Cs) 236, 604
municipal governments, sponsorship
     by 382–3
mutuals 573–4
National Co-operative Business
     Association 110
privatization 189
profit maximization 14
retail co-operatives 379
rural co-operatives 188

savings and loans sector 105, 148, 150–2,
     155, 573
  demutualization 573
  financial crisis of 2008 573–4
  mutuals, amalgamation with 573–4
  Savings and Loans Crisis 148
size of co-operatives 109
small-sized enterprises 148, 270
utilities 109, 188–9
Weaver Street Market 379–80
wholesale distribution co-operatives 579
worker co-operatives 240, 591
United States, employee ownership in 114–27
20ᵗʰ century, key developments in the 120–4
American Revolution 114, 116
autonomy in decision-making 212
best employers 220–1
broad-based ownership 115–21, 125
capitalism 121, 125, 212, 214–18, 221–2, 223
  firm outputs, relation with 212, 214–18,
     221–2, 223
  shared 212, 214–18, 221–2, 223
Christianity 121
cod fishery and profit-sharing 114–15, 116
  American Revolution 114
  colonies 114–15
  inclusive capitalism 114
  profit-sharing 114–15, 116
  tax credits 115
collective bargaining 123
colonies 114–15, 119
combinations of worker ownership and
     profit sharing xxix, 212
co-monitoring by workers 219–20
Constitution 123
corporate ownership shares 118
culture xxix, 213, 216–17, 220–2, 224
democracy 117–18
economic importance xxvii
Eligible Worker Owned Cooperative
     (EWOC) 126
Employee Retirement Security Act of 1974
     (ERISA) 126
ESOPs xxvii, 120, 122–7, 213, 214, 221–3
  Employee Retirement Security Act of
     1974 (ERISA) 126
  fairness 127

United States, employee ownership in (*Cont.*)

    Great Depression 123–4, 126

    tax incentives 126–7

  fairness 127

  field experiment on profit sharing in fast-food franchises 213, 223–4

  financial performance 213, 224

  founding fathers 114–18, 125

  free riders 218–19

  General Accountability Office (GAO) (US Congress) 212, 213, 223

  General Social Survey (GSS) (US government) 214–16, 219

  Goldman School of Public Policy study 213, 224

  government sponsorship 212

  Great Depression 123–4, 126

  hard, willingness to work 216

  highest paid workers 127

  high-tech companies xxvii

  historical perspective xxvii, 114–27

  homestead legislation 117–18, 124–7

  industrialization 117–20

  inequality 115–18

  innovation, culture of 217

  land ownership 115–18, 125

  large groups of workers xxix, 214, 220

  Louisiana Purchase 117

  loyalty and pride in firm 215–16

  management reports 213

  metastatistics 211–12

  middle-class ownership society 115, 125

  Northwest Ordinance 116–17

  older workers 127

  participatory ownership culture, importance of 221–2, 224

  pay 217–20

  pension plans 223

  political economy 117–21

  profit sharing xxix, 120–1, 123–4, 211–12, 213–21, 223–4

  property ownership 115–17, 125

  public policy 117, 125

  quality of output 213, 224

  research xxix, 211–26

  Shared Capitalism Research Project (NBER) 213, 214–20

  size of workplace xxix, 214

  stock ownership 212, 215–21, 223–4

  suggestions, willingness to make 216–17

  tax 121, 123–4, 126–7

  trade unions 119–20, 123

  Trust Index 221

  turnover of workers 213, 215, 224

  UK Treasury study 212, 223

  welfare capitalism 122

  work conditions 217–18

United States, home care industry in 386–97

  agencies 387–8, 389–92

  attitudes of workers xxxii, 389–95

  caregivers, characteristics of 390–1

  Certified Home Health Agencies 389–90, 531

  chain-affiliated agencies 387–8

  conventional for-profit businesses xxxii, 387–90, 392–6

  Co-operative Home Care Associates (CHCA) 387, 389

  co-ordinators 391, 393

  daily environments 391

  education and training 390–3, 395

  environment 387–91

  ethnicity 388, 390

  Fair Labor Standards Act 388

  governance xxxii, 387, 389

  High Performance Work Systems (HPWS) 388, 395

  homogeneity 387

  industry factors 387–8

  job satisfaction xxxii, 392–4

  Licensed Home Care Services Agencies 389

  Medicare 387–8

  minimum wage 388

  not-for-profit businesses xxxii, 387–8, 390, 392–6

  ownership structures 389

  pay 387–8, 392–5, 531

  poverty 388, 394

  private agencies 387–8

  profit-sharing 390

  quality of jobs xxxii, 387, 392, 394

  quality of workforce 388, 391–2

  reporting 387

  routines 391

self-interest 395
shortage of workers xxxii, 386–7
trade unions 392–3, 394–5
training 387
turnover of workers xxxii, 388, 391
type of work 388
websites 390
women 386, 388, 390
worker co-operatives xxxii, 387, 389–96, 531
United States, shared capitalism in 361–73
401k retirement plans, company stock
  in 368–9
broad-based worker-ownership
  plans xxxii, 361–7, 370
capitalism 361, 370
cash profit-sharing 362–3
citizen's shares 363–4, 369–70
employee ownership 364–72
  incidence of worker owners 364–5
  policies to encourage work
    ownership 367–72
  stock ownership 362–5, 368–9, 370–1
equity-sharing 362–4, 367, 370, 372
  joint stock-companies 362
  performance shares 362
  restricted stock shares 362
  stock market shares 362–3
ESOPs xxxii, 363–72
executive pay
  broad-based worker-ownership
    plans xxxii
  performance-related pay 370
  tax code, reform of xxxii, 370
expansion of worker ownership xxxii
extent of broad-based ownership 361–7
gain-sharing 362–3, 368
General Social Survey (GSS) 361–7
Office of Broad-Based Capitalism, proposal
  for xxxii
policies to encourage work
  ownership 367–72
profit-sharing 362–3, 367–8, 370
restricted stock, grants of 368–9
sectors 365–6
size of companies 365
small businesses to employees,
  encouragement of sale of xxxii, 371–2

ESOPs 371–2
  retirement xxxii, 371–2
  Subchapter T worker co-operatives 372
  tax incentives 371–2
Subchapter T worker co-operatives 372
tax code, reform of xxxii, 370
tax incentives 367–72
  broad-based worker-ownership
    plans xxxii
  executive pay xxxii, 370
  federal business tax subsidies xxxii, 367
  subsidies of unshared capitalism 370
wage substitution 364
worker co-operatives 369–70
United States, worker co-operatives
  in 527–38
advantages 532
anchor institutions 534
business skills 532–3
capitalism 528–9
categories of co-operatives based on
  motivation 535
Centre for Family Life (CFL) 534, 535–6
change 532–5
cities, support from 536
Cold War 529
communal values 527
conversions 534
credit unions and co-operative banks 534
culture 532
definition of worker co-operatives 530
democracy 532–7
Democratic at Work Institute 530–1,
  534, 537
Democratic at Work Network
  (DAWN) 534
demographics 531
Division of Self-Help Co-operatives 529
economic motives 535–7
education and training 533–4
Evergreen co-operatives 534, 535–6
extent 530–1
financial crisis of 2008 530–1, 533
grants 529
grass-roots initiatives 534
Great Depression 529
growth 532–4

United States, worker co-operatives
    in (*Cont.*)
  health and safety 134
  historical perspective xxxv, 527–30
  home care industry, women in 531
  ideological conflicts 529
  ideological motives 535–7
  immigrant
      communities 533, 536
  indigenous people 527
  individualism and self-reliance 532
  industrialization 527
  inequalities 530, 537
  infrastructure, lack of 533
  internal and external pressures 529
  joint stock companies 135
  Knights of Labor 528–9
  labour exchanges 529
  labour republicanism 528
  Mondragón co-operatives 533
  New Deal 529
  number of co-operatives 528
  number of employees 133
  ownership 531
  pay 531, 536–7
  perverse supply response 137
  poverty 534, 535–6
  regional organizations 529–30
  rural areas 534
  self-interest 535
  size of co-operatives 529, 530–1
  small co-operatives 529
  social change 535–7
  social democratization 530
  states 530
  strikes 527–8
  trade unions 528
  US Federation of Worker Co-operatives
      (USFWC) 530, 534–7
  women 531
  workshops 527–8
universal basic income (UBI) 375–6
urbanization 82–3
Uruguay 133–4, 137–8, 336
utilitarianism 22–3
utilities *see* public utilities, co-operatives
    providing

Valentinov, VL 165
values *see* principles and values
Vamstad, J 86
van der Hoff, Frans 472
Van Parijs, Phiippe 376
Vanek, J 57, 65, 134–5
veil of ignorance 57
Venezuela 335
vertical integration concept 163, 164, 167
Vidal, I 88
voice rights *see* participation and
    voice rights
Volksbank xxxii–xxxiii, 146–7, 401,
    404–5, 408
voluntary associations
  capitalism 588
  democracy 90, 589
  individual commitment 588
  multi-stakeholder organizations 89
  relations with 81
  socially sustainable enterprises xxxvi,
    587–9, 590
  trust, creation of 89
  work to rule 588
voting *see also* one person one vote principle
  consumer co-operatives 576
  credit unions and co-operative banks 145,
    146, 153
  participation 47

wages *see* pay/equity compensation
Walker, John Amasa 119
Walras, Leon 98
Ward, B 63, 65
Washington, George 114–17
water 184, 188–90
Webb, Sidney and Beatrice 98
Weitzman, Martin 36
Welch, Jack 7
welfare services
  asymmetric information 88
  capitalism 34
  competitive advantage 89
  co-production services 86–7
  democracy 47, 87, 90
  enterprise form 241
  globalization 41

multi-stakeholder co-operatives 87
property-owning democracy 34–5
public policy 175
quality 88
retrenchment 82, 84, 90
social and political dimensions xxvi,
    76–7, 83–91
social and solidarity
    co-operatives 175–7, 179–81
staff and clients, promotion of dialogue
    between 88–9
trust, creation of 89
unemployment benefit, preserving 140
Weltmann, Dan 217
WGZ-Bank AG 400
Whyte, Kathleen 289
Whyte, William 289
Wicksteed, P 22–3
Wikipedia 60
Wilkinson, R 592
Williams, Raymond 445–6, 449, 452, 454
Williamson, OE 68
wind energy 188, 321, 323–4
women 456–61, 463–7
    consumer co-operatives 581
    custom 457
    development and sustainability of
        communities 354–5
    gender dynamics 460–1
    home care industry 531
    social and political dimensions 81
    social capital 465
    socio-economic status 456–7
work to rule 588
worker co-operatives 131–44 see also United
    States, worker co-operatives in
    access to capital, impediments on 380
    democracy xxxii, 383
    behavioural differences 68–9
    capital 131–2, 134–7, 141
    capitalism 102, 137
    CICOPA 579–80
    commitment 380, 395–6, 532
    communities, role in xxvii, 132, 139–42
    conceptions 134–7
    consumer co-operatives xxxii, 379–82
    control 131, 138–9, 141

co-operative law, role of 541
co-ordination mechanism, co-operation
    as 57, 68–9
creativity 139
credit unions and co-operative banks 594
decline 579–80
definition 132
demand shocks 131–2, 136–8
democracy 35
disabilities, workers with 177
disadvantaged workers 176–9
discrimination 176–7
economic democracy xxvii–xxviii, 139–41
economic theory 131–2
employee ownership 591–2
enterprise form 234, 239–41
externalities 139–40
finances 132
financial crisis of 2008 xxxvi, 571–2,
    579–80, 582
governance 381, 580
health and psychiatric disorders 140–1
historical perspective 99, 102
information asymmetries 139
institutional sponsorship 380, 382–3
internalization of decisions xxvii, 131, 139
Internet 380
jobs, provision of good, reliable xxvii,
    135, 141
joint stock corporations 135
market economy, role in 131
market failures 134, 138
moral hazard on behalf
    of managers 139
municipal governments, sponsorship
    by 382–3
number of co-operatives 131, 132–3, 579
number of employees 133
objectives 137–9
organizational degeneration 380
ownership metaphor 591–2
participatory models 380
pay 68–9, 131–2, 138–9
percentage of businesses in market, as 133
perverse supply response 131, 137–8
priority 76
privatization 135, 136

worker co-operatives (*Cont.*)
profit buy-back rule,
    compulsory 135–7, 139–41
profit maximization 68, 137, 139
public support 142
public works contracting 102
reasons for creation xxvii
research xxvii, 131–4
resilience 579–80
retail co-operatives 379–80
sectors 133
security of employment 138–41
self-extinction 135
short-lived, idea as being 131
size of co-operatives 131, 133, 134–5
small and medium-sized enterprises 133
small, idea as co-operatives as being 131,
    133, 134–5
social and political dimensions 76, 88–9
social and solidarity co-operatives 172,
    176–9, 181
social capital 381
social inclusion 176–7
socially sustainable enterprises 591–2, 594
solidarity xxxii, 383
special, as 131–3, 141
spillover effects in communities xxvii,
    131, 139–42
stability xxvii, 135, 141
stakeholders 131
strategy, control of firm xxvii, 139

sustainable jobs xxvii, 131, 139–41
taxi services 380
trade unions 381–2
tradeable shares 135–6
travel accommodation 380
trust, creation of 89
under-investment 131–2, 134–7, 141
unemployment benefit, preserving 140
work integration 176–9, 181
worker ownership *see* **employee ownership**
World Co-operative Monitor (ICA/Euricse)
2014 Report 266–71
Alliance with the Global 300 263, 266
Euricse xxx, 262–74
European co-operatives 272–3
ICA xxx, 262–74
methodological issues 263–6, 273–4
Metrics Framework Structure 265
size of co-operatives xxx, 262–74, 578, 607
types of organizations 264
Wu, B 517–18

Xu, X 517–18

Year of the Co-operative (UN) xxiv
Yu, K-H 482–3
Yuan, P 513, 523

Zachernuk, T 517
Zhang, L 514, 519
Zhao, Li 513, 523

Lightning Source UK Ltd.
Milton Keynes UK
UKHW030726040119
335008UK00006B/7/P